A MILITARY HISTORY OF THE
COLD WAR, 1944–1962

CAMPAIGNS & COMMANDERS

GREGORY J. W. URWIN, SERIES EDITOR

A MILITARY HISTORY OF THE COLD WAR, 1944–1962

JONATHAN M. HOUSE

UNIVERSITY OF OKLAHOMA PRESS : NORMAN

Also by Jonathan M. House

Toward Combined Arms Warfare: A Survey of 20th-Century Tactics, Doctrine, and Organization (Fort Leavenworth, Kans., 1985)
Military Intelligence, 1870–1991: A Research Guide (Westport, Conn., 1993)
(with David M. Glantz) *When Titans Clashed: How the Red Army Stopped Hitler* (Lawrence, Kans., 1995)
(with David M. Glantz) *The Battle of Kursk* (Lawrence, Kans., 1999)
Combined Arms Warfare in the Twentieth Century (Lawrence, Kans., 2001)

This book is published with the generous assistance of the McCasland Fund, Duncan, Oklahoma.

Library of Congress Cataloging-in-Publication Data

House, Jonathan M. (Jonathan Mallory), 1950–
    A military history of the Cold War, 1944–1962 / Jonathan M. House
    p.   cm.
    Includes bibliographical references and index.
    ISBN 978-0-8061-4262-3 (hbk. : alk. paper)
    1. Cold War. 2. Military history, Modern—20th century. I. Title.
    D842.2.H68 2012
    355.0209'045—dc23

2012008651

A *Military History of the Cold War, 1944–1962* is Volume 34 in the Campaigns and Commanders series.

The paper in this book meets the guidelines for permanence and durability of the Committee on Production Guidelines for Book Longevity of the Council on Library Resources, Inc. ∞

1 2 3 4 5 6 7 8 9 10

Respectfully dedicated to those who served on both sides,
and especially to veterans of the following units,
with whom my wife and I served:

4th Battalion, 37th Armor
19th Engineer Battalion (Combat)
245th Engineer Detachment (Utilities)
Headquarters, 2nd Infantry Division
Headquarters, 24th Infantry Division (Mechanized)
2nd Combat Intelligence Company
102nd Military Intelligence Battalion (Combat Electronic Warfare
and Intelligence)
124th Military Intelligence Battalion (CEWI)
375th Chemical Company (Processing) (Type B)
316th Chemical Detachment (Decontamination) (Team FA)
436th Chemical Detachment (Decontamination) (Team FB)
326th Area Support Group

CONTENTS

ILLUSTRATIONS

FIGURES

PREFACE

The voluminous literature of the Cold War tends to two extremes
of magnification: some authors choose to write macro accounts
about national security and diplomatic history, while others chron-
icle the individual experiences of soldiers, commanders, and political leaders. Both bodies of literature are valuable, and I have availed
myself of them to a considerable extent, but I do not pretend to have
mastered the historiography of either extreme. Because this is not
intended as a work of diplomatic history or as an account of individual combat, those subjects are included only where necessary to
provide context.

Instead, I focus on the vast, often neglected middle ground in
which politicians and military officers designed, organized, and
equipped military organizations and then committed those units to
operations. It is an attempt to cover not only the conventional and
unconventional conflicts of the Cold War but also the long periods
of semimobilization and heightened alert, when millions of soldiers,
sailors, and airmen became, to use Keith Laumer's mocking term,
the "Veterans of Unfought Wars." Even those who never fired a shot
in anger suffered significant physical and psychological damage from
years of exercises, alerts, cruises, and patrols. Being a soldier is hazardous to your health even in "peacetime." In describing the military
aspects of the conflict, I have attempted to give some sense of the
psychological atmosphere in which events occurred, an atmosphere

in which mistakes and misunderstandings might transform peace into war in seconds. This atmosphere, though difficult to convey to those who did not experience it, explains many decisions that would otherwise appear inflammatory or ill considered.

My purpose is twofold. First, these military developments, well known to specialists but not necessarily to most historians or general readers, deserve study for their own sake. This is not detail for the sake of detail, but rather variations that illustrate important and frequently overlooked complexities. Cold War insurgencies, for example, did not always have the same outcome. There were successful revolutions (China and Indochina), unsuccessful revolts (Greece, the Philippines, Malaya, and Kenya), and occasionally a military failure that nonetheless led to political victory (Algeria). Similarly, and contrary to some recent studies,[1] the North Atlantic Treaty as a political alliance did not automatically lead to the elaborate military structure of the North Atlantic Treaty Organization. Moreover, one cannot fully understand the current American involvement in the Middle East without viewing that involvement in the context of the Suez Canal (1956) and Lebanon (1958) crises.

Second, these events provide an extended case study of the Clausewitzian relationship of policy to the military. Although national policy should always determine military actions, the interaction between the two became especially difficult during this period of limited wars and ideologically motivated insurgencies. It is no coincidence that Samuel Huntington and other academics attempted to codify the nature of civil-military relationships at precisely the time when the traditional delineation between the two became porous, when politicians and soldiers alike had to think constantly of the political and economic implications of warfare. Most students of the Cold War are aware of the instances in which generals engaged in policy confrontations with their governments. However, there are numerous other cases in which political leaders, such as Anthony Eden, Nikita Khrushchev, and John Kennedy, made military decisions that hamstrung and ultimately thwarted their own political goals. Similarly, governmental national security policies had military implications that took on a life of their own, quite apart from diplomatic or domestic political considerations during the Cold War. The invasion of South Korea convinced European policy makers that they needed credible forces to make deterrence and containment effective. The perceived need to make the North Atlantic alliance viable militarily at a time when Britain and France were fighting insurgencies elsewhere accelerated the rearmament and sovereignty of West Germany. The result was a host of military commitments around the globe, accompanied by expensive atomic and conventional armed forces, which in turn inevitably produced nuclear weapons accidents and aerial reconnaissance confrontations. In such a pressure-cooker, hothouse atmosphere, politicians as well as soldiers felt an instinctual preference for military solutions to political problems. To gloss over all this is to omit large portions of the Cold War.

The practical requirements and limitations of military operations influenced national policies quite as much as the reverse. Most obviously, all participants in the Cold War found themselves hampered by the realities of space and time, realities that made it difficult to project military force to the desired locations in an effective and timely manner. Thus, Mao Tse-tung committed the Chinese People's "Volunteers" to the Korean War not when the United Nations (UN) forces were most vulnerable, but rather when Mao's generals felt they had sufficient air and logistical support to project their forces a short distance into Korea. Nikita Khrushchev deployed short-range missiles to Cuba in 1962 partly because he was unable to field effective intercontinental missiles as a nuclear deterrent, and partly because without such a deterrent he could neither ensure Soviet security nor advance his domestic economy.

The vast scope of this topic forced me to omit certain topics that I considered less than essential to the military conduct of the Cold War. For example, the 1946 U.S.-Soviet confrontation over Iran was a key step in the diplomatic or national security chronology of the Cold War but did not involve significant military actions. The 1948 Arab-Israeli conflict, while important to the later development of the Middle Eastern problem, did not, unlike subsequent regional wars, involve Great Power support or actions, so I chose to bypass it in the interests of brevity and clarity.

By contrast, I have included a number of neglected conflicts that were essential to the story of European decolonization and counterinsurgency. In this regard, the Mau Mau in Kenya and EOKA (National Organization of Cypriot Fighters) in Cyprus provide valuable comparisons to the supposedly flawless British counterinsurgency techniques in Malaya. In addition, these colonial campaigns put stress on British and French military resources, thereby exacerbating Western security concerns in the National Atlantic Treaty Organization (NATO) and the Middle East, yet the colonial issues are rarely mentioned beyond broad generalizations.

As with all authors, I am indebted to the staffs of numerous libraries, including those of the Pentagon, Gordon College, and the Command and General Staff College. I also owe considerable thanks to several of my colleagues, including Gary Bjorge, Sean Kalic, John Kuehn, and Joseph Fischer, who generously provided their expertise by reviewing portions of the manuscript.

I need to say a word about transliterations. Linguistic experts will undoubtedly object to my use of obsolete and even archaic versions of foreign names, such as the Wade-Giles system that transliterates the Nationalist Chinese People's Party's name as *Kuomintang* rather than the current pinyin system, which uses *Guomindang*. There are similar transliteration issues regarding Korean and Arabic names. For important names and organizations, I have chosen to use the transliterations most commonly employed in the West at the time of the events in question, rather than introduce anachronistic modern transliterations. In the case of Chinese terms, I have included the pinyin transliteration in parentheses immediately after the first use of the Wade-Giles term, for ease of reference.

Although I was a cold warrior for many years and continue to teach for the U.S. Army Command and General Staff College, this book is entirely my own and does not represent the official position of any government or agency. Finally, in a survey work of this kind, it is inevitable that I would inadvertently overlook key facts and interpretations; all such errors are solely my responsibility.

Fort Leavenworth, Kansas
August 2011

A Military History of the
Cold War, 1944–1962

1

PROLOGUE
A Tale of Three Cities

The mission would have been risky even if the city had not been defended by anti-aircraft guns and obscured by the smoke of a dozen fires.[1] Polish, British, and South African air crews had to fly a 1,750-mile round trip from Italy, crossing an occupied continent with more Axis night fighters than navigational beacons. With the short nights of high summer, at least part of the trip had to be in daylight, even though some of the B-24 Liberator and British-built Lancaster crews were so shorthanded that their nose machine guns were unmanned. In the middle of this odyssey, the aircraft had to fly one at a time down the Vistula River, pass two bridges, turn hard left, and then locate the faint diamond and T-shaped lights of the drop zone in Krasinski Square. In the smoke and darkness over Warsaw, hitting that square required each airplane to drop down to 500 feet above ground level and slow to a stalling speed of 140 miles per hour. But the Polish resistance was fighting the Germans with their bare hands, and someone had to deliver weapons to them.

The first plane in the stream that night was flown by Captain N. Van Rensburg of No. 31 Squadron, South African Air Force. German searchlights reached up to find the plane, quickly followed by a web of colored tracers from machine guns and 20mm anti-aircraft positions. At such low speeds, the crew felt as if they were hanging in midair. Unable to locate the drop zone on the first pass, Van Rensburg wrenched the lumbering four-engine aircraft around and flew the gauntlet a second time. Finally, the Liberator lurched upward as thirty-six containers spilled out of the bomb bay, their parachutes blossoming unseen to float downward in the darkness. Van Rensburg's plane made it home almost unscathed, but others were not so lucky. Out of twenty-eight aircraft sent to Warsaw that night, three were shot down and a fourth had to crash-land in the Ukraine. Most of the other planes came home with flak damage. Over the course of five moonlit nights in August, the Allied Air Forces in Italy dispatched ninety-two planes to Warsaw, of which seventeen were lost outright and three more crashed on the way home. Reduced to only eight crews, No. 31 Squadron had to stand down from further operations. Despite such sacrifices, less than half of the weapons containers reached their intended recipients.[2]

The obvious question is, Why was such a suicidal mission necessary? Perhaps more to the point, why did these airmen have to fly halfway across Europe to help the Poles when their mutual allies of the Soviet Union's Red Army were only a few kilometers away?

The Warsaw Uprising of 1944 was in many ways the curtain-raiser for the Cold War.[3] The resistance forces in Poland, known as the Armia Krajowa (Home Army, or AK),were led by professional soldiers loyal to the London-based Polish government in exile of Prime Minister Stanislaw Mikolajczyk. Neither the leaders in Warsaw nor those in London had forgiven the Soviet Union for helping Nazi Germany defeat Poland in 1939. The Soviets insisted that they were only recovering territory lost in 1920, territory that was ethnically non-Polish and therefore belonged under Soviet control. In July 1941, Prime Minister Winston Churchill had persuaded the Polish exile government to establish diplomatic relations with Moscow, but even those fragile ties had ended two years later, after the revelation that the Soviets had murdered thousands of Polish prisoners of war in the Katyn Forest.[4]

From Joseph Stalin's viewpoint, the London government and its Home Army were nuisance groups that would never accept Soviet annexation of eastern Poland. They might, in fact, become a threat to the postwar security of the Soviet state. This was precisely why Stalin's secret police, the NKVD, had murdered 14,500 Polish officers and cadets at Katyn and elsewhere in 1940 and then attempted to blame the Germans for the massacre.[5] Four years later, when the Red Army reentered eastern Poland, the Soviets quickly arrested leaders of the Home Army while drafting their followers into the Moscow-controlled First Polish Army. On July 27, 1944, Lieutenant General Tadeuz Komorowski, commander of the Polish resistance forces, told his London government that such action "indicates that the Soviets want to destroy the Home Army."[6]

The failed attempt to assassinate Adolf Hitler on July 20, 1944, encouraged the Poles to believe that Germany was close to collapse. At the same time, the Red Army appeared on the verge of taking Warsaw. In five weeks, the huge encirclements of Operation Bagration had destroyed more than thirty German divisions while moving the battle lines three hundred kilometers westward. The Germans were clearly in retreat, and had even begun to withdraw from the Polish capital. This Soviet victory placed General Komorowski in a quandary. The temptation was to seize control of Warsaw, defeating the hated occupiers and giving the London government some stature in future negotiations with Stalin. Unfortunately, Komorowski had previously sent most of his scarce weapons to the eastern provinces, where the first battles of liberation would occur as the Red Army advanced. This left the Warsaw branch of the Home Army almost unarmed. At most, there were 1,000 carbines, 67 machine guns, 35 anti-tank launchers, and 1,700 revolvers to equip 40,000 Warsaw members of the AK. Such a collection of light weapons might have been sufficient to launch an urban terror campaign, but not to seize control of the city. As one resistance officer wrote later, "It was easier to part with a girl[friend] than with a rifle."[7]

If Komorowski did nothing, however, the Soviets would occupy the Polish capital and impose their own puppet government, ending any chance for what he and his assistants defined as Polish liberty. To further complicate his calculations, Komorowski knew that the AK was a hodgepodge of political groups that might desert the organization if their leaders stood idle in the crisis. After five years of occupation, the Poles were more interested in striking at the hated Germans than in debating policies about the arriving Soviets.

The exile government in London was not only far from the battlefield but also leaderless at the moment of decision. In late July 1944, Prime Minister Mikolajczyk left for Moscow in a vain effort to reach some accommodation with Stalin. Before his departure, Mikolajczyk had authorized his political representative inside Poland, J. S. Jankowski, to order a rising on his own initiative if the circumstances seemed favorable. The Polish commander-in-chief, General Kazimierz Sosnkowski, had also abdicated his responsibility. Sosnkowski had privately encouraged the Home Army to make its own decisions without waiting for civil authority. Fearing that Mikolajczyk would concede too much to the Soviets, the senior Polish military leader deliberately put himself out of communication with the prime minister and the Home Army so that he could not be ordered to surrender to the Soviets. At the end of July, Sosnkowski embarked on an inspection tour of Polish exile units in Italy and ignored repeated urgings to return to London. By some accounts, the general had forbidden any uprising without a prior agreement with the Soviets; unfortunately, the London government had censored these statements out of its messages to Warsaw.[8]

The British and American governments were equally unhelpful. Both Churchill and President Franklin Roosevelt had reluctantly concluded that Stalin's forces would inevitably control Poland at the end of the war, and both had encouraged the exiled Poles to reach an accommodation based on that reality. The U.S.-British Combined Chiefs of Staff had not even recognized the Home Army as part of their forces, saying that Poland fell outside of their strategic sphere.[9]

Left to decide on their own, Komorowski and his staff hesitated for several days in late July. Broadcasting in Polish, Soviet radios called on the Poles to rise up against the occupation. A rival communist resistance group, the People's Army, issued a proclamation on July 29, falsely claiming that the AK leadership had deserted Warsaw and again calling on the populace to rebel. On the afternoon of July 31, the AK staff, dressed in nondescript civilian clothes, assembled at their secret headquarters in Warsaw to learn of the prime minister's trip to Moscow. They hoped that this would initiate cooperation between the AK and the Red Army. Then the AK commander for the city, Colonel Antoni Chrusciel, arrived with a report that Soviet tanks were entering Praga, a Warsaw suburb on the eastern bank of the Vistula. With the Red Army seemingly only hours away, it appeared imperative that the AK seize the capital and establish its own, pro-London government before the Soviets could introduce their puppets. Komorowski summoned the underground political leadership, including Jankowski, who endorsed the military's plan to begin the uprising at 5 P.M. the next day, August 1, 1944. They confidently expected that the British and Americans would force the Soviets to come to their aid.[10]

The result was an epic of missed opportunities and gallant futility. The Home Army failed to secure the four bridges across the Vistula, without which it had little hope of linking up with the Soviets. After the first few days of fighting, the Germans were able to regain control of major routes through the city, dividing the rebels into five separate segments that were systematically defeated, block by block. Outraged by the Polish rising, Heinrich Himmler ordered various SS police units, composed in equal parts of violent criminals and Soviet turncoats, to subdue the city. The result was a crime wave that horrified not only the Polish population but even the German governor, SS general Erich von dem Back-Zelewski. Back-Zelewski had been heavily involved in genocide killings, but he eventually countermanded Hitler's orders to execute women and children, and demanded that the worst SS thugs be withdrawn. Ultimately, the German commander even offered surrendering AK partisans the legal status of prisoners of war.[11]

While the Germans cleared block after block of Warsaw, the defenders waited in vain for reinforcements. With complete disregard for the staggering distances and logistical problems involved, Polish commanders demanded that the British and Americans deliver to the battlefield not only weapons but also whole formations of the Polish exile army and air force. The best that the British could provide was a forlorn stream of long-range bombers dropping weapon containers over the stricken city, hoping that at least some of those containers would reach the Home Army.

The rising that was supposed to hold out for a few hours or days dragged on for weeks, and still the Red Army did not arrive. In hindsight, Komorowski and the other soldiers commanding the AK should have realized that, at the end of a three-hundred-kilometer mechanized advance, the Soviet spearheads had already expended most of their ammunition, fuel, and manpower. Major General N. D. Vedeneev's 3rd Tank Corps reached a point within fifteen kilometers of Warsaw on July 30, but there a German counterattack struck Vedeneev's depleted spearheads. Most of the German armored units involved were also severely under strength. In the crisis, however, the Germans assembled more than one hundred self-propelled guns normally assigned to police security units. These guns ambushed Vedeneev's lead elements outside Warsaw. Then, over the next few days, the German defenders were joined by 4th Panzer Division and 5th SS Division Viking severely mauling Vedeneev and other elements of the Soviet Second Tank Army. By August 5 the Soviets had lost the initiative and were stalled east of Warsaw. They did not resume the advance until late August, and did not approach the suburbs of Warsaw until September 13, six weeks after Colonel Chrusciel had announced their imminent arrival. In fact, Warsaw did not finally fall into Soviet hands until January 1945.[12]

Churchill repeatedly urged Stalin to aid the Home Army, but with little success. On August 5, the Soviet leader replied to one such appeal from the British prime minister: "I think that the information which has been communicated to you by the Poles is greatly exaggerated and does not inspire confidence. . . . The Home Army of the Poles consists of a few detachments which they incorrectly call divisions. They have neither artillery nor aircraft nor tanks. I cannot imagine how such detachments can capture Warsaw."[13]

Following their defeat in early August, the Soviets apparently did make further efforts to relieve the defenders of Warsaw.[14] Yet, to overcome the German defenses in the area, the Red Army would have had to abandon its future plans and completely reorient its troops and supplies to break into the capital. A pause was inevitable to allow time for the Soviet units to rebuild their strength. Even if they had succeeded, the Russians would have faced a bitter struggle to clear the Germans from the ruined city, a city that would have formed an unsuitable base from which to launch a new offensive. Long after the events, the memoirs of Soviet commanders continued to blame the Poles for failing to communicate and cooperate with the Red Army, whereas both sides were equally at fault.

If relieving Warsaw was impractical, there was still little military justification for the Soviet failure to aid the defenders and thereby wear down the Germans. In particular, the Western Allies asked for permission to use a preexisting system, known as Operation Frantic, to supply the Poles. Under Frantic procedures, B-17 Flying Fortresses of the U.S. Army's Eighth Air Force regularly conducted shuttle raids, flying from Britain over Germany to bomb deep targets and then continuing on to an airfield in the Ukraine. A few days later, the process would be reversed. However, the Soviet government initially refused to authorize the use of the Frantic base to aid the Home Army. On August 16, Deputy Foreign Minister Andrei Vyshinsky replied to such a request by saying that the Soviets "decidedly object to American or British aircraft, after dropping arms in the region of Warsaw, landing on Soviet territory, since the Soviet government did not wish to associate themselves either directly or indirectly with the adventure in Warsaw."[15]

Stalin finally relented in mid-September, but by that time the partisan enclaves had become so reduced in size that they were too small to serve as drop zones, especially for high-altitude delivery. One hundred and seven B-17s dropped a total of 1,284 weapons containers over the city on the 18th, but only 228 of those containers actually reached the Home Army.[16] In late September, the Soviets themselves flew air cover and dropped some supplies to the defenders, although this assistance arrived far too late.

The Home Army held out until October 4, 1944, a total of sixty-three days. Without adequate arms, the Poles nonetheless tied up more than 21,000 German troops. The Warsaw Uprising cost at least 17,200 Poles killed or missing, and inflicted almost equal casualties on their better-equipped and -trained foes.[17]

At the time and for decades thereafter, the Western Allies reproached the Soviets for not doing enough to help the Home Army. Such criticism of the Red Army, which suffered half a million casualties to reach Warsaw, became a self-fulfilling prophesy. The issue simply confirmed Stalin's belief that the Home Army and the London exile government were implacable foes of the Soviet Union, and thus the deaths of Poles and Germans alike only simplified the task of conquering Poland in order to provide for postwar Soviet security.[18]

ATHENS, GREECE, DECEMBER 11, 1944

Field Marshal Harold Alexander had just become the Allied Commander-in-Chief for the Mediterranean Theater, but his first duty had nothing to do with defeating Germany. Instead, he flew into an airfield outside Athens in an attempt to resolve a weeklong struggle between the liberating British forces and the dominant resistance organization in Greece, an alliance of left-wing groups known as the National Popular Liberation Army, or ELAS. The British were convinced that ELAS was a wholly owned subsidiary of the Greek Communist Party. When

Alexander asked for transportation from the airfield to the capital, he learned that he needed an armored vehicle because the route was under sniper fire from ELAS. Moreover, ELAS controlled the telephone system between the two British enclaves. As Alexander related later,

> Not a happy welcome! However, the Communists obligingly put through my call to the commander of our troops in Athens, [Lieutenant] General Ronald Scobie, who by now had some 5,000 men at his disposal, and in due time two armoured-cars arrived to take us the six or seven miles to Athens. We bought a lot of bullets on the journey—we could hear them hitting the outside of my armoured-car—but we were not stopped.
>
> When I arrived at General Scobie's headquarters . . . I learnt that the Communists were in control of most of the city, and that only the centre, an area which embraced British Military headquarters and the British Embassy, was still in our hand . . . I was told that we had only three days' supply of food.[19]

Thus, while World War II still raged a few hundred miles to the northwest in Italy, Greece was convulsed by what the British regarded as a communist-inspired civil war, an apparent attempt by the Soviet Union to extend its control into the Mediterranean. As Churchill wrote on December 22, "If the powers of evil prevail in Greece, as is quite likely, we must be prepared for a quasi-Bolshevised Russian-led Balkan peninsula, and this may spread to Italy and Hungary."[20]

The reality was far more complex than Churchill, a longtime opponent of communism, was willing to acknowledge. The Moscow government had almost no contact with or interest in ELAS, which was a home-grown product of the many different forces and long-standing political divisions in Greek society. Instead, the Communists and other elements of ELAS were justifiably concerned that the British-backed right-wing government would resume its prewar persecution of all leftists.

Prior to the Axis occupation of 1941, Greece had experienced a long history of social unrest and political upheaval. Despite efforts at land reform, the majority of Greeks remained desperately poor. After a series of coup attempts, a republican government ruled the country from 1923 until 1935, when the monarchy was restored. Only a year later, dreading a Spanish-style left-wing civil war, King George II dissolved Parliament and gave dictatorial powers to retired General Ioannis Metaxas.[21] This dictatorship not only emasculated the mainline political parties but also tainted the monarchy in the eyes of many Greeks. Most of the leadership groups in Greek society lost their legitimacy and shared suffering reduced prewar social distinctions. Small wonder, therefore, that during World War II, the Greek Communist Party and other left-wing groups formed the effective resistance force ELAS and its political counterpart EAM, or that many in the resistance opposed the return of King George and his British-backed exile government. Recognizing this, in February 1942, George officially terminated the dictatorship and restored the 1911 constitution. Still, the exile government was so averse to popular movements that it never encouraged the resistance at home.[22]

In March 1943, major units of the exiled government's army and navy mutinied in Egypt, although there was no direct connection between this mutiny and ELAS. Royalist officers and the British Army crushed the mutiny, but King George recognized the popular dissatisfaction involved and promised that he would not return to Greece until a plebiscite decided the future of the monarchy.

In May 1944, EAM/ELAS, the noncommunist National Republican Hellenic League (EDES), and the exiled politician George Papandreou reached an uneasy deal to share power in the so-called Lebanon Agreement. This agreement did not prevent a violent struggle over spheres of influence between ELAS and the much smaller EDES. In July, a Soviet inspection team arrived in Greece, where the visitors found ELAS to be much weaker than Yugoslav communist leader Tito's equivalent force. To the Soviets, therefore, ELAS had little chance of establishing communist rule by force. The leader of this mission, Lieutenant Colonel Grigorii Popov, told EAM/ELAS leaders to seek compromise with the Papandreou government. By the Caserta Treaty of September 26, 1944, ELAS and EDES agreed to take orders from the British commander when the Allies reentered Greece.[23]

A related issue was the fate of the security battalions that had helped the Axis occupiers fight the resistance. Depending on one's political hue, these men were either fascist traitors serving the oppressor or protectors of the innocent from the depredations of communist bandits. When the Germans began to evacuate Greece in the fall of 1944, ELAS troops massacred both the security battalions and the

Greek villagers who had supported them. The left was outraged when, upon returning from exile, the Papandreou government and its British allies not only protected veterans of the security battalions but appointed some of them to lead the new paramilitary National Guard.[24] Meanwhile, a royalist underground organization known simply as X began to assassinate leftists in Athens. Liberals as well as Communists feared that the right-wing officers of the returning government and their peers in the security battalions would reimpose a repressive, royalist regime.

Given this background, conflict was probably inevitable. As early as November 7, 1944, Churchill wrote to his foreign secretary, Anthony Eden, that "I fully expect a clash with E.A.M., and we must not shrink from it."[25] The British believed that they were restoring legitimate constitutional democracy in the teeth of a communist conspiracy, a conspiracy that violated Stalin's promise to Churchill that the British would have predominant influence in Greece.[26] Yet, for many Greeks, communist or otherwise, the exile government was scarcely more desirable than the Axis occupiers, and EAM and ELAS were the only hope for a democratic future. ELAS leaders did not plan to seize power in late 1944, but neither were they willing to let the right wing resume its dominance in Greek politics.

To prevent violence, Churchill and General Scobie pressed for the demobilization of all resistance formations, which would have left power in the hands of the British Army and the royalist government. The ELAS commander, General Stefanos Sarafis, insisted that he would obey operational instructions from Scobie in accordance with the Caserta Treaty, but that demobilization was a domestic matter to be settled by the Greeks. Understandably, ELAS/EAM leaders did not trust either the British or Papandreou to create a fair, democratic society in Greece. To compound the matter, the British had withdrawn most of the Special Operations Executive (SOE) officers who had worked with the Greek resistance during the Axis occupation, thereby depriving Scobie of the people best qualified to understand and negotiate with ELAS. In late November, various compromise proposals were discussed, including one that would have created a new national army in which the number of ELAS veterans would match the total strength of units from the royalist government and EDES. Sarafis, however, wanted all three forces to be integrated down to company and platoon level so that the ELAS force might not be ordered away from the capital while the right-wing units seized power. The British officers, trained to think in terms of unit identity and cohesion, interpreted this as a demand for complete dissolution of the royalist army, and negotiations foundered.[27]

On December 2, 1944, the pro-EAM ministers resigned, and the remainder of the cabinet voted to dissolve all guerrilla groups and order all officers, including those serving with ELAS, to report to the War Ministry for reassignment. The next day, the Greek Communist Party (KKE) called a mass meeting in Syntagma Square in Athens, defying a government ban on such activities. A violent confrontation ensued in which as many as twenty-eight people died, with the blame attributed mostly to excessive force by the royalist police. Since most Greeks still despised the police because of their collaboration with the Axis occupiers, the policemen feared for their lives. After this clash, Papandreou attempted to resign, but Churchill refused to allow it. Civil war seemed inevitable, and Churchill told Scobie, "Do not hesitate to act as if you were in a conquered city where a local rebellion is in progress."[28]

General Scobie was hardly in a position to obey this instruction, however. Weakened by the 1943 mutinies, the Greek royal government's forces were ill prepared for confrontation. This government had brought only a few loyal units back to Greece, specifically the Rimini Mountain Brigade, the all-officer Sacred Band of near-battalion strength, and a few hundred paramilitary policemen. The British III Corps was scarcely better prepared. Scobie had a nominal strength of 26,500, supported by five British and Greek fighter squadrons. However, most of the British troops were engineers and other specialists, scattered about the countryside in an effort to feed the people and restore the shattered infrastructure of Greece. When violence broke out, many of these soldiers and their precious supply dumps and motor vehicles were promptly captured by ELAS. In mid-November, the British had decided to divert two brigades of the 4th Indian Division, en route from Italy to Egypt, to Greece. Even when these brigades arrived, however, the actual combat power of the British was initially quite limited.[29]

At the time, ELAS had an organized strength of almost 49,000, but its effective force was considerably less. ELAS, like the British Army, was spread throughout the country, while many of its soldiers wanted nothing more than an end to violence. Moreover, Athens was not the only flashpoint; in mid-December, General Safaris led three divisions—15,000 of his best troops—to northwest Greece to defeat the conservative EDES. In any event, ELAS was essentially an amateur guerrilla force, not a true army. Major General Manolis Mandakas, the ELAS commander in the capital area, had as many as seventy artillery pieces, primarily captured from the Italians, but he was short of artillery ammunition and lacked junior leaders with the training necessary for sustained urban combat. A planned ELAS attack on the night of December 15–16 failed because the insurgent commanders could not coordinate their units inside the city.[30]

What the British did not know, or at least refused to believe, was that EAM/ELAS was acting entirely without orders from Stalin. In the midst of the December confrontation, Petros Roussas, a member of the central committee of the Greek Communist Party, attempted to travel to Moscow to get support. Instead of welcoming him, Stalin had Roussas arrested and deported![31] This rebuff, combined with remaining hopes for a peaceful solution, may explain ELAS's failure to press the battle before British reinforcements arrived.

In mid-December, a lull in the fighting occurred as both sides consolidated their forces, and Sarafis attacked EDES in the west. On December 17, Churchill asked Alexander if there was any danger of a British surrender in Athens. After a failed attack on the 18th, ELAS captured Kiphassia Airfield outside Athens on December 20, taking 250 prisoners from the Royal Air Force. Meanwhile the British and various Greek factions fought house to house in Athens and the nearby port of Piraeus. During this bitter struggle, Field Marshal Alexander flew in the commander of X Corps, Lieutenant General John Hawksworth, to assume tactical control. Scobie remained in overall command because of his standing with the Greek royalists. In addition to 4th Division, the British eventually deployed a tank regiment and two brigades of 46th British Division. On the 20th, Scobie warned the populace of Athens to take shelter before Hawksworth launched a counterattack. ELAS sustained significant casualties and its morale suffered. In six days of heavy fighting, the British gradually gained the initiative in the Athens area, but Alexander told his prime minister that only a political settlement would resolve the conflict. Anxious to focus his limited forces on the ongoing Italian campaign, Alexander reminded Churchill that the Greek resistance had kept at least six Axis divisions busy for years.[32]

For ten days, Alexander, British Minister for the Mediterranean Harold Macmillan, and Ambassador to Greece Reginald Leeper all urged that Archbishop Damaskinos of Athens head a temporary government as regent. Damaskinos had a national reputation for defying the German occupation, having openly denounced the forced deportation of Jews and Greek laborers. His appointment would be a clear gesture that King George would not return home without popular approval. Neither Churchill nor King George wanted to make such a compromise. Further complicating matters, many Americans believed the British were supporting authoritarian monarchists versus the true democrats in Greece. The newly appointed U.S. secretary of state, Edward R. Stettinius, made a speech in which he indirectly criticized British policy in Greece.[33]

Churchill finally decided to see the situation in person, flying to Greece on Christmas Day 1944. Shells were still falling the next day when he traveled to central Athens, and leftists tried to plant a bomb in the sewers underneath the Grande Bretagne Hotel where he was expected to meet with local leaders. Despite these obstacles, the British succeeded in assembling a broad group of leaders for the Athens conference, December 26–28, 1944. Representatives of all parties participated, including three EAM leaders ironically dressed in British-supplied field uniforms. Even General Nikolaos Plastiras, leader of the 1923 republican coup, was present. In addition to British civil and military officials, Churchill carefully included both the U.S. ambassador and the Soviet representative, Colonel Popov. Archbishop Damaskinos, whose considerable height was increased by the cylindrical black hat of his office, chaired the meeting. Churchill began by appealing to the Greeks for compromise, and Field Marshal Alexander remarked icily that Greek troops should be fighting the Germans in Italy rather than the British at home. Then Churchill led the foreigners out of the room, leaving the Greeks to debate among themselves.[34]

For three days the arguments and recriminations raged, covering more than two decades of violent politics and four years of Axis occupation. At one point, General Plastiras and the acting head of the Greek Communist Party, George Siantos, almost came to blows, threatening each other with the gutter language they had learned while growing up in the same village. The only consensus of the meeting was to recognize the archbishop as interim ruler.

While conference participants struggled in vain to reach agreement, the fighting continued, with ELAS gradually losing ground. On the 29th, after the conference terminated, General Hawksworth's troops overran the headquarters of the ELAS 13th Division, effectively clearing the city. By December 31, the Greek royalist and British forces had overcome the last ELAS stronghold in the area, on Mount Parnassus.[35]

Churchill returned to England impressed by Damaskinos's presence and fervent anticommunism. Nonetheless, George II remained opposed to appointing a regent, which would impede his own return to power. The nocturnal prime minister followed his usual practice, staying up all night on December 30, until those around him, including the Greek monarch, were exhausted. At one point, Churchill told George that if he did not agree, Britain would abandon the king and recognize a new Greek government under the archbishop. By dint of such badgering, the British leader finally persuaded George to appoint Damaskinos. To add insult to injury, Damaskinos in turn named the republican General Plastiras as prime minister.[36]

Having gained the upper hand both militarily and politically, General Scobie was able to impose a truce in mid-January 1945, after which the regent's government met with EAM/ELAS delegates in early February. The misperceptions of the right wing were evident when the government representatives initially demanded to negotiate only with the Greek Communist Party, not understanding the multiparty coalition of EAM. After considerable efforts by Macmillan and Leeper, however, the two sides reached the Verzika Agreement of February 12, 1945. Under a simultaneous military agreement with the British, General Sarafis demobilized ELAS and surrendered large numbers of weapons, although die-hards concealed other guns for future action. In return, the Greek government declared an amnesty and an end to martial law, and promised both a purge of security forces and a referendum on the future form of Greek government. The leftists were either too weak or too naïve to insist on complete immunity from prosecution, however, and outside of Athens the agreement did not even require arrest warrants to apprehend those accused of lawbreaking. Still, war-torn Greece returned to an uneasy peace, and the KKE was a legal political party for the first time since 1936.[37]

The Battle of Athens, sometimes known as the second act of the Greek Civil War, was the wrong fight at the wrong a time. The hesitant, halfhearted actions of EAM and ELAS strongly suggest that this was not a planned revolution but rather an accidental conflict resulting from the clash of the left-wing resistance with the reactionary leaders of the British and exiled Greek governments. For its part, the British Army had committed 75,000 troops to Greece and lost 237 soldiers killed and more than 1,800 wounded, a tragic waste at a time when every man was needed in Italy.[38] Bitter feuds of the interwar and occupation eras had come to a boil while World War II still raged, and few Greeks believed that these issues had been resolved.

Saigon, September 26, 1945

There were simply too many foreigners in Southeast Asia.[39]

First, of course, were the French, who in 1862 had established a colony with Saigon as its capital. By 1885 they had taken over most of Southeast Asia, including what is now Laos, Cambodia, and Vietnam, and codified their conquest in a treaty with the imperial Chinese government. That did not mean that the local population accepted the occupation, of course—frequent uprisings occurred throughout the history of the colony. Still, French rule continued even after Nazi Germany had conquered France in 1940. In defeat, the French nation split into two factions—the majority, including most of the administration of French Indochina, remained loyal to the so-called Vichy regime that collaborated with the Germans, while more adventurous souls supported the exile or "Free French" government of acting Brigadier General Charles de Gaulle. A few brave men and women remained within the Vichy administration while secretly working for the Allies.

Next came the Japanese. Taking advantage of Vichy's weakness, during 1940–1941 Japan demanded concessions from French Indochina. Local French forces suffered eight hundred casualties resisting the Japanese invasion and eventually had to bow to the stronger foe.[40] By the time Tokyo attacked the United States in December 1941, there were 50,000 Japanese troops on bases in the French colonies of Southeast Asia. For five years, Tokyo permitted the Vichyite administration to continue functioning, provided that it furnished the Japanese with raw materials and transportation. To keep the French off balance, the Japanese also provided some encouragement to Vietnamese resistance groups, including the local Communists. All this changed on March 9, 1945, when increasing French resistance efforts and the approach of Allied forces prompted the Japanese to seize complete control of what is now Vietnam. Thousands of French soldiers and administrators were imprisoned, while others escaped into the interior and retreated northwest toward China. Two days after the coup, Vietnam's traditional ruler, Emperor Bao Dai, proclaimed an independent government that was actually a Japanese puppet. This sequence of events, in which the hated European masters had first submitted to an Asian power and then were imprisoned by it, had a profound effect on public opinion in Asia. Vietnamese nationalists saw that the Europeans were vulnerable, and French colonial rule was permanently discredited. As Peter Dunn has observed, "The French . . . surrendered the Mandate [of Heaven] when they were humiliated by the Japanese in March 1945, although it took some time for them to understand that."[41]

On August 11, 1945, it was Japan's turn to sue for peace, declaring an armistice. Yet, with the exception of those troops fighting the British in Burma, the Japanese forces in Southeast Asia remained a formidable enemy; their commanders obeyed Emperor Hirohito's order to cease hostilities, but they were by no means convinced that they had lost the war. Furthermore, the victors held the Japanese responsible for maintaining order until Allied troops could arrive. Because of this precarious situation, General Douglas MacArthur, the overall commander for the occupation of Japan, instructed other Allied forces to delay any occupation of the region until the surrender had been formalized in Tokyo, an event that did not occur until September 2. During the late summer and fall of 1945, therefore, Japanese forces remained in position in Indochina while French colonial administrators and Allied prisoners of war languished in Japanese camps. Even after Allied troops arrived belatedly, the Japanese remained armed and active in shaping political developments.

The Allies were another force in the region, but they were divided by both geography and policy. In October 1944, an Allied agreement allocated responsibility for Southeast Asia to the newly created China Theater, where Lieutenant General Alfred C. Wedemeyer was both the U.S. forces commander and chief of staff to Chinese Generalissimo Chiang Kai-shek (Jiang Jieshi). Wedemeyer attempted to continue the preexisting U.S. policy that opposed postwar colonial rule by France. Most American leaders had no interest in expending people or resources to help their allies—British, French, Greek, or Chinese—reimpose the imperial or dictatorial governments that had existed before the war.

President Franklin Roosevelt was particularly suspicious of Free French attempts to regain control of its Indo-Chinese colonies. Thus, when the Free French created a special unit of soldiers to infiltrate Vietnam, the United States refused to provide transportation for this unit and impeded Free French efforts to operate out of China. Similarly, the United States gave little help to those French troops who escaped from northern Vietnam after the Japanese takeover.[42] Otherwise, official U.S. policy was to avoid involvement in the area, although the Office of Strategic Services (OSS), America's wartime organization for espionage and covert operations, frequently violated that neutrality.

By contrast, Vice-Admiral Lord Louis Mountbatten and his Southeast Asia Command (SEAC) were much more interested in encouraging resistance to the Japanese in Vietnam and in helping the French regain control of their colonies. Although Vietnam belonged on paper to the China Theater's area of operations, Mountbatten believed that he had an agreement with Chiang Kai-shek that permitted British support for resistance forces in the region. In retrospect, it appears that Chiang never communicated this agreement to his own chief of staff, Wedemeyer, thereby compounding the confusion. The two allied commands disagreed about this matter for months in 1944–1945, with tragic consequences. The British and American governments had radically different plans for Indochina, contributing to the ultimate breakdown of order. In addition, when Mountbatten tried to supply resistance forces in the region without Wedemeyer's knowledge, U.S. night fighters apparently shot down several Royal Air Force aircraft by mistake. In May 1945, Wedemeyer finally asked for clarification on the issue from the two governments and the U.S.-British Combined Chiefs of Staff. With the death of President Roosevelt, however, Washington was no longer willing to oppose a French return to the former colonies. At the Allied Potsdam Conference of July 1945, the British tried to transfer the entire region from Wedemeyer in the China Theater to Mountbatten in SEAC but finally compromised on a plan that divided the region horizontally along the 16th parallel. Once the Japanese surrendered, this division meant that the Chinese Army would occupy the northern portions of Vietnam and Laos, while the rest of the region became the responsibility of SEAC.[43]

SEAC was caught off guard by the sudden Japanese armistice. The command had always been last in priority for Allied resources, and now both the U.S. and British governments wanted to demobilize as quickly as possible. Mountbatten found himself short of the essentials he needed to assume control of the vast region of Southeast Asia and what is now Indonesia—transportation, civil affairs experts, signal corps units, combat forces, and even spare parts. Only the under-strength 20th Indian Division was available to reoccupy southern Vietnam, and Mountbatten lacked the aircraft and ships to move this division rapidly. Moreover, as noted above, SEAC had to negotiate a surrender with the numerically superior and generally resentful Japanese forces in the region. A medical team with some supplies parachuted in to assist the prisoners of war, but the first British troops did not arrive in southern Vietnam until September 6. On that date, a tiny advance party, including less than one platoon of infantry, landed at Tan Son Nhut Airbase. A larger British force, consisting of four companies of infantry plus a brigade and division tactical headquarters, arrived by air starting on September 13, but they were still far outnumbered by the Japanese.[44]

Vietnamese resistance movements, and especially the Viet Minh organization of Ho Chi Minh, exploited the contradictions and interstices between these various foreign groups. Ho (previously known as Nguyen Ai Quoc) served for decades as an agent of the Communist International; he was unquestionably a devoted exponent of Marxism-Leninism, although he probably came to that belief through his desire to free his country from the French.[45] Regardless of his true motivations, Ho had accepted aid from almost every domestic and foreign group, building up a political and military structure within Vietnam during the war. Like ELAS, the Viet Minh was a broadly-based patriotic front whose leadership was heavily communist; "Viet Minh," in fact, was a shortened version of the Vietnamese for "League for the Independence of Vietnam."

Despite the official American policy of "hands off" Indochina, Ho found ways to get at least the appearance of American support in 1944–1945. Operating from China but outside of Wedemeyer's control, OSS Detachment 202 worked with various Southeast Asian groups, including the Viet Minh. At first, the United States restricted itself to rescuing downed Allied aircrews, but eventually the OSS provided training and weapons for the anti-Japanese guerrillas. The fact that such guerrillas would also oppose the French was of little concern to Americans interested in defeating Japan but not in restoring French power.[46]

The Indo-Chinese Communist Party (ICP) numbered fewer than 5,000 members in 1945, but with both the French and the Japanese defeated, the ICP was able to rally Vietnamese nationalists of all different political hues. On August 16, the ICP convened a Viet Minh People's Congress at Tan Trao; the meeting was sometimes referred to as the "Lightning Session" because it met and adjourned so quickly that many non-Communists did not arrive in time to participate. This "congress" endorsed Viet Minh calls for independence and general insurrection with a ten-point program of foreign and domestic policies that included giving land to the peasants. Beginning on August 19 in Hanoi, the Viet Minh orchestrated vast nationalist demonstrations while hit squads assassinated potential opponents. By the 23rd, Bao Dai decided to abdicate after a nominal reign of only five months. The day before the abdication, a joint OSS-Army Air Force team led by Major Archimedes Patti arrived in Hanoi, ostensibly to collect information and evacuate Allied prisoners. Major Patti quickly concluded that any French attempt to reassert control would precipitate a civil war. Perhaps unwittingly, the presence of a few OSS officers in uniform gave the appearance of U.S. support to Ho's patriotic proceedings.[47]

Charles de Gaulle wanted to reassert French sovereignty as quickly as possible. He intended to prepare the Indo-Chinese colonies for eventual autonomy within a French federation but failed to make this intention clear in public, thereby tying the hands of his representatives. With British assistance, three-man teams of Free Frenchmen, originally intended to reconnoiter the situation, parachuted into Vietnam in late August in a foolhardy attempt to regain control. The division between the China and Southeast Asia Theaters again produced different results. In the north, the Viet Minh captured all seven teams, executing most of the men involved. In the south, where similar teams fell into Japanese hands, Mountbatten telegraphed the Japanese commander that their leader, Colonel Cedille, represented both the French government and SEAC. With this backing and considerable audacity, Cedille escaped Japanese house arrest and almost succeeded in restoring government in Saigon, but lacked the strength to hold what he had seized.[48]

On September 2, Japan formally surrendered in Tokyo Bay. At the ceremony, General MacArthur told the French representative, General Philippe Leclerc, to move into Indochina as quickly as possible to regain control. Leclerc had been asking for airlift to do just that for months, but he was too late.

On the same day as the Japanese surrender, Ho Chi Minh appeared on the balcony of the Hanoi Opera House. Speaking to a crowd estimated at half a million Vietnamese, he declared the independence of Vietnam. Deliberately appealing to Western traditions of liberty, Ho's declaration began with the "Life, Liberty, and the pursuit of Happiness" passage from the American Declaration of Independence, followed by a litany of accusations against the French that closely paralleled the American grievances of 1776. Not all Americans were impressed by this declaration, however. On September 20, Brigadier General Philip Gallagher reported from Hanoi that Ho Chi Minh "is an old revolutionist . . . a product of Moscow, a communist."[49]

In Saigon, however, a similar effort ended in disaster. Different Vietnamese groups quarreled with each other, and a vengeful mob murdered six Frenchmen. This shattered the illusion of Viet Minh control over the country and paved the way for growing antagonism between the Vietnamese forces on one side and the British and French on the other.[50]

In the midst of this power vacuum, the OSS arrived in southern Vietnam. Operating out of Mountbatten's base in Ceylon, OSS Detachment 404 sent its own intelligence and observer element, known by the codename "Embankment," to accompany the British. Like its counterpart in the north, Embankment was supposed to evacuate American prisoners, gather information, and avoid involvement in the postwar political situation. Again like its northern counterpart, Embankment achieved the first two missions but failed to remain neutral.

On September 1, even before the British arrived, a prisoner of war evacuation team from Embankment parachuted near Saigon, where it was treated respectfully by the Japanese. This tiny group, led by 1st Lieutenant Emile R. Connasse, witnessed the riots of September 2 and attempted to protect French civilians in the city. On the 4th, the main body of Embankment arrived under the command of Major A. Peter Dewey. In his efforts to protect civilians and gather information, Dewey established close contacts with local leaders of the Viet Minh. Major General Douglas D. Gracey, the British commander of 20th Division and head of the Armistice Control Commission in the south, understandably resented this activity on the part of a junior American officer. In Gracey's mind, Dewey's dealings could be interpreted as official U.S. recognition for and even support of the Viet Minh. On the 14th, Gracey ordered the Embankment team to cease all intelligence activities until its mission was clarified, an order that Dewey apparently ignored.[51]

Meanwhile relations deteriorated between the British and French forces on one side and the Viet Minh and its supporters on the other. It took days of negotiation for Colonel Cedile, the French representative, to arrange the release of his compatriots from Japanese and Viet Minh prisons. The Japanese, who far outnumbered the European forces, allowed various local groups to attack Frenchmen with impunity. To prevent further violence and casualties, General Gracey launched a coup on the night of September 22–23, 1945, to evict the Viet Minh from power in Saigon. Fifteen hundred Indian Army troops, supported by three hundred Frenchmen, including ex-POWs and armed civilians, seized control of key installations in and around the city—communications, prisons, police stations, and the like. The coup was successful, but the Vietnamese nationalists were enraged. On the night of September 24–25, a Vietnamese mob murdered almost 150 French civilians in north-central Saigon.[52]

The fact that the French used American uniforms and equipment may have been partly responsible for the sequel to this coup on September 26. On that date, Major Dewey and his executive officer, Captain Herbert Bluechel, were stopped at a Vietnamese roadblock that they had previously passed without difficulty. The operators of this roadblock—apparently a band of the Avant Garde youth, a Viet Minh front organization—opened fire. Dewey reportedly leaped from his jeep, announcing in French that he was an American, but was cut down and died immediately. A wounded Bluechel escaped to an OSS villa nearby, where the Americans fought off another attack until a company of the 1st Gurkha Rifles relieved them and dispersed the attackers.[53]

Although numerous Americans, especially aircrew members, had died in Southeast Asia during World War II, Peter Dewey is often described, with considerable justification, as the first American to die in the Vietnam conflict. His assailants may have mistaken him for a Frenchman, but he was certainly part of the lethal cocktail of different nationalities and political beliefs that sparked the violence in which he died. His body was never recovered.

Within a month, the British and French were openly at war with the Viet Minh while the increasingly demoralized units of armed Japanese soldiers continued to complicate the situation. General Gracey's strong action expelled the Viet Minh from Saigon, giving the French a more secure base of operations than they enjoyed in the north. Between October 1945 and January 1946, the 20th Indian Division and other British forces suffered at least 40 killed and 110 wounded, while the estimated Vietnamese deaths during the same period exceeded 1,700.[54] By the time the last British Commonwealth forces left in 1946, the First Indo-Chinese War was in full swing.

The struggles in Warsaw, Athens, and Saigon all involved confrontations between local resistance forces and the Allied troops supposedly arriving to liberate them. Moreover, in all three cases the U.S. government proved reluctant to become involved, while Britain, in its waning days as a world power, struggled to maintain order. Indeed, many of America's World War II allies had to bear the violent cost of resolving prewar conflicts that carried over into the postwar period.

All three situations involved fundamental misunderstandings and misperceptions. The Polish Home Army thought that its uprising would force the Soviet Union to recognize and even support its fight; instead, that uprising doomed the Polish nationalist movement. The British and Greek royalist forces regarded ELAS as nothing more than a front for the Greek Communist Party and ultimately for the Soviet Union. In fact, Moscow had no interest in the battle of Athens, and many members of ELAS acted not to advance communism but to prevent a return of right-wing dictatorship. Like the Poles, the failure of their rebellion only facilitated the seizure of power by their worst enemies. The Vietnamese rebels thought of themselves as nationalist freedom fighters and expected American support as a matter of course. Despite the advent of a Socialist Labour government in London in mid-1945, British commanders remained cynically convinced that all opposition to "legitimate" exile governments was communist-inspired, an attitude that helped drive nationalist and democratic groups into the arms of the Marxists. Nationalism, Marxism-Leninism, conservatism, fascism, and democracy may be clearly differentiated in theory, but they were hopelessly confused in practice. Well-intentioned Poles, Britons, and Americans, both politicians and soldiers, often found themselves unintentionally contributing to political events for which they felt little sympathy.

2

ORIGINS, INTERESTS,
AND FORCES

As the battles in Warsaw, Athens, and Saigon suggest, the Cold War was inextricably connected to the political and military events that preceded it. The eminent Cold War historian John Lewis Gaddis has written that World War II "had been won by a coalition whose principal members were already at war—ideologically and geopolitically if not militarily—with one another."[1] Yet this generalization does not by itself explain the nature and outcome of the confrontations that followed. Initial points of friction arose for a number of reasons in places where the victorious Allied armies occupied former Axis territories at the close of World War II. In addition, the experiences of that war and of its antecedents strongly colored the perceptions and attitudes of decision makers on both sides.

AGGRESSION AND SUBVERSION

By 1945, most Western politicians and soldiers believed implicitly that the greatest war in history could have been avoided or materially shortened if their predecessors had opposed Axis expansion when it first appeared. The Japanese invasion of Manchuria in 1931, the Italian conquest of Ethiopia in 1935, the German reoccupation of the Rhineland in 1936, and a half-dozen other events appeared in retrospect to be missed opportunities to stop the aggressors short of full-scale global conflict. Instead, at least according to conventional wisdom, too many governments had sought to appease the apparently reasonable demands of the aggressors in a vain effort to avoid war. With the benefit of hindsight, future cold warriors dismissed as unimportant the fact that these appeaser governments had no choice because their armies were unready and their populations unwilling to fight.

Joseph Stalin and his successors undoubtedly shared this perception. Indeed, during the 1930s, the Soviet Union had called in vain for collective security to stop the Axis and believed that many Western leaders would have been quite content to stand aside while the Fascist and Marxist regimes bled each other to death. Moreover, the Soviets like the French were acutely sensitive about any postwar measures that might permit Germany to rise from the ashes and threaten European peace yet again.

In short, one of the few principles on which everyone agreed was that trouble deferred was trouble multiplied—aggression must be nipped in the bud by a firm, confrontational approach to international affairs. Two generations of leaders on both sides of the Iron Curtain were quick to perceive threats to their vital interests, and almost equally quick to take action—diplomatic, military, economic, or otherwise—in response to those threats. Of course, in any given situation, the two sides would disagree completely as to who was the aggressor and who the defender of world peace. In the mid-1970s, for example, the Voroshilov Academy, providing the Soviet Union's highest level of military education, taught its students that American and British foreign policy was designed to aggravate the instability of the Middle East, and that Israel supported Western imperialistic capitalism by defeating the "progressive" regimes of Egypt and Syria. The Soviets viewed themselves as the stabilizing factor in the region, a view that most Americans would have considered absurd.[2]

This is not to suggest that either side was trigger happy or determined to force war on its opponent. In fact, given the shared perception of the "lessons" of World War II, what is astonishing is not the number of battles that occurred during the Cold War, but rather the fact that conflict was not more frequent, more widespread, and more deadly.

Although both sides were agreed on the need to halt overt aggression, they were completely at odds on the role of internal subversion and revolution. By definition, Marxists regarded the 1917 Russian Revolution as the first step in the coming proletarian victory that would destroy capitalism throughout the world. Between the two world wars, the Third or Communist International Working Man's Association, known as the COMINTERN, was the Soviet Union's chosen instrument to advance the cause of that revolution. Founded in 1920, the COMINTERN demanded that all socialist parties and their associated labor unions acknowledge the leadership of Moscow, the first communist regime. In turn, the COMINTERN provided political indoctrination, training, financing, advisors, and if necessary weapons to help its members disrupt economies and overthrow hostile regimes throughout the world. Based on Lenin's view of imperialism as the final, desperate stage of capitalist exploitation, all actions that disrupted capitalist control of markets and resources, even in the most underdeveloped colonies, would hasten the ultimate revolution.

Thousands of Soviet advisors and exiled dissidents received training in Soviet schools. Those groups that received aid from the COMINTERN were by no means always dedicated socialists, of course. Indeed, the Marxist analytical framework, which assumed that all agrarian societies must first pass through the capitalist, bourgeois stage before they could reach the proletarian revolution, often prevented Stalin and others from seeing the potential for immediate revolution in the Third World. During the 1920s, for example, Soviet advisors and aid continued to help the republican, Nationalist Chinese government even after Chiang Kai-shek had repressed the Chinese Communists and demanded that the Soviets stop teaching Marxism in Chinese military schools. In this instance, Moscow was content to advance its influence on the "progressive" Chinese government even at the expense of the local Communists.[3]

The specter of Moscow-supported subversion was very real between the world wars. As a gesture of Allied unity, Stalin dissolved the COMINTERN in 1943. Nonetheless, many Western leaders believed with considerable justification that the Soviet Union continued to encourage unrest and insurrection in many forces. As illustrated by the Battle of Athens, men like Churchill were quick to perceive Stalin's hand even in situations where the local Communists were acting in defiance of instructions from Moscow.

PATTERNS OF INSURGENCY

The Polish Home Army, Greek ELAS, and Viet Minh were all examples of the innumerable resistance movements that thrived both during and after World War II. The repressive nature of Axis domination had inspired such movements in almost every country that experienced occupation during the war.

Local communist and socialist groups were at the forefront of most of these movements. The German invasion of the Soviet Union in June 1941 prompted the COMINTERN to call on all Communists to organize resistance activities in their own countries. Their training and experience in operating undercover gave local Communists in France, Greece, China, Southeast Asia, and many other areas a great advantage over moderate or right-wing insurgents. In many instances, the Communists appeared more interested in recruiting and indoctrinating fighters than in actually attacking the occupying forces, a fact that prompted their rivals to accuse the Communists of preparing for a postwar struggle at the expense of the current resistance effort. In fairness, however, one should acknowledge that the British SOE and American OSS, which supplied and advised the resistance movements, often counseled those groups to avoid conflict and remain hidden until the eve of Allied liberation.

Such advice or direction reflected the very limited role that Allied commanders allocated to unconventional warfare. Although guerrilla forces had existed for centuries if not millennia, they had normally acted as auxiliaries rather than war-winning forces in their own right. To cite one famous example, during the peninsular campaigns against Napoleon, the conventional British-Portuguese Army of Arthur, Duke of Wellington, had benefited enormously from the irregular efforts of Spanish guerrillas. Together, these two very different forces posed a military dilemma, sometimes referred to as Compound Warfare, for which the French Imperial armies had no solution. To control the guerrillas, the French needed to disperse throughout the peninsula, whereas to defeat Wellington, they needed to concentrate their troops in one mass.[4] With some justification, therefore, World War II commanders believed that resistance fighters needed outside supplies or weapons—an outside sanctuary—and ultimately organized conventional forces to achieve major results. The premature uprising of the Polish Home Army, operating far from British and American bases of support, seemed to confirm the general belief that resistance groups by themselves could not stand up to conventional armies. By contrast, resistance groups in France, the occupied Soviet Union, the Philippines, and many other locales had been very effective when operating in cooperation with the conventional Allied forces sent to liberate them.[5]

In sharp contrast to this limited view of insurgency was the theory of protracted, revolutionary warfare developed during the 1930s and 1940s by men such as Mao Tse-tung (Mao Zedong) in China and Vo Nguyen Giap in Indochina. This theory stressed the fundamentally *political* nature of insurgent war, which would involve three stages of development. In Phase I, the insurgent developed popular support among the people and thereby built up his infrastructure while avoiding serious contact with the occupying forces. In many instances, the insurgent appealed to the aspirations of the population for national self-determination, land reform, and the like. If necessary, the insurgent would intimidate or eliminate those members of the population who objected to this program. Without ever firing a weapon, the resulting network of sympathizers provided the small group of armed rebels with intelligence, recruits, food, and concealment.

This political development would continue throughout the protracted struggle for power, but two subsequent phases would in theory superimpose themselves on top of Phase I efforts. In Phase II, the insurgents conducted a prolonged period of unconventional or guerrilla warfare. Although Mao's entire form of revolutionary warfare is sometimes termed "guerrilla" war, guerrilla tactics were largely confined to this second phase. The insurgents attacked only when they had concentrated overwhelming force against an isolated element of their conventional opponents; if forced to fight under adverse circumstances, the insurgents would break contact as quickly as possible, dispersing their forces to fight another day. So long as the insurgents were not completely destroyed, they continued to wear down the enemy's forces and political will. Finally, after a prolonged series of pinprick attacks had weakened and demoralized the occupier or counterrevolutionary government, the growing insurgent forces would enter Phase III, change their tactics to more conventional ones, and seek to destroy the enemy and capture key political terrain, such as the capital city. Regional and even local bands would transition to become part of the revolutionary army, often augmented by defections from their opponents. This was the fundamental *military* innovation of Mao's revolutionary warfare: the idea that an insurgent force did not need an outside conventional army to achieve final victory because it could "grow its own" such force in Phase III.[6]

Such was the theory, at least, of protracted revolutionary warfare, allowing a poorly equipped but well-motivated insurgent to defeat a much stronger opponent over years if not decades of struggle. In practice, of course, the insurgent commander might misjudge the local situation, usually when human impatience and optimism prompted the insurgents to launch a premature effort to seize power. Under such circumstances, the commander might need to retreat from Phase III (semi-conventional, offensive operations) back to Phase II (guerrilla warfare) or even Phase I (political preparation of the population). The keys to eventual success were political determination and persistence rather than firepower and numbers.

During the 1940s, most Western politicians and soldiers were slow to understand or accept this theory of protracted warfare. To a great extent, the difficulty was a political one. Because the defender viewed the insurgent as a Moscow-trained interloper whose Marxist ideas would be of interest only to a few malcontents, that defender often ignored the political issues behind the conflict. Instead, the legal government or occupying power would deny the insurgents' political purpose, branding the rebels "bandits" or "criminals" whose eradication was a matter for the police rather than the armed forces. Even in European colonies, the occupiers convinced themselves that the majority of the population was content with the political situation and would only support the insurgents when coerced.[7] By refusing to address the political, economic, and social issues on which the insurgents based their popular support, the governments in power abandoned the struggle for the "hearts and minds" of the local peoples. Later, when the conflict escalated to Phase II, the government turned to military solutions without in some cases including political or social reforms to satisfy the concerns of the populace. If the government inflicted civilian casualties through excessive force or deliberate reprisals, these casualties only increased the population's hidden support of the insurgents.

Eventually, of course, the political nature of such insurgencies became evident to all concerned. Unfortunately, this realization caused some professional soldiers to become political partisans themselves, as evidenced by the extremism of the French Army in Algeria (see chapter 10). Moreover, conventional soldiers and their political masters were unimpressed with the value of "civic action" efforts to provide better education, public health, and security to the population.

The success of such operations was difficult to measure. Nonetheless, most of the effective counterinsurgency campaigns—in Malaya, the Philippines, and even to some extent Greece—owed their success largely to a government that helped its people and convinced much of the population to support the existing regime, or at least refuse to side with the insurgents.

The Western Allies

The political and diplomatic origins of the Cold War have produced a voluminous historiography, which is beyond the scope of this military study. Nonetheless, a brief examination of the causes of the war is necessary to explain the national and military strategies of the participants. Few historians today would contend that "communist aggression" was the sole or even the primary cause of the Cold War, although it certainly appeared so to many Western observers in the 1940s and 1950s. Instead, the confrontation evolved from a combination of conflicting national interests and misperceptions.

In 1945 Germany and Japan were prostrate while France and Italy were still recovering from four years of occupation and war. There were, therefore, only three states that could claim to be Great Powers. The two obvious powers were the United States and the Soviet Union; the third candidate was Great Britain.[8]

Two world wars in thirty years had reduced Britain from the wealthiest, most powerful nation-state in the world to an exhausted, nearly bankrupt shell. After suffering years of Luftwaffe bombings and U-boat blockades, the British people had had to contend with the V-1 and V-2 missiles in 1944. Although the actual deaths caused by these attacks were limited, the missiles destroyed so many windows that the population, especially in metropolitan London, suffered severe heat loss during the winter of 1944–1945.

By the end of the war, British military power was greatly overextended, with troops trying to maintain order and rebuild society in dozens of countries. Commonwealth countries including Canada, Australia, New Zealand, and South Africa had also exerted their maximum efforts during the war and were anxious to return to peace. Moreover, the British Empire, already restless in the 1930s, was poised for a new series of efforts toward independence, efforts that Britain was ill prepared to resist. The empire and commonwealth had helped

London win World War II, but that war had also accelerated the empire's demise and the weakening of commonwealth ties.

Given this state of national exhaustion, an objective observer might have expected postwar Britain to minimize its overseas commitments and concentrate on rebuilding its economy. Yet, it was precisely that exhaustion that drove British leaders, especially Churchill, in their efforts to restructure the postwar world and achieve some tangible successes in return for all their sacrifices. While few British politicians supported the continuation of the British Empire with Churchill's fanaticism, most could see the need for Britain to remain involved in world affairs. In particular, the prospect of a Europe dominated by Moscow appeared to them to be trading one form of totalitarianism for another. They were prepared to compromise, to recognize the natural Soviet desire for security in Eastern Europe but not to allow total Soviet domination. Instead, Britain sought to be a model democracy, to lead and inspire other European states while maintaining its worldwide influence. In connection with this basic goal, Britain was still saddled with maintaining order between Hindus and Muslims in the Indian subcontinent, and between Jews and Arabs in Palestine. Even after the 1945 election brought the Labour Party to power, British leaders were willing not only to use their own efforts but also to leverage American resources to achieve this goal of a peaceful world where Britain still had influence.[9]

Thus, within the constraints of near-bankruptcy, London attempted to maintain the military and intelligence structure that it had developed during the war. From a peak of 5.1 million men under arms, Britain conducted a gradual demobilization, hampered by the continued need for imperial policing. These requirements meant that the army continued to absorb more men and funds than the Royal Navy or Air Force. Indeed, the shortage of troops for this function undoubtedly hastened the British withdrawal from India and Pakistan in 1947. Although the Labour Party came into office in 1945 with the intention of ending conscription, "national service" had become such a way of life that it continued until 1960; the only immediate change was an end to conscripting women and coal-mining labor.[10] The continued demand for troops throughout the world kept British Army strength above 700,000 in 1949 and in excess of 400,000 into the 1950s. The regular army included seventy-seven infantry and thirty armored battalions, augmented by three Royal Marine Commandos and eight battalions of Gurkhas. Thus the British maintained a post-war force only slightly smaller than the U.S. Army of the same era.[11]

The brilliant wartime record of British intelligence agencies ensured that those agencies would continue into the postwar period with little reorganization, albeit with sharply reduced manpower and budget. The only casualty was the Special Operations Executive, which in 1946 transferred its covert operations responsibilities to the Secret Intelligence Service, sometimes inaccurately referred to as MI6. In addition to resource constraints and somewhat antiquated structure, however, British Intelligence was hampered by the unwitting presence of several highly placed Soviet "moles," of whom the most infamous was "Kim" Philby.[12]

If Britain appeared to be in decline in 1945, the United States was obviously the greatest power in history and the sole possessor of atomic weapons. The U.S. Navy and U.S. Army Air Forces were the largest and most capable such forces in the world, with ninety-nine fleet and escort aircraft carriers and thousands of aircraft.[13] In order to man these services and especially to provide the civilian labor force for the "Arsenal of Democracy," the U.S. Army contained only eighty-nine divisions, plus another six Marine divisions.[14] Although this ground force was far smaller than its Soviet counterpart, the U.S. divisions were lavishly equipped, combat-hardened formations with better artillery support and more motor transportation than any army in the world. In addition, after six years of invasions and aerial bombardments, the United States possessed the only intact, fully functional industrial plant in the world. U.S. Lend-Lease aid, in terms of both weapons and food, had been critical to the continued operations not only of Britain and the Soviet Union, but also of France, China, and numerous other allies.

Of course, a significant number of isolationist politicians, led by men such as Republican Senator Robert Taft of Ohio, resisted the trend toward American involvement in world affairs. Yet, the experience of the previous four years had broadened the horizons of millions of Americans, who appeared willing to perform in their role as a world power even if not yet aware of the cost of that role.

Long before victory in 1945, the U.S. armed forces had developed plans for a robust postwar establishment to maintain that role in world affairs. In January 1944, for example, President Roosevelt approved Joint Chiefs of Staff document 570/2, which called for a worldwide network of airfields for years after the war. That same year, the U.S. Navy had reluctantly reduced its original demobilization plan to what it considered a barebones plan for 550,000 men with a potent aircraft carrier force.[15]

Unfortunately for these plans, U.S. political will and military power were largely ephemeral. As so often before and since, the first instinct of the American people when they had won a great struggle was to demobilize the forces that had made victory possible. Not only were the vast American armies, navies, and air forces doomed to be dismantled, but they didn't even return home as intact units. Instead, in an effort at fairness, official policy allowed individual soldiers to return home by seniority, based on a complicated system of "points" awarded for overseas service, time in combat, and other factors. Consequently, the most experienced divisions became, in a matter of months, skeletons filled with a mixture of veterans and recruits from many other units—strangers to each other who would have been hard-pressed to fight effectively as teams. To cite one example, the 113,000 soldiers, airmen, and Marines who were assigned to the contentious China Theater at the end of 1945 had dwindled to only 12,000 by the end of the following year.[16] Meanwhile, the National Guard and Reserve units that had provided the framework for mobilization in 1940–1941 were in most cases completely dissolved by the individual rotation system, leaving the United States with fewer citizen soldier units than at any time in the previous fifty years. The reserve components had to rebuild themselves from scratch in an environment of public opinion that saw little use for them. By mid-1946, the eighty-nine army divisions of 1944 had withered to sixteen divisions more suited to occupation than to combat, and even this number continued to shrink, bottoming out at fewer than ten divisions in late 1947. The Army Air Forces' 213 combat aircraft groups of 1945 had declined to 63, of which only 11 were fully operational, while the U.S. Navy shrank from 1,166 combat vessels to only 353 ships. The active duty Marine Corps maintained one understrength division with supporting aircraft on each coast.[17]

President Roosevelt and his successor, Harry Truman, were both acutely aware of the irresistible public demand to demobilize. As a founding member of the Reserve Officers Association, Truman made a major political effort in 1945–1946 to enact the longtime goal of many such citizen soldiers, Universal Military Training. UMT was a plan to build a pool of trained soldiers in peacetime through conscripted training followed by part-time service in the reserve components, but the public had no interest in such sacrifices. Both isolationists and well-intentioned pacifists, such as the Friends Committee on National Legislation, labored to thwart the UMT plan. They succeeded but inadvertently worked against their own long-term goals. UMT, after all, was intended to provide for a full mobilization, another world war. Instead, what the United States increasingly needed was a smaller, partial mobilization. By defeating UMT, its opponents actually ensured a revival of the draft (see chapter 4), which was much more flexible as an instrument to provide labor for the sustained readiness of the Cold War.[18]

Meanwhile, Truman felt compelled to slash defense spending to offset the national debt incurred during the depression and the war, a debt that peaked at $269 billion in June 1946.[19] The president was so concerned about the national debt and the accompanying prospect of a renewed depression that he insisted on massive reductions in defense spending throughout the later 1940s. In effect, Truman had not really adjusted to the requirements necessary to function as a world power.

Nor was the U.S. nuclear monopoly the wonder weapon it had first appeared to be. In mid-1946, the entire U.S. stockpile consisted of nine implosion-type atomic weapons, a figure that did not even reach fifty until two years later.[20] The United States had even fewer specially modified "Silver Plate" B-29 bombers and trained assembly crews to deliver these bombs. Moreover, with a maximum range of 5,300 miles, any B-29 attack on major targets in the Soviet Union would be a one-way, near-suicidal mission.

Intelligence was, as always, a necessary adjunct to national power, but here, too, the demobilization atrophied American capabilities. Throughout the war, the OSS had failed to reach an effective working relationship with the military intelligence agencies and the Federal Bureau of Investigation. The unexpected Japanese capitulation in the summer of 1945 threw many issues, including the future of the intelligence community, into sudden disorder. The new president was harried by hundreds of momentous decisions, and he also disliked OSS Director William Donovan on a personal level. Truman therefore accepted the advice of his budget director, Harold D. Smith, to disestablish the OSS and transfer its analytical functions either to the

State Department or to the military services. Executive Order 9621 abruptly implemented this plan, effective October 1, 1945.[21] Within weeks, the continued need for some form of national-level intelligence operation became obvious, but in this as in other bureaucratic matters, the Department of the Navy resisted any form of centralization. As a compromise, on January 22, 1946, President Truman created the Central Intelligence Group (CIG) under Rear Admiral Sidney W. Souers, the former deputy director of naval intelligence. Initially, however, the CIG was primarily an analytical office limited to collating intelligence for the president and his cabinet.[22] Meanwhile, the field intelligence collection units, most of them consisting of uniformed personnel, dissolved as quickly as the combat forces; only a vestigial Strategic Studies Unit survived in the War Department.[23] During the early years of the Cold War, therefore, American strategic intelligence about the Soviet Union and other potential adversaries was at best uneven and at worst nonexistent.

In short, the United States was in no position to confront the Soviet Union at the end of the war. Americans might believe in the value of democratic capitalism and individual liberty, but they initially saw no need to fight for those beliefs. In any event, Franklin Roosevelt had attempted to satisfy internationalists who opposed such a confrontation. Throughout the war Roosevelt tried to establish a relationship of trust with Stalin, to allay Soviet suspicions and to recognize the overwhelming Soviet needs for economic aid and buffer states as security against future invasion. The president was not naïve about Soviet intentions, but he apparently felt, with considerable justification, that he was unable to prevent Soviet occupation of Eastern Europe and must therefore follow diplomatic avenues to moderate Soviet policy in the region. In his efforts to convince Stalin, Roosevelt openly distanced himself from Churchill, much to the latter's dismay. In the spring of 1945, just before his death, the apparent failure of this policy may have prompted Roosevelt to be less yielding with the Soviets. Within a month of succeeding Roosevelt, Truman also turned to a firmer policy, seeking to deter the Soviets from what he viewed as unjustified aggrandizement.[24]

Roosevelt's conciliatory approach inevitably brought the U.S. government into conflict with the British in 1944–1945. For example, the Roosevelt administration favored such drastic actions as the Morgenthau Plan to eliminate all heavy industry from postwar Germany.

This plan was dear to the Soviets and French but obviously hazardous to the future of a pro-British, democratic Europe, which could hardly survive the removal of its German industrial heart. In truth, many American officials felt no compunctions about thwarting British wishes. Conservative American politicians often claimed that the British had manipulated the United States into entering World War I in 1917, and conspiracy-minded Americans also suspected that Roosevelt and Churchill were responsible for the surprise at Pearl Harbor. Once in the war, senior U.S. officials and military officers frequently found the British outmaneuvering them on strategy, resulting in the 1942–1943 invasions in the Mediterranean at a time when American planners wanted a direct invasion of France. The fact that the British had reason to fear high casualties in a premature cross-channel invasion did not diminish the frustration felt by senior members of the U.S. government. As the war neared its end, British efforts to restore monarchies and colonial regimes further irritated American policy makers who did not wish to expend blood and treasure for objectives that appeared contrary to American beliefs and national interests. Thus, British stabilization efforts in Greece, Vietnam, and elsewhere frequently occurred without U.S. support.

With diplomacy failing, the British alliance fraying, and American intelligence and military structure withering away, perhaps the only leverage that the United States had in the immediate postwar period was economic—the promise of unlimited production to aid its friends in rebuilding a shattered globe.

THE SOVIET ENIGMA

Soviet motivations and national interests under Stalin were far less obvious than those of Britain and the United States, and indeed may never be fully explained. What is clear in retrospect is that Stalin and his government were not fanatically seeking the worldwide triumph of the proletarian revolution. As so ably analyzed by Randall Woods and Howard Jones, ideology was only one of at least three interrelated considerations that drove Soviet policy.[25]

The most basic consideration—the single interest that trumped all other motivations—was not Marxism but Russian national security. Coming after centuries of foreign invasion, the German occupations of western Russia in both world wars fueled a desire bordering on mania for absolute safety against any future attack. The Soviet armed forces officially lost 29.6 million killed, wounded, and missing during the war, to which must be added at least seventeen million dead civilians, many of whom died as German slave laborers.[26] This trauma drove the Soviet government and population to maintain armed forces and control buffer territories to preclude another invasion. It also prompted a crash project to match the United States in nuclear weapons.[27]

Patriotic desire and hatred of the Germans rather than theoretical Marxism motivated most Soviet soldiers in World War II. In the process, however, the Soviet government gained a new legitimacy in the eyes of its people as defender of the Motherland, and the Communist Party of the Soviet Union received an influx of six million new members who had earned their party cards in battle.

Meanwhile, the suffering of the war had left the Soviet Union far too weak to undertake any new risks in the immediate postwar era. Twenty-five million Soviet citizens were homeless in 1945. Stalin had to invest enormous efforts in rebuilding the industry and physical plant lost during the conflict, which explains in large part the postwar Soviet pillaging of factories in Germany and China. Not until 1952 did the average Soviet worker, working seventy-hour weeks, regain the 1940 standard of living.[28] A drought in 1946 further complicated economic recovery, producing near-famine conditions. In addition, Ukrainian and Lithuanian insurgents resisted the reimposition of Soviet rule throughout the later 1940s, a fact that Moscow naturally did not advertise.

In practical terms, therefore, the Soviet Union had clearly defined national security goals in 1945. These concerns included Soviet control over Eastern Europe, reparations to help rebuild the Motherland, and a Germany that could never again attack to the east. In addition, Stalin and other Soviet leaders believed that their overwhelming contribution to the defeat of Germany had earned them a major international role, a role that the Western powers should acknowledge and reward. In this respect, Stalin's view of national strategy was more appropriate to the eighteenth century than the twentieth.[29]

While national interest prompted Moscow to seek security in all directions, that same interest argued strongly against foreign adventures outside the Soviet buffer states. Stalin could and did press his former allies for postwar concessions, in part because he believed that the West did not respect the true scope of Soviet sacrifices to the war effort. Indeed, it is important to recognize that many of the issues that Moscow raised during the 1940s were as much about respect and prestige as they were about ideology or security. In any confrontation, however, the Soviet dictator was too cautious to risk open conflict.[30]

Under these circumstances, the second Soviet motivation—Marxist ideology—sometimes had to take a back seat to national security. Dedicated Marxists like Stalin sincerely believed that the proletarian revolution would eventually displace capitalism throughout the world. If Moscow saw an opportunity to disrupt capitalist, imperialist world trade by supporting a local insurrection, it was clearly an international socialist duty to hasten the collapse of capitalism by aiding those rebels. Such, in essence, was the argument that Stalin gave to his confidants to explain why he had provoked a minor crisis by his reluctance to withdraw Soviet forces from northern Iran in early 1946. Quite apart from oil concerns, he believed that supporting a group of communist-led ethnic Azerbaijanis in the area was both ideologically correct and a useful lever for Soviet power. Only when the United States and Britain cited the continued Soviet presence in Iran as an excuse to maintain their own troops in Greece, China, and elsewhere did he authorize the withdrawal of his troops, ending an unnecessary crisis.[31]

In an ideological argument dating back to the 1920s, Stalin and his henchmen were unwilling to support socialist revolts abroad when such revolts might jeopardize the security of the first socialist state. Vladislav Zubok and Constantine Pleshakov, two recent Russian historians of the Soviet leadership, have argued that this formed the basis for the compromise between national security and ideology, a compromise they termed the "Revolutionary-imperial paradigm" of Soviet foreign policy.[32] This compromise, in which cautious self-interest usually trumped Bolshevik idealism, was reflected in a host of decisions taken during the later 1940s, including the lack of Soviet support for the Greek Communist uprising. Although the Soviet Union was certainly willing to extend its influence wherever the Americans would permit, it was not the centralized, methodical aggressor responsible for every disturbance in the postwar world.

Marxist ideology did, however, contribute to the advent of the Cold War by causing misunderstandings on both sides. Many Westerners believed Moscow's rhetoric about the proletarian revolution and regarded every socialist or leftist uprising in the world as part of a Moscow-directed conspiracy. Consequently, Western policy makers frequently misunderstood the motivations of both the Soviet government and the (admittedly left-wing) national liberation movements of the world. Conversely, Stalin and his supporters had ideological blinders that prevented them from understanding the motivations of their capitalist counterparts. Certainly, they had reason to be suspicious of longtime anticommunists such as Churchill. Yet, Stalin had no understanding of the nature of British or American democracy, believing it to be a sham to conceal control by wealthy capitalists. Thus, he dismissed Roosevelt's attempts to explain the workings of congressional and public opinion on matters such as the postwar Polish government, believing those explanations to be a smokescreen for Roosevelt's own class-based interests. If anything, he expected that Roosevelt would be satisfied with the *appearance* of Polish democracy rather than any real self-government.[33]

National security and ideology were thus central to Soviet foreign policy, but in addition, Stalin had to satisfy the interests of various institutions within Soviet society. Like any successful dictator, he understood the importance of playing off one center of power against another so that they would not cooperate against him personally. In his case, the two most powerful institutions in the Soviet Union were the Red Army (renamed the Soviet Army in February 1946) and the Communist Party of the Soviet Union (CPSU). Each of these institutions was deeply interested in the creation of satellite states in Eastern Europe and Asia. For the army, such satellites were not only an essential security measure to protect the Motherland but also a source of useful, interesting career opportunities. To cite one example, Marshal of the Soviet Union Konstantin Konstantinovich Rokossovsky, one of the most brilliant field commanders of World War II, was for many years thereafter the minister of defense in the Polish government, ensuring Polish loyalty to Moscow. Similarly, officials of the CPSU could applaud the creation of the socialist states of Eastern Europe for both philosophical and personal reasons. On the one hand, these states and their attendant communist parties represented the advance of world socialism. On the other, CPSU officials found it personally rewarding to be able to advise and sometimes dominate their Eastern European counterparts with frequent visits to countries that had consumer goods unavailable in Moscow. Thus, for national, ideological, and institutional reasons, Stalin was committed to the creation of buffer states in Eastern Europe and the Far East. Beyond this basic goal, however, postwar Soviet policy was often driven by mutual misunderstandings as well as the interaction of the three different factors in Soviet behavior.

For Moscow, as for London and Washington, one of the most urgent tasks in 1945 was the demobilization of its armed forces. Because the Red Air Force and Navy were relatively small auxiliary services, this meant primarily the demobilization of the Red Army, a force of some 520 division equivalents and 11,365,000 men in 1945. Although this manpower was desperately needed to rebuild the Soviet economy, the Soviet leadership was careful to maintain a large conventional force, manned by a cadre of veterans. Still, five million men returned to civilian life within the first year, and by 1948 the Soviet Army had shrunk to an official total of 175 divisions and 2,874,000 men, although Western observers believed it to be considerably larger. Thus, while the U.S. Army cased the colors on 90 percent of its combat divisions, the Soviets created a peacetime force structure that was roughly 30 percent of its wartime peak. Moreover, the inactivated units were almost entirely conventional, foot-mobile rifle divisions, leaving the tank and motorized rifle units—the cream of the wartime maneuver force—predominant in the peacetime Soviet Army. By 1948, the U.S. Army in western Germany contained one infantry division and the equivalent of a mechanized cavalry division (the Constabulary), but its counterpart in the Group of Soviet Forces, Germany (GSFG), included eight tank, ten mechanized, and four rifle divisions, the latter in the process of being motorized. Like their American counterparts, many of these units were short on manpower and current weaponry. Moreover, the Soviet divisions were designed for relatively short combat life, with less repair and sustainment capabilities than their U.S. equivalents. Overall, however, the Soviet Army retained considerable more capability than the U.S. Army.[34]

Soviet intelligence efforts also continued unabated after the defeat of the Axis. Building on a centuries-old tradition of Russian human intelligence and counterintelligence, Soviet agents were remarkably ruthless and effective both during and after World War II. The wartime People's Commissariat for State Security (NKGB, not to be confused with the internal NKVD) was redesignated as the Ministry for State Security (MGB) in 1946, which in turn became part of the

Committee for State Security (KGB, or Komitet Gosudarstvennoy Bezopasnosti) in 1954. These changes in headquarters organization did not cause any abatement in field collection. In addition, the Soviet military's Main Intelligence Directorate (GRU, or Glavnoye Razvedovatel'noye Upravlenie) was equally active if less well known.[35]

The struggle against the Axis had given the Soviet intelligence services extraordinary opportunities to recruit agents. Committed Communists entered into various trusted positions within Western governments and armed forces, while noncommunist, patriotic men and women in similar positions could see nothing wrong in sharing sensitive information with their Soviet allies. As Lieutenant General Mikhail Milstein, head of the GRU at the end of the war, later recalled, "In that period all our intelligence activities . . . relied essentially on the so-called liberal cadres, that is, the ones who sympathized with the Soviet Union . . .[and who] worked not for cash, but for the idea."[36] When Soviet espionage first became public immediately after World War II, some politicians, notably Senator Joseph R. McCarthy (Republican, Wisconsin), made a career out of exaggerating the threat and often charging innocent people without proof. Such false charges made thinking people question the very existence of the alleged espionage. In retrospect, however, Western governments were aware of the scope of the threat since at least the fall of 1945, when a Soviet code clerk defected in Canada and revealed the extensive espionage penetration of the Manhattan Project, whose mission it was to develop the first atomic weapon. Much of the proof of such activities was not released at the time because it came from a successful U.S. Army Security Agency effort to decrypt Soviet communications, the so-called VENONA project.[37] In a postwar world where the United States had the only atomic weapons and the only intact industrial plant, Stalin used human intelligence as a major equalizer.

FRICTION POINTS I: GERMANY

As illustrated by events in Greece and Southeast Asia, friction was inevitable at almost every point where Western troops encountered communist-led forces during the final defeat of the Axis. The most significant but by no means the only such point of contact was in central Europe as the Allied armies overran the last vestiges of the Third Reich.

Soviet Control, 1945

N
W E
S

Norwegian Sea

ICELAND

SWEDEN

FINLAND

NORWAY

North Sea

DENMARK

Baltic Sea

USSR

North Atlantic Ocean

BRITAIN

NETH.

Soviet Zone

POLAND

GERMANY

BELGIUM

CZECHOSLOVAKIA

FRANCE

SWITZ.

AUSTRIA

HUNGARY

ROMANIA

ITALY

Trieste

YUGOSLAVIA

BULGARIA

Black Sea

PORTUGAL

SPAIN

GREECE

TURKEY

TUNISIA

Mediterranean Sea

MOROCCO

ALGERIA
(French North Africa)

LIBYA

EGYPT

MAP 1. Europe, 1945

For several years prior to this, the Allies had worked on a plan for the division of Germany into zones of occupation. Originally, these zones were supposed to be only a temporary measure pending a definitive peace treaty; apparently the authors had never heard the aphorism that in government, nothing is so permanent as a "temporary" measure. At the Quebec Conference of 1943, Roosevelt and Churchill had proposed this division, with roughly 40 percent of Germany occupied by the Soviet Union while the western 60 percent would fall to the British and Americans. Eventually, Churchill insisted that France should also have an occupation zone, which was carved out of the British and American areas. Berlin, which would fall inside the Soviet zone, was similarly divided into four sectors. Considering that the Western Allies had yet to land in northwestern Europe, they had reason to anticipate that the Soviet Union might well conquer all of Germany. Therefore, the proposed occupation zones, combined with an agreement in principle that the Western zones would export industrial goods to the Soviet zone in return for food, seemed about the best arrangement that London and Washington could obtain.[38]

By the spring of 1945, however, the sudden German collapse in the west offered an opportunity for the Western Allies to advance much farther into Germany than originally envisioned. Prime Minister Churchill and the commander of 21st Army Group, Sir Bernard Law Montgomery, both urged the American leaders to advance toward Berlin, arguing that "tactical zones" need not be identical to postwar occupation zones. Yet, Truman and his field commander, Dwight D. Eisenhower, had no interest in incurring extra casualties and in the process offending their Soviet allies. While the British worried about the postwar situation in Europe, American strategic attention was increasingly focused on the looming campaign against Japan, for which the United States needed Soviet assistance. On March 31, 1945, Eisenhower sent a message (Supreme Commander Allied Forces [SCAF] message 252) to Stalin via the U.S. Embassy in Moscow. Eisenhower felt justified in seeking to coordinate the military junction of the various armies conquering Germany; there had already been an incident on March 18 when the U.S. Army Air Forces had shot down two Soviet fighters that the American pilots had mistaken for Germans. SCAF-252 outlined Eisenhower's future plans, which focused on eliminating any Nazi "final redoubt" in southern Germany, leaving Berlin to the Soviets. To this end, Eisenhower had already detached General William H. Simpson's Ninth U.S. Army from Montgomery's control and directed the remaining British and Commonwealth force of 21st Army Group to advance on Hamburg and Denmark rather than Berlin. In his response to this message, Stalin enthusiastically approved of the proposed plan and disingenuously suggested that Berlin was no longer a major target.[39]

The British were scandalized by this exchange of messages, which they attributed to American political naïveté, although Chief of Staff George C. Marshall had approved Eisenhower's action.[40] In fact, conquering Berlin was so psychologically important to the Soviet people that the Red Army incurred unnecessary casualties in a desperate rush to get there before the Western Allies. In retrospect, therefore, the British plan to push eastward would have incurred not only additional casualties but additional ill will with their Soviet allies.

After the German surrender, a number of unsavory dramas played out in Europe. Up to fourteen million ethnic Germans were expelled from East Prussia, the Sudetenland, and other areas being transferred permanently to foreign governments, thereby eliminating the irredentist issues that Hitler had exploited so cleverly in the 1930s. In return for regaining their own captured soldiers that had fallen into Soviet hands, the British and Americans forcibly returned all Soviet citizens, including those who had served the Germans in anticommunist forces, to Soviet control. The same fate awaited thousands of noncommunist refugees from the Baltic States, Yugoslavia, and other Eastern European countries. Eleven former Soviet soldiers who had served in Andrei Vlasov's anti-Soviet army committed suicide to avoid their inevitable fate in Soviet hands. On Stalin's orders, the Soviet Baltic Fleet occupied the Danish island of Bornholm, controlling the entrance to the Baltic Sea, while Soviet diplomats pressured Norway to grant a twenty-five-year lease for a naval base in the extreme northern part of the country, where the Soviets had evicted the Germans.[41] Meanwhile, the Allied Control Commissions responsible for temporary administration of the eastern countries generally deferred to Soviet wishes, while the continent almost starved in the winter of 1945–1946. Soviet proconsuls, both Red Army commanders and senior officials of the Communist Party, in effect governed most of these countries.[42]

Friction Points II: Trieste

While Eisenhower's forces cautiously made contact with their Soviet counterparts and settled into the prearranged occupation zones of Germany and Austria, a more complex scenario developed in the area of Trieste, the ethnic boundary line between Italians and Slavs along the Yugoslav border. Logically enough, it was here that General Alexander's Mediterranean Theater made contact with the first true Soviet surrogate army of the Cold War, the Yugoslav Army of ex-partisan commander Josip Broz, aka Tito. In 1945, the Yugoslav-Soviet split was still well in the future, and Tito was the recipient of extensive aid from the Red Army. In addition to light infantry weapons, the Soviets delivered thousands of guns and mortars, and trained a Yugoslav tank brigade and three air regiments, which participated in the final liberation of northern Yugoslavia.[43] To assert Yugoslavia's political claims to the Trieste region, in late 1944, Tito's Slovenian followers established control over the communist-led partisans of northeastern Italy.

Churchill, who had earlier switched British support from conservative Yugoslavs to Tito because the communist partisans were more effective, had tried and failed to reach a political arrangement with the new Yugoslavian government in 1944. As the war ground to a close, Alexander visited Belgrade in February 1945, seeking a limited agreement regarding military cooperation in the region.[44] The Yugoslav dictator reluctantly agreed that Trieste could serve as the base, under a British-American military government, for a projected invasion northward into Austria. This agreement became virtually irrelevant two months later, however, when total German collapse was visibly imminent.

On May 1, 1945, the Fourth Yugoslav Army occupied Trieste, murdered or deported a number of Italian leaders, and conducted dubious "elections" of communist local governments in the area. The German garrison of the port understandably preferred to surrender to General Bernard C. Freyberg, whose 2nd New Zealand Division arrived the next day. A tense standoff ensued, with the chief of staff of Fourth Yugoslav Army demanding that Freyberg withdraw immediately across the Isonzo River. Alexander tried to avoid confrontation at the end of a tenuous supply chain, but Churchill was adamant.

The British soon rejected the Yugoslav local "government" as ineffectual. The U.S. Secretary of War, Henry L. Stimson, advised Truman not to become involved in a matter that they both regarded as serving British political interests.[45] Yet, the United States was involved, if only because the allied military governments in all occupied Italian areas were combined British-American teams.

In June, all sides agreed to another "temporary" solution in Belgrade, again pending a final peace agreement. By this agreement, Britain and the United States would administer "Zone A," consisting of Trieste and (initially) an enclave around the small port of Pola to the south, while Yugoslavia governed "Zone B," the much larger rural area around these cities. De facto, the British-American force, which included the understrength U.S. 88th Infantry Division, became the protectors of the ethnic Italian population against the deprivations of angry Yugoslavs, who had experienced systematic discrimination in the area. For several years thereafter, Trieste remained a hot spot, punctuated by violent demonstrations from both ethnic groups as well as the 1947 murder of a British brigade commander by an ultra-nationalist Italian. At one point, Tito orchestrated a general strike in the ports and then complained when United Nations relief supplies did not arrive in Yugoslavia.[46]

Stalin sympathized with Tito but was unwilling to risk a confrontation about the issue. As the situation cooled, Western troops withdrew from Trieste, but the local government anomaly remained. The British sought to create a Free Territory of Trieste but were unable to get the United Nations Security Council to endorse this solution. In 1954, the Security Council belatedly agreed to allow Italy and Yugoslavia to continue administering the two zones without any settlement as to sovereignty over the area. Thus the Trieste issue, which at one time held the promise of immediate armed conflict, faded into a peaceful if odd accommodation between the two sides.

Friction Points III: Northeast Asia

At the Yalta Conference in early 1945, Stalin had confirmed his promise that the USSR, which had maintained its neutrality with Japan throughout the Pacific conflict, would attack Japanese forces on mainland Asia within three months of the end of hostilities in Europe. Soon after midnight on August 9, 1945, the Red Army fulfilled

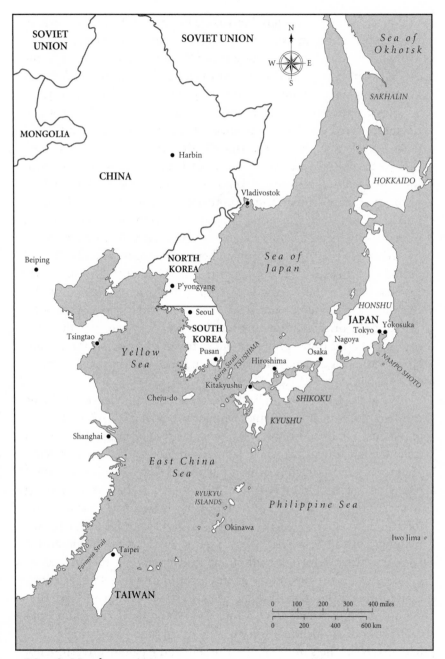

Map 2. Northeast Asia

that promise. After redeploying 10,000 kilometers from the German heartland, more than 1.5 million Soviet troops attacked on a front of 4,400 kilometers, overrunning some of the most barren terrain in the world to capture Manchuria. Within a week, the Soviets had defeated 1.2 million Japanese and satellite troops of the Kwantung Army.[47]

Having limited its own ground forces to ninety-five divisions, and having suffered enormous casualties at the hands of fanatical Japanese defenders of the Pacific islands, the United States considered this Soviet assistance almost indispensable. To ensure that support, the United States continued Lend-Lease aid to the Soviet Far East region even after Truman had abruptly terminated that aid in Europe.[48] Indeed, by some accounts, the Soviet entry into the war weighed even more heavily than the atomic bomb in Japan's decision to surrender.[49]

Yet, once that intervention and surrender occurred, the United States and its allies had to deal with the sudden reality of Soviet involvement in the Pacific war. First, the United States pointedly excluded the Soviet Union from the occupation of Japan, thereby avoiding the divisive problems that Germany experienced. Initially, the British and other allies provided token occupation forces, but Japan was never divided into occupation zones like those in Germany and Austria.

Next, the United States had to reach an accommodation about the future of the Korean peninsula, which the Soviet 25th Army invaded on August 10. In addition to shipping 400,000 Japanese and Korean prisoners off to work as slave laborers in Siberia, the Soviets occupied the industrialized northern portion of Korea and immediately began to seize machinery, fertilizer, and minerals.[50] The task of choosing another "temporary" line of demarcation between U.S. and Soviet forces fell to Colonel Charles Bonesteel and Major Dean Rusk, two members of the Strategic Policy Section of the army's Operations Division. Rusk, a former staff officer for General Joseph Stillwell in China and a future secretary of state, could find no natural demarcation line on the map. Instead, the two proposed the 38th parallel (38 degrees North Latitude), a line that would leave the traditional capital, Seoul, inside the southern (American) zone. Unwittingly, they had arrived at the same line the Russian and Japanese governments had selected for spheres of influence in 1896, so Moscow was quite willing to accept this as a temporary demarcation. Unfortunately, the 38th parallel was nothing but a line on a map. Militarily, it was indefensible, especially because it came so close to Seoul while cutting across the Ongjin Peninsula in west-central Korea, transforming the southern tip of that peninsula into a virtual island of southern territory. Economically, the line was even more dysfunctional because it left most of Korea's heavy industry, fertilizer production, and coal in Soviet hands. Still, it was the best that could be achieved on short notice. Lieutenant General John Hodge's XXIV U.S. Corps, led by the veteran 7th Infantry Division, began to land in Korea on September 8, 1945, and quickly found itself engulfed by a variety of issues and conflicts with both the Soviets and the Koreans. To cite one example, when an OSS mission arrived in Pyongyang, it found the Soviets so firmly in control that the United States had to threaten to withhold rice from the north before the Soviets would release enough chlorine to stop a cholera epidemic in the south.[51]

The Red Army's presence in northern China produced one of the most complex situations in the immediate postwar period. For reasons that become clear in chapter 6, the Chinese Communist Party (CCP) was not Moscow's highest priority in the region, although certainly the Soviets surreptitiously turned over some captured weapons and other supplies to the People's Liberation Army. Instead, Stalin tried to advance Russian national interests in the region without openly confronting the United States, a difficult task at best. On August 14, 1945, while the Soviets were rolling over the Japanese Kwantung Army, the Nationalist Chinese foreign minister, T. V. Soong, signed a Sino-Soviet Friendship Treaty. In return for China's de facto recognition of the independence of Soviet-dominated Outer Mongolia, Moscow promised not to aid the CCP in the looming civil war with the Nationalist Chinese government. The sudden Japanese defeat therefore left Chiang Kai-shek's nationalists to deal with both the CCP and the Red Army in Manchuria and northern China. Fortunately for Chiang, the United States at first continued its support for the Nationalist government, providing air and sealift to move substantial Nationalist troops into the region before the CCP could fully exploit the situation. Although the Soviets did pose some practical obstacles by asserting their renewed power in the region, in the fall of 1945, they avoided open confrontation with Chiang and the United States even when the United States interposed Marines in the area.[52] Here, as in Europe, Stalin appeared willing to maintain the wartime alliance if he could do so without compromising Soviet national interests. This ambivalent situation did not survive more than a few months, however, leading to renewed fighting between Red and Nationalist Chinese.

The destruction of the Axis in 1945 eliminated the principal reason for U.S.-British-Soviet cooperation but did not lead to immediate confrontation, despite their conflicting goals at the end of the war. As the armed forces of these three powers contacted each other over the corpses of the German and Japanese empires, misunderstandings and friction irked local commanders, but no one was willing to plunge immediately into another war. All three powers had overwhelming economic and social needs for demobilization, but only the United States fully indulged that urge. All three powers also had issues of internal stability and continuity at home—there were major leadership turnovers and espionage scandals in the United States and Britain, while Stalin felt it necessary to reassert ideological purity and launch additional purges of those he imagined were conspiring against his power.

Thus, diplomacy and national security were not always the highest priority for the Great Powers, although each had goals in that arena. For the British and Soviets, the immediate postwar period was a long series of improvised efforts to maintain their military power in order to achieve a postwar world worthy of their sacrifices. For the United States, the same period was an effort to find some nonmilitary lever to reach its own vaguely defined national objectives.

3

THE GREEK CIVIL WAR

GENESIS

On May 30, 1945, an emaciated man stepped off a British transport airplane, returning to his native Greece after surviving the Nazi concentration camp at Dachau. Nicos Zachariadis, secretary-general of the Greek Communist Party (KKE) for the previous twelve years, had lost neither his passion for Marxism nor his loyalty to Stalin and the Moscow party line. He immediately began preaching opposition to British occupation, no compromise with monarchists or fascists, and expansion of legal activities such as labor unions.[1]

Having lost the Battle of Athens five months before, the KKE was weak and discredited, and its central committee was split over whether to focus on national concerns or follow the Moscow line. Strongly anticommunist elements of the paramilitary Greek National Guard and the illegal, right-wing X Group harassed former leaders of ELAS, arresting thousands while 3,000 other diehard Communists and their supporters moved to Yugoslavia rather than submit to the new government.[2] Government military and police forces excluded ELAS leaders in violation of the Varzika Agreement, which had ended the 1944 confrontation, but at least the KKE was a legal party for the first time since 1936.

At the time, the traditional politicians of the Greek government, supported by British and some American officials, sincerely believed that the KKE was a threat to Greek and indeed European liberty. Both sides agreed that the poverty and misery of postwar Greece seemed fertile ground for communist expansion. In 1945–1946, however, Zachariadis and most of his subordinates continued to work for legal rather than violent seizure of power. In retrospect, some historians have argued that conservative persecution forced the KKE into renewed rebellion. Even Zachariadis was threatened with prosecution for "spreading malicious rumors."[3]

Despite this persecution, in 1945–1946 the KKE was still ambivalent, seeking to keep its options open. The KKE leadership felt too weak to seek an immediate revolution and got no support from the Soviet Union. In his wartime agreement with Churchill on spheres of influence, Stalin had formally recognized the British-backed regime in Athens. Tito's Yugoslavia, hoping to gain control of Greek Macedonia, was more supportive. On December 15, 1945, representatives of the KKE and the Yugoslav and Bulgarian general staffs met in Petrich, Bulgaria. The representatives agreed to create what became the Democratic Army of Greece (DAG) but subordinated that force to the Yugoslav military, which promised more aid than it actually delivered. Meanwhile, the former supply service of ELAS revived, quietly establishing a network to collect and hide weapons. In February 1946, the KKE Central Committee endorsed the creation of a guerrilla force but still hedged its bets between legal and illegal means. As historian Lawrence Wittner wryly observed, "Greece's communist leaders faced the crisis of 1946 with the same fatal indecision they had shown in 1944."[4]

The crisis arose when the British and American governments, having pressured the Greek government into a partial amnesty for ELAS, insisted that the conservative Athens government hold parliamentary elections on March 31, 1946. This would be followed on September 1 by a referendum on the continuation of the monarchy. The KKE chose to boycott these elections, and the right wing undoubtedly manipulated some of the results despite the presence of 1,200 foreign election observers. Some historians claim that the combination of right-wing security forces and private gangs made a fair election impossible. Nonetheless, it appears that many Greeks, especially the tradition-minded farmers of the countryside, genuinely feared a renewal of violence and perhaps a communist dictatorship, and voted accordingly. With no communist candidates, the right-wing

Nationalist United Front received 55.2 percent of the vote in the March election, and King George was finally able to return after the September referendum endorsed the monarchy by 68.2 percent. These elections, however questionable the numbers, doomed the KKE's efforts to gain power legally, and additional veterans of ELAS went into exile.[5]

MARKOS AND THE DAG

Small groups of guerrillas took to the field in the spring of 1946, raiding their first town on March 30. The real success of the DAG began in August when, responding to intense internal pressure from its members, the KKE Central Committee appointed Markos Vaphiadis to command the new organization. At age forty, "General Markos" was a veteran member of the KKE and a political officer of ELAS. Despite his lack of practical command experience, Markos had apparently learned a great deal from observing Sarafis, the noncommunist war-time leader of ELAS. Indeed, Markos proved to be a master of unconventional warfare, and much of the success of the DAG can be attributed to his guidance. Like Mao Tse-tung and Vo Nguyen Giap, Markos deviated from the traditional Marxist emphasis on proletarian revolution, believing that the KKE could lead the rural peasants of his country to victory over the upper classes.[6]

Instinctively, Markos realized that the DAG must follow true guerrilla tactics, decentralizing into small groups that assembled only long enough to launch a sudden attack before dispersing to deny the government's forces a target. He established a system of messengers and later high-frequency radios to coordinate the operations of his bands without the normal hierarchy of command and control. Most of his staff and logistical operations were initially located on Yugoslavian and Bulgarian bases, inaccessible to the Greek government forces.

In late September 1946, the DAG symbolically responded to the king's return from exile by attacking a series of villages near the Yugoslav and Albanian borders. In each case, a few hundred rebels launched a night attack to overwhelm the local defenders, then seized food supplies and dispersed, often across the border, before government relief columns arrived. The last and largest of these attacks struck the industrial town of Naoussa in Macedonia, at a considerable distance from the frontier. This time, the local army and police

MAP 3. Greece

garrisons put up a spirited defense that finally drove off the attackers, who dispersed into the mountains.[7]

Even the defeat at Naoussa advanced Markos's goals by spreading fear throughout most of the country. Politicians demanded garrisons to defend the towns in their districts, thereby pinning down most of the government's limited manpower in a dispersed, passive defense that left the initiative to the insurgents. This proved to be a recurring problem not only throughout the Greek Civil War but also in most other counterinsurgency campaigns of the Cold War.

When the guerrillas first reappeared in the spring of 1946, the Athens government, again like other governments in similar situations, attempted to treat the matter as a police problem—a form of organized banditry—rather than a political rebellion. Although this policy was intended to deny credibility to the rebels, it also tied the hands of the government forces by requiring police to operate within the (admittedly minor) constraints of civilian law. Very quickly, however, it became clear that the DAG outnumbered and outgunned the paramilitary police or gendarmerie of Greece. The British Army was in the process of training a 92,000-person Greek National Army (GNA), but neither the GNA's equipment nor its training was complete. Moreover, half of the GNA was equipped for conventional, motorized warfare rather than for the light infantry and mountain operations necessary to defeat the insurgents. The government in Athens sought British aid to increase the army to 200,000 as well as to create rural self-defense or MAY units. The British could not afford such a massive increase in aid and compromised on a temporary increase in the GNA to 135,000 plus limited supplies of obsolescent equipment for the MAY self-defense force.[8]

Unbeknownst to the British and conservative Greek leaders, the DAG was already suffering its own manpower problems. When Markos assumed command in August 1946, the DAG had only about four hundred armed men in the field inside Greece, plus perhaps 3,000 more in camps across the border. His initial successes won him considerable acclaim, and by October the DAG numbered approximately 6,000 in the field. In January 1947, the GNA General Staff estimated the total insurgent strength, both inside and out of the country, at 10,800. Most of these initial recruits were genuine volunteers, communist and noncommunist veterans of ELAS who regarded the Athens regime as a dictatorship that deprived the Greek people of political and economic freedom. Other recruits may have been more reluctant but were hounded into resistance by government persecution. Yet, to succeed, Markos estimated that he needed a total strength of 50,000; as he sought to expand the DAG toward this goal, he quickly ran out of true volunteers among the conservative rural population. Almost from the beginning, therefore, the DAG impressed young men as well as ELAS veterans from the areas it controlled, and these draftees were often less than enthusiastic. Six hundred DAG soldiers deserted by the end of 1946. Although DAG troop strength peaked at approximately 25,000 in the fall of 1948, more than half of these men and women were unwilling participants. Moreover, Markos lacked weapons for many of his followers; in order to get arms and other support from neighboring communist states, he had to promise various concessions including border adjustments at Greece's expense.[9]

These weaknesses were not initially apparent, however. Despite the harsh winter weather, the pace of guerrilla attacks rose markedly in January-March of 1947. The Athens government was clearly on the defensive while the DAG was gaining ground. In the spring of that year, Markos moved portions of his headquarters, training, and support structure into two remote areas inside Greece—the Grammos Mountains on the border with Albania and the Vitsi Mountains at the tri-border intersection of Albania, Yugoslavia, and Greece.

For at least a year after the formation of the DAG, the KKE followed a dual-track strategy, fomenting rebellion while continuing to function as a legal political party within Greece. However, its meetings were frequently disrupted by violent right-wing attacks and police interference; the conservatives would make no gesture at compromise.

THE TRUMAN DOCTRINE

Renewed violence and the expense of the growing conflict contributed to a rapid decline of the Greek economy during 1946. This decline made the Athens government increasingly dependent on foreign aid to prosecute the war. Under British and American pressure, in January 1947, the Greek cabinet reshuffled itself to include more representatives of the political center, but conservatives continued to dominate the government, violating the civil rights of those who opposed it.

The Labour government of Great Britain was concerned by both the failures on the battlefield and the continuing cost of the war.

Given its own economic problems and ongoing commitments else-where in the world, London could not afford to support the war by itself. The obvious solution was to seek American assistance. On February 27, 1947, Chancellor of the Exchequer Hugh Dalton pres-sured Foreign Secretary Ernest Bevin to send a diplomatic note to Washington. This note hinted broadly that Britain was on the verge of withdrawal from Greece.[10]

The British message spoke directly to America's perceived interests in Greece. Like the Bevin government, most members of the Truman administration regarded the Greek Communist insurgency as a deliber-ate Soviet policy. Privately, senior leaders were aware that the Soviets were providing little direct support to the DAG. Yet, even if Stalin were not directly involved in the insurgency, a communist victory there would, it appeared, inevitably give the Soviet Union bases and influence in the region. More generally, the United States feared the power vacuum that would occur when Britain withdrew not only from Greece but also from Palestine and Egypt. The United States had already been trying to reinforce Turkey, both to defend it against perceived Soviet expansionism and to provide bases for possible U.S. bombing raids against the Soviets in case of war.[11] In short, Truman was motivated by geopolitical interests as well as by ideology. Infla-tion and the huge American national debt continued to limit U.S. spending, but the president decided to make a major appeal to gain public support for a new policy of intervention in the Mediterranean. He pitched the appeal not in terms of self interest but rather in defense of democracy, a winning message both at home and abroad.[12]

As part of this public campaign, Truman addressed a joint session of Congress on March 12, 1947. In the speech, he announced what became known as the Truman Doctrine: the United States would support "free peoples" who resisted attempted subjugation not only by external aggression but also by internal armed minorities. Although Truman did not refer directly to the Soviet Union or to the Commu-nists, everyone in the audience knew the opponent's identity.[13] In the short run, this meant primarily military and economic aid to the Greeks and Turks. More generally, the Truman Doctrine drastically widened the previous U.S. definition of aggression, including not only open invasion but also subversion and guerrilla warfare. As such, this speech was the intellectual precursor to American involvement in the subsequent counterinsurgency campaigns of the Cold War.

At the time, the president's speech did not win universal support. Liberals questioned the degree to which the right-wing, monarchist Greek government really represented its people, while many Europeans were alarmed by the apparent extension of U.S. influence on their continent. The administration had considerable difficulty getting the aid bill through Congress, and Secretary of State George C. Marshall had to virtually draft the Greek government's request for assistance. In keeping with Stalin's hands-off policy on the matter, however, Moscow made no public comment on the speech.[14]

The Truman administration initially underestimated the magnitude of the task in Greece, believing that a combination of economic and military aid would be sufficient to help the Greeks triumph over what appeared from Washington to be a small minority of Communists. Secretary of War Robert P. Patterson told a congressional committee that he anticipated sending no more than forty U.S. soldiers to determine Greek military requirements and then supervise the transfer of the equipment involved. Much of the aid was supposed to be economic rather than military, which may explain why Truman initially appointed a civilian, former Nebraska Governor Dwight Griswold, to head the American Mission for Aid to Greece. Griswold, like the president, had been an artillery captain in World War I and had performed well in the post–World War II administration of western Germany. He and other American officials apparently believed that they could pressure the Greek government into various political, economic, and military reforms that would permit the Greeks to quickly defeat the insurgency.[15]

A small military staff, the U.S. Army Group in Greece (USAGG), arrived in Athens on May 24, 1947, sixteen days after Congress passed the aid package. Commanded by Major General William G. Livesay, USAGG began with fewer than fifty personnel, whereas the British had a 14,000-man garrison plus 1,380 advisors to the GNA. The first requisitions for U.S. supplies were sent on June 10, with the first shipment arriving on August 2. By early September 1947, the United States had delivered 174,000 tons of supplies, especially trucks to improve GNA mobility and logistics.[16]

High Tide of the Insurgency

While the Americans established a logistical pipeline, the Greek National Army and gendarmerie struggled desperately to hold their own during

MAP 4. Northern Greece

most of 1947. The government forces always seemed to arrive too late to catch their opponents, who retained the initiative. Moreover, until American aid arrived in quantity, the GNA was equipped with surplus British and captured German arms, and often found itself outgunned by DAG heavy machine guns. Morale was low, especially among older reservists who were forced to serve repeated tours of active duty.

Despite these handicaps and the continued demands for defensive garrisons, the GNA planned to defeat the Communists as quickly as possible. Lieutenant General D. Jiandzis, commander of the GNA's 1st Army, wanted to clear the DAG from south to north, leaving the gendarmerie to mop up and secure areas behind the advancing army. He attempted this strategy in April 1947 with the government's first major offensive, Operation Terminos, which was intended to encircle and clear a mountainous area of central Greece. Snow and freezing temperatures slowed the movement of 16,000 government troops assembled for the operation but also made the rebels underestimate the magnitude and danger of the attack. The battle turned into an eleven-day pursuit across the mountains, during which the GNA suffered 120 casualties while estimating that it had killed more than 600 rebels and captured 412 more. However, a shortage of troops combined with the difficulties of terrain and weather allowed most of the DAG forces to escape. Elsewhere the DAG continued its sudden raids; on April 23, for example, the rebels wiped out a company of ninety-three gendarmes at Mt. Parnon in the Peloponnesus area of southern Greece.[17]

Unfortunately, the continuous demand for defensive garrisons prevented the GNA from following up on its initial success; most of the forces assembled for Terminos were dispersed, and the initiative reverted to the rebels. The DAG grew in numbers, prestige, and weaponry during this period. To encourage his sometimes reluctant conscripts, Markos began to assign young, dedicated communist women to combat units rather than restricting them to support roles. Indeed, for some women, the DAG represented a welcome opportunity to escape the traditional female roles in rural Greece.[18] Moreover, at the cost of additional concessions to the Yugoslav government, Markos obtained an increased supply of artillery and other heavy weapons from the border communist states. This was dramatically illustrated on May 22, 1947, when DAG anti-aircraft guns shot down a government

Spitfire. Of equal importance was the invisible growth of Markos's YIAFAKA network of unarmed sympathizers, the essential framework that provided intelligence and supplies to the guerrilla bands. In July, a DAG team even attempted to kidnap the British commander, General Scobie, while he was on a hunting trip.[19]

Emboldened by their rapid success, the political leaders of the KKE decided to increase the pace of their struggle. The governments of Albania, Yugoslavia, and Bulgaria all urged Zachariadis to declare an independent government in the field, a government to which the communist states could give diplomatic recognition and open military assistance. Unfortunately, creating such a government meant that the DAG had to take and hold a town large enough to serve as the capital of the new state. In May 1947, the KKE Central Committee overruled a reluctant Markos and directed him to capture a suitable capital. In so doing, the politicians committed the common mistake of abandoning Phase II guerrilla operations prematurely in favor of a more conventional, full-scale civil war. Between late May and July 1947, Markos made at least six different attempts to seize such a town, only to be repelled by the dedicated younger commanders who were emerging in the GNA.[20]

After a brief reversion to guerrilla tactics, Markos tried again in October. This time, his target was the town of Metsovo, sitting in a valley of the Grammos Mountains near the Albanian border. The defenders, Colonel Konstantinos Dovas's brigade of the 11th GNA Division, had three infantry battalions spread out to secure the supply route through Metsovo. Anticipating a DAG attack, the Greek General Staff used some of the first American aid trucks to redeploy a fourth battalion into the area. The reinforcing battalion arrived on the afternoon of October 18, 1947. Soon after midnight that same evening, an estimated 5,000 insurgents attacked the scattered garrisons totaling 2,000 defenders. North of Metsovo, the GNA 584th Battalion repelled the first attack, but in the darkness and fog, insurgents managed to bypass the defenders and occupy portions of the town. In the ensuing eight days, October 19–27, the town changed hands at least four times in desperate fighting. Farther south, the defenders of nearby Karakoli had to be resupplied by airdrop when they ran short of ammunition. On October 20, the defending commander, Colonel Dovas, melodramatically radioed, "Our men and I will fall to the last man, but Metsovo will not become Markos's capital." Dovas made good on his promise, and the DAG withdrew on the 27th.[21]

GOVERNMENT REFORM

As in so many other struggles of the Cold War, political developments were at least as important as battlefield results. In particular, the government's harsh treatment of suspected dissenters discredited the Athens regime while forcing more Greeks into the enemy camp. Such actions far exceeded the excesses of the American McCarthy era. Under the Security Law of 1946, the Greek government banished suspects to remote islands without formal charges or trial; 7,200 were banished by April 1947, while thousands more went to prison. Large numbers of women and children were detained under primitive conditions simply because their male relatives were considered "red." The authorities often apprehended socialists under the accusation that they were fellow travelers of the Communists. At least 3,136 Greeks suffered legal execution between 1946 and 1949, and many others were murdered without trial. Even Churchill, no friend to the Communists, protested the mass executions. At one point, the military classified Jehovah's Witnesses as an "offshoot" of the KKE. The U.S. government sanctioned the mass arrests of July 1947, arrests that drove the remaining KKE leaders into the hills and eliminated any chance of compromise. In late August, however, the backlash over these measures led to the resignation of Prime Minister Dimitrios Maximos, replaced by the aged liberal Themistoclis Sophoulis, who presided over a broader center-right coalition. This, in turn, produced some reforms in the gendarmerie. Nonetheless, violations of civil rights continued throughout the conflict. Such abuses obviously weakened the government's legitimacy and provided recruits for the DAG.[22]

Equally controversial was the change in monarch. On April 1, 1947, King George II died, succeeded by his brother Paul I. Paul believed in a more active role for the monarchy, and he was heavily influenced by his wife, Frederika, who was a granddaughter of the German Kaiser Wilhelm II and had been a youth leader in Hitler's Germany. Both the king and queen were staunch anticommunists, and Paul repeatedly intervened to make the government more effective if sometimes more ruthless. In particular, Paul worked to make

General Alexander Papagos, who had defeated the Italian invasion of 1940–1941, commander-in-chief with near-dictatorial powers.[23]

U.S. officials were equally concerned by the need for change. Despite Markos's failure to seize and hold a suitable capital, the DAG was clearly winning in the fall of 1947. Meanwhile, although the British continued to train and advise the GNA, the British military garrison shrank sharply in size. In October, the U.S. Army's director of military intelligence, Major General Stephen J. Chamberlin, concluded an on-site inspection with a report that the GNA was demoralized and disorganized, and faced an efficient, Soviet-supported foe. Without consulting either Griswold or General Livesay, Chamberlin recommended an expanded American advisory effort.[24] The perceived insurgent threat had already eroded the initial American reluctance to expand government forces; in September, the Greek General Staff and General Livesay, the USAGG commander, had agreed on a plan to expand the GNA to a total of 150,000 men, soon increased to 200,000. The new army would form eight infantry divisions, three separate brigades, and a number of commando or LOK (Lochos Oreinon Katadromon) units, derived from the Greek exile Mountain Brigade. These LOK special forces units eventually reached the size of an additional division. Beyond this, the United States agreed to expand the National Guard to a total of one hundred battalions, each composed of five hundred reservists, policemen, and local volunteers. Although it took almost a year to build up this force, the National Guard eventually freed much of the regular army for offensive operations. Total Greek government armed strength exceeded 260,000 by the end of the 1940s. Moreover, the demand for manpower meant that for the first time the Greek government began to conscript suspected leftists rather than leaving them free to join the rebels. Some of these leftists ended up in penal units and island concentration camps, but the effort further restricted the manpower pool from which the DAG could draw.[25]

The dire situation also prompted the United States to reconsider its initial plan to send only a few officers to oversee the supply of military aid. On November 4, 1947, President Truman approved General Chamberlin's recommendations to create a Joint U.S. Military Advisory and Planning Group (JUSMAPG) of approximately two hundred officers and men. The principal purpose was to assist the

Greeks in staff planning, but eventually a few of these soldiers became advisors in combat. Some American observers believed, probably falsely, that the GNA was reluctant to close with the enemy and needed encouragement. Although such advisor groups were later quite common, JUSMAPG represented an extraordinary commitment on the part of the United States at a time when only a few other countries, such as the Philippines, had American advisory groups. The political as well as military role of the new organization was apparent from the fact that Secretary of State Marshall personally selected its commander. Acting on the advice of General Eisenhower, Marshall chose James A. Van Fleet to head JUSMAPG. The candidate had already proven himself in combat during the European campaigns of World War II—commanding a regiment, two different divisions, and finally a corps. Van Fleet received a promotion to lieutenant general when he went to Greece in February 1948. General Livesay remained in country, but his role was restricted to the logistical aspects of American assistance.[26]

The United States even briefly considered the deployment of combat troops—either Americans or survivors of the Polish exile army—to Greece. However, General Chamberlin helped persuade Defense Secretary James Forrestal of the political cost of such foreign troops.[27]

Balance of Forces

Meanwhile, the communist quest for a revolutionary capital continued. In late September, a series of DAG attacks pushed various government garrisons out of the border towns that separated Albania and Yugoslavia from Markos's base areas in the Grammos Mountains. Then, in mid-December 1947, the insurgents tried again. Various false reports prompted the Greek government to shift six battalions of the 8th GNA Division to defend Ioannina, a major town 40 kilometers south of the Grammos. Instead, on Christmas Day, Markos personally directed an attack on Konitsa, a town of 5,000 in the foothills just south of the mountain stronghold. Thousands of insurgents deployed to delay the advance of government relief columns, while 7,000 men of the DAG 16th and 32nd Brigades, supported by two batteries of mountain howitzers plus anti-aircraft machine guns, attacked the town. The initial predawn assault failed to surprise the defenders but overran two infantry companies west of the town. The defending brigade commander, the ubiquitous Colonel Dovas, was wounded when his jeep hit a land mine, yet the defenders held on. On the northern ridge overlooking Konitsa, the reinforced 584th GNA Battalion beat off a series of attacks over the next four days. Although rain hampered the arrival of reinforcements, the GNA shocked the attackers with a hail of fire from newly issued American weapons. On New Years' Eve, the DAG withdrew, seriously bloodied. That same day, two GNA companies infiltrated into the town over seemingly impassible mountain routes. The relieving force found 240 dead and 77 wounded rebels left behind, while the GNA lost the equivalent of a battalion—513 men—killed, wounded, and missing.[28]

Even before the battle of Konitsa began, the KKE had prematurely declared itself to be a provisional government. On December 24, 1947, a DAG radio station in Albania announced the membership of the new government, in which all but one cabinet minister were members of the KKE Central Committee. Although General Markos was increasingly at odds with Zachariadis about the abandonment of guerrilla tactics, his great prestige made the DAG commander prime minister and defense minister. To the KKE's chagrin, however, not even communist states recognized the new government diplomatically.[29]

In fact, the KKE found itself increasingly ignored if not abandoned by the communist bloc. Stalin and his Yugoslav counterpart, Tito, had often disagreed, but in the spring of 1948, their rivalry escalated rapidly. With some justification, Stalin feared that Yugoslavia, Albania, and Bulgaria might form a federation. Tito responded politely to Stalin's written accusations but refused to back down. In June 1948, a meeting of the Communist Information Bureau (COMINFORM, the successor to the COMINTERN) in Bucharest condemned the Yugoslav Communist Party for abolishing "democracy" and deviating from the Moscow line. Bordering on the Soviet Union, Bulgaria had no choice but to fall back into the Stalinist camp. Tito responded to the COMINFORM accusations by publishing his correspondence with Stalin, a move that inflamed Yugoslav patriotism and helped the dictator foil a pro-Soviet military coup. This left the KKE in a delicate position, torn between Tito, who was supporting the Greeks, and Stalin, who controlled most of the communist bloc but had never favored the Greek revolution. For some months, Tito continued to support the

KKE. Eventually, however, his need for Western economic aid to replace lost Soviet help would prompt him to abandon his Greek foster children.[30]

While the ideological struggle played out, the DAG continued raids throughout northern and central Greece, and the GNA planned for a summer effort in the Grammos Mountains. In preparation for this offensive, on February 28, 1948, the 8th GNA Division launched Operation Pergamos, seeking to clear the Mourghana ridge line, which lay on a north-south line just to the west of the Grammos. The attack, using one LOK commando and seven infantry battalions, failed dismally, due largely to a lack of artillery to deal with the DAG pillboxes defending the ridge. For the first time, the DAG had defeated the government in pitched battle, a defeat that helped confirm American suspicions that the GNA troops were reluctant to close with the enemy. General Van Fleet insisted on a new attempt, codenamed Falcon, in early April, but this was equally unsuccessful. These two operations cost the GNA 590 killed or wounded and 178 soldiers missing, while greatly increasing the prestige of Markos's insurgents.[31]

The GNA reorganized its command structure before renewing summer operations. General Constantine Ventiris, who had been in charge of counterinsurgency operations during the previous year, became chief of the Greek General Staff, and his Northern Army headquarters was dissolved. In February 1948, the British and Americans pressured the civilian government into ceding more power to the military. The British and U.S. commanders sat in on all meetings of the Supreme National Defense Council. Meanwhile, the Greek field army reorganized into five corps rather than three. The Ministry of Public Safety had a number of successes in breaking up the communist YIA-FAKA intelligence and supply network in Athens, Salonika, and other major cities.[32]

In the course of 1948, JUSMAPG grew to a total of 450 U.S. soldiers—advisors who became increasingly involved in planning and even directing Greek operations. At least three U.S. officers were killed in action implementing General Van Fleet's pressure on the Greeks to "Get out and fight!" Although this attitude sometimes offended his Greek counterparts, Van Fleet achieved results. Both American and Greek officers displayed a sort of crusading zeal for anticommunism. In the process, the American commander argued successfully to increase military aid at the expense of economic assistance. Eventually, Van Fleet's desire to help the Greeks even at the cost of ignoring diplomats and budgets offended Dwight Griswold, the civilian head of the American Mission for Aid to Greece. In late July 1948, Griswold recommended that the general be reassigned despite his visible success. Secretary of the Army Kenneth Royall went to Athens to investigate the conflict of personalities. Queen Frederika charmed the secretary while praising the general, and Royall recommended that Van Fleet remain in place. Griswold resigned, and the U.S. ambassador to Athens assumed his duties.[33]

Turnover

Van Fleet's influence was evident in a series of government offensives conducted in the spring and summer of 1948, but the main impetus came from the Greek officer corps itself, as a new generation of successful field commanders emerged. The first offensive was Operation Dawn, aimed at surrounding and clearing rebels in the Roumeli Mountains of central Greece. Three infantry divisions, two LOK battalions, and four battalions of police and National Guard, supported by artillery and a battalion of armored cars, encircled the mountains on land while the Greek Navy patrolled the coastline. Greek Air Force Spitfires and AT-6 Harvard trainers flew 370 armed sorties in support. Again, improved government firepower inflicted casualties on the DAG and reestablished communications between Athens and the northern part of the country. Between April 15 and May 26, the government claimed 610 guerrillas killed, 310 wounded, and 995 captured. Despite this success, Dawn failed to completely eliminate the DAG threat in the rough terrain of central Greece.[34]

After the failure at Konitsa in December, Markos had argued for a return to guerrilla tactics. Yet, Zachariadis and the provisional government insisted on more conventional tactics—standing to fight against the new government incursions. This decision proved costly to both sides in the summer of 1948. Beginning on June 14, the GNA launched Operation Coronis (Crown) against the main DAG stronghold in the Grammos Mountains. Six government divisions—40,000 men—attacked the Grammos, considerably outnumbering Markos's 12,500 men in the area. The DAG was well prepared in two lines of fortifications with minefields, and security leaks gave Markos the Coronis plan well ahead of time. The stubborn communist defense stopped the initial GNA assault cold while guerrillas raided supply lines in the government's rear areas. This rebuff forced the GNA to reconsider and adjust its plans. General Ionnis Kitralakis, the 2nd Corps commander and former operations chief during the Greek-Italian War of 1940–1941, decided to concentrate on the southeastern approaches to the Grammos, abandoning efforts to conduct concentric attacks from various directions. When the assault resumed on June 28, the GNA improvised various solutions to its tactical problems, such as forcing herds of animals to cross suspected minefields and thereby detonate the mines. For the first time, the Greek pilots used U.S.-supplied napalm, although the twenty-five-pound bombs were often too small and inaccurate to hit the concealed DAG bunkers. However, the air force more than tripled its sortie rate and began to develop more expertise in ground support.[35]

The insurgents contained this second effort, but morale declined as they realized the extent of government power and American aid in comparison to their own lack of communist bloc support. Some rebels began to openly criticize their leadership, wrongly blaming Markos for the decision to stand and fight. By July 25, the government had restructured the tactical command and renewed its attacks, this time assaulting simultaneously from the northeast and southwest. On the latter front, the fortified hill of Kleftis repeatedly changed hands between the DAG and troops of General Thrasyvoulos Tsakalotos's I Corps. Tsakalotos, the charismatic former commander of the exile army's Mountain Brigade, energized his troops for more aggressive operations. By August 20, General Markos realized that the battle was lost and ordered a retreat. That night, Markos broke out of the encirclement on the northern side, allowing the provisional government, fifty artillery pieces, and a large number of wounded insurgents to escape to Albania. The remaining 8,000 defenders withdrew northward to their bastion in the Vitsi Mountains. The GNA had lost 801 killed and 31 captured or missing, whereas the DAG suffered 3,128 killed, 589 captured, and 603 deserters. As in previous operations, the government was left in possession of the battlefield but had failed to destroy its opponent.[36]

Despite the communist defeat, the KKE leadership continued to insist on conventional tactics. General Markos disagreed so vehemently that KKE political officers reportedly attempted to assassinate him during the retreat from Grammos.[37] In June, Zachariadis traveled to Moscow to appeal for more aid, especially heavy weapons to conduct his increasingly conventional war against the American-equipped GNA. Andrei Zhdanov, the leading Soviet expert on ideology and party affairs, flatly refused. However, Zachariadis appealed directly to Stalin, who agreed to provide some assistance. While the Soviets remained skeptical of the KKE's chances for victory, they could not afford to appear to desert their ideological comrades at a time when the upstart Tito was providing so much aid. Moreover, by 1948, the confrontation between east and west had become so overt that Stalin was less concerned about challenging his former allies in the Balkans.[38]

Although Markos was still too popular to be dismissed openly, Zachariadis continued to push his own ideas for the conduct of the war. The failure of the DAG combined with the sense that its manpower was slowly drying up prompted him to push for a military decision before the government's forces could fully absorb American weaponry and training. To this end, during the latter half of 1948, the DAG abandoned its loosely connected bands in favor of a more conventional military organization. Divisions consisted of three brigades, each of three to four battalions. Nominally, each battalion contained 430 men and women, 6 mortars, and 29 machine guns. Political officers were active at every level down to platoon. In practice, of course, many of these new units were lacking in manpower, weapons, and above all trained leaders and staff officers. Indeed, a conventionally organized DAG could not hope to compete in terms of equipment with the U.S.-backed GNA. Still, the reorganization permitted Markos to place his best officers in charge of the new units.[39]

In the midst of these struggles, a true Greek tragedy unfolded as both sides resorted to forcible evacuations to control the population. The government had already moved 310,000 people out of contested areas during 1947 and continued the process in newly cleared areas during 1948. Meanwhile, Yugoslavia, Romania, Hungary, Bulgaria, and Czechoslovakia all accepted Greek children whom the DAG had evacuated. By the end of the war, more than 23,000 children had been separated from their families in this manner. Each side insisted that it was protecting the population from the other side, while accusing the opposition of hostage-taking and brainwashing.[40]

After the communist escape from the Grammos Mountains in August, the government left one division to occupy the area and shifted four other divisions northward to the DAG stronghold in the Vitsi Mountains. This left General Tsakalotos with only one division to clear the troublesome defenses of the Mourghana ridge. After failing in his initial effort, on September 14, 1948, Tsakalotos launched his four best battalions on a pincer movement, seeking to cut off the ridge at the Albanian border. When field guns based inside Albania fired on this attack, Tsakalotos ordered counterbattery fire and sent an infantry company in a brief raid across the border—the only time in the war when the Greeks openly violated the DAG's sanctuary. By the 16th, I Corps had captured Hill 1806, the key to the Mourghana area.[41]

The government was less successful in its attack on the Vitsi Mountains. Indeed, the fall of 1948 proved to be the nadir of the government's defensive effort. Kitrilakis, the commander of the GNA 2nd Corps, was a brilliant theoretician but not an inspirational leader. He failed to isolate the Vitsi area from reinforcements, and his initial attacks accomplished little. On September 14, the same day that Tsakalotos seized the initiative on the Mourghana, two of Kitrilakis's demoralized battalions broke and ran under fire. Seventy-eight men were executed for desertion, and the GNA had to withdraw and regroup. General Van Fleet's criticism of the Greek effort almost created an international incident, but eventually he smoothed over the situation. The LOK commandos seized Mount Vitsi on October 18, but during the rest of that month, the DAG gradually pushed the GNA back. Thirteen thousand insurgents had thwarted 50,000 government troops, while both fighters and civilians became increasingly war-weary.[42]

On December 11–12, 1948, the insurgents again demonstrated their power in a raid on Karditsa, far removed from the Grammos. Four DAG infantry brigades overran the town, whose refugee-swollen population had reached 50,000. The attackers ravaged Karditsa, abducting nearly 1,000 civilians, then withdrew, leaving the roads mined to hamper the belated government reaction. The government was able to thwart several other attacks in November-December, but the rebels had regained the initiative, seizing towns for as long as five days. The only bright spot during this period was again provided by Tsakalotos, whose I Corps headquarters was transferred to south-central Greece, conducting another clearing operation that broke the back of resistance there during late December.[43]

The Athenian politicians and their American and British allies recognized the crisis they faced. In January 1949, Secretary Marshall endorsed the idea of a centralized military command under Alexander Papagos, the hero of the 1940–1941 war. On January 20, most of the moderate and right-wing political parties joined in a new "Government of National Salvation" whose first act was to recall Papagos to active duty as commander-in-chief. Papagos was given the power to replace commanders, introduce martial law, and bypass civilian leaders. He also brought back General Ventiris, whom the previous administration had dismissed as chief of staff. In effect, Papagos had almost unlimited powers, supplanting civilian control of the war. Despite heated arguments, however, Papagos failed to get U.S. backing for another increase in troop strength.[44]

Instead, the new commander-in-chief threw his troops into battle with a ruthless urgency. He authorized officers to shoot anyone who was negligent or faint hearted. Beginning in the south and moving steadily northward, a series of search and clear operations gradually sanitized the country outside of the mountain redoubts. In addition to capturing armed rebels, the police detained suspected Red sympathizers everywhere. This continued violation of civil liberties claimed many innocent victims, but it also deprived the DAG of much of its intelligence and support network, making the insurgents blind and nervous.[45]

Meanwhile, Zachariadis contributed mightily to his own defeat. General Markos had already lost control of the DAG, but on February 4, the Provisional Government relieved Markos and his principal supporter, the head of the clandestine network, for supposed ill health. Three days later, the government ordered the arrest of six of Markos's best generals, one of whom was executed. To compound his errors, Zachariadis returned to the official Moscow line that Macedonia should be independent from Greece, a decision that outraged nationalist sentiments throughout Greece. At the same time, the Tito-Stalin controversy reached its final conclusion. Yugoslav and Albanian aid declined steadily, and on July 10, 1949, in response to British and American economic pressure, Tito announced the gradual closure of the frontier. The 16,000 DAG soldiers inside Albania and Yugoslavia were interned, leaving their comrades virtually isolated inside Greece.[46]

In late spring, Zachariadis closed down most training centers and ordered a return to guerrilla tactics. By this time, however, the populace was tired of war in general and of the DAG's demands in particular, and began to betray the rebels to government forces. Still, those rebels retained considerable strength, having reoccupied their redoubts in the Grammos and Vitsi Mountains with some 12,000 troops.

Their hopes to hold out until winter were dashed when the government launched Operation Pyrsos (Torch) in August 1949. One LOK and seven regular divisions concentrated around the two areas, with considerable U.S. equipment and nearby forward air strips to support them. Farther to the east, III Corps controlled an additional two divisions plus supporting troops for a simultaneous clearing operation along the Bulgarian border. General Kitrilakis orchestrated a deception to suggest that the GNA would attack the Grammos Mountains first, then struck at Vitsi on August 10. Up to 169 air sorties per day plus U.S.-supplied mountain howitzers provided fire support to five separate attacks against this stronghold, allowing the GNA to clear most of the Vitsi in a single week.[47]

Although most of the I and II Corps had redeployed around Grammos by August 22, Papagos delayed an additional three days to permit the Greek Air Force to bring fifty newly arrived Helldiver aircraft into service. On the 25th, the GNA moved rapidly to seal off Grammos from neighboring Albania. The next day, the Albanian dictator Enver Hoxha followed Tito's lead, halting artillery fire from inside his country and announcing that anyone crossing the border would be interned. Although he did not attempt to disarm the DAG troops, he did threaten to cut off food supplies if they returned to Greece. By the end of the month, all resistance had ceased in the Grammos Mountains, leaving the GNA in possession of 40 field guns, 600 machine guns, and 200 mortars, as well as 1,000 dead DAG fanatics.[48]

The Greek Civil War virtually ended with Operation Pyrsos. Zachariadis and his supporters tried to continue the struggle, but on October 16, the DAG radio announced a unilateral ceasefire. On the 17th, King Paul promoted Papagos to field marshal. President Truman described Van Fleet as "tops in my book . . . I think he is one of our ablest men,"[49] leading to the general's subsequent command in Korea. Most of the remaining rebels were rounded up by the end of the year.[50]

Conclusion

An estimated 158,000 people died in the course of the Greek Civil War.[51] It would be simplistic to ascribe the government's victory to the advent of American military aid and advice, although the presence of such aid, when contrasted with the eventual end of communist bloc assistance, had both a material and a psychological effect on all participants. It also insulated the anticommunist Greek military from political control for decades after the war. A politicized officer corps seized power in April 1967, and the resulting purges demoralized the Greek Army by the early 1970s.[52]

Nor was the success due solely to tough-minded commanders like Dovas, Tsakalotos, and Papagos, although the government's military leaders generally outclassed their DAG opponents, with a few exceptions such as Markos Vaphiadis, in professional skill and knowledge. Certainly Nicos Zachariadis hastened his own failure by sidelining his best commander and prematurely abandoning guerrilla tactics in favor of conventional warfare that gave the government targets to defeat. Under these circumstances, the rebellion was literally outspent by the United States, which provided $760.7 million in economic aid and $476.8 million in military support during the three fiscal years from July 1947 to June 1950. Indeed, American officials came to regard Greece as a kind of model for dealing with European Communists. In December 1947, when the Allies were about to withdraw from Italy, the administration depleted U.S. Army war stocks to ensure that the Italian armed forces had enough weapons to repress the left.[53]

American aid, by itself or in concert with the civilian Zachariadis's mistakes, might not have won the war. Fundamentally, the majority of the Greek population was either neutral or openly opposed to the communist regime. Despite the frequent abuse of power by the Athens government, its populace apparently concluded that the Communists posed a greater threat to their future happiness. No doubt the Orthodox priests of this deeply religious nation contributed to this opposition of the Communists, as did the general war-weariness of all concerned. The importance of public opinion in insurgencies was a lesson that had to be repeatedly relearned by both sides.

4

ARMED FORCES IN AN ATOMIC AGE

Despite all the points of potential and actual conflict during the first three years after World War II, the Great Powers attempted to avoid major confrontation. In this lull, the organization and civil-military relations of the two sides evolved generally in parallel. Each side experienced significant civil-military strains while attempting to balance national defense and economic security. Such friction contributed to more serious conflicts between soldiers and civilians when subsequent conflicts revealed the effects of peacetime economies.

THE INCREDIBLE SHRINKING U.S. ARMED FORCES

In 1945–1946, almost everyone in the U.S. armed forces wanted to get home as quickly as possible. After a decade of depression and four years of war, too many private lives had been put on hold for too long, and the veterans were eager to start careers and families. The government had introduced the Servicemen's Readjustment Act of 1944, popularly known as the G.I. Bill of Rights, which offered unprecedented opportunities for education and home ownership, but only if the serviceman could get discharged. Yet, leaving aside any concerns about the Soviet Union, the United States needed to maintain occupation forces in Germany and Japan, so it could discharge veterans only to the extent that replacements arrived to take their places.

This, in turn, meant continuing the Selective Service System even after victory was assured.[1] Although the navy (and in the future, the Army Air Forces) was confident that it could fill its ranks with volunteers, the same was obviously not true for the Army Ground Forces, the essential "boots on the ground" of occupation. For that matter, conscription for the army had often motivated "volunteers" for the other services. Yet the one-year extension of conscription that became law in May 1945 limited the draft to men aged nineteen to twenty-six, the very pool of replacements that had been virtually fished dry in 1944–1945. Responding to public pressure, Congress did not wish to draft men who had just turned eighteen, even though they formed the largest available group of potential conscripts.

By the end of that year, Selective Service was unable to meet its monthly quota of new conscripts, and the process of discharging experienced veterans began to slow down. When this problem became public knowledge, there were considerable protests and at least one riot of troops overseas. President Truman received scores of petitions from soldiers and politicians, asking for the early discharge of specific groups.[2] These protests were critical in convincing Congress to extend the draft through March 31, 1947, while continuing to limit the liability to those aged nineteen or older. The extension also reduced the term of service from twenty-four to eighteen months. This extra year enabled the army to bring the veterans home, but political opposition to the draft continued, and Truman's efforts to replace it with Universal Military Training failed dismally. As a consequence, the president allowed conscription to lapse in April 1947, a clear indication that despite civil wars in Greece, China, and elsewhere, he was still hoping to avoid military confrontation with the Soviet Union.[3] Congress had previously authorized enlistment bonuses to attract volunteers, and a surprising number of men did step forward. Still, the prospects for maintaining the 684,000-person army of June 1947 were dim, with the last draftees leaving active duty at the end of that month.

In the rush to demobilize, entire divisions dissolved without even a ceremony to mark their passing, leaving their equipment unsupervised and unmaintained. In 1947, the U.S. Army had more than 370,000 unserviceable motor vehicles on its books. In 1950, only 6,600 of the 28,000 tanks on hand in 1945 still functioned.[4] Spare parts, including batteries for tactical radios, were almost unattainable.

The equipment problem seriously affected the capability of the reserve components. By the end of 1946, the Truman administration had authorized the reestablishment of twenty-seven (later twenty-eight) National Guard and twenty-five Reserve divisions. The National Guard formed twenty-six infantry and two armored divisions, while the Organized Reserve was allocated four airborne, three armored, and eighteen infantry formations. The political influence of the National Guard ensured that the Reserve had a lower priority for funding and equipment.[5] However, all reserve component units had serious equipment deficiencies even four years later when they were recalled for Korea. Although the officers and senior noncommissioned officers of these units had a wealth of wartime experience, they were understrength in junior enlisted men. Moreover, prior to 1957, there was no requirement for reserve component recruits to undergo active duty basic training, so that men who joined after the war had little training.[6]

Whether volunteers or draftees, postwar inductees were on average far less trained than their predecessors. During World War II, the standard basic training cycle, usually conducted by a division as it trained for deployment, consisted of seventeen six-day weeks. In the immediate postwar era, the public backlash against wartime strictness reduced basic training to as little as eight five-day weeks, although by 1948, this was increased again to thirteen weeks. The reduced training still included qualification with individual weapons. Gone, however, was the so-called "Battle Indoctrination Training," where trainees crawled forward while live machine-gun and artillery fire passing over their heads, or advanced across a range while firing live ammunition and grenades. The headquarters of Army Ground Forces and its successor, Army Field Forces, intended that live-fire combat training would resume after the start of a national emergency. In fact, of course, the Korean conflict occurred without warning; twelve days after U.S. troops entered combat, Army Field Forces reinstituted live-fire training.[7]

Overall, the average age, maturity, and discipline of the peacetime army inevitably declined. By January 1947, Lieutenant General John R. Hodge, commander of the shrinking XXIV Corps that still occupied South Korea, regarded his callow enlisted troops as a menace to public order. He described them as young men who thought that the army should provide them "a vacation with pay while they earned a free education" under the G.I. Bill.[8]

Part of the problem was psychological. With the advent of the atomic bomb, many people considered ground forces to be obsolete, suitable only for occupying territories already conquered from the air. The U.S. Army's only claim to participate in the high-technology future was a deliberately concealed effort to develop missile technology. This effort had begun in 1945 with U.S. efforts to exploit captured German scientists, engineers, and other specialists, including German intelligence officers concerned with the Red Army. The British and Soviets made similar efforts. One part of the multifaceted American exploitation was Operation Paperclip, the clandestine shipment of hundreds of German scientists to the United States. Among this privileged group were more than one hundred individuals, including the later-famous Wernher von Braun, who were veterans of the German missile program. Ignoring possible involvement in slave labor and other war crimes, U.S. Army intelligence and ordnance officers asked these men to continue their studies at Fort Bliss, Texas, and the newly established White Sands Proving Ground in New Mexico. At the latter location, an experimental army battalion worked with the Germans using a ragged collection of captured V-1 guided rockets and V-2 ballistic missiles. These missiles often proved erratic when tested, however; during one month in 1947, three V-2s went off course, one of them landing less than three miles from the heavily populated city of Juarez, Mexico.[9] Still, the testing continued, with some of the data shared with the navy. Meanwhile, the U.S. Air Force used a different group of German scientists and engineers; based on the swept wings of the Me-262 jet fighter, the air force began to develop F-84 and F-86 fighters with better aerodynamics and therefore higher speeds than its initial, straight-wing jets.

Although the U.S. Navy experienced fewer recruiting problems in the immediate postwar era, it was also the subject of radical reductions in funding and capability.[10] In the administrative chaos after the unexpected Japanese surrender, the Navy Department was hard-pressed to determine its postwar requirements and size. Its first attempt at an annual proposed budget was $6 billion, at a time when the Truman administration wanted the *entire* defense budget to total only $5 billion.

In the general rush to demobilize, the navy had to provide vessels to move the other services home from overseas. Once-proud aircraft carriers became floating hotels under Operation Magic Carpet, with predictable losses in efficiency and capability. Because the regular navy officer corps had remained very small throughout the war, the reserve officers who staffed major headquarters and most ships' crews evaporated in a matter of months. By the middle of 1946, the fleet had been reduced from 99 to 23 aircraft carriers and from 412,000 to 24,000 aircraft. Although the first three ships of the new Midway class fleet carriers were completed in 1945–1946, the navy put 2,600 other ships into mothballs with dehumidifiers to extend their lives at the moorings. Many of the vessels still in commission lacked competent crews to put to sea.[11] Despite this, the navy like the other services still had many overseas obligations.

Nor was the U.S. Navy's sea power invulnerable. In 1946, naval analysts became concerned that the Red Navy might field the improved German Type XXI submarine, a true submersible whose underwater speed of sixteen knots rendered existing USN anti-submarine warfare tactics and equipment obsolete. In fact, the Soviets were slow to capitalize on this captured German technology, but the possibility alone prompted crash projects that led to improved sonar and anti-submarine weapons in 1947–1948.[12]

STRATEGIC AIR COMMAND

Although buffeted by the same public demand for demobilization that plagued the U.S. Army and Navy, the Army Air Forces (AAF) was comparatively well off, albeit few of its senior officers would have acknowledged their advantage at the time.

In planning prior to the end of hostilities, Army Chief of Staff George C. Marshall had insisted that the AAF reduce its postwar strength from 105 groups to 70 groups and 54 separate squadrons. This figure, which seemed laughably small in the context of the world war, in fact proved too large for the air force to achieve at any time before the Korean War.[13]

From the beginning in the 1920s, advocates of air power had always insisted on centralized, independent control of that power. During the later Pacific war, for example, AAF head General Henry H. Arnold had created a separate organization, the Twentieth Air Force headquartered on Guam. For the bombardment of Japan, Twentieth Air Force was under the direct control of the AAF's Strategic Air Forces, rather than that of the theater commander, Admiral Chester Nimitz.

By the end of the war, the public perception of the power of strategic bombing, even before the advent of atomic weapons, helped the future U.S. Air Force stake its claim to both independence and military preeminence in technology and budgets.

Still, the first step after victory, as for the other services, was to bring a large portion of the air units home from overseas. This task fell to the Continental Air Forces, which accepted and processed 5,462 aircraft and 73,643 airmen between May and August 1945, followed by 734,715 additional personnel in the next six months. As in the other services, men received discharges based on longevity, with little concern for the postwar capabilities that would remain after their departure.

Once the initial rush of redeployment finished, however, General Arnold set out to create the nucleus of a future independent air force. In the spring of 1946, he divided the continental assets of the AAF into three components: a Strategic Air Command (SAC), a Tactical Air Command (TAC), and an Air Defense Command (ADC). Pride of place went to SAC, which assumed control not only of the bombardment groups of 2nd Air Force but also of two of the four fighter groups that remained operational in the United States. ADC had such a low priority that it received few operational flying units.[14]

As part of this reorganization, on March 31, 1946, the Continental Air Forces was redesignated as SAC, with headquarters at Bolling Field in Washington D.C., although it soon moved to Omaha, Nebraska. General George C. Kenney, who had already persuaded General Douglas MacArthur to merge all Pacific AAF elements into a single command, soon assumed command of SAC. Yet, Kenney was distracted by other projects, including advising the newly formed United Nations, leaving his deputy, Major General St. Clair Street, to build the new force from scratch. Meanwhile, the AAF had difficulty retaining highly skilled airmen, who were in demand for civilian airlines.

Like the rest of America's postwar military, SAC was a hollow shell. Only the 509th Composite Group had the actual training, equipment, and experience to drop atomic bombs. By 1947, this group of "Silverplate" B-29s was joined by five other B-29 groups, not all of which were fully equipped or trained even for conventional operations, let alone atomic bombing. The early atomic weapons were so large (up to 10,500 pounds) that a special ground crew had to build a concrete-lined pit, place the components of the weapon on a hydraulic lift inside that pit, and then taxi the specially equipped aircraft over it so that the weapon could be assembled and lifted inside the bomb bay.[15] At the end of 1945, there were forty-six Silverplate-configured B-29s but far fewer atomic bombs or trained bomb assembly crews. Thus, in the event of war, most of SAC would have had to use conventional bombs.

Because of the prestige and secrecy attached to the atomic bomb, even government planners were unaware of these limitations. To cite one example, in November 1945, the Joint Intelligence Committee, reporting to the Joint Chiefs of Staff, nominated some 20 Soviet industrial plants for atomic bombing in the event of confrontation. At the time, the entire U.S. stockpile was two atomic bombs, and the AAF itself estimated a 52 percent attrition rate on bombers before they reached their targets.[16]

In 1946, President Truman ordered the expenditure of two scarce atomic bombs to evaluate their effect on military targets. Operation Crossroads was conducted at Bikini Atoll in the Pacific in July. A fleet of ninety ships sat at anchor around the island to determine the effect of the A-bomb on those ships. In the first test, "Able," a B-29 air-dropped the bomb but missed its aiming point and therefore destroyed only five ships. The second or "Baker" test involved the detonation of a bomb suspended ninety feet below the surface of the water. This explosion destroyed eight ships and contaminated many more with radioactive salt water.[17]

Based on this experiment, the Joint Chiefs of Staff concluded that the United States needed to be on constant alert to reduce the chance of surprise attack, and that atomic bombs were so scarce that targets must be carefully selected. This scarcity dominated SAC planning for the next several years.[18]

The atomic weapons were so prestigious that they became the subject of a serious custody battle during the later 1940s. In the fall of 1945, Truman suggested internationalizing nuclear energy under the U.N., including sharing information with the Soviet Union. Of course, this sharing was conditional upon the Soviets permitting on-site inspection to ensure that they were not secretly producing atomic weapons; this proviso made an otherwise utopian solution unacceptable to the Soviets.[19] Civilian officials of the Atomic Energy Commission (AEC) convinced President Truman that atomic energy was too broad and important a capability to be left in military hands. Executive Order

9816 transferred all the Manhattan Engineer District's wartime property, including the atomic bomb stockpile, to the AEC effective January 1, 1947. The AAF understandably wanted control of the bombs to facilitate deployment in an emergency, and so the debate continued within the government for several years. This controversy forced the AEC to conduct a practice drill for custody transfer, known as Operation Unlimited, in November 1948. Not until 1951 did the growing atomic stockpile and increasing international tensions lead the AEC to share control with the military.[20]

Despite all these obstacles, in 1947, SAC began to practice overseas deployments, seeking to position its B-29s and B-50s (improved versions of B-29s) within range to bomb the Soviet Union. At first, the SAC leadership, composed as it was of veterans of Twentieth Air Force in the Pacific, had no use for European bases, which they thought would fall quickly to the enemy in the event of war. Their old bases in the Far East were far better equipped, but also farther from potential Soviet targets. Although the polar route was the shortest way to reach the enemy, extreme weather and navigation problems in this region severely stressed the early SAC crews. In August 1947, for example, the 47th Bomb Group deployed to Ladd Field, outside Fairbanks, Alaska, on a short-notice drill. Of sixteen bombers that took off from the Continental United States, eleven turned back due to navigation problems. During 1946–1947, several B-29s crash landed and one disappeared without a trace while operating in extreme northern latitudes. Meanwhile, the limited budget prevented the air force from addressing these navigational issues.[21]

THE UNIFICATION DEBATE

Still, the power of the atomic bomb coupled with a carefully cultivated image of being a modern, technologically advanced force gave the AAF considerable leverage in postwar restructuring discussions. The World War II structure—separate War and Navy Departments cooperating through various ad hoc planning boards, such as the Joint Chiefs of Staff and dozens of joint agencies, while theater commanders argued for scarce resources—obviously needed revision. It was a foregone conclusion that the air force would become a separate service, but the overall organization of America's armed forces was open to debate. The result was the first of numerous instances of civil-military friction.

This debate was colored by personalities and perceptions, many of the latter being false. In the eyes of many army leaders, President Roosevelt, a former assistant secretary of the navy, had a significant bias in favor of that department. He had appointed retired Admiral William D. Leahy as "chief of staff to the President." Although Leahy had no clearly defined authority, he chaired the improvised U.S. Joint Chiefs of Staff (JCS), which consisted of the chief of staff of the army (Marshall), the commanding general of the AAF (Arnold), and the Chief of Naval Operations (CNO Admiral Ernest King). Thus, in simplistic terms, the wartime JCS was divided evenly between two army and two navy flag officers, a situation that hamstrung them in their negotiations with the well-coordinated policies of their British counterparts.

With the death of President Roosevelt, the presidential bias appeared to shift. President Truman was a reserve colonel of field artillery and also had a personality conflict with the brilliant secretary of the navy, James Forrestal. Truman, the small businessman from the Midwest, was very uncomfortable around the Princeton-educated Wall Street financier. Therefore, Forrestal and senior naval officers believed that the new president was inclined to favor the army in decisions about postwar military structure. In reality, of course, Truman had little patience with senior officers of any service. He admired the honor code of professional soldiers, but his populism and his own experience as a citizen soldier made him resent the implied claim that academy graduates were an elite. Still, his obvious reluctance to include Forrestal in his inner circle coupled with the eventual replacement of Leahy by a series of distinguished army officers appeared to confirm his supposed pro-army bias.[22]

One of the few exceptions to Truman's low opinion of career officers was George Marshall. Before his retirement as army chief of staff in the fall of 1945, Marshall had argued eloquently for the need to have a single defense department, presided over by a civilian secretary, a single chief of staff, and a unified military staff. Truman even endorsed such a plan in a message to Congress on December 19, 1945. Marshall's successor as chief of staff, General Eisenhower, was equally interested in reducing duplication. In early 1946, he sent a memo to the other Joint Chiefs suggesting that the marine corps should be reduced to a small auxiliary of the navy since large combined-arms marine units would simply duplicate the army. Given the Army Air

Forces' doctrinal belief in centralized control of aircraft, senior AAF commanders were inclined to agree with Marshall and Eisenhower, always under the proviso that the air force would be a separate but equal part of this new structure. In fact, Arnold's successor in command of the AAF, Carl Spaatz, made an "off-the-record" speech in March 1946 that questioned the very need for a navy, given the importance of strategic bombing and the fact that the potential adversary, the Soviet Union, had such a limited maritime force.[23]

Needless to say, such intemperate suggestions by Eisenhower and Spaatz alarmed the uniformed and civilian heads of the Navy Department, who feared being reduced to impotence with the skeletal marine corps while naval and marine air elements were subordinated to the air force. Nor was this fear groundless, considering that when the British Royal Air Force had become independent at the end of World War I, it took control of the Royal Navy's air arm, setting back British sea-based airpower by at least a decade.[24] During the centuries of naval warfare before radio communications, the navy had developed a tradition of decentralization and cooperation— allowing the naval commander to make decisions on the spot rather than being directed from Washington. In naval eyes, performing their worldwide missions required decentralization of control, plus naval air and marine air-ground combat teams to extend their influence ashore. Moreover, Forrestal believed that coordination between the services was far less important and difficult than inter-agency issues, and sought to coordinate all the foreign and defense policies of the United States.[25]

Given these considerations, Forrestal and most admirals preferred something on the lines proposed in October 1945 by the navy secretary's former business partner Ferdinand Eberhardt. The Eberhardt Plan called for three coequal service departments that would coordinate their efforts through various boards, including a national security council and a national security resources board.[26] When the Senate Military Affairs Committee was unable to reconcile such dissimilar plans by the end of 1945, a special subcommittee assumed the thankless task. Major General Lauris Norstad, an aviator who served as the army's director of plans and operations, and Vice Admiral Arthur W. Radford, Deputy Chief of Naval Operations for Air, advised the subcommittee. After nine drafts failed to produce agreement, in May 1946, Truman gave identical letters to Forrestal and Secretary of War

Robert R. Patterson, urging them to reach a resolution by June 15. Even this impetus achieved little in the face of conflicting service definitions of national security, so the president personally directed a compromise solution. There would be four civilian secretaries— for Defense, Army, Air Force, and Navy—but only the first of these would sit in the cabinet. The marine corps would retain its independence and tactical aviation, although wherever possible land-based aviation units would be manned by the air force.[27]

Even the president's intervention did not completely resolve the matter. In the fall of 1946, Congress and the public supporters of the marine corps demanded further compromises. Predictably, the army, with its advocacy of centralization and perceived irrelevance in the atomic world, had to make most of the concessions. Norstad and Radford drafted a final plan, signed on January 16, 1947, by their respective service secretaries and therefore known as the Patterson-Forrestal Agreement. After further negotiations in Congress, the plan became law on July 26, 1947.

In many ways, the National Security Act (NSA) of 1947 reflected an American acknowledgement of the need to restructure for prolonged involvement and confrontation in foreign affairs.[28] The act created the National Security Council (NSC), a resources board, and a Director of Central Intelligence supervising both the intelligence community and a new Central Intelligence Agency (CIA). It also gave statutory existence to the Joint Chiefs of Staff, although that body remained in its weak World War II configuration. It would consist of the army and air force chiefs of staff, the Chief of Naval Operations (CNO), and ("if there be one") the chief of staff to the Commander-in-Chief. In other words, there was no chairman of the Joint Chiefs.

Contrary to popular conception, the 1947 act created a secretary of defense but *not* a Department of Defense. Instead, it substituted a loose organization, obviously inspired by Forrestal and Eberhardt, known as the National Military Establishment. The organization included a variety of coordinating bodies, such as the Munitions Board, the Research and Development Board, and the War Council, the latter including the secretary, the three service secretaries—Army, Navy, and Air Force—and their uniformed chiefs of staff. Although the secretary of defense was defined as "principal assistant to the president in all matters relating to the national security," his powers were strictly limited, with all functions not specifically delegated to him assigned to the secretaries of the three service departments.[29] This meant in practice that the defense secretary could control military budgets only to the extent that the president supported him. The three service secretaries were excluded from the line of presidential succession, making them de facto subcabinet officers, yet if they objected to any decision of the defense secretary, they could so inform him and appeal directly to the president. The secretary of defense was authorized three assistants but no deputy or undersecretaries. The JCS consisted of no more than one hundred officers due to a lingering fear of the pernicious dangers of general staffs on the Prussian/German model. Rather than a unified defense establishment, NSA 1947 preserved many of the inefficiencies of the previous situation.

To use an historical analogy, the 1947 act was similar to the Articles of Confederation developed during the Revolution, which denied power to the central government/secretary of defense in favor of the individual states/service departments. Such a compromise set the stage for numerous legislative and executive adjustments between 1949 and 1986. The result was a patchwork that often increased service rivalries and civil-military discord.[30]

The greatest loser in this debate was the State Department, which never regained its pre-1941 control over U.S. foreign policy and intelligence. Moreover, Truman was unwilling to cede any control to the newly created National Security Resources Board and other mobilization structures, and Eisenhower eventually did away with these boards.[31]

President Truman asked Robert Patterson, the champion of unification, to become the first defense secretary, but Patterson wanted to return to private life. Thus, in one of the most painful ironies of American history, James Forrestal, the great opponent of a centralized defense establishment, became the first secretary of defense (July 1947–May 1949). While it would be simplistic to blame his subsequent suicide on the difficulties of his new position, the stress of trying to coordinate a large and loosely structured government organization undoubtedly exacerbated his condition. Indeed, in late 1948, Forrestal confessed to Truman that he had been wrong to insist on a weak secretary of defense.[32]

ECONOMICS AND BUDGETS

The new law did not resolve many of the issues of national security; it only changed the venue of the arguments. Truman himself had little interest in the resulting national security structure. Thus, the first Director of Central Intelligence (DCI), Admiral Roscoe Hillenkoetter, did not have the authority to coordinate the service intelligence branches.[33] During the later 1940s, however, policy debates in Washington centered not on intelligence or even defense per se, but rather on economic and budgetary issues.

As already noted, the United States' great advantage in comparison to the rest of the world appeared to be its industrial strength. Yet, Truman's attempts to wield this advantage ran into difficulties. Acting under congressional mandate, he had abruptly ended Lend-Lease aid to the Soviet Union as soon as Germany surrendered, an action that he later regretted.[34] Moreover, the United States and its allies wanted to preclude future German aggression by dismembering the German industrial and scientific base. Yet, diplomatic officials, most notably Assistant Secretary of State Dean Acheson, argued that the European and American economies could only prosper under a general resumption of trade, including some economic recovery for Germany.[35] Given this conflict of intentions and the growing antagonism between the former allies, no concerted policy developed with regard to Germany. So long as the European economies languished on the edge of collapse, they appeared more likely to succumb to communism than to serve as major trading partners for the United States.

When retired General Marshall became secretary of state in February 1947, he again tried to use the economic element of power. The result was the June 1947 Harvard University speech in which he announced the Marshall Plan, an invitation for European governments to present their plans for economic reconstruction; if the United States agreed with the plans, it would fund the cost. To explore this proposal, that same month all the European governments, including those of the Soviet Union and Eastern Europe, met with Marshall for a Council of Foreign Ministers meeting in Paris.[36] Even the Soviet foreign minister, Vyacheslav Molotov, attended, apparently hoping to get a much-needed loan while encouraging differences of opinion among the Western nations. Yet, after several days of intense negotiations, Molotov abruptly condemned Marshall's offer as a trick and withdrew from the conference. Although Stalin's motivations were often obscure, it appeared that participation in the Marshall Plan would have required the Soviets to expose the incredible weakness of their economy, an action they understandably feared. Moreover, instead of simply negotiating a much-needed loan directly with Washington, the Soviet government found that it would have to participate in a highly structured European economic plan that was of necessity beholden to the United States. Rightly or wrongly, the Soviets feared that the new European Recovery Administration (ERA) would mean surrendering their influence in Eastern Europe. As a result, although the ERA did help Western Europe recover from the war, it failed in its more basic political purpose of ensuring open cooperation across the Continent. Instead, for Stalin it was a final proof that he could no longer cooperate with the United States.[37]

While the ERA stimulated the American economy by placing large production orders, it also increased the possibility of inflation. After fourteen continuous years of deficit spending for the Great Depression, World War II, and its aftermath, the U.S. economy appeared vulnerable to inflation or even another depression. The large expenditures involved in the Marshall Plan only reinforced Truman's determination to balance the budget by cutting defense spending. In December 1947, the president sent Congress a budget request for fiscal year 1949, scheduled to begin in July 1948, of $4 billion for the European Recovery Program and only $9.8 billion for defense spending.[38] Although a sizeable supplemental request eventually increased this allocation, the austere nature of such a budget, which included cutting personnel authorizations by 13 percent, is self-evident. Despite rising tensions with the Soviet Union during the next several years, Truman and his defense secretaries continued to fight for restraint in defense spending. Under these circumstances, the temptation to rely on atomic bombing as the primary instrument of military power was almost overwhelming.

The principal loser in the budget battles was the U.S. Army, which continued to shrink in both manpower and capability. As vice chief and then chief of staff of the army from 1947 on, J. Lawton Collins proposed a gradual program to build the army up to twelve active and thirteen high-priority national guard divisions by fiscal year 1952. However, the continued budget cuts prevented the army from even maintaining its ten existing divisions as anything but shells.[39] Moreover, without fuel, spare parts, and specialized ammunition, commanders found it difficult to conduct meaningful training. It is no exaggeration to say that the army's inadequate performance at the start of the Korean War can be traced primarily to lack of resources during the preceding several years.

The great winner, of course, was the U.S. Air Force. The first secretary of the new department, W. Stuart Symington, argued with much justification that the air force needed considerable funding for new bombers and jet-fighter interceptors, the essential components of an air power-oriented defense posture. When budget cuts forced reductions in air elements, the air force responded by transferring units away from the control of various regional unified commanders in order to reinforce the SAC organization.[40] When Forrestal and others tried to maintain a balanced defense capacity across the four services, Symington implied to Congress that the administration was neglecting the air force. A number of defense studies, most notably the Finletter Report of January 1948, supported Symington's position, arguing for air power to the virtual exclusion of the other services.[41]

New aircraft were enormously expensive; for example, the average B-17 in World War II cost $218,000 to build, whereas SAC's new flagship, the Convair B-36, went for $3.6 million each by 1949, when the air force requested hundreds of them.[42] The B-36 was the final stage in the long evolution of propeller heavy bombers that included the B-17 and B-29. This huge aircraft had a wingspan of 230 feet. It was powered by six rearward-pushing propeller engines, supplemented in 1949 by four jets, so that the result was sometimes referred to as "six turning and four burning." With a bomb capacity of up to 86,000 pounds, using air-to-air refueling the B-36 could travel anywhere in the world to perform SAC's mission. However, the aircraft was very expensive to build and maintain, and its survivability against sophisticated air defense systems with jet fighters was debatable.

ROLES AND MISSIONS

It was in this environment that the navy's uniformed leaders reached a crescendo of frustration about the future of national defense. Naval officers noted that the submarine blockade of Japan had driven that nation to the brink of collapse even before conventional and nuclear bombing took effect. As for the future, naval officers believed with some merit that the air force's plan for strategic atomic bombing might well prove indecisive in the case of war, and that the government needed the flexibility of aircraft carriers. Without rejecting the idea of strategic nuclear bombing, naval aviators wanted to be able to supplement such bombing with seaborne strikes against military targets.

In turn, this meant that the navy needed carrier aircraft capable of delivering atomic bombs, which was difficult in an age when the only existing bombs were very scarce and very large. By late 1946, the first such aircraft, the AJ-1 Savage, had undergone redesign to permit it to carry the 10,300-pound Mark III "Fat Man" out to a combat radius of 864 miles. To provide longer ranges, however, the carrier admirals wanted a new class of larger aircraft carriers, dubbed the *United States* class after the proposed first ship to be built. This class featured a flush-deck design without the characteristic "island" of previous carriers in order to accommodate aircraft with wider wing-spans. The design would also better withstand the high winds of a near-miss atomic attack.[43]

The air force was as irritated by the navy position as vice versa. Although few air force leaders wished to absorb naval aviation, they regarded aircraft carriers as an obsolescent weapon of limited capacity. To expend scarce defense dollars building vulnerable ships that would launch even scarcer atomic bombs against tactical, short-range targets appeared as a colossal waste at a time when only the B-36 could carry the fight to the presumed enemy in Moscow. In an atmosphere of increasing animosity, during 1948–1949, each service encouraged press reports favorable to its position and even attempted to plant spies inside each other's offices.[44] In late 1948, Navy Secretary John L. Sullivan and CNO Admiral Louis E. Denfield went even farther by creating a new office to defend naval policy interests. Heading the newly formed OP-23 as Assistant CNO for Organizational Research and Policy was Captain Arleigh Burke, already legendary as a destroyer commander in the Pacific conflict. Burke has also served as chief of staff to the Fast Carrier Task Force during the latter half of the war, making him unusually qualified to articulate the navy's conception of present and future warfare.[45]

Defense Secretary Forrestal was unable to dissipate the pressure built up by restricted budgets and rival atomic delivery systems. He did, however, make two successive attempts to negotiate an agreement that would delineate service roles and missions, in order to reduce rivalry and duplication. The first of these negotiations occurred in Key West, Florida, between March 14 and 19, 1948. Secretary Forrestal sequestered himself with the army and air force chiefs of staff and the navy chief of operations; once they reached some limited agreement (without any formal minutes of the meeting), the principals returned to Washington, where a JCS "Functions Paper" summarized the results of the meeting. Some of these results were significant, in that the Joint Chiefs of Staff as a group now had more responsibility for and involvement in combat operations and budgetary proceedings; the latter was particularly necessary at a time when the defense secretary had little control over departmental budgets. In the event of future combat, the JCS would designate one of its members as the primary "agent" to coordinate all aspects of a particular mission— for example, the army became the executive agent for the Korean conflict when it began.[46]

Superficially, the functions identified at Key West seemed to be comically self-evident: the army was responsible to produce forces for sustained combat on land; the navy had responsibility for sea warfare; the marine corps was the primary proponent for amphibious warfare, land operations to defend naval bases, and support to a naval campaign; and finally the air force was responsible for strategic air warfare, air defense of the United States, and both air and logistical support of ground forces. Beyond that basic division of functions, two or more services were to cooperate on functions that crossed service boundaries, including amphibious landings, air defense, and strategic air attacks. This last provision seemed to recognize the navy's argument that it should retain a role in atomic air operations. The principal loser, again, was the army. For the next fifteen years, the air force held a virtual veto over the design and employment of army aircraft while retaining sole responsibility for armed air support of the army. Unfortunately, given the ever-tightening budgets of the later 1940s, the air support function inevitably took a back seat to more visible missions, such as strategic bombing, continental air defense, and air transport. In December 1948, Hoyt Vandenberg, the air force chief of staff, felt forced to economize further at the expense of air support by combining Tactical Air Command with Continental Air Defense Command. When senior army commanders protested this apparent neglect of their requirements, Vandenberg appointed a board to investigate the issue. This board was headed by Lieutenant General Elwood "Pete" Quesada, a legendary air support commander in World War II, and thereby mollified the army leadership in the short run.[47]

Although the Key West Agreement was significant in many areas, it failed to resolve all the issues of interservice rivalry, particularly those between the navy and the air force. Five months later, on

August 20–22, 1948, Forrestal tried again, inviting the joint chiefs to meet with him at the Naval War College in Newport, Rhode Island. This conference clarified the air force's primacy in strategic warfare by specifying that the navy would not be excluded from atomic weapons, in return for which the navy dropped its opposition to "interim" air force control of the joint program for the handling of nuclear weapons. In effect, therefore, the Newport agreement kept alive the navy's argument that it could use atomic weapons both for tactical targets and to complement SAC's strategic program. In addition, Forrestal overcame JCS objections to the creation of a Weapons Systems Reevaluation Group to provide more objective advice on the use of such weapons.[48]

The Revolt of the Admirals

Despite these two landmark agreements, the issue of air force versus navy delivery of atomic weapons continued to cause friction between the services and on Capitol Hill. Each side sincerely believed that its doctrinal position was correct, but Truman's efforts to restrict defense spending exacerbated the issue.

By the time the matter came to a head in 1949, Louis A. Johnson had become the second secretary of defense. Johnson was a forceful and even abrasive personality, a man of strong opinions about defense preparedness and great ambition who owed his appointment in part to his success in raising funds for Truman's reelection. During the later 1930s, two successive secretaries of war had found him a disruptive influence, and he had been too inflexible to support the president's policy of providing aircraft to Britain ahead of the U.S. Army. As a result, Johnson had to resign as assistant secretary of war in 1940.[49] He came into office as defense secretary determined not only to restrict defense spending but to accelerate the cuts originally mandated by President Truman. From the navy's perspective, Johnson was doubly biased against carrier air power. Not only was he a veteran of the World War I army who had remained a reserve officer between the wars, but he had served on the board of directors of Consolidated Vultee, the primary contractor for the B-36. Whereas Forrestal had occupied a modest office in the Pentagon, his successor immediately moved into the E-Ring suite originally built for the secretary of war when the entire building had been devoted to that one department.

Johnson also appointed principal assistants with little experience of government or the military, increasing the chances for friction.[50]

Louis Johnson benefited from a belated reform of the defense structure. During 1947–1948, former President Herbert Hoover chaired a reorganization commission that endorsed Forrestal's recognition that the 1947 National Security Act was unworkable. In August 1949, therefore, President Truman signed a major amendment to the 1947 National Defense Act. The 1949 amendment formally created the Department of Defense and a nonvoting chairman of the JCS. It also demoted the three service secretaries in relationship to the president and gave the defense secretary control over the new department, including its budget.[51] These changes further reinforced Secretary Johnson's autocratic style.

While this reform was still going through Congress, Johnson brought the navy-air force disagreement to a sudden crisis in April 1949. The immediate issue was the fate of the new supercarrier *USS United States*, whose keel was laid down on April 18. Johnson had promised Navy Secretary John Sullivan not to make an immediate decision about the carrier. However, after consulting General Eisenhower but *not* the senior naval officers, on April 23, the defense secretary abruptly terminated construction of the ship, apparently believing that it represented an unaffordable luxury. Sullivan resigned in protest, thereby depriving his department of its political voice in the administration.[52] To succeed Sullivan, Johnson chose Francis Matthews, an official with no military experience who believed that naval officers should confine their opinions to protests through channels. Johnson thought he had mollified such protests when he agreed that the navy could convert several existing carriers to accommodate atomic-capable aircraft, but this only deferred the issue for a few months. In repeated rounds of budget cutting that summer, the navy absorbed two-thirds of the total reductions demanded by Johnson.[53]

Meanwhile, the B-36 program encountered considerable criticism, much of it instigated by the navy through an anonymous document passed to a congressman. The fact that Defense Secretary Johnson and other officials had an apparent conflict of interest in awarding the contract coupled with real doubts as to whether the huge bomber could penetrate modern air defenses led the House Armed Services Committee to conduct hearings on the matter beginning in August 1949. During the first round of such hearings, Air Force Secretary

Symington, Chief of Staff Vandenberg, and other senior air force officials assured Congress that the B-36 could fly so high and bomb so accurately that no defenses could halt it. Symington also exposed the author of the anonymous report as a civilian employee of OP-23, thereby discrediting the navy's position. Amidst mutual recriminations, the House committee recessed its hearings for several months.[54]

During the recess, a naval officer leaked the written opinions of several senior admirals to the effect that navy morale was seriously damaged by the ongoing budget cuts and policy decisions. Secretaries Johnson and Matthews considered such criticism to be disloyal and were concerned that the B-36 hearings had divulged sensitive information about the limitations of that aircraft. Matthews made numerous efforts to delay or cancel the hearings altogether so as to prevent further public wrangling between the services. Yet, when the committee hearings resumed in October, Chief of Naval Operations Denfield believed that he had to defend his service's position, even if it meant defying civilian authority. Admiral Denfield told the committee that in his opinion the budget cuts imperiled the fighting strength of the navy and marine corps, and that he supported the criticisms made by naval aviators against the B-36 program and the policies of the Defense Department. He bluntly described these policies as being based on "the erroneous principle of the self-sufficiency of air power."[55] The commandant of the marine corps, General Clifton B. Cates, was equally frank with the House committee, alleging that the army wanted to eliminate the marines and take over the amphibious mission.

The cumulative effect of this uniformed opposition to Johnson's policies became known as the "Revolt of the Admirals." General Omar Bradley, the chairman of the JCS, condemned the admirals as undisciplined, encouraging civilian officials to take action against them. Secretary Matthews had already nominated Denfield for another two-year term as chief, but under pressure from Johnson, he dismissed the admiral, who retired rather than accept a lesser position. His designated successor, Admiral Forrest P. Sherman, immediately dissolved OP-23, which appeared to be the center of naval opposition. Not content with this, Matthews instructed a navy selection board to remove Captain Burke from the promotion list for rear admiral. Fortunately for the interests of fairness, Truman's naval aide convinced the president that Matthews lacked the authority to remove a name from a promotion list, and Burke was reinstated.[56]

In the short run, the so-called revolt cost the navy dearly. The number of carrier battle groups declined from twenty-four (including eleven attack carriers) in fiscal year 1949 to only nine groups (including six attack carriers) for fiscal year 1951, which was scheduled to begin in July 1950. Admiral Sherman was unable to start construction of a new aircraft carrier until early 1951. Overall, the Revolt of the Admirals became a symbol of the severe budget cuts of the later 1940s, cuts that significantly weakened the United States as it entered the Korean conflict.

The British armed forces underwent many of the same debates in the later 1940s. As Chief of the Imperial General Staff from 1946 to 1948, Field Marshal Viscount Montgomery's notoriously irascible personality hampered him in bureaucratic politics. He lobbied hard to keep conscripted service at eighteen months, but succeeded only in offending most of the cabinet and his peers. Montgomery tried and failed to centralize planning in the Chiefs of Staff Committee, the equivalent of the U.S. JCS. The Royal Air Force asserted its need for large budgets to acquire a new generation of jet fighters and bombers, and argued with the army and Royal Navy, respectively, for control of air defense missiles and coastal aircraft. The Royal Air Force (RAF) and the British Army, like their American counterparts, were skeptical of the Royal Navy's desire to build new aircraft carriers. Perhaps the only thing the service chiefs agreed upon was their dislike for the Labour minister of defence.[57]

Postwar Soviet Forces

As described in chapter 2, the Soviet defense structure retained much of its capability while partially demobilizing during the later 1940s. Although 8.5 million men of thirty-three conscript age groups had returned to civilian life by 1948, the Soviet Army retained 97.5 percent of those officers with advanced military schooling.[58] Indeed, the smaller Soviet Army was able to motorize or mechanize most of its units, virtually eliminating foot-mobile infantry divisions. The first Soviet armored personnel carrier, the wheeled BTR-152, entered production in 1945, although even the infantry in some tank divisions was still truck mounted until the mid-1950s.[59] By 1948, a Soviet mechanized division consisted of three motorized rifle regiments and a medium tank regiment (12,000–13,000 men), equipped on a scale that the Soviets could rarely afford during the war. Group of Soviet Forces, Germany (GSFG), the headquarters controlling the occupation of eastern Germany, had a total of twenty-two divisions. Behind GSFG were further divisions, generally less well equipped, stretching back across Central and Eastern Europe in great depth. The Soviet intention was probably defensive, but this massive assembly of mechanized forces gave the impression that Moscow was holding Western Europe hostage. In September 1947, National Security Council Memorandum 57 (NSC-57) ratified a Defense Department plan for preemptive use of atomic weapons as the only way to halt a Soviet attack in Western Europe.[60]

Yet, the shattered Soviet economy demanded every available effort for reconstruction, so Soviet divisions like their Western counterparts increasingly consisted of veteran cadres controlling large numbers of young, half-trained conscripts. DOSAAF, the Voluntary Society of Assistance to the Army, Air Force, and Navy, provided the equivalent of several weeks of premilitary training for Soviet teenagers, including orientation in small arms and chemical defense. Thus, except for specialized technicians and junior sergeants, the conscripts received little in the way of centralized basic training once they reported for duty. Instead, the draftees found themselves assigned directly to tactical units, in which the quality of training depended considerably on the leaders and on the other missions assigned to the unit. To cite one example, the Soviet Army had to clear 13.7 million mines and unexploded shells or bombs from the Ukraine alone; elsewhere the troops continued the traditional practice of growing their own food or assisting in the civilian harvest.[61] Because Soviet youth had less experience with motor vehicles than their Western counterparts, maintenance and operation of a unit's tanks and trucks consumed a large portion of the available training time.

Nuclear Proliferation

While the Soviets maintained a large and relatively modern army, they had to struggle with issues of airpower and atomic weapons. Publicly, Stalin insisted that the atomic bomb meant little and that mechanized forces would still win wars. Privately, however, he directed a number of crash projects to close the technological gap with the West.

Although Stalin's reasons were, as ever, obscure, he was apparently motivated not just by fear of the U.S. bomb but also by a desire to have the prestige of the very latest weapons.

Legend has it that the Soviet nuclear effort began with a brilliant young physicist, Georgiy N. Flerov. When the German invasion hit a lull in February 1942, Flerov got some time off from his Red Air Force unit. He visited a nearby university library to review the Western scientific journals, searching for acknowledgement of his own contributions to theoretical physics. What he discovered was that all the American scientific leaders in his field had suddenly stopped publishing in the professional journals. His conclusion was that these men must all be involved in a secret project to develop an atomic bomb. Supposedly, Flerov wrote first to a senior Soviet scientist, urging his government to imitate the Americans. Receiving no immediate response, the young physicist then wrote directly to the Soviet dictator, who launched the Soviet effort parallel to the Manhattan Project.[62]

Of course, Flerov's discovery was hardly the first sign that the West was embarked on a nuclear plan, but it may have helped confirm information coming from the British nuclear program. The Soviets had a number of agents in this program, of whom the most infamous was Klaus Fuchs, an idealistic communist refugee from Nazi Germany. Beginning in the fall of 1941, Fuchs sent reports about the nuclear program through his GRU controller.[63]

Regardless of the significance of Flerov's letters or Fuch's reports, the Soviets had indeed begun working on their own atomic weapon long before Truman informed Stalin of the bomb in 1945. As in so many other technical fields, Soviet efforts were hampered by the fact that promising young scientists were often imprisoned or executed as part of the great political purges. Still, in 1942, Flerov and other physicists resumed work on the question, while the NKVD placed a priority on collecting information about the U.S.-British atomic program. Faced with a shortage of fissionable material for experimentation, in 1943, Moscow had the effrontery to ask the United States for eight tons of uranium oxide ore under the auspices of the Lend-Lease program. Needless to say, this request was one of the few that the Americans did not honor, but the Soviet physicists continued their experiments.[64]

In 1945, most Americans considered the Soviets to be hopelessly backwards in scientific and technical terms, anticipating that it might take twenty years for Stalin to acquire an atomic bomb. In fact, the Soviets took only forty-nine months, detonating their first device in 1949. The Soviet espionage effort in the West had indeed developed rapidly, both before and during World War II. This became acutely obvious in September 1945, when code clerk Igor S. Gouzhenko defected from the Soviet embassy in Ottawa, bringing with him 109 documents showing the scope of NKVD collection efforts. Although Gouzhenko had little direct knowledge of espionage inside the United States, his defection gave J. Edgar Hoover, the notoriously anticommunist director of the Federal Bureau of Investigation, ample grounds to pursue the matter further.[65] British, American, and Canadian counter-intelligence officials apprehended numerous agents over the next five years, but the damage had already been done.

The Red Scare paranoia of the era naturally concluded that spies must have given the entire U.S. program to the enemy. Yuli B. Khariton, a leading designer at the Arzamaas-16 weapons laboratory, later claimed that, under intense pressure to produce a bomb, his colleagues copied the U.S. Nagasaki weapon to produce their first atomic detonation.[66] Still, while espionage undoubtedly provided the design concept, the technical details of atomic weapons design and construction were so voluminous that it is unlikely that the Soviets obtained complete plans. Some of the most famous spies, such as Ethel and Julius Rosenberg, were more effective in copying electronics developments than in the atomic project. What the Western information did do was to guide the Soviet physicists along the most efficient path to develop a weapon. As Steven Zaloga concluded,

> Espionage saved the Soviets considerable time in the basic research and advanced development phases by removing the need to explore fruitless, expensive, and unproductive alternative technologies. . . But the role of espionage should not be exaggerated. The location, mining, and processing of sufficient uranium is a gargantuan process involving tens of thousands of workers and scientists, and requiring considerable technological competence. Spying made it possible for the Soviets to design the bomb sooner and develop it less expensively than had they undertaken Operation Borodino [the atomic project] without the aid of espionage. The Soviets could have developed an atomic bomb without the espionage material, but it probably would not have been available until the early or mid 1950s.[67]

Given the highest priority in the Soviet state, Operation Borodino plunged forward in the later 1940s. Lavrenti Beria, head of the NKVD (redesignated MGB after the war) from 1938 to 1946, personally supervised the project, including the assistance of captured German scientists working in the so-called "First Circle" of the GULAG of concentration camps. Stalin pressured Beria for a bomb within two years, and in turn Beria browbeat the head of the project, Igor Kurchatov. In August 1948, when the first plutonium breeder reactor failed, Kurchatov only barely succeeded in dissuading Beria from arresting the "culprits." Unlike the U.S. program at Los Alamos, all information in Operation Borodino was strictly compartmentalized, making scientific and engineering collaboration far more difficult. Nor was the project immune from periodic purges and demands for political correctness over accurate science. Nonetheless, on August 29, 1949, Kurchatov set off the first atomic device in the desert south of Semipalatinsk in Kazakhstan. Beria was so suspicious that he insisted that a team of Soviets who had witnessed a U.S. nuclear test verify that Kurchatov's detonation was equivalent.[68]

Ironically, Stalin's persistent contention that the atomic weapon had only limited military significance meant that the Soviets were slow to adjust to the doctrinal changes inherent in such a weapon.[69] Other states, however, were quick to recognize the potential shift in the power balance. Edward Teller, a refugee Hungarian physicist, had campaigned since 1946 for the United States to go to the next step by developing the fusion or hydrogen bomb. He used the Soviet detonation as a lever to persuade Congress and President Truman to the same conclusion, despite the adamant opposition of J. Robert Oppenheimer and other leaders of the nuclear physics community, who considered the enormous destructive power of a hydrogen bomb to be too indiscriminate for use as a weapon. General Bradley and the JCS argued that the United States had to obtain the hydrogen bomb both to avoid a Soviet advantage in this area and to sober those who tended to advocate the use of nuclear weapons. Early in 1950, Truman secretly authorized pursuit of this new weapon.[70]

The result was another form of arms race. Beria, one of the few Soviet leaders who understood the theory of nuclear physics, continued to push his scientists so hard that the first Soviet hydrogen fusion detonation occurred less than six months after the United States achieved the same result in November 1952 (see chapter 13). In the process, Beria built closed scientific cities and industrial complexes in a country that was otherwise far behind the West in technology.[71]

The Soviet detonation also energized the ongoing British effort to develop their own atomic bomb. Britain had provided a major portion of the theoretical expertise for the World War II Manhattan Project, as well as facilitating American efforts to obtain uranium ore from various African locations. Yet, the wartime British economy had been unable to match the vast industrial effort involved in producing the U.S. bomb. Like Stalin, British leaders came to regard possession of this weapon as a matter of prestige, an affirmation of their great power status. In 1947, the British government established a formal goal of achieving a nuclear weapon within five years. The next year, the United States reluctantly agreed to a deal with the British, whereby the Americans would supply detailed nuclear information while the British gave up their claim to veto any U.S. use of a bomb and allocated two-thirds of African uranium production to the United States[72] In October 1949, Klaus Fuchs, by now the head of theoretical physics for the British Atomic Energy Research Establishment, was unmasked as a Soviet agent, bringing unwanted publicity to the British effort. Under the supervision of William Penney, the British finally succeeded on October 3, 1952, using an improved version of the U.S. "Fatman" design to vaporize a test vessel anchored off the coast of Australia.[73]

THE SOVIET AIR FORCE

Concurrently with the effort to develop an atomic device, Moscow also struggled to develop an air force that could defend against and deliver such a device. In 1946, for example, the Soviet research budget was five billion rubles, twice the allocation for 1945.[74]

First was the need for an effective air defense. Like the Americans, the Soviets moved many German experts to the Soviet Union— reportedly more than 3,000 in October 1945 alone. With them came the aircraft factories used to build advanced German aircraft— teams from the Soviet aircraft industry dismantled the factories and reassembled them one hundred kilometers northwest of Moscow. There the Soviets tested early German jet and rocket aircraft, including the Arado 234 twin-jet bomber and the Me-163 and Me-262 fighters. Although considerable long-term research continued in both rockets and jet propulsion, Soviet designers at the Mikoyan-Gurevich Design Bureau were immediately interested in the gas turbine engines produced by BMW and Junkers. The results were the MiG-9 and Yak-15, the first Soviet jet aircraft, which appeared at the 1946 May Day celebration. However, these first efforts were simply adaptations of existing propeller aircraft; for example, the Yakovlev design team mounted a Junkers Jumo engine on the superb Yak-3 fighter design to produce the Yak-15.[75]

These early aircraft lacked power and speed, and the Soviet factories had difficulty with quality control. Then, in September 1946, the British government made an ill-considered effort to improve both relations and trade with Moscow. Prime Minister Clement Attlee authorized the sale of ten Nene-2 gas flow turbine engines, which the Soviets were able to copy. The Mikoyan engineers used these engines to produce the MiG-15, a true sweptwing jet fighter, which flew for the first time in December 1947. Although the MiG-15 had a relatively short range and proved to be an unstable gun platform, it could climb and turn faster than the American fighters it would encounter in Korea. Soviet industry cranked out 15,000 of these fighters between 1948 and 1956.[76] The Western airpower displayed during the Berlin Blockade (see chapter 5) undoubtedly encouraged Stalin to redouble these efforts. Together with German-designed radar systems, the MiG-15 gave the Soviet Union a rudimentary air defense system by 1950. However, all-weather fighter interceptors and surface-to-air missiles took another decade for fielding. National Air Defense forces, known as PVO-Strany (Protivovozdushnoi Oborony Strany), grew in importance and size until 1954, when the head of PVO became a commander-in-chief and deputy defense minister, equal to the heads of the other armed services.[77]

Air defense had always held a high priority in the Soviet Union, but strategic bombing was another matter. During the Great Patriotic War, neither the Red Air Force nor the German Luftwaffe in the east had conducted much that might be described as strategic bombing. In 1946, however, the Red Air Force reestablished its Long Range Aviation (Dal'nyaya Aviatsiya—DA) branch. At first, Long Range Aviation was little more than a name since its aircraft were still twin-engine medium bombers. Although Soviet engineers were perfectly competent, they had little experience in designing or mass-producing large bombers. In 1944, three U.S. Army Air Force B-29s had made forced landings in Siberia at a time when the Soviet Union remained officially neutral in the war with Japan. The U.S. air crews eventually came home, but their aircraft remained behind, interned. In a remarkable feat of reverse engineering, the design bureau of Andrei Nikolaevich Tupolev, the Soviet leader in multi-engine aircraft, copied the B-29 and produced a Soviet version, the Tu-4 (NATO codeword Bull). Although Soviet industry could not yet reproduce certain items, such as the plexiglass canopy and wing tanks, the Tu-4 gave the Soviets a true strategic bomber for the first time. Due to an apparent error by an air controller, when the first Tu-4s participated in the 1947 May Day parade, they flew over the city at an altitude of only two hundred meters, allowing U.S. observers to confirm the detail of the copy. By 1953, Stalin had almost 1,000 TU-4s, but by that time, such propeller-driven aircraft were obsolete.[78]

Soviet airmen recognized this, but again the problems of engine design and production limited their options. The first true jet bomber, the Ilyushin Il-28 (Beagle), flew in 1948. It was equipped with a "Russianized" version of the same Rolls-Royce engine, the Klimov RD-45. As such, it had a maximum speed of five hundred miles per hour and a range of some 1,600 miles (2,520 kilometers). Moreover, this aircraft was initially too small to carry the primitive nuclear weapons of the day, although it later became a workhorse tactical bomber. The next effort, the Tupolev Tu-16 (Badger), entered production in 1954, but it also fell short, being approximately equal in speed (six hundred miles per hour) and range (3,500 miles or 5,600 kilometers) to the Boeing B-47 that SAC had fielded three years earlier. Almost simultaneously with the Badger, the Soviets began to produce the Mya-4, designed by Vladimir Myasishchev. Designated Molot (Hammer) by the Soviets and Bison by NATO, the Mya-4 fulfilled a commission issued by Stalin five years earlier to build a truly intercontinental bomber that could transport the first Soviet atomic weapons. It used the same engines as the Tu-16 but achieved slightly higher speed and much greater range (6,000 miles or 9,600 kilometers). Unfortunately, this aircraft was expensive to build and quite vulnerable to air defense, so relatively few were ever fielded. Instead, Long Range Aviation depended primarily on Tu-16 bombers with air-to-air refueling and air-to-surface missiles.[79]

Butting Heads

Just as in the United States, in the Soviet Union there were serious postwar conflicts between senior officers and the political leadership. In this instance, however, the issue was more political than doctrinal or budgetary.

Stalin had contributed materially to the victory of his regime over Germany and well deserved his self-promotions to marshal of the Soviet Union and then generalissimo. For the rest of his life, he wore a marshal's uniform on most public occasions. Unfortunately, he believed that his political control depended upon being recognized as the principal if not only savior of his country, to the detriment of his generals' reputations. Given the emotional importance of the Great Patriotic War, the increased prestige of the Soviet Army, and the influx of millions of combat veterans into the Communist Party, he may have been correct to worry about his image relative to the field commanders. On the other hand, it is entirely possible that this dictator, like other megalomaniacs, really believed his own press. Regardless of the reason behind his policy, every study of the war published during his declining years was careful to include a chapter describing how the great Stalin had saved the country. This culminated in 1951 when his longtime henchman, Marshal K. Y. Voroshilov, published a book, *Stalin and the Armed Forces of the USSR*, which attributed the 1945 victory almost exclusively to Stalin's brilliant leadership.[80]

In February 1946, Stalin warned the senior generals in his speech on the anniversary of the founding of the Red Army. While recognizing the achievements of the army during the war, the dictator also emphasized the contributions of the people and the Communist Party. A month later, he imprisoned much of the senior leadership of the Red Air Force, including Chief Air Marshal Alexandr A. Novikov, the man who had completely revitalized the air force in 1942–1943. Novikov was accused of libeling Vasilii Stalin, an air force officer and son of the dictator, while some of Novikov's subordinates were blamed for allegedly inferior aircraft during the war.[81]

A number of other generals and admirals were imprisoned and tortured into confessions, but perhaps the biggest fish was Georgi Konstantinovich Zhukov, Stalin's deputy supreme commander and chief troubleshooter during the war. While several other men contributed at least as much to the Soviet victory, none was more prominent and publicized than the aggressive, bullet-headed Zhukov. If, in fact, there was any soldier who could challenge Stalin's grasp of power, it was Zhukov, although there is no indication that he ever plotted to do so. During the war, the Defense Commissariat's Counterintelligence Directorate (colloquially known as SMERSH, an acronym for "Death to Spies") had compiled allegations against Zhukov under the code name Gorodetz (Arrogant Man).[82] Using additional "evidence" coerced from Novikov and others, MGB chief Beria accused the marshal of inflating his own role in the war and criticizing Stalin. At a meeting of the Supreme Military Council and Politburo in June 1946, Zhukov's own rival and deputy as land forces commander, Marshal Ivan Stepanovich Konev, denied any illegality but criticized his commander's style of leadership. Zhukov found himself demoted to command of the insignificant Odessa Military District, while the former political officer Konev replaced him in Moscow. In December 1947, the disgraced hero was summoned back to Moscow to face more of Beria's charges, but the strain caused him to have a heart attack. Stalin dismissed the charges, contenting himself with assigning the marshal to the even more remote Urals Military District in Sverdlovsk. There Zhukov remained until the dictator's death, at which time he was rehabilitated as a deputy defense minister. This allowed him to personally arrest Beria and later to endorse Khrushchev's clique in internal power struggles.[83]

By humiliating Zhukov and encouraging divisions among his senior commanders, Stalin quashed any army criticism of his wartime role. To further limit military influence, in 1946, Stalin appointed Nikolai A. Bulganin, a party leader and political officer with no command experience, as defense minister, promoting him to Marshal of the Soviet Union.[84]

After four years of total warfare, it was inevitable that priorities and attention would shift away from the armed forces of the victorious allies to other aspects of their societies. Stalin and Attlee labored to bring their countries back from the precipice of economic collapse, while Truman, blessed with a fully functional industrial plant, nevertheless felt that he had to cut defense spending to avoid a return to the Great Depression. That shift alone would have resulted in some civil-military friction, but there were greater issues involved. During the later 1940s, the armed forces of the three Great Powers continued to perform worldwide commitments but with significant shortages of personnel and funding. At the same time, the examples of incinerated Japanese cities and of advanced German rockets and jets prompted all those involved to seek more atomic weapons and faster, longer-range aircraft to deliver or thwart delivery of those weapons. Within the constraints of economies returning to peace, the major powers therefore invested considerable resources, including significant numbers of German engineers, in a continuing arms race. In turn, these programs took on a life of their own, in which growing diplomatic friction encouraged growing arms developments and vice versa.

5

CONFRONTATIONS
AND ALLIANCES

In the later 1940s, all the major powers were struggling to develop cutting-edge aircraft with speeds approaching that of sound and ranges expressed in thousands of kilometers. It is therefore ironic that the first great confrontation of the Cold War should be decided by lumbering transports such as the C-47, designed in the mid-1930s and cruising at 170 miles per hour. Fortunately for world peace, using these old transports avoided a shooting war over Berlin.

CZECHOSLOVAKIA AND CONSCRIPTION

For four centuries, Westerners had regarded Europe as the political, economic, and military center of the world, dominating the rest of humanity regardless of cultural sophistication. Throughout the Cold War, British, American, and Soviet leaders considered Europe to be the primary zone of competition and confrontation, even though an unbiased observer might well have argued that the continent was exhausted and increasingly irrelevant.

It was predictable and natural that the Soviet Union would seek to control as much of Europe as possible, for the strategic, ideological, and organizational reasons described in chapter 2. In response to Winston Churchill's famous "Iron Curtain" speech in 1946, Stalin published an interview in *Pravda* stating with unusual candor that the issue in Eastern Europe was not freedom but security—eliminating governments hostile to the USSR.[1] Moscow was particularly determined to occupy Germany as well as the USSR's immediate neighbors in Poland, Romania, and Bulgaria. In 1945, Austria, like Germany, was divided into sectors by the Allied Powers,[2] while adjacent Hungary, being a natural corridor to the West, also endured close Soviet control. Yugoslavia, as we have seen, had produced its own robust communist insurgency, which at first seemed to be a loyal satellite, though later, Tito very publicly went his own way, obtaining Western aid to counterbalance the distant Soviet threat.[3]

After Soviet foreign minister Molotov rejected the Marshall Plan in 1947, the Soviet leadership redoubled its efforts to ensure control of Central and Eastern Europe. Because Stalin had concluded that the wartime alliance with the West was definitively terminated, he no longer hesitated about asserting complete control within his sphere. The chosen mechanism for this control was a reincarnated COMINTERN, this time called the Communist Information Bureau or COMINFORM. On September 22–28, 1947, two of Stalin's loyal subordinates, Andrei Zhdanov and Georgi Malenkov, organized the COMINFORM at a secret meeting held in Szklarska Poremba, a small town in Poland. A few months later, when Tito showed signs of independence, Zhdanov and the COMINFORM led the vain effort to force the Yugoslavs back into the Marxist fold.[4]

Among other issues, the COMINFORM brought Czechoslovakia back to the "front burner" for Stalin. Czechoslovakia occupied a special place in Western perceptions because the British and French had permitted its robust democracy to be dismembered by Hitler in 1938–1939. Thereafter, the German occupiers had played on the longstanding rivalries between Czechs and Slovaks, occupying the former while turning the latter into a separate satellite state. After Hitler attacked the Soviet Union in 1941, Communists in both halves of the compound state became actively involved in anti-Nazi resistance, although pro-Western Czechs later accused their communist peers of betraying them to the Germans.[5]

In Slovakia, Communists and Westerners formed an underground national council and in early August 1944 sent representatives to ask for Soviet assistance in throwing off the German yoke. What followed was a variation on the theme of the Warsaw Uprising.

On August 29, 1944, the Slovaks rose up in rebellion and called on the Red Army, then about one hundred miles (160 kilometers) away, for help. Over the next two months, the Soviets did fly in 2,800 members of the (pro-Soviet) exiled Czech armed forces, as well as significant numbers of exiled Slovak Communists. Yet the West had to provide arms to the uprising, and once again the Allies (this time in the form of the American OSS) had to get Soviet approval to fly inside their sphere of control. Eighteen tons of American weapons arrived on October 7, but this was too late, and the Slovak rising, like its Polish counterpart, collapsed in late October.[6]

Although elements of the U.S. Third Army entered western Czechoslovakia in early May 1945, Eisenhower once again respected the Yalta Agreements, withdrawing those forces in favor of the Red Army. Prague was, in fact, the last major European capital to fall that month, but by December all foreign troops had left the country. In their place remained the Soviet-controlled I Czech Corps (actually the size of a large brigade). The corps commander was General Ludvik Svoboda, a former Czechoslovak officer (and future president of the republic) who had somehow convinced the Soviets to trust him. Perhaps inevitably, Svoboda (whose name ironically means "freedom" in a number of Slavic languages) became defense minister in the postwar government. In turn, it was natural that he would choose his own former officers to lead the revived Czech Army, excluding many officers who had served the exiled Czech government in London. It was also unsurprising that Svoboda established a system that paralleled that of the Soviet political officers. After the fact, many pro-Western Czechs regarded this as a deliberate communist conspiracy, for which Svoboda was roundly vilified. In fact, his subsequent performance in 1968 suggests that he was at least as much of a patriot as a Marxist; in any event, the Czech Communists kept track of noncommunist officers in the military, making any Western conspiracy difficult.[7]

Far more serious was the Czech Communist Party's growing control over the police and security apparatus of the revived state. For several years, the Czechs attempted to walk a neutral line.[8] The Czechoslovak-Soviet Treaty of Friendship and Military Alliance (December 12, 1943) bought them some freedom of maneuver, at least until the Soviets sought to tighten controls after the Marshall Plan. When the crisis came in 1948, however, there was no nucleus within the government to defend the democratic Czech Republic. In late February, the Soviet deputy foreign minister, Valerian Zorin, visited Prague, a visit that the West generally regarded as directing the actions of the Czech Communists. Led by Klement Gottwald, this party demanded that President Edvard Benes appoint them to form a new government. With the noncommunists in disarray at home and the Group of Soviet Forces, Germany, visibly prepared to invade, Benes had to acquiesce. The famous pro-Western foreign minister Jan Masaryk died in March by the traditional Czech method of being pushed or jumping out of an upper-story window. By May, Gottwald had rewritten the constitution and rigged elections to ensure communist control, and Benes resigned.[9]

Unlike the previous takeover of East European governments, the February 1948 coup in Prague was the shockingly public overthrow of a staunchly democratic regime. Although Moscow's exact role in the coup was never clear, internal communist takeovers were now an obvious threat to democracy in Europe. This helped persuade Western governments that they had to take a harder line with the Soviets and their allies. The U.S., British, and French governments issued a joint declaration deploring the "establishment of a disguised dictatorship of a single party."[10]

The Czech crisis convinced President Truman that he had to address the dwindling manpower situation of the U.S. Army. He had failed to persuade Congress of the need for Universal Military Training, and the army had great difficulty enlisting volunteers. In early 1948, Army Secretary Royall reported that recruiting was attracting only 12,000 per month instead of the 30,000 needed. More troops were necessary, if only to maintain the credibility of Truman's promise to defend Europe. The JCS advocated resumption of selective service as the quickest way to bolster American military capability.[11]

Not only was the public reluctant to renew the draft, but African-American civil rights advocates wanted to preclude the kind of discrimination that had occurred under conscription in both world wars. Although Truman's handpicked civil rights commission had called for an end to military segregation in 1947, Black labor leader A. Philip Randolph lobbied Congress to force the issue. A new draft law in 1948 forbad discrimination on the basis of race, a provision which the Selective Service system immediately implemented. Yet, the president went even farther under pressure from Randolph. On July 30, 1948, Truman issued Executive Order 9981 outlawing military segregation in any form. In practice, however, the segregated units did not suddenly disappear because there was no procedure for reassignment between units until the crisis of 1950 forced integration of individual replacements.[12]

The new draft law, signed in June 1948, authorized two years of conscripted service. In addition to providing actual draftees, the law had the usual effect of encouraging voluntary enlistments to avoid the draft. Active army voluntary enlistments doubled in fiscal 1949, while the Army National Guard gained 60,000 men, or almost 20 percent of its strength, in the second half of 1948.[13]

Over the next twenty-four years, the demand for draftees rose and fell repeatedly. As the postwar "Baby Boomers" came of age, the supply of potential conscripts far exceeded demand even at the peak of the Vietnamese conflict, so that the draft truly became "selective service." The result was a perception of inequity that eventually doomed all forms of conscription, leading to a professional volunteer force.[14]

Divided Germany

Germany remained a blasted hole in the middle of the continent. In the wake of firebombing and ground fighting, the Soviet Union disassembled and removed many of the German factories, even in the western zones, as war reparations. The forcible expulsion of ethnic Germans from neighboring states left Germany, already prostrate and starving, with at least ten million additional mouths to feed.[15]

At the summit conferences during World War II, Roosevelt, Stalin, and Churchill had never reached agreement as to the postwar disposition of Germany. They agreed that Germany must never rise again as an aggressive military power, but beyond that there were a host of different opinions as to how to treat the country. In general, Moscow and Paris sought maximum reparations to rebuild their own countries while weakening Germany; Washington and London soon realized that reparations must be balanced against the need for the Germans to at least feed themselves and perhaps participate in the postwar European economic recovery.

The continued friction between the former allies precluded any peace settlement or serious plan for Germany's future, but the military occupation zones in effect dismembered the country into dysfunctional parts. As some wag observed, the occupation sectors gave the industry to Britain, the food to the Soviet Union, and the scenery to the Americans.[16] Despite agreements to trade resources between

MAP 5. Occupied Germany

occupation zones, very little was actually exchanged, and the German zones became four amputated limbs.

Stalin expected that by thwarting economic recovery he would eventually obtain a neutral or even pro-Soviet Germany. Unfortunately, the Soviet leadership did not recognize that their own policies operated against this outcome in two ways. First, Soviet repression and exploitation alienated most Germans, making it difficult to create a pro-Soviet state. Not only had the Soviets made little effort to prepare for a military government, but as Marxists, they had no real understanding of how a capitalist economy operated. Second, the longer that the Soviets blocked economic progress, the more they encouraged their former allies to accept the division of Germany as permanent and create a West German state.

It is traditional, and completely accurate, to deplore the manner in which the Soviets raped eastern Germany literally as well as economically.[17] Certainly the conquerors took anything they wanted and printed worthless occupation currency to pay for some of it. For similar reasons, France was also determined to keep Germany prostrate. Indeed, during the three years after the end of the war, Paris often aligned itself with Moscow to block any recovery. In fairness, of course, the British and American policies were also rather harsh, at least initially. In the absence of permanent agreement about the future of Germany, the U.S. sector was governed by JCS Order 1067 of September 1944, as modified by President Truman on May 11, 1945 (JCS 1067/8, indicating the eighth version of the order). The original intent of this regulation had been to prevent recovery and fraternization; the British occupiers were bound by similar regulations. In both instances, however, the military governors softened these restrictions within months. Although some sense of humanitarianism may have prevailed, the primary motivation for the United States was to complete the occupation process as rapidly and cheaply as possible. This, in turn, meant permitting some measure of German economic and political recovery.[18]

Berlin was a particular bone of contention. Early Soviet efforts to prevent the Western Allies from coming to the city and to strictly regulate movement across the Soviet zone into West Berlin appeared in retrospect to be part of a longstanding conspiracy to annex the city. For example, when Colonel Frank Howley attempted to lead the first echelon of American military government across the Soviet zone in late June 1945, Soviet officers limited him to 112 men and 50 vehicles, citing a nonexistent "Berlin Agreement" about the matter. Then, when he reached the city in early July, Howley had to present the Soviets with a fait accompli, taking over the six boroughs of the American sector during the night because the Soviets were dragging their heels.[19] In practice, however, the Americans may have exaggerated the reasons for Soviet obstructionism. Any military commander would naturally wish to control others, however friendly, operating inside the area for which he was responsible. Regardless of the cause, from the very beginning, there was friction, often played out in the Allied Control Council, consisting of the four military governors of Germany. In September 1945, the Soviets agreed to permit ten trains per day to cross their zone from the western occupation zones into West Berlin, but the United States had to threaten armed guards on the trains to prevent the Soviets from stopping them to check the identity of passengers. On November 30, 1945, the Allied Control Council established three air corridors leading from the three western sectors into West Berlin; these corridors became critical when the situation came to a boil in 1948.[20]

As time went on, the British and Americans came to see that Germany had to recover to some extent, if only to feed itself and facilitate the sluggish European recovery. Yet, economic recovery required both German self-government to regulate business and a reliable currency—the Soviets, who had no interest in the success of Germany or of capitalism, were opposed to both measures. In October 1946, the Soviets did agree to relatively free municipal elections in all portions of the former capital, although within their own sector, they insisted that socialists and Communists merge into a Socialist Unity Party (SED). Much to their chagrin, the SED polled less than 20 percent of the votes city-wide (and not much more even in the eastern sector), as compared to 48 percent for the middle-of-the-road Social Democratic Party (SPD) and 22 percent for the Christian Democratic Union (CDU). These embarrassing results prompted Moscow to oppose any further elections. By one account, in fact, the SED leaders eventually convinced Stalin that he should force the West out of Berlin to eliminate moderate opposition in future city elections.[21]

For the United States, the man responsible for dealing with this vexing situation was Lieutenant General Lucius D. Clay, who had been in charge of military government since April 1945. In his previous career, Clay had been frustrated by his inability to get combat assignments in either world war. Instead, he had spent most of his career as an engineer officer working on construction projects and economic mobilization, during which time he served with civilian luminaries, such as future Secretary of State James F. Byrnes. This experience together with the fact that he was the son of a senator from Georgia equipped him superbly to deal with the economic, political, and diplomatic issues of German recovery.[22]

Initially, however, Clay attempted to follow U.S. policy, which was to cooperate with the Soviets as allies. Thus, he agreed with a proposal that Zhukov presented to the effect that the Allied Control Council must make all decisions on the basis of unanimity, giving the Soviets veto power over all major aspects of occupation policy.[23] Similar "gentlemen's agreements" between the Allied military governors resolved a number of conflicts in 1945–1946, but over time the friction between the Great Powers coupled with local issues, such as Soviet agents operating in West Berlin, reduced the sense of cooperation to almost nothing. Both the Soviets and the French, devastated by German occupation, were understandably preoccupied with the dual questions of gaining reparations to rebuild their economies and preventing Germany from recovering power. Thus, the French unilaterally attempted to absorb the coal-mining region of the Saar into their domestic economy, to the detriment of overall German recovery.[24]

As a result, the Allied Control Council, like the Council of Foreign Ministers that met periodically, accomplished nothing. The uncertain occupation policy was exacerbated by internal conflicts within the Truman administration, resulting in four secretaries of state and as many undersecretaries between 1945 and 1949. The diplomatic deadlock prompted American military leaders to make numerous decisions on their own. In the absence of coherent guidance from the State Department, General Clay became a forceful advocate within the administration. In one instance, the State Department had failed to inform Clay of a change of U.S. policy and then reprimanded him for following his previous instructions.[25] Meanwhile Clay and his British counterpart, General Brian Robertson, concluded by July 1947 that the 1946 interallied plan to remove additional German factories as reparations would leave their two sectors unviable economically.

They began to urge their respective governments to delay further reparations until the four powers had established procedures to operate
Germany as a unified economy.[26] By late 1947, Clay also called for a
policy of open commitments to the Germans, promising them self-
government and continued U.S. defense support so as to give them a
stake in rebuilding their economy and society. He encountered considerable American criticism for favoring anti-Soviet labor unions
and slowing the disassembly of the industrial cartels that were widely
blamed for past German aggression.[27]

At the December 1947 London meeting of foreign ministers,
Molotov made what might have been concessions about reparations
and economic cooperation between zones. By this time, however,
Secretary of State Marshall, having been rebuffed about his offer of
economic aid, had lost patience. Molotov's fear that the European
Recovery Plan would lead to American dominance in Western Europe
was fast becoming a self-fulfilling prophesy. Marshall was apparently
determined to restore the German economy solely in the western
sectors, and primarily in the British and American zones.[28]

The Czech coup in February 1948 reinforced Western perceptions
that they faced an intransigent and possibly aggressive Soviet Union,
invoking the perceived lessons of appeasement from the 1930s. In
March, British Foreign Minister Ernest Bevin explicitly compared the
Soviet actions to "our experience with Hitler" and invited the United
States to enter into talks to create what became the North Atlantic
Alliance (see below).[29]

More pragmatically, the British and Americans sought to formalize
their cooperation to restore the West German economy, if only to make
it self-sustaining. Even prior to the Czech coup, the two military
governors, Clay and Robertson, had outlined a process for reestab-
lishing the economy and local government, including issuance of a
new currency, in the so-called "Bizonia" of their two occupation zones.
They called together the minister-presidents (governors) of the eight
German *lander* (provinces or states) in Bizonia and began establishing
a legislative council, high court, and administrative departments. To
avoid Soviet retaliation, the minister-presidents pretended that they
were being forced to accept these measures by economic necessity.[30]
Later that spring, the British, Americans, and (reluctantly) French agreed
to these organizations in a London meeting. Acting on instructions

from Moscow, the Soviet representative to the Allied Control Council, Marshal Vasili Sokolovsky, used this London meeting between the three Western Allies as an excuse to declare the Control Council dead at its March 20, 1948, meeting; as the council's chairman for the month, he adjourned the body without scheduling a further meeting.[31]

Immediately after the Czech coup, the ubiquitous army director of intelligence, Lieutenant General Chamberlin, had visited General Clay and warned him that further Soviet actions were likely in the near future. Chamberlin noted that the U.S. Army in Germany, consisting of only one infantry division plus the division-sized U.S. Constabulary, was completely inadequate to defend its sector. During 1947–1948, the Constabulary had reconfigured itself and retrained to emphasize tactical operations, but it remained a lightly armored body of division size with shortages in weapons such as anti-tank recoilless rifles. After Chamberlin departed, General Clay sent a "back channel" message to him, reemphasizing their mutual concerns: "For many months, based on logical analysis, I have felt and held that war was unlikely for at least ten years. Within the last few weeks, I have felt a subtle change in Soviet attitudes which I cannot define which are now giving me a feeling that it [war] may come with dramatic suddenness."[32]

This message touched off a minor war scare, in which Secretary Forrestal and the armed services seriously contemplated the possibility of nuclear conflict with the Soviet Union. Director of Central Intelligence Admiral Hillenkoetter gave the president a cautiously worded assessment that indicated no Soviet preparations for war but noted the continued possibility for miscalculation on the part of Moscow. Truman responded by addressing Congress about the "growing menace" of Soviet expansion, a statement that undoubtedly contributed to the sense of crisis in both capitals. Yet, despite a U.S. Army staff study about the possibility of blocking access to Berlin across the Soviet zone, few officials anticipated the nature of the crisis that eventually arose.[33]

In April, Churchill, as opposition leader, privately proposed that the West take advantage of its temporary nuclear monopoly by threatening atomic war if the Soviet Union did not withdraw from Berlin and East Germany. Foreign Secretary Bevin and Prime Minister Attlee ignored him, but the very suggestion reflected the growing tension of the time.[34]

BLOCKADE

Access to Berlin across the Soviet zone had been an issue since 1945. Periodically, the Soviets attempted to search each train and vehicle moving through their zone, something which the Western Allies generally resisted. On January 23, 1947, for example, the British escorting officer refused to allow the Soviets to demand passes from Germans riding on a train from Berlin to the west. In retaliation, the Soviets simply uncoupled the railroad cars in question, leaving them motionless on a siding.[35] Beginning on March 30, 1948, however, the Soviets interfered with road and rail traffic by redoubling their demands to identify all travelers. The American lieutenant in charge of one train made the mistake of permitting the inspections, for which he was almost court-martialed. Clay immediately protested the Soviet policies and succeeded in forcing through one freight train without stopping. He also shifted much of his personnel movements to C-47 aircraft of the 61st Troop Carrier Group, United States Air Force (USAF). On April Fool's Day, a squad of Soviet soldiers attempted to set up a roadblock near Gatow Airport in the British sector; four hundred British infantry with armored cars "persuaded" them to withdraw. The next day, when the Soviets posted armed guards around their railway operations office in West Berlin, Colonel Howley and General Clay responded with so many military police and infantry that all the Soviets withdrew.[36]

This game of cat-and-mouse harassment quickly turned deadly, however. The Soviets had periodically attempted to interfere with flight operations into and out of the western sectors of Berlin. In a typical such move on April 5, a Yak-3 fighter aircraft buzzed a British European Airways flight that was on its approach run to Gatow Airport. The Russian pilot apparently misjudged the clearances involved and crashed into the British plane, killing the crew and seven passengers. General Robertson, followed quickly by Clay, ordered fighter escorts for future transports, an action that temporarily cooled Soviet aggressiveness.[37] After initially apologizing, the Soviets began to blame the British for the incident. At the time, this appeared to be implausible propaganda; in retrospect, however, the Soviets were arguing for the procedure with which they were most comfortable, under which their ground controller would have had positive control over the British aircraft.

During this period of time, the commanders of the three western sectors of Berlin conferred about stockpiles and other precautions

to ensure that their troops would be supplied if the transport inter-
ruptions continued. Few expected the Soviets to cut off *all* movement into the western sector.

The final straw was currency reform, a move that would definitively sever the eastern and western zones, and end the blank check
of worthless Soviet-printed occupation currency. The Soviets considered such currency to be a legitimate part of their reparations from
Germany; certainly they did not understand the principles of mone-
tary supply in the same way that Western economists did and therefore
resented the unilateral Western action. In a January 1947 memorandum
on the subject, Soviet Finance Minister Arseni G. Zverev had claimed
that the Western Allies were trying to "impose control over the amount
of our expenditures on the occupation and reparations."[38]

On June 18, the Western Allies introduced a new currency in West
Germany but not in Berlin, which they still regarded as an area of joint
administration. The Soviet response was to further restrict traffic,
followed on June 22 by the issuance of their own "East Mark" in
Berlin. The Americans and British therefore distributed specially
marked "B" marks in West Berlin, arranging for the population to
exchange its old money between June 25 and 27. The Soviet riposte
was almost immediate: on June 24, they stopped all road, rail, and barge
traffic between West Berlin and western Germany, and cut electrical
power to portions of the western sector. The official excuse was a temporary need to rebuild bridges, but in effect West Berlin was isolated.[39]

COUNTERMEASURES

That same day, Stalin issued the so-called Warsaw declaration, stating
his terms. These terms included restoration of four-power control over
Germany, creation of a unified German government, and eventual
withdrawal from a neutralized Germany. Neither the British nor the
American government was prepared to make such concessions, although
they were careful not to sever any of the remaining diplomatic and
military channels. The French government was willing to negotiate,
but its allies were adamant. In Germany, Generals Clay and Robertson
had already persuaded their French counterpart, General Pierre Koenig,
of the need to defy the Soviet actions. The question was, how?[40]

From a vantage point sixty years later, the Berlin Airlift appears
to be the obvious response to the Soviet move: it unified the Western

Allies, inspired the downtrodden Germans, and handed Moscow a major propaganda defeat by upholding Western values of democracy and free enterprise. At the time, however, the airlift was by no means a certainty. On the contrary, it was a high-risk operation, betting the prestige of the United States (and more specifically the United States Air Force) to protect an isolated, nonessential city filled with people who had been the hated enemy only three years before. No one had ever succeeded in an aerial supply operation of such magnitude before; most observers were inclined to think that all the airlift could do would be to prolong the inevitable loss of Berlin at the price of American prestige and German starvation.

Although both the U.S. and British staffs had previously contemplated aerial resupply of their Berlin garrisons, they had taken no preparations for an airlift, and no one was optimistic about supplying an entire city. Such a task would involve far more than just moving food—it would require coal and petroleum products to provide heat and power to 2.5 million people. In addition, at least some movement of civilian passengers and manufactured goods was necessary to maintain the shaky West Berlin economy. At the time the blockade began, West Berlin had perhaps a thirty-six-day supply of food and forty-five days of coal on hand.[41] Moreover, the available airfields both in West Germany and in Berlin were far from ideal. The British field at Gatow had been a German training base that lacked the ground facilities for transshipping and storing bulky supplies. Three years before, the Americans had repaired their air base at Tempelhof with pierced steel planking to provide a barely functional runway. Worse still, a series of apartment houses and a four-hundred-foot-tall smokestack complicated the landing approaches to Tempelhof. Instead of the recommended flat glide path in which an aircraft would descend only one foot for every four hundred feet of flight, the actual approach was one foot for every sixteen feet.[42]

As soon as the Soviet action was announced, General Clay turned to Lieutenant General Curtis LeMay, then commander of U.S. Air Forces in Europe (USAFE). USAFE had only about one hundred transport aircraft, primarily twin-engine C-47s, on hand but began aerial supply operations within twenty-four hours of the Soviet move. On the 16th, President Truman directed a full-scale effort, and the air force began assembling more aircraft and pilots from all over the world.

The British had already started their own airlift but were hampered by maintenance and equipment limitations.[43]

The airlift was by no means the only Western response. Encouraged by Foreign Secretary Bevin, the 301st Bombardment Group (thirty B-29s) flew to West Germany on July 2; two other groups deployed to England after a formal invitation by the British government. All of this was done with full publicity as a show of force, concealing the fact that none of these groups was equipped for atomic bombing. Despite its request for assistance, the Attlee government was concerned that an atomic attack launched from their soil might call down a Soviet retaliation on Britain. The one fully functional Silverplate unit, the 509th Bombardment Group, remained in the United States on twenty-four-hour alert. On training missions, its aircraft flew no farther east than Labrador. Logistical problems delayed the deployment of additional fighters to Europe, although eventually an F-80 jet fighter group arrived.[44]

During the early weeks of the blockade, Clay and his British and French counterparts developed a contingency plan whereby an armed force would attempt to push a convoy of trucks through to Berlin. This task force would be built around a Constabulary regiment plus engineers, British infantry, French anti-tank guns, and two hundred trucks. Undersecretary of State Robert Lovett, who had disagreed with Clay on previous issues, scoffed at the idea, arguing that it would be easy for the Soviets to block bridges and other chokepoints, thwarting the effort. When the JCS contacted their British counterparts about the convoy plan, the latter replied that they considered a convoy to be "militarily unsound and politically undesirable." In any event, the Soviets gave no indication of wanting to force the issue by armed conflict, and the United States was equally unready for war, so the ground convoy plan was never implemented.[45]

Within the city, conflicts ranged from the comic to the tragic. On June 26, two days into the blockade, a U.S. armored car stopped General Sokolovsky, the Soviet commander, while he was speeding in the American sector. When Sokolovsky's bodyguards pointed their weapons, the U.S. sergeant in charge of the patrol put a pistol to the general's stomach, creating a standoff until an American officer released the Soviets.[46] Other incidents were not as harmless. The West Berlin public repeatedly demonstrated against Soviet actions and on September 9 assaulted Soviet troops who tried to block the demonstration; twelve civilians were wounded, one fatally. The Soviet Military Adminis-tration offered to feed the entire city if the West Berliners would register in the Soviet sector, but since the Soviets had notoriously failed to feed even East Berlin, this propaganda ploy fell flat. Deputy Mayor Ferdinand Friedensburg, a Christian Democrat who had pre-viously sought to bridge the gap between the two sides, now fired the pro-Soviet chief of police, Colonel Paul Markgraf, in favor of his deputy, Johannes Stumm. Markgraf refused to give up his office in East Berlin. The result was a de facto split into two police departments, although for a long period Stumm's noncommunist police served without pay.[47]

Berliner resistance was based on a growing confidence in the Allied airlift. This airlift did not spring full blown overnight but suffered considerable difficulties. In the early days, there were insufficient aircraft and sometimes dangerous haste in operation; LeMay reduced the peacetime safety margin of twenty-five minutes between aircraft flight times to only five minutes. Soviet fighters repeatedly buzzed the transport aircraft. In any but fair weather conditions, the flight was risky at best; the USAF transports navigated by radio beacons and dead reckoning, and had to take steep approaches into Tempelhof. Accidents began to mount up, with a C-47 crew dying in a crash in West Berlin on July 25. At first, the U.S. effort was coordinated by Brigadier General Williston B. Palmer, who was responsible for army logistics in Germany. By the end of July, however, the airlift had become so complex that Major General William Tunner, deputy com-mander of the Military Air Transport Service, arrived from Washing-ton to take control. Because he had directed air ferry operations from India to China over "the Hump" during World War II, Tunner was one of the few officers qualified to organize the Berlin effort.[48] After initial British resistance, in August a Combined Airlift Task Force (CALTF) headquarters began operations, with Tunner in command and Air Commodore J. W. F. Merer as his British deputy.

The first issue was, of course, to find sufficient aircraft to con-duct the operation. Virtually all French airlift assets were already committed to the fighting in Indochina, so the Americans had to supply the French as well as themselves. Each C-47, whether British or American, could carry only about one-half ton of supplies, so the USAF sent fifty-four of the newer C-54s, which carried an average of 9.5 tons. After Clay went to Washington to plead for either a ground convoy or increased airlift, Truman agreed to send seventy-five additional C-54s and to fund construction of another airfield at Tegel in the French sector. U.S. Navy aircraft eventually joined the airflow. The British, with a limited supply of "Dakotas" (C-47s), turned to other expedients, including the York, a transportation version of the Lancaster bomber, and even Sunderland flying boats, which landed on the Havel Lake in Berlin over Russian protests. Given the salt-water protection of these aircraft, their initial cargo of anodized salt was a logical use of an unusual asset. Under RAF control, Australian, New Zealand, and South African aircrews soon flew down the corridors to Berlin. Eventually, the British chartered a number of civilian airliners to supplement their efforts, although the use of civilian aircrews further complicated the problem of navigation and control for the airlift. By contrast, the only civilian airline supporting the United States was Pan American Airways, whose DC-4 pilots had extensive military backgrounds.[49]

This multiplicity of aircraft complicated operations because each had different speeds not only for flying but also for loading and unloading. This, in fact, was the principal reason why the USAF rarely used the newest and largest aircraft, such as the C-124 Globemaster, in the actual missions to Berlin, preferring to use them on transatlantic flights for which scheduling was not as critical. The British solved the problem of flying speeds by having the Yorks fly at a lower altitude than the Dakotas. For the United States, the larger number of aircraft eventually led to complicated schedules that allowed different aircraft to arrive at a steady interval of four minutes, such as that in use during August 1948.[50]

Both the USAF and RAF soon based only one or two types of aircraft at a specific airfield to simplify maintenance, loading, and scheduling. They installed lights, access roads, and other infrastructure improvements to make airfields at both ends more effective. With Clay's approval, Tunner hired a former Luftwaffe maintenance specialist, General Hans von Rohden, to recruit German mechanics and arrange translation of the relevant technical manuals.[51] Gradually, Operation Vittles changed from an improvised show in which pilots routinely violated the rules to a smooth, efficient process. The initial sputtering became a steady drone of engines, every four minutes, giving the lie to the blockade.

Once the airlift became a real operation, the Soviets did not permit it to continue unchallenged. On August 26, Soviet-instigated demonstrations disrupted a meeting of the Berlin town council (Magistrat), but that evening 30,000 Berliners counterdemonstrated. On numerous occasions, the Soviets announced that they were conducting "usual exercises" by the Red Air Force, which often involved fighter planes passing dangerously close to transport aircraft or firing live ammunition at towed targets. Power outages were a daily fact of life in West Berlin, but on October 2 the Soviets cut off power to Gatow Airfield in an attempt to stop the British effort; the British promptly cut power to the Soviet airfield and Radio Berlin, which caused the electricity to come back on at Gatow! Because the Soviets had announced that the (Soviet-dominated) German government controlled Radio Berlin, the French sector commander, General Jean Ganeval, did not bother to inform the Soviets that the radio's broadcast towers, located inside the French sector, obstructed the new airfield under construction at Tegel. After the puppet government ignored his requests to move the towers, on December 16 he sent combat engineers to dynamite those towers, outraging the Soviets.[52]

Poor visibility, long flying hours, poor navigation equipment, and Soviet harassment took their toll. Transporting fuel and other flammable materials was especially hazardous. On September 14, two USAF pilots bailed out over the Soviet zone after their C-47 engines failed, but friendly Germans helped them escape. Others were less fortunate. Two C-47s collided in midair on August 24, killing four crew members. Five C-54s crashed between December 5, 1948, and January 18, 1949. In the course of the airlift, at least forty Britons (half of them civilians) and one Australian died, along with one U.S. Army, one U.S. Navy, and twenty-nine USAF fatalities.[53]

Yet, despite mounting losses, the airlift gradually succeeded. For a long time, the actual tonnage lifted was not published, giving the Soviets the opportunity to scoff at the Allied effort. On September 10, for the first time, the combined RAF-USAF total reached 5,000 tons of supplies in a single day. Eight days later, despite Soviet fighter harassment, the daily total reached a record 6,988 tons, although the daily average over the month was much lower. The peak was on April 15, 1949, when Tunner called for an all-out effort in honor of Air Force Day and to supply the Berliners for the approaching Easter. On that day, 1,398 flights lifted a total of 12,941 tons.[54]

Such figures belie the fact that the airlift could not keep pace with the actual needs of an entire city. Dehydrated foods reduced the bulk that had to be transported, but Berliners, who were already under-nourished before the blockade, continued to lose weight. Still, because their diet had now become a matter of national priority for the Western Allies, the Berliners probably ate better and more regularly than at any time since the war.[55]

As winter approached, coal was a particular problem. The USAF and RAF packed the coal in duffle bags to speed the process of loading and unloading aircraft, and reduce the coal dust left on the aircraft. Unfortunately, the users in Berlin often did not return the empty bags, causing a crisis in containers. The western city government estab-lished public warming shelters to maximize the heating potential of scarce fuel.

What saved the operation was an exceptionally mild winter. After a cold September, temperatures were generally above average, reducing the need for both heating fuel and calories to keep warm. By spring, it was apparent that West Berlin had weathered the storm literally and figuratively, and that the Soviets had missed their chance to starve out the Allies.

All this time, extensive negotiations had gone on at the United Nations (UN) in New York, in Moscow, and between the city sector commandants on the spot. None of these negotiations really accom-plished anything, however. Even when the Soviets made gestures of compromise, the Western diplomats had become too suspicious to accept them. The end to the long crisis came abruptly. The deputy U.S. representative to the UN, Philip Jessup, had engaged in months of fruitless negotiations with Soviet Ambassador Yakov Malik. On May 4, 1949, the two reached a simple agreement in New York that terminated restrictions on movement into and out of Berlin effective May 12, with a Conference of Foreign Ministers meeting to follow in Paris on the 23rd. Geoffrey Roberts has suggested that this was, in fact, Stalin's goal throughout the confrontation: to cause the Allies to abandon their tripartite efforts in London and return to diplomatic negotiations to determine the future of Germany.[56] Yet, this argument is unconvincing. By creating the Berlin Crisis and continuing it long after the Allies had shown any sign of wavering, Stalin had virtually guaranteed that West Germany would become an independent state without Soviet involvement; the foreign ministers meeting could be nothing more than a face-saving gesture in return for the Soviet concessions on Berlin.

Although the blockade formally ended in May, the Western Allies had to consider the possibility of a resumption in the future, especially after the diplomatic meeting failed to produce any agreement on Germany. NSC 24/2, produced on June 1, 1949, planned for stockpiles in Berlin while maintaining the capability to resume the airlift. Although the document urged a warning to Moscow against another blockade, there were no provisions for armed force. Meanwhile, the airlift continued on a reduced basis for months after the crisis.[57]

The Berlin Crisis crystallized the emerging conflict that became known as the Cold War. For many Westerners, it eliminated the remaining desires and hopes for accommodation with the Soviet Union. More significantly, it changed the public perception of the German people, making them seem more like victims than a threat. The new face of Germany was not goose-stepping aggressors but little children near the airfields of West Berlin, scrambling to catch the candy bars that American pilots dropped by handkerchief "parachutes" as their C-47s landed. For their part, many Germans began to have some confidence in American support against further deprivation.

War Plans

This first great confrontation of the Cold War prompted considerable change in the war plans of the respective powers.

Perhaps because the United States still had a nuclear monopoly, Moscow did not try to force a military confrontation. At no time during the ten-month crisis did the Group of Soviet Forces, Germany (GSFG) go on full alert, even though Soviet intelligence accurately assessed the weakness of British and American forces in Germany. However, Sokolovsky, as commander of GSFG, did issue an order on March 25, 1948, that assigned fifteen rifle battalions (seven from Third Shock Army and eight from Eighth Guards Army) to secure the interzonal border. In retrospect, therefore, General Clay's proposed blockade-busting convoy would almost certainly have provoked armed conflict.[58]

Moscow was even more concerned by the possibility of USAF bombing, although there is no clear evidence as to whether Stalin knew that the deployed B-29s were not atomic capable. On June 30,

1948, the Politburo appointed Marshal L. A. Govarev as commander-in-chief of PVO-Strany (the national air defense command) and ordered Defense Minister Bulganin to restructure the Moscow Air Defense Region. Eight fighter aircraft divisions and other units redeployed to protect the capital.[59]

Ironically, a crisis sparked in part by Soviet fear of a revived Germany also accelerated Soviet efforts to resurrect the German Army. Since the fall of 1946, the occupiers had been organizing "Alert Police" units to maintain order and secure the borders of the Soviet occupation zone. Many of the officers of this new police were German prisoners of war who had been "reeducated" in Siberia, then given a choice between serving in uniform or digging in the Soviet mines. Once the Berlin Blockade began, the Soviets accelerated the creation of the Alert Police. Forty units of 250 men each formed during the summer of 1948. American intelligence reports in 1948–1949 indicated that these "police" were training with mortars, machine guns, and anti-tank weapons, while Soviet officers observed the process. Clearly, the Alert Police had a paramilitary role to bolster the occupiers in the event of conflict. Two hundred senior police leaders attended Soviet military schools over the next several years, and by 1955 this organization, having been redesignated as the Barracked People's Police, finally emerged as the East German National People's Army.[60]

The first Berlin Crisis also prompted considerable adjustments in American war planning. Not surprisingly, the initial postwar plans for future conflict, collectively called the "Pincher" plans, had assumed a replication of World War II, with the Soviet Union rapidly overrunning West Germany and France, and attacking Turkey and the Middle East. The air portion of the Pincher plan originally was a purely conventional approach, focusing on Soviet petroleum production facilities, although General Curtis LeMay prepared a separate nuclear annex. In a variety of regional contingency plans drawn up in 1946–1947, the Joint War Plans Committee assumed that the United States and its allies would counterattack in the Middle East and Mediterranean, while using Egypt, Britain, and other familiar bases for strategic air attacks. Britain had agreed in June 1946 to permit U.S. use of such bases, and the necessary bomb assembly pits for B-29s were ready by mid-1947.[61] In 1949, the United States also quietly provided funding to lengthen runways at Abu Sueir in Egypt. Unfortunately, rising Egyptian nationalism jeopardized British control of its Suez bases, and the Joint Chiefs of Staff felt too overextended to commit U.S. forces to the Middle East. Thus, the U.S. government frustrated the British by remaining noncommittal about this vital region through the late 1940s and early 1950s.[62]

Part of the problem of planning was the constantly weakening state of American military power. In February 1947, the Joint Planning Staff submitted an outline War Plan (JCS 1725/1) to the joint chiefs to obtain guidance as to the planning parameters for future conflicts. Again, like the Pincher plans, this document envisioned a repetition of the recent war experience. For example, the services assumed that thirty-six months into the conflict they would have largely replicated the 1945 situation, with 90 army divisions, 264 air groups, and 21 fleet aircraft carriers. For the first time, JCS 1725/1 explicitly envisioned the atomic bombing of the Soviet Union, calling for thirty-four bombs (far more than the actual inventory on hand) aimed at major cities in the first strike.[63]

Until 1949, President Truman regarded atomic warfare as a last resort. As conventional forces continued to shrink, however, the planners increasingly turned to the atomic option as the only means of compensating for overall military weakness. During the summer and fall of 1947, the joint staff planners produced two plans—Broiler, an emergency plan if war occurred before July 1948, and Charioteer, a slightly longer-range plan. Both of these plans depended on the air force's vaunted strategic airpower, including widespread use of atomic weapons as well as conventional bombing. The planners clearly saw the difficulty of holding key bomber bases—in Britain, the Middle East, India, and Okinawa—but had no other immediate solution.[64]

All of these plans were largely staff exercises with little or no guidance from political authority. The Berlin Blockade belatedly caused civilian decision makers to focus on the imminent possibility of war at a time when the United States was extremely weak. In September 1948, the National Security Council produced a policy statement on nuclear weapons known as NSC-30. This was the only such statement until at least 1959. While asserting the president's absolute control over the employment of atomic bombs, NSC-30 clearly recognized the USAF position that atomic bombs were the primary means of attack in case of war. Curtis LeMay, who became head of the Strategic Air Command at the end of 1948, seized upon this document as authorization to press forward with a bomber force that would always be prepared for worldwide employment.

The American government as a whole began to produce more frequent and detailed war plans throughout the second Truman administration, as the president reluctantly came to see the increased importance of nuclear weapons. In 1949, he authorized the first of several increases in the capacity to produce fissionable materials. Meanwhile, improved bomb design meant that standardized yields grew from twenty kilotons (Mark 3, 1948) to five hundred kilotons (Mark 18, 1952).[65]

THE NORTH ATLANTIC TREATY

For Britain, the Berlin Blockade had underlined the limits of its military capabilities near home while its forces were still spread across the globe. In turn, this reemphasized the need for an alliance with the United States that would ensure continued American involvement in Europe while giving the British government some opportunity to influence decision making in Washington.

The process of achieving such a transatlantic partnership was well underway in mid-1948; indeed, the prospect of such an alliance may have been part of Stalin's motive in forcing a confrontation over Berlin. If so, the decision backfired badly. Given America's long tradition of isolationism and opposition to "entangling alliances," it is difficult to imagine how a formal alliance could have come about without the shared experience and urgency of the Berlin Airlift.

Today, we tend to assume that the entire purpose of this new pact was to create the military alliance that confronted the Soviet Union and its allies for the next four decades. At the time, however, European nations were almost equally concerned by the prospect of a revived Germany. If restoring the European economy depended on restarting its industrial heart in Germany, it was equally true that none of its neighbors could be sanguine about the prospect of a resurrected German state, however limited that state might be. Only the United States could achieve the twin tasks of counterbalancing the natural tendency of Germany to dominate Western Europe while impeding Soviet influence in the region.[66]

British Foreign Minister Ernest Bevin, who had already been instrumental in bringing about the Truman Doctrine of 1947, was the principal architect of the new alliance. For months, he had been talking about a Western European Union built on the Treaty of Dunkirk, an alliance that he had signed with his French counterpart, Georges Bidault, in March 1947. In January 1948, Bevin presented his concept to Parliament, and within weeks Bidault and he were negotiating with the governments of Belgium, the Netherlands, and Luxembourg to form a loose alliance. On March 17, the five governments signed the Brussels Pact, creating the Western Union.

Five days later, parallel negotiations came to a head when British and Canadian representatives arrived at the Pentagon for ten days of talks about a possible Atlantic security system. The talks were generally positive but did not result in a formal alliance. Although Secretary of State Marshall generally supported Bevin's efforts, he felt that the immediate goal should be to reassure France by integrating Germany into the European economy. Marshall therefore advised Truman to downplay any American military commitment for fear that such talk would interfere with congressional funding for the European Recovery Plan.[67]

On June 11, 1948, however, the Senate voted overwhelmingly to approve Resolution 239, the "Vandenberg Resolution," which endorsed U.S. "association" with regional agreements for collective self-defense. With this support and the impetus of the Berlin Blockade, British, French, and American officers held a series of conferences in an effort to design a combined command structure, possibly headed by General Clay or some other American senior officer. Meanwhile the French, with most of their forces committed to Indochina, pleaded for both an immediate U.S. commitment to defend Europe and increased American military aid to prepare for a potential conflict. In September, President Truman authorized the transfer of equipment and spare parts to bring three French divisions in Germany up to combat readiness. This was a matter of some concern to the JCS because such military aid appeared to be cutting into war stocks that the United States needed for its own defense. In October, the Western Union created a Permanent Military Committee chaired by Field Marshal Montgomery and invited the United States to designate representatives to the committee as well as to the Western Union's Equipment and Armament Committee.[68]

The issue of a formal treaty continued for some time, with the European governments seeking a strong obligation for mutual defense while the U.S., mindful of congressional sensibilities, sought a weaker commitment that left each signatory to determine how it would assist in meeting an attack. As finally signed on April 4, 1949, Article 5 stated that:

> The Parties agree that an armed attack on one or more of them in Europe or North America shall be considered an attack against them all; and consequently agree that, if such an armed attack occurs, each of them . . . will assist the Party or Parties so attacked by taking forthwith, individually and in concert with the other Parties, such action as it deems necessary, including the use of armed force, to restore and maintain the security of the North Atlantic area.[69]

Thus the North Atlantic Treaty or Treaty of Washington concerned attacks only in a specified portion of the world and allowed each nation considerable latitude as to how it would respond to an attack. This phraseology was clearly intended to satisfy the U.S. Senate about American commitments in Europe; no one could have foreseen that the first time this provision would come into force would be for the commitment of NATO-crewed aircraft to defend the United States after the terrorist attacks of September 11, 2001.

Once signed, this document still had to be ratified. In European eyes, the treaty was important primarily to increase military assistance to rearm their forces. The undetermined cost of such aid troubled both the JCS and Congress, but the Truman administration succeeded in persuading Congress to consider foreign aid and the treaty as separate matters. The Senate ratified the treaty on July 21, 1949, and it went into effect on August 24th.[70]

Thus, the North Atlantic Treaty came into being as a political alliance with some limited obligations for the United States to help arm the European forces. As a political statement, it was the most far-reaching Western response to the Berlin Blockade, representing an American attempt to deter aggression by committing itself in advance, something it had not done in 1914 or 1939.[71] What remained to be done was to implement this political agreement into a functioning military alliance.

World War II had ended with a divided Germany, and that division in turn had provoked the first major confrontation of the Cold War.

Any chance for the continued cooperation of the victorious Allies was long gone by 1949. With a few exceptions, such as Yugoslavia, Europe was divided into two increasingly armed camps. While the West had won the first confrontation, on the other side of the globe the most populous nation in the world was entering the communist camp.

6

THE CHINESE CIVIL WAR

Zhang Xueliang (Chang Hsueh-liang) was an unlikely Chinese patriot. As the eldest son of Manchurian warlord Zhang Zuolin (Chang Tso-lin, also known as the Old Marshal), he had led a privileged youth punctuated by violent pranks. Tradition has it that the younger Zhang earned expulsion from Hamilton College by shooting out most of the dormitory windows in the central quadrangle. Returning to Manchuria, the young man enjoyed a life more notable for debauchery and drug abuse than military prowess. Nonetheless, he succeeded to power when a Japanese time bomb killed his father in 1928. Like many other warlords, "Young Marshal" Zhang Xueliang came to terms with the growing power of the Nationalist Chinese republic led by Chiang Kai-shek, but that republic's drive to eliminate foreign dominance of China put the Young Marshal in the bad graces of Tokyo and contributed to the Japanese occupation of Manchuria in 1931. Forced south along with his army, Zhang was in and out of favor with the Chinese republic. In October 1935, however, Chiang Kai-shek appointed Zhang as deputy commander of the Northwestern Bandit Suppression Headquarters, charged with liquidating the remnants of the Chinese Communist Party (CCP). Zhang's forces had to turn ninety degrees away from the Japanese threat in Manchuria in order to fight their fellow Chinese.

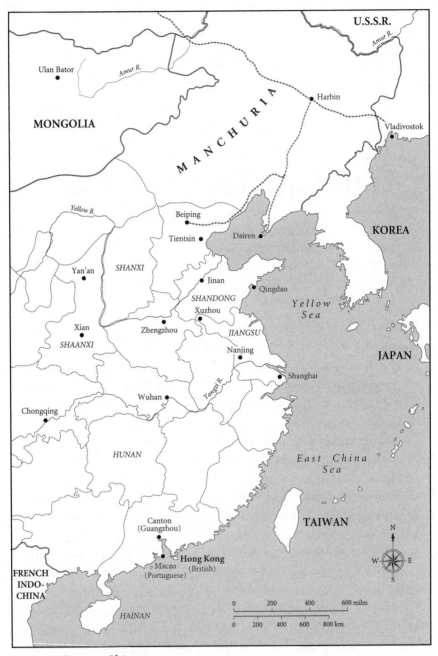

MAP 6. Eastern China

134

Secretly, Zhang negotiated with the Chinese Communists, seeking to reach a truce so that they could confront the common enemy.[1]

In December 1936, an angry Chiang arrived at Zhang's headquarters in the city of Xi'an (Sian) in north-central China. The commander-in-chief directed renewed attacks to finish off the CCP, but Zhang and his supporters decided otherwise. Early on the morning of December 12, Zhang's troops burst into the visitor's quarters, killing several bodyguards and at least one general. Chiang escaped in his nightshirt, leaving behind his uniform and false teeth. He injured his back and suffered cuts from brambles before being apprehended by Zhang's men. Zhang wanted his nominal commander to make peace with the CCP and focus on Japan, a position he made clear in telegrams to the other Chinese warlords. For days, however, all the Chinese generalissimo would do was defy his captors and threaten Zhang with the consequences of his actions. Meanwhile other nationalist generals, convinced that their leader was dead, launched air and ground attacks on Xi'an.[2]

Zhang was stymied. His political advisor, the Australian journalist William H. Donald, tried to negotiate a compromise, and after a few days Chiang's influential, Wellesley-educated wife, Soong Mei-ling, arrived to further the negotiations. Finally, the communist political leader Chou En-lai (Zhou Enlai) also came to Xi'an, under instructions from the COMINTERN to promote a nationalist-communist alliance against the Japanese. Chiang Kai-shek grudgingly gave a verbal promise to cease attacking the CCP and focus on the Japanese; on the strength of that promise, he and his wife flew out of Xi'an on Christmas Day, 1936. The Young Marshal, nattily attired in a padded jacket and golfing trousers, voluntarily accompanied his commander, seeking to put the best face on his mutiny. Within a few days, he was arrested, court-martialed, and placed under house arrest for what turned out to be fifty-five years, until both Chiang and his successor were dead.[3]

The reasons behind this comic opera were as complicated as the Chinese Civil War itself. Bruce Elleman has suggested that the entire incident might have been an elaborate ruse, designed to allow Chiang to compromise with the Reds and fight the Japanese without losing face for backing down against the CCP.[4] Some have depicted Zhang Xueliang as a true Chinese patriot, while others argue that he was acting in his own selfish interests, aiming not so much at Chiang himself as at a violent secret society of Chiang's followers, the Lixingshe, whose arbitrary actions threatened Zhang as much as the Communists.[5] Moscow obviously wanted the Chinese to contain Japanese expansionism, but its policy varied between supporting a separate CCP state and urging a united front with the nationalists. Mao Tse-tung may well have negotiated the deal not to satisfy Moscow so much as to ensure that Chiang's armies would be decisively engaged against Japan, which is in fact what happened.[6] Regardless of the motivations, the Xi'an Incident led to the so-called Second United Front, an uneasy truce between the Chinese Communists and Nationalists that prevailed for most of the next eight years. Once Japan was defeated, the civil struggle resumed almost as if the war had never happened, leading to a communist victory in 1949.

THE CHINESE REVOLUTION, 1911–1927

To understand the 1945–1949 Civil War, one must first consider the situation that produced it. China in the early twentieth century was the helpless victim of foreign and domestic elites. Thirty-three different foreign governments had extorted agreements that negated Chinese sovereignty, allowing these foreigners to maintain their own armies, navies, and police forces to protect their citizens who entered China on business or as missionaries. A complicated economic situation led to the concentration of most Chinese farmland in the hands of a small number of landlords, reducing the traditional peasantry to share-croppers, hired hands, or vagrants. The last imperial dynasty sputtered to a halt in 1911, replaced by a republic that had little actual power. Politically, warlords like Zhang Xueliang dominated large portions of the country; one of these warlords, Yuan Shikai, hijacked the presidency of the republic in 1912 and tried to make himself emperor before dying in 1916.[7]

This situation produced not only an angry, dispossessed peasantry but an equally angry, nationalistic intelligentsia that sought to restore order and regain their sovereignty from the foreign occupiers. Out of a range of political groups, the most influential republican reformers were the Nationalist or Kuomintang (KMT) Party (sometimes Romanized as Guomindang or GMD) founded by Sun Yat-sen (Sun Zhong-shan), who was intermittently head of the republic until his death of cancer in 1925. In the early 1920s, Sun sought the support of various Western governments in order to strengthen his republic against the warlords, but in 1923 only the COMINTERN would provide advisors, weapons, and funds.

Like many reform-minded Chinese, Sun admired the manner in which the Bolsheviks had mobilized the Russian people for a revolution; he was therefore willing to work with the Communists but only on condition that he retained leadership of the KMT. In theory, this meant that all members of the Chinese Communist Party joined the KMT as individuals; nonetheless, both the COMINTERN and the CCP intended that these individuals would have dual membership, forming a bloc within the KMT. The resulting alliance was called the First United Front.[8]

In 1924, the CCP was still a relatively small party, having formed only in 1920 through the action of a handful of radical intellectuals including Mao. Following Marxist doctrine, it focused on the small industrial labor force of China, which was concentrated in Shanghai, Canton, and a few other cities. After all, according to Marx, China was still in the agricultural or feudal phase of economic development, decades or centuries away from development of the capitalist bourgeoisie and industrial proletariat that would eventually lead to a communist revolution. It therefore made sense to cooperate with "progressive bourgeois" reformers, such as the KMT, in hopes of hastening the long-term economic and political growth of China. As a practical matter, Moscow wanted to support the KMT in order to counterbalance Japanese and Western influence in the region.

The Soviet Union sent several notable veterans of the Russian Civil War, including Vasily K. Bluecher and A. I. Yegerov, to China. Russian and Japanese military and political instructors became essential to the Whampoa (Huangpu) Military Academy, the nursery of future officers for the KMT's army. This academy grew rapidly from a three-month candidate course to a two-year military college. The commandant of the academy was Chiang Kai-shek, a leading military reformer who had joined the KMT in 1923, with Liao Chung-k'ai, a non-Marxist leftist, as his political officer. Recognizing the importance of a modern military for political purposes, Sun Yat-sen had sent Chiang to the Soviet Union to study warfare. While he valued the assistance of foreign advisors, Chiang resisted efforts to indoctrinate the cadets as Communists. In March 1926, Chiang arrested a number of Chinese Communists and placed some Russian advisors under house arrest, accusing the Communists of seeking to kidnap

and deport him to the Soviet Union. After this crisis, the senior
Soviet advisor, Andrei Bubnov, redoubled efforts to cooperate with
the KMT's army, but Chiang was adamant that Communists be
excluded from command positions in that army.[9]

In 1927, Chiang led the new army on the so-called "Northern
Expedition," an advance from the KMT stronghold in the southeast
that culminated in the capture of key cities including Shanghai and
Nanjing (Nanking), which later became the new capital of the republic.
Yet the internal friction continued. Chiang claimed to have intercepted orders from Stalin instructing the CCP to undermine the
general's authority. Regardless of the truth of this allegation, the
army's political commissars, many of whom were Communists, often
disagreed with Chiang's commanders. In March 1927, several commissars encouraged KMT troops to attack foreigners in Nanjing. Although
this was popular among Chinese reformers, it only increased foreign
opposition to the KMT's efforts to unify the country. Chiang was
particularly embarrassed that he had to use the KMT 7th Corps (a
Chinese organization often referred to as an army) to purge Communists from his own 1st Corps in Nanjing.[10]

By this time, Chiang had used his personality and control of officer
assignments to gain mastery of the army; its successes in the Northern
Expedition had made him popular with all reformers in China. Therefore, although the CCP-dominated central committee of the KMT
voted to reduce his authority, the Communists did not act decisively.
Instead, Chiang struck first. On April 12, 1927, KMT soldiers and
allied local gangsters attacked the union halls and other CCP centers
in Shanghai and Canton. The French government and local merchants
helped arm this attack in order to dispose of pro-Soviet labor unions.
At least 8,000, and possibly many times that number, died in the attacks.
At Whampoa, Chiang executed 350 cadets on suspicion of communist
sympathies. A series of battles between KMT factions, warlords, and
Communists ensued, and at one point Chiang resigned and went
home to demonstrate his importance to the party. Eventually he
emerged as the commander-in-chief of the KMT army, the Soviet
advisors departed, and the CCP went into full retreat.[11]

THE LONG MARCH AND MAO TSE-TUNG

In ensuing years, the Chinese Communist leadership exhibited its
military incompetence, repeatedly trying to fight conventional battles

against Chiang's much stronger forces. Fortunately for the future of the CCP, Chiang was not able to concentrate on them but instead became involved in fighting warlords and trying vainly to eliminate Soviet control of the Manchurian railroads. To counterbalance the Soviets, the KMT government in Nanjing invited Japan to intervene in Manchuria. This invitation plus the threat of increasing Soviet power may have contributed to the eventual Japanese occupation of that province.[12]

To replace the departed Soviets, Chiang turned to Germany. In 1928, the Germans established a military mission to train and equip the nationalist army. The most famous German advisor was Hans von Seeckt, the man who had rebuilt the German Army after World War I and institutionalized the tactics that made that army so formidable in the next world conflict. Following Seeckt's advice, the KMT build hundreds of blockhouses, linked by roads, to hem in the communist base areas in south-central China. Communist leaders unwisely attacked these forts, suffering significant losses. Using the line of forts as a base, Chiang's "Fifth Encirclement Campaign" forced the remnants of the CCP out of their strongholds in southern China in October 1934.[13]

The resulting "Long March," a circuitous strategic retreat by three communist "armies" along multiple routes, lasted for 369 days. After the first six weeks, there was little significant fighting, although the sheer distance involved—6,000 miles—resulted in numerous losses along the way. This retreat, represented in Chinese Communist accounts as an epic victory, culminated when the survivors arrived in northern Shaanxi province in late October 1935. There, in the remote area of Yan'an (Yenan), the CCP established an austere headquarters that directed its activities for the next dozen years. Of equal importance was the gradual emergence of Mao Tse-tung as leader of the CCP. Although he still encountered internal opposition after the Long March, it was this experience that gave him the political leadership and military experience to direct the Chinese Communist revolution.[14]

As suggested previously, Mao Tse-tung was innovative and even heretical in two different ways, one political and one military. Politically, Mao argued that in the unique circumstances of China, Karl Marx's famous sequence of agricultural feudalism to capitalist industrial society and finally to proletarian revolution was not immutable. Instead, Mao contended that it was possible for the CCP to mobilize the peasantry that made up 73 percent of the Chinese population and achieve a communist revolution far sooner than Marx had predicted. This did not mean that he expected to stop the economic development process, but only that this development could reach its fruition after the Communists had seized political power. This idea scandalized the more orthodox Marxists in the CCP, men who continued to oppose the concept of a peasant revolution for years. Perhaps one reason for Mao's ideological success was simply language. In German and English, the term "proletariat" clearly connoted urbanized, industrial workers; in China, however, "proletariat" was translated by the ideographs for "property-less class," a term that described the downtrodden rural peasants quite as much as it described any factory worker. By promising land reform at the expense of the landlords of China, Mao had a foolproof platform to gain the loyalty of the rural Chinese populace. Ironically, therefore, many of his followers thought they were achieving ownership of their own farms, only to learn after 1949 that the further development of socialism meant agricultural collectivization.[15]

Mao was not a military tactician and usually left field command to subordinates. In fact, he probably borrowed many of his tactical ideas from Zhu De, a former warlord who was the military commander of the southern base area in which Mao was the political leader from 1927 to 1931.[16] Mao was, however, a gifted politician who accurately analyzed the CCP's situation within China and used the concepts of others to construct a military solution to that situation. Mao's military statements reflect a knowledge of the Chinese theorist Sun Tzu and bear resemblances to many of the ideas of Carl von Clausewitz and Antoine-Henri Jomini. Like Clausewitz, he stressed the importance of political goals in war.[17] Although Mao's military thought evolved over about a decade, as early as 1929 he emphasized the fundamentally political nature of revolutionary warfare, asserting that "the Chinese Red Army is an armed body for carrying out the political tasks of the revolution."[18] In addition to treating the peasants with respect, the army's main function, even at the expense of military operations, was to proselytize and assist the peasantry. Even his most famous instructions on guerrilla tactics, written in 1930, were actually part of a larger passage emphasizing politics:

> Divide our forces to arouse the masses, concentrate our forces
> to deal with the enemy. The enemy advances, we retreat; the

enemy camps, we harass; the enemy tires, we attack; the enemy retreats, we pursue.

To extend stable base areas, employ the policy of advancing in waves; when pursued by a powerful enemy, employ the policy of circling around.

Arouse the largest number of the masses in the shortest possible time and by the best possible methods.[19]

Perhaps Mao's greatest originality was to place these traditional guerrilla tactics in the dual context of political support and unlimited time. While Westernized armies always sought quick and decisive victory, Mao recognized that the only hope for his weak forces was protracted conflict, causing both attrition and demoralization among his enemies.[20] Only after a prolonged struggle would the revolutionary forces move on to Phase III mobile or conventional warfare, and even then those forces would be supported by the mobilized populace and local guerrilla bands.

These, in essence, were the tools that Mao used. He was not a field commander for any significant time period. Nor, despite his belief in the people growing their own armed forces, was he completely unsupported in his efforts to wear down the KMT. Following the outbreak of full-scale hostilities between China and Japan in the summer of 1937, the Japanese Army unintentionally performed many of the functions of the conventional army in a nineteenth-century compound force (see chapter 2), wearing down the KMT while the Communists husbanded their strength for the ensuing struggle with Chiang's forces. Once the United States entered the Pacific war, both Communists and nationalists tended to avoid risky offensive actions, leaving the Americans to defeat Japan and clear the way for the subsequent power struggle. During this time period, both the communist and nationalist armies tried to build up their strength. Chiang Kai-shek's army received extensive training and equipment from the Americans, while in Yan'an, Lin Biao with scant Soviet assistance trained his own army of disciplined regulars, including limited numbers of artillerymen and communications specialists. On occasion during the war, such as the "New Fourth Army Incident" of 1941, Chiang used force in a vain attempt to assert his nominal control over the Red Army, but even this did not completely end the truce between the two parties.[21]

In the contest between these two groups, Mao had better human materials. While there were undoubtedly some venal and oppressive leaders among the Communists, overall their ideological focus made them self-policing and generally honest. The KMT also had a significant number of competent soldiers and sincere politicians. Unfortunately, Chiang's party was in the same situation that European rulers had found themselves three centuries before, when they too began to build modern states. In each case, the new central regime lacked both the authority and the trained leadership to establish a modern government throughout the country. Forced to cover a much larger area than the Communists, the KMT necessarily made compromises with warlords and other independent power groups, whose interests were far more selfish than nationalistic. Because of this influx of warlords, the senior officers of the nationalist army were often far less competent technically than their Whampoa-trained subordinates. Wartime expansion diluted the quality of the junior officers as well; by 1944, only 27 percent of such leaders had any formal training. Moreover, the Whampoa military clique controlled the central army, mistrusting even those regional generals who proved to be competent.[22] As a result, the best intentions of the KMT often floundered in a swamp of incompetence and corruption. Government inefficiency was so great that the KMT could not take military advantage of its large population nor care for its wounded, and by 1945 the country was wracked by inflation.[23] The incident at Xi'an was a precursor of the innumerable problems that prevented the KMT from achieving its high ideals of a united and efficient national republic.

This inefficiency and corruption coupled with Chiang's preference for fighting Communists rather than the Japanese exasperated U.S. officials and advisors during World War II. The senior U.S. officer in theater, the irascible General Joseph Stillwell, advised cutting off aid and even overthrowing Chiang to force the Chinese to fight. His more politic successor, Lieutenant General Wedemeyer, was sympathetic but still pessimistic about Chinese Nationalist capacities.[24] Even Franklin Roosevelt, long the defender of the KMT as the legitimate government of China, had lost patience by 1944. To promote Chinese cooperation against the common enemy, in July 1944 the United States sent a liaison team, the so-called Dixie Mission, to Yan'an. In dealing with this mission and with the U.S. ambassador to China, Mao and Zhou Enlai cleverly presented themselves as reasonable men interested in friendship with America and defeat of the Japanese. The U.S. mission provoked outrage in the KMT government but also helped legitimize the CCP as a diplomatic player.[25]

The Soviet Union, neutral against Japan until 1945, also paid lip service to the Second United Front. Stalin was irked by the independent-mindedness of the CCP and Mao, and was as always willing to sacrifice the Chinese Communists to advance Soviet security interests. Moreover, in the long run it was to his advantage to keep China weak by recognizing the nationalist government while still giving limited support to the Chinese Communists.[26]

MANCHURIA, 1945

Still, by 1945 Chiang commanded an army of 2.5 million men, including thirty-nine divisions equipped and trained by the United States. The KMT's center of gravity was in southern and western China. By contrast, the Chinese Red Army numbered perhaps 900,000 full-time soldiers, most of them in base areas in northern and north-central China.

The great prize was Manchuria, where neither Chinese force had any significant presence, and where the Soviet Red Army shattered the Japanese and puppet Manchukuo defenders in August 1945. Repeated Russian and Japanese aggression had made restoration of Chinese sovereignty in Manchuria a matter of national prestige, and both sides raced to fill the power vacuum caused by the Japanese surrender. The KMT felt that it had to take control, but its own centers of power in the south and west were so remote from the northeast that this race overextended Chiang's forces. The CCP saw a great opportunity in the region and therefore rushed into Manchuria with little preparation.

The Soviet occupiers initially favored the KMT government as part of Stalin's continued efforts to ensure Soviet interests while cooperating with the United States. At the Yalta Conference in January 1945, Stalin again pledged to attack Japan and support Chiang Kai-shek's government, in return for which the United States made a vague recognition of Soviet "preeminence" but not annexation of Manchuria. In Stalin's mind, this apparently meant that China would become a buffer state between the Soviet sphere of influence in northern Asia and the American sphere in the Pacific. After Roosevelt's death on April 12, the Truman administration at first tried to continue

MAP 7. Northern China

144

this policy of cooperation but soon began to support Chiang's ambassadors in tough negotiations in Moscow. The resulting Sino-Soviet Treaty, signed on August 15, 1945, was a series of compromises. Stalin settled for limited restoration of Russian economic control of the Manchurian railroads and ports, plus de facto Chinese recognition of Soviet domination in Outer Mongolia. In return for these concessions, the Soviets implicitly renewed their promises not to support the CCP against Chiang but instead to turn Manchuria over to the KMT.[27]

Once Japan sued for an armistice, Chiang, with American backing, demanded that Japanese forces in China surrender to him as the legal government of the country. Outside of Manchuria, the Imperial Japanese Army remained strong and undefeated, reluctant to surrender to anyone, let alone the nonuniformed "rabble" of the Chinese People's Liberation Army (PLA). Japanese commanders continued to control large portions of northeastern China and even to campaign against the Reds for some weeks after the armistice. Months after the war, the Japanese remained in control of Shanghai, looting at will. In Beiping (as the KMT had renamed Beijing in 1928), the local Japanese commander threatened to negotiate with the Communists unless he and his staff received money and special privileges from the nationalist regime; his troops set off explosions to convince the populace that only the Japanese could defend them from the Communists. In some instances, local KMT commanders actually hired individual Japanese soldiers or entire units to help them control the countryside. By some accounts, 80,000 Japanese troops fought for the KMT as late as 1947, which further contributed to the poor public image of the nationalist regime.[28]

In Manchuria itself, the Soviet Red Army reigned supreme. Just as in East Germany, the invaders had invested relatively little effort into planning their occupation after fighting ceased. Vast rural areas saw no Soviet troops at all, while elsewhere Soviet conduct toward the population and the CCP varied from open hostility to wary cooperation. The Soviets treated all Japanese-owned factories as war booty, subject to confiscation just as in Germany. Some Russian officers disarmed all partisans, including Communists, while others cooperated quietly with the CCP. On September 6, 1945, elements of the communist Eighth Route Army bluffed their way past the new occupiers into the major city of Shenyang, marching in under propaganda banners that proclaimed the Soviet mission to restore the region to KMT control! Four days later, the local Soviet commander, General Kovtun-Stankevich, told his red counterpart that the communist troops must depart but did not force the issue. Meanwhile, several thousand men of the "Northeast Anti-Japanese Army," a group of Soviet-trained and equipped Chinese, joined the CCP forces; these men were more loyal to the Moscow party line than to the independent communist regime of Yan'an. Despite Soviet and KMT directives to the contrary, during August-September the CCP seized 300,000 rifles, 138,000 machine guns, and 2,700 mortars and artillery pieces from the Japanese, making the PLA well armed for the first time in its history.[29]

While confusion prevailed in the northeast, diplomatic negotiations continued. Believing that the Soviets would support his claim to be part of a coalition government, on August 29 Mao began negotiations with the nationalists in the wartime KMT capital of Chongqing (Chungking), but these talks went nowhere. For the first time ever, on September 14 a Soviet delegation arrived in Yan'an, but its main purpose was to insist that the CCP must follow the Moscow line in implementing the Sino-Soviet Treaty.[30] Meanwhile, Chiang apparently relied on Soviet promises with regard to Manchuria and chose to reoccupy the coastline of southern and central China before moving northward.

In late September, the Soviets tightened their control over remaining Japanese arms supplies while informing the local Chinese Communists that the Russians would withdraw within two months, in accordance with the treaty. Both the Yan'an (CCP) and Chongqing (KMT) regimes redoubled efforts to deploy their own troops and officials into Manchuria before the Soviet departure. In Chiang's case, however, he was suspicious of regional units that were not fully under his control. He therefore delayed matters by sending troops from his own central army. Although the United States obliged with sealift and airlift for the KMT troops, this delay gave Mao more time to occupy Manchuria and proselytize the local population. One nationalist field army commander was so insulted that he defected to the Communists, an omen of future such losses.[31]

Between October 6 and 29, 1945, the U.S. Fourteenth Air Force airlifted the 92nd Chinese Nationalist Corps (CNC, sometimes referred to as an "army") to Beiping from central and southern China, and moved the 94th CNC to the Tientsin area closer to the coastline. Each of these corps or "armies" consisted of two small divisions, each of which in turn had three infantry regiments but only one artillery battalion and limited logistical components. Such a corps totaled between 25,000 and 35,000 men. Admiral Thomas Kinkaid's U.S. Seventh Fleet prepared to transport at least three other CNCs, some from as far away as Haiphong, Vietnam, directly to ports on the Manchurian coast. This would allow the nationalists to take control quickly as the Soviets departed. By late October, however, the Soviets began objecting to any Nationalist Chinese presence in the port of Dalian (Dairen), where Moscow was attempting to reassert the old Russian concessions. Moreover, the People's Liberation Army had occupied one of the target ports, Yingkou. Once it became clear that the CCP and possibly the Soviets would oppose the nationalist landings, the U.S. commanders felt required to bow out. Admiral Kincaid and General George C. Stratemeyer, who was the U.S. forces commander in the temporary absence of Wedemeyer, informed Chiang on October 27 that their orders precluded involvement in possible combat operations.[32] Instead, the navy redirected the 13th CNC to Chinwangtao, just south of the Great Wall and therefore a logical base for operations into Manchuria. From there, the nationalists had the much more difficult task of occupying Manchuria along the vulnerable railroad lines of the region. As Chiang's chief of staff, Wedemeyer had previously recommended consolidating control of northeastern China before moving into Manchuria, but Chiang felt compelled to move in as the Soviets left and thereby deny the area to the CCP.[33]

The presence of the U.S. Marines' III Amphibious Corps in the Tientsin–Beiping area greatly facilitated the movement of the KMT into the northeast. On August 10, a Joint Chiefs of Staff directive ordered General Wedemeyer to assist the nationalist government in arranging the surrender and repatriation of Japanese troops, but without becoming involved in the nationalist-communist struggle.[34] Within 48 hours of Japan's suing for peace in August, Admiral Chester Nimitz, the Commander-in-Chief, Pacific Ocean Areas, had ordered this corps to prepare to move into China, which would put it under Wedemeyer's command. Although the U.S. desire to contain the Soviets figured prominently in these decisions, it is equally true that more than 600,000 Japanese soldiers and civilians were located in northeastern China, requiring disarmament and repatriation. On September 30, the main amphibious convoy of III Corps began unloading at the mouth of the Hai River. Major General Keller Rockey, the corps commander, moved the 1st Marine Division into the area of Tientsin and Beiping, while the 6th Marine Division (minus the 4th Marine Regiment, which went to Japan for occupation duty) attempted to secure the ports and railroad along the coastline. The corps was supported by a marine air wing of four groups plus additional U.S. Navy aircraft, all of which made an imposing show of force. The local populace and foreign nationals in the area, remembering the marine presence in China before 1941, welcomed the arrival. Still, the Chinese Communists in the area, including 170,000 regulars from the 8th Route Army, were rightfully suspicious of this intrusion. Marine pilots took periodic ground fire while patrolling the railroads but could not retaliate without permission from headquarters. A series of minor incidents and firefights also occurred in October-November.[35]

The transportation of nationalist troops as well as the deployment of the marines reflected a conclusion within the War and Navy Departments that the United States must support Chiang no matter how inadequate his leadership might be. From the perspective of Washington, the nationalists were the legal government of China, while Moscow apparently controlled the Chinese Communist Party. Nonetheless, the United States was determined to avoid involvement in the looming confrontation between nationalists and Communists, a confrontation that seemed insignificant by comparison to growing friction in Europe. In November 1945, the JCS admonished Wedemeyer to ensure that the U.S. forces remained nonpartisan.[36] Yet much of what those forces did, such as airlifting troops, securing Japanese weapons, and protecting mines and railroads, effectively aided the nationalists in their struggle. As a marine corps historian so eloquently remarked, "Set down in the midst of a fratricidal war with ambiguous instructions to abstain from active participation while 'cooperating' with Central Government forces, the Marines walked a tightrope to maintain the illusion of friendly neutrality."[37]

On November 27, 1945, the secretaries of war, navy, and state met to determine how and when to withdraw the marines from China. They concluded, rather illogically, that the marines must remain to facilitate the nationalist movement into the northeast, while at the same time the United States should negotiate a peace between the two Chinese regimes. In effect, the United States wanted to avoid distractions from the pressing problems of European reconstruction.[38]

THE MARSHALL MISSION

General of the Army George Catlett Marshall has already appeared several times in this narrative, but chronologically the China crisis marked his first major role in the Cold War. A graduate of Virginia Military Institute rather than West Point, Marshall might never have received a commission had it not been for the army expansion during the Philippine Insurrection of the early 1900s. He was among the first generation of officers to benefit from the professional educa-tion system established within the army prior to World War I, becoming a consummate staff officer who rose to chief of staff of the Army on September 1, 1939. As the military head of both the ground forces and the Army Air Forces for the next six years, General Marshall had more responsibility than any officer since Ulysses S. Grant. His perfor-mance in the role was nothing short of brilliant. Not only was he an expert manager and advisor, but he had a unique understanding of how to represent the army to both Congress and the public. In the ordinary course of events, this superb soldier, universally respected by all, should have commanded the Normandy Invasion and gained the acclaim accorded to Dwight Eisenhower. Instead, Franklin Roosevelt kept him in the Pentagon, allegedly explaining that "I didn't feel I could sleep with you out of Washington."[39]

In 1945, Marshall was sixty-five years old. Six years of constant strain had left him grey, jowly, and exhausted. President Truman finally permitted him to retire formally on November 26, 1945, only to sum-mon him back to duty the next day as special representative to China. Yet, everyone in Washington agreed that only someone of Marshall's reputation could convince both sides to sit down and talk.

From the start, Marshall was determined to curb Chinese Commu-nist influence; given Stalin's professed support for the Chiang govern-ment and suspicion of Mao, this appeared a possible if difficult mission. Arriving in China in December, Marshall insisted on the nationalist government's sovereignty over Manchuria while offering the CCP the right to participate legally in government and politics. As usual, Zhou Enlai acted as the reasonable man, open to compromise when talking to the American general, although Marshall remained skeptical.[40]

Still, both sides were uncertain about the future, and Marshall wielded great influence in controlling military and economic aid to the stricken country. In two months, he achieved remarkable results. On January 10, 1946, both sides agreed to an immediate cease-fire and to establish a tripartite "Executive Headquarters" in Beiping to work out the details of enforcing that armistice. On January 31, a Political Consultative Conference including KMT, CCP, and other representatives agreed to a National Assembly to meet in May and redraft a constitution. Finally, and most astonishingly, on February 25 Marshall got the two sides to agree to gradually demobilize their forces over a period of eighteen months, leading ultimately to an army of fifty KMT and ten PLA divisions that would be integrated and distributed across China.[41]

Unfortunately for China, neither party honored these agreements because neither regarded them as an acceptable path to achieve its goals. In particular, the Nationalist Army continued to advance into communist-held areas of Manchuria. After achieving tactical victories in mid-May 1946, the more right-wing KMT officers believed that they could settle the matter by force and thwarted Marshall's further efforts to negotiate a renewed agreement. These generals blamed Marshall for imposing a short-lived cease-fire in late June 1946, at a time when the Communists were retreating in Manchuria, but the Nationalist Army was already overextended, and it is unlikely that it could have decisively defeated the Communists even if the fighting had not paused for two weeks. When the United States continued to transfer surplus equipment to the nationalists, Yan'an rightfully criticized this as American support of one side in the dispute. To address this criticism, in August 1946 Marshall got the State Department to cease issuing export licenses for munitions going to China. The general continued his fruitless efforts at negotiation until the end of 1946, then returned home to become secretary of state.[42]

Open Conflict

The People's Liberation Army (PLA) was hard-pressed in 1945–1946. Surprised by the sudden Soviet invasion and Japanese surrender, the CCP had made several major decisions. First, it would shift soldiers from the more southern base areas into northeastern China and Manchuria; this was the so-called "advance to the north, defend in the south" strategy.[43] Because the first contacts with the Russians had been favorable, the PLA troops expected to acquire Japanese weapons and winter uniforms once they arrived at their new locations. Thus, the party center in Yan'an ordered 60,000 troops to move from Shandong to Manchuria but to take only 20,000 weapons with them.[44] Simultaneously, the CCP apparently decided that it was time to go beyond guerrilla tactics and move to "mobile warfare" or Phase III conventional operations, a policy confirmed by orders from the party center in Yan'an on September 19, 1945. It is worth noting that at that time, Mao was away, negotiating in Chongqing. This shift to more conventional operations again assumed that the PLA could obtain heavy weapons and supplies in Manchuria. The new communist force included many transfers from the Eighth Route and New Fourth Armies, but its official name was the Northeast People's Autonomous Army, under the command of Lin Biao (Lin Piao).[45]

The CCP and PLA hurried into the region without their usual political base. A group that had depended on rural peasants for a decade suddenly found itself moving into the cities of Manchuria and northeast China, where most Japanese supply dumps and Soviet troops were located. In the long run, this decision proved to be successful, but in 1945–1946 the Communists were very vulnerable, lacking popular support and dependent on inconsistent Soviet aid. Moreover, they became associated in the Chinese public mind with the excesses of the Soviet occupiers, which did not simplify their task.

To further complicate matters, the newly arrived PLA enlisted local troops, including former units of the Japanese puppet regime, for the communist cause without extensive political training. These troops often had better equipment and weapons than the veteran fighters from the south, yet, because they lacked indoctrination, many of the new recruits defected to the Nationalist Army, taking their weapons with them. Consequently, the veteran troops often felt that they were treated unfairly. One commander telegraphed to Mao that the situation could be described as "seven no's—no party organization, no mass support, no political power, no grain, no money, no medicine, no shoes or clothing."[46]

It is worth noting that the nationalist forces suffered the same handicaps in terms of poor political and logistical support in Manchuria. The KMT had originally been a popular mass political party like the CCP, but from 1937 to 1945 the government had been effectively exiled from its base of support in southern China. It had no more political base in Manchuria than did the CCP and depended on Soviet, American, and Japanese support to gain its initial control of the southern half of that province. Like Yan'an, Chongqing had been caught off guard by the Japanese collapse and took some time not only to deploy troops but also to construct a new government for the northeast. On August 31, 1945, Chiang Kai-shek created a clumsy structure in which his son, Chiang Ching-kao, was the diplomatic representative to the Soviets while two other officers were in effect rivals—one as head of the Northeast Headquarters of the Military Affairs Commission (Hsiung Shih-hui) and the other as troop commander in the region (General Tu Yu-ming). Friction was inevitable, and the nationalist government never established effective control of northeastern China and Manchuria.[47] Nor did the nationalists follow their successful tactics of mid-1934 by cordoning off and eliminating PLA base areas. Instead, the nationalist units remained tied to the major cities and connecting railroads.

Despite such handicaps, the Nationalist Army had considerable success during the spring and summer of 1946, when it outnumbered and outgunned the Communists. After long delays, in March of that year the Soviets belatedly began to withdraw from Manchuria. Although often uncooperative, they generally followed the letter of their 1945 agreements, turning the southern and central cities of the province over to the advancing nationalists. Falling back to the north, the defending Chinese Communists methodically destroyed railroad and other bridges to delay the nationalist advance. In the second half of April, the defenders made a stand at Ssup'ing, a key rail junction midway between the major cities of Shenyang (often known by its Mongol name of Mukden) and Changchun. This defense cost the PLA heavily but allowed the CCP to occupy much of rural northern Manchuria.[48]

For both sides, this campaign like much of the Chinese Civil War was a matter of conventional warfare, using numerous mortars and artillery pieces, and on the nationalist side, limited air support. Although both armies were dependent on large numbers of human laborers for their supplies, battles often focused on control of the scarce railroad lines. The CCP had decided to shift to Phase III mobile warfare, and its principal commander in Manchuria, Lin Biao, was a product of the Whampoa Academy who had always been skeptical about the value of guerrilla tactics.[49] This is not to say that guerrilla warfare no longer existed. Indeed, throughout the three years of struggle in the later 1940s, local and regional communist forces continued to harass the nationalists in many parts of China, generally restricting them to major cities and railroad lines in disputed regions such as Manchuria. By one calculation, the Reds destroyed 10,250 miles (16,400 kilometers) of railroad line between 1945 and 1947, while the nationalists only repaired 3,700 miles (5,920 kilometers).[50] Such attacks not only tended to immobilize the nationalists but also steadily deprived them of supplies. For their part, the Communists also had to battle small bands of bandits, Japanese stragglers, and dissidents in their own rear areas. Nonetheless, the climatic struggles of the Chinese Civil War were more conventional battles than insurgent raids.

TURNING THE TIDE

The revolutionary nature of Mao's forces was more apparent in the villages than on the battlefield. As part of the race to take Manchuria, the Chinese Communist Party had sent not only regular soldiers but also 10,000 party workers led by nineteen of the seventy-seven members of the party's central committee. The presence of so many outsiders created some tensions in Manchuria, where the newcomers often encountered resistance from village elders and other traditional elites. To reduce such problems, the party at first moved very carefully, seeking coalitions with local leaders. Uncertain of its long-term success in Manchuria, the CCP initially operated under the cover name of the All-Circle People's Federation and was careful to place its few reliable Manchurian Communists in prominent leadership roles. This federation advocated land and education reform, and a variety of other changes that earned widespread support. In 1946–1947, the CCP gradually gained control of much of eastern and northern Manchuria, building a base of support that ultimately proved decisive in comparison to the isolated nationalist troops. The presence of the trained and ideologically committed PLA accelerated this process, advancing the political mobilization of northeastern China in a hothouse manner by using both force and persuasion to overpower opposition. This is not to deny that many Manchurians were as war-weary as their counterparts behind nationalist lines, but the CCP was much more effective at generating popular support.[51] The CCP launched similar efforts in other parts of China, encouraging peasants in increasingly violent attacks on landlords from mid-1947 onward. Mao himself later explained that the goal was not so much land redistribution as breaking down traditional patterns of local society and mobilizing the peasantry to support the war.[52]

The KMT army had reached its high-water mark in the fall of 1946, occupying most cities in southern and central Manchuria while controlling much of central and southern China. Already, however, it was stretched thin in towns and along railroad lines, leaving much of the Manchurian countryside to the Reds. Standing passively defensive, the nationalist troops lost their fighting edge while some of their commanders engaged in the usual corruption and business speculation. That fall, Lin Biao began to infiltrate into the more rural areas of southern Manchuria, occasionally striking at his opponents. In October, Lin's troops wiped out the Nationalist 25th Division at Tungliao, west of Ssup'ing, while the 184th (Yan'an) Division defected to the Communists in the southern portion of the province.[53]

In China proper, the nationalists had more success in 1946–1947. After great efforts and a fortuitous defection on the part of a Red commander, the Nationalist Army regained control of the railroads and much (but not all) of the rich coastal province of Shantung, south of Tientsin, forcing Mao to withdraw much of the regular PLA forces from the area.[54]

Yet the nationalist cause again suffered from war-weariness within its own ranks and in the general population. After eight years of fighting against Japan, the troops saw no prospect of being discharged, and lost heart or offended the populace by looting. Reports of KMT officers kidnapping and mistreating men for the army were widespread.[55] Once Japan surrendered, much of the Nationalist Army reverted to the prewar tradition of regional identity, making it difficult to redeploy troops from one province to another. Communist attacks often focused on the few central army units that were the primary nationalist combat force. Inflation and corruption dogged the KMT regime. The Whampoa clique, with its suspicion of outsiders, further undermined unity of effort, and Chiang maintained a truly Byzantine command structure to prevent any rivals to his power. When regional commander Pai Chung-hsi won victories in central China, for example, the government regarded him as a threat rather than an asset and put limits on his forces.[56]

Technically, the Nationalist Army also suffered from a multiplicity of different weapons made by Germany, Japan, the United States, the Soviet Union, and other arms manufacturers. According to some accounts, the U.S. arms embargo of 1946–1947 further hampered the Nationalists by depriving them of spare parts for vehicles and crew-served weapons.[57] Overall, however, the KMT had ample supplies of weapons and probably lost more to capture, defection, and poor planning than to maintenance failure. A 1950 classified evaluation by the Nationalist Ministry of National Defense accurately assessed the issue: "We have never heard it said that our military defeat in recent years resulted from a lack of ammunition or an insufficiency of other supplies. Rather, we inadequately understood bandit-suppression and anticommunism; we had insufficient morale; and our government, economy, and programs completely failed to provide clear support for the bandit-suppression military effort."[58]

At the same time as the U.S. arms embargo, the KMT regime received unprecedented foreign aid. China was the largest single recipient, to the tune of $658.4 million, of United Nations Relief and Rehabilitation Aid (UNRRA), with the United States paying 72 percent of all UNRRA costs. Millions of additional dollars came from Canada, the Export-Import Bank, and other sources. While the United States did block arms shipments in 1946–1947, it simultaneously gave or sold China another $200 million worth of "nonmilitary" wartime surplus trucks and other equipment, often at advantageous rates. Yet, little of this aid achieved its intended purpose of improving the Chinese economy.[59]

The actual size and equipment of units on both sides varied widely, but a typical nationalist army corps might total up to 35,000, divided into two or three often understrength infantry divisions. Due to American aid, the nine infantry battalions in each division had ample machine guns and light mortars, and the division as a whole usually had an artillery battalion with twelve to eighteen 75mm howitzers and perhaps eight 4.2-inch heavy mortars. The most highly favored corps sometimes had an additional nondivisional battalion of 105mm howitzers, as well as eighteen light tanks, usually U.S.-manufactured Stuarts.[60]

The Nationalist Navy and Air Force were also well equipped but again suffered from corruption and inefficiency. The navy consisted of gunboats and a few larger surface vessels but proved unable to interdict arms smuggling because many commanders accepted bribes to supplement their meager salaries. The air force, originally trained by the United States, had a peak strength of 200 fighters (P-40s, P-51s, and later some P-47s), 30 bombers (B-24s and B-25s), and 120 transports (C-47s and some C-46s). These aviation units also suffered from poor morale and coordination; the transports were perhaps the most effective part of the air force, and air power rarely proved decisive in battle.[61]

The People's Liberation Army forces lacked such refinements, fielding a rudimentary air force late in the war. On the ground, the closest equivalent to a nationalist corps was the "column," consisting of two or three lightly equipped infantry divisions. Not only were these divisions less well endowed with crew-served machine guns and mortars, they also typically had only one or two batteries each of 75mm howitzers. As the campaigns of 1947–1949 wore on, however, desertion, defection, and capture brought the PLA a steady increase in U.S.-built heavy weapons and trained crews.[62]

The Communists also received significant aid from the Soviet Union, although Stalin was careful to avoid overt involvement. In addition to the Japanese arms in Manchuria, the Soviets transferred extensive captured Japanese and German weaponry, as well as experienced Korean and even Japanese soldiers (the latter prisoners of war), from North Korea to help equip and train the growing Red force. Civilian Soviet specialists assisted the CCP with railroad operation, public health, and other specialties. Determined to maintain his independence, however, Mao paid for this largess with food shipments that caused shortages in Manchuria and elsewhere.[63]

In March 1947, with Lin Biao already making inroads in Manchuria, Chiang Kai-shek sent General Hu Zongnan (Hu Tsung-nan) with 150,000 nationalist troops to expel the Communists from their political capital in Yan'an. Jung Chang and Jon Halliday have suggested that Hu was a longtime communist sympathizer, whereas other accounts attribute treachery to his personal secretary. In either event, this expedition accomplished nothing but an empty propaganda gesture. Given ample warning of the advance, Mao ordered the town evacuated, leaving each dwelling neatly swept. On March 16, the 1st and 29th Chinese Nationalist Corps approached Yan'an from the south and west. Mao assigned the defense of the town to Peng Dehuai, future commander of Chinese forces in Korea. Although significantly outnumbered, Peng delayed the attackers until the morning of March 19, when the 1st Corps entered an empty town. Over the next month, Mao proceeded to burnish his military credentials by ambushing two of Hu's regiments, each left suspiciously isolated and unsupported, and then capturing a major nationalist depot to resupply the Red troops in the area. Although Peng actually conducted operations, Mao clearly intended these actions to lessen the propaganda impact of Yan'an's fall. For the next year, the communist leader and his entourage remained tantalizingly close to the KMT troops around Yan'an but were never intercepted. In any event, the communist field command was sufficiently decentralized so that this disruption in its administrative operations did not significantly impede the war effort.[64]

In mid-1947, a communist offensive achieved startling success in the core KMT area of the central plains, one of the wealthiest regions of China. The plains had sustained considerable damage during the Japanese conflict, but in 1947 it suffered a new man-made disaster. With U.S. engineering assistance, the nationalist government had diverted the Yellow River in the spring of 1947, thereby uprooting 100,000 people. This well-intentioned but misguided project provided a ready-made base of support for the opposition. Commanded by the ruthless Liu Bocheng, with Deng Xiaoping as his political officer, in July communist regulars isolated and destroyed a number of the Nationalist Army's best regiments in the central plains. The 2nd and 4th Chinese Nationalist Corps lost the bulk of their forces—80,000 casualties—while Liu and Deng lost only 10,500. A jubilant Mao cited the central plains battles as the turning point of the war. To avoid KMT pursuit, Liu continued to advance southwestward to the old, pre-1934 base area in the Dabie Mountains. After completing a five-hundred-kilometer march in August-September 1947, however, the Communists found the former base area devastated by years of oppression, making it a poor bastion for future operations.[65]

Meanwhile in the northeast, the combat power of the U.S. III Amphibious Corps continued to decline in 1946–1947. By April of 1946, virtually all the combat veterans who had arrived the previous fall had rotated home, being replaced by dwindling numbers of inexperienced new recruits. In June, the III Corps headquarters itself folded into a reinforced 1st Marine Division that numbered less than half the original 50,000 troops. As the marines and the nationalists visibly weakened, the PLA in the Tientsin-Tsingtao area grew bolder. On July 13, 1946, the Communists captured seven marine bridge guards, releasing them only after much propaganda. A more serious incident occurred on July 29, when the Reds ambushed a platoon-sized marine patrol at Anping, along the route from Tientsin to Beijing, resulting in four dead and eleven wounded. Communist propaganda alleged that the marines were fighting alongside KMT troops, although no KMT soldiers were present.[66]

The shrinking marine force was only the most visible indication that the United States was distancing itself from Chiang's regime. General Marshall's departure at the end of 1946 led to the dissolution of the US-KMT-PLA headquarters that was supervising the nonexistent agreement in Beiping. This in turn permitted the departure of most of the marine forces, something that Marshall had long advocated. By the spring of 1947, only two battalions and three air squadrons of marines remained in the Tsingtao area, primarily to guard a U.S. Navy training activity there. Clashes continued, however. On the night of April 4–5, 1947, the Communists successfully raided a marine ammunition depot at Hsin Hao, killing five sentries and wounding eight. When a reaction force moved from Tsingtao to relieve the depot, it ran into a land mine and ambush. The marines belatedly turned remaining ammunition over to the Nationalist Army. Although some marines remained in north China until the final evacuation in early 1949, their once-potent presence had become ineffectual much earlier.[67]

Manchuria Falls

Despite his defeat in the central plains during 1947, Chiang Kai-shek wisely refused to transfer forces to that area, correctly anticipating that northeastern China and Manchuria would prove to be the next major contest with the PLA. Unfortunately, the regional, almost feudal structure of the KMT's forces prevented reinforcement of even this threatened region. Superior intelligence provided by the local population allowed the PLA to gain the initiative in Manchuria during May-June 1947, expanding its control southward by up to 240 kilometers. Only at Ssup'ing did the Communists fail, suffering 40,000 casualties while besieging the town during June 1947.[68]

During the second half of the year, Lin Biao conducted a war of attrition, attacking the railroads and outposts of southern Manchuria that provided the logistical lifeline to the only major nationalist holdings remaining in the province—the cities of Harbin, Changchun, Shenyang, and Chinchow. Chiang changed commanders and reinforced

Manchuria at the expense of the neighboring Beiping area, but to little avail. The economic situation in KMT-controlled regions of China continued to worsen, and for prestige reasons Chiang refused to evacuate the beleaguered cities of the northeast and Manchuria. By the end of 1947, even nationalist sources admitted that overall their forces numbered 2.7 million to 1.15 million full-time communist soldiers; the actual ratio was probably even less favorable to the KMT, which of necessity had relied on superior numbers during the previous two years.[69]

For the fall of 1947, Lin Biao wanted to conduct a major pincers operation to cut off the supply lines of the nationalist forces in Manchuria's southern cities. Mao hesitantly agreed, and during the freezing weather of late September Deng Hua's 7th Column struck the 49th Chinese Nationalist Corps, newly arrived from Jiangsu Province in east-central China. Deng virtually wiped out the 49th but suffered such heavy casualties that Lin resisted Mao's urgent demands for a follow-up offensive.[70]

Three months later, Lin finally responded by broadening an intended local attack into another attempt to pinch off railroad connections. This time the PLA isolated the primary railroad junction of Shenyang. Bad flying weather prevented the KMT forces from detecting the communist troop movements until just before the scheduled attack date of January 14, 1948. Lin's troops routed the 5th Corps, demoralizing the defenders and forcing them to strip forces from other towns in order to concentrate on the defense of Shenyang. Some of the best units in the nationalist camp, including the New 1st and New 6th Armies, succeeded in stabilizing the situation temporarily. However, by February the PLA had cut the railroad lines and seized the port of Yingkou, leaving many of the nationalist forces in Manchuria to depend on the limited airlift capacities of the Nationalist Air Force and civilian air lines. In March 1948, Major General David Barr, the senior U.S. military advisor remaining in China, urged Chiang Kai-shek to take advantage of this lull and begin a gradual withdrawal from Manchuria, or at least evacuate outlying garrisons into Shenyang. For reasons of prestige, however, the Chinese generalissimo would agree to evacuate only Kirin, a town near Changchun. In China proper, the Communists reoccupied Yan'an in mid-April 1948 and easily defeated demoralized nationalist troops in the Shantung peninsula that spring.[71]

Lin Biao's next target in Manchuria was the junction at Ssup'ing, site of many previous battles. The veteran 88th Nationalist Division, whose cadre had fought together throughout the war against Japan, defended the town desperately but finally succumbed on March 13, 1948. The KMT now held only a few pockets in Manchuria around the major cities of Chinchow, Shenyang, and Changchun.[72] The Communists possessed the initiative in Manchuria and indeed throughout China.

Despite this success, Lin Biao remained cautious, preferring to wait until winter so as to train and concentrate more forces before resuming the offensive. As always, Mao Tse-tung focused on the political and psychological trends rather than an objective calculation of military forces. Mao badgered Lin with frequent telegrams, forcing the PLA into an offensive several months before Lin had intended. This decisive campaign for Manchuria, often referred to as the Liaoshen Campaign because it was fought in the Liaoning province and climaxed in the capture of Shenyang, began on September 12, 1948, although Lin did not make a decisive commitment until early October.[73]

For this campaign, Lin had assembled nearly 600,000 troops, of whom almost half were recently promoted militiamen and other local volunteers with limited training. First, he cleared the remaining outposts along the railway line from Shenyang and Chinchow, then concentrated on the latter city with 65,000 regulars. The 31st CNC, which arrived belatedly from Taiwan, failed to fight its way into the city from the south. On September 25, Chiang Kai-shek directed Wei Lu-huang, the latest in a series of nationalist commanders in Manchuria, to send a relief column westward out of Shenyang, thence south to Chinchow. Wei resisted until Chiang flew to Shenyang to enforce his orders. By the time this column had advanced halfway to Chinchow, the PLA had captured the city on October 17. Much of the relief force was destroyed as it withdrew back toward Shenyang. Two days later, the northernmost nationalist outpost, the city of Changchun, also fell. Here the Nationalist 60th Corps, long condemned to short rations by the isolated position of the town, mutinied, helping disarm the New 7th Corps and complete the capture of the city.[74]

Meanwhile the bulk of the Shenyang garrison, consisting of elements of five corps, had advanced southward along the rail line to restore communications and attempt to recapture Chinchow. Commanded by General Liao Yao-hsiang, this formidable force of experienced troops made considerable progress but left behind only the 52nd CNC and two regiments of the 207th Youth Division to garrison the vital rail junction. Seizing the opportunity, Lin Biao left two columns to delay any nationalist advance northward from the port of Hulutao. Instead of attacking Chinchow as the KMT expected, Lin swung his main force of eleven columns, totaling 200,000 men, in a wide flanking movement east of the railroad, cutting off Liao's armies from the rear. Such a movement was only possible because the PLA had thousands of Manchurian laborers to move supplies and the wounded. Liao himself died early in the battle, which lasted from October 27 to 30, 1948, and resulted in the complete destruction of his army, with an estimated 25,000 dead. Recognizing reality, the garrison commander of Shenyang, General Chou Fu-cheng, defected to the communist side, and the city fell on November 1–2. Also on the 2nd, the port of Yingkow fell; the remaining nationalists evacuated their bridgehead at Hulutao, southwest of Chinchow, on the 9th. In less than two months, the PLA had cleared all of Manchuria. Seven corps, totaling twenty-nine divisions and 400,000 men, had disappeared from the nationalist order of battle, and many of these troops now served their former opponents.[75]

DENOUEMENT

As the Liaoshen Campaign ended, the PLA was preparing an even greater effort in central China. Between November 9, 1948, and January 10, 1949, the Communists progressively dismembered and destroyed the largest formation in the Nationalist Army, the Xuzhou Bandit Suppression Headquarters, which was in essence an army group. This headquarters controlled four field armies, four lightly equipped pacification area headquarters, and a variety of specialized units. Overall, this organization had twenty-three corps and a total strength of 800,000 men and two hundred tanks. On paper, therefore, superior nationalist fire support, heavy equipment, and numbers should have been more than a match for the two PLA armies opposite them, which totaled perhaps 510,000 main-force soldiers. What equalized the situation were the PLA's popular roots that could tap into another half a million local and regional militiamen, at least as many unarmed transport laborers, and extensive human intelligence sources. By contrast, the nationalist troops were increasingly demoralized, for all the reasons previously suggested—war-weariness, especially for southern soldiers fighting far from home; frequent defeats at the hands of the PLA; and a sense that their officers did not provide pay, supplies, medical care, and other essential support.

What followed was arguably the largest single battle of the entire Cold War. The Communists caught the Seventh KMT Army redeploying from one set of fortified cities to another. The bulk of Seventh Army might have extricated itself had it not been for the sudden collapse of the 3rd Pacification Area, a two-division force located northwest of the Seventh's new concentration area. This in turn prompted other units to withdraw in a panic, exposing the Seventh Army to attacks from both sides.[76] Disasters like this overcame the competence of several nationalist commanders, and the entire army group headquarters fell into communist hands after a series of battles in the snow.

After the successive disasters in Manchuria and the central plains, the nationalist cause was doomed. When PLA forces attacked the remaining nationalist forces around Tientsin on January 14, 1949, the 130,000 defenders promptly surrendered. On the 23rd, General Fu Tso-yi, the commander of nationalist forces in northern China, surrendered the 200,000 troops in the Beiping area and allowed the communist forces to enter the city. With nationalist forces north of the Yangtze River thus eliminated, the stage was set for a communist offensive into southern China. As he had done previously, Chiang Kai-shek resigned the presidency and called for negotiations to settle the civil war. The Communists responded with harsh conditions that would have meant the end of nationalist rule; when an agreement was not reached, on April 21 communist forces crossed the Yangtze. Nanjing, the capital of the KMT movement, fell to the Communists four days later. When a British gunboat, HMS *Amethyst*, appeared to evacuate foreigners from the city, communist gunners shelled it and forced it to run aground, with the loss of fifty British sailors including the vessel's commander. In July, the *Amethyst* escaped, but the Royal Navy was humiliated and the British public enraged.[77]

Britain, which had reoccupied Hong Kong at the end of August 1945, now had to contemplate the threat of war with the PLA. Believing the colony to be indefensible, the Australian government declined to provide assistance, although New Zealand promised modest naval support. Thus, at a time when the British Army was severely stretched in world commitments, it had to prepare to defend Hong Kong as well. Two Gurkha battalions from Malaya joined a Royal Marine Commando and a tank battalion from the Middle East as reinforcements, so that by late 1949 the garrison numbered 30,000 troops backed by land- and naval-based air. Fortunately, the CCP chose not to press the issue immediately, and the next year London recognized the new communist government, effectively defusing the situation.[78]

Nationalist troops in the northwest still inflicted some sharp reverses on the PLA in the summer of 1949, but for all practical purposes the civil war was over, with the CCP building a new government in Beijing and the KMT withdrawn onto the island of Taiwan.

There were many recriminations, especially by Republicans in the United States, concerning who was responsible for "losing China." These partisan accusations undoubtedly contributed to the fact that for the next two decades, the United States continued to recognize Chiang's regime as the only legitimate government of China, an absurd state of affairs that in turn helped produce the Chinese-American struggle in Korea.

In fact, from the beginning, Moscow and Washington had tacitly agreed not to make China a major bone of contention. Both the Soviets and the Americans had strong reservations about the ideology and the practical ability of their Chinese counterparts, so neither Great Power provided sufficient aid. Using popular support, the PLA was able to maneuver more freely and gather intelligence far more reliably than the well-trained nationalist commanders. Under the circumstances, the CCP, which had become a major tool for peasant mobilization, inevitably generated more support than the KMT, which had ceased to be a mass political party in all but name. Mao's focus on the political nature of the war served him well and gave his theories of insurgency an exaggerated reputation. Nonetheless, the Chinese Civil War, like the long struggle in Vietnam, actually ended in a conventional campaign of conquest rather than a guerrilla war of insurgency.

7

THE KOREAN CONFLICT

TAEJON, KOREA, JULY 20, 1950

The North Korean 3rd and 4th Divisions tore the 24th Infantry Division apart. A month before, the 24th along with the other three divisions of Eighth U.S. Army had been on occupation duty in Japan. Like most units in the postwar army, the 24th had only two, instead of three, battalions in each infantry regiment and two, instead of three, batteries in each artillery battalion. The division mustered about 11,300 of its authorized 18,500 strength, and it was even weaker in tanks and other heavy weapons.[1] In a policy that dated back to fighting the lightly armored Japanese tanks of World War II, Eighth Army infantry units were equipped with the 2.36-inch bazooka anti-tank rocket rather than the much more effective 3.5-inch rocket used against the well-armored German tanks. Although the senior officers and noncommissioned officers in the 24th Infantry were veterans of World War II, the bulk of the division was composed of half-trained peacetime soldiers. During 1949–1950, the commanders of Eighth Army had conducted platoon-, company-, and some battalion-level training to improve their readiness, but the more complex tasks, such as battlefield maneuver or adjusting artillery fire, had not yet been mastered. The densely populated Japanese islands provided little opportunity for such training. In any event, budget shortages deprived Eighth Army of the ammunition, spare parts, and other "expendables" necessary to train effectively.

164

Once North Korea invaded the south on June 25, the 24th Infantry Division drew the mission of deploying to slow down the enemy advance. Transfers from the other three divisions made up some of its critical personnel shortages, but the sudden reassignment of so many strangers damaged unit cohesion in both the gaining and the losing divisions.

Nor did the division deploy as a single unit; the U.S. Navy and Air Force, also hampered by budget cuts, were hard-pressed to assemble the transportation needed to move the troops to Korea. The 24th Division's first echelon, Task Force Smith, consisted of only one reduced-strength infantry battalion (1st of the 21st Infantry Regiment) with attached 4.2-inch mortars and one howitzer battery. The latter carried thirteen rounds of 105mm high-explosive anti-tank (HEAT) shells, the entire supply on hand in the 24th Division.[2] This forlorn hope deployed in a defensive position south of Suwon on July 5, but the North Koreans, many of them veterans of the Chinese Civil War, rolled right over the task force, inflicting 153 killed and captured in a matter of hours. Except for the scarce 105mm rounds, all U.S. anti-tank weapons proved ineffective against the Soviet-supplied T-34/85 tanks leading the North Korean attack.

Subsequent attempts by larger elements of the 24th to halt the advance southward were equally ineffective. Whenever they encountered a U.S. blocking position, the North Koreans halted, deployed, found open flanks, and bypassed the defenders with the skill of long experience. The two-battalion regiments of the 24th were operating without a strong reserve force and often without communications with higher headquarters. Moreover, their air support was limited or nonexistent. The USAF had placed a low priority on air-ground cooperation since 1945, and most available fighters were based in Japan with relatively short flying ranges, giving them little time to loiter over the battlefield. The navy's one available aircraft carrier and the air force did conduct deeper attacks against the North Koreans that month, but such raids had little effect on the battlefield. On several occasions, in fact, fighters strafed American fugitives by mistake.[3]

The division's luck ran out at Taejon, where it tried to make a stand. The 34th Infantry Regiment with an attached, battered battalion of the 19th Regiment established a thinly held defense on the north side of the city. On July 19, the 34th contained initial probes of the North Korean People's Army's (NKPA) 3rd and 4th Divisions, although the situation was so desperate that the 24th Division commander, General William F. Dean, exhausted himself moving from place to place, directing the fire of individual light tanks rather than controlling the entire battle. Early the next morning, the 3rd Division (to the northwest) and the 4th (from the north and northeast) bypassed and encircled the 34th Regiment. While the NKPA tightened its encirclement on the city, fighting dissolved into chaotic urban confrontations. By this time, the first few 3.5-inch rocket launchers had arrived by airlift, and Dean and other senior commanders repeatedly took a few men with launchers off to knock out individual T-34s. On the evening of the 20th, as convoys of survivors tried to break out of town to the south, General Dean himself took a wrong turn and encountered an enemy roadblock, forcing him to escape on foot. The North Koreans finally captured him on August 25, although they did not announce this fact until December 1951.[4]

Between July 5 and 20, 1950, the 24th Division lost 1,624 men killed, wounded, and missing, although almost one hundred of the latter found their way back to friendly lines. Among the losses were not only the commanding general but also the majority of regimental and battalion commanders in the division. When Dean returned from captivity after the 1953 armistice, he learned that President Truman had presented his presumed widow with a Congressional Medal of Honor, recognizing his individual bravery if not his battle command.[5] Despite this disastrous baptism of fire, the troops of Eighth Army recovered within three months, only to be ravaged a second time when China intervened in Korea in November 1950.

Other conflicts in the Cold War lasted longer and attracted greater historical study. At least two other crises—the Cuban missile confrontation in 1962 and the Yom Kippur War in 1973—came closer to nuclear holocaust. In retrospect, however, the Korean War was the longest high-intensity interstate conflict of the era and carried within it perhaps the greatest potential to expand into a world war.[6]

DIVIDED KOREA

Historian Allan Millett has summarized the Korean problem by remarking that "Like the history of modern China, the Korean people divided into two revolutionary factions, split by their conflicting visions of a modern Korea long before World War II."[7] Both groups were staunchly nationalistic, but one was influenced by the West, including Christian missionaries, while the other owed allegiance to the Communist International. Neither side really accepted the concept of democracy. There were significant divisions even within these two factions, making it more difficult for an outsider to comprehend the complexity of their politics.[8]

At the time, Soviet leaders undoubtedly assumed that the United States controlled the noncommunist, Christian political elements within Korea, but that assumption was a gross oversimplification. Even the eventual dictator of South Korea, Syngman Rhee (Yi Sungman), who had been out of touch with his countrymen during decades of exile in the United States, rarely bent his principles to accommodate Washington. On the contrary, Rhee and other Korean leaders angered the United States by demanding immediate independence in 1945, rather than accepting the need for foreign help to rebuild a nation devastated by decades of Japanese exploitation. In the fall of 1946, a violent leftist uprising in South Korea led to the deaths of eighty-two policemen and four hundred civilians, many at the hands of the U.S. occupation force restoring order. As a result, numerous Korean political groups depicted the U.S. commander in Korea, Lieutenant General John Hodge, as a near-fascist even as he struggled to create a demo-cratic government.[9] Rightly suspecting the Korean National Police (KNP) of ties to antidemocratic rightists, Hodge created an alternative organization, the "police reserve" or constabulary, which eventually became the Republic of Korea Army (ROKA). Unfortunately, the ROKA nurtured within its ranks a number of communist agents.

Lieutenant General Ivan M. Chistiakov, the able commander of Soviet Forces in North Korea, had his own political factions. Ulti-mately, the Soviets facilitated the rise to power of Captain Kim Il-Sung (born Kim Songju), but even he was not a docile puppet, nor neces-sarily their initial choice for leader. Kim was a former guerilla who had fought (under Chinese command) against the Japanese in Manchuria during the 1930s. Moreover, he at first had to cooperate with the Yan'an faction as well as with domestic leftist peasants.[10]

The larger question was the reunification of Korea. At the Moscow foreign ministers' conference of December 1945, Stalin's government agreed to leave the matter up to a joint US-Soviet military commis-sion, which predictably never reached agreement. Instead, the Soviets used the Moscow agreement to dissolve any political groups in the north that opposed the commission, a principle that applied to most of the noncommunist parties. Meanwhile XXIV Corps, like its counterpart III Amphibious Corps in China, withered away as part of the American demobilization. By 1947, the continued strain and expense of occupation prompted the United States to turn the matter over to the U.N. General Assembly. Moscow protested this action, which bypassed the deadlocked Security Council; instead, the Soviets prevented free elections in their zone and tried to hamper them in the south.[11]

In April 1948 National Security Council document 8 approved U.S.-supported elections to permit an independent South Korea but carefully limited U.S. support to preserve the resulting independent state.[12] By 1949, both the Soviet and U.S. Armies had withdrawn their troop units from their respective zones, leaving only advisors and trainers to support the armies of the two rival governments. On the surface, at least, Stalin had preserved the Korean peninsula as a buffer zone without a strong U.S. presence.

Yet the U.S. departure did not mean that peace descended on the peninsula. On the contrary, Millett argues that the Korean War actually began on April 3, 1948, when communist attacks erupted on the island of Cheju and soon spread to almost all the provinces on the mainland. Over the next two years, the south's security forces—KNP and ROKA—lost 7,235 dead, along with at least 30,000 civilians and three American advisors. The rebellion included significant mutinies by pro-communist elements within the constabulary that was evolving into the ROKA. The constabulary eventually arrested or discharged more than 1,500 of its members, while almost 2,000 mutineers died fighting. Although the rebel leaders were Marxists from the South Korean Labor Party, the new government in Pyongyang encouraged the rebellion with arms and propaganda.[13]

In the midst of this widespread insurgency and elections of dubious authenticity, the Republic of Korea came into existence in May 1948 and elected Rhee as its head. By April 1950, the KNP and a purged ROKA had stamped out open rebellion; in the process, their troops acquired considerable experience although the senior officer corps remained arrogant and sometimes inept. At the same time, an escalating series of firefights and other incidents occurred along the 38th Parallel. In May 1949, for example, the North Koreans seized five hilltops south of the parallel in the isolated Ongjin peninsula, and a multiregiment ROKA counterattack met only partial success. Still, the United States was unwilling to provide significant defense assistance to the new republic. The U.S. military aid budget was extremely tight, and American leaders were afraid that heavy weapons would help Rhee invade the north. Worse still, the "abandonment" of China prompted an angry Congress to reject the Truman administration's entire request for aid to Korea in January 1950.[14]

PREPARATION FOR INVASION

Meanwhile, the North Korean security forces paralleled the growth of their counterparts to the south, but these units were designed for mid-intensity combat rather than counterinsurgency. As it departed Korea, the Twenty-Fifth Red Army transferred not only many Soviet weapons but also most of the equipment of the former Japanese occupiers. By June 1950, the North Korean People's Army consisted of at least 180,000 men, including ten infantry divisions, a motorcycle reconnaissance regiment, and the 105th Tank Brigade.[15] Between them, these latter two units had 173 T-34 tanks and thirty armored cars. To spearhead the offensive, such elements could break up into smaller, battalion-sized units intended to function as "forward detachments," the Soviet concept of mobile units that exploited rapidly into the enemy rear areas. Forward detachments bypassed centers of resistance to reach key objectives and dislocate the enemy's defenses. Typical division organization included three infantry regiments of three battalions each, one 122mm and two 76.2mm artillery battalions, and numerous anti-tank and self-propelled guns. A significant number of the NKPA troops were veterans of the Soviet and Chinese armed forces, in some cases transferred to North Korean command as complete units. The NKPA was supported by forty-eight propeller-driven YAK-9 fighters and IL-10 light bombers plus a navy of twenty fast attack boats.[16]

All this Soviet equipment was not a gift; on the contrary, the Pyongyang regime had to take out loans with the Soviets and transfer gold, silver, radioactive thorium, and other valuable materials.

Having failed in his efforts to overthrow the Republic of Korea by insurrection, Kim Il-Sung was determined to seize the south by invasion. Although more cautious, Mao Tse-tung eventually supported

Kim, apparently believing that the United States would not wish to become embroiled in a situation that from his viewpoint was analogous to the Chinese Civil War.[17]

There remains the mystery of why Stalin supported the North Korean invasion at the risk of confrontation with the United States Having achieved his basic goal of keeping the peninsula out of U.S. control, the Soviet dictator had little to gain by such an invasion. As late as March 1949, the Soviet dictator categorically rejected Kim's proposal for even limited attacks, but in January he acquiesced. In the interim, of course, the Soviet Union had gained a measure of psychological confidence by detonating its first atomic device, and the CCP had come to power in China. Stalin did warn Kim not to expect direct Soviet participation in the war and instructed the Korean leader to consult with Mao before proceeding. Apparently, Stalin believed that the prospect of the new Chinese government, allied to Moscow, would discourage the United States from responding to an attack on the peninsula. He may also have sought to increase the antagonism between China and the West by such a confrontation. In any event, the North Korean government was determined to fight, and a refusal by Stalin would have reduced Soviet influence relative to that of China.[18]

Traditional analyses often emphasize the misleading nature of a January 1950 speech in which Secretary of State Acheson omitted any mention of Korea in describing the U.S. defensive perimeter in Asia. In fact, the purpose of that speech was to stress the limits of U.S. support to Nationalist China on the island of Taiwan as part of the administration's ongoing partisan argument concerning the "loss" of China.[19] Communist leaders in Moscow, Beijing, and Pyongyang apparently concluded that this foreign policy failure had left the United States in disarray and retreat. A better understanding of democratic politics would have shown them that the China "failure" virtually guaranteed that President Truman would respond strongly to what appeared to Americans as open aggression in Korea.

INVASION

In June 1950, the ROKA consisted of eight understrength infantry divisions, of which only four had even a single battalion of howitzers, with only two-thirds of the infantry regiments having anti-tank companies.

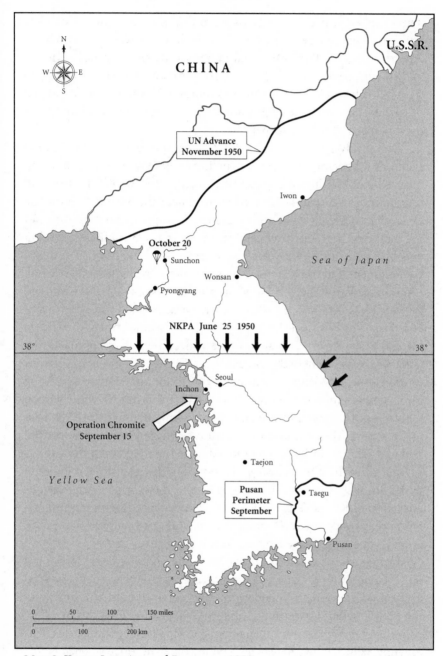

N
W E
S

CHINA

U.S.S.R.

UN Advance
November 1950

Iwon

October 20
Sunchon

Sea of Japan

Wonsan

Pyongyang

NKPA June 25 1950

38°   38°

Seoul

Inchon

Operation Chromite
September 15

Yellow Sea

Taejon

Pusan
Perimeter
September

Taegu

Pusan

0   50   100   150 miles
0   100   200 km

MAP 8. Korea: Invasion and Response, 1950

The primary anti-tank weapons were the same 2.36-inch bazookas and small-caliber recoilless rifles that later proved ineffective in American hands. The ROKA had a total of only eighty-nine howitzers and twenty-seven armored cars, with most of its infantry equipped with M1 rifles and 60mm and 81mm mortars. The "air force" consisted of twenty-two unarmed light aircraft, and the navy of a handful of patrol craft and minesweepers.[20]

Soviet advisors provided a draft "Preemptive Strike Operational Plan" that became the basis for the initial NKPA attack.[21] This plan ensured ample numerical superiority against its opponents, who had only four of their eight divisions arrayed near the 38th Parallel while the remainder continued to repress the insurgency farther south. In the isolated Ongjin peninsula, a regiment of the 6th NKPA Division and a border constabulary brigade overwhelmed the ROK 17th Infantry Regiment. On the Kaesong-Munsan valley corridor leading to Seoul, the remainder of the 6th Division plus the 1st NKPA Division and forward detachments from the 105th Tank Brigade easily outnumbered the thinly spread 1st ROK Division. Twenty miles (thirty-two kilometers) east of Munsan was the widest avenue of approach, the Chorwon Valley, where the 3rd and 4th NKPA Divisions, both veterans of the Chinese conflict, faced the ROK 7th Infantry Division. Led by tanks and engineers, the immediate goal of this attack was the road junction of Uijongbu, future site of the fictional 4077th MASH. East of Ch'orwon, the mountainous terrain restricted both sides, yet the 2nd and 7th NKPA Divisions moved light infantry down the valleys against the 6th ROK Infantry Division. Finally, the three regiments of the 8th ROK Infantry Division were spread out to cover the eastern coastline of Korea. The NKPA 17th Motorcycle Regiment and 5th Division attacked south along the coastal road, supplemented by amphibious landings, engaging each ROK unit in turn.[22]

Despite later recriminations, both the U.S. Far East Command (FEC) G2 and the fledgling Central Intelligence Agency developed an accurate order of battle concerning the North Korean buildup along the 38th Parallel. Unfortunately, neither General MacArthur, the FEC commander, nor his intelligence officer, Major General Charles Willoughby, believed that the Soviet Union would authorize an open North Korean invasion of the south. Their disbelief can be traced back to the fact that the United States regarded the 38th Parallel as the border between two states, whereas the North Koreans and Chinese considered it a temporary dividing line in a civil war. This difference in perspective goes far to explain the surprises of June and November 1950.[23] In addition, Willoughby attempted to control all intelligence collection in his theater but dismissed reports from agents that he had not recruited. Worse still, once the invasion began, FEC had few agents in North Korea and only two photo reconnaissance squadrons to track the enemy's advance.[24]

The ROKA fought well but was outnumbered and outgunned. The 2nd and 7th ROK Divisions attempted to counterattack on the 26th near Uijongbu but accomplished little without artillery support. A difficult situation became impossible at 0215 hours on June 27, when the ROKA prematurely destroyed the main bridges across the Han River south of Seoul, trapping troops and supplies still north of the river. Because the charges were detonated without warning, several hundred civilians and soldiers died in the explosion or drowned as a result.[25] Thereafter, the ROK retreat became disorganized and chaotic.

Meanwhile, the U.S. government reacted far more quickly and decisively than Moscow or Beijing had anticipated. At Acheson's suggestion, President Truman persuaded the UN Secretary-General, Trygve Lie, to convene an emergency meeting of the Security Council in New York; because of the international dateline, this meeting occurred on the afternoon of June 25, 1950. The Soviet Union was boycotting the council because of America's insistence that the nationalists were the legal government of China and thus was not present to veto the proceedings. Instead, by a vote of thirteen to zero with Yugoslavia abstaining, the Security Council called on North Korea to stop its attack and withdraw to the 38th Parallel. Two days later, with Moscow still absent, the United States persuaded the Security Council to go even further. The council called on members to help repel armed attack, as provided for in Chapter Seven of the UN Charter.[26] The United States used this resolution to create a UN Command, the first such collective security force of the Cold War.

Even before the second vote, Truman had authorized the use of air and naval forces in Korea. As the ROK forces crumbled in late June, he reluctantly concluded that the United States must commit ground troops, resulting in the debacle of the 24th Infantry Division in July. Three of the four divisions in Eighth Army—the 24th and 25th Infantry and the 1st Cavalry—moved to Korea and entered the fray piecemeal during July and August. Recognizing the gravity of the situation, in mid-July President Rhee conceded command of all ROKA troops to MacArthur, who in turn subordinated the Koreans to Lieutenant General Walton H. ("Johnny") Walker, who as head of Eighth Army became the tactical commander of the Korean defense. This allowed the United States to begin an act of desperation that eventually became a mainstay of the Korean conflict—the Korean Augmentation to the U.S. Army (KATUSA). The three divisions deploying from Japan each received several thousand South Koreans to fill out their ranks. The 7th Infantry Division, which initially remained in Japan and was reduced to a cadre to fill the other units, had to absorb 8,600 Korean civilians, most of whom could not speak English. In the short run, the presence of so many disoriented, untrained foreigners in their ranks further hampered the performance of U.S. Army units in the summer and fall of 1950. Eventually, however, these men became a vital part of every American unit in Korea, providing hard work and language skills that few Americans could match.[27]

Many tragedies played out during this painful retreat. One of the most serious arose out of the North Korean practice—learned during the Chinese Civil War—of dressing in civilian clothes in order to infiltrate through enemy front lines. The Americans were already bedeviled by infiltration, and they responded with an illegality of their own—requesting the U.S. Air Force to fire on any large groups of civilian-garbed individuals who approached UN lines. On July 26, the refugees of two small Korean villages reached a roadblock manned by elements of 1st Cavalry Division near the bridge at No Gun Ri, a town on the main road southeast of Taejon. According to the refugees' later recollections, the American soldiers searched them and then directed them onto the nearby railroad line, where the Koreans suffered first air attack and then U.S. ground fire over the next several days, killing a large number of civilians.[28] Understandably, the survivors believed that the soldiers, having determined that they were not a threat, had nonetheless directed air strikes and other attacks against them. In fact, there was so little air-ground coordination at this stage of the war that on July 27 an F-80 mistakenly strafed the command post of the 1st Battalion, 7th Cavalry Regiment, near the railroad overpasses in question.[29] It is more probable that a U.S. aircraft attacked the villagers in accordance with the standing request from the army, which does not excuse either this attack or the subsequent ground fire.

In later years, the chaotic retreat of Eighth Army and especially the fate of Task Force Smith have often been cited as the ultimate example of unpreparedness. Yet, whatever criticisms one may level at the ROKA or Eighth Army, these forces managed to delay the North Korean advance long enough to set up a defensive perimeter in southeastern Korea while redeploying forces from the United States for a counteroffensive.

THE BUILDUP

Reinforcements came in three forms. First were individual soldiers to strengthen existing units and replace casualties. The first group of such fillers began movement on July 18, with more than 7,300 reaching Japan by the end of the month. Second, MacArthur asked for formed units to bring his divisions up to wartime strength, a daunting task in itself that required four tank battalions, twelve separate tank companies, eleven infantry battalions, and eleven 105mm howitzer batteries. Some of these units were readily available, in the form of two battalions of the 29th Infantry Regiment in Okinawa plus the 5th Regimental Combat Team (RCT) from Hawaii. These units were no stronger in numbers or equipment than the original components of Eighth Army and suffered accordingly when they entered combat. Armored units were more difficult to come by, especially since the entire army had virtually no formed tank battalions.[30]

More significant were MacArthur's requests for additional large formations to conduct the war. In early July, he asked for at least two additional infantry divisions, a marine division, an engineer special brigade for amphibious landings, an airborne infantry RCT, four anti-aircraft battalions, and a variety of specialized units. The Joint Chiefs of Staff agreed, but the strategic reserve was so weak that they sought and got Truman's approval on July 7. The 2nd and 3rd Infantry Divisions, 2nd Engineer Special Brigade, 187th Airborne RCT, and other smaller units soon began to deploy, with the 2nd Infantry Division's lead regiment reaching the battlefield within a month of alert.[31] The understrength 1st Marine Division formed a provisional brigade to deploy immediately, with other units to follow.

In turn, the government undertook a partial mobilization. In order to satisfy political concerns, the administration chose reserve component units from throughout the country, including four National

Guard infantry divisions and two separate RCTs.[32] Other guard divisions were mobilized later. Yet, although thousands of individual reservists and some specialized companies and battalions were soon en route to Korea, most of the mobilized National Guard units initially stayed at home. The first major guard combat formation sent to Korea, the 45th Infantry Division, did not arrive there until the end of 1951. In part, this reluctance to send the guard units to Korea was due to the need to rebuild the strategic reserve. More fundamentally, however, the Truman administration thought that the Soviets might have intended the entire Korean attack as a distraction in preparation for a future operation in Europe or elsewhere. In fact, Truman's first public announcement of support to the Republic of Korea also included increased military assistance to counterinsurgency efforts in the Philippines and Indochina.[33] During July, the one aircraft carrier battle group in the western Pacific, Task Force (TF) 77 built around *USS Valley Forge*, had to dash back and forth between bombing North Korea and providing a naval presence in the Taiwan Straits.[34] Thus, from the beginning of the Korean conflict, Washington conducted it as a limited war that might not have first priority on available resources.

While Washington felt a shortage of military resources, London's cupboard was completely bare, with only one brigade—the 29th—in strategic reserve at home. Indeed, the British chiefs of staff initially recommended that no British ground forces participate in the UN operation, but this was a political impossibility. In what became a recurring pattern of the post–World War II world, the British Army stretched itself to support the American alliance. Because 29 Brigade needed several months to assemble and deploy by sea, the British responded to American pressure by sending 27 Brigade, with only two infantry battalions and an anti-tank troop (platoon), directly from Hong Kong. This threadbare force arrived on August 28 and immediately went into the line. It was dependent on U.S. logistics and artillery, and justly complained that American commanders often deprived it of necessary fire support and failed to inform it of changes in plans. An Australian infantry battalion joined the brigade from Japan in October, followed by a New Zealand artillery unit, prompting the group to be renamed 27 Commonwealth Brigade. By the time 29 Brigade arrived from Britain, the need was again so great that both brigades remained in Korea. In July 1951, these two brigades combined with other units from Australia, New Zealand, and Canada to form the

1st Commonwealth Division in Korea, the last major instance of Commonwealth solidarity in war.[35]

Other third-party contributions were even more difficult to obtain. Although a few air elements, such as the F-51s of Royal Australian Air Force No. 77 Squadron, arrived within days, most governments initially hesitated to commit ground troops. Eventually, however, the need to fulfill the concept of collective security prevailed. A Turkish brigade entered combat in October. Battalion- and company-sized units from thirteen other nations followed, although the United States generally insisted on reequipping such units with American weapons to simplify logistics. Most of these smaller units were at various times attached either to the two British/Commonwealth brigades or to American infantry regiments. Another five nations provided medical support. Overall, however, the United States and the Republic of Korea provided the bulk of ground forces, with 51 and 43 percent of ground forces, respectively.[36]

Operation Chromite

By August 4, 1950, the defenders had withdrawn into the Pusan Perimeter, a rectangular-shaped bridgehead approximately twenty miles (thirty-two kilometers) east to west and thirty miles (forty-eight kilometers) north to south. The battered survivors of five ROK divisions manned the northern and northwestern faces of this defensive position, while the three U.S. divisions faced eastward from an area just north of Taegu down to the coast. This latter front generally paralleled the Naktong River, a shallow water boundary that constituted the last natural defensive position to protect the vital ports of Pusan and Pohang. When more fully manned units such as the 1st Marine Brigade arrived, they became the counterattack forces to block various NKPA attempts to break through the perimeter. These attacks continued throughout August and early September, while reinforcements and supplies slowly built up behind the front lines. The defenders numbered roughly 125,000 ground troops, while the North Koreans had no more than 70,000 effectives at the front. However, the previous battles plus an underestimation of enemy casualties caused the defenders to exaggerate their foes.[37]

While General Walker directed the stiffening defense of Pusan, his superior, MacArthur, was planning a counteroffensive.[38] As evidenced by his initial request for forces, MacArthur had put his staff to work on such a plan as early as July 4. By August 12, this crystallized into Operations Plan 100B, an outline for an amphibious landing at the port of Inchon. The plan was dubbed Operation CHROMITE.[39] To complete detailed planning, MacArthur used two marine mobile training teams that happened to be in Japan when the war began. Although Major General Oliver P. Smith, the 1st Marine Division commander, arrived in Tokyo on August 22 with part of his staff, they were soon preoccupied with the needs of the marine brigade at Pusan. Thus the training teams together with the amphibious group headquarters of Rear Admiral James H. Doyle did most of the planning.

The technical problems were daunting. Vast mud flats and shallow water limited any assault on Inchon to a few hours twice each day, at high tide. The approach to the port was through a twisting, thirty-four-mile-long channel that at night could only be navigated by ships equipped with sonar and radar. In the landing area, there were no beaches in the conventional sense, only piers and seawalls that could be crossed with great difficulty, using improvised scaling ladders. Moreover, the fortified island of Wolmi-Do dominated these beaches. Even if the landing force established a beachhead, Inchon was a poorly developed port of limited capacity located at the end of a narrow peninsula. Thus, it would be difficult to bring in additional forces, and a determined enemy might contain the invaders in a small area.

The risks involved in the proposed plan raised serious concerns in the minds of Smith, Doyle, and their staffs. These concerns were echoed by Army Chief of Staff J. Lawton Collins and Chief of Naval Operations Forrest P. Sherman when those two men traveled to Tokyo in late August to represent the JCS. Nonetheless, MacArthur insisted on his plan and provided reasonable responses to their objections.

The command structure for Operation Chromite was equally controversial. Rather than subordinating the invasion force to Eighth Army or to some marine headquarters, MacArthur created a new organization, X Corps, answering directly to him. The corps commander was Major General Edward M. Almond, who would simultaneously continue as chief of staff of Far East Command. The X Corps staff included only ten marine and two naval officers for liaison.

Given the rapid buildup of forces, the troop list for the invasion was also improvised. Because the 1st Marine Division had only two infantry regiments (1st and 5th), the ROK Marine Regiment became the third maneuver element. Similarly, the 11th Marine Artillery Regiment was short one battalion, a deficiency made up by attaching the U.S. Army's segregated 96th Artillery Battalion of towed 155mm howitzers. Meanwhile, Navy Secretary Francis P. Matthews had directed that no seventeen-year-old marines would participate in the assault because of the negative political effect if they became casualties. More than five hundred such young marines remained behind at Kobe, Japan, under control of the recently reactivated 1st Armored Amphibious Tractor Battalion. Instead, Company A of the Army's 56th Amphibious Tank and Tractor Battalion led the landings on Blue Beach, while the 2nd Engineer Special Brigade provided overall amphibious support. In total, the 1st Marine Division that went ashore at Inchon consisted of 19,494 marines and naval personnel, 2,786 ROK marines, and 2,760 U.S. Army soldiers.[40] X Corps was rounded out by the 7th Infantry Division, which was almost 50 percent KATUSA. Fortunately for later events, the 7th also received a large influx of noncommissioned officers from the infantry and field artillery schools, giving the division a quick infusion of technical knowledge.

Still, marine planners were understandably reluctant to use the 7th Infantry Division in any critical role during the Inchon landing. This became a major issue on September 1, when General Walker protested the release of the 5th Marines from its role in the Pusan Perimeter. The marine officers refused Almond's suggestion to substitute the 7th Division's 32nd Infantry Regiment for the 5th Marines at Inchon. Finally, MacArthur approved a compromise whereby another green unit of the 7th Division, the 17th Infantry Regiment, would remain on ships near Pusan as a floating reserve while the 5th Marines withdrew to participate in the landing. The marines were equally reluctant to rely on an untried army unit, the 1st Special Operations Company, to seize Wolmi-Do the night before, preferring to divert a scarce rifle unit, the 3rd Battalion, 5th Marines, to that task. The special operations company instead tried vainly to seize Kimpo Airfield on the day after the Inchon invasion.

Transportation was another problem, given that the U.S. Navy had only ninety-one amphibious vessels worldwide. The Military Sea Transportation Service-Western Pacific chartered four Japanese-owned and twenty-six American merchantmen to augment its own thirteen ships. The assault landing was made possible because MacArthur's occupation administration had kept thirty aging Landing Ships, Tank (LSTs) in commission outside the naval force structure. These LSTs were manned in many cases by veterans of the Imperial Japanese Navy, including at least one former battleship captain. The ships had to accelerate their loading process and sortie from port several days early to avoid a typhoon.

Airlift was even more strained, with available planes still dedicated to bringing troops and supplies from the United States. On August 26, Far East Air Forces (FEAF) formed two provisional squadrons of C-47 transports to lift a projected airborne operation in support of the invasion. However, the 187th Airborne RCT did not arrive in Japan until September 21, too late for the Inchon landing.[41]

Despite multiple problems and security leaks, Operation Chromite succeeded. After a prolonged naval and air bombardment, the 3rd Battalion, 5th Marines, landed on Wolmi-Do at 0622 on September 15, 1950, and secured the island within two hours. The defending NKPA 18th Division plus four separate regiments proved inexperienced and uncoordinated.[42] At the next high tide (5:31 that afternoon), the remainder of the 5th Regiment attacked past Wolmi-Do to the seawalls of Inchon itself. Rain squalls, smoke, and a shortage of Navy guide boats caused some confusion when the 1st Marine Regiment landed south of the city, but both landings achieved footholds, allowing eight LSTs to nose ashore. All night, the 2nd Engineer Special Brigade controlled unloading so that the LSTs could depart on the next morning's high tide.

Generals MacArthur and Almond went ashore frequently beginning on D plus 1, and on September 21 X Corps headquarters established itself ashore, formally ending the joint amphibious landing. Marine-army friction continued during the next several days. First, the 7th Infantry Division's axis of advance led it away from the 1st Marine Division, exposing the marine flank; subsequently, Almond divided the city of Seoul and assigned the eastern and southern portion to the 7th Division, causing further coordination issues. General Smith became enraged by General Almond's habit of bypassing the division headquarters and giving orders directly to regimental commanders. Nonetheless, X Corps finally cleared Seoul on September 27 despite strong local counterattacks by the NKPA.

The day after the Inchon landing began, Eighth Army launched a general counterattack to break out of the Pusan perimeter and retrace its steps northwestward toward Seoul. Despite numerical superiority, the UN forces were still severely limited in ammunition, complicating their task. The NKPA around the perimeter, apparently unaware of the landing in its rear, initially fought desperately against this attack. Within seven days, however, the breakout was complete.[43]

In late August, Mao Tse-tung had warned the North Koreans of a possible invasion at Inchon. The Soviets had prodded Kim to mine the likely invasion ports, but for bureaucratic reasons the Inchon channel remained open.[44] Intent on victory, both Kim and his Soviet advisors were slow to grasp the significance of the UN landing and therefore missed any opportunity to withdraw before their troops were trapped in a pincer between X Corps and Eighth Army. Then Pyongyang lost communications with its forward commanders. Almost before he realized it, Kim's forces had gone from the brink of victory to headlong defeat and destruction. By October 1, both Stalin and Kim were asking Mao to intervene to stem the tide of UN victory.[45]

PURSUIT AND DECISION

Conducted in the teeth of so much criticism, Operation Chromite not only reversed the course of the war but also made MacArthur's military judgment appear infallible. The North Korean People's Army's weaknesses, long concealed by its initial advantages of surprise and equipment, became apparent in the chaotic retreat that followed. Poor communications, inadequate supplies, and lack of competent staff officers took their toll, with much of the NKPA collapsing into flight in a matter of weeks.

In short order, the UN forces launched a general pursuit northward. By the end of September, the ROK Army had advanced up the eastern half of the peninsula, reaching Wonju in the center and even farther north on the east coast. Eighth Army was almost equally swift, using two newly created corps headquarters to control its divisions in the march northwestward to Seoul. The 1st Cavalry Division's 7th Regiment, energized by a new commander, William Harris, led the way. To speed the pace, Harris formed Task Force Lynch, built around Lieutenant Colonel James H. Lynch's 3rd Battalion, with attached tanks, engineers, reconnaissance, and tactical air control elements. Given the state of Korean roads, leading an advance with tanks could and frequently did produce collapsed bridges. Still, beginning on September 26, Task Force Lynch, followed by the rest of Harris's regiment, raced up the main road to make contact with X Corps south of Seoul. After a wild night that included firefights with bypassed enemy T-34s and infantry, on the morning of the 27th the task force made contact with the 7th Infantry Division's 31st Regiment just north of Osan. The contact was at first bloody, with the 31st opening fire on the strange approaching force, but after one unfortunate American death this movement closed the pincers of MacArthur's offensive.[46]

Not everything in the improvised UN forces went well. On September 23, 27 Commonwealth Brigade, attached to the 24th Infantry Division, encountered serious resistance from the NKPA 10th Division near Taejon. When both the British and the North Koreans displayed the same aircraft recognition panels, three F-51s mistakenly attacked the British, inflicting sixty casualties.[47] Such incidents indicated that some portions of the NKPA would continue to fight and that the UN forces were still unable to coordinate complex operations. Both Walker and Almond frequently relieved regimental commanders, ruthlessly seeking the men who could somehow control their inexperienced troops.

Nonetheless, by the beginning of October UN forces were approaching the 38th Parallel. With echoes of the "lessons of appeasement" in their ears, American leaders did not wish to allow "aggression" to go unpunished or to appear weak when confronting China and the Soviet Union. Moreover, there was no question that Syngman Rhee intended his ROK Army to continue the pursuit, uniting the peninsula under Seoul's government. Yet, even the entire UN force—just under 200,000 troops—would be inadequate to occupy the vastness of northern Korea.

Everyone recognized that such an action carried a serious risk of conflict with China or the Soviet Union. As early as July 17, President Truman had asked the National Security Council for recommendations as to whether or not UN troops should cross the 38th Parallel to reunify the entire country. The resulting study (NSC-81, dated September 11) proposed that non-Korean troops should not approach the Chinese or Soviet borders. With Truman's approval, on September 27 the JCS directed MacArthur to submit a plan for the occupation of North Korea but placed certain limitations on such a plan. No air, land, or naval forces would cross into Manchuria or the Soviet Union, and no non-Korean troops would operate in the area near the borders. MacArthur promptly replied with a plan to cross the 38th Parallel in force in the second half of October. Eighth Army would continue to advance northward to seize Pyongyang, while X Corps re-embarked at Inchon to attack Pyongyang from the west. As an alternative, Almond's force could travel by sea around the southern end of Korea and then invade the east coast port of Wonsan at the narrowest part of the peninsula. Meanwhile, the ROK Army would continue to drive northward in the eastern and central portion of the country. The Truman administration endorsed this plan, and George Marshall, now secretary of defense, privately wrote to MacArthur that the administration wanted it to appear as if crossing the parallel was a military necessity rather than a political decision.[48]

It was indeed a logical military decision because the UN forces needed to pursue the beaten enemy to prevent reorganization and liberation of captured prisoners. In pursuit of the latter goal, on October 20, 1950, the 187th Airborne Regimental Combat Team parachuted onto drop zones near Sukch'on and Sunch'on, about twenty-six miles (forty-two kilometers) north and northeast of Pyongyang. The intent of this operation was to rescue a reported trainload of friendly prisoners of war and possibly trap elements of the NKPA and North Korean government. In fact, however, MacArthur had delayed the operation several times so that when the 187th jumped, all but one enemy regiment had already withdrawn farther north, and there were no prisoners to liberate.[49]

THE CHINESE INTERVENTION

In retrospect, many observers argued that the UN pursuit into North Korea was a reckless operation done despite repeated Chinese warnings of dire consequences. On September 30, Zhou Enlai announced that the Chinese "would not tolerate" foreign aggression, by which he clearly meant an attack on the North Korean regime. Two days later, Zhou repeated this to the Indian Ambassador to Beijing, K. M. Panikkar, and New Delhi immediately passed this warning to Washington. Perceiving the danger, the British government asked the United States to propose a compromise with North Korea. Thus, so the argument goes, the advance into North Korea forced the Chinese to act in their own defense.[50]

A number of factors make this explanation incomplete at best. First, the Indian government was so desirous of achieving peace that Washington considered its reports, especially those emanating from

Ambassador Panikkar, to be unreliable. On previous occasions, he had reported that China was on the verge of invading Taiwan (when in fact the US intervention in the Taiwan Straits prompted Mao to suspend such an invasion) and that Chinese troop movements in Manchuria were purely routine (which was far from true). Second, the United States did respond to the warning. In early November, Secretary of State Acheson tried repeatedly to contact the Chinese in order to guarantee a buffer zone along their border. By that time, however, the Chinese were unwilling to respond.[51]

In fact, Mao Tse-tung almost certainly would have intervened even if only ROK troops had crossed the 38th Parallel. He was already frustrated that the United States had reversed its policy by interposing naval vessels in the Taiwan Straits, preventing the final defeat of Chiang Kai-shek. To Mao, Korea was another revolutionary war failure that would embolden the United States throughout northeastern Asia; stopping the United States was both a national security imperative and a response to counterrevolution. He also believed that a successful war would improve the CCP's standing within China and China's standing within the region, while continuing the revolutionary mobilization of his own people. Thus, as early as July 7, the Chinese Central Military Commission (CMC) directed the movement of crack troops to the Manchurian border. By July 13, this had expanded to become a new command—the Northeast Frontier Force (NFF) consisting of four infantry corps and three artillery divisions for a total of 255,000 men. By the end of July, the NFF had closed up along the border. For the next two months, former KMT officers trained by the United States during World War II taught PLA troops how the Americans fought. At a time when the NKPA still appeared on the verge of victory at Pusan, Mao was preparing for intervention in Korea.[52] In other words, the widely held belief that China intervened because the U.S. advance threatened its borders was an exaggeration if not a myth.

As the war in the south continued and U.S. involvement increased, Mao redoubled his preparations. On August 26, Zhou chaired a meeting that identified two additional field armies for possible movement to Manchuria, directed the creation of extensive medical facilities in the province, and earmarked 100,000 other soldiers as replacements for anticipated casualties. The next day, Mao ordered that eight additional corps be sent to Manchuria. On September 8, still a week before the Inchon invasion, Mao resubordinated the Ninth Army directly under the CMC and alerted both it and the Nineteenth Army for a possible move to the border.[53]

In early October, the Chinese leader repeatedly authorized diplomatic warnings and otherwise suggested that he might yet refrain from intervention. Although he undoubtedly disliked the idea of renewed war so soon after his victory at home, Mao's principal motivations for these gestures were practical ones. He apparently sought to persuade other Chinese leaders that he had tried all reasonable measures to avoid the conflict. At the same time, when Zhou visited Moscow he discovered that Stalin was having second thoughts about the risks of a confrontation over Korea. The Soviet dictator appeared to renege on promises of jet fighter cover for the Chinese intervention force. On October 12, Mao ordered a final pause in deployment, both to appease his politburo and to pressure Stalin. Two days later, Stalin agreed to dispatch sixteen air regiments, approximately 120 MiG-9s and -15s, to Manchuria, although he severely restricted their use in Korean airspace. With this support assured, Mao finally committed four infantry corps with supporting artillery to move into North Korea. To avoid open war with the United States, Beijing adopted the transparent fiction that these units were all "volunteers," although the UN commanders always referred to them as the Chinese Communist Force (CCF). The first troops crossed the Yalu River on October 19, and each man removed the red star, the symbol of the PLA, from his cap before crossing. Contrary to later legend, UN air elements detected the logistical support involved in this movement and quickly destroyed two hundred scarce trucks.[54]

Lin Biao, the victor of Manchuria and China's most distinguished general, had argued that China should focus on problems at home and that engaging the United States in Korea had only limited chances of success. He therefore declined the offer of command, although for months U.S. intelligence assumed he was the leader of the "volunteers." Su Yu, an equally renowned commander, was seriously ill. Mao therefore turned to Peng Dehuai, the self-taught guerrilla leader from Mao's own province who had risen to command of the Northwestern Military Region. Unlike his rivals, Peng loyally supported Mao in leadership meetings in early October and entered the war with considerable confidence in his success.[55]

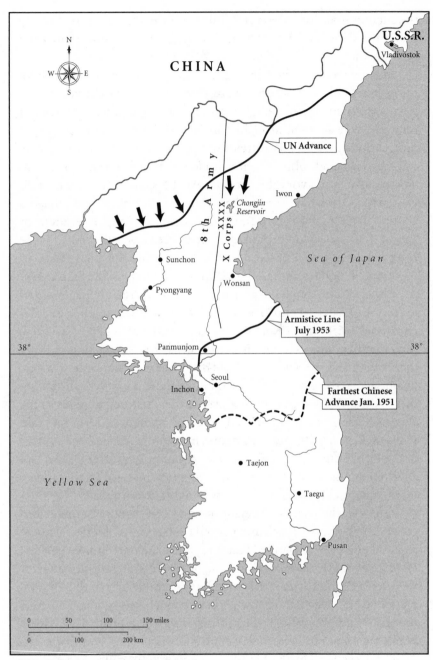

MAP 9. Korea: Chinese Intervention

Movement to Contact

Meanwhile, the UN movement into North Korea continued unchecked. Eighth Army pushed northward from Pyongyang, with Major General Frank W. Milburn's I U.S. Corps making the main effort. Walker had selected Milburn, one of his more experienced and aggressive commanders, and in turn gave I Corps priority for units and staffing.[56] In late October, this corps consisted of the 1st Cavalry and 24th Infantry Divisions, the 1st ROK Division, and 27 Commonwealth Brigade. It pushed northward across the open Chongchon River Valley with II ROK Corps (6th and 7th ROK Divisions) on its right and IX U.S. Corps following behind.

MacArthur's decision to re-embark X Corps at Inchon in order to conduct further amphibious operations produced a giant snarl of logistical problems and backlogs. Its first objective, Pyongyang, fell to I U.S. Corps before Almond's force was re-embarked. By the time X Corps appeared off its next target—the east coast city of Wonsan— on October 20, I ROK Corps, led by the ROK Capital Division, had already reached the area. A large minefield delayed even the administrative landing of the corps at Wonsan. 1st Marine Division did not complete disembarkation until the last day of October, followed during the first half of November by the newly arrived 3rd U.S. Infantry Division, which like its predecessors had absorbed large numbers of U.S. replacements and untrained KATUSAs to bring it up to strength. Although eight Japanese minesweepers cleared most of the Wonsan area, mines remained a problem for weeks—on November 16, an army tug and crane barge struck a mine and sank with the loss of thirty men. Finally, the U.S. 7th Division diverted to land at Iwon, one hundred miles (160 kilometers) to the northeast of Wonsan. Again, however, I ROK Corps had already passed this point. This prolonged sea movement tied up scarce shipping, to the detriment of Eighth Army's supply requirements. Moreover, because the Korean peninsula widened considerably north of Wonsan, X U.S. Corps, with I ROK Corps on its right (eastern) flank, advanced northward, spreading troops extremely thinly in an effort to occupy the entire area and prevent the NKPA from regrouping. Engineers and transportation were also in short supply. Almond in effect became a separate field army commander with the ROK corps subordinated to him. As his force pushed northward, it found that the NKPA was by no means beaten and continued to conduct strong delaying actions.[57] As a result, the U.S. and ROK units of Almond's command were even more vulnerable than 8th Army to the eventual Chinese counteroffensive.

In the general advance, some commanders succumbed to the lure of being first to the Yalu River. In Eighth Army, this honor fell to the reconnaissance platoon of the 7th Regiment, 8th ROK Division, II ROK Corps. This reinforced platoon with a U.S. advisor reached the river at Chosan on the morning of September 26. Because of the longer distance involved, X Corps units did not reach the border until a month later. There the successful element was the 7th Division's 32nd Infantry Regiment. Task Force Kingston, a company-sized cluster of units built around Lieutenant Robert C. Kingston's platoon from Company K, reached Singalpajin on November 28, followed by most of 3rd Battalion, 32nd Regiment.[58]

Neither of these units could stay at the border because by this time the Chinese intervention was an accomplished fact; the only remaining issue was its scope and mission. Peng and his corps commanders quickly persuaded Mao that all four corps should establish blocking positions in front of the enemy since anything less would risk defeat in detail. Chinese commanders were acutely aware of their weaknesses in firepower and anti-aircraft defenses, but Mao was adamant about engaging the enemy. Initially, the 39th, 40th, and 38th Corps (from west to east) deployed in front of Eighth Army on a line approximately fifty miles (eighty kilometers) south of the Yalu, while the separate 42nd Corps deployed in front of X Corps east of the Chongjin Reservoir, often referred to by its Japanese name of Chosin.[59] Intent on speed, the UN forces, like those of Chiang Kai-shek a few years before, tended to move along the few roads and railways in the area, and the Chinese proved quite adept at blocking these avenues in front of a unit and then walking the ridgelines to attack the enemy's flanks and rear. This was not an easy task, but the Chinese were well trained and so lightly equipped that they could make such movements more readily than their opponents.

Mao had instructed Peng to attack the ROK units first, both because they were weaker and to gain experience before dealing with the Americans. The first such attack occurred on October 25, approximately fifteen miles (twenty-four kilometers) northeast of Ulsan. The 3rd Battalion, 2nd Regiment, 6th ROK Division, dismounted from its trucks to deal with what it thought was a small NKPA roadblock, only to find itself surrounded by two regiments of the 40th CCF Corps. Half the battalion, including its U.S. advisor, Lieutenant Glen Jones, fell captive. The regiment's 2nd Battalion almost suffered a similar fate that night but managed to break free. When the Chinese attacked the rest of the regiment in force at 0330 on the 26th, that regiment quickly disintegrated, although most of its soldiers eventually reached friendly lines. The 7th Regiment of the same division, which had reached the Yalu on October 26, lost the bulk of its strength in ambushes as it retreated. Within five days, the 6th ROK Division lost most of its organization and combat power, and its parent II ROK Corps fell back, opening a gap with the neighboring I U.S. Corps.[60]

Meanwhile, the ROK 1st Division had a similar surprise encounter with the 39th CCF Corps near Unsan. The ROK division commander, General Paik Sun Yup, had served under Japanese command in Manchuria and positively identified the enemy dead and prisoners as Chinese troops. To reinforce the light weapons of the ROK units, the 1st Cavalry Division's 8th Regiment moved into Unsan on November 1. That night, two full divisions of the CCF fell upon the ROK 15th Regiment and two battalions of the 8th Cavalry Regiment at Unsan. Supported only by light mortars, the attackers quickly closed to hand-grenade range and overran the ROK and U.S. positions. Chinese tactical communications, using whistles and bugles rather than radios, confused and unnerved the defenders. The ROK regiment held firm for two hours, but its eventual collapse exposed U.S. artillery and supply elements. The 8th Cavalry's commander, Colonel Hallett Edson, attempted an orderly withdrawal using his uncommitted 3rd Battalion as a rear guard, but the CCF destroyed all coherent defenses. By daylight on November 2, the 8th Cavalry had become a mass of individual fugitives, having abandoned all its vehicles and twelve howitzers of the supporting artillery battalion. When the survivors reassembled, the 8th had lost eight hundred men, one-quarter of its strength. The rest of I Corps closed up into defensive positions and waited for further attacks. Perhaps equally alarming was the appearance of MiG-15 fighters over northern Korea on October 31.[61]

In the X Corps area, on October 29 the ROK 3rd Division captured sixteen members of the 370th Regiment, 124th Division, 42nd CCF Corps. General Almond personally witnessed the interrogation of these prisoners and informed MacArthur that he believed their account of large Chinese units in Korea. The 7th Marine Regiment assumed the advance from the ROK troops and encountered Chinese resistance in regimental strength. Twenty miles (thirty-two kilometers) to the east, the 31st Infantry Regiment of 7th Infantry Division encountered the CCF 126th Division, and prisoners identified the third division as the 125th, of 42nd Corps.[62]

After these startling first encounters, the CCF suddenly broke contact on November 6 and seemingly melted away. Optimists in Tokyo hoped that the enemy had decided not to contest the UN occupation. Others have argued that the Chinese government had made an initial show of force and then paused to see whether the UN would cease its northern advance. As a practical matter, however, Peng's troops were so short of firepower and supplies that they failed to destroy even small UN units and had therefore broken contact to reorganize.[63]

The American and British governments were at least as responsible as MacArthur, the theater commander, for allowing this strategic surprise concerning Chinese intentions to occur. One should note, however, that MacArthur and his intelligence officer, Willoughby, had resisted efforts by the CIA to develop its own intelligence sources in the region. Therefore, as late as October 12, the CIA echoed Willoughby, telling President Truman that there were "no convincing indications" of Chinese intent to conduct a full-scale intervention. On November 6, however, a National Intelligence Estimate finally acknowledged that Chinese Communist ground and air forces had engaged the UN troops and that they had the capacity to halt or even push those troops southward.[64]

UN RESPONSE AND RENEWED ADVANCE

When he had met Truman on Wake Island on October 15, General MacArthur had assured the president that the Chinese were unlikely to intervene and that if they did so, U.S. airpower would isolate and destroy them in a matter of days. When MacArthur tried to make good on that promise, however, he set off a controversy within the government. On the morning of November 6 (Washington time), Air Force Secretary Thomas Finletter learned that MacArthur had ordered the Far East Air Forces to launch a series of attacks designed to cut off the Chinese incursion, including bombing the North Korean ends of all the bridges across the Yalu. Given the inaccuracy of aerial bombardment, such an attack risked destruction to Chinese and Soviet territory, and would violate the spirit of an agreement with London to consult before making any attacks on Manchuria. With the concurrence of the president and Secretary Marshall, Deputy Defense Secretary Robert Lovett had the Joint Chiefs of Staff instruct MacArthur to avoid any attacks within five miles of the border until further instructions. MacArthur's response to this restriction was almost panicky: "Men and materiel in large force" were "pouring across all the bridges over the Yalu from Manchuria," he wrote, and demanded that the president be informed of his protest. Under these circumstances, Truman authorized the bombing, again deferring to the general on the spot.[65]

MacArthur's reaction not only shocked leaders in the Pentagon but also intensified the ongoing debate as to the nature of the war in Korea. From the beginning, most members of the Truman administration regarded this war as a dangerous distraction from Europe. Therefore, the administration wanted to limit the conflict to the Korean peninsula and certainly did not wish to risk open conflict with China or the Soviet Union in that region.[66] MacArthur had consistently argued against such restrictions, but the new threat brought the issue to the forefront and began the process that led to his relief from command five months later.

When the Chinese broke contact, MacArthur and his troops regained their balance and began to prepare for a renewed advance. Eighth Army reshuffled its forces to present a more coherent advance in northwestern Korea and began to move cautiously forward. In the process, Milburn's I Corps in the west gave up units to its neighbors, retaining only the 24th Infantry and 1st ROK Divisions. General Walker inserted Major General John B. Coulter's IX Corps between I U.S. and II ROK Corps, with the 25th and 2nd Infantry Divisions advancing generally up the Chongchon River Valley, supported by the newly arrived Turkish brigade. In 8th Army reserve, the damaged 1st Cavalry Division followed in support, securing the supply route. Similarly, II ROK Corps advanced parallel to Coulter's forces, with the 7th and 8th ROK Divisions abreast and the weakened 6th ROK Division following.[67] Only the difficulties of bringing supplies forward prompted Walker to delay a renewed offensive until late November. In addition to shortages of fuel and rations, the U.S. Army lacked sufficient cold-weather clothing for such a large force. In the cold days of a war that seemed to be almost over, discipline declined about matters such as carrying full ammunition loads and digging defensive positions in the frozen ground.

In the interim, the enemy also reshuffled its forces, bringing in five additional corps across the border and moving the 42nd Corps from the Chongjin Reservoir westward to the eastern flank of Eighth Army. Mao had approved Peng's plan to prepare large-scale ambushes close to the Chinese border, while leaving one division in each corps farther south to delay the enemy and raid its rear areas. The ultimate goal was encirclement of large UN units. By Thanksgiving, two corps belonging to Thirteenth CCF Army were aligned opposite each of Walker's three UN corps—the 50th and 66th in the west, opposite Milburn's I Corps; the 39th and 40th in the center opposite Coulter's IX Corps; and the 38th and 42nd barring the way to General Hue's II ROK Corps. Farther east, the newly arrived Ninth CCF Army, consisting of three corps, had replaced the 42nd Corps opposite Almond's force.[68]

In retrospect, it seems incredible that U.S. commanders were unaware of the scope of Chinese forces opposite them. Interrogation reports and other data had identified at least six Chinese corps, totaling as many as 400,000 troops, in Korea, but few senior leaders seemed to have formed an accurate picture of the threat. General Walker was concerned but uncertain, while his G2 officer, Lieutenant Colonel James Tarkenton, claimed only a few thousand Chinese were actually in Korea. Generals Almond and MacArthur apparently had a more realistic understanding of the numbers, if not the capabilities, of their opponents. Traditionally, Willoughby, MacArthur's G2, gets the lion's share of blame for an estimate that, as late as November 24, credited the Chinese with only 60,000 to 70,000 troops in Korea. Some of this error may have been due to willful refusal to credit unwelcome reports, but it is also fair to note that the Chinese troop movements were well concealed from aerial reconnaissance, and in North Korea there were few friendly civilians to confirm enemy troop strengths. MacArthur himself appears to have believed that the Chinese would contest his renewed advance to the Yalu but that a rapid advance supported by airpower would overcome them.[69]

DISASTER

In the bright if chilly sunlight of November 24, Eighth Army cautiously resumed its advance. For the first two days, resistance was limited, except in the II ROK Corps on the right. On the other flank, a regimental operations officer in the 66th CCF Corps deserted to the 1st ROK Division, providing complete information about the strength and distribution of Thirteenth Army, including the fact that it intended to ambush the UN forces near Taechon. General MacArthur remained optimistic, however. In a typically brave gesture, he flew in an unarmed transport to reconnoiter northwestern Korea, then returned to Tokyo to argue, on the basis of this flight, that there was no defensible line short of the Yalu River itself. By this, MacArthur was serving notice that he would disregard the prohibition against non-Korean troops near the border. In the same message to the JCS, the general spoke confidently of the end of the war, including redeploying U.S. troops to Japan and paroling the captured NKPA troops.[70]

Behind MacArthur, however, Eighth Army encountered a determined and confusing enemy. With UN vehicular movement confined to the valleys, flanks unavoidably became exposed to the light Chinese troops who moved along the high ground at night. In addition to a number of tactical penetrations between UN regiments, the entire 38th Corps made a flank march to penetrate between the 7th and 8th Divisions of II ROK Corps. By the night of November 28–29, the 113th Division of 38th Corps had marched south and then westward, occupying the town of Kunu-ri behind the 2nd U.S. Infantry Division. Infiltrated from the front and cut off from the rear, the 2nd Division tried to break out to the south, while the 1st Cavalry Division attempted to push through to relieve it, but the Chinese doggedly held their position. In the final days of November, the 2nd Infantry Division almost dissolved into chaos. The Turkish brigade, assigned to protect the division's right flank, took heavy losses in a gallant stand. Most of the division escaped, but it left behind almost all its vehicles and heavy weapons, as well as 2,400 POWs.[71] Similar incidents elsewhere left the Eighth Army reeling in retreat down the inadequate roads it had just used to move north.

The further advance of X Corps was the subject of much debate in November. Almond had been operating under instructions to clear all enemy forces while securing northeastern Korea, but the Far East Command G3, Brigadier General Edwin Wright, thought differently. Wright wanted Almond to attack in a northwestern direction so as to cut Chinese supply lines and close up with Eighth Army. While this may have made sense at an operational level, it was virtually impossible in the harsh terrain of North Korea. Almond's staff engineer estimated that it would take six battalion-months of engineer effort just to improve the primitive road leading to the Chongjin Reservoir, and that was only the first stage in Wright's proposed advance. After considerable discussion, MacArthur decided in Wright's favor on November 24 and directed X Corps to advance northwestward as soon as possible. In turn, this meant that Almond had to shift the 7th Infantry Division westward so as to relieve the marines who would spearhead the advance. The first stage of this adjustment involved Task Force Faith, built around the 1st Battalion, 32nd Infantry, 7th Infantry Division. This task force was supposed to relieve the 5th Marine Regiment east of the reservoir on November 26 but had to scramble to arrive in time. Thus, the 1st Marine and 7th Infantry Divisions were strung out along roads, still redeploying when the CCF attacked two days later.[72]

The ensuing battles were so disjointed and confused as to defy brief explanation. Some army units, such as Company D, 10th Engineers, fought well, but others, composed of miscellaneous Americans and KATUSAs with little unit cohesion, fell apart under extremes of weather and enemy action. Commanders at every level had to make heart-wrenching choices between saving their units and trying to evacuate their wounded and frostbitten casualties. The Chinese 80th Division, 27th Corps, virtually destroyed Task Force Faith, equivalent to an understrength regiment, on November 27–28, with only a few survivors reaching marine lines. The 1st Marine Division, being a more homogeneous and coherent organization, performed much better but was hampered by a shortage of motor vehicles in comparison to its army equivalents. Moreover, army and marine communications equipment was often incompatible. Close air support and more than 1,200 tons of parachuted supplies kept the marines functional in late November, but the weather was so bad December 1–3 that the marines were left on their own, without air cover. Weapons malfunctioned frequently in the extreme cold. When the weather and air cover improved on December 4, the remaining elements of X Corps and I ROK Corps fought their way back to the port of Hungnam, north of Wonsan. From Hungnam, most of Almond's command evacuated by sea during the second half of December.[73] So ended what Adrian Lewis has identified as the last offensive campaign of the American citizen-soldier.[74]

Peng Dehuai handed the United States one of its greatest defeats in history in November-December 1950. U.S. casualties totaled 1,970 killed in action, 2,500 prisoners of war, 4,000 missing in action (of whom at least 1,200 died), and more than 4,000 wounded.[75] Yet, this victory cost the Chinese as much as the UN forces. UN airpower could not stop the Chinese attacks, but it did exact a price in terms of casualties and lost supplies. Among the casualties was Mao's eldest son, Anying, killed by a U.S. airstrike on a Chinese command post on November 24–25.[76] Moreover, the Chinese suffered quite as much from cold as did their opponents. By the time the second offensive was over, the Ninth Army in the east had 30,000 frostbite cases, including 1,000 deaths. The entire Ninth Army was out of action for three months to recover its health and combat power. Meanwhile, on December 8, 1950, Peng asked Mao for permission to pause in the pursuit and suggested that the CCF confine its operations to the area north of the 38th Parallel. For political reasons, however, Mao insisted that Peng continue southward. Indeed, the poor American performance in November-December had confirmed Mao's prejudices and given him a false idea of Chinese ability to defeat the UN forces. Mao's desire for total victory, in part to inspire his own populace, lasted long after the initial Chinese advantages had failed. He apparently never recognized that the army that suffered defeat in North Korea was not a typical American force—it was filled with half-trained Americans and KATUSAs, and caught by surprise when the war seemed over. Once it recovered its nerve and cohesion, subsequent battles were different.[77]

Change of Command

For the moment, though, the UN Command was in full retreat. On November 30, Truman publicly suggested that the United States might use nuclear weapons to stem the Chinese tide, but this trial balloon evoked a furious British and European response.[78] Four days later, the JCS refused MacArthur's request for major troop reinforcements. Generals Walker and Wright spoke gloomily of withdrawing back to the Pusan Perimeter. In the interim, after a conference of commanders MacArthur issued Commander-in-Chief, UN Command, Order Number 5 on December 8. This order laid out a series of nine defensive lines, with instructions for Eighth Army to delay progressively at these lines while withdrawing southward when necessary. Walker insisted that while he would hold Seoul as long as possible, he needed the freedom to withdraw if necessary to preserve his force from what appeared to be an overwhelming new enemy. At least, after much argument, X Corps finally merged under Eighth Army command.[79]

General Walker did not live to see this change, however. On the morning of December 23, a Korean truck driver accidentally forced the Eighth Army commander's jeep off the road north of Uijongbu, with fatal results. For months, General MacArthur had lobbied Washington to get Lieutenant General Matthew B. Ridgway, the U.S. Army's deputy chief of operations, to succeed or possibly even replace Walker. Now, with an urgent need for a new field commander, MacArthur got his way, and Ridgway was en route to Korea within twenty-four hours of notification.[80]

Both Walker and Ridgway were highly competent soldiers who had commanded corps in World War II, but there the resemblance ended. Through no fault of his own, Walker was associated with the early defeats of the Korean War, at a time before the U.S. supply "pipeline" was fully established to support operations. By contrast, his successor arrived with a mandate to rebuild the Eighth Army and a charismatic reputation to match. Moreover, Walker had reached the height of his career in Korea, whereas the younger Ridgway was on a career path that would take him to the highest positions in the U.S. Army. Although Ridgway had served under MacArthur at West Point after World War I and again briefly in 1945, he was respectful of but not awed by the Far East commander. Ridgway had a close connection to the Joint Chiefs of Staff and understood the Truman administration's policies in a manner that his new boss never did.

From the moment Ridgway arrived in Japan, he wanted to counterattack to take advantage of the enemy's overextension. However, a whirlwind tour of headquarters and units in the last week of 1950 convinced him that the U.S. Army and ROK elements of the UN force needed to regain their confidence and aggressive spirit. Only a few units, such as 27 Commonwealth Brigade, and a few commanders, like Almond, were prepared to attack. Some of this lack of will Ridgway attributed to an absence of public support at home, and he asked General Collins to explain the Korean conflict more forcefully to the American public. Meanwhile, Ridgway focused on the basic expectations of the troops, such as mail, food, and warm clothing. He insisted on aggressive patrolling to improve intelligence data and demanded that commanders at all levels lead from the front to reassure their troops. Ridgway told President Rhee that he had no intention of abandoning the peninsula or the Korean people. The new commander demanded that the units get off the roads and secure their flanks on the hills of Korea, making contact with neighboring units to prevent flanking maneuvers.[81]

Eighth Army was still recovering and X Corps had not yet finished its redeployment when the CCF and NKPA began their third offensive in late December. The first blow fell in the east, where the North Korean 5th Corps attacked the ROK Army frontally while the NKPA 2nd Corps penetrated the mountain gaps of the ROK 3rd and 9th Divisions to block their rear south of Hongchon. Although the 2nd U.S. Infantry Division was still recovering from its ordeal a month before, Ridgway sent the 23rd RCT from that division northward into battle, blocking this threat. Farther west, on New Year's Eve, the CCF 39th Corps crossed the frozen Imjin River and cracked the defenses of the ROK 1st Division north of the capital. The newly arrived 29 British Brigade slowed the enemy advance, but it was obvious that the UN forces would have to withdraw again, evacuating Seoul on January 2–4, 1951. Unlike the sad scramble of December, however, this withdrawal was made in fairly good order, with careful control of bridge demolitions. Still, Ridgway was angered by the failure to inflict more damage on the enemy and had to intervene personally to ensure that British and other rearguard units were not abandoned. By January 7, the UN defenses were tied back in along Line D, thirty-five miles (fifty-six kilometers) south of Seoul and near the 37th Parallel. X Corps had inserted itself into the line in the center of the peninsula, greatly reducing the opportunities for enemy infiltration.[82] The Chinese commander, Peng, wrongly concluded that his opponents must have brought in major new units that prevented a repetition of his previous success. Yet, he encountered criticism from Kim Il-Sung and the Soviet ambassador to Pyongyang, neither of whom could understand the practical difficulties faced by the weakened CCF.[83]

Eight days later, Eighth Army began a series of reconnaissance in force actions designed both to determine the enemy dispositions and to restore American confidence. Each such operation included considerable air, artillery, and tank support to ensure local superiority of forces. Beginning with a single regiment, on January 25 this effort blossomed into Operation Thunderbolt, by which I and IX Corps each sent out a reinforced division to probe the enemy. Ridgway himself made innumerable low-level flights over the battle area so that he had a complete grasp of the difficult terrain he asked his troops to attack. Gradually, the UN troops pushed northward toward and in some instances beyond the Han River.[84]

The Chinese and North Korean forces, although undersupplied and understrength, did not submit tamely but instead contested the UN advance at every turn. One of the most famous such actions occurred at Chipyong-ni, a town approximately forty miles (sixty-four kilometers) east of Seoul, in mid-February. Colonel Paul Freeman's 23rd Infantry RCT of the 2nd Infantry Division, at the time subordinated to X Corps, included not only attached tanks, artillery, and engineers, but also the French battalion contributed to the UN force. Regiments from four different CCF divisions surrounded this force on February 13–14, 1951, seeking to dislodge it and gain access to the valley leading south from Chipyong-ni. Almond and Ridgway had anticipated this effort and provided a steady stream of air strikes and aerial resupply to support Freeman's defense. By the time 27 Commonwealth Brigade and the 5th Cavalry RCT reopened the supply route to Chipyong-ni, an estimated 5,400 Chinese lay dead.[85] Thereafter, Ridgway launched a number of limited attacks that were intended to inflict maximum enemy casualties.

In late February, Peng returned to Beijing and attempted to explain to Mao the differences between this new war and the Chinese Civil War. Far from their home bases, the CCF troops had difficulty getting reinforcements or even food, and lacked training in the use of captured enemy weapons. Above all, UN airpower hampered every movement and resupply effort.[86] Unable to compete logistically, the Chinese and North Koreans reluctantly pulled back northward, and for the final time Seoul changed hands on March 16, 1951.

Cautiously exploiting his success, Ridgway continued to push ahead, with I Corps launching Operation Courageous, the advance to the Imjin River north of Seoul, on March 22, 1951. On the morning of the 23rd, the 187th Airborne RCT's parachutes once again spilled out of C-119s, this time onto drop zones near the key road junction of Munsan. They encountered only limited rearguard resistance from the NKPA 9th Division and elements of the 28th CCF Corps. The I

Corps commander, General Milburn, improvised a regimental-sized mechanized formation by borrowing tanks and self-propelled artillery from various other units. This Task Force Growden, named for the commander of the 6th Tank Battalion who commanded it, linked up with the airborne the same evening. In the ensuing days, Milburn turned both the paratroops and the armor eastward, advancing to the valley due north of Uijongbu in an unsuccessful attempt to cut off the retreating Chinese.[87]

MacArthur's Relief

Although the UN forces had recovered from their worst defeat, the Korean situation kept the Truman administration on tenterhooks throughout the winter and spring of 1951. On the one hand, President Truman did not want to abandon South Korea and allow the communist states a major victory. On the other, he and his advisors continued to regard the conflict as a diversion of resources that might well escalate into a larger war. Nor could American intelligence be certain that the Chinese or Soviets would not risk such an escalation. This concern came to a head in early April 1951, when more than seventy Soviet submarines concentrated in Pacific waters, apparently threatening the vital supply route between Japan and Korea. Under the circumstances, the Joint Chiefs believed that the United States needed to prepare in case Stalin expanded the war. For a year, Strategic Air Command (SAC) bombers had carried the nonradioactive casings for nuclear weapons; now the JCS asked the president to transfer nine fissionable bomb cores from the Atomic Energy Commission to air force control. Reluctantly, Truman approved the action, placing atomic weapons in SAC's hands for the first time since 1946. The air force moved bomb components as far forward as Okinawa, but Truman would not allow Silverplate B-29s to deploy beyond Guam. Still, the seriousness of the situation is reflected in the fact that these movements were done in secrecy.[88]

Nor were America's allies and UN partners united about Korean policy. As the UN forces again approached the 38th Parallel in March, President Rhee pushed hard for a renewed effort to unite the entire peninsula, while a British minister stated publicly that the UN would not advance north of the parallel without full intergovernmental coordination. Few officials in Washington or the European capitals were willing to risk escalation or face the human cost of a renewed advance deep into the north.[89]

In the delicate balance of diplomacy and war, Truman again planned to make crossing the parallel a military rather than a political decision but also hoped to use Ridgway's renewed success as an opportunity to propose a cease-fire. Unfortunately, MacArthur repeatedly thwarted this goal with public statements that alarmed friend and foe alike. In December 1950 and January 1951, he even suggested bombing Manchuria, blockading China, and importing Chiang Kai-shek's troops to bolster the UN defenses. Any of these actions would certainly have brought forth a stronger enemy response and could not have been effective without bombing Soviet targets as well. On January 12, the JCS recommended a number of more modest measures, including a blockade if the UN were expelled from the peninsula, but Truman did not make a decision. By March, Truman was planning to offer a cease-fire, but MacArthur continued to undercut such policies in public and private.[90]

It was these public comments, in defiance of repeated directives to clear statements with Washington, that ultimately led to MacArthur's dismissal. This was not simply a matter of the general's ego and political ambitions. In fairness to MacArthur, he not only believed deeply in the necessity of stopping communism but also had spent much of his career operating in political and diplomatic arenas as theater commander, occupier of Japan, and the first United Nations commander in history. Although he was insubordinate by ordinary standards, he believed that he had a right and duty to express his opinions on such matters.[91] He never seriously accepted the idea of a war fought for something less than victory.

The final straw was a letter written by MacArthur to a congressman, a letter that violated the spirit if not the wording of the previous gag order. Truman had endured repeated challenges from flag officers in the previous five years and understandably felt it necessary to reassert civilian control. Not only did this letter clearly defy government policy, but the presence of a successful Ridgway provided an immediate replacement for the troublesome general. After consulting with Secretary Marshall and the Joint Chiefs, Truman relieved the Far East commander effective April 11, 1951. The JCS nominated Ridgway to succeed MacArthur, with Lieutenant General Van Fleet to command Eighth Army. The administration faced a hail of congressional and public criticism, but there was really no alternative if Truman were to maintain control of foreign policy and avoid escalation.[92]

STALEMATE

The communist forces did not wait for Washington to resolve its civil-military problems. During the spring of 1951, Mao insisted on two additional major attempts before he accepted Peng's estimate that they could not expel their opponents from the peninsula. The first such attack, known as the fourth Chinese offensive, was a counteroffensive in February that, as we have seen, was unable to halt Ridgway's own operations. By late April, however, the CCF Ninth Army had recovered from frostbite, while additional reinforcements had made the dangerous trek southward to strengthen the Chinese north of Seoul, so that Peng had twenty-seven divisions ready to attack. Anticipating this, IX Corps pushed northward up the Chorwon Valley in early April, almost reaching the town of that name along a perimeter that Eighth Army planners labeled Line Wyoming. From Chorwon east to the Sea of Japan, the other UN corps—X U.S., III ROK, and I ROK—also fought forward to Wyoming, on a line generally twenty to twenty-five miles (thirty-two to forty kilometers) north of the 38th Parallel. Because of the difficulty of crossing the Imjin River farther west, however, I Corps remained much closer to Seoul, along Line Kansas.[93]

Thus, when the Chinese fifth offensive began on April 22, 1951, it was the westernmost part of the UN line that was at the greatest risk. Major General Robert Soule's 3rd U.S. Infantry Division, with various attached UN forces, had to defend the twisting Imjin River in this sector. In particular, 29 British Brigade with an attached Belgian battalion was overstretched to defend twelve miles (nineteen kilometers) at the point where the Imjin formed an S-curve, creating several fords. Although senior UN commanders had expected an offensive, the Chinese had broken contact and pulled back up to twenty miles, making it difficult for the UN to gather tactical intelligence about the enemy. Expecting to advance northward, most of the British brigade had dug only minimal defenses and was caught off guard by the attack.[94]

Major elements of the CCF 63rd and 64th Corps suffered heavy casualties in crossing the Imjin River fords between April 21 and 23, but eventually the 63rd's 187th and 189th Divisions cut off and surrounded the 1st Battalion, the Gloucestershire Regiment, on the 24th. Brigadier Thomas Brodie, the British brigade commander, asked Soule for support, but the first attempts to relieve the Gloucesters failed. Soule decided to wait for morning to mount another relief effort, relying on Brodie's belief that his men could hold out. Instead, on the night of the 25th, the "Glosters" were overrun and their commander killed despite a gallant defense. Significant portions of the battalion escaped from the Chinese trap, only to be mistaken for Chinese and engaged by other UN forces. Overall, 29 Brigade suffered 1,091 killed, captured, and missing, about 20 percent of its strength. The Gloucesters alone lost 530 captured out of an original strength of 773 men.[95]

Despite this tragic loss and a temporary breakthrough in the mountains of eastern Korea, at the boundary between X U.S. and III ROK Corps, the Chinese succeeded only in pushing back the UN forces. UN forces fell back to the so-called "No-Name Line" just north of Seoul and halted the enemy there, then counterattacked. Peng's objective had been to destroy the 3rd Infantry Division, three separate brigades, and several ROK divisions.[96] Instead, he had to settle for the Gloucester battalion and a few ROK regiments. By June, the CCF and NKPA were farther north than they had been before the fifth offensive.

The Chinese were unable to repeat their previous success for a number of reasons. First and foremost, the UN forces had regained their confidence and had acquired a measure of discipline and competence under Ridgway's and then Van Fleet's command. Growing air and artillery support gave the defenders a decisive edge. Indeed, one of Van Fleet's first acts as commander was to require an increase in the standard rate of fire for artillery. Instead of firing thirty to fifty rounds per artillery tube per day, as specified in doctrine, Van Fleet wanted five times that many shells. In one twenty-four-hour period, X Corps alone fired 43,000 rounds. This "Van Fleet Day of Fire" placed great stress on the ammunition supply but weakened the attackers.[97]

Far East Air Forces contributed to this fire superiority. In addition to countless close air-support missions, the USAF bombed newly rebuilt airfields in North Korea on April 17–23, thwarting the plans of Chinese air commander Liu Ya-lou to deploy fighter bombers in support of the ground offensive.[98] In turn, the overwhelming UN fire superiority demoralized the attackers. By this point in the war, China had committed large numbers of former KMT troops that had been co-opted in the course of the Chinese Civil War. Such troops were more likely to fall back or even surrender in the event of failure. During this offensive, the Chinese lost 17,000 prisoners of war, the bulk of such POWs during the war.[99]

After a year of mobile warfare, the two sides settled down to a bloody but immobile form of conflict. Although the United States might have exerted enough force to break this stalemate, the risks and costs of such an effort far outweighed the potential benefits. Instead, for the next two years, the Korean conflict came to resemble World War I, with massive expenditures of firepower and significant casualties for relatively minor changes in the terrain. While both sides conducted guerrilla operations behind the lines, the CCF and NKPA effectively abandoned their tradition of mobile, infiltration tactics in favor of field fortifications and raids. The situation allowed the U.S. Army to capitalize on its longstanding expertise in central direction of artillery fire. When the communist side attacked a U.S. outpost, pre-planned fires descended like a horseshoe around that outpost, preventing any enemy reinforcements. At Pork Chop Hill in 1953, this trend reached its peak. During one twenty-four-hour period, nine artillery battalions fired a total of 39,694 rounds to protect a single company—less than 200 men—of the 179th Infantry Regiment, 45th Division.[100]

THE AIR WAR

Just as in World War I, stalemate on the ground gave greater prominence to air operations. The Korean conflict was not only the first war between jet aircraft but also the first opportunity for a comparison of air weapons and tactics in the Cold War.

For the first five months of the war, the UN forces had uncontested air superiority. However, most aircraft were based in Japan or on carriers because of the difficulties of maintenance and operations on the unimproved airfields of South Korea. This plus the short range of aircraft such as the F-80 (1,090 miles, or 1,744 kilometers) made it difficult for fighters to operate over extreme northern Korea. Moreover, Far East Air Forces had relatively few of the best fighters in the U.S. arsenal, the F-86. In addition to the 1st Marine Air Wing, operating off small, World War II–era escort carriers, the U.S. Navy built up to an average strength of three carrier air groups, although not all of them were on station at the same time.

In November-December 1950, the Soviet Union secretly deployed 1,186 anti-aircraft guns and eight fighter divisions to China to defend against a possible U.S. expansion of the war in Korea. Stalin also sent ten tank regiments as a symbol of protection. Most of the initial Soviet aircraft were the marginally effective MiG-9s, but Mao again appealed to Stalin for more modern defenses. The 151st Guards Fighter Aviation Division, commanded by Major General Ivan M. Belov, received the newer MiG-15 because it was scheduled to turn over its own aircraft to the fledgling Chinese People's Liberation Army Air Force (PLAAF).[101]

Nervous about direct involvement in the conflict, Stalin initially ordered the Soviet Air Force simply to defend Chinese airspace; it is possible that MacArthur's major effort against the Yalu bridges caused Belov and other Soviet commanders to believe that China was at risk of attack, justifying the first Soviet air operations in the war. Even when Stalin reluctantly permitted his fighters to intervene in Korea, he insisted on a number of precautions, including eliminating Soviet markings on the aircraft and insisting that they fly only over friendly held territory, so that no shot-down flyers would fall into UN hands. This latter restriction led to the term "MiG Alley," referring to the area of northwestern Korea where most Soviet pilots flew. On November 15, Moscow directed that Colonel Aleksey V. Pashkevich take his 50th Fighter Aviation Division to Manchuria for air operations over Korea. Soviet fighters operated over extreme northern Korea during November–December 1950, making UN air attacks, especially by B-29s, much more costly.[102]

In response, the USAF's 4th Fighter-Interceptor Wing established a forward operating base for its F-86s at Kimpo Airfield, between Inchon and Seoul, in mid-December. So began the long duel for air control between the MiG-15 and the F-86. Each side's airfields were in sanctuaries, not open to air attack by the other, so only aerial combat and ground fire could affect the struggle. As is so often the case with aerial combat, the rival claims of the opposing pilots are impossible to balance—each side claimed a favorable kill ratio. However, after the Soviet Union dissolved, a Russian staff study acknowledged losing

336 aircraft and 120 pilots in the Korean conflict. Total Soviet casualties were 146 officers and 153 enlisted men.[103]

Meanwhile, the PLAAF, with no experience in air operations and little "stick time" as pilots, attempted to form a Chinese People's Volunteer Air Force that in fact absorbed most of the available resources of the PLAAF. By 1952, this force had developed some proficiency, counterbalancing the declining quality of Soviet units as Moscow rotated its less-experienced airmen to the conflict. Sensing this decline, in the spring of 1953 a number of USAF pilots violated official policy by flying over Manchurian airfields, ostensibly in hot pursuit but actually to force an engagement with enemy fighters. The PLAAF flew more than 29,000 sorties in the war, less than half the number of Soviet sorties, and acknowledged losing only 224 MiG-15s, 7 other aircraft, and 116 airmen in combat, plus an additional 168 aircraft lost to other causes.[104]

The USAF was frustrated by political limitations on its actions. Not only was it restricted to attacks within the Korean peninsula, but even major population centers required Washington's approval as targets. UN air interdiction could slow but not stop enemy troop and resupply movements and was a costly operation with reservist aircrews and obsolescent aircraft such as the B-26. Attempting to increase pressure on the Communists during the prolonged armistice negotiations, General Ridgway gained JCS permission for a major raid on Pyongyang in July 1951, but poor weather caused many of the aircraft to divert to secondary targets. Only the B-29s were able to get through using the radar bombing that improved their accuracy while lowering vulnerability to enemy fighters.[105]

In mid-1952, a new bombing campaign began, inspired by Brigadier General Jacob Smart, the FEAF head of operations. Coordinated navy-air force air efforts, sometimes supported by Commonwealth air units, attacked North Korean industrial plants, including a major power plant that also provided electricity to Manchuria. Leaflets dropped before the raids warned the population to abandon target areas, but the enemy still used these raids for propaganda purposes. These bombing efforts devastated much of North Korea, contributing materially to the pressure for an armistice. Thus, despite considerable criticism from the army about the quality of close air support and extensive squabbling about interservice cooperation, the USAF felt that it had been remarkably successful in Korea.[106]

Prisoners of War

Negotiations to end the indecisive war began on July 8, 1951, at Kaesong and continued intermittently for two years, with much gamesmanship, at nearby Panmunjom. Although the issues involved were many and varied, none was so intractable as the question of prisoners of war (POWs).

As befits a war that in the minds of both sides was largely ideological in nature, the fighting did not stop when a man was captured. Chinese and North Korean captors used threats, persuasion, and isolation to undermine the resistance of American POWs, many of whom were psychologically unprepared for such manipulation. Despite the bravery and self-sacrifice of some prisoners, discipline broke down in many instances. POWs murdered their wounded or ill comrades and made propaganda statements without any physical coercion. Thirty-eight percent of U.S. Army soldiers taken prisoner died in captivity, and about one-third of all surviving POWs collaborated with their captors to some degree. No American escaped successfully from a permanent POW camp, and twenty-one American POWs eventually chose not to return to freedom at the end of the war. Downed pilots were tortured to get them to "confess" to ludicrous charges of biological warfare, designed to counteract the bad publicity when communist prisoners elected not to return home. By contrast, prisoners from the U.S. Marine Corps (USMC) or other UN armed forces had greater discipline and identity, and therefore resisted their captors more effectively. After numerous courts-martial and a thorough investigation by the Defense Department, in 1955 the president promulgated a Code of Conduct for future POWs.[107]

There were many more communist prisoners in UN hands, and they created an even bigger headache. The huge numbers—eventually 170,000 military and civilian prisoners—were crowded into vast camps on Koje Island. Many of these POWs were South Koreans or former KMT soldiers who had been co-opted into the NKPA or CCF, respectively, and had no interest in returning to the north at the end of the war. As a result, one of the key issues in armistice negotiations was the UN insistence that every prisoner must be free to choose whether or not he would be repatriated.

Unlike the communist treatment of UN prisoners, the U.S. captors offered education and vocational training on a voluntary basis only.

Within the camps, militant Communists organized to dominate other prisoners, holding secret courts and executing those who attended education classes or expressed a desire not to be repatriated. When in the summer of 1952 the United States began to screen and release civilians who had been imprisoned along with soldiers, the communist negotiators at Panmunjom complained bitterly.[108]

Increasingly, the communist leaders blocked their captors from conducting screening or in fact any other activity within the compounds. On May 6, 1952, the prisoners took Brigadier General Francis T. Dodd, the camp commandant, hostage when he came to hear their grievances. The prisoners released Dodd only after gaining various propaganda concessions. Finally, on June 10, the 187th Airborne Regiment, backed by medium tanks, overran the most militant compound at a cost of one U.S. soldier and thirty-one prisoners killed, with many more injured. Thereafter, prisoners were dispersed and placed under tight control, but the incident had been a public relations black eye for the UN.[109]

Armistice

Dwight Eisenhower won election as president in November 1952 with a clear promise that he would resolve the Korean conflict. After visiting the peninsula as president-elect, he pushed his new foreign policy team to find ways to resolve the situation, including asking the JCS for a plan to end the war militarily, if necessary using atomic weapons.[110]

In May 1953, the new administration sent public and private messages indicating that it might resume active operations and perhaps use nuclear weapons against China. General Mark Clark, who succeeded Ridgway as UN commander in May 1952, ordered the truce talks recessed for a week, giving the other side a clear message that further intransigence would lead to an end to negotiations.[111]

Although the opposition probably took such messages seriously, the Chinese appeared willing to risk nuclear attack. Fortunately, other factors contributed to a change in the North Korean-Chinese negotiating position. The economies of both countries had suffered heavily from the war, and renewed USAF bombing of irrigation dams added to the North Korean misery in 1953. The Soviet government wanted to reduce tensions in Europe, a desire accelerated by Stalin's death in March 1953. Mao had finally concluded that he had achieved maximum political value out of the war and could settle for less than total victory.[112]

Both sides compromised and finally signed the armistice on July 27, 1953, an armistice that never led to a peace treaty. By a complicated process, representatives of neutral nations screened all POWs to determine their desire for repatriation. Twenty-one Americans, one British soldier, and 325 Koreans elected to remain in China or North Korea. By contrast, 21,835 communist soldiers, including 14,235 of the 21,700 Chinese POWs, chose not to return home.[113]

The Korean people were undoubtedly the greatest sufferers in the conflict. In the larger sense of the Cold War, however, Korea was a draw. China could boast that it had halted the power of the United States, but only at enormous cost. Between 1950 and 1953, the Chinese suffered 1,010,700 casualties, including 152,000 dead, 833,000 wounded or hospitalized, 21,700 POWs, and 4,000 missing in action.[114] The Chinese economy, already damaged by decades of continuous war, suffered even more. Mao had caused the focus of the Cold War to shift both physically—to East Asia—and intellectually—to ideology.[115] Of equal significance, the confrontation with the United States delayed normalization of relations and deprived China of its UN Security Council seat for two decades. As for the Soviet Union, Stalin's efforts to embroil the United States in Asia backfired. The Korean conflict prompted the United States to launch a massive rearmament campaign and negotiate a series of regional alliances that the Soviet Union was ill prepared to match.

8

EUROPEAN ALLIANCES
AND ARMAMENTS

I think none of us has ever believed for an instant that the
United States could, over the long term (several decades), build
a sort of Roman Wall with its own troops and so protect the
world. Not only would the ultimate cost be excessive; equally
important is the adverse reaction that inevitably springs up in
any country where foreign troops are stationed. . . . To the natives,
American troops are representatives of the richest and most
powerful nation on earth, and consequently remind the native
that he is unable to solve all his national problems for himself.

Dwight Eisenhower, 1953[1]

On November 1, 1948, at the height of the Berlin Blockade crisis,
Field Marshal Sir Bernard Law Montgomery left his post as chief
of the Imperial General Staff to become the first chairman of the
Western European Union Commanders-in-Chief Committee. It was
a weak position in a weak alliance—the European effort to coordinate its own defense at a time when the United States had no treaty
obligation to help. As chairman, Montgomery was not even the designated wartime commander of the union, though his instructions told
him to plan for that possibility. The French, Belgians, and Dutch had
accepted him primarily to get British involvement in continental
defense, only to find that the British government shied away from
a formal commitment.[2]

The blunt, egotistical Montgomery, who had already failed at the politics of senior British defense planning, was hopelessly ill equipped for the diplomacy required to establish a new multinational alliance. Still struggling to rebuild their economies, none of the Western Union's members was willing to make the defense expenditures necessary to organize a credible defense, and Montgomery was not the man to cajole them into incremental improvements. His own nominee for land component commander, General de Lattre de Tassigny, openly criticized and defied him. After three months in his new position, the field marshal told Foreign Minister Bevin that West Germany must be included in both the Western Union and the still-developing North Atlantic alliance.[3] By November 1949, he summed up the situation in a memorandum to his former peers, the British chiefs of staff:

a) The French Army is in an appalling state; this is no exaggeration. The French are cutting down Western Union expenditures and 'stall' as soon as efforts are made to implement the practical requirements of the Cs-in-C [Commanders-in-Chief] War Organization.

b) The Belgian Army is making no progress. The Belgian Defence organization flounders about in uncertainties.

c) The Dutch Army progress is practically NIL. . . .

e) The Americans decline to use the great influence they could bring to bear to hasten practical progress.[4]

Fortunately for Montgomery's peace of mind if not his bruised ego, he was about to be superseded by his former wartime boss, Dwight Eisenhower, as the Korean War powered both the United States and the North Atlantic Treaty into an unprecedented peacetime defense buildup. Then it would be the Soviets' turn to take measures to balance the growing resurgence of the West, a resurgence they had unwittingly provoked in Berlin and Korea.

FROM NORTH ATLANTIC TREATY TO NATO

The trials of the Western European Union illustrate the oft-forgotten fact that simply signing an alliance does not ensure the integration of the allies' command, control, and troop units. Historically, very few alliances have actually organized for war while still at peace; one would have to look back to the Delian League (476 B.C.), a naval alliance of

Legend:
- Nato, *c.*1960
- Neutral
- Warsaw Pact

N
W E
S

Norwegian Sea

ICELAND

SWEDEN

FINLAND

NORWAY

North Sea

Baltic Sea

DENMARK

USSR

Soviet Zone

BRITAIN

NETH.

POLAND

North Atlantic Ocean

BELGIUM

GERMANY

CZECHOSLOVAKIA

FRANCE

SWITZ.

AUSTRIA

HUNGARY

ROMANIA

Trieste

ITALY

YUGOSLAVIA

BULGARIA

Black Sea

ALBANIA

PORTUGAL

SPAIN

GREECE

TURKEY

TUNISIA

Mediterranean Sea

ALGERIA

MOROCCO

LIBYA

EGYPT

MAP 10. NATO and the Warsaw Pact, c. 1960

Greek city-states against ancient Persia, to find a precedent for the eventual structure of the North Atlantic Treaty Organization (NATO).

Given the close proximity and apparent strength of the Soviet forces in East Germany, all the signatories of the North Atlantic Treaty agreed on the need for military forces ready to fight on short notice. The issue was who would provide the troops and equipment. Indeed, by common consent American politicians had deferred a discussion of this question until after they had ratified the treaty on July 21, 1949.[5]

Still recovering from World War II, the European members understandably expected the United States to provide the lion's share of both troops (to ensure that the U.S. nuclear umbrella was committed to Europe) and weapons (to supply the threadbare European forces, many of them already using Lend-Lease equipment). France, which should have provided the bulk of troops for European defense, was deeply involved in Indochina (see chapter 10). In Washington, Truman and the State Department preferred to have the Europeans defend themselves with U.S. equipment, while the Defense Department and especially the U.S. Army objected that such aid would come at the expense of America's own defense needs, just as it had done in 1940–1942. Congress was still reluctant to spend money on defense, but the news of the first Soviet atomic detonation ensured passage of an initial $500 million in assistance.[6]

Meanwhile, although many officials might have privately agreed with Montgomery on the need for West German rearmament, that was so politically sensitive as to be almost unthinkable in some European capitals. The creation of the Federal Republic of Germany (FRG) in September 1949 brought the issue to a head. The Christian Democrat Konrad Adenauer became its first chancellor and pressed the Allies for authority to create a federal police force. When he first raised the matter diplomatically in April 1950, Adenauer's principal concern was the need for public order in the new federal capital of Bonn. However, the outbreak of the Korean conflict raised a new specter—the possibility that, as in North Korea, the Soviet-backed East German "Alert Police" might invade the FRG while Moscow denied all responsibility for such an "internal revolutionary conflict." Reinhard Gehlen, the former head of Germany's wartime analysis of the Soviet Union who had sold his services to the Central Intelligence Agency, contributed to the fearmongering by exaggerating the threat.

The British government, which otherwise had little use for Adenauer, encouraged him in the push for paramilitary federal police.[7]

It was only a short step from police to soldiers, but although Washington and London came to see the need for this, some German officials in Bonn were opposed. Adenauer feared a return of German militarism but was willing to have some form of defense force in return for regaining German sovereignty. Paris was understandably alarmed about the resurrection of a German military and especially a German General Staff. In October 1950, Jean Monnet, the great advocate of European integration, quietly suggested to Premier René Pleven that France create a Pan-European army. This army, under international control, would maximize the use of available resources, including those of West Germany, without permitting the Germans to have independent major units or a revived general staff. Pleven persuaded his parliament to vote for this plan, later known as the European Defense Community (EDC), with integrated arms forces and headquarters. In Pleven's view, the largest unit of any one nationality should be a battalion, grouped into multinational divisions.[8]

BUILDING THE BUNDESWEHR

As a practical matter, it would require years to create an effective multinational force because of language and training barriers. The United States and many Europeans did not think they could wait for this, and the Germans understandably wanted a greater say in their own defense. Moreover, the British government had no interest in joining a federal system.[9]

Secretary of State Acheson skillfully played a compromise position, in which the United States argued to begin forming German regiments immediately while recognizing the French intent to convene a conference to negotiate what later became known as the EDC. In December 1950, North Atlantic Council meetings in Brussels approved this dual approach, permitting the first steps in the formation of West German units. Almost simultaneously, the French achieved their parallel goal of creating the supranational European Coal and Steel Community (ECSC), which would make secret German rearmament impossible because of European oversight of steel production.

In May 1952, the members of the ECSC signed an EDC treaty in Paris, but after much delay France, the originator of the plan, rejected it in August 1954.[10] As French military power was drained in Indo-china, Paris felt that it could not counterbalance a rearmed Germany in Europe, even with British and American promises of their con-tinued presence there. Moreover, French nationalists objected to the EDC, which placed supranational controls on troops and arms production not only in Germany but in France as well. Despite the efforts of President Eisenhower's secretary of state, John Foster Dulles, the EDC never came to fruition. After the French rejection, British Foreign Secretary Anthony Eden led a successful effort that modified the WEU to include German and Italian units, thereby legitimizing German rearmament.[11] West Germany officially joined NATO in 1955.

Initially, the sense of imminent Soviet threat had prompted the Germans to plan on creating their army within two years, but quite apart from the holdups and confusion caused by the EDC effort, various factors caused extensive delays. The Eisenhower administra-tion was determined to support Adenauer because of German political opposition to rearmament. Still, U.S. military aid budgets and produc-tion capabilities could not begin to match the initial German demand for 7,500 tanks, 8,400 armored personnel carriers, and a host of smaller weapons and devices. Moreover, the Bonn government repeatedly tried to pass the entire cost of rearmament along to the United States, whereas the normal aid situation was for the United States to provide only what the partner government could not procure by itself.[12]

The FRG also experienced great internal difficulties in its rear-mament.[13] In retrospect, it almost appeared as if politicians were so determined to root out Prussian militarism that they eliminated Ger-man efficiency at the same time. Chancellor Adenauer himself had little interest in military matters, beyond a general belief that the FRG must have effective armed forces to assert its sovereignty and earn its place in NATO. He therefore delegated the details of rearmament to a shadow defense ministry. On a British recommendation, Adenauer named former General of Panzer Troops Gerhard Graf [Count] von Schwerin as the first head of this office in May 1950. Schwerin's creden-tials as both a soldier and an opponent of Nazism were impeccable, and he immediately laid the groundwork for future rearmament. Unfortunately, Schwerin was no politician; the chancellor reluctantly dismissed him after only five months when the general bluntly told reporters that conscription might be necessary to man the new armed forces.[14] Schwerin's successor was Theodor Blank, a left-wing member of Adenauer's Christian Democratic Union. Because the shadow defense office had a title that was impossibly long even by German standards, it was thereafter known as the "Amt [Office] Blank." Unfortunately, Blank was not only poor at management and suspicious of professional soldiers but also as inept with the press as his predecessor. His office was chronically understaffed and lacked a single military head to coordinate planning. Although the cost of rearmament far exceeded the initial estimates, Blank was unwilling for political reasons to request additional funds. At the same time, however, he sought to please Pan-Europeanists by purchasing the French-built Noratlas transport aircraft instead of the cheaper and more capable American C-119. To add insult to injury, in 1955 a secretive personnel board, composed entirely of civilians, rejected a number of key members of Blank's staff who had applied for commissions in the new Bundeswehr. This arbitrary action demoralized the already disorganized staff.[15]

In 1950, Schwerin had assembled a number of former Wehrmacht officers to plan the new armed forces. The resulting study was known as the Himmerod Memorandum because their deliberations took place in the Benedictine Abbey at Himmerod. The memorandum called for an army of 250,000 men in twelve armored divisions, an air force of 831 fighter and reconnaissance aircraft, and a limited navy of minesweepers, torpedo boats, and landing craft. Except for its underestimation of the eventual size of the air force, this study proved to be remarkably prescient and became the basis for the future Bundeswehr.[16] On a less attractive note, the memorandum insisted that the Adenauer administration should release convicted war criminals in return for the service of ex–World War II officers in the new force. This was an early stage in a successful effort to exonerate the German officer corps for its crimes.[17]

Amt Blank lacked both the funds and the organizational ability to implement this ambitious plan. By April 1956, only two-thirds of the scheduled 66,000 men had been brought on active duty, due largely to a lack of barracks space to house them. U.S. military commanders engaged in creative financing to rehabilitate enough facilities to allow German rearmament to begin at all. The new German air force was particularly hard-pressed because several generations of air technology had been compressed into the decade since the former Luftwaffe pilots had last flown. U.S. Air Force Europe not only provided hundreds of instructors and support personnel but also literally produced the plans for the new air force after Amt Blank proved unequal to the task.[18]

Ultimately, these repeated near disasters produced a clamor for Blank's dismissal. In October 1956, Adenauer appointed Franz-Josef Strauss as defense minister. Strauss promptly established an effective organization but felt forced to revise the original, ambitious schedule for rearmament. Instead of a planned three-year process, the actual elapsed time was eight years, 1953–1961.[19] Even with added time, certain aspects of West Germany's remobilization proved too ambitious. This was particularly true of a 1958 decision to arm the air force with F-104 Starfighters built in Germany under U.S. license. German factories found it difficult to manufacture such a complex aircraft, and West Germany's air force lacked experienced pilots and mechanics to operate it. The result, in 1963, was a scandal in which German F-104s crashed at a rate of almost one per week.[20] The Bundeswehr eventually became a formidable force, but the path to that stage was surprisingly long and difficult.

The Rise of NATO

While the Germans labored ineffectually to rearm themselves, the North Atlantic Treaty evolved into an organized force. As Timothy Ireland has persuasively argued, the Korean War motivated the United States to convert a political treaty into a true military alliance. In turn, the involvement of U.S. forces gave the French sufficient reassurance that they reluctantly agreed with Acheson.[21] Thus Kim Il-Sung's ill-considered attack on South Korea, reinforced by the Chinese intervention, was a direct cause of the creation of NATO that included German troops.

The integration of the FRG into NATO is often depicted as a key political decision, but it also had significant military consequences. Clearly, German troops could not be motivated by a war plan that conceded most of the FRG's territory to an invading enemy. France was equally interested in halting the attacker as far east as possible. NATO became committed to a forward defense strategy, determined to contest every meter of German soil along the interzonal boundary with the east. This in turn made it impossible to trade space for time and helped impel the alliance toward use of nuclear weapons to compensate for a shortage of maneuver space and conventional troops.

At the December 1950 Brussels meeting, Secretary Acheson suggested that the North Atlantic Council should name a military leader for the defense of Europe—the Supreme Allied Commander, Europe (SACEUR). To no one's surprise, the consensus nominee was Dwight D. Eisenhower, whose wartime record of building a multinational armed force to defeat Germany made him the natural candidate.

Although the Department of Defense had done some preliminary planning, Eisenhower had to begin almost from scratch to accomplish two simultaneous goals: first, to create a multinational command and staff structure to integrate the defense of Europe, and second, to encourage all members of the pact to contribute effective forces to that defense.

Whereas his World War II headquarters had been primarily a bilateral British-American force, he now had to build a structure that integrated the forces of twelve different nations.[22] Just as in 1943, Eisenhower created a fully integrated staff, with each department consisting of officers from multiple nations and armed services, rather than trying to govern by the committee method favored by the British and by the Western European Union. The resulting staff took the name Supreme Headquarters, Allied Powers Europe (SHAPE), with the same shoulder insignia as its 1944 predecessor. The SHAPE chief of staff, U.S. Army Major General Alfred Gruenther, was a skilled military diplomat who sent staff officers to Europe to begin preliminary planning even before Eisenhower received his official appointment. In order to demonstrate a commitment to defending all of Europe, the new headquarters had to be on the Continent, with France as the logical choice. In the early spring of 1951, the staff assembled in the Hotel Astoria in Paris, with its communications located in the nearby blockhouse built by the Germans when they occupied the city. Using his usual charm, Eisenhower had considerable success in persuading his new staff officers to think internationally, to the point of not communicating NATO plans to their own governments. He also mandated French language classes to provide a second common language for the staff. The headquarters eventually moved to a new location in the suburb of Saint-Germain-en-Laye. This complex included "SHAPE Village," apartments that not only encouraged interallied contact but also reduced the inevitable comparisons based on differing national pay scales for the officers involved.[23]

Looking at the defense of Western Europe, an operations area stretching from Norway to Algeria and eventually Turkey, Eisenhower had to construct a multinational command structure in addition to the basic headquarters. In effect, he divided this responsibility into a central land mass on the European mainland, flanked by a northern and a southern area that each involved a mixture of land and sea defenses. British Admiral Sir E. J. Patrick Brind initially headed Allied Forces Northern Europe, located in Oslo, Norway, while U.S. Admiral Robert B. Carney commanded Allied Forces Southern Europe, with headquarters in Naples. In turn, these commanders had component chiefs of various nationalities, including Norwegian and Danish in the north and Italian in the south. Given the significance and weakness of the center, Eisenhower retained overall command of that region, with French Marshal Alphonse Juin as the Allied Land Forces commander. Eisenhower and his successors often had to engage in a complicated balancing act, to the point of creating unnecessary command positions to satisfy national pride and ensure full participation.[24] When Turkey and Greece became members of NATO in February 1952, their mutual antagonisms prevented them from participating in the same exercises and command structure.

Eisenhower's other task was even more difficult. While Montgomery, once again in his wartime role as deputy supreme commander, applied his talents to training the available troops, Eisenhower had to cajole member nations to provide more such forces for their mutual defense. Even the United States required tact—Eisenhower regularly provided reports to President Truman and his special NATO representative, W. Averell Harriman. The first SACEUR also had to spend considerable time entertaining visiting Congressmen, a distraction that was more useful for his future role as president than his present task as commander.[25]

In the atmosphere of continued urgency that arose during the Korean War, his efforts bore fruit. The 4th U.S. Infantry Division, reactivated as part of the Korean buildup, reached Europe in May 1951 as the down payment on an increase that eventually brought three additional divisions to Germany. Unlike the Eighth Army in Korea, which was wracked by personnel instability with twelve-month combat tours, the Seventh Army in Europe slowly developed into a relatively stable, conventional opponent to the Soviet Army.[26] A supplemental appropriation for fiscal 1951 included more than $3 billion for military equipment to NATO, including 2,300 tanks, although these took more than a year to produce and deliver.[27] Meanwhile, SHAPE plans were expressed in terms of required troop levels, endorsed by the North Atlantic Council. The original goal was for fifty divisions, half of them active duty, by 1952; in that year, the target mobilization time for the remaining reserve divisions was cut from ninety to thirty days. In 1953, the council reported an actual inventory of thirty-five divisions, with a goal of seventy divisions and 5,500 jet aircraft by the end of 1954.[28]

Goals were one thing, accomplishments quite another. Although NATO forces grew during the early 1950s, there was a limit to what the European states could afford. Moreover, the threat of Soviet attack appeared to recede in the mid-1950s, so that NATO was far from even minimum defense capacity until the West German divisions began to form.[29] The United States was still distracted by the Korean conflict, while France had most of its experienced troops fighting in Indo-china. This diversion became even more serious when, in 1955, the French began to deploy large numbers of troops to repress the Algerian rebellion. Thus, while the four French divisions in West Germany were at 94 percent strength in 1951, the remaining divisions in France proper had only 60 percent, of which no more than 9 percent were career officers and Noncommissioned Officers (NCOs). Moreover, the eighteen-month conscription limit meant that at any given time new draftees made up 28 percent of a French division.[30]

The British Army of the Rhine had perhaps the most difficult problem because its four divisions provided the principal force to defend the north German plain that offered an inviting axis for Soviet advance across Europe. Despite assistance from the Belgians, Dutch, and Danes, this was a clearly impossible task using conventional forces. Moreover, whereas the French had a single major military commit-ment overseas, the British had a number of smaller conflicts, including their involvement in Korea and low-level insurgencies in Malaya, Cyprus, and the Suez Canal. Even with conscription, Britain could not hope to meet its NATO goals of 300,000 men. Such realities led NATO to turn increasingly to tactical nuclear weapons during the mid-1950s. Military Committee (MC) 48, the alliance's 1954 statement of force requirements, called for the same number of ready conventional units for the initial battles but lowered the goal for reserve units that might be irrelevant once nuclear exchanges began.[31]

Developing air forces was an even greater problem, as the German case illustrated. It involved not only expensive jet aircraft and pilot training but also the construction of airfields within NATO member states. The Western European Union had started this process with a plan to build thirty-five airfields, a plan that expanded greatly when NATO came into being. Prolonged negotiations led to a program to build airfields over a period of years, with the United States providing 41 percent of the cost. By 1954, the United States had contributed almost $10 billion to the alliance.[32] In this, as in other aspects of infrastructure and joint procedures, NATO went far beyond any previous alliance in its efforts to create an effective combat force.

Although Eisenhower was the obvious choice for SACEUR, the subject of an American Supreme Allied Commander, Atlantic (SACLANT) proved more controversial. The Joint Chiefs of Staff and U.S. Navy considered it essential to have a single unified commander to protect the supply lines from the United States to Europe from Soviet submarines. The British chiefs of staff reluctantly concurred. However, when President Truman nominated an American admiral as the first SACLANT in February 1951, it became a partisan issue in London. For a year, Winston Churchill adamantly insisted that Britain had to control its own sea lanes, but eventually he conceded the point to superior American naval resources.[33] The matter became embroiled in ongoing British efforts to create a British-commanded Middle East pact that would be equivalent to NATO (see chapter 12). In the fall of 1951, the United States and Turkey agreed to such a pact in return for British support of full NATO membership for Greece and Turkey.[34]

Eisenhower also had occasional conflicts with the U.S. Joint Chiefs of Staff. In theory, regional joint commanders like MacArthur in the Pacific had operational command over their forces, but the JCS was loath to concede that it had no authority over those forces. The situation was complicated by the fact that Eisenhower, unlike his successors as SACEUR, was not simultaneously the head of U.S. European Command (EUCOM), the regional unified headquarters located in Frankfurt, Germany. The issue came to a head in August 1951, when the JCS approved an emergency war plan called Ironbark that included specific tasks for EUCOM troops. The JCS insisted that it was "vested with statutory responsibility for the safety of U.S. forces throughout the world." Eisenhower protested vehemently, not least because such a unilateral U.S. plan was a bad precedent when he sought to persuade the other NATO members to confide their forces to his control. The most that the JCS would agree to was to direct U.S. commanders in Europe to coordinate their plans to support SACEUR.[35]

On June 1, 1952, General Eisenhower left command in Europe to enter the presidential race at home. His successor, Ridgway, continued to work for greater readiness, including increased ammunition stocks and better logistical infrastructure. As the NATO forces matured in the crucial center, Ridgway relinquished direct command of that region in favor of Marshal Juin, thereby assuaging French concerns about American dominance of the alliance.[36] (In 1954, the French government fired Juin for his outspoken opposition to the EDC.) The U.S. government also made Ridgway the commander of the U.S. EUCOM, a move that simplified his relationships with the Defense Department but also lessened his status as a truly international commander for NATO. Nonetheless, Eisenhower, Ridgway, and their successor, Gruenther, all made significant contributions to the delicate diplomacy of transforming the North Atlantic Treaty into a viable military force.

NSC-68

The U.S. investment in NATO was only the most prominent and long-lasting aspect of an overall military buildup that grew out of the challenge posed in Korea. At the heart of this transformation was a study drafted before that war even began, National Security Council document 68 (NSC-68). This document was the brainchild of Paul Nitze, appointed by Secretary Acheson to head the State Department's Policy Planning Staff in January 1950. Although Nitze used many preexisting studies and worked with representatives of the JCS and of Defense Secretary Wilson, the overall result was something unprecedented: a single statement of U.S. national security policy.[37]

In the words of Dean Acheson, "[t]he purpose of NSC 68 was to so bludgeon the mass mind of 'top government' that not only could the President make a decision but that the decision could be carried out."[38] NSC-68 therefore painted a somber picture, simultaneously projecting a long confrontation with the Soviet bloc and urging rapid rearmament to meet that threat. For Nitze, the Soviet leadership clearly intended to expand its control throughout and even beyond the Eurasian land mass. The document therefore argued that "The United

States, as the principal center of power in the non-Soviet world and the bulwark of opposition to Soviet expansion, is the principal enemy whose integrity and vitality must be subverted or destroyed by one means or another if the Kremlin is to achieve its fundamental design."[39] The American authors estimated that, by 1954, the Soviet Union would probably have two hundred atomic weapons, a sufficient number to successfully attack the United States.[40]

Therefore, Nitze argued, the United States must use every means, including diplomacy, alliances, economics, foreign aid, and the military, to contain the threat. Military force was essential as a deterrent and as a basis for negotiations, but not as the only instrument of foreign policy. In particular, the United States needed to take advantage of the window of opportunity while it still had nuclear superiority, using the time to restore its armed forces and defense economy. The document avoided giving any cost estimates, but the obvious implication was a major shift in government spending. In short, NSC-68 was not only a defense strategy but also a set of talking points to motivate public support for sustained defense efforts.

None of these ideas was particularly original, but NSC-68 stated them in a single, coherent program with a sobering sense of urgency. Moreover, Nitze recognized that to some extent the balance of power depended upon not only actual military and economic capabilities, but also public perceptions of those capabilities. Thus, the United States and its allies must not only be strong enough to contain the Soviets, they must be *perceived* as being strong in order to reduce the risk of conflict by misunderstanding or misperception.[41] Such an observation seems commonplace today, but in the relatively complacent world of post-World War II Washington, it was a remarkably sophisticated revelation.

The North Korean attack, two months later, seemed to confirm these dire projections. Viewed from the West, that attack seemed to be Soviet expansionism based on a misperception of American resolve. One of the first casualties of the war was Defense Secretary Louis Johnson, whose budget-cutting efforts in support of Truman's austerity campaign earned considerable blame when American unpreparedness became apparent in Korea. He was succeeded in September 1950 by George Marshall, called yet again to provide leadership for his country. Marshall, however, was exhausted by years as chief of staff and further years as a diplomat and secretary of state. He therefore leaned heavily on his deputy secretary and eventual successor, Robert A. Lovett. Lovett had the perfect background for his position, having been at various times a naval aviator, an international banker, assistant secretary of war for air, and undersecretary of state.[42] It was this team together with Secretary of State Acheson that presided over the defense buildup forecast by NSC-68 and mandated by the Korean conflict.

The result was a frantic period of budgetary maneuvering in 1950–1951. Fiscal year 1951, which began six days after the North Korean invasion, originally projected only $13 billion for the defense budget, with an authorized U.S. Army strength of 630,000 and an overall uniformed strength of 1.5 million. The navy was to have fifteen carriers of all types, while the air force had forty-two combat and six troop carrier wings. The initial defeats and the Chinese intervention provided the impetus for four successive supplemental budgets over the next six months. By the time the smoke had cleared, the Defense budget had reached $48 billion, equal to the total of the four previous fiscal years. Uniformed strength authorizations more than doubled to 3.24 million troops, including eighteen army and two and one-third marine divisions, twenty-seven carriers, and eighty-seven combat and troop carrier wings.[43] Despite the partial mobilization of the reserve components, none of the services actually reached these authorized strengths by the end of the fiscal year in June 1951.

Behind closed doors, the armed services argued for even larger appropriations and troop strengths over the long haul. In September 1950, the Joint Chiefs and service secretaries responded to an initial request for estimates concerning military implementation of NSC-68 with a coordinated proposal for $260 billion over fiscal years 1951 through 1955. Although Secretary Marshall was sympathetic to the basic thrust of this request, Lovett and he repeatedly asked for reduced estimates. Based on the experience of 1940–1942, Marshall felt that too much money spent at one time would not only be wasteful but also would lead to a future peak and then reduction of industrial orders rather than a steady schedule over the long period envisioned by NSC-68. Even after Marshall retired, Truman followed this basic approach, "stretching out" the defense buildup over a number of years. By the time he left office, the planned strength of the forces was twenty army and three marine divisions, twenty-seven aircraft carriers of all types, and ninety-eight air force wings.[44]

Overall, the defense budget and the armed forces grew phenomenally during the years of the Korean conflict. However, Eisenhower won election in 1952 based in part on a promise of significant reductions in defense spending. Eisenhower, Secretary of State John Foster Dulles, and the prominent businessmen who made up most of the Eisenhower cabinet all believed that the economic health of the United States was more significant in the long term than numbers of conventional weapons systems or troop units. Indeed, one of Eisenhower's major reasons for running for the presidency was his belief that the Truman approach to national security was unsystematic and wasteful. Upon taking office, he established a formal system using the National Security Council and various supporting committees to produce logical government policies. In the spring of 1953, Project Solarium examined three different approaches to dealing with the Soviet Union, ranging from the status quo to an aggressive rollback. This study provided the raw material for the administration's new policies.[45] The resulting "New Look" aimed at using all American resources—diplomatic, military, economic, and covert intelligence.[46] The policy's most visible aspects, however, were greater reliance both on regional alliances and on nuclear weapons, the so-called "Massive Retaliation" policy described in chapter 13. When Eisenhower submitted his budget for fiscal year 1955, it called for defense spending of $31 billion, three-quarters of the final Truman budget proposal in January 1953.[47]

A contradiction in the New Look prevented further reductions: in order to encourage the regional alliances to field their own armed forces, the United States found that it could not reduce its own troop strength in Europe nor be too explicit in its promises of nuclear support in the Middle East. Similarly, the Eisenhower administration could not reduce military aid to its allies, who felt the pressure of tight budgets at the same time that the post-Stalin USSR appeared less threatening, and were therefore reluctant to rearm themselves. Thus, for example, even though the JCS proposed a major redeployment of forces back to the United States, the administration was unable to make any significant reduction except from Korea.[48]

Meanwhile, the armed forces fluctuated during the 1950s. As a percentage of pre-Korean strength, the U.S. Navy and Marine Corps actually grew more than the other services in 1950, increasing in authorized strength from 461,000 to 718,000, or 55.7 percent.[49] Although often invisible to the ground troops, carrier strikes and shore bombardments contributed materially to interdicting Chinese and North Korean supply and troop movements. Like the other services, however, the navy remained focused on the Soviet threat in Europe and the Mediterranean.

The army's growth had come with only marginal improvements in technology, but during the early 1950s the U.S. Navy completed its transition from World War II propeller aircraft to jets, bringing with them greater speed and capacity but also higher risks in take-offs and landings. By 1957, the navy arrived at a total of fifteen attack carriers as the basis for sustained operations in a state of semimobilization. This figure permitted two carriers in the western Pacific and three or four in the Atlantic and Mediterranean at all times, with the remainder being in port, training, or transiting to and from the forward deployment areas. Until a new *Forrestal* class of super carriers was ready, the navy had to rely on the *Essex* and *Midway* classes built during the mid-1940s, with nine of the former having their decks reinforced to handle heavier loads.[50]

The perceived intelligence failures of 1950 in Korea also produced significant changes in the fledgling U.S. intelligence community. In October of that year, Eisenhower's wartime chief of staff, General W. Bedell Smith, replaced the experienced but unfortunate Hillenkoeter as Director of Central Intelligence. Smith's rank and organizational ability revitalized the CIA. Meanwhile, the wartime precedent of the OSS was renewed in the Office of Policy Coordination (OPC), a covert action unit that was assigned to the CIA but took instructions from the secretaries of Defense and State. OPC went from 302 personnel and $4.7 million in 1949 to 5,954 people and $82 million in 1952. Concurrently, OPC developed a host of projects in political, psychological, paramilitary, and economic warfare, the basis of the CIA's subsequent and very sinister reputation.[51] In November 1952, Truman issued an executive order centralizing operational control of the various armed services cryptologic units under a new National Security Agency (NSA).[52]

U.S. ARMY IN THE 1950s

Troop strengths, especially in the army, reflected the high and low tides in government spending during the 1950s. The initial deployments in response to the North Korean invasion had left only the 82nd Airborne Division and the gutted, undermanned 11th Airborne and 2nd Armored Divisions in the Continental United States. In September 1950, therefore, the government mobilized four National Guard divisions (the 28th, 40th, 43rd, and 45th Infantry). The Chinese intervention led to the activation of the 31st and 47th Infantry Divisions four months later, followed in early 1952 by the 37th and 44th Infantry. Because the organized reserve divisions had a lower priority for funding, the Defense Department only activated non-divisional reserve units. However, even the National Guard divisions lacked equipment, training, and personnel, varying between 8,000 and 9,500 men each, as compared to an authorized force of 18,800. As a result, the army had to fill these guard units with draftees and in several cases reduced their authorized strength to 14,500. Beginning in 1952, the states that had furnished these mobilized guard divisions were able to activate duplicate divisions, so that (on paper at least) most of the mobilized units were replaced in the force structure even before the Defense Department returned the guardsmen to their civilian lives.[53]

Meanwhile, the Defense Department continued to reactivate dormant Regular Army divisions. In addition to the eight National Guard divisions on active duty, by early 1952 the Regular Army had two armored (1st and 2nd), two airborne (11th and 82nd), and eight infantry (1st Cavalry fighting as infantry, plus 1st, 2nd, 3rd, 4th, 7th, 24th, and 25th Infantry) divisions. Beyond this peak of twenty divisions, there were another eleven "divisions" that were actually training cadres for the growing influx of draftees and volunteers; in the mid-1950s several of these, including the 3rd Armored and 101st Airborne Divisions, converted to combat status after the guard divisions returned to inactive duty.[54]

As with its European counterparts, the U.S. Army found it difficult to maintain effective forces due to a rapid turnover in draftees. Transferring individual soldiers from the United States to overseas locations contributed to this readiness problem and also meant that at any given time a significant number of soldiers were in training or in transit between units. One solution to this situation was Operation Gyroscope, by which entire divisions in Germany and the United States swapped equipment and bases in a large troop movement. Between 1955 and 1958, fourteen divisions participated in Gyroscope, but the expense and difficulty finally led to a halt in the process.[55] A related problem was reserve component training. Although the armed services sought to ensure that discharged combat veterans served in troop units, the public considered this unfair. Instead, in 1955, Congress created a new system whereby six months' active duty and seven and one-half years' reserve service could substitute for the customary two years of conscript active service.[56]

More fundamentally, the U.S. Army had to adjust to the threat of a nuclear battlefield. The 1954 revision of the army's Field Manual 100-5, *Operations*, reasserted the importance of ground troops in a limited war, arguing against Massive Retaliation. Two successive army chiefs of staff, Ridgway (1953–1955) and Maxwell Taylor (1955–1959), tried in vain to dissuade President Eisenhower from reducing ground forces. Although Ridgway never publicly disagreed with Eisenhower's cuts, he also refused to endorse them, providing ammunition for Democrats in Congress. This opposition cost Ridgway the customary second two-year term as the army's senior officer.[57] After his retirement, Taylor criticized the paradigm, arguing that the army and the nation needed more options and more flexibility in dealing with future limited wars like that in Korea.[58] This viewpoint formed part of the Democratic campaign position in 1960, leading to the Flexible Response doctrine of the 1960s. In the interim, however, the army as an organization addressed the nuclear battlefield in two ways: tactical nuclear weapons and divisional reorganization.

It took more than a decade to develop atomic weapons that were sufficiently small and reliable to be fired from 155mm howitzers. During the 1950s, the available weapons were so bulky that the army's first nuclear delivery weapon in 1953 was the M65 "Atomic Cannon," a massive 280mm gun based on German World War II designs and requiring two large tractors to move it. The Korean conflict led to a crash project to create a smaller, more maneuverable nuclear-armed rocket launcher. The M13 Honest John Rocket, launched from a self-propelled truck chassis, entered service on an emergency basis in 1952 and officially became a standard weapon two years later.[59] Subsequent refinements in the Honest John during the 1960s produced a lighter version with a maximum range of 24.8 kilometers and various warheads up to forty kilotons. As an unguided rocket, it was far less accurate than missile- or aircraft-delivered weapons but gave army corps and divisions their first reliable nuclear system. In 1961, a smaller version known as the XM-51 Little John took the field. This variant had a range of only 17.6 kilometers, which meant that the firing unit had to take precautions against the radiation and other effects of its own nuclear detonation. Still, the Little John permitted air-deployable units or even individual infantry battalions to have a nuclear capability.

Organizationally, the Honest John rocket was only part of a major restructuring of the U.S. Army in the later 1950s. Given the Eisenhower administration's emphasis on nuclear warfare, the army sought to develop a doctrine and organization that would allow ground units to function on a nuclear battlefield. This meant that units had to be self-contained combined-arms formations, without vulnerable logistical trains, while being able to disperse widely throughout the battle area. Moreover, in contrast to the Soviet Army, which was fighting only on the Eurasian land mass, the U.S. Army's infantry divisions had to be lightly equipped so that they could deploy rapidly to any potential trouble spot.

The resulting structure was called the Pentomic Division, a public relations term meant to convey the idea of a unit that could function in both nuclear and conventional conflicts. The key change involved was to eliminate the regiment, which had been the basic maneuver element since the American Revolution (regimental designations were retained for purposes of unit identity but had no tactical significance except in a few specialized forces such as the armored cavalry). In place of three infantry regiments, each controlling three infantry battalions, the Pentomic infantry or airborne division was built around five oversized battalions called "battle groups." Each battle group had four (later five) rifle companies, a heavy mortar company, and attached tank, artillery, and engineer elements. Even the infantry squad changed, increasing from nine to eleven men subdivided into two fire teams, each with an automatic rifle. In theory, therefore, the division commander could maneuver these battle groups throughout the battle area while avoiding presenting lucrative targets for enemy atomic attack.[60]

Yet this new structure had many weaknesses. First and foremost was command and control. By eliminating the regiment as a headquarters, the Pentomic Division gave the commander an impossible span of control, including five battle groups, the tank battalion, the armored cavalry (reconnaissance) squadron, and a new division trains headquarters. The only option available to this overworked commander was to place some of his units under a single brigade headquarters led by the assistant division commander. Each battle group commander had a similarly wide span of control, so that the loss of any one headquarters in battle could result in hopeless confusion. There were also issues regarding the manner in which artillery and armored personnel carriers supported the infantry.

The Pentomic changes were much less drastic in the armored divisions and non-divisional armored cavalry regiments. Overall, however, the resulting ferment about doctrine and organization caused more confusion than improvement, especially when American commanders contemplated using the resulting structure against the armor-heavy Soviet forces. Perhaps the only positive effect was that the smaller Pentomic divisions permitted the Eisenhower administration to quietly reduce actual troop strengths in Europe by 16,000. However, when Defense Secretary Charles Wilson tried to drastically reduce the army's strength in 1957–1958, he encountered resistance from both the European allies and General Norstad, the Supreme Allied Commander, so that the U.S. commitment remained almost constant in the later 1950s. In effect, this delicate balance between budgets, conventional forces, and growing reliance on tactical nuclear weapons meant that NATO never really embraced Massive Retaliation. Instead, it arrived at a form of flexible response, including both conventional and nuclear war planning, in the later 1950s.[61]

RISE OF THE WARSAW PACT

Although the details were classified, the entire world was aware of the effects of NSC-68 on U.S. and NATO defense capabilities during the early 1950s. The same cannot be said for Soviet defense policy during the same period. Joseph Stalin's intentions and beliefs may never be completely clear to historians.

Stalin's natural paranoia increased in his old age, prompting him to launch renewed internal purges. Even his loyal foreign policy agent, Molotov, was not immune—in 1948, Andrei Vishinsky replaced Molotov after the latter's wife was sent to Siberia for suspected "Zionist" activities.[62] Cautious Soviet officials catered to the dictator's known predilections. For example, when George Kennan's influential "X" article appeared in the journal *Foreign Affairs* in 1948, Kennan's plan for the "containment" of the Soviet Union appeared in Stalin's translation as "strangulation."[63]

Nonetheless, although the Kremlin protested the North Atlantic Treaty in 1949, Stalin was not at first concerned or impressed by the West's attempts to band together; Moscow took no military measures in response to the treaty.[64] What did alarm Stalin was the accelerated rearmament of the United States, Western Europe, and above all West Germany in response to the Korean conflict. In a vain attempt to prevent the rearmament of the hated enemy, Stalin's government repeatedly proposed a peace treaty to be negotiated with a unified, neutral Germany. However, the West insisted that such a Germany be headed by a democratically elected government, and neither side was willing to contemplate having a unified German state join its opponents, so this initiative went nowhere.[65] For propaganda purposes, the Soviet Union supported various European efforts to ban nuclear weapons, but such agreements did not have a decisive effect. Instead, the persistent Soviet propaganda about the allegedly aggressive intentions of NATO came to have a subliminal effect on Eastern European leaders who should have known better, giving them a vague sense of being threatened by NATO, a sense that lingered into the twenty-first century.

There were occasional threats to Soviet leadership, of course, especially in Poland. In 1945, the occupiers declared that all prewar Polish officers in the rank of captain and higher were unsuitable, clearing the way for the rapid rise of dedicated young Communists, such as the future strongman Wojciech Jaruzelski. In 1947, Stalin insisted that the remaining pro-Western Polish officers be purged and sent in a number of officers like K. K. Rokossovsky to remodel the Polish Army on the Soviet style.[66]

With the COMINFORM dominating the various communist parties and loyal officers controlling key satellite military forces, Stalin did not see any need for a collective security alliance. Soviet diplomats negotiated bilateral defense agreements with Hungary, Bulgaria, Romania, and Finland in 1949, but went no farther. Then in 1955, the wartime allies reached a rare agreement on evacuating a unified, neutral Austria. Because many of the existing bilateral treaties authorized Soviet occupation until a final peace was arranged, this meant that Stalin's successors had to rethink their diplomatic and military arrangements. The inclusion of West Germany in NATO reinforced the need for greater defense structure. Moreover, historian Vojtech Mastny has suggested that Nikita Khrushchev, the emerging leader of the Soviet Union, may have hoped that an Eastern European defensive alliance could be used as a diplomatic bargaining chip to negotiate the dissolution of both NATO and its counterpart.[67]

On May 1, 1955, the Soviet Union and its satellites—Albania, Bulgaria, Hungary, East Germany, Poland, Rumania, and Czecho-slovakia—signed a Treaty of Friendship, Co-operation, and Mutual Assistance that became known as the Warsaw Pact. This agreement superficially resembled the North Atlantic Treaty, and in fact cited both that treaty and the WEU to justify its existence. The Warsaw Pact noted the right of self-defense included in the United Nations Charter of 1945 as further reason for its existence. The core of the pact was a mutual promise that in the event of attack upon any of its members, the other members would consult immediately and take such steps as each thought necessary to defend its allies.[68]

In reality, however, the Warsaw Pact never developed the type of political and consultative structure that arose from the North Atlantic Treaty. The Political Consultative Committee never functioned as the kind of deliberative body that the North Atlantic Council became. A secret command plan gave control of the satellite armed forces to Soviet commanders, who for decades used a heavy hand in ordering their allies about. This crude Soviet influence extended beyond military exercises and personal relationships to include directing the organization and stationing of the satellite armed forces. For example, the Soviets reversed the Hungarian government's efforts at shrinking its army. Instead, six Hungarian infantry divisions, two mechanized divisions, and two air divisions came under direct Soviet control in 1955.[69] Similarly, the Soviet military rarely shared its detailed plans with satellite staffs, conducting separate, Soviet-only nuclear planning sessions even in the context of multinational Pact exercises.[70]

Moscow's influence over Eastern European defenses extended even to industry. The vehicle for coordinating weapons production was the Council for Mutual Economic Cooperation (COMECON), formed in January 1949 as a pale substitute for the Marshall Plan. Beginning in 1956, Stalin's successors used COMECON as an umbrella organization to ensure that the different national arms industries did not duplicate each other. The satellite countries could produce their own small arms, but heavier and more sophisticated weapons were determined by Moscow. Unfortunately for those involved, the industrial planning decisions were not based on availability of raw materials or other considerations that would have determined where new factories were built under a capitalist system. As a result, areas such as Slovakia acquired heavy industries that were not economically efficient. However, this system did permit Moscow to farm out truck and tank production to Czechoslovakia, anti-aircraft and antitank weapons to Bulgaria, and so on, so that Soviet industry could focus on high-technology applications, such as missiles, lasers, and space research. Stalin, seeking to establish himself as a great communist theoretician, even announced the "law of systematic politico-economic development," which argued that heavy industry and raw materials must take precedence over consumer goods in order to develop the socialist state quickly. This aspect of the Warsaw Pact was essential for the Soviets to compete against American superiority in technology and production.[71]

Poland, with its long history of being an invasion corridor for the Germans, consistently supported the Pact and even encouraged Soviet efforts to institute stronger controls. Other governments, particularly that of Rumania, resisted central direction, rightly fearing that Moscow might commit them to war without prior consultation.

The Soviet Armed Forces in the 1950s

Meanwhile, the Soviet armed forces evolved in a manner that somewhat paralleled that of their principal adversaries.

So long as Stalin lived, the Soviet Army continued to perfect the organization and tactics of the Great Patriotic War, emphasizing armored and mechanized operations. In 1951, the Soviets added a fifth regiment, consisting of heavy tanks and self-propelled guns, to the mechanized division, bringing it to an authorized total of 14,244 men, 197 medium and heavy tanks, and 117 towed and self-propelled artillery pieces. Motorized rifle divisions acquired a similar tank/self-propelled gun regiment, together with 76mm self-propelled gun batteries to support each rifle regiment. The authorized number of vehicles in a rifle division rose from 419 in 1944 to 1,488 in 1948. Such an organization was probably too unwieldy for effective maneuver, given the degree of training and experience of junior officers and peacetime conscripts. Further complicating matters, in mid-1950 Stalin reestablished military councils at every level of command, giving political officers the command authority they had lost in 1942.[72]

When Georgi Konstantinovich Zhukov returned to power after Stalin's demise, he introduced a number of changes that reflected the Soviet version of America's "Pentomic" concerns. Accepting strategic surprise and nuclear warfare as likely possibilities, Zhukov moved to simplify the Soviet force structure while at the same time emphasizing armored protection against the effects of atomic weapons. He was ably supported in this by Vasily Sokolovsky, who as chief of the general staff from 1952 to 1960 provided the doctrinal basis for the new force structure. The unwieldy mechanized divisions and armies disappeared, as did the remaining dismounted infantry and horse cavalry units in the Soviet force structure. In their place, the basic building blocks became smaller tank and motorized rifle divisions (MRDs), as well as a limited number of airborne rifle divisions. A typical combined-arms army was built around two or three MRDs and one tank division; a tank army might contain four tank divisions and in some cases a heavy tank regiment to provide an independent mobile group. The massive towed artillery so common to Soviet offensives during World War II declined in Soviet planning, due largely to a sense that such guns would provide lucrative targets for NATO atomic weapons. Instead, Soviet theoreticians envisioned nimble mechanized formations exploiting the effects of their own nuclear attacks. Missile-equipped artillery and air defense units gradually replaced many of the conventional artillery tubes. Overall, the Soviet Army and Navy declined from 3.62 to 2.14 million men between 1955 and 1958, making more personnel available for the ever-growing air defense and strategic air arms. By 1958, the tank divisions had lost the motorized rifle battalions previously included in their tank regiments. As a result, a tank army of four divisions had only twelve infantry battalions, all mounted in armored personnel carriers.[73]

Zhukov had unprecedented political influence because of his wartime record and because Stalin's successors initially needed him to ensure their own control. In October 1957, however, he fell from power again after prolonged disagreements with Khrushchev. One aspect of this conflict was Khrushchev's desire to further reduce the size of the army in favor of newer weapons systems; another issue was Zhukov's efforts to limit the influence of political officers within the armed forces, something that Khrushchev, a devoted Party man and former political officer, could not tolerate. To some extent, this drama was also a continuation of wartime relationships, in which

Zhukov and Alexander Vasilevsky represented the central Stavka (and therefore to some extent Stalin himself), while Khrushchev, as a senior political officer, had been associated with the field commanders at Stalingrad.[74] One of this latter group, Marshal Rodion Y. Malinovsky, replaced Zhukov as defense minister for the next decade (1957–1967). Malinovsky reduced the army to 140 divisions but attempted to maintain a balance between traditional, large army advocates and Khrushchev's vision of a much smaller conventional force that exploited the effects of nuclear fires. Malinovsky continued to assert the validity of conventional warfare and to insist that Communist Party control must not interfere with the operational effectiveness of the units. This disagreement contributed to Khrushchev's own eventual downfall.[75]

Meanwhile, the perceived threat that Zhukov posed to Communist Party control led to a reemphasis on political education in the army. Political officers criticized commanders in a manner that undermined discipline, so that in November 1958, Malinovsky issued a pointed warning to the political officers.[76]

The Soviet Navy labored under even greater constraints than the army. Virtually destroyed during the Russo-Japanese War, the Russian and later Soviet Navy had never gone beyond the role of "helper" for the Red Army, providing riverine and coastal patrols, including limited amphibious operations, to support the land forces. Most Soviet surface vessels were relatively small and limited in capability. The navy's principal striking power was focused on submarines, while advocates of Alfred Thayer Mahan's theory of sea power were discouraged and in some instances purged during the 1920s and 1930s.[77]

After 1945, the Soviet Union's new status as a world power coupled with the perceived need to counter American naval power led Moscow to contemplate a compromise in naval affairs, adding a modest fleet to the traditional coastal defensive forces. In 1950, Stalin approved a major building program that would include four large aircraft carriers.[78]

Once the dictator died, however, this program was doomed, in large measure because Khrushchev was unwilling to dedicate resources to a construction program at a time when it seemed much cheaper to rely on nuclear weapons and thereby redirect Soviet industry toward consumer goods.

On October 29, 1955, the battleship *Krasnodar*, an ex-Italian vessel, exploded at anchor near Sebastopol, killing 599 sailors. Khrushchev used this disaster to purge N. G. Kuznetsov, head of the Soviet navy, and other ocean-going navy or blue-water advocates.[79] Khrushchev insisted that only submarines, destroyers, and torpedo boats were relevant in the nuclear age.

The great advocate of Soviet sea power, Admiral Sergei G. Gorshkov, had to contend with this issue when he became military head of the navy in February 1956. Gorshkov kept a cruiser construction program alive and argued strenuously for equality with the army but could not stop repeated manpower and budget cuts. In 1957 alone, the Soviet Navy had to reduce its strength from 600,000 to 500,000, mothballing 375 warships. Naval aviation also suffered cuts, and a number of uncompleted ships went to the scrap heap. Gorshkov did not receive the resources to build a navy until the 1962 Cuban Missile Crisis exposed Soviet weakness at sea.[80]

SATELLITE UPRISINGS

While senior Soviet and satellite leaders jockeyed for power, their populations continued to suffer from the ill effects of World War II and from the distortions of centrally directed, planned economies. Worse still, in the aftermath of Stalin's death, his successors made well-intentioned attempts to mitigate the worst problems of socialism, and these attempts encouraged frustrated workers to demand more change. Inevitably, this provoked sometimes violent opposition to the governments in power. Thus, the Soviet and satellite armies configured for mechanized war against the West found themselves increasingly involved in repressing "counterrevolutionary" rebellions in the streets of Eastern Europe.

The first major unrest occurred in the great Skoda arms factory at Plzen, Czechoslovakia, on June 1, 1953. The immediate issue was a forced currency exchange that would leave the workers with worthless money, but the crowds soon demanded free elections. Only Czech tanks halted the disturbance.[81] Sixteen days later in East Germany, a protest against unreasonable production quotas and food rationing soon spread. Here, the usual eastern bloc problems of industrial workers were complicated by a failure of food production, due in large measure to the flight of East German farmers to the western zones.[82] While the West saw primarily the violence in East Berlin, in fact the disorders spread to four hundred towns and cities in East Germany. The poorly armed police were unable to curb these demonstrations, suffering at least seventy-nine policemen injured and two missing in Berlin alone.[83]

While surprised, the new collective leadership in the Kremlin responded strongly, using Group of Soviet Forces, Germany, armor to help the police repress the demonstrations with considerable violence. The three divisions of Second Mechanized Army moved into East Berlin late on the 17th, putting down disorders with a heavy hand. Three other field armies sent tank and mechanized regiments to occupy other major cities, resulting in 209 civilians killed or wounded and another 3,351 arrested in thirty-six hours. The operation carried some risk of widening into a bigger conflict, of course, especially because the West Berlin population was incensed by the repression and demonstrated vociferously. On the morning of June 18, 1953, East German "People's Police" at the Brandenburg Gate claimed that they had received fire from the west; they shot back, killing a West Berlin policeman.[84]

Unfortunately for future events, the Soviet leadership drew several faulty lessons from the 1953 demonstrations. Politically, only Secret Police Chief Lavrentii Beria recognized the depth of Central European anger at the Soviets; other civil and military leaders were convinced (and remained so even forty years later) that the entire incident was a plot of the Western intelligence services. In reality, although Eisenhower had won election in part because of his call to "roll back" the communist empire, the United States was unprepared to risk another confrontation, and so the Soviet leaders were able to put the lie to American radio broadcasts urging Eastern Europeans to rebel.

Militarily, the incidents appeared to be easily suppressed by Soviet armor; the key challenge was to get the tanks to urban areas as quickly as possible. In fact, the spontaneous worker protests had never contemplated organized resistance. Moreover, the reduction in the proportion of infantry in Soviet units during the 1950s meant that their armor would be unprotected if they ever encountered an urban enemy determined to fight at close quarters.

Three years later, therefore, the opposition to the Soviet Union and the socialist system was much more difficult to repress, particularly because Stalin's successors had unintentionally encouraged reformers by cautiously criticizing the previous regime.

This time, the trouble began in Poznan, the great industrial city of western Poland. On June 28, 1956, the workers went on strike for better wages, demanding "Bread and Freedom." The rally turned violent, freeing political prisoners from the city jail and calling for an end to dictatorship and Soviet occupation. Some Polish officers tried to avoid bloodshed, and there were instances of soldiers refusing to shoot at the demonstrators. Ultimately, however, the paramilitary police of the Internal Security Corps (KBW) and units of the Polish Army opened fire, killing fifty-three and wounding more than two hundred. Thereafter, elements of the KBW, disgusted by the repression, supported ongoing reform movements within the Polish government. Khrushchev condemned Poznan as foreign provocation rather than recognizing the fundamental unrest in the satellites.[85]

The Soviet leader was particularly concerned by the prospect of the anti-Soviet Wladyslaw Gomulka, imprisoned without trial in 1948 but recently rehabilitated, coming to power in Warsaw. In an attempt to forestall this, in October 1956 Khrushchev invited himself to a meeting of the politburo of the Polish United Workers' Party (PZPR). Gomulka's supporters preempted this by appointing him as first secretary of the PZPR. The next day, Khrushchev, Molotov, and a large political and military delegation, including Warsaw Pact commander Marshal Konev, arrived at the Warsaw airport in an attempt to intimidate the Polish Communists into obedience. Tense discussions ensued. Gomulka assured the Soviets that Poland would remain within the Warsaw Pact but demanded withdrawal of most of the Soviet "advisors," including Rokossovsky, who had taken the Polish armed forces outside the control of the PZPR. While the discussions were going on, Gomulka learned that the Northern Group of Soviet Forces, the headquarters of Soviet troops in Poland, was moving combat troops toward the capital in an obvious move to press for conformity. As Polish defense minister, Rokossovsky controlled the levers of power, preventing the Polish Army from responding. To his chagrin, however, the KBW security troops began to take up blocking positions around Warsaw, raising the possibility of fighting between Soviets and Poles. Frustrated, Khrushchev ordered the Soviet troops back to their barracks, and the Soviet delegation returned to Moscow. Over the next several weeks, Gomulka repeatedly assured the Kremlin of his loyalty in external affairs but eventually forced Rokossovsky out of his Polish government positions. The Polish Army returned to the control of its own government while remaining part of the Warsaw Pact.[86]

The Hungarian Uprising, 1956

The Khrushchev administration had reluctantly accepted this compromise because it faced an even graver threat in Hungary. Here, the Soviets were to some extent responsible for their own problems. In the immediate aftermath of Stalin's death, Georgi Malenkov and Lavrenti Beria had sought to appease unrest by forcing the high-handed Stalinist leader Matyas Rakosi out of office. His successor, Prime Minister Imre Nagy, was a very moderate reformer, but his reputation was enhanced in 1955 when Khrushchev, seeking to stop liberalization, dismissed Nagy in favor of Rakosi. By the summer of 1956, the Poznan riots had encouraged unrest among Hungarian students and intellectuals, to the point where a visiting Soviet troubleshooter, Anastas Mikoyan, again forced Rakosi out of office in favor of Erno Gero, who did nothing to address public discontent.[87]

Meanwhile, the Soviet headquarters in west-central Hungary—the so-called Special Corps in Szekesfehervar—prepared for possible unrest. A group of senior officers from Moscow arrived in mid-July and helped the corps commander, Lieutenant General Piotr N. Lashchenko, draw up the Volna (Wave) contingency plan that would reinforce the Special Corps to provide a massive Soviet force in the event of disorders.

Gomulka's apparent success in Poland produced such disorders on October 23, 1956. Students and eventually workers formed large crowds. While there is some question as to whether the initial demonstrations were peaceful or not, they ceased to be so that evening, when the Hungarian State Security Police (Allamvedelmi Hatosag or AVH) opened fire on crowds seeking to enter the state radio station and party newspapers. An Hungarian Army battalion sent to the radio station went over to the demonstrators' side. A nervous Gero desired Soviet assistance but couldn't get his government to agree on a formal request. Meanwhile, on the afternoon of the 23rd both the Soviet ambassador, future leader Yuri Andropov, and the senior Soviet military advisor, M. F. Tikhanov, asked Moscow to intervene militarily. Even before the Presidium in Moscow approved the action, the 2nd Guards Mechanized Division in Hungary and the 128th Guards Rifle Division in the Soviet Carpathian Military District received alert orders.[88]

Unfortunately for the Soviets, the 1953 experience had conditioned them to believe that unsupported tanks could easily disperse demonstrations. The Soviet Army had no specific training in civil disorders, and its armor-heavy configuration meant that each regiment might have as few as six hundred infantrymen to protect the armor or control the crowds. Moreover, the Soviets found that they had to act almost alone in Budapest; while only a few units of the Hungarian Army actively supported the rebels, the army as a whole had poor morale and was undergoing a major reorganization.

The first Soviet unit, the 2nd Guards Mechanized, reached Budapest at dawn on October 24 and quickly occupied various key points including the radio station, Parliament, and the Defense Ministry. Only the 87th Tank/Assault Gun Regiment failed in its mission of securing a railroad station and the nearby Corvin Cinema; the latter became a center of rebel resistance throughout the crisis. On that first day, an estimated twenty-five protestors died and two hundred were wounded. On the 25th, the situation spun out of control when Ivan A. Suslov, the chairman of the Soviet KGB, ordered a company of the Soviet 6th Mechanized Regiment, 2nd Division, to "clear the square" of protestors outside the Hungarian parliament. The soldiers began with warning shots but quickly escalated to machine-gun and even tank main gunfire, killing sixty-one people. By the end of the day, the 33rd Guards Mechanized Division and the leading regiment of the 128th Guards Rifle Division had reached Budapest, but the Soviets began to suffer significant casualties. Without accurate intelligence or active Hungarian military support, the invaders were unable to establish control of the city. The bewildered Soviet soldiers wrongly believed that they were fighting Hungarian fascists, leading to atrocities on both sides. A few Hungarian units, including the 8th Mechanized Regiment, some anti-aircraft batteries, and three heavy construction battalions, defected over the next few days, providing the rebels with more military expertise and weapons than the Soviet planners had anticipated. In the narrow streets of the capital, Soviet tanks, unsupported by infantry, fell prey to the ironically named Molotov cocktails. The thin-skinned, open-topped BTR-152 personnel carriers were even more vulnerable. Moreover, the haste with which operations were conducted contributed to Soviet vulnerability. Early on the morning of October 28th, for example, six Soviet tanks and 360 Hungarian infantrymen assembled for an attack, but there was no communication between the two groups. When the Special Corps headquarters nonetheless insisted on an attack, the tanks went off unescorted. As a result, three T-34 tanks were burned, and a T-54 was severely damaged.[89]

The divided and uncertain role of the Hungarian armed forces caused problems outside of Budapest as well. In the countryside, 6,500 Hungarian soldiers arrested various demonstrators on the 24th, although reformers in the Defense Ministry later ordered these people released, causing further confusion. That afternoon, Hungarian troops fired warning shots over the heads of a crowd at Szekesfehervar. Misunderstanding the nature of this firing, Soviet soldiers then fired into the crowd, killing seven.[90]

Despite this bloodshed, both the Hungarian and the Soviet leadership were divided within themselves. On October 25, the politburo of the Hungarian Workers Party met and, bowing to popular pressure, chose Nagy as premier. In Moscow, Stalin's successors were using the crisis as a bargaining tool. Khrushchev was willing to have Nagy remain within the government (if not actually as premier) but sought assurances of Hungarian loyalty to the Soviet bloc. On October 30, the Soviet leaders temporarily agreed on a partial troop withdrawal and negotiations with the Nagy government.

Yet the pressure on both leaderships was immense. Signs of unrest in Rumania and Czechoslovakia as well as the emerging Suez crisis (see chapter 12) encouraged Moscow to seek a quick end to the situation. Even Soviet students began to speak out. Imry Nagy, who began the crisis as a loyal if reforming Communist, found himself pushed day by day to more extreme measures to satisfy the rebels. On October 30, the freedom fighters formed a national guard, which Nagy recognized, and a disgraced major general, Bela Kiraly, became president of a defense committee and de facto minister of defense. Kiraly used the staff of the Hungarian Fourth Army headquarters to organize a Public Safety Command and restore some order in rebel-held portions of the city. On October 31, the U.S.-financed Radio Free Europe called on the freedom fighters to reject communist rule.[91]

While the politicians negotiated, the Soviet armed forces continued to pour into Hungary. As Warsaw Pact commander, Marshal Konev attached a number of regiments to the Special Corps. General Mikhail Malinin, first deputy chief of the Soviet General Staff, assumed command of the intervention forces, which soon totaled seven mechanized divisions, two motorized rifle divisions, one tank division, and two understrength airborne divisions. Two Soviet fighter divisions (159 aircraft) were available for close air support, while two bomber divisions were also on alert, despite the fact that their weapons were far too indiscriminate for use in urban warfare.[92]

By October 31, Nagy was demanding the withdrawal of all Soviet troops from Hungary and stating his intention to withdraw from the one-year-old Warsaw Pact. KGB Chief Suslov and Soviet Deputy Premier Mikoyan agreed to these demands, in return for which the Hungarian leadership promised not to permit their country to be used as an anti-Soviet base. However, the Presidium in Moscow could not permit such an extreme solution and decided on November 2nd that renewed military force was necessary.

So Zhukov and Konev launched their final offensive, Operation Whirlwind. Konev arrived in the country to assume personal control of the operation. This time, the Soviets made careful preparations before attacking, including positioning elements of two elite airborne divisions. Their reconnaissance of Budapest was so obvious that General Kiraly warned the Hungarian government of an impending attack. Nagy repeated his previous instructions not to resist, but Kiraly and most of the freedom fighters rejected his orders. On the evening of November 3rd, the KGB arrested several senior Hungarian officers who thought they were negotiating for a Soviet troop withdrawal— in the process, the Soviets seized a map of Hungarian defenses.[93]

In the best Soviet tactical style, the main attack was preceded by small advance detachments assigned to seize key points and dismember the Hungarian defenses. The most important such attack came at 4:30 A.M. on November 4, when a dozen tanks and 165 men of the 3rd Battalion, 108th Airborne Regiment, led by Major L. A. Donchenko and accompanied by KGB officers, seized the Hungarian Defense Ministry without firing a shot. This raid netted thirteen generals and decapitated the already chaotic Hungarian defense structure. Similar detachments struck elsewhere, while 170 artillery tubes and mortars fired a wartime preparatory attack against the Hungarian construction engineers and freedom fighters in the Corvin Cinema.[94] Assault detachments used flamethrowers, satchel charges, and the other arcane instruments of urban warfare. While the 2nd and 33rd Mechanized Divisions, reinforced with more armor, reoccupied key points in the capital, other Soviet troops disarmed large portions of the Hungarian Army outside the capital.

Despite overwhelming manpower and careful planning, Operation Whirlwind did not succeed without serious losses and missteps. On November 5, freedom fighters ambushed and wiped out a reconnaissance company of the 128th Rifle Division. The same day, an anti-aircraft battery of the 128th shot up and looted the Egyptian delegation offices. Two days later, despite Soviet attempts to control the Hungarian anti-aircraft batteries, the latter shot down an IL-28 bomber over Budapest, killing three crew members. Although the fighting in Budapest attracted world attention, resistance in eastern Hungary was equally fierce; between November 4 and 8, the Eighth Mechanized Army suffered thirty-three killed in action, forty-nine wounded, and six missing. Although the Soviets officially ended operations on November 12, sporadic resistance continued for at least five more days.[95]

The true scale of the Hungarian fighting may never be known. Between October 23 and December 1, 1956, Hungarian hospitals treated 12,791 wounded, including 1,458 outside Budapest. An estimated 2,000 Hungarian civilians died, plus several hundred Hungarian troops and police fighting on both sides. After the fighting ended, Nagy and 350 other leaders were executed, with perhaps 10,000 imprisoned and 200,000 others, many of them highly educated, fleeing to the West. As for the Soviets, at least 670 invaders were killed, 1,500 were wounded, and 67 became missing in action. On December 18, the Soviet Presidium indirectly acknowledged the ferocity of resistance by awarding its highest combat decoration, Hero of the Soviet Union, to twenty-six soldiers—fourteen of them posthumously.[96]

Apart from the suffering of the Hungarian people, the Soviet Union paid a considerable political price for its victory, including widespread discontent within its bloc and a United Nations General Assembly motion calling for its withdrawal. Khrushchev and his colleagues undoubtedly felt that they had no choice once Nagy, unlike Gomulka, tried to secede from the Warsaw Pact. Nonetheless, the two weeks of Hungarian resistance left a pall over Europe and provided momentum for Western containment efforts throughout the world.

9

THE PHILIPPINES
AND TAIWAN

During the 1950s the Cold War became intertwined with the rapid collapse of Europe's overseas empires. The Marxist governments in Moscow and Beijing provided both ideological encouragement and material aid to various anticolonial movements. For that reason, the United States and its allies often dismissed the true economic and political concerns of the so-called Third World, blaming such movements on communist agitators.

The indecisive conflict in Korea, coupled with the equally frustrating and ultimately failed defense of French Indochina (see chapter 10), seemed to demand greater American efforts in the Pacific region. Right-wing politicians and, in some instances, flag officers pushed the Truman and Eisenhower administrations to defend remaining "free" lands and perhaps even "roll back" the perceived advance of Chinese-backed communism. Such figures bristled at State Department officials who tried diplomatic compromises to separate China from the Soviet Union. Instead, the domestic right wing preferred to push for action and possibly limited nuclear war in Asia. Even Eisenhower's secretary of state, John Foster Dulles, advocated such confrontations.[1]

Although the two presidents successfully resisted pressures for renewed war in Asia, they did try to form a series of agreements for regional containment. Mutual defense treaties with Japan (1952), South Korea (1953), and the nationalist Republic of China (1954) committed the United States as firmly as the North Atlantic Treaty

243

had done in Europe, without gaining equal support from local allies. In September 1954, after the French defeat in Indochina, Dulles organized the Southeast Asia Collective Defense Treaty with representatives of Australia, France, Great Britain, New Zealand, Pakistan, the Philippines, and Thailand. The resulting defensive organization, known as the Southeast Asia Treaty Organization (SEATO), never developed the capabilities of NATO but nonetheless provided a framework for regional cooperation, including eventual allied support in Vietnam.

Beyond these treaties, Washington gave extensive military aid to repress Chinese-backed insurrections in French Indochina and the Philippines, while repeatedly confronting Beijing over the continued independence of the Nationalist Chinese government in Taiwan.

A Tradition of Insurgency

Since the arrival of the Spanish colonizers in the sixteenth century, the Philippine Islands have rarely been without rebellion or insurgency of some type. The anti-Spanish rebels of the mid-1890s soon became the anti-American insurgents of 1900, and the U.S. Army defeated them only with considerable effort and much violence.[2] Although President Theodore Roosevelt declared victory in 1902, intermittent fighting occurred for years thereafter. Indeed, the predominantly Muslim southern islands continued to resist the U.S. presence almost indefinitely, just as they had opposed Spanish control. Moreover, the economic disparity between landowners and peasants gave rise to periodic rebellions in other parts of the archipelago, such as that of 1934 in the center of Luzon, the largest island.

Like other colonies, the Philippines became the target for Communist International agitation between the world wars. Nationalism and economic unrest provided fertile ground despite the announced U.S. policy of eventually granting independence. The National Peasants Union formed in 1922 and five years later associated itself with the COMINTERN. The Communist Party of the Philippines, founded in 1928–1930, went underground after a 1931 police raid and was banned in 1934. In 1938, Commonwealth president Manuel L. Quezon pardoned Crisanto Evangelista and other communist leaders on the promise of good behavior; these leaders soon merged with the local socialist party.[3] This was a common phenomenon of the late 1930s, when the leftist parties in many countries formed a united front, ostensibly against fascism. Frequently, however, the well-disciplined Communists followed the Moscow party line to seek control of the resulting mergers.[4]

With the Japanese conquest of 1942, Americans and Filipinos became allies in yet another insurgency against the new occupier. This alliance was not always cordial, however. In particular, the communist-led Hukbong Bayan Laban Sa Hapon (People's Anti-Japanese Army, abbreviated as Hukbalahap or the "Huks") in central and southern Luzon refused to subordinate itself to American command and sometimes detained members of rival American-led resistance groups.[5] Although the Japanese caught and executed Evangelista in 1942, other Huk leaders developed a potent guerrilla force. Luis Taruc, a socialist leader of peasant origins who had joined the Communists as part of the 1938 united front, emerged as the Huk field commander. By 1943, the Huks had reached a peak strength of perhaps 10,000 people. However, their military activities provoked both Japanese reprisals against civilians and increased Japanese sweeps of the countryside, disrupting Huk organization. The insurgent leaders apparently decided to focus on building popular support, minimizing attacks on the Japanese until the U.S. invasion of Luzon in January 1945. U.S.-backed guerrillas followed a similar policy of wait and see, but after the fact the Huks claimed to have borne the brunt of the fighting. To complicate matters, groups of bandits sometimes posed as guerillas.[6]

UPRISING

The war derailed the Philippine economy, created enormous destruction, and brought a large influx of Japanese and American small arms, which made a subsequent insurrection possible. Just as in Greece, the returning exile government and American forces wanted little to do with left-wing guerrilla bands. The Huks had indeed aided the American war effort, including the famous raid to rescue American prisoners at Los Banos. Despite this, U.S. Army intelligence officers, heavily influenced by conservative Filipino landlords and politicians, portrayed the Huks as communist thugs who had collaborated with the Japanese. General Douglas MacArthur, a staunch opponent of communism, ordered that the Huks be disarmed, while many veterans of the U.S-led insurgents became Philippine policemen with veterans' benefits.[7] The United States also encouraged landowners to employ private security forces.

MAP 11. Central Luzon

By 1946 the newly independent Philippine government had to focus on recovery and could scarcely spare attention to deal with either peasant economic issues or potential insurgents. In the elections of that year, six members of the left-wing Democratic Alliance, including Luis Taruc, earned seats in the Philippine Congress. President Manuel Roxas engineered the exclusion of these representatives, claiming that the former Huks had employed terror to coerce the voting. Roxas thereby gained the gratitude of conservatives as well as ensuring that his own party had an ironclad majority in the lower house.[8] By that time, the U.S. Army's Counter Intelligence Corps and the Philippine Military Police (later redesignated Philippine Constabulary) had chased most of the surviving Huks into the hills of Luzon, where they reconstituted their wartime command structure.[9]

By themselves, the true Filipino Communists were too few to mount a serious threat to public order. However, before, during, and after the Japanese occupation they had a natural constituency in the central plains of Luzon, north of Manila, and centered on the sanctuary provided by 3,400-foot-tall Mount Arayat. Of the sixteen million inhabitants of the Philippines, 1.5 million lived in this region, with most of them being rice and sugar sharecroppers. This area was particularly suited to growing cash crops, and U.S.-backed surveying and land registry had ignored peasant traditions of common ownership. During the interwar period, rapid population growth increased the misery of these peasants. Of equal significance was the fact that in place of the traditional paternalism of the Filipino landlords, a new generation of landowners operated their holdings on a strictly business proposition, charging their tenants as much as 50 percent interest to borrow rice between harvests. Postwar American efforts to restore the Philippine economy to 1941 standards did nothing to address the issues of the hard-pressed sharecroppers.[10]

The first government response to the new insurgency played into the hands of communist propaganda. As in Greece, the Philippine armed forces were rebuilding themselves for external defense and had no interest in fighting the insurgents. Instead, the initial counterinsurgency effort involved only 3,000 Philippine Constabulary troops with limited arms and training. While some of the constabulary were combat veterans, others were motivated by personal gain, including exploiting the people they were supposed to protect. Such problems in the constabulary only mirrored corruption in the government as a whole, making the general population reluctant to trust government forces.

In 1948, hardliner president Roxas died unexpectedly. His successor, Elpidio Quirino, offered an amnesty to the Huks and entered into negotiations with Luis Taruc. Both sides violated the spirit of this de facto cease-fire. Still, the amnesty period allowed the insurgents to expand and consolidate control over much of rural Luzon, reaching an estimated total of 15,000 armed men with 100,000 active supporters. Eventually, the Communists broke off negotiations and renamed the movement Hukbang Mapagpalaya sa Bayan (People's Army of Liberation), although the term "Huk" remained in general use.[11]

The outnumbered constabulary continued to fight a generally ineffectual campaign against the insurgents, who had enough local support to thwart intelligence efforts. The 5th Battalion Combat Team (BCT) of the Philippine Army received orders to support the constabulary but accomplished little. Only a few government elements, including Colonel Napoleon Valeriano's "Force X" from the 16th Constabulary Company, had tactical successes. By posing as Huks, Valeriano's men infiltrated the enemy and spread mistrust.[12] His special units became known as "nenita" or "skull squadrons" for their ruthlessness. Overall, however, the insurgents continued to rule the countryside. In many towns, local government officials fled to the capital, returning to their posts only in daylight and under armed escort. Whenever government troops attempted to move against the Huks, local sympathizers used runners, lights, and drums to warn the insurgents, eliminating any chance of surprise. Eventually, the Huks began to form battalions or "Field Commands" of up to seven hundred men, a precursor to a general uprising.[13]

Although there had been some Chinese influence on the Philippine Communists before and during World War II, there was no real indication that the Huks had foreign support or direction. For the United States, therefore, the issue was not ideological opposition to the Communists so much as control of a strategic base in the volatile Pacific rim. (U.S. air and naval bases were essential to regional defense until their final evacuation in 1992.) Yet, as so often during the Cold War, Washington appeared to be playing a losing hand, backing a government in which corruption and ineffectiveness seemed to doom the counterinsurgency effort. President Quirino's party openly manipulated the 1949 elections to its own ends, making the Huks seem the only avenue for reform. Moreover, in the years immediately after World War II, few Americans understood the unique nature of politicized revolutionary warfare. As a consequence, the Joint U.S. Military Assistance Group (JUSMAG) for the Philippines was ill equipped to advise its local counterparts in the Philippine government.[14]

Then, on August 28, 1949, the Huks blundered by ambushing and murdering the popular wife and daughter of former President Quezon. Under public pressure, Quirino belatedly acted to increase counterinsurgent forces, merging the constabulary with the Philippine Armed Forces. In addition to a unified logistical command, the reorganization fielded ten infantry BCTs that had some success in 1949 but were still untrained in civic action and counterinsurgency. Underpaid troops continued to extort money from the peasantry, while charges of excessive force and massacre were widespread, especially after the Philippine Air Force began to attack ground targets with P-51 and AT-6 aircraft.[15]

Magsaysay and Lansdale

The opposition had its own problems. In addition to insufficient funds, weapons, and rebels, there were significant rifts between the urban political wing, the Partido Komunista ng Pilipinas (PKP), and the peasant-based rebel army.[16] Still, given the limited size of the Philippine Armed Forces and the continued corruption at all levels of the government, the long-term outcome of this conflict would probably have been an insurgent victory. Two men—a Filipino leader and his American advisor—are usually credited with reversing this trend.

Ramón Magsaysay (1907–1957) remains a larger-than-life, charismatic figure to this day. During World War II, he rose to the rank of major in the U.S.-backed guerillas, and MacArthur recognized his ability by making him military governor of Zambales, a province on Luzon. Elected to the Philippine Congress after the war, Magsaysay was a tireless advocate for both veterans' rights and military action against the Huks. As chairman of the House Committee on National Defense, in April 1950 he traveled to Washington, where he convinced the Truman administration and the U.S. Congress to allocate $10 million in scarce military aid. At the suggestion of the JUSMAG commander, Major General Leland Hobbs, President Quirino named Magsaysay secretary of defense effective September 1, 1950. Magsaysay accepted the position on condition that he would have a free hand to deal with both the armed forces and the insurgency.[17]

While Magsaysay is generally recognized as a national hero, his American advisor, then-Lieutenant Colonel Edward Lansdale (1908–1987), has a more sinister image, perhaps because of his reputation as a kingmaker in both the Philippines and South Vietnam. Growing up between the world wars, Lansdale had been an advertising man and sometime reserve officer in San Francisco. He spent much of the war working as a civilian analyst for both the army and the Office of Strategic Services before finally going overseas in October 1945 as a major, Deputy G2 for the U.S. Army Philippines-Ryukus Command. Lansdale quickly made himself an expert on the Philippines, fearlessly traveling alone and talking with peasants and even Huks in an effort to understand local conditions. His advertising background made him unusually sensitive to issues of psychology and propaganda in dealing with the insurgency. By 1949, he had transferred to the newly created U.S. Air Force, where he taught in an intelligence school in Denver. In November of that year, Lansdale transferred again to the Office of Policy Coordination (OPC), the covert operations group directed by a panel of Defense and State Department officials. As such, the OPC was not technically controlled by the Central Intelligence Agency, although Lansdale later operated in support of CIA goals. In 1949–1950, he put his understanding of advertising and public opinion to work on various psychological warfare projects. Lansdale first met Magsaysay during the latter's 1950 visit to Washington, creating such a favorable impression that the new Filipino defense head asked for him as an intelligence advisor. Lansdale arrived back in the Philippines the same month that Secretary Magsaysay took office.[18]

The exact extent of Lansdale's influence in Filipino policy is difficult to determine. Indeed, as his biographer Cecil Currey has noted, Lansdale was so sensitive about local dignity that he was careful to ensure that new policies always appeared to emanate from Filipino decisions rather than American recommendations. In 1953, when Lansdale's role became an issue in Philippine politics, he left the islands temporarily, traveling to Vietnam as part of a U.S. inspection team. There is little doubt, however, that the low-key American colonel had extensive influence with the flamboyant Philippine defense secretary, to the point where Magsaysay shared a room with Lansdale in the American compound when the Huks threatened to assassinate the Filipino leader.[19] The result was a uniquely effective partnership. Although Lansdale often irritated the conventional American advisors in the area, Ambassador Myron Cowen acknowledged the USAF officer's contribution in a 1951 cable to the secretary of state:

> Colonel Lansdale has been the right hand of the Secretary of National Defense Magsaysay and he has in a large measure been responsible for Magsaysay's success in breaking the backbone of the Huk military forces. . . . It is inconceivable to me that the Philippine situation would be as favorable as it is without Colonel Lansdale's superb performance. He has lived day and night with Magsaysay at very real risk to himself. He has guided and advised him. He has provided a driving power and when necessary a restraining one and furthermore he has been a better source of intelligence than all the rest of our intelligence efforts put together.[20]

TURNAROUND

The remarkable partnership between the Filipino politician and the American advisor had a number of different aspects. Militarily, Magsaysay improved the constabulary's quality and reduced its poor image by completely integrating it into the regular armed forces. He weeded out at least some poor leaders and soldiers with highly publicized courts-martial for corruption and summary dishonorable discharges for incompetence. He more than tripled the rations allowance (from thirty centavos to one peso per day) so that the troops would have no reason to extort food from the peasants, and in fact could afford to have a beer with the locals. To ensure a more accurate record of enemy casualties, Magsaysay issued cameras to every unit to be used in verifying the enemy dead, although in some instances where the camera failed, troops cut off ears to prove their claims. Some enterprising intelligence officers used the cameras for another purpose. On occasion, they would leak advance notice of a raid on a barrio, giving Huk sympathizers time to leave town. On the appointed day, the government soldiers would photograph the (presumably loyal or neutral) people who remained in the barrio; on subsequent, unannounced raids, anyone who had NOT been photographed previously was immediately interrogated as a possible insurgent.[21] This was only one of many methods evolved, by trial and error, to build up a complete order of battle of the enemy. Eventually, Filipino intelligence officers knew so much about their opponents that aircraft-mounted loudspeakers could address the Huks by name, prompting the enemy to suspect that there were traitors in their midst.

In addition, Magsaysay recruited up to 10,000 villagers as volunteers to defend their own barrios, freeing the small number of army troops from guard duty so the BCTs could relentlessly pursue the insurgents.[22] A typical BCT consisted of three small rifle companies, a heavy-weapons company, a reconnaissance company, and on occasion a 105mm artillery battery. Although equipped and organized on U.S. tactical lines, the BCTs increasingly conducted squad and platoon commando operations. Such a patrol might consist of one officer and fifteen to thirty men, with two Browning automatic rifles, a radio, and the ubiquitous camera. These patrols operated on a schedule and routes that intersected with other patrols at fixed intervals. Slowly during 1951 and 1952, such patrols began to beat the enemy at his own game. By April 1952, at least 35 percent of the Huks who had been active in 1950 had left the fight through death, capture, or surrender.[23]

At the same time, Magsaysay moved to separate the guerrillas from their peasant base by addressing the economic and political concerns of the Luzon farmers. The government undertook numerous reforms and improvements, many administered by the so-called Economic Development Corps but with obvious involvement by the Philippine Army. In Luzon, these efforts included health clinics in the barrios, agrarian courts for grievances, government-backed credit for farmers, new schools, bridges and irrigation projects.[24] More daringly, at Magsaysay's suggestion the republic offered free land, with government help to develop it, on the southern island of Mindanao. Initially, only about 950 families, of which perhaps 250 were surrendered Huks, moved to this new and difficult frontier. As the news of this project spread, getting a plot of land became the standard price that each guerrilla asked for when he surrendered. When Manila provided generators for electricity in the Mindanao tracts, irritated British officials complained that Malayan rebels had begun to ask for electricity when *they* surrendered (see chapter 11). Although the numbers involved in this experiment were relatively low, the very act of making this offer eliminated the principal appeal of the PKP. Moreover, the involvement of the Philippine Army in these improvements paid strong dividends as the rural populace came to regard the army as a positive and trustworthy element.[25] Aided by the U.S. Information Service, the Philippine armed forces assigned psychological teams who lived with the people, building schools and other projects.

The final step was an unusually honest election held in 1951, which further contributed to government legitimacy. Magsaysay refused to campaign during this election, enhancing his reputation for nonpartisan effectiveness. Instead, the secretary provided such effective security at the polls that he stymied Quirino's efforts to rig the results.[26] Lansdale brought in American experts, who showed the Filipinos techniques such as thumbprints to validate ballots. He also distributed forged, supposedly Huk propaganda, urging the rebels to boycott the elections.[27]

With his enormous popularity and control of the armed forces, the defense secretary could easily have taken power illegally. In 1953, however, he resigned after President Qurino denigrated his influence. The charismatic leader then ran for president on the Nationalist Party ticket, promising to eliminate corruption as an essential step in the process of repressing the insurrection. Magsaysay's landslide victory (2.9 million votes versus 1.3 million for the opposition) solidified his ability to prosecute the counterinsurgency.[28]

All these efforts, military and civilian, took far more money than the infant Philippine government could afford. Between 1950 and 1955, the United States provided $500 million in aid, of which $383 million went for economic assistance and $117 million for military aid.[29] This aid did not always arrive in a timely manner, especially because the conflicts in Korea and Indochina had a higher priority. Moreover, Ambassador Cowen and other officials in the Truman administration repeatedly objected to providing the Philippine Air Force with napalm, arguing that such a weapon would cause too many civilian casualties.[30] Eventually, Lansdale convinced his government to provide even this unwieldy weapon to help Magsaysay. U.S. aid allowed the Philippine Armed Forces to expand to a total of twenty-six battalion combat teams, of which one served in Korea.

The internal divisions within the PKP contributed markedly to the final defeat of its organization. The politburo and secretariat of the party became convinced that the proletarian revolution was at hand by 1950; in the words of Luis Taruc, "The secretariat's triumphant mood reached a state of delusion."[31] In the process, many leaders became lax about security, operating openly in Manila rather than hiding in the hills. In a series of raids during October 1950, Magsaysay captured most of the political leaders of the party, complete with their records. In a reprise of the problems of the Greek Communist Party, the PKP leadership was in such a rush to gain victory that it overruled and then virtually relieved its field commander, insisting on party loyalty over combat performance. Taruc repeatedly urged a return to guerrilla tactics and sought to continue cooperation with other leftist movements. By contrast, the politburo demanded immediate revolution and condemned all other political parties. PKP attempts to spread the revolution to other areas of the Philippines had little success because of the many local variations in ethnicity and economic issues.

Meanwhile, Magsaysay's forces launched a series of sweeps to keep the enemy off balance and isolated from the support of the barrios. A surprise attack in January 1951 captured two additional members of the PKP leadership and scattered the others; Taruc himself lost his weapon in the scramble to escape, an event that greatly embarrassed him. In April 1952, Taruc barely escaped another raid in which his third wife died.[32]

The End of the Huks

After several attempts at negotiations, Taruc surrendered on May 16, 1954. The government negotiator, future liberal martyr Benigno Aquino, Jr., had promised him amnesty, but instead the guerrilla leader was imprisoned on charges of executing collaborationists during World War II. By this time, scarcely 2,000 of the original 15,000 Huks remained in the field; with the decline in public support, they had to support themselves by banditry, which further damaged their credibility. Scattered insurgents continued to struggle even during the 1960s; renewed uprisings ensued periodically thereafter, but none approached the dangerous scope of 1950–1951.[33]

The Philippines was obviously a successful counterinsurgency, but observers disagreed as to the reasons for that success. Coming after the anticommunist success in Greece and the failure in Indochina, the Philippine episode seemed to offer a simple recipe for success: a charismatic, reforming local leader, with expert American advice and extensive foreign aid, seemingly could defeat a revolutionary insurgency in a matter of months.[34] In fact, of course, Magsaysay and Lansdale won because of a number of special circumstances, not least the fact that the Philippine archipelago was easily isolated so that the rebels had no foreign assistance or sanctuary. In addition, Magsaysay had provided at least the appearance of progress in addressing political and social concerns, something that other government leaders would be hard-pressed to achieve. Nor were these local concerns as complex and intractable as those of some other former colonies. Honest elections, government reforms, civil improvements, skillful propaganda, resettlement, and kind treatment of prisoners, supported by small-unit military operations based on Magsaysay's own guerrilla experience, contributed to a victory that would be difficult to replicate elsewhere.[35]

THE OFFSHORE ISLANDS

Although Ramón Magsaysay brought the Philippines at least temporarily to a state of representative government, the same could not be said of Chiang Kai-shek and his Nationalist Chinese government. As described in chapters 6 and 7, the combination of domestic American politics and the Chinese intervention in Korea forced the Truman administration to defend Chiang long after Mao had won the civil war in China.

From the start of the Korean conflict, Washington was committed to preserving the Kuomintang (KMT) government in exile on Taiwan, an island often referred to by its Japanese name, Formosa. The United States resumed arms sales to Chiang in 1951, with the proviso that such weapons be used only for defensive purposes.[36] The issue was whether America had any obligations to defend other KMT-held territory. When it withdrew from the mainland in 1949, Chiang's government retained a string of islands along the central and southern coast of China. In the spring of 1950, the Chinese People's Army seized a number of these outposts, notably the large southern island of Hainan, but other islands remained in KMT hands. Some of the remaining islands, such as Quemoy (Kinmen) were literally in the harbor mouth of Chinese ports. These small nationalist enclaves could serve both to interdict trade to nearby ports and to launch raids and guerillas against the mainland.[37]

In Dwight Eisenhower's first State of the Union address, he satisfied Republican demands that the United States "unleash Chiang

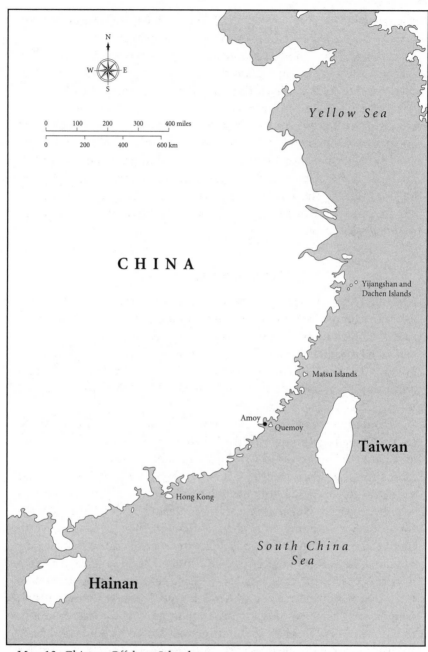

MAP 12. Chinese Offshore Islands

Kai-shek" by announcing that the Seventh Fleet would no longer "shield Communist China" from the KMT. This meant little at the time except for a slight increase in nationalist bombing and amphibious raids on the mainland. Senior officials at the Defense and State Departments repeatedly discussed the dangers of an aggressive Nationalist China and therefore decided to provide obsolescent F-84G fighters rather than the F-86s that had performed so well against MiG-15s in Korea. Eisenhower considered Chiang to be a man in eclipse but hoped that limited KMT raids would help pressure Beijing into moving closer to the United States and away from the USSR. In fact, however, these attacks only fueled Mao's irritation with the United States for its interference in Asian affairs. Once the Korean armistice was signed, Beijing was able to focus on the offshore islands, which became a flashpoint.[38] Moreover, the new administration instructed Admiral Arthur W. Radford, the outgoing Commander-in-Chief, Pacific (CINC-PAC), to plan for the defense of Formosa. This change in mission had consequences later when, as chairman of the JCS from 1953–1957, Radford adopted a very aggressive attitude about confronting Beijing on Chiang's behalf.

After the end of the Geneva Conference on Indochina in 1954 (see chapter 10), government propaganda in China began to demand recovery of the offshore islands. On September 3, 1954, the People's Liberation Army (PLA) started shelling Quemoy, arousing alarm in both Taipei and Washington. Six-thousand artillery rounds fell on the islands that first day, wounding among others two American military advisors. Two days later, the U.S. Navy had assembled three carriers, a cruiser, and several dozen destroyers to repel a supposed invasion of Quemoy, even though there was little evidence that the PLA was prepared to conduct such an attack. On September 9, Vice President Richard Nixon presided over an inconclusive meeting of the National Security Council on the matter. Admiral Radford, now chairman of the JCS, argued that the KMT could not hold Quemoy without American support and that such a loss would be detrimental to nationalist morale and U.S. prestige in the region. He believed that air and naval support alone could hold the islands, although General Ridgway, army chief of staff, questioned the entire proposal and suggested that a U.S. infantry division would be necessary to hold Quemoy.[39]

While the United States worried about Quemoy, the regime in Beijing focused on the northernmost KMT outposts, the Yijiangshan and Dachen (or Tachen) Islands, as its immediate objectives. By 1954, the nationalists had about 1,000 troops on the two tiny Yijiangshan islands, with about 20,000 (one division plus a number of raiding units) on the Dachens. Because these islands were 360 kilometers north of Taiwan, the nationalist Republic of China Air Force (ROCAF) found it difficult to provide air cover there.[40] On May 15, 1954, the PLA seized four small islands in the Dachens group, prompting the U.S. Military Advisory and Assistance Group (MAAG) in Taipei to recommend reinforcements for the remaining islands, but Chiang hesitated. This hesitation had the desired effect of causing the Eisenhower administration and especially Secretary Dulles to fear a loss of face as well as territory.[41]

In an unrelated incident in July, the USS *Philippine Sea* launched aircraft to search for survivors after the Red Chinese shot down a British DC-4 airliner near Hainan. Fighting in one of the last purely propeller air encounters, two Chinese La-7 fighters attacked two U.S. Navy A-1 Skyraiders and an F4U Corsair; the more experienced American pilots promptly shot down both Chinese aircraft, further ratcheting tensions.[42]

Beginning on November 1, 1954, the Communists launched a series of air attacks on the two northern island groups. However, because the fledgling People's Liberation Army Air Force (PLAAF) had little experience in air-to-ground attacks or over-water navigation, these missions initially had little effect. Even by its own optimistic accounting, in three months of intermittent attacks the PLAAF lost nineteen aircraft to anti-aircraft fire while delivering only 35.9 percent of its bombs on target. Still, these attacks did assist the PLA in an improvised landing of 4,000 troops that occupied Yijiangshan on January 18, 1955.[43] While insignificant in itself, this landing permitted the PLA to bring the main Dachens under artillery fire from Yijiangshan.

Diplomatically, the United States allowed Chiang Kai-shek to control the crisis. On December 2, Chiang obtained a formal mutual defense treaty with the United States, although the treaty did not specifically address the offshore islands. Once the PLA seized Yijiangshan, Eisenhower felt compelled to respond diplomatically. Within two weeks, both houses of Congress had passed, by near-unanimous votes, the so-called "Formosa Resolution," a remarkable grant of executive power that set an unfortunate precedent for future confrontations.

The resolution authorized Eisenhower to use American forces to defend not only Taiwan but also "such related positions and territories of that area now in friendly hands . . . as he judges to be required or appropriate." Thus, Eisenhower had staked his personal as well as national prestige on being able to defend Nationalist China.[44]

Having made a diplomatic statement, the Eisenhower administration was wise enough to recognize that the Dachen Islands were untenable. To obtain Chiang's agreement to this evacuation, on January 31 Eisenhower secretly promised to help defend the remaining islands, Quemoy and Matsu, thereby stretching the Formosa Resolution to the utmost. Beginning on February 5, the Seventh Fleet assisted the nationalists in moving more than 27,000 troops and civilians from the Dachen Islands to Taiwan. U.S. Navy demolition teams destroyed most of the island defenses before departing. During this evacuation process, the PLAAF shot down a U.S. Skyraider southeast of the Dachens, but the pilot was rescued, so that Eisenhower was able to downplay the incident.[45]

Even this did not end the diplomatic crisis. On the contrary, Secretary Dulles and other officials continued to make bellicose statements during March and April 1955, hinting that Washington suspected Beijing of preparing a direct attack on Formosa. Foster Dulles viewed the Cold War and especially East Asia in an intensely passionate, moralistic manner that envisioned no compromise.[46] At a March 10 meeting of the NSC, Dulles asserted that the government needed to begin preparing the public for U.S. involvement in hostilities, possibly including nuclear weapons, to defend the offshore islands. Admiral Radford wholeheartedly agreed, remarking that the JCS had instructed the Strategic Air Command (SAC) to develop a target list for an atomic offensive against China. By that time, SAC had deployed a wing of B-36 bombers to Guam, with another wing on alert for deployment. It was in this context that Dulles made his famous policy statement about Massive Retaliation.[47] The secretary of state may have been attempting to provoke the Chinese into an overt move that would justify an American nuclear response. Although less sanguine about the use of such weapons, in late April Eisenhower sent Radford and Assistant Secretary of State Walter Robertson with a further proposal. If Chiang would abandon the untenable islands of Quemoy and Matsu, the U.S. Navy would blockade the Chinese coast to prevent the buildup of a force to invade Taiwan. Fortunately for regional peace, Chiang refused the offer, feeling he could no longer trust the changing policy of the Eisenhower administration. Meanwhile, opposition politicians in the United States and allies in Europe pressured the administration to downplay its confrontation with Beijing. On April 23, Chinese Foreign Minister Zhou Enlai, discouraged by Soviet opposition to the crisis, effectively ended the confrontation by announcing that Beijing did not want war with the United States The shelling gradually declined, but U.S.-Chinese talks in Geneva later in 1955 reached an impasse.[48]

Both Chinas had profited from the crisis. Beijing could claim to have retaken territory in the teeth of U.S. opposition, while Taipei ensured major U.S. support for its future survival. Thus, Chiang and Mao between them had maneuvered the United States into a commitment that went far beyond Taiwan itself.

ANOTHER BUILDUP

The end of the crisis did not mean an end to friction and trouble. For years thereafter, the U.S. Navy maintained sea and air patrols in the crowded Formosa Straits, and such sustained operations had costs. In August 1956, Chinese fighters shot down a Navy Mercator intelligence aircraft on a night mission in the straits. Even when hostile forces were not involved, the grinding routine of standing patrols took its toll on naval forces in the area, known as Task Force 72. In the peacetime navy, many of these vessels were manned at only 60 to 70 percent of authorized strength, with resulting exhaustion and accidents for the crews. Sustained air operations were, as always, particularly risky—in one week in 1957, *USS Midway* lost three aircraft and two pilots in accidents off Taiwan.[49]

Meanwhile, from 1955 onward, both sides improved their defenses while continuing to spar about the offshore islands. The United States had already given Chiang $1.6 billion in economic and military aid by 1954,[50] but now the scope of such aid and of American military assistance grew rapidly. Among the U.S.-supplied weapons were hundreds of landing craft, ostensibly to resupply the offshore islands but potentially to conduct an amphibious landing on the mainland. The Republic of China's armed forces were already ludicrously strong for such a small population base but continued to grow to a total of 600,000 men, including an army of at least 400,000 men in twenty-one divisions. With American backing, beginning in 1956 this army insisted that all conscripts serve a full two years with the colors, after which they moved to reserve units. By 1958, the KMT divisions began reconfiguring to follow the U.S. Pentomic model. The U.S. advisory effort, redesignated in 1958 as a joint military assistance command, grew apace, eventually including a signal battalion to communicate with other U.S. agencies. The United States also deployed a Nike-Hercules air defense battalion, although by 1962 the KMT army assumed control of that mission.[51] As head of the Taiwan Defense Command, Vice Admiral Roland N. Smoot controlled all U.S. forces, including advisors, in the area.

Still, the United States did not believe that the nationalists could defend themselves without U.S. support. In 1957, the United States announced that it would deploy nuclear-capable Matador missiles to Taiwan. In a Joint Staff study completed in May 1958, the JCS concluded that the United States would have to use naval and air forces, including nuclear weapons, in the event of limited war in the area.[52] This conclusion was almost unavoidable, considering that the U.S. Seventh Fleet in the Far East had only two aircraft carriers, and that most U.S. ground forces were already earmarked for the defense of Korea and Western Europe.

Beijing was equally diligent in preparing for a future crisis. Recognizing that air superiority would be the first prerequisite in any such operation, the PLAAF began building and repairing airfields in 1956. By the summer of 1958, it had reached the point where its 1st Air Corps, operating out of Fujian (Fukien) in eastern China, possessed a command structure and a limited network of radars, anti-aircraft guns, and searchlight troops. Beginning on July 27, 1958, veterans of the Korean air conflict transferred from the 5th to the 1st Air Corps and moved into Fujian. The PLAAF assembled six fighter regiments in first line and seventeen regiments (including two regiments of bombers) in support, for a total of 520 aircraft. Among these planes were a significant number of MiG-17Fs, equipped with afterburners and generally faster and more stable than the MiG-15s of the Korean conflict. Three PLA field armies, each numbering about 46,000 men, were also in Fujian, as compared to 86,000 nationalist troops on Quemoy and another 23,000 on Matsu.[53]

THE SECOND TAIWAN STRAIT CRISIS

Given these relative figures, it seems clear that Beijing did not intend a ground invasion of the offshore islands. However, after extensive debates in the Military Commission from May through July 1958, that government launched a renewed propaganda campaign for the "liberation" of Taiwan, accompanied by the PLAAF redeployment described above. A combination of factors was probably behind this escalation. First, Taiwan was a significant irritant to the Chinese, especially since the nationalists periodically launched guerrilla raids and propaganda leaflet drops on the mainland. Next, beginning in May 1958, the United States was visibly distracted by a prolonged crisis in Lebanon (see chapter 12). On July 15, U.S. Marines landed in Beirut; three days later, Mao directed the redeployment of air elements to Fujian by the 27th. Third, the Chinese leadership apparently calculated that it could force the surrender of Quemoy and Matsu by prolonged interdiction of supplies, a calculation shared by many Western military planners. Finally, as he did so often in his career, Mao Tse-tung deliberately provoked a crisis simply to galvanize the youth of China and thereby perpetuate the revolutionary fervor that he so highly valued. He may also have been trying to embarrass Moscow since its efforts at reconciliation with Washington looked like appeasement to Beijing.[54] As in the Korean War, the Chinese Communist leadership apparently considered that U.S. nuclear attacks were unlikely or at worst survivable; nonetheless, they avoided either invasion or direct attacks on U.S. vessels.

On July 17, 1958, the Nationalist Chinese armed forces went on alert and increased reconnaissance flights along the coast. Within restrictive rules of engagement, the redeployed PLAAF aggressively defended its air space. On July 29, four MiG-17Fs tangled with an equal number of F-84Gs, downing two of the nationalist aircraft. The appearance of the MiG-17 in Chinese hands was an unpleasant shock for both the ROCAF and the USAF. On the advice of Admiral Smoot, the United States decided to supply Chiang with the more modern F-86 fighter, equipped with Sidewinder missiles, but such an action required time for shipment and transition training. Therefore, on August 3, the USAF deployed new F-100 fighters to Taiwan to temporarily offset the MiG-17s. Neither this action nor the dispatch of a U.S. carrier battle group to the area reassured Chiang Kai-shek, who insisted that his outposts were under imminent threat of invasion. While these responses were developing in early August, a much-publicized visit to Beijing by Nikita Khrushchev and his defense minister concerned Western observers. CIA analysts correctly interpreted this visit as a sign of discord rather than solidarity between the two great communist states, but Eisenhower and especially Foster Dulles considered the visit a threat. In retrospect, it appears that the Soviets had little influence over Beijing's planning of the crisis, although Khrushchev loyally offered specialized equipment for an invasion.[55]

The possibility of renewed attack placed the Eisenhower administration in a quandary. The offshore islands had no value in themselves and were certainly not a vital interest of the United States. Despite its ambiguous wording, the Formosa Resolution of 1955 did not provide clear authorization for the United States to defend those islands. Moreover, both Admiral Smoot, the local commander, and the CIA reported that there was no strong indication that Beijing was actually preparing to invade those islands. On the other hand, the fall of these islands would cost the United States considerable prestige and might well demoralize the nationalists to the point of collapse of the Taiwan government.

After waiting three weeks for the nationalists to either attack the mainland or withdraw from the offshore islands, on August 23 China resumed heavy bombardment of Quemoy. Before doing so, however, Mao summoned the local commander, General Ye Fei, to ensure that these attacks would cause few American casualties. As everyone had anticipated, the nationalists were unable to resupply the islands under fire. On August 24, communist PT boats sank one KMT supply ship and damaged another. During August, the PLAAF also flew in IL-28, Tu-4, and IL-10 bomber regiments in anticipation of an escalated struggle. However, the Red Chinese fighters averaged only five sorties each over a period of twenty-three days in August, indicating continued problems with maintenance and logistical support.[56]

As in the previous crisis, Secretary Dulles took a hard line, although this time he left room for negotiations. With the backing of the JCS and the president, on September 4 he made a public statement indicating that the defense of Quemoy and Matsu was "increasingly related to the defense of Taiwan," and that the United States would intervene if the nationalists were unable to defend the islands. He also wrote to British Prime Minister Harold Macmillan, indicating that such an intervention would probably not succeed without the use of nuclear weapons. More publicly, that same day General Curtis LeMay, the air force vice chief of staff and flamboyant former commander of SAC, departed to visit Taiwan, an obvious indicator that the United States was considering nuclear attack. Eisenhower himself, however, was even more reluctant to use nuclear weapons than he had been three years previously.[57]

Meanwhile, U.S. military actions had a practical effect on the crisis, particularly with regard to resupply of the offshore islands. The United States persuaded the nationalists to preload their landing craft for rapid offloading of supplies when they reached an island. More importantly, with the approval of the JCS, U.S. cruisers and destroyers escorted these landing craft in international waters, although they had to turn back upon reaching a point three miles from the islands. Because the PLA did not wish to engage the United States directly, this escort limited interdiction fire to the final three-mile dash and unloading time, thereby greatly facilitating resupply and allowing the island garrisons to hang on. The United States also supplied eight-inch (203mm) howitzers to strengthen counterbattery fire from the islands. These measures combined with a growing U.S. suspicion that the Taipei government was exaggerating the supply issue reduced the sense of crisis in early September. The United States consistently opposed nationalist plans to bomb the mainland in retaliation. Nonetheless, as a precaution the USAF kept a small number of B-47s, its newest bombers, on alert in Guam throughout the confrontation.[58]

By September 1958, the Lebanon crisis had subsided, so that the U.S. Navy could assemble a force of at least five carriers in the Taiwan area. Elements of the USAF's quick-reaction force, the Composite Air Strike Force, began to arrive at regional airfields in early September. This gave the USAF and USN a combined total of two hundred nuclear-capable aircraft. At the behest of the new CINCPAC, during September the Military Airlift Command and contract commercial aircraft delivered more than 5,000 tons of conventional bombs and other supplies to airfields in Guam, the Philippines, and elsewhere.[59] At the same time, the PLA's artillery fire, which had initially been overwhelming, slackened and became intermittent, perhaps due to shortages of ammunition.

On September 6, the People's Republic of China (PRC) foreign minister, Zhou Enlai, announced that he was prepared to resume the ambassadorial discussions previously held in Geneva. Although the Eisenhower administration believed that Beijing had backed down, it would probably be more accurate to say that the Chinese had concluded, based on U.S.-escorted resupply efforts, that they could not capture the offshore islands at that time. The next day, September 7, Khrushchev weighed in with a letter to Eisenhower, accusing the United States of having seized the islands from the people of China. The wording was so undiplomatic that the U.S. Embassy returned it to the Soviet foreign ministry without comment. Khrushchev may well have written this letter to mollify the Chinese rather than to seek confrontation with the United States[60] Chinese and American representatives did meet in Warsaw in mid-September but only restated their irreconcilable positions concerning the islands.

Despite these diplomatic gestures, the struggle to interdict the offshore islands continued for some time. Beginning on September 21, the nationalists used C-46 transport aircraft to air-drop supplies to Quemoy. After several successful airdrops, however, the PLAAF came up with an effective counter. On October 3, the nationalists dispatched 24 C-46 transports, protected by twice as many F-86 fighters. Their opponents sent 48 MiG-17Fs to distract the ROCAF fighter escorts at high altitude while four other MiGs flew in low to a point where they could pop up and shoot down two transports. This tactic made further airdrops too risky.[61]

Three days later, the PRC minister of defense (and former commander in Korea), Peng Dehuai, declared a seven-day cease-fire, supposedly out of consideration for the civilian populace of the islands. This action virtually ended the chance to starve the islands into submission, and the United States promptly stopped escorting resupply convoys, further reducing the chances of confrontation. In a bizarre touch, Beijing later announced that the PLA would shell the offshore islands only on odd-numbered days, thereby permitting resupply on the even days. In response, Washington decided that U.S. vessels would escort transports only on the even-numbered days. This situation, which Eisenhower rightly described as a "Gilbert and Sullivan War," continued intermittently for years, and there were occasional air battles. Generally speaking, however, the PLAAF now controlled its own airspace, while the ROCAF, backed by the USAF and USN, had the advantage over the straits.[62]

Both sides had been surprised by the crisis. In a number of speeches after the fact, Mao admitted that he had underestimated the American response. As for Eisenhower and Dulles, Richard Immerman has observed that "the speed and psychological pressures of a crisis situation brought both men dangerously close to shooting from the nuclear hip over stakes they knew were nowhere near commensurate."[63] Five times in one year, President Eisenhower rejected military advice to use nuclear weapons in the crisis.[64]

While Beijing and Washington maintained their prestige in the second crisis, Chiang Kai-shek was less successful than in the previous confrontation. The United States pressured him to reduce both the garrisons of the offshore islands and the scope of attacks on the mainland. Nonetheless, forty years later, these outposts together with Taiwan remained a bone of contention for the Beijing regime.

Regional Allies

Although the Huk insurrection and the Formosa Straits grabbed headlines, the United States had a number of other issues in East Asia during the 1950s. In particular, American policy makers found that their Pacific alliance system required periodic maintenance and adjustment.

Nowhere was the change more dramatic than in Japan. Article 9 of the U.S.-inspired 1947 Constitution specifically renounced war and forbad the creation of armed forces. Yet, as early as 1948, General MacArthur felt the need to create a paramilitary police force, beginning the same process of rearmament that had occurred in both Germanies. The sudden deployment of virtually all of Eighth Army to Korea during the summer of 1950 combined with an aggressive North Korea and communist China made defense of the Japanese islands an urgent issue. With JCS approval, MacArthur immediately began the creation of a coast guard and four Japanese light infantry divisions, initially described as the "Japanese national police reserve" and later as the "national safety force."[65] U.S. weapons and advisors for Japan increased steadily, limited only by the demands of the Korean conflict.

These forces became a purely Japanese responsibility with the signature, in September 1951, of both a peace agreement and a security treaty between Japan and the United States. A national safety agency supervised the creation of what eventually became the Self-Defense Forces. However, Japanese public opinion was at best ambivalent about rearmament; like the Germans, many Japanese had decided to renounce armed force after the painful experience of World War II.[66] In 1955, the redesignated Japanese Defense Agency established a six-year plan to form six army divisions, four separate brigades, thirty-three air squadrons, and a small navy. However, the Japanese Diet (legislature) frequently cut budgets and otherwise restricted rearmament, so that only six divisions, two brigades, and four air squadrons took shape by 1957.[67]

Moreover, the continued and unrestricted American use of bases in Japan rankled the Japanese. In particular, U.S. control of the Ryuku Islands as well as open American discussion of the use of nuclear weapons offended many Japanese. Under pressure from Prime Minister Nobusuke Kishi, in late 1957 the United States decided to withdraw the one remaining army unit, the 1st Cavalry Division, for relocation to Korea as part of the overall reduction of the army. Similarly, U.S. Marine units left Japan proper for Okinawa, and eventually the final ground combat element, an Honest John missile battalion, shifted to Korea as well. The United States thereby reduced its presence in Japan by at least 40 percent, although air and naval bases, as well as army logistics elements, remained.

After prolonged and difficult negotiations, the two governments signed a new, more equitable defense treaty in 1960. In particular, the Japanese government established its right in principle to decide on major changes in U.S. force presence and activities on the home islands, although separate diplomatic notes indicated that this did not apply to routine unit rotations and minor adjustments.

Once the 1953 armistice went into effect, a similar evolution occurred in American relations with the Republic of Korea (ROK). Because the United Nations Command was the official signatory of the armistice, it had to remain in existence in some form, as did Eighth Army headquarters as its ground component command. However, by 1956, the U.S. forces in the peninsula had shrunk to two infantry divisions, a fighter-bomber wing, and supporting troops, for a total of perhaps 60,000 Americans. KATUSAs continued to fill out the ranks of most American units. The main burden of defense fell on the ROK.

Even during the war, Syngman Rhee had major policy disagreements with the United States. With the end of open hostilities, Rhee understandably wanted greater equality in the relationship. At the same time, the ROK military sought to evolve in the direction of a more professional, capable force. Despite the enormous strain on the Korean economy, Rhee's government wanted to make its armed forces more modern but not necessarily smaller. Although the armistice agreement

forbad the introduction of new weapons and units into the peninsula, apparent Chinese violations of this agreement led to a May
1956 UNC announcement that it was suspending the "neutral"
inspection of South Korean ports.

After prolonged negotiations in 1957–1958, the Eisenhower
administration moved U.S. nuclear-capable weapons to the peninsula
and undertook limited modernization, including conversion of three
ROK fighter squadrons to jet aircraft. In return, Rhee agreed to maintain his eighteen active infantry divisions on a reduced manning level
but would not accept conversion of such divisions into reserve formations.[68] Although both governments considered reductions in the
ROK Army during 1960, tensions on the peninsula argued against
any major change. These tensions periodically reached a crescendo,
most notably in the late 1960s when the United States seemed distracted by Vietnam.

Overall, therefore, the liberal expenditure of military aid and periodic
deployment of armed forces maintained the U.S. Pacific defense perimeter during the 1950s. The same could not be said of its erstwhile
European allies, however, which spent the decade fighting a series of
frustrating and often unsuccessful counterinsurgency wars.

10

THE TWENTY-YEAR WAR
France, Indochina, and Algeria

Captain Jean Pouget's career epitomized the best aspects of the French Army after its defeat in 1940.[1] Graduating from the Saint Cyr military academy in December 1942, Pouget had joined the anti-German resistance rather than the Vichy army. Reintegrated into the regular forces in 1944, he had been wounded while serving with the First French Army in the campaign that finally defeated Hitler. Next, he volunteered for the French expeditionary corps in Indochina, where he fought in several campaigns, served as aide to the French commander-in-chief, and parachuted into the doomed fortress of Dien Bien Phu three days before it fell in 1954. Like thousands of other Frenchmen and their colonial allies, he suffered torture and brainwashing in the Viet Minh prisons, learning the intensely political lessons of his enemy. Pouget finally returned home, emaciated and ill, in late 1954. By that time, the next conflict in Algeria was already under way.

His career earned him promotion to *chef d'escadron* (cavalry major) far earlier than his more conventional contemporaries. Yet he was sick in spirit as well as in body. An entire generation of young officers not only had suffered humiliating defeat but felt that their government had forced them to abandon the local inhabitants who had fought beside them against the Communists. While convalescing,

Pouget reread Carl von Clausewitz's classic study *On War* and was struck by the Prussian's famous observation that "war is merely the continuation of policy by other means."[2] Taking out his notebook, the French officer wrote, in the best style of his Cartesian education,

> Theorem: The Viet Minh won the war because their military operations, whether successes or failures, rigorously followed a political line clearly traced and firmly imposed.
>
> Corollary: The principal cause of the defeat of the [French Army in the Far East] was the congenital incapacity of the Fourth Republic to conceive and impose a correct policy in Indo-China.[3]

Standoff

During the desperate days of World War II, officials of the Gaullist exile government had developed an enlightened policy that they hoped would allow the declining French Empire to survive as a federated "French Union" in which different national groups would have local autonomy while following Paris in foreign and defense matters. As the most populous and wealthiest of France's colonies, Indochina was a critical test case for this so-called "Brazzaville Policy." Unfortunately, this model of self-government within a French framework was unacceptable to both sides. Although Ho Chi Minh made concessions, he wanted more independence than France would grant, while many French colonial officials and officers openly sabotaged a policy they found naïve and ill conceived.[4] Thus, after more than a year of negotiations and tentative agreements, the truce between the Viet Minh and the French broke down in late 1946. What followed was a conflict that can best be described as the First Indo-Chinese War.[5]

Both sides were nervous and trigger-happy, but the actual fighting began on November 20, 1946, when the French attempted to control the movement of fuel oil in the Red River Delta near the northern port of Haiphong. The local French commander, Colonel Debres, used Vietnamese resistance as an excuse to seize key points in the port city at a cost of 240 Vietnamese and seven French killed. Three days later, Debres ignored the orders of his immediate commander by pushing the issue even further. French land and naval guns bombarded the local Viet Minh headquarters, while French Air Force Spitfires

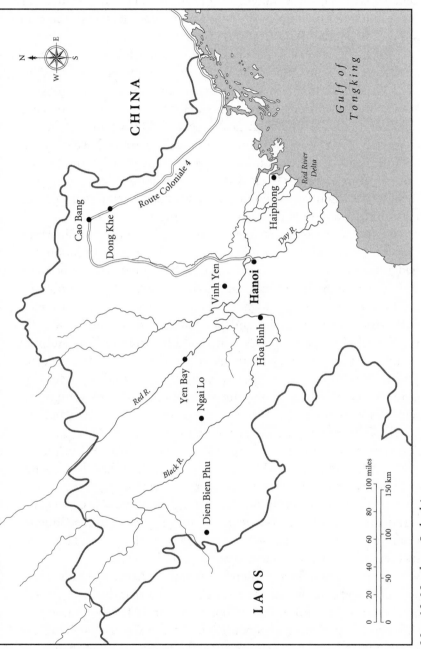

MAP 13. Northern Indochina

reportedly strafed fleeing refugees. The total casualties of this incident are still in dispute, ranging from the official French estimate of
three hundred killed up to the Viet Minh claim of 60,000; the true
number was probably several thousand.[6]

A standoff ensued for the next few weeks, while one last round
of negotiations took place. On the evening of December 19, 1946,
the so-called Vietnamese Vespers attacks began after an explosion
knocked out electricity and darkened Hanoi. Even at this late date,
however, the leadership of the self-proclaimed Democratic Republic
of Vietnam (DRV) was divided, so that the orders to attack were issued,
countermanded, and then muddled. Warned in advance, the French
used superior firepower to clear the city, but not until January 17 did
the last Viet Minh regular units withdraw under cover of morning fog.
Local militia continued to resist into February.[7]

Neither side was prepared for the conflict. Although Ho Chi Minh
was convinced that he controlled the majority of the population, his
fledgling DRV was woefully unprepared. Its regular army of perhaps
40,000 was supplemented by approximately the same number of
local militiamen, not all of whom acknowledged central government
authority. There were also independent militias associated with
various religious groups. Ho's army had little ammunition and virtually no radios or heavy weapons; most of its leaders were recent
graduates of training courses that were as short as three weeks in
duration. One Chinese Communist regiment that took temporary
refuge in Vietnam during 1946 provided some additional instruction,
but the Chinese were preoccupied with their own war. Although Ho's
government had begun to stockpile supplies in rural areas in October
1946, by the spring of 1947 French sweeps threatened these base areas.[8]

On December 22, in the midst of the initial fighting in Hanoi, the
DRV publicly predicted a protracted struggle in three phases, roughly
parallel to those of Mao Tse-tung. Yet, in comparison to the Chinese
Communists, the DRV began with a much smaller numerical base and
less territory in which to maneuver and elude the enemy.[9]

Some analysts have depicted the French Army as being over-
confident and complacent about its ability to defeat the insurgents,[10]
and certainly the initial French operations in 1946–1947 came as a
shock to inexperienced opponents like Ho and Vo Nguyen Giap, his
field commander. Moreover, throughout the conflict, the French referred
to their opponents as "outlaws" (hors la loi), which reflected a refusal

to acknowledge the political issues involved. French officials also tended to underestimate the strength of Vietnamese nationalism. Yet, General Jean de Lattre de Tassigny had advised his government to seek a political solution, and the French garrison in the later 1940s was severely limited in size and capability. When the fighting began, there were approximately 75,000 troops in Indochina, including not only Frenchmen but also Algerians and other colonial regiments as well as the Foreign Legion, which at the time contained many fugitive German and French fascist soldiers. The size and budget of this force was constantly subject to conflicting demands, such as the diversion of troops en route to Vietnam to put down a rebellion in eastern Madagascar in 1947. The Fourth French Republic, with its fatal division of political parties, lacked the unity and stability to develop and implement bold policies. The government in Paris was struggling to restart the economy and rebuild French defenses at home, and inevitably regarded Indochina as less important. In December 1947, for example, just as the war intensified in Southeast Asia, French legislators demanded that the commander reduce his total troop strength. In 1950, the budget directed a further reduction of 9,000 men in Indochina and forbad the deployment of French conscripts outside of Europe. Needless to say, the French Communist Party attempted to block prosecution of the Indo-Chinese war, including propaganda, opposition to funding, and strikes to delay shipment of troops and supplies.[11]

Under the circumstances, the French expeditionary corps never had sufficient troops to control the country. The movement of troops to the north in 1946–1947 left the southern part of Indochina dangerously exposed to insurgents. The French did recruit a significant number of local troops under the auspices of an autonomous "State of Vietnam," which Paris created after much debate in 1948–1950 under the perennial emperor Bao Dai. Dedicated right-wing and other anticommunist Vietnamese made great efforts to defeat the DRV. Similarly, with French support, the monarchs of Laos and Cambodia granted constitutions and held elections in 1947, becoming associated states of the French Union.[12] However, none of these states achieved the popularity and legitimacy of the DRV. The French refusal to permit these governments to operate their own armed forces and diplomatic services only reinforced their images as puppets.

The years 1947–1949 passed without a clear decision. The French won numerous tactical victories but could never secure the countryside of Indochina. They launched massive encirclement operations using a combination of mechanized, airborne, and amphibious forces but rarely trapped the enemy. The Viet Minh operated in relatively small units, often with only one full-time, main force battalion in a regiment of part-time guerrillas, while the DRV gradually established political control in much of northeastern Vietnam. At a meeting of leaders in May 1949, Giap announced that he expected a protracted war to continue for some years.[13]

Although the first Viet Minh "division," the 308th, traced its creation to June 1948, Giap did not actually begin organizing his army into larger units until 1949–1950. Initially, these divisions had only light weapons, such as locally produced rocket launchers and a few 57mm recoilless rifles.[14] Moreover, despite their later reputations, Giap and the other leaders had little experience or understanding of large-unit operations. Without foreign aid, the revolutionary struggle might well have continued for decades.

Foreign Aid

By the end of 1949, France had suffered 16,270 casualties and was spending $500 million per year on the Indo-Chinese conflict. Such losses obviously affected France's economic recovery as well as its ability to participate in NATO. The fact that Paris had to maintain such a large force in Indochina also meant that the French were even more uncomfortable about rearming West Germany. Moreover, by the spring of 1950, the Truman administration had come to view Indochina as another part of the global communist threat, or at least another area where Republicans might criticize Truman as "soft" on communism. Reluctantly, therefore, his administration came to accept the need for U.S. military and economic aid to this war. This policy became official in April 1950, when President Truman approved NSC-64, followed soon thereafter by U.S.-French discussions on military aid.[15]

Fortunately for the Vietnamese revolution, the success of the Communists in the Chinese Civil War made good on the deficiencies of their southern neighbors. In January 1950, the People's Republic of China (PRC) became the first state to recognize the DRV, followed a few weeks later by the Soviet Union. That month, Ho walked for seventeen days from his rural base area to China, then traveled to Beijing and Moscow looking for assistance.[16] The PRC was more than willing to help; in addition to the ideological bonds of socialism, Mao Tse-tung regarded Indochina together with Korea and Taiwan as key national security interests where China must confront the United States. Stalin was less forthcoming; just as in the case of Kim Il-Sung, the Soviet dictator referred Ho to Beijing for assistance. This policy, as noted above (chapter 7), was probably due to a combination of Marxist prejudice against preindustrial societies and a pragmatic desire to get Red China fully committed as a Soviet ally. Still, the Soviets provided at least seven hundred trucks, which were essential to the logistics of the growing Viet Minh force.

Ho Chi Minh and Vo Nguyen Giap have become justly famous as practitioners of protracted revolutionary warfare, but in the later 1940s they were still amateurs in large-unit operations. Recognizing this, Ho asked Beijing not only for arms but also for advisors and even unit commanders. Conscious of Vietnamese national sensitivities, however, the Chinese wisely declined to assume command and did not contemplate committing their own troops to Indochina unless the United States intervened there. By July of 1950, Mao had provided both a flood of supplies and a Chinese Military Advisory Group (CMAG), including seventy-nine experienced senior officers of the PLA. The Viet Minh 308th Division spent the summer of 1950 in southern China, receiving equipment and training. Meanwhile, even before the CMAG deployed as a whole, the CCP Central Committee sent one of its own members, General Chen Geng, to Vietnam in early July 1950. Chen was an early graduate of the Whampoa Military Academy who had risen to command an army group during the civil war. Disguised as a Viet Minh officer, Chen rapidly assessed the situation and concluded that the Vietnamese insurgents were too inexperienced for major operations. Instead, he recommended that they begin by attacking small French outposts as a means to improve their confidence and tactical ability. He also prepared a comprehensive critique of Viet Minh strengths and weaknesses, ranging from the underutilization of women to a tendency to conceal bad news from higher headquarters. Although such critiques were probably valid, they did not endear the Chinese advisors to Giap and his fellow Vietnamese Communists.[17]

Nonetheless, the Viet Minh followed his advice. In an effort to reduce cross-border movements, the French Army had established a series of fortified outposts, connected by Route Coloniale 4, along the northeastern border of the country. The insurgents had repeatedly interdicted supply columns along this route, to the point where the French contemplated abandoning the farthest posts, but under Chen's guidance the Viet Minh went even further. On September 16, 1950, the 308th Division attacked the small outpost of Dong Khé. The attackers made numerous errors, such as beginning at dawn rather than dusk, which forced them to suspend the attack temporarily when French air support arrived. Still, by the 18th, Dong Khé had fallen. This, in turn, made the larger post at Cao Bang logistically unsupportable, setting the stage for a major French defeat.[18]

The stretch of Route Coloniale 4 between the two outposts was particularly difficult to traverse, with steep hills, deep gorges, and tropical rain forest. The entire route was therefore a natural ambush site. The commander of Cao Bang's Foreign Legion garrison, Lieutenant Colonel Pierre Charton, further complicated the task of withdrawal by encumbering his column with all his supplies and impedimenta, as well as a significant number of friendly refugees. As Charton slowly withdrew on October 3, 1950, a relief column under Lieutenant Colonel Marcel Lepage attempted to retake Dong Khé and thereby open up the withdrawal route. Instead, the 308th Division, reinforced by the 209th Separate Regiment, severely mauled Lepage's force. When Lepage radioed for help, Charton abandoned some of his supplies, trying to strike across country to catch the enemy in flank. The two French forces were caught in the jungle and defeated in detail, with both commanders falling captive. The 1st Foreign Legion Parachute Battalion, dropped in an effort to distract the enemy, was pushed into a gorge and virtually destroyed. In addition to this battalion, three Foreign Legion, one local partisan, and three Moroccan battalions were shattered. Overall, the French lost 6,000 troops, thirteen artillery pieces, and hundreds of trucks and lighter weapons, sufficient to equip an entire Viet Minh division.[19]

STAY OF EXECUTION: DE LATTRE DE TASSIGNY

Both sides read too much into this unfortunate encounter. Panicky French commanders evacuated the rest of Route 4 and even considered abandoning Hanoi and Haiphong. Coming within weeks of the Chinese intervention in Korea, this campaign gave the appearance of a centralized plan to throw the West out of Asia. The Truman administration responded predictably, expanding its military assistance group under Brigadier General Francis G. Brink and increasing the flow of military and economic aid.[20] For his part, a jubilant Giap thought that victory was at hand and planned a full-scale attack on the remaining French positions in northern Vietnam.

In the crisis, the French government sought a new commander for Indochina at the end of 1950. After several more senior and likely nominees declined the opportunity, the choice fell to General Jean de Lattre de Tassigny. De Lattre, who had commanded First French Army during 1944–1945, had a reputation as a showman, a prima donna, and a commander who was ruthless with subordinates—his nickname in the army was "King John." He demanded and got unprecedented power, being the first French military commander in Indochina who was simultaneously governor-general of the region. Arriving on December 17, 1950, de Lattre immediately relieved several officers, including the commander of the honor guard that received him. He appointed a number of young colonels who had performed well for him in 1945 and held a parade in Hanoi to reassure French supporters of their military strength.[21]

In addition to inspiration, de Lattre recognized the need to "sell" the war to Frenchmen, Americans, and the Indo-Chinese populations. He asserted that the conflict was not a colonial war but part of the worldwide struggle against communist totalitarianism. In an April 1951, speech to the Vietnamese, he insisted that "I have come to achieve your independence, not to limit it. The French Army is here only to defend it." A few months later, lobbying the Americans for more aid, de Lattre telescoped the famous domino theory down to a single statement: "Once Tonkin [North Vietnam] is lost, there is no barrier until Suez."[22] The general's energy combined with the shock of the frontier defeat prompted the French military to form true national armies in the associated states of Lao, Cambodia, and Vietnam; the latter had 120,000 men in training by the end of 1951.

While de Lattre was still encouraging morale and foreign support, Giap began a carefully planned attack on the Red River Delta, the core of remaining French positions in the north. On January 14, 1951, the 312th Division surrounded Mobile Group 3, a mechanized formation of brigade size, near the town of Vinh Yen, at the apex of the delta; the veteran 308th Division positioned itself along a major road, expecting the French relief column to advance on land, as it had done in the frontier campaign. Instead, General de Lattre flew to the spot personally and airlifted five of his scarce airborne battalions from southern Indochina to relieve the mobile group. The French Air Force used newly supplied U.S. napalm to inflict more than 6,000 casualties on the Viet Minh, who faded away after several days of intense fighting.[23]

Giap shifted to the northeastern corner of the delta, sending three divisions against French outposts on the night of March 23–24, 1951. Again, the insurgents achieved some initial success, often through human wave attacks, but key French strongpoints held out, inflicting hundreds of casualties. Undeterred, Giap tried a third attack, this time on the southern flank of the delta at the end of May. Two Viet Minh regiments infiltrated into the delta ahead of time to disrupt French relief efforts after the 304th, 308th, and 320th (minus) Divisions struck frontally. One company of nationalist Vietnamese troops, commanded by de Lattre's son Bernard, held fast to its blocking position, but in the process Lieutenant de Lattre was killed. (Like most professional armies, the French Army was very much a family affair; at least forty-two other sons of generals fell in Indochina and Algeria.) Viet Minh bazookas and recoilless rifles ambushed the improvised riverine craft coming up the Day River to support the defenders. Again, however, General de Lattre responded promptly with four brigades and extensive air and artillery support. By mid-June, the Viet Minh withdrew, having suffered 12,000 casualties and shattered crack divisions from three vain attacks on the Red River Delta.[24] These units withdrew to the rain forest, where Chinese advisors worked to rebuild their organizations. For a time, in fact, the Viet Minh were short of food and other basic supplies.

Encouraged by his success and seeking a propaganda victory, de Lattre decided to reoccupy the city of Hoa Binh (which ironically means "Peace" in Vietnamese) in the fall of 1951. His plan was to create another meat grinder that would chew up his opponents in the same manner as the delta campaign. Instead, the French suffered unsustainable casualties in a series of ambushes and outpost defenses. In November, Giap sent the 304th, 308th, and 312th Divisions to besiege Hoa Binh, while the 316th and 320th harassed the supply lines. On January 12, 1952, a riverine convoy on the Day River suffered a catastrophic ambush, ending water resupply to Hoa Binh. Only very belatedly did the French, who had heavy engineer equipment, clear away the brush along Route Coloniale 6, the remaining land supply route, to reduce the chance of ambush. In late February 1952, the French had to evacuate Hoa Binh, withdrawing back to the delta.[25]

General de Lattre did not live to see this defeat, however. Suffering from cancer of the hip, he went home after a year in command and died on January 11, 1952. The French government posthumously promoted him to marshal of France. Despite his inspirational leadership and short-term successes, however, it is unlikely that even de Lattre could have reversed the long-run trends of French numerical inferiority and wavering political support.

DOWNWARD SLIDE

De Lattre's successor, Raoul Salan, was on paper the best man for the job. He had spent decades studying the languages and culture of the Orient, and was nicknamed "the Mandarin." However, he was unable to change the pattern of events. While the Viet Minh reverted to guerrilla tactics, Salan launched Operation Lorraine in October 1952, another elaborate, carefully orchestrated pincers campaign that failed to eliminate the insurgent base areas.[26] His commanders continued to seek opportunities for conventional battles in which French firepower could overwhelm the rebels. The defenders did have some success thwarting the terror tactics of Nguyen Binh, the Viet Minh leader in southern Vietnam, but could not eliminate the insurgency even there.

General Chen, who had planned the initial Viet Minh success along the northern frontier, had departed Vietnam in mid-1951 to become deputy commander of the volunteer forces in Korea. His successor, Wei Guoqing, suggested that the DRV concentrate its efforts in northwestern Vietnam, near the border with Laos. French forces in the region were weak, and the long flight times between coastal airfields and the interior of the country would hamper French resupply and air support. There followed extensive discussions with both Beijing and the DRV leadership, involving a prolonged visit of Ho Chi Minh to China from September to December. Eventually, Wei won his point, including not only tactical plans but also the necessity for Viet Minh cultural sensitivity to the minority groups of the northwest. On October 10, 1952, eight Viet Minh regiments began to move westward. Following Wei's proposals, the insurgents captured Nghai Lo in mid-October, after which the French abandoned most of the northwestern region to them. By this time, the Viet Minh main force units had acquired numerous Chinese-supplied automatic weapons, so that they actually had more firepower than their opponents. Major Marcel Bigeard's 6th Colonial Parachute Battalion was sacrificed as a rear guard for the French withdrawal, although Bigeard and about 40 percent of his men survived an epic forced march. In one cheap stroke, Ho Chi Minh had gained a vast new source of support while positioning his troops to aid the neighboring Communists of Laos, who by 1953 controlled much of that isolated kingdom.[27]

The Viet Minh did not have the northwest entirely to themselves, however. In December 1951, General de Lattre had organized the Composite Airlanding Commando Groups (Groupements de Commandos Mixtes Aéroportés, or GCMA), small teams of French noncommissioned and junior officers who led local anticommunist guerrillas, often based on the various minority groups that suffered discrimination by lowland ethnic Vietnamese. The GCMA commander was then-major Roger Trinquier, a colonial parachute officer with long service in Asia who eventually became one of France's foremost theorists of counterinsurgency. With some equipment from American special operations officers, Trinquier built up the GCMA to the point where it claimed to control 20,000 anticommunist insurgents. While this figure may appear inflated, at least ten Viet Minh battalions were diverted to tracking the insurgents, and at one point Giap had to ask for Chinese help to suppress the GCMA threat in the border area. Even after winning independence, the North Vietnamese government publicly acknowledging killing 183 insurgents and capturing 300 more between July 1954 and April 1956.[28]

Still, political events continued to evolve in a manner unfavorable to the French. Over time, the associated states of Indochina asserted increasing autonomy from France as the price of assuming a greater share of the military burden. By April 1954, Paris had granted independence to the anticommunist government centered in southern Vietnam, and Ngo Dinh Diem was emerging as a national leader of considerable credibility. In the process, the absentee Emperor Bao Dai was discredited, as were right-wing political leaders such as Nguyen Van Tam.[29]

In 1953, General Henri Navarre, with no experience in the region, succeeded Salan as commander-in-chief of Indochina. Navarre asked for and got a vast increase in American aid, hoping to build up a large

Vietnamese national army that would take the offensive by 1955. This so-called Navarre Plan also involved more reinforcements from France, as well as reorganizing all the French troops into coherent divisions rather than a hodgepodge of brigade groups. American diplomatic and military officials saw merit in Navarre's ideas but were dubious about his prospects. In an August 28, 1953, memorandum to the secretary of defense, the Joint Chiefs observed that "a basic requirement for military success in Indochina is one of creating a political climate in that country that will provide the incentive for nations to support the French."[30] Still, when the French government could not pay for the new Vietnamese battalions, the Eisenhower administration persuaded Congress to almost double military assistance for the war.[31] In the short run, Navarre felt that he had to seize and maintain the initiative against Giap. In January 1954, he launched Operation Atlante, a vain effort to clear southern Vietnam so that he could turn the region over to the new Vietnamese Army.

To reassert control in northwestern Vietnam, Navarre also began Operation Castor in November 1953. By parachute and airlanding, he inserted 11,000 French and French Union troops into the valley of Dien Bien Phu, 275 kilometers (170 miles) west of Hanoi. The site already contained an airstrip constructed by the Japanese. The original intent of Castor was to build a hedgehog, a center of resistance from which strong patrols would fan out to interrupt Viet Minh logistics and troop movement in the region. By this time, the Chinese- and Soviet-equipped insurgents had developed an extensive network of motorized logistics, but that network was supplemented by so many human porters that, just as in the Chinese Civil War, it was largely invulnerable to interdiction. Moreover, Giap reacted quickly, establishing a loose cordon around Dien Bien Phu. Instead of an offensive base, the valley with its airfield now became a besieged fort, but visitors noted the flimsy nature of most field fortifications.[32]

If the Viet Minh had rushed into battle, they might well have suffered defeats similar to those of 1951. By this time, however, Giap had learned enough patience to wait until conditions were ripe. The 351st Division, a heavy formation created to manage Giap's limited artillery and engineer assets, received considerable influxes of Chinese equipment and advisors during the winter of 1953–1954. By one account, China provided 200 trucks, 100 artillery and anti-aircraft pieces, 3,000 other guns, and 60,000 artillery shells for the siege of

Dien Bien Phu.[33] Mao Tse-tung became involved personally, planning the creation of additional heavy divisions for future campaigns. Perhaps equally important, after the August 1953 armistice in Korea, Beijing could focus more attention on Indochina. Experienced Chinese officers from the Korean campaign advised the Viet Minh on building and camouflaging artillery positions. Before launching their attack, the insurgents dug hundreds of kilometers of trenches and numerous hardened artillery positions. This made it difficult for the French to conduct counterbattery fire when Giap attacked Dien Bien Phu in the spring of 1954. By contrast, the French built only temporary sandbag and log bunkers around the airfield, without any concrete.

Dien Bien Phu had a number of other weaknesses.[34] Operationally, it was so far removed from French bases that air support and resupply were extremely difficult, particularly during the monsoon season. The situation was complicated by the fact that throughout the siege, other Viet Minh forces attacked French Union positions in Laos, the Red River Delta, and southern Vietnam distracting available reserves and support away from the northwest. Thus, from the start of the siege, the French were critically short of ammunition, especially hand grenades and mortar rounds. Similarly, although French estimates of Viet Minh numerical strength were relatively accurate, the planners of Operation Castor had believed that Giap could not supply more than two divisions with limited artillery in this remote location.

Tactically, while the need for an airfield may have necessitated establishing the base in a valley, the French failed to control high ground nearby. Moreover, more than one-third of the entire French force, including three infantry battalions, several artillery batteries, and a platoon of tanks, were in Strongpoint Isabelle, seven kilometers (4.3 miles) south of the main position, where they could provide only limited support to that position. Three of the eight battalions in the main position were supposed to provide a quick reaction reserve, but all three were committed early to the defense of outposts at the northern end of the valley. The more numerous and better-emplaced Viet Minh artillery overwhelmed their French counterparts, who had only two battalions of 105mm and one battery of 155mm howitzers.

Although historians commonly speak of the defenders as being French, in fact the garrison of Dien Bien Phu reflected the multinational nature of the war. Bernard Fall calculated that the original garrison of 11,000 men consisted of one-third Vietnamese, one-quarter Foreign

Legionnaires, one-fifth African colonial troops, and slightly more than one-fifth (22 percent) soldiers from metropolitan France. During the battle itself, five more battalions—three French, one Foreign Legion, and one Vietnamese—parachuted into the doomed position. In addition, approximately 1,530 other soldiers, of whom half were Vietnamese and 680 had never before parachuted, voluntarily jumped in as individual replacements.[35] These figures suggest that, belatedly, France had convinced some former colonists that the Viet Minh were a threat to their future.

Giap's own account of the battle is expressed with the abstract precision of a staff study, although the reality was more confusing.[36] Between March 13 and 17, 1954, the attackers seized two hills north of the main positions. During the next month (March 30 to April 30), they succeeded in capturing a number of hills overlooking the main position. Each time, the attackers concentrated overwhelming superiority and firepower against a single position, although resolute French counterattacks meant that two key positions were shared by the opposing sides, separated by only a few yards of no-man's-land. Napalm and low-altitude explosive bombs inflicted considerable casualties, but the monsoon weather and hours of darkness severely hampered air support. By mid-April, the airfield was no longer usable, and replacements and supplies had to arrive by the unpredictable means of parachute landing.

As the danger to Dien Bien Phu increased, so, too, did French requests for American aid. In January 1954, the French government not only sought additional bombers, transports, and spare parts but also asked the United States to provide mechanics to maintain the French aircraft. Despite a public outcry about this, President Eisenhower agreed to provide more than two hundred mechanics, although he gave reporters the impression that these airmen were really part of the U.S. advisory effort.[37] Eventually, the CIA's front airline, Civil Air Transport, transported French paratroops and parachuted supplies into Dien Bien Phu, but the United States stopped short of a shooting role.

In March, General Paul Ely, the French chief of staff, consulted with JCS Chairman Radford about the possibility of a U.S. air strike to save the beleaguered garrison, or at least to strike a psychological blow. The Joint Advanced Study Committee even drew up a contingency plan to employ three tactical nuclear weapons at Dien Bien Phu, a proposal that USAF Chief of Staff Nathan Twining supported as a deterrent to future communist "aggression." Army Chief of Staff Ridgway together with the president and secretary of state opposed such a drastic measure, but the JCS did commission a contingency plan known as Vulture to provide U.S. carrier air support around Dien Bien Phu. In April, two fleet aircraft carriers, USS *Essex* and *Boxer*, moved into the South China Sea and flew 2,600 sorties over Vietnam and even southern China, while Radford tried to convince Eisenhower to implement Vulture. The Joint Chiefs instructed the Pacific, Far East, and Strategic Air Commands to plan for possible Chinese aggression in Indochina or Korea. In late April, General Joseph Caldara, commander of the Far East Air Force's bomber force, personally reconnoitered the area and drew up a plan for a major B-29 strike. By this time, however, the French and Vietnamese forces were at such close quarters that even conventional bombing, let alone atomic attack, would have been an act of desperation.[38]

Ultimately, Eisenhower did not intervene, although he provided French Union forces with more equipment and financial support than they could use. Subsequent scholarship suggests that while Foster Dulles was willing to go to war, Eisenhower and other members of his administration apparently hoped that the mere threat of American intervention would cause the Viet Minh to break off the siege. If this was their intent, it failed, and Congress was unwilling to give Eisenhower the kind of broad mandate it had so recently granted about Taiwan. Having just ended one land war in Asia, U.S. public opinion and some senior commanders such as Ridgway were not inclined to enter another such conflict. Any U.S. intervention would have required both British support and French sharing of command, neither of which was forthcoming. However, the debate did produce Eisenhower's famous analogy, first articulated at a press conference on April 7, of a row of dominos in which the fall of Indochina might lead to other failures.[39]

Finally, during the first week of May 1954, the attackers used their massive artillery support and hilltop positions to achieve fire superiority and systematically take the main French position. General Christian de Castres, the commander, and his headquarters fell into enemy hands about 5:30 P.M. on May 7. Of the 15,000 defenders, approximately 3,000 were killed during the battle, and 2,000 Thais decided to switch sides. The remaining 10,000 men became prisoners, with no medical attention, little food, long forced marches, and relentless political reeducation. For their part, the Viet Minh lost an estimated 20,000 killed taking the position.[40]

CONSEQUENCES

Objectively speaking, Dien Bien Phu did not mean a decisive defeat for the French military; no more than 3 percent (albeit perhaps the best trained 3 percent) of the total French Union forces were involved. Yet, coming on top of six years of World War II and then eight years of frustrating and indecisive combat in Southeast Asia, this defeat effectively ended the French search for victory on the battlefield. The presence of such a large number of prisoners of war also provided a powerful inducement to compromise. In Geneva, Switzerland, the Great Powers were already conferring about the issue even before Giap won his victory. Dulles tried to prevent any concessions by the Western powers, but France had had enough. In June, Pierre Mendes-France came to power as prime minister by pledging to extricate France from the problem. The resulting Geneva Accords of July 1954 divided Indochina into four states: Laos, Cambodia, North and South Vietnam. The latter two were supposed to be divided only temporarily, pending a 1956 free election by secret ballot to determine their future government. The United States did not sign this agreement, arguing that only the United Nations could conduct a fair election. Under the accords, French forces abandoned Hanoi in October 1954 and began a massive sealift of 700,000 refugees, many of whom were Catholic, out of North Vietnam. By contrast, no more than 90,000 Viet Minh moved northward, leaving large numbers of supporters in the south. The last French troops did not depart Indochina until April 1956, and French instructors remained in the newly christened Republic of [South] Vietnam for another year.[41]

Long before that, however, American advisors had assumed the French role as the trainers and equippers of that republic's armed forces. In early 1954, the two Dulles brothers (John Foster at the State Department and Allen at the CIA) had also sent Colonel Lansdale, the anointed American expert on insurgency, to Saigon. Lansdale immediately set to work sabotaging Viet Minh operations and spreading propaganda to discredit that regime—propaganda that contributed to the flow of refugees from north to south. Moreover, he began to work with Ngo Dinh Diem as the obvious "Magsaysay" figure in Saigon. While Diem himself was a man of considerable credibility, his wife's family became notorious for their corruption.[42] In retrospect, the path to American involvement in the next Indo-Chinese War was already clear before the French had departed.

Meanwhile, thoughtful French officers developed an elaborate theory of how to fight an insurgency, a theory often referred to as *la guerre révolutionnaire* (revolutionary war). Belatedly, these officers and especially those who had been Viet Minh prisoners recognized the political nature of Maoist insurgencies. To combat this, they planned to control the population both physically and intellectually, fighting the information war against future insurgents.[43] Such officers entered the next insurgency, which was already brewing in Algeria, with a much greater preparation for their roles in that struggle.

Unfortunately, making professional officers politically conscious led down a slippery slope to making those officers politically *partisan*. As early as 1956, General Navarre's memoirs accused politicians of allowing the French Army "to be stabbed in the back," the famous phrase by which the German Army had avoided responsibility for its defeat in 1918. That same year, a disgruntled General Jacques Faure attempted to plan a coup against the Fourth Republic, but his amateurism defeated his purpose.[44] Quite apart from the suffering and dishonor of defeat, many French veterans believed that their government had forced them to abandon loyal anticommunist forces, such as the GCMA. A dangerous contempt for politicians in general and the Fourth Republic in particular infected influential portions of the career armed forces, especially the senior noncommissioned officers and battalion commanders who had borne the burden in Indochina. These professional soldiers felt isolated from French society by their sacrifices. At the same time, the officer corps as a whole became more ingrown, with more graduates of the Saint Cyr military academy being the sons of officers and NCOs.[45] The coming struggle in Algeria would only intensify this alienated, contemptuous attitude.

SOURCES OF THE ALGERIAN CONFLICT

The causes of the Algerian rebellion were many and varied, and are relevant here only to the degree that the French government understood (or misunderstood) those causes. Beginning with its first invasion

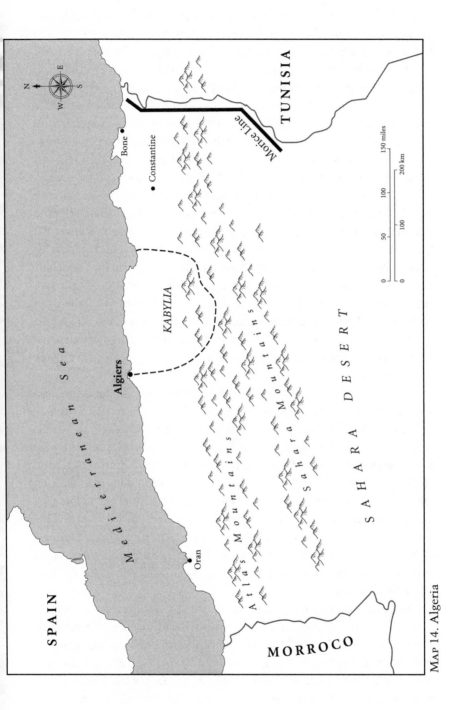

MAP 14. Algeria

287

in 1830, that government encouraged European settlement in Algeria, expropriating land from the locals on numerous occasions. A long series of French governments hoped to colonize and impose French culture on the country, but in the absence of sufficient Frenchmen, Algeria admitted large numbers of Spanish, Maltese, and Corsican immigrants. By 1954, the European population of Algeria, variously called *colons* (colonists) or *pieds noirs* (black feet), had reached one million people, of whom the majority were not ethnically French. These Europeans had extensive political and economic privileges in comparison to the local population. Although the colons could easily qualify for French citizenship, there were many barriers to citizenship for the local population. In order to become a citizen, the applicant had to renounce Islamic law (*sharia*), an act that bordered on apostasy for a devout Muslim. By 1936, only 2,500 Muslims had actually "assimilated" and achieved citizenship.[46] Towns with a significant European presence had elected councils in which three-fifths of council seats were reserved for the Europeans, while towns with few Europeans were governed by French-appointed officials. Efforts by educated, moderate Algerians to gain greater equality and self-government met bitter resistance from the colons, who feared a loss of their own privileges and position.[47]

The rapid growth in local population made a bad situation worse. The Berber and Arab population doubled after 1906, reaching 8.4 million by 1954. Such an increase made the existing economic situation, with widespread landlessness, underemployment, and malnutrition, intolerable. By the mid-1950s, one million locals, including one-quarter of the urban population, were completely unemployed, and another two million were seriously underemployed. The average colon had an income almost thirty times that of his local counterpart.[48] The frustrations of inferior social status and poverty fueled a resurgence of Islam among the population. Indeed, one of the leading organizations seeking national autonomy was the Association of Algerian Ulema (religious teachers).

In short, Algerian rebels were motivated by discrimination, unemployment, cultural encroachment, and rudimentary forms of nationalism and radical Islam. Most French officers recognized the need to improve the quality of life for the inhabitants but discounted the power of Algerian nationalism. Many Frenchmen found it difficult to accept that the Algerian populace as a whole was hostile to the French presence. Instead, the French tended to believe that a small minority of rebels was coercing the majority of the population into supporting the resistance. French officials and officers exaggerated the role of international communism and Pan-Arabism in provoking rebellion. In this regard, one of the principal French motivations for invading Egypt during the 1956 Suez Crisis (see chapter 12) was the mistaken belief that by overthrowing Pan-Arab leader Gamal Abdel Nasser, they would strike a major blow against the Algerian rebels.[49]

CONTROLLING ALGERIA

Despite the Indo-Chinese experience, the French government was slow to respond to the first attacks of the newly formed Armée de Liberation Nationale (Army of National Liberation, or ALN) on November 1, 1954. As is typical of the early stages of an insurgency, the government came up with numerous theories to avoid recognizing the political legitimacy of a rebellion. The November 1 attacks were variously attributed to organized crime, Berber separatists, and nationalists from nearby Tunisia, where the French government had recently exiled the monarch. The French National Assembly did not declare a state of emergency until March 31, 1955, five months after the insurrection began. Meanwhile, in response to the initial attacks, 20,000 soldiers and twenty companies of paramilitary security police deployed from France to reinforce the 54,000-man garrison of Algeria, which launched a number of sweeps, especially in the mountains of Kabylia, a largely Berber area with extremely difficult terrain.[50] In the process of these operations, the French used both helicopters for troop transport and fixed-wing aircraft for attacks on suspected insurgent concentrations.[51] Indiscriminate air strikes and mass arrests eliminated significant portions of the ALN but also increased the population's support for the rebels.

After the initial round of activity, a lull ensued. The ALN was a small force, limited in both numbers and weapons. Contrary to French perceptions at the time, the Nasser regime in Egypt held the rebels at arm's length, although Cairo did offer a haven to the exiled leaders of the political wing, the National Liberation Front or FLN, and subsequently provided small amounts of weapons.[52] Moreover, the ALN had made little effort to develop popular support in advance, relying on a combination of public dissatisfaction with France and fear of terrorist attack. The French Army, for its part, was still reorganizing after its withdrawal from Indochina and was not prepared for major operations in Algeria.

In 1955, Jacques Soustelle, an intellectual and former head of the Free French secret service during World War II, became governor-general of Algeria. With him came the French Army, in force. Based on its experience in Indochina, the French Army undertook a four-pronged approach to counterinsurgency.

First were the seven hundred Sections Administratives Specialisées (Special Administrative Sections, SAS), which acted as local government, civic action, and propaganda teams throughout the countryside. A typical SAS consisted of one or two company-grade officers, a noncommissioned officer, a medic, several civilian employees, and thirty to fifty Algerian militiamen for security. In some instances, teachers also provided free public education (in French). By 1960, there were 2,000 French soldiers, 3,700 civilians, and 19,000 local militiamen assigned to the SAS. These offices and their urban counterparts, the Sections Administratives Urbaines (SAU,) worked for both the civilian government and the military chain of command. Many of the officers involved were acutely aware of the political dimension of insurgency and labored to gain the trust and support of the local populace. They were advocates of the doctrine of guerre révolutionnaire like Colonel Antoine Argoud, who argued that to win the support of the undecided population, it was necessary to "Protect Them, Involve Them, and Control Them."[53]

In addition to the SAS, a significant portion of the French Army was also dedicated to territorial control, usually by dividing populated areas into a grid system (quadrillage) for occupation. This eventually involved two hundred light infantry battalions, composed primarily of reservists and conscripts who lacked training or equipment for counterinsurgency. Still, some of the commanders of these units were quite sophisticated in their approaches. One such example was Major Jean Pouget, the Indo-Chinese veteran introduced at the beginning of this chapter. In 1956–1958, Pouget commanded the 584th Support Battalion (Bataillon du Train) in a remote region of mountainous desert where he applied his hard-won knowledge of the political dimension of insurgency.[54] He not only shaped his mutinous mob of Parisian reservists into an effective combat force but also helped the local SAS to get full cooperation from the local population. Pouget demanded that his troops show complete respect for the locals and would only garrison a town upon the request of the tribal chiefs. By the time he left command in early 1958, Pouget had achieved such close coopera-tion with the populace that the FLN acknowledged that it could no longer operate in the 584th's area of operations. Although few qua-drillage commanders were as effective as Pouget, overall these units seriously hampered the insurgents.

Secondly, in addition to physical control, the occupiers tried infor-mation control. Much of the theory of guerre révolutionnaire revolved around propaganda and psychological action. A new staff section, G5, assumed responsibility for psychological action, civil affairs, and public information at every headquarters from division upwards. Thousands of officers and NCOs were trained in these ideas at the "Center for Training and Preparation in Counter-Guerrilla Warfare." The French Army also produced a large-circulation newspaper, *Le Bled* [*The Outback*], that depicted the ALN as throat-cutting thugs who ruled by terror. All of this was intended to present the government's viewpoint and contrast Western values to those of the insurgents.[55]

The third prong of French strategy was to isolate Algeria from arms and reinforcements. In this regard, the occupiers followed the well-recognized principle that successful counterinsurgencies, such as those in Malaya, the Philippines, and Greece, had all controlled the borders to isolate the insurgents. In Algeria, the French Navy patrolled the coastline to interdict arms smuggling. In 1957, the French finished construction of the Morice Line along the border with Tunisia, which had become a sanctuary for training and equipping the ALN. The Morice Line included barbed wire, high-voltage fences, antipersonnel mines, and ground surveillance radar. It was backed with roving patrols and, eventually, a cleared no-man's-land that extended several kilo-meters into Algeria. In the spring of 1958, the ALN launched a series of attacks escalating up to battalion size but failed to penetrate the barrier. This failure cost the ALN at least 6,000 casualties while leaving a further 12,000 rebel troops trapped inside Tunisia.[56]

Finally, the military conducted more conventional operations, with a mixture of fixed security posts and cordon and search efforts. Such operations sometimes inflicted casualties on the enemy, espe-cially during the first two years when the insurgents forgot their guerrilla tactics and tried to fight conventionally. By comparison to parachute insertions, the skillful use of helicopters significantly improved

French chances of encircling and trapping an insurgent force. However, government attacks also caused collateral damage, which sometimes undid the good will accumulated by the SAS. SAS officers often disagreed bitterly with the more conventional tactics of the rest of the army. Moreover, the majority of French troops became tied down on defensive tasks, including 80,000 guarding the Morice Line, leaving relatively few reserves for offensive actions.

More controversially, in order to isolate the insurgents, the French Army moved up to half a million Algerians out of their homes into resettlement camps.[57]

Because Algeria was legally part of France, successive governments in Paris were free to use conscripts and reservists in the war, an option that had not been available in Indochina. In 1956, for example, France doubled its troop strength in Algeria to a total of 390,000 by recalling reservists to active duty and extending military conscript service from eighteen to twenty-seven months.[58] Added to more than 100,000 local military and paramilitary troops, this meant that France, with a population of about forty-seven million, had half a million armed men to control the 9.4 million people and 2.4 million square kilometers of Algeria. (By way of comparison to a recent conflict, Iraq in 2003 had 26.7 million people in an area less than one-fifth that of Algeria.[59]) French troop strength remained at this level for the next four years.

The rebels had their own difficulties, quite apart from successful French attacks. There were divisions between the external leadership in Cairo, led by Ahmed Ben Bella, and the younger rebel colonels commanding various interior zones (Wilaya). In 1956, the French Air Force forced a civilian airliner carrying Ben Bella and several associates to land in France, where the French imprisoned these men for the remainder of the conflict. Meanwhile, the ethnic divisions between Berbers and Arabs generated considerable mistrust, which the French were sometimes able to exploit. The Algerian Communist Party (PCA) first condemned the FLN and then, when it saw initial rebel successes, tried to compete with it. After many recriminations, the PCA finally agreed to merge with the ALN, which needed its numbers and bomb-making expertise to extend terror attacks into Algiers and other cities. Predictably, the Communists then tried to take over the revolution. In response, ALN leaders deliberately sacrificed PCA squads in vain attacks and accused the communist leaders of betrayal. The insurgents did, however, begin systematically appealing to the population to widen their popular support.

THE BATTLE OF ALGIERS

Although the rural battles resembled a classic Maoist insurgency, Algeria also saw an increase in urban terrorism. The bombings and assassinations in Algiers prompted the French Army to conduct a major operation against the terrorist cells in the city, especially the structure of Yacef Saadi, head of the Algiers "Autonomous Zone" of the ALN. In January 1957, Governor-General Robert Lacoste gave General Jacques Massu, commander of the 10th Parachute Division, virtually unlimited powers to deal with the terrorists in Algiers. Massu was frustrated by the indecisive war and by the recent French failure in Egypt, where he had been the assault force commander. Massu's chief of staff, Colonel Yves Godard, was a great advocate of guerre révolutionnaire. Godard set out to make himself an expert on the Algiers underground, organizing spies and double agents against the rebels. He was aided by the three-man-cell structure of the urban insurgents, which meant that interrogators could be certain that each prisoner could provide two or three other names to pursue. The 10th Parachute Division spent most of 1957 systematically ferreting out and crushing the rebels. In the process, Massu and Godard used illegal methods to break a Muslim protest strike and sanctioned the use of torture to obtain information. Eventually, they captured Saadi and most of the bomb makers of Algiers, but alienated not only the local population but also many French liberals. The so-called Battle of Algiers caused great damage to French prestige worldwide.[60]

Given their own experiences in Indochina, a few French officers were quick to use torture to obtain information from captured insurgents. In France, public opinion was particularly susceptible to reports of torture because of the horrible experiences of German occupation. It was especially abhorrent to learn that some of the torturers were German members of the French Foreign Legion. Many of the French officers in Algeria had themselves been victims of harsh treatment by the Germans or Vietnamese and were therefore very conscious of the issue. Pouget, for example, severely punished his troops for abusing prisoners and insisted that he got more information by decent treatment. Yet, some officers felt compelled to use extreme measures to protect the population from terrorist attacks.[61] Moreover, even though the occupiers unquestionably tortured and murdered prisoners, the rule of law was never completely ignored. At the height of the Battle of Algiers, for example, an Arab on trial repudiated his confession on the grounds that he had been tortured. When his defense attorney displayed the welts and burns on the man's back, the court acquitted him.[62] Overall, the use of torture caused divisions within the officer corps while compromising the moral authority of the French Army.[63]

POLITICS AND THE CHALLE PLAN

Although the government had considerable tactical success in 1955–1958, the prolonged war caused increased unrest both in France and in diplomatic circles. Ben Bella and the other leaders of the FLN played skillfully on the image of France, the great advocate of liberty and equality, denying both to the Algerians. In September 1955, the Arab states arranged to have the UN General Assembly publicly debate the Algerian problem; the French ambassador walked out in protest, insisting that it was a French domestic issue.[64] The FLN carefully linked military action with this political campaign; each November, insurgent activity would reach a crescendo to coincide with the General Assembly meetings.[65]

In addition, over time the FLN established control of several remote areas that had escaped French rule. In 1958, the FLN declared itself to be a provisional government and persuaded a few Arab states to recognize it. Belkacem Krim, the "foreign minister" of this phantom regime, skillfully played on Cold War rivalries. Nikita Khrushchev granted the FLN de facto recognition as a propaganda gesture to the Third World, while Krim used the threat of a communist Algeria to pressure the French to negotiate.[66]

By 1958, French domestic opposition was growing, prompting both the pieds noirs and many of the career soldiers of the army to dread a French capitulation to the rebels. The two groups converged in their opposition to government policy. In February 1958, army leaders authorized an illegal air raid on the village of Sakiet, Tunisia, to protest government softness about the ALN. This outrage prompted American and other foreign demands for France to negotiate with the rebels. After a series of efforts in Paris to reach a compromise solution with the FLN, right-wing parties, pieds noirs, and schoolboys combined to launch a violent demonstration in Algiers on May 13, 1958. When the riot police proved incapable of containing the demonstration, sympathetic paratroopers stood aside and let the mob seize the government offices. Some career officers joined the protestors in forming a Committee of Public Safety under Massu. The commander-in-chief, Salan, refused to obey government orders. This near-mutiny in Algiers was followed by widespread demonstrations, including a coup in Corsica by the 11th Parachute Shock Demi-brigade, a legendary special operations unit. The island would allegedly serve as the staging base for Operation Resurrection, a military takeover in Paris.[67]

Although this plan may have been more bluster than fact, it had the desired effect, which was to bring an end to the Fourth Republic. Prior to the events of May, few officers were overt Gaullists, but de Gaulle's representatives in Algeria, especially Leon Delbecque, hinted that once in power the general would keep Algeria under French control.[68] In the crisis, de Gaulle returned from his self-imposed retirement to become prime minister, after which he obtained public votes approving both a new Fifth Republic and his own election as president of that republic. Once in power, he toured many units in Algeria and informally promised the officers to keep Algeria French.

De Gaulle then took a step that gratified many die-hards, making Air Force General Maurice Challe the military commander in Algeria in December 1958. De Gaulle's prime minister, Michel Debré, told Challe that the government needed quick results not just for political reasons but also because France was about to experience a manpower shortfall; the reduced birth rates during the German occupation of 1940–1944 were reflected in smaller groups of military conscripts coming of age starting in 1959. The so-called Challe Plan galvanized the counterinsurgency effort that year. First, Challe built on the idea of his predecessor, the ubiquitous General Salan, who had created a dozen "hunter" companies—mixed formations of French and local soldiers. These companies used unconventional tactics to locate and relentlessly track enemy forces, calling in air support and conventional units to destroy the enemy. Second, after carefully reshuffling his available forces, Challe freed up three divisions—the 10th and 25th Parachute and the 11th Infantry—to act as a general reserve, available for rapid deployment against enemy concentrations. (One should note that each French division consisted of only four to five maneuver battalions.) In a series of nine operations over the first seven months of 1959, these forces worked systematically from west to east through Algeria, clearing areas, pushing active insurgents eastward, and reducing ALN strength by at least 40 percent. General Challe personally supervised these sweeps from his helicopter. The operations killed two of the six wilaya commanders. Finally, Challe worked to extend the effectiveness of police intelligence and SAS to gain greater control over the population.[69]

<h2 style="text-align:center">FAILURE</h2>

By late 1959, the French military had defeated their opponents in the field and established a good if imperfect control of the native population. While military force alone could not eliminate the causes of the insurgency, large portions of the country were effectively under French rule. Unfortunately, this military victory did not translate into political success, for a variety of reasons.

First, the continued efforts of the minority European or pied noir population neutralized all attempts to provide better treatment and more civil rights for the Berbers and Arabs. For much of the Algerian conflict, French officials, soldiers, and especially colons apparently believed that they could simply turn back the clock, repress the rebellion, and reestablish Algeria as French territory with few if any changes. Given the virulence of the Algerian resistance, this definition of the desired end state was unrealistic as early as 1955. Not until 1958 did France offer any compromise concerning the rights of the local population, and by that time the FLN's support was too well entrenched.

Second, the FLN skillfully manipulated international perceptions to place France at a disadvantage morally and politically. Put simply, the insurgents won the battle for information and perception, and they did so before the advent of the twenty-four-hour-television news cycle. Regardless of the terror bombings in the cities and the murder of collaborators in the countryside, the French forces rather than the insurgents appeared to be the amoral oppressors. The image of France as a repressive colonial power made it impossible for the British and American governments to provide public support.[70]

Third, Paris found it politically difficult to sustain a prolonged counterinsurgency effort. The widespread use of conscripts and casualties among French citizen-soldiers brought the war home to the French populace. Coming on top of defeat and occupation during World War II, failure in Indochina, and economic sluggishness at home, the prolonged counterinsurgency struggle in Algeria eventually aroused considerable political dissent in France. The Algerian War was a major issue in French society that also hampered France's participation in the NATO defense of Europe.

For all these reasons, Charles de Gaulle became convinced that the Algerian conflict could not continue indefinitely. Despite his own strong sense of nationalism and French glory, de Gaulle had the clarity of vision to extricate France from an open-ended struggle. He therefore decided to capitalize on Challe's successes, hoping to create an autonomous Algeria that was in some way still linked to France. On September 16, 1960, he announced that a referendum would allow the Algerians to determine their future. Despite widespread opposition by the pieds noirs, the vote occurred on January 8, 1961, with most non-Europeans voting for some form of independence.[71]

This decision brings us to the final reason for the French defeat, the politicization of the French Army. Having lost in 1940 and again in 1954, many career soldiers were emotionally committed to maintaining Algérie Francaise as a matter of honor. Once they mastered the political dimension of revolutionary war, they became politically partisan themselves. In particular, these soldiers had made personal commitments to protect the Algerian nationals who served the French Army and were justly concerned that these nationals would suffer if France abandoned them. Some, such as Trinquier, had already experienced this betrayal in Indochina, and they did not wish to repeat that situation.

These professional soldiers had expected de Gaulle, well-known as a conservative nationalist with a highly defined sense of honor, to support their position. They consequently felt betrayed by the referendum. Within weeks of the vote, a secret society known as the Organisation de l'Armée Secrète (Secret Army Organization, OAS) formed in Madrid, beginning years of terror attacks inside France. More openly, on April 21, 1961, a group of officers backed by the 1st Foreign Legion Parachute Regiment seized power in Algiers, hoping to reproduce the revolutionary crisis of 1958. General Challe, whose military victory earned him a leadership role in the putsch, announced that "The high command [of the coup] reserves the right to extend its action to the métropole [Metropolitan France] to reconstitute a constitutional and republican order which has been gravely compromised."[72] Yet, this praetorian attitude affected only a small portion of the French Army in Algeria. By radio broadcast, De Gaulle appealed directly to the troops, and the coup collapsed. This coup did, however, weaken the French position in negotiations with the FLN. On March 18, 1962, the two sides signed the Evian Accords to grant independence, and a cease-fire took effect the next day. As the French military rebels had feared, thousands of militiamen and other supporters of French rule suffered torture and murder at the hands of vengeful former rebels.

Algeria officially became independent on July 3, 1962, although the last French troops did not depart the country until 1968. In August 1968, de Gaulle amnestied all those who had rebelled against the government, apparently seeking army support in the face of wide-spread youth riots in France.[73]

For decades thereafter, the French armed forces remained deeply divided by their experiences in Indochina and Algeria. The theory of guerre révolutionnaire was discredited by the images of torture and military revolt. As part of its depoliticization, the army had to eliminate its G5 and other information control measures, abandoning its hard-won experience in counterinsurgency. Although the French Army remained very active in its former African colonies, it generally sought to establish short-term order rather than long-term political outcomes.[74]

11

THE DECLINE OF EMPIRES

JERUSALEM, JULY 22, 1946

The terrorists disguised themselves as hotel waiters and laborers; the 350 kilograms (770 pounds) of TNT entered the building's basement concealed in milk containers.[1] Although the attackers had telephoned a warning of their attack, that warning did not reach decision makers in time to prevent a tragedy; contrary to legend, the government did not reject the threat as ridiculous. Even after security forces discovered the intruders, the situation seemed to be a matter of crime, not terrorism.

The explosives, set off by an acid timer, erupted with a huge roar at 12:37 P.M. The left wing of the King David Hotel, which housed the British government in Palestine, collapsed completely, killing ninety-one Britons, Palestinians, and Jews. The National Military Organization (Irgun Zvai Leumi), a radical group seeking Jewish independence, had achieved its greatest coup against the occupying power. Ironically, the author of this attack was Menachem Begin, who as an Israeli politician would spend much of his life battling Palestinian terrorism.

Even before this attack, the British were in an impossible position in Palestine. Given the antagonism between Jews and Palestinians, and the widespread Western sympathy for the victims of the Holocaust, there was literally no political solution to the problem. Instead, British policemen and soldiers, including the flower of the postwar army, the 6th Parachute Division, struggled to maintain order for another twenty-two months after the King David Hotel explosion. Ambushes and bombings occurred frequently. Ultimately, neither the British nor the United Nations could resolve the situation, and in May 1948 the British withdrew as the two sides dissolved into war.

The failed British government in Palestine was a school of hard experience that equipped soldiers, policemen, and administrators for subsequent conflicts throughout the dwindling British Empire. Indochina and Algeria were, after all, only two of the innumerable counter-insurgencies fought in connection with the decline of European empires after World War II. In some instances, such as the former British Empire, the divestiture occurred in a relatively orderly manner, although even the British had their failures, contrary to the Anglophile spin on the period. In other cases, such as the Dutch and Belgian colonies, which had little preparation for independence, significant conflicts broke out either before or after they were set free. As in the case of the French colonies, however, the Cold War complicated these struggles, with the two blocs conducting surrogate conflicts in many portions of the Third World. This chapter cannot hope to discuss all of these conflicts, but a few of them—especially in the Dutch, British and Portuguese colonies—deserve further study. What many of these cases have in common is the interaction and sometimes confusion of political and military ideas about the correct means and ends of counterinsurgency.

INDONESIAN INDEPENDENCE

Chronologically, one of the first such conflicts was the fight for Indonesian independence.[2] Like the French in Indochina and the British in Malaya, the Dutch lost not only their colonies but also much prestige when Japan overran Southeast Asia in 1941–1942. The Japanese occupiers encouraged a limited degree of Indonesian nationalism, including armed paramilitary groups led by the nationalist leaders Sukarno and Muhammad Hatta. On August 17, 1945, the defeated Japanese permitted Sukarno to declare an independent Indonesian republic. The Japanese sponsorship of this government only reinforced Dutch beliefs that Sukarno and Hatta were puppets, and that the vast majority of residents in the Netherlands East Indies wanted nothing more than a restoration of Dutch rule.[3]

MAP 15. Southeast Asia

Like the French, the Dutch had inadequate armed forces to reassert their ownership; even a year after the Japanese surrender, the Dutch military in the East Indies numbered only 30,000, consisting primarily of a U.S.-trained Dutch marine brigade and a reconstituted, lightly armed Royal Netherlands Indies Army (Koninklijk Nederlands Indisch Leger). At first, the Dutch had to rely on the quarter of a million Japanese troops to maintain order. Thereafter, The Hague depended upon Britain to protect their interests and colonists. The British wished to aid their ally and maintain order, but they were overstretched and could not provide forces to control the vast archipelago.[4]

Against Dutch wishes, the British attempted to negotiate with the republicans, but "Pemoeda" paramilitary gangs and the newly formed republican army resisted British efforts to occupy the cities of Java and Sumatra. The Pemoedas went even further, harassing and in some instances murdering Dutch civilians and former POWs. Matters came to a head when the British 48th Brigade tried to establish order in Surabaya, the east Javanese city that is the second largest in Indonesia. A stray bullet killed the British commander, Brigadier A.W.S. Mallaby, on October 30, 1945. This prompted the British to land the entire 5th Indian Division, supported by tanks and the RAF, in the Surabaya area; the ensuing battle killed some 250 British soldiers as well as thousands of Indonesians. Overall, as many as six hundred British and Indian soldiers died, most of them protecting the Dutch population in Java.[5]

Under some pressure from London and Washington, the Dutch negotiated with the republicans but persisted in regarding them as a tiny minority of troublemakers. Beginning in February 1946, the Dutch pushed for the creation of an Indonesian commonwealth, united with the Dutch crown but with no recognition of the republican government. To satisfy the British and Americans, in March 1947, the Dutch negotiators signed the so-called Linggadjati Agreement that conceded autonomy to the republic in certain portions of the archipelago and promised peaceful negotiations to create a federation by 1949.

In fact, the Dutch did not regard the agreement as binding. Once they were able to increase their military forces, they tried to wipe the republic off the map in the vain hope of establishing security that would attract American investment to the colony. On July 21, 1947, 100,000 well-equipped Dutch troops launched Operation Product, a conventional "police action" that seized control of the key ports, cities, and oil fields of Java and Sumatra. Armored vehicles, air support, and naval gunfire—much of it provided through American military aid—ruthlessly enforced Dutch control. The numerous but poorly armed defenders (recently redesignated as the national army of Indonesia or TNI) were no match for this conventional attack and instead slipped away to begin guerrilla actions.[6] The Dutch soon experienced the frustrations of fighting an indecisive counterinsurgency against foes who did not have to meet the same behavioral standards expected of the Europeans.

The growing sense of a global Cold War, reinforced by public criticism of Dutch imperialism, led the Truman administration to press for renewed negotiations. The colonial government, believing that time was on its side, tried to obstruct the U.S.-chaired UN "Good Offices Committee," sent to reach an agreement. The Dutch military regularly violated the resulting Renville Agreement of January 17, 1948, continuing to seize republican territories. Meanwhile, Washington became aware that, contrary to Dutch claims, Sukarno's republic was a legitimate government. In mid-September 1948, the army's G2, General Chamberlin, noted that the republic had considerable popular support and predicted that the Indonesian Communist Party might well gain power from the nationalists if the Dutch continued to stonewall. Later that month, a leftist-inspired revolt broke out in the east Java city of Madium. The immediate issue was that the TNI was reorganizing into a smaller, more professional force, causing many of the troops to be discharged. The U.S. government was impressed when Prime Minister Hatta promptly used central police and troops to crush the revolt, reinforcing Chamberlin's arguments for U.S. support of Sukarno.[7]

Despite an obvious shift in British and American views of the matter, the Dutch government tried again to eliminate the republic by military action. Operation Kraii (Crow) began on December 19, 1948, because The Hague believed that it could achieve victory while the United Nations was in Christmas recess. Recognizing that he could not defeat the thousands of republican soldiers and guerrillas in the archipelago, Dutch commander Simon Spoor aimed to seize the republican leadership by a coup de main against its capital, the central-Javanese city of Djokjakarta. The Dutch Special Forces Regiment parachuted onto a nearby airfield, after which the Dutch air force flew in reinforcements that fanned out to control the city. Sukarno, Hatta, and other leaders decided to wait for the Dutch to arrest them rather than fleeing ignominiously. The TNI put up more resistance than it had shown the year before, but Dutch air support broke up these defenses, forcing them to again turn to guerrilla warfare.[8]

This Dutch "second police action" was only marginally more effective than the first. It aroused enormous criticism in Europe and the United States, to the point where it endangered the Truman administration's efforts to create the North Atlantic alliance. The Dutch attack seemed a clear violation of the right of self-determination championed by the Truman Doctrine. Secretary of State Acheson bluntly indicated that the Dutch share of Marshall Aid was endangered, and The Hague reluctantly accepted a cease-fire and granted Indonesia independence. The frustrated Dutch military withdrew in 1949, leaving behind an unstable new republic.

THE MALAYAN EMERGENCY: THE PROBLEM

British Malaya, French Indochina, and the Dutch East Indies had many things in common besides proximity. Each had been a multiethnic agricultural economy with a strong drive for independence. In each, the Japanese conquest had discredited the European rulers while encouraging local insurgents. In all three cases, when the former colonial power returned, it attempted to establish local autonomous governments but ran into widespread opposition. While converting to a political party, the Malayan People's Anti-Japanese Army, like the Greek KKE, concealed weapons in anticipation of a possible future conflict.

One significant difference was the presence in Malaya of large numbers of ethnic Chinese. Most of them had immigrated in the 1920s and 1930s as unmarried young men working in tin mines, rubber plantations, and other difficult, dangerous jobs, so that they lacked any family or community structure to stabilize them. The Depression and subsequent Japanese occupation threw them out of work, turning 600,000 Chinese into squatter farmers working on the edge of starvation. Such a discontented, rootless minority provided a fertile recruiting ground for postwar communist agitation. It also meant that the vast majority of insurgents belonged to a single ethnic minority. This could be an advantage in identifying likely insurgents, but it also exposed the Chinese to government coercion and discrimination.[9]

MAP 16. Malaya, 1950

In the period immediately after World War II, Malaya appeared to be dissolving into chaos. After years of warfare, the civil service and police forces were in ruins, unable to ensure food supplies or maintain order. Robbery, piracy, and violent strikes were commonplace.[10] The British government offended both the Malay and Chinese populations by a series of proposals for federation of the local native states. The economy remained sluggish at best, and the British decision to end the use of Japanese currency angered many who lost their savings in the currency shift.[11]

This environment seemed custom-made for exploitation by the small Malayan Communist Party (MCP). After carefully hiding about 20 percent of the weapons it had received during the war, the MCP, like its counterparts in Greece and the Philippines, attempted to take power by legal means, campaigning as a political party and organizing hundreds of often violent labor actions, including a 1947 general strike in Singapore. Despite the fact that a Labour government was in power in London, British officials acted strongly to thwart these nominally legal leftist activities.[12]

Having withdrawn from Indonesia and Palestine, and transferred the Greek problem to American responsibility, the British government in the late 1940s remained beset by tight budgets and by the need to reestablish defenses in Europe. In retrospect, therefore, it was somewhat surprising that London decided to contest the MCP takeover of Malaya. The reason was twofold. First, Malayan tin and rubber were extremely important and lucrative exports, and the owners of these enterprises had considerable political influence. Of equal or greater significance was the British belief that violence in Malaya was part of a Moscow-directed effort to take over Southeast Asia. Unfortunately for the British, neither the United States nor the Commonwealth agreed with this assessment, at least prior to the invasion of South Korea.[13] As a result, Britain had to deal with the Malayan situation alone for the first two years of the growing emergency.

Given the seemingly favorable situation and British opposition on the legal route to power, it was probably inevitable that the MCP should turn to insurgency. In addition, the ongoing civil war in China, where the Communists were on the verge of victory over the KMT, inspired ethnic brethren in Southeast Asia. Yet, contrary to the perceptions of contemporary Western observers, there is no clear evidence that the COMINFORM ordered the Malayan Communists to rebel.[14]

Instead, during the spring of 1948, radicals within the MCP pushed the party leadership into premature initiation of hostilities, indicated by a series of violent attacks on Europeans and officials. On June 16, 1948, armed Chinese gangs murdered three European planters and two of their Chinese employees.[15] The British declared a local state of emergency the same day and expanded it to cover the entire peninsula by June 18.

This prompt British response caught the rebel leaders unprepared, before they had completed either their planning or their recruitment of the populace. Chin Peng, the head of the MCP, later acknowledged that his party had not expected the British to take action until at least September; as a result, the Central Committee had not yet met to finalize its war plans.[16] In fact, on July 16, a routine police raid in the western state of Selangor unwittingly interrupted a planning meeting of the insurgent force, killing the overall commander, Lau Yew, and disrupting rebel coordination. The British rapidly expanded their police force from 10,000 to 40,000 and brought in several hundred veterans of the wartime British guerrilla advisors (Force 136) and of the Palestine police. Among the latter was Colonel W. N. Gray, a Royal Marine officer and former inspector-general of police in Palestine who became police commissioner in Malaya. This force was backed by eleven infantry battalions (three British, six Gurkha, and two Malay) and was soon reinforced by another battalion from Hong Kong, the 4th Hussars, an armored car regiment, as well as the 2nd Guards Brigade from Britain. Emergency legislation permitted arrest without trial and required the registration, including photographs and fingerprints, of all residents over the age of twelve.[17]

This heavy-handed approach prevented an early victory for the insurgents, but it also alienated much of the population. Hiring policemen was relatively simple; training them to use minimum force and to obtain useful intelligence from the population took years of effort. Convinced that the rebels represented a minority in a population that was essentially loyal, government officials initially made little effort to address the causes of discontent. Tactically, the troops and police had difficulty distinguishing between insurgents, supporters (known as the Masses Organization or Min Yuen), and innocent civilians—all Chinese were treated harshly, and eager junior officers sometimes destroyed houses without due process. When a patrol entered a village unexpectedly, the security troops could not distinguish between foe and civilian, with the result that anyone who moved suddenly or fled might well be shot. Thousands of Chinese squatters were forcibly "repatriated" to Nationalist China, which their families had left decades before. Under these circumstances, many ethnic Chinese residents concluded that they had no alternative but to support the rebels, who eventually renamed themselves the Malayan Races Liberation Army (MRLA). Even among the ethnic Malays, the government forces appeared to be a disruptive element rather than a source of security.[18] The High Commissioner for Malaya, Sir Henry Gurney, observed in December 1948 that he was "not at all satisfied that the government cause is helped by adopted methods likely to make criminals and CTs [Communist Terrorists] out of people who were deprived of their livelihood and suffer destruction of their property."[19]

The MRLA had its own problems. Despite its 1945 stockpiling, weapons and ammunition were in short supply. Because there were no radio communications, couriers offered the only means to disseminate directives, requiring weeks or months to implement a change in policy. Although as many as four hundred insurgents were involved in a few early attacks, the British found it easy to track down such large formations, prompting the MRLA to disperse into small units hiding in jungle camps close to squatter villages. In fact, the first British military commander, Major General Sir Charles Boucher, seemed to regard his enemy as a conventional foe and deliberately pushed that enemy into the jungle, making subsequent pursuit more difficult.[20] For much of the emergency, the MRLA operated in "platoons" of twelve to fifty men; despite the MCP's impatience for victory, its campaign never got beyond the early part of a Phase II Maoist insurgency. The leadership of the MCP and MRLA was as rigid as the government in its view of race, excluding ethnic Malays who might have sympathized with their cause. In December 1949, the MCP Central Committee belatedly concluded that it must concentrate on expanding the Min Yuen and otherwise developing public support, something that the Chinese Communist model required before beginning the armed struggle.[21]

Thus, neither side was prepared when the conflict began. During the later 1940s, British security efforts remained decentralized, with police, soldiers, and civil administrators sometimes working at cross purposes while failing to share information with each other. Incoming troop units eventually sent cadres ahead to learn at a jungle warfare center, but the units themselves suffered from considerable turnover and resulting lack of numbers and training. Conscripts spent so much of their national service time in basic training or on troop ships going to and from the Far East that they had little time on station; regular army volunteers on three-year enlistments also turned over frequently. One British infantry battalion in 1949 had only 250 of its authorized 637 men, and even the Gurkha units had a high percentage of new recruits.[22]

Meanwhile, the MRLA continued its attacks. Although most accounts speak of 6,000 to 8,000 insurgents in the field, the initial numbers were probably considerably less; even some of the veterans of the anti-Japanese campaigns refused to go back into the jungle. In the spring of 1949, Chin Peng and his colleagues attempted to mass troops near the mountain of Gunong Tahon, seeking to create a liberated base area. The British detected this troop movement, however, and counterattacked so strenuously that the MRLA had to abandon its plans and return to small-unit operations.[23] Still, by 1950, both the number of insurgent troops and the number of violent incidents were growing rapidly, focusing on the Malay population and on disrupting the economy. The British continued to conduct large-unit sweeps that did not achieve any lasting results. In May of that year, the monthly total of such incidents reached a new high of 534. This figure shocked Commissioner Gurney into requesting a military expert as "Director of Operations." London sent Lieutenant General (retired) Sir Harold Briggs.[24]

BRIGGS AND TEMPLER

It is customary to attribute much of the eventual British success to Briggs, although some of this success was the result of cumulative learning by the entire counterinsurgent force. Briggs was a brilliant individual whose service as an Indian division commander in the Burma campaigns of World War II had equipped him to understand jungle and unconventional operations. Upon arrival in Malaya in June 1950, he quickly analyzed the situation and proposed both military and civil solutions. Militarily, Briggs ensured the establishment of police-military-civil coordinating committees at every level, including joint military-police operations rooms to share intelligence information. He also began the process of separating the insurgents from their civilian support base in a number of ways. First, Briggs insisted that

A MILITARY HISTORY OF THE COLD WAR, 1944–1962

food be strictly controlled; in many areas, rice was only sold already cooked, making it difficult to transfer from civilians to rebels. The British also began a controversial program (eventually named "New Villages") that by the end of 1951 had resettled 400,000 squatters, mostly ethnic Chinese, into villages guarded first by police and later by the villagers themselves. Briggs contended that such home guards would free the police and soldiers for offensive action. As a general rule, the government built these villages first in southern Malaya, then added new ones as the secure zone moved progressively northward. The military attempted to sweep and clear the country from south to north. This massive resettlement effort involved irksome interference in personal lives and required coordination with employers so that employees were grouped in villages near businesses. It also necessitated construction of a huge infrastructure of roads, buildings, communications, and government offices.[25]

The New Villages reflected Briggs's belief that success required achieving public confidence and support. He constantly pressed the police and civil administration to provide more services to the populace, particularly in the new settlements, in order to convince the former squatters that the government could not only protect but also assist them. As Briggs argued:

> Successes against bandit gangs, though essential to security and morale, were in effect only a "rap on the knuckles." It is at this "heart" we must aim, to eliminate the Communist cells among the Chinese population to whom we must give security and whom we must win over. . . . One of the most vital aims throughout the Emergency must be to commit the Chinese to our side, partly by making them feel that Malaya and not Red China is their home. Without their co-operation it will indeed be difficult to bring the Emergency to a successful conclusion.[26]

To ensure compliance, the security forces often conducted the resettlements by surprise raids. Squatters were given only a few minutes to gather their belongings, after which the raiders burned their homes to prevent reoccupation. Although the MCP issued a circular encouraging the squatters to oppose resettlement, these brusque British tactics prevented such resistance.[27]

Such a goal was necessarily a long-term effort; although the food control and resettlement programs made some progress in 1950–1951, Briggs lacked the authority to fully coordinate and implement his plan. Consequently, the counterinsurgent forces received little if any information from the populace and had few Chinese-speaking personnel in any case. Commanders spoke vaguely of bandit groups, with little precise order of battle information; as a result, large-scale clearing operations often came up empty-handed. Intent on keeping the insurgents moving, army units rarely stayed in one place long enough to develop local knowledge and contacts. Most British intelligence during the first half of the emergency was based upon examination of corpses, prisoners of war, and captured documents.[28]

On October 7, 1951, this indecisive state of affairs was shattered by the assassination of Commissioner Gurney. When his small convoy was ambushed north of Kuala Lumpur, Gurney exited his car to draw insurgent fire away from his wife and died within seconds. The ambushers did not even know the identity of their victim but were simply attacking a target of opportunity. Sixteen days later, another, less publicized MPLA ambush wiped out an entire British platoon, leaving sixteen men killed and as many wounded.[29]

These events galvanized government attention and coincided with Winston Churchill's return to power in the 1951 parliamentary elections. Indeed, one of the campaign issues in Britain had been solving the impasse in Malaya. After a reexamination of the entire question, the new government decided to appoint an overall director for the war effort. General Briggs's ill health ruled him out, and in fact he died soon after leaving his post the next year. Instead, the new high commissioner was General Sir Gerald Templer, who had become familiar with government policy as vice chief of the Imperial General Staff under Montgomery. The youngest British corps commander during World War II, Templer had also served in intelligence and military government positions, preparing him for his new role. He was a short, slight, forceful infantry officer with the standard British military mustache and a reputation of being an extremely exacting commander. When Churchill interviewed him for the position, the general bluntly asked what the government desired as the political end state for Malaya. Impressed, Churchill insisted that Templer be the unified head of the military, police, and civil administration, although some expressed trepidation at putting a soldier in charge of so many civil functions.[30]

Like Briggs, Templer understood the central importance of winning hearts and minds. In his first speech to the Legislative Council in 1952, he argued that the emergency made it more rather than less urgent to develop local self-government.[31] Indeed, the British promise of independence for Malaya deprived the insurgents of their greatest propaganda advantage. In the meantime, however, Templer toured the country, insisting that all aspects of the administration and the populace must cooperate to eliminate the communist threat and hasten self-government. Like Briggs, he repeated that "The answer lies not in pouring more troops into the jungle, but rests in the hearts and minds of the Malayan people."[32]

The new commissioner tried many routes to achieve this goal. He emphasized providing services and improving the lives of the transplanted squatters, eventually arming Chinese employees of the tin mines to defend those mines as part of the home guard. Templer sought to bring all the benefits of British society to Malaya, including Boy Scouts, the Red Cross, and other volunteer activities for women and youth. He even sponsored museums and the construction of middle-class suburbs.[33] In 1952, Police Commissioner Arthur Young sent a letter to every member of his force indicating that future promotions depended upon providing kindness and service to the civilian population. At the same time, the British redoubled controls on food supplies. Nor did Templer hesitate to use coercion when it seemed appropriate. In a famous incident in March 1952, the commissioner publicly criticized the leaders of a community that in his mind had tolerated a number of CT attacks in their midst. He refused to allow these leaders to remain neutral in the struggle. After imposing a curfew on the town for twenty-two hours out of every day, Templer gave the inhabitants the opportunity to provide information anonymously, which led to the arrest of forty suspects and the end of the curfew. By the end of 1952, the number of incidents had dropped by almost one-quarter in comparison to the previous year, as the insurgents became increasingly isolated from the populace. Moreover, as the security forces eliminated the MRLA from certain areas, Templer ended irritating restrictions on personal conduct by declaring the cleared locales to be "White Areas." This provided a genuine incentive for the population to cooperate with his administration.[34]

Templer benefited from the efforts of many who had come before him, not least General Briggs's ideas and the slow development of police Special Branch intelligence about the MPLA and Min Yuen. Templer also commanded a force of more than 40,000 trained police and twenty-five maneuver battalions, as compared to an enemy that peaked at 8,000 in 1951 and declined to 3,000 four years later. The Korean conflict aided the counterinsurgent effort in several ways. It provided a booming demand for Malayan exports and therefore both employment for the poor and tax money to fund the war effort, at least during Templer's first year in office. In addition, Australia and New Zealand adopted the British view that Malaya was part of a wider communist effort in Asia. In response, the Commonwealth provided air and eventually ground units to help in Malaya.[35]

With all these resources, Templer still was the essential leader who provided both motivation and coordination.[36] In constant visits throughout the peninsula, the new commander berated some and congratulated others but convinced both the security services and the population that his administration was genuinely concerned about them. His checklist of services for the New Villages included adequate farm land, property titles for homes, sanitation, hygiene, and schools. Well attuned to perceptions and psychology, Templer created a Director-General of Information Services to coordinate not only appeals to the insurgents but also general information and broadcasts to the public. He also imposed unified intelligence and military structures, the latter headed by General Hugh Stockwell as both General Officer Commanding Malaya and commander of the Federation Army.[37]

Templer set the tone throughout the peninsula but obviously did not act alone. An operational research team analyzed each action, while surrendered CTs advised the British on how to improve tactics. In 1952–1953, a multiethnic Alliance Party emerged that belatedly offered the ethnic Chinese a future in the emerging Malaysia.[38]

ENDING THE EMERGENCY

Special Branch intelligence eventually captured an MCP circular, dated October 1951, indicating that the Communists were already on the defensive at the time of Gurney's ambush. Chin Peng later acknowledged that the Communists had been unable to stop the resettlement process and were gradually losing their sources of food, information, and recruits.[39]

Despite the improved situation in settled areas, the British-led forces still had to invest thousands of hours in small-unit patrolling to track down the dwindling MPLA. This was easier said than done, for in the dense, muddy jungle, it was difficult to make any headway at all. The British quickly learned that they could not wear helmets, radios, field packs, and other heavy equipment normal in conventional operations.[40] Gradually, the troops and police special units shed their heavy gear and became experts at jungle operations. The struggle became one of small-unit actions by junior officers, with security patrols often operating in radio silence, out of touch with their headquarters. These patrols soon learned that the MPLA had convinced aborigine groups that the rebellion was in their interests; in some instances, the aborigines apparently believed that the Japanese were still in control! Aborigines replaced squatters as sources of food and information for the insurgents. At first, the British attempted to resettle the aborigines just as they had done with the Chinese, but 8,000 of the primitive people sickened and died when removed from their native environment. Instead, therefore, the counterinsurgent planners decided to win aborigine confidence and create "jungle forts" to deny these areas to the MPLA. These forts had to be hacked out of the jungle and supplied entirely by air.[41]

Transport and resupply were, in fact, the primary roles of the Commonwealth air forces in the emergency. Weather and a shortage of hardened airfields limited offensive air support. Fog and jungle made navigation so difficult that even with accurate intelligence, the Royal Air Force bombers could rarely hit the kind of small targets offered by the insurgents. In one instance in 1956, the RAF conducted three separate air strikes totaling more than 350 tons of bombs before finally killing four CTs of an MPLA platoon. Aerial reconnaissance was more effective, locating hundreds of insurgent camps and farm plots.[42]

Still, aerial resupply and medical evacuation proved invaluable. British, Australian, and New Zealand air crews, primarily flying C-47 twin-engine transports, made it possible for isolated outposts and patrols to operate almost indefinitely in pursuit of the elusive enemy. Parachute supply drops into small clearings were not only difficult but also hazardous to the aircrews, who suffered higher casualty rates than the infantry they supported. Helicopters also provided much resupply as well as medical evacuation for 5,000 wounded and sick people—both security troops and aborigines. In January 1953, U.S. military assistance provided ten S-55 helicopters, each capable of lifting ten troops

or four litters. Anticipating the U.S. actions a decade later, Commonwealth helicopters sprayed defoliant chemicals on dozens of suspected
CT farm plots to deny food to the enemy. Finally, aircraft delivered
millions of surrender pamphlets to suspected guerrilla hideouts.
Because these pamphlets took time to develop and print, they generally proved less effective than airborne loudspeaker appeals.[43]

By the time Templer handed over command to his deputy in May
1954, more than 1.3 million Malayans resided in secure "White"
areas and elected councils governed 209 of the New Villages.[44] The
insurgents had clearly failed, but a few hundred continued the struggle. In 1955, Chin Peng offered to negotiate a settlement, but the
British and the developing Malayan government would not agree to
a legalized communist party even under a different name, and the
struggle continued at least on paper until 1989. In the interim, Chin
and his few remaining adherents operated along the Thai border, the
only place where he could find the kind of sanctuary that his Greek and
Vietnamese counterparts had so often exploited. Malaya became independent in 1957, and the emergency officially ended three years later.[45]

Many observers have cited Malaya as a model of how to defeat a
protracted revolutionary insurgency, and certainly techniques such
as the control of population, food, and propaganda are worthy of study.
Yet, the British methodology involved oppressive control of the populace and racial politics that would be difficult to replicate today even
if one wished to do so. The government deliberately incited the Malay
and Indian populations to stereotype and resent the Chinese minority,
although that minority eventually received civil rights. Even Kumar
Ramakrishna, an advocate of General Templer's positive role, acknowledged that Templer and his subordinates did not comprehend the
culture and politics of the Chinese in Malaya, and Templer repeatedly commented that he did not understand why the enemy refused
to surrender.[46] Hearts and minds often took a back seat to coercion.
As the distinguished British historian Hew Strachan has remarked,
"In Malaya there was a competition for authority, which was not
necessarily a competition for everybody's affection."[47]

One should also note the advantages that the British side possessed. After World War II and Palestine, Britain was blessed with a
supply of able and sophisticated people to deal with the situation. As
in the Philippines, the insurgents had only limited sources of weapons
and popular support. The geography of a narrow, isolated peninsula

favored a policy of progressively clearing and holding the jungle while pushing the rebels away from their support base. Except on the remote Thai frontier, the MRLA had no outside aid or sanctuaries. Because the British were technically the invited guests of traditional Malayan leaders, and because they were able to move toward creation of a democratic government, they offered politically conscious inhabitants a viable alternative to the MCP. Finally, thanks to a booming Malayan economy and the role of Gurkha and Commonwealth troops, London was able to conduct a sustained campaign without compromising public support at home. In short, while "it was a famous victory," that victory was neither simple nor clean, nor necessarily a model for others.

CYPRUS

Numerous other British counterinsurgencies overlapped the long struggle in Malaya. Perhaps the oddest of these was the British attempt to repress the Ethniki Organosis Kyprion Agoniston (National Organization of Cypriot Fighters, or EOKA), a group of fewer than three hundred rebels who forced Britain to relinquish the island of Cyprus after four years of terror attacks.

Before coming into British hands in 1878, the island of Cyprus had many rulers, including the Byzantine Empire, various Crusader organizations, Venice, and finally, after 1571, the Ottoman Empire. This mixed heritage has made modern Cyprus a constant bone of contention. Some 80 percent of the population in the 1950s considered themselves to be ethnically Greek, while the government of Turkey stood as the protector of the Turkish minority.[48]

For eighty years, Britain had ruled Cyprus by benign neglect, punctuated by periodic protests and demands for *enosis* (unification with Greece). In particular, the Greek Orthodox Church insisted on its leadership of the Greek Cypriots and thwarted British efforts to establish local constitutional rule. Even the local communist party came to embrace enosis as a popular goal.

In the 1950s, the declining British presence in the Middle East suddenly thrust Cyprus into prominence. After evacuating Palestine (1948) and the Suez Canal Zone (1954) under pressure, London found itself losing influence in other countries such as Jordan, where in March 1956 local agitation forced King Abdullah to dismiss the British officer commanding the Arab Legion. Although Cyprus lacked major port facilities, its airfields and geographic location made it a natural base for continued British presence in the Middle East. Unfortunately for the British, the agitation for enosis was already reaching a crescendo, while Turkey strongly opposed such a solution.

Field Marshal Alexander Papagos, the victor of the Greek Civil War, became prime minister of his country in 1952 but was reluctant to force the issue of Cyprus. Instead, he tried to maintain good relations with Turkey, Britain, and the rest of NATO while quietly seeking a compromise on the matter. Papagos's attempts were thwarted by Archbishop Makarios III, who as leader of the Greek Cypriots orchestrated anti-British protests in Greece, the United States, and the UN General Assembly.[49]

Even Makarios hesitated to challenge the British militarily, although he was fully informed about plans for a terror-based insurgency in Cyprus. The leader of this insurgency was Colonel George Grivas. Born on Cyprus in 1898, Grivas had a long career in the Greek Army, including fighting guerrillas in Turkey and organizing his private resistance force, X, during the Axis occupation. Grivas was always associated with right-wing nationalist causes, especially the redemption of territories such as Cyprus that he considered to be historically Greek. Beginning in 1951, he carefully planned an insurgent campaign on the island and persisted in assembling arms and recruits despite discouragement from Marshal Papagos and vacillation by Archbishop Makarios.[50]

At first glance, Cyprus seemed an unlikely site for effective insurgency. A small island of 140 by 60 miles (225 by 96 kilometers) offered little concealment for insurgents and was subject to Royal Navy blockade as soon as attacks began. Grivas relied upon the support of the population to conceal his small band of men, using various Christian groups to organize the Greek Cypriots. Grivas also identified at least twenty Greek Cypriots within the local police force who were willing to spy for him. Early in his terror campaign, the colonel directed the murder of all officers involved in Special Branch intelligence, thereby demoralizing and blinding the police force.[51]

The British played into Grivas's hands. The London government refused to discuss any change in sovereignty over the island, making negotiations about local government impossible. After various bombing attacks and attempts at compromise, on March 9, 1956, the British exiled Makarios to the remote Seychelles Islands, where he remained as a martyred figure under house arrest.[52]

The British governor-general, Field Marshal Sir John Harding, was a distinguished soldier whose career had culminated as chief of the Imperial General Staff. However, given the political restrictions placed upon him by London and his own temperament, he was unequipped to deal with an insurgency. He regarded EOKA as simply a security threat to be resolved by force. Grivas's attacks began on March 31, 1955, and in November a rash of bombings compelled Harding to declare a state of emergency and request reinforcements. By March 1956, the British garrison included 17,000 soldiers in fourteen maneuver battalions, controlled by one Royal Marine and three army brigade headquarters. Among the troops was the 16 Parachute Brigade, intended as Britain's strategic reserve for the Middle East but quickly drawn into the insurgency.[53]

The British attempted to follow the Malayan model, integrating the police, army, and civil government. Unfortunately, the first of these forces was a slender reed, unable to provide useful intelligence or security. When Greek Cypriots refused to join the police, Harding hired large numbers of poorly educated Turkish Cypriots, expanding the total police force from 1,386 constables in 1954 to 5,878 hastily trained men two years later. A commission of senior policemen from Britain recommended that Harding disband the new auxiliary police, but he refused. Many of these new recruits were guilty of corruption, torture, and other abusive behavior; when EOKA killed a Turkish policeman, his peers stood aside while a Turkish mob attacked Greeks. Rightly or wrongly, the Greek majority accused British troops of the same types of abuse, eliminating any chance that the government forces would gain public support against the terrorists. As James Corum has observed, "The abusive behavior of the Cyprus Police was a godsend to the insurgents, who made the actions of the security forces a central theme in their international propaganda campaign."[54] Thus, although the total British security force approached 40,000 soldiers, sailors, airmen, and police in 1956, they were unable to track down three hundred terrorists amidst 400,000 Greeks.

The insurgents used not only force but also peaceful means to embarrass the British. School children demonstrated frequently, tying down security forces in the cities. When Harding would not permit schools to fly the Greek flag, all but 81 of 499 elementary schools

closed rather than risk EOKA reprisals. The British further antago-
nized the clannish population by imposing collective fines and curfews
on villages where explosions occurred. Grivas may have been arrogant
and paranoid, but his methods were effective.[55]

The security forces had some successes using systematic searches
and logical deductions. The commander of 16 Parachute Brigade noted
that there were few security incidents near the Kykko Monastery in
the mountains of western Cyprus, suggesting that the rebels might
be using this area as a sanctuary. In May 1956, therefore, a reinforced
brigade launched Operation Pepperpot to search this area. An army
patrol fired on but failed to catch Grivas; the British did seize and
publish his diary, which documented Archbishop Makarios's involvement and the ruthless nature of EOKA plans.[56]

Gradually during the later 1950s, a new group of British intelligence officers built up a knowledge of EOKA, including Grivas's system
for message drops to pass out instructions. At one point, the British
believed that they had located Grivas's hideout, but Prime Minister
Macmillan vetoed any attempt to arrest him because of the possibility of collateral casualties.[57] Just as in Algeria, international perceptions were on the side of the insurgents despite their many terror
attacks. Eventually, Britain had to make a compromise that left Cyprus
ruled by a joint Turkish-Greek government, with Britain retaining
several military bases. In 1959, having achieved the impossible, Grivas
left the island on board a Greek national aircraft; upon his arrival in
Athens, the government promoted him to lieutenant general. This
singular victory was overshadowed by his later defeats, however. Archbishop Makarios managed to outmaneuver not only Grivas but also
the governments of Greece, the United States, and Britain during the
struggle between Greek and Turkish Cypriots that culminated in a
Turkish invasion on July 19, 1974.[58]

Mau Mau

The same strengths and weaknesses shown in Malaya and Cyprus
characterized the British repression of the Mau Mau movement in
Kenya between 1952 and 1956. Although this uprising did not, in fact,
have a direct relationship to the Cold War, the British experiences here
interacted with those in Malaya and elsewhere, sometimes leading
to false beliefs in a communist threat in Kenya.

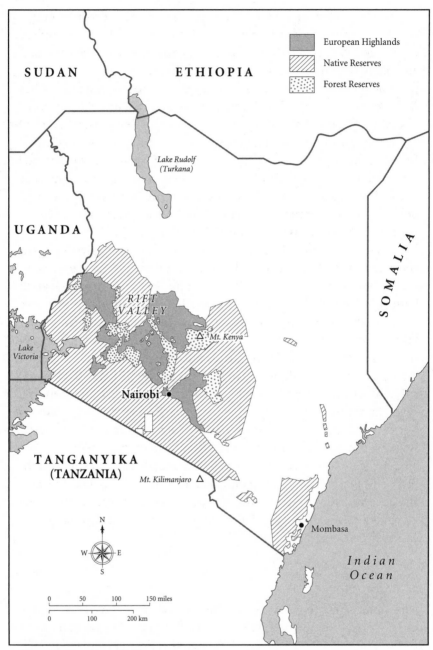

MAP 17. Kenya, c. 1953

320

The causes of this movement are still in dispute, reflecting the British difficulty in distinguishing between agitators and genuine issues. Essentially, a large portion of the native population of Kenya believed, rightly or wrongly, that European settlers had stolen the best farmlands immediately after World War I. In fact, the settlers generally took unoccupied lands. However, the Kikuyu tribe grew from 300,000 to 1,300,000 in the first half of the twentieth century, creating an enormous land hunger. Just as in Malaya, a large population of marginal squatter farmers developed, providing a ready audience for advocates of violent change.[59]

The population and especially the Kikuyus were divided concerning the best means to rectify this situation. Some senior tribal chiefs remained loyal to Britain, and a few radicals advocated violence. In the middle were many reformers led by the Western-educated Jomo Kenyatta (born Kamau wa Ngengi). European settlers had gained considerable wealth and influence during World War II and felt threatened by African challenges, however peaceful, to their vision of Kenya as a "White Man's Country." From their viewpoint, Kenyatta was a troublemaker, especially since in his youth he had visited the Soviet Union and joined the Communist Party. In reality, Kenyatta was skeptical of all European political ideas but was working to use the Kikuyu tribe as the basis for an independence movement.[60] The alarmed settlers heavily influenced British official views of the situation, lumping Kenyatta in with the radical Mau Mau society.

The Mau Mau had begun in secret during the 1930s and by the late 1940s used intimidation tactics to force Kikuyu tribesmen to swear loyalty and secrecy. The group was particularly active in the area southwest and west of Mount Kenya, where native and settler lands were intermixed. Kenyatta's Kikuyu Central Association (KCA) undoubtedly encouraged the Mau Mau but did not fully control the movement. Yet, the British apparently drew a false analogy between the KCA and the communist parties of places such as Malaya. When the Kenyan Emergency officially began in October 1952, the government arrested Kenyatta and other KCA leaders, trying them as the supposed leaders of the Mau Mau. Thus, the British missed an opportunity to co-opt local leaders into the government and in fact may have driven more Kikuyu into the radical camp.[61]

The prospect of a native secret society swearing oaths to eliminate the European presence stirred basic, irrational fears among the settlers.

Oaths were essential to Kikuyu society, and once an individual swore to support the Mau Mau goals, he could not go back on his word without being ostracized. The European settlers were particularly horrified by instances in which their own servants betrayed planters who were then literally butchered by the Mau Mau.[62] Yet, these same settlers insisted that their own servants were loyal, interfering with police efforts to interrogate and arrest suspects. The British governor, Sir Evelyn Baring, felt compelled to take official action to preempt unrestrained settler violence. For much of the insurgency, therefore, British officials and commanders had to deal with settlers who demanded extreme repression and armed guards for their farms rather than effective operations to address native issues and neutralize the threat.[63]

After a series of murders including that of a loyalist chieftain, Baring declared a state of emergency on October 20, 1952. That night, a British infantry battalion arrived by air from the Middle East Command to join three battalions of the King's African Rifles (KAR). Troops with fixed bayonets patrolled Nairobi to reassure the settlers. The government mobilized all police reservists as well as the Kenya Regiment, the latter composed of European reservists. This action was accompanied by all the draconian restrictions applied in Malaya, including detention without trial for thousands of inhabitants and the execution over the next two years of 290 men for possessing arms and 45 for administering unlawful oaths. Yet, the government again lacked detailed police intelligence about the opposition.[64]

Organizationally, the government in Kenya went through the same halting steps as those taken in Malaya. Major General W.R.N. Hynde arrived in January 1953 as director of operations but was only an advisor to the governor; Hynde sympathized with the settlers, which made it difficult to take an independent, objective view of the situation. As Briggs had done in Malaya, Hynde created a hierarchy of coordinating committees among the various security military forces, but this left no one in charge. Violence continued to escalate, culminating on March 26, 1953, when the Mau Mau surrounded and burned the loyal village of Lari, northwest of Nairobi, killing eighty-four and wounding another thirty-one. That same night, the rebels overran a nearby police station, seizing weapons and freeing 173 prisoners.[65] This massacre motivated many law-abiding Kikuyu to oppose the Mau Mau more strongly and led in June to the arrival of General Sir George Erskine as the newly created commander-in-chief for Kenya. Unlike

Templer in Malaya, however, Erskine had only limited control over the police and auxiliary forces.[66]

Erskine had three British and five KAR battalions, plus an armored car regiment and a few AT-6 training aircraft that could drop small bombs. By the end of the year, he received another two battalions in the form of 49 Infantry Brigade, plus an engineer unit, giving him a total of some 10,000 combat troops. Even this left him outnumbered by the estimated 12,000 active Mau Mau, although fortunately only about 1,500 of the rebels had firearms.[67]

As in Malaya, even light aircraft had difficulty finding and attacking insurgents in the forest, and the available intelligence rarely allowed time for preplanned air strikes. Without air-ground communications, the AT-6 sometimes attacked friendly patrols and reported them as enemy! Lincoln bombers attacked predetermined map coordinates but rarely achieved significant results. Perhaps the most successful air support came from the small, privately owned aircraft of the Kenya Police Reserve, who dropped food to patrols and hand grenades to the Mau Mau. Beginning in 1954, a few helicopters provided resupply, but in general air support had limited effect.[68]

During the second half of 1953, General Erskine launched a number of sweeps in different areas; the troops again had to develop proficiency in such operations, but they had enough success that an amnesty campaign known as "Green Branch" led to eight hundred surrenders by early 1955. In April 1954, Erskine devoted four battalions to a cordon and sweep operation of Nairobi, an effort that screened the entire population and arrested some 16,500 on suspicion of supporting the Mau Mau. This Operation Anvil shattered the Mau Mau hierarchy and its communications between the forest and the city, but numerous innocents suffered and families were broken up. Thereafter, registration papers and frequent police checkpoints kept the capital under control. Some observers considered Anvil to be the turning point of the entire campaign.[69]

Following Anvil, the government forces began to systematically clear various Kikuyu districts, turning them over to civilian authority as they became secure. The army cut mile-long trails into the forest and established base camps at the end of those trails, depriving the insurgents of any warning that the troops were about to enter a specific area. Such operations at least kept the insurgents on the move, separating them from the rest of the population and encouraging further surrenders. At the same time, Erskine took the calculated risk of expanding and arming the Kikuyu Guard. Originally a group of loyalist natives, this force soon became so strong that it challenged the Mau Mau but also used violence for its own self-interest. So the government selectively transferred the more reliable members of this guard into the Tribal Police, which then served to hold the perimeter of various areas being searched by regular troops.[70]

Success in the field as well as a rapid development of police intelligence gave the government an obvious advantage by mid-1955, so that the majority of the population supported the efforts to find the remaining rebels. This support increased when the British governor, over settler protest, included moderate African leaders in the Kenyan administration. In October,1956, a government-organized "pseudo gang" wounded the last major Mau Mau leader, Dedan Kimathi, who later died at the hands of a tribal policeman. Thereafter, the army withdrew from the field, leaving the police to hunt down the remnants of the rebellion.[71]

Ten thousand British and African soldiers, 21,000 police, and 25,000 Kikuyu Guards had taken four years to defeat an organization that had no outside support, little structure, and few weapons. In the process, the administration had to contend not only with the rebels themselves but also with major instances of security forces abusing and torturing prisoners. Although the Mau Mau failed in the short run, their rebellion undoubtedly hastened independence not only in Kenya but also in other African colonies.[72] In turn, the wave of independence in Africa contributed to political instability during the 1960s and 1970s, an instability that often involved struggles between surrogate organizations backed by the two sides in the Cold War. Fortunately, Kenya itself avoided this instability for several decades, based largely on its experience with the Mau Mau.

THE PORTUGUESE EMPIRE

Nowhere in Africa was the violence more intense nor more prolonged than in the Portuguese empire.[73] The Soviet Union, China, and their allies became deeply involved in these rebellions, achieving success through protracted revolutionary conflicts that wore down Lisbon's will. As such, these rebellions were an essential part of the Cold War

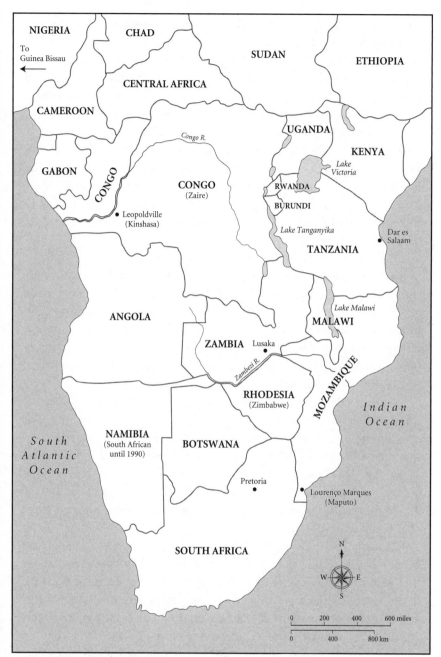

NIGERIA

To
Guinea Bissau ←

CHAD

SUDAN

ETHIOPIA

CENTRAL AFRICA

CAMEROON

UGANDA

KENYA

GABON

CONGO

Congo R.

CONGO
(Zaire)

Lake
Victoria

RWANDA

BURUNDI

● Leopoldville
(Kinshasa)

Lake Tanganyika

Dar es
Salaam ●

TANZANIA

Lake Malawi

ANGOLA

MALAWI

ZAMBIA Lusaka ●

Zambezi R.

RHODESIA
(Zimbabwe)

MOZAMBIQUE

*Indian
Ocean*

*South
Atlantic
Ocean*

NAMIBIA
(South African
until 1990)

BOTSWANA

Pretoria
●

● Lourenço Marques
(Maputo)

SOUTH AFRICA

N
W E
S

0   200   400   600 miles

0   400   800 km

MAP 18. Southern Africa

rivalries of the 1950s and 1960s, and set the stage for even greater, more conventional violence after Portugal withdrew.

Having been the first to colonize the continent in the late 15th century, Portugal was also the last European power to give up its colonies. Holding onto these colonies for centuries was by no means easy, with frequent outbreaks of native and settler unrest. Still, for most of the 450 years of Portuguese rule, Lisbon had been able to make do with a tiny force in each colony—often no more than 1,000 Europeans and 5,000 native troops, backed by a militia drawn from loyal tribes. Given the ferocious attrition that disease imposed on European colonists and soldiers, native troops with either local or European officers seemed the most cost-effective way to maintain order in the colonies.[74]

After 1945, the three remaining Portuguese colonies—Mozambique on the east coast of Africa and Guinea and Angola on the west—were indeed thriving economies. In 1959, for example, Angola exported $50 million in coffee and $20 million in diamonds, and was just beginning to exploit its petroleum reserves. Much of this production was only possible because of forced African labor, although Lisbon never officially condoned racial discrimination. The colonial wealth balanced Portugal's own trade deficit.[75]

Antonio de Oliveira Salazar, the dictator of Portugal from 1932 until 1968, considered these colonial possessions to be essential not only for the economic well-being of the home country but also as justification for Portugal's claim that it was still a major power. In December 1960, the UN General Assembly voted to condemn Lisbon for this policy, but the Lisbon government insisted that, just as in the case of Algeria, its African possessions were not colonies but integral parts of the Portuguese nation.

During the 1950s, many of the educated residents of Angola and Mozambique disagreed with Salazar; encouraged by the wave of colonies gaining independence as well as by the Marxist-Leninist message of the Soviet Union and China, these Africans attempted labor strikes and protests to no avail. By 1960, they had concluded that Lisbon would never willingly release its possessions.

Still, not all residents of the colonies actively sought independence, and even those who did so were divided on cultural, ideological, and sometimes tribal lines. In 1956, for example, the Marxist, assimilated radicals in Luanda, Angola, founded the Movimento Popular de Libertacao de Angola (Popular Movement for the Liberation of Angola, MPLA). Not only did the Portuguese police persecute the group, but these radicals found they had little in common with the peasantry. By contrast, Holden Roberto's Uniao das Populacoes de Angola (Union of Angolan Peoples, UPA) first took shape in the early 1950s, based on the rural Bakongo tribe on both sides of Angola's northern border with the Belgian Congo. Roberto was a nationalist inspired and eventually supported by the independence movement in the Congo. As a result, the UPA was neither culturally Portuguese nor ideologically Marxist. In Portuguese Guinea, the Partido Africano da Independencia da Guine et Cabo Verde (African Party for the Independence of Guinea and Cape Verde, PAIGC) had fewer rivals, but its leader, the well-educated nationalist Amilcar Cabral, had considerable difficulty recruiting the prosperous farmers of this swampy region. Cabral ruefully admitted that only personal grievances among rootless young men, not Marxism or anti-imperialism, attracted supporters. Mozambique, by contrast, had numerous splinter radical groups.[76]

Having studied the ongoing struggles in Algeria, Malaya, Cuba, and elsewhere, by 1960 the Portuguese civilian and military leadership was well aware of the possibility of insurgency in its colonies. Lisbon undertook modest reinforcements of its colonial security forces in anticipation of trouble.

REBELLION

The first outbreak came in 1961, in Angola. On February 4, the MPLA inspired a violent crowd that attacked the police and prisons in Luanda. The government broke up this demonstration, but on March 15, Holden Roberto launched his poorly armed force of 4,000 to 5,000 across the border into northern Angola. Given the low population density and scattered security posts of Angola, there was little to stop this group, which resembled a mob more than an army. Over the next six weeks, Roberto's UPA attacked some seven hundred farms and one hundred government posts, killing at least five hundred Europeans and thousands of Africans. At first, the attacks were formless acts of thuggery, but in the late spring Roberto imposed sufficient control that his troops began to systematically destroy economic assets in northern Angola. Eventually, the local militias of both Europeans and peace-loving natives succeeded in containing the rampage, some fifty kilometers north of the capital, until reinforcements arrived from Portugal. At the same time, some European vigilantes took out their frustrations on innocent Africans and Protestant missionaries, whom they blamed for encouraging a desire for independence.[77]

The UPA onslaught was a great psychological shock and gave rise to an attempted military coup against Salazar. Salazar suppressed the coup on April 13 but in the process disrupted reinforcement efforts by replacing virtually the entire leadership of the defense ministry. The Lisbon government now faced a major insurrection at a time when its armed forces and defense funding were far more meager than what was available to France, Britain, and other counterinsurgent actors. Moreover, it would have to project and sustain military power at a distance of more than 7,000 kilometers from metropolitan Portugal. By late June, Lisbon had increased the garrison of Angola to almost 50,000 men while reinforcing its other colonies. However, given the poor road network in Angola, the rebels were able to delay and ambush the advancing Portuguese forces. One hundred thirty-four security personnel died in the 1961 counteroffensive. Because the dry winter season in Angola was limited to the period from May to August, it took all the Portuguese efforts, including the profligate use of napalm, to push the UPA back to the northern border area before the rains returned. By that time, more than 400,000 local inhabitants had become refugees, many of them in the two neighboring Congos; this loss of labor seriously affected coffee production for the next several years.[78]

During those years the UPA and its successor group, the Frente Nacional de Libertacao de Angola (National Front for the Liberation of Angola, FNLA), made little progress beyond raids across the northern border. In 1966, however, two other groups widened the war zone by attacks in eastern and northeastern Angola, respectively. The Marxist MPLA, headed by the hard-liner Agostinho Neto and backed by Soviet and East German aid, became an effective military force; the cotton economy of eastern Angola was devastated, and many locals became alienated from a Portuguese administration that was unable to protect them. The much smaller Uniao Nacional para a Independencia Total de Angola (National Union for the Total Independence of Angola, UNITA) received aid from China and took on the trappings of a Maoist insurrection.

The opposition movements in the other two colonies predated the rebellion in Angola and soon took to the bush as well. In 1963 the PAIGC began a series of efficient raids across the borders into Guinea, tying down a disproportionate number of Portuguese forces in that relatively small, poor area. Along the coastline, rivers, and swamps of Guinea, the Portuguese Navy was intimately involved in fighting the guerrillas and resupplying isolated outposts, often using inflatable boats with outboard motors. Last, extensive communist-bloc support facilitated a major insurrection in Mozambique, although the local leaders retained their independence from their patrons. Here, the dominant rebel movement was the Frente de Libertacao de Mocambique (Mozambique Liberation Front, FRELIMO), formed in 1962 by the merger of three splinter groups. After two years of preparation, FRELIMO attacked northern Mozambique from training camps in neighboring Tanzania. After the Portuguese successfully contained this threat, in 1968 FRELIMO moved into Zambia and opened a new front in the northwestern part of Mozambique.[79] Meanwhile, both the Soviets and the Chinese provided advisors (often Cuban) and extensive training, including year-long courses for some leaders. By 1973, PAIGC had even acquired 122mm artillery pieces and surface-to-air missiles, the latter bringing down four Portuguese aircraft in one month.[80]

However, these movements never approached the Phase III or mobile/conventional stage of protracted revolutionary warfare. Their operations tended to be minor raids and ambushes with the frequent use of mines. In contrast to the Vietnamese and Cuban revolutions, the anti-Portuguese revolutionaries generally tried to avoid terror attacks and other civilian casualties; the sole exception was the assassination of hundreds of tribal leaders for intimidation purposes. Within their small "liberated" base areas, these rebels, especially PAIGC and FRELIMO, provided health care and other basic services but made little effort to impose collectivization or other practices that would challenge traditional norms. Only PAIGC approached the status of a successful revolutionary government, eventually influencing but not controlling much of Guinea's hinterlands and having diplomatic relations with eighty states. Cuban military and medical aid contributed to this success. Otherwise, the various movements adhered to a strategy of attrition since they were incapable of defeating their opponents in the field.[81]

PORTUGUESE RESPONSE

By most measurements, the Portuguese response to the insurrections was impressive if sometimes clumsy. By 1971, Lisbon maintained a ground force totaling 142,000 soldiers in Africa, supported by significant air and naval components. Forty percent of this army, including significant numbers of junior officers, was African, a sign that the Portuguese leadership had succeeded in convincing some of its colonists to support its policies. To these figures must be added at least 10,000 police and 35,000 part-time militiamen recruited to protect their communities, thereby freeing the army for more offensive tasks. Almost half of the national budget went for the colonial effort, supplemented by major incomes from the colonies themselves.[82] On occasion, the military launched large clearing operations. The most famous of these was Operation Gordion Knot in 1970, when 10,000 Portuguese troops attacked FRELIMO bases east of Lake Malawi (or Nyassa). Portuguese commanders claimed that this operation killed more than four hundred guerrillas, reduced FRELIMO's forces from 8,000 to 4,000, and discouraged the Makonde tribe that had hitherto supported FRELIMO.[83] Most of the time, however, operations were on a much smaller scale.

The military did have problems with chain of command. In each colony, there were component commanders for the respective services who were often senior in rank to the overall commanders-in-chief, the latter having been selected for effectiveness rather than seniority. There was also occasional conflict between military and civilian officials. In July 1969, each colony's commander-in-chief received government authority over all military operations, curbing the powers of the civilian governors-general.[84]

Portuguese intelligence efforts were at least partially effective. The PIDE (Polícia Internacional e de Defesa do Estado), later redesignated as the DGS (Direcção General de Segurança), was heavy-handed but effective in tracking and countering the efforts of the various insurgent movements; in several instances, the PIDE arranged the assassination of rebel leaders, although this usually failed to disrupt their organizations.[85] The PIDE and some army commanders, notably General Kaulza da Arriaga in Mozambique, had great success in persuading rebels to surrender and freely join the counterguerrilla forces. Among the deserters were at least five central committee members of FRE-LIMO as well as mid-ranking military commanders. These defectors were often motivated by factionalism within the rebel movements, especially between pro-Soviet and pro-Chinese leaders.[86] The government was also quite successful in playing tribal groups off against each other.

Taking a leaf from the British experience in Malaya, the Portuguese constructed hundreds of fortified villages.[87] The effort began as a means to resettle the populace displaced during the 1961 UPA attacks but expanded notably in both Angola and Mozambique, especially after 1967. Ultimately, more than a million Angolans, or 20 percent of the population, were displaced, as were another million (15 percent of the population) in Mozambique, and 150,000 (30 percent) in Guinea-Bissau.[88] Portuguese leaders began with the intention of protecting and isolating the populace from the guerrillas but soon found that concentrating residents in this manner made it easier to provide health, education, and other services to the population.

Unfortunately, the implementation of this massive resettlement left much to be desired. Some of the displacements began before building materials, security, and safe water were available at the new sites. Moreover, because the army tended to regard the guerrillas as a foreign-based threat, it constructed fully fortified villages only along the northern and eastern frontiers of Angola, and the northern boundary of Mozambique; resettlement sites in the center of the colonies often lacked defenses to repel insurgent attack. Portuguese soldiers had to perform the roles of civil administrators, teachers, and health professionals. Frequently, people were moved to land that was dissimilar and less fertile than the land they had left. When the moves occurred after planting season, the affected people lost their old crops without time to plant and harvest in the new location. Africans particularly resented resettlements in which the Lisbon government gave their former farms to discharged European soldiers. For these and similar reasons, the resettlement effort was at best a mixed blessing, increasing rather than preventing disaffection in some instances and failing to provide stable labor forces in others.[89]

Nonetheless, the Portuguese government did undertake significant social and economic reforms because its counterinsurgency doctrine recognized the primacy of such operations in what it termed "conquering hearts and minds."[90] Beginning in 1961, the government eliminated all legal distinctions between indigenous and Portuguese citizens, and outlawed the use of forced labor. In 1971, a new Portuguese constitution designated Angola and Mozambique as autonomous states with their own budgets and elected assemblies, much like those the French had established in Indochina two decades earlier.[91] Massive road construction projects not only facilitated troop movements but also enhanced and unified the economies of the Portuguese colonies. These projects added more than 5,000 miles (8,460 kilometers) of asphalt highway in Mozambique alone in a six-year period. In southern Mozambique, guerrilla attacks failed to delay the construction of the massive Cabora Bassa Dam on the Zambesi River, designed to provide electric power both for the colony and for sale to South Africa.[92]

STRATEGIC CONTEXT

Strategically, however, the insurgencies were a virtual stalemate. By 1973, the Portuguese had suffered an estimated 12,000 soldiers dead due to combat, illness, and accident in Africa.[93] The Portuguese army could not be defeated but neither could it destroy its enemies completely. So long as the MPLA, PAIGC, and FRELIMO remained in the field, however battered they were at a tactical level, the rebellions presented their opponents with an open-ended, insoluble threat. For a relatively small investment in weapons, advisors, and training, Moscow, Beijing, and Havana had created a running sore that damaged NATO unity and the Western image of promoting democracy.

Internationally, Portugal stood almost alone. In the fall of 1961, the UN General Assembly again condemned Lisbon's colonial policies. The United States was also critical and reduced military aid to Lisbon but could not afford to take a hard line because it needed continued access to the airbase on the Portuguese Azores islands. Although the Caucasian regimes in Rhodesia and South Africa supported the counterinsurgency efforts in Mozambique, newly independent states such as the former Belgian Congo, Zambia, and Tanzania provided sanctuary and encouragement to the rebels. Lisbon did not risk major incursions to eliminate these sanctuaries. Even the Rhodesians and the Boers, with their largely Caucasian forces, looked down upon the Portuguese effort to fight as a multiracial army.

Thousands of miles away, Portugal suffered a stinging symbolic blow in the loss of its three tiny enclaves on the Indian subcontinent—vestigial colonies that it had refused to surrender to the Indian government. On December 17–18, 1961, the Indian Army overwhelmed the garrisons of Goa, Daman, and Diu. Although defense of these enclaves was impossible, the Salazar government court-martialed and cashiered the surviving commanders when they surrendered after a stiff fight. Career soldiers rightly felt that the government had made them scapegoats for the defeat in India and would do the same in Africa. Yet, this loss to India only encouraged hard-core Portuguese nationalists to fight all the harder in Africa.[94]

As the insurgencies continued without resolution, Portugal's underdeveloped economy suffered from the constant drain of heavy defense expenditures and four-year conscription for its young men. Salazar suffered a stroke and retired in 1968, but his corporatist, fascist economy continued to labor under the strain. At the same time, the proportion of Portuguese exports going to its colonies declined from 43 percent in 1960 to only 10 percent thirteen years later. In 1972, the economy took a sharp downturn. The war was draining Portugal without providing significant economic return.[95]

The Armed Forces Movement

On March 15, 1974, the DGS police, aided by the right-wing Portuguese Legion, raided a meeting of officers at the Military Academy in Lisbon. This raid led to the arrest of forty officers and the dismissal of two senior generals on charges of disloyalty. This time, however, the government's efforts to thwart opposition only accelerated revolutionary change. One month later, army units seized the government and communications offices of Lisbon, overthrowing the fascist regime and ushering in a period of turbulent but democratic politics in Portugal.[96] The Armed Forces Movement (Movimento das Forcas Armadas, or MFA) quickly ended Portugal's rule in Africa, turning over the former colonies to varied fates, including civil war in Angola.

Observers have suggested a variety of explanations for this stunning change. Some alleged that the career officers were angered by a recent government decision to give equal pay and promotions to officers conscripted for the colonial struggle, although in fact this grievance was apparently used as a cover story for the officers to meet while conspiring against the government.[97] Others have chalked up the April 25 revolt as a victory of the African insurgents' Marxist propaganda, and certainly some members of the MFA called for a socialist government at home. Yet, the actual causes went considerably deeper.

This Portuguese military action was, in fact, almost a mirror image of the French Army's mutinies in 1958 and 1961.[98] Where the Fourth French Republic was ineffectual and indecisive, the fascist regime established by Salazar forty years earlier was brutally repressive and incredibly stubborn in trying to continue the counterinsurgency struggle. In the long run, the French Army could not thwart the wishes of its people, whereas the Portuguese Army was the only institution that might articulate and implement popular desires to end the war. Where career French officers and NCOs had become increasingly isolated from their parent nation, the officer and enlisted ranks of the Portuguese armed forces had become the most democratic and representative bodies in the entire country. While university-educated French reserve officers served a few years in Algeria and then left active duty to enter politics, conscripted Portuguese university graduates spent as long as eight years in the colonies, unable to leave active duty or publish criticisms of the war. In fact, as Douglas Porch has observed, "The armed forces remained the only place where a man could keep his own counsel, albeit discreetly."[99] The shortage of applicants willing to enter the Portuguese officer corps was so acute that men of all classes and political opinions became academy graduates. Under the pressure of an open-ended colonial commitment, both academy graduates and conscript officers came to share a sense that their country was headed in the wrong direction and that they must act not to preserve the colonies but to divest their nation of that burden. By April 25, a majority of the officer corps in its various services shared this belief, making it impossible for the regime to find enough loyal defenders to halt the revolt and continue the war.

Contrary to popular belief, protracted revolutionary insurgency does not always win, as evidenced by the Greek, Philippine, and Malayan examples. Successful insurgencies usually require not only a deeply held cause but also outside assistance and sanctuaries, as well as a kind of patient persistence that is contrary to human nature. For the same reasons, successful instances of *counterinsurgency* usually involve superior financial and numerical resources, the ability to isolate the rebels from outside aid, and a willingness to continue the war of attrition—a willingness usually based upon a government that addresses at least some of the basic needs of the populace and works closely with its field commanders. In the case of an outside power, this also requires the sustained support of its own citizenry. Given these considerations, the failure of the Netherlands, France, and Portugal to defend their empires is not nearly so surprising as their national abilities to sustain the struggle for so long.

12

THE UNITED STATES ENTERS THE MIDDLE EAST

For the past three months, Major General Paul D. Adams, U.S. Army, had been the de facto ruler of Beirut—at the time a prosperous city of multiple religious confessions that seemed threatened by political radicalism. To maintain order, he had issued tough but effective rules of engagement to his troops:

1. Do not shoot until fired upon;
2. If fired upon, raise the hostiles one weapon [i.e., use the next larger or heavier type of weapon] and put a stop to the firing;
3. If they match your weapons, raise them one again and again until the firing ceases.[1]

This aggressive policy had enabled Adams to accomplish his mission with only one American soldier killed in action. With a friendly general installed as president of Lebanon in September 1958, the "Switzerland of the Middle East" once again appeared to be peaceful and secure.

By October, the initial U.S. Marine landing forces were long gone, and the U.S. Army had almost completed its withdrawal. On his last day in command, General Adams had his official sedan, prominently marked with American flags, drive through the volatile Basta quarter of northern Beirut before his departure. Instead of hostility, this defiant gesture provoked nothing but scattered applause from the Lebanese spectators.

The United States had completed its first postwar intervention in the Middle East with all the outward appearance of success;
subsequent deployments were not nearly so cheap or effective as
Adams's operation.

Strategic Situation

Between the two world wars, Great Britain had been the dominant
power in the Middle East, with France controlling Syria and Lebanon.
By 1945, however, Britain was nearly bankrupt and repeatedly sought
U.S. funding to maintain its position in the region. Moreover, postwar
Egyptian nationalism produced rising violence against the center of
British military force in the region, a complex of bases along the
Suez Canal. Even before London evacuated these bases in 1954, its
presence in the region was based largely on a bluff—a promise to aid
friendly regimes in Jordan and Iraq in the event of a Soviet offensive
into the region. At the same time, both London and Washington were
reluctant to provide such regimes with weapons that might be used
against Israel.[2]

The United States had established a network of airbases and
supply depots in the region during World War II, but these atrophied
along with the rest of the U.S. armed forces in the later 1940s. Nonetheless, the Middle East remained critical not only for its petroleum
supplies but also for its potential role as a bomber base in case of war
with the Soviet Union. In July 1954, NSC policy paper 5428 concluded that U.S. vital interests would be "critically endangered" if
the Middle East passed under Soviet control.[3]

Despite this, the United States was reluctant to remain involved
after 1945; when the British asked for funding and support, Washing-
ton consistently replied that this was a British responsibility.[4] At a
North Atlantic Council meeting in Ottawa in September 1951, the
Truman administration agreed in principle to a combined Middle East
Command (sometimes called the Middle East Defence Organization)
with a British supreme commander equivalent to the Supreme Allied
Commander, Europe, but neither the Eisenhower administration nor
the Arab states was interested in implementing such a plan. Australia,
New Zealand, and South Africa offered to commit troops to the region
in case of war, just as they had done in World War II. However, with
the spread of conflict in Southeast Asia, the governments in Canberra

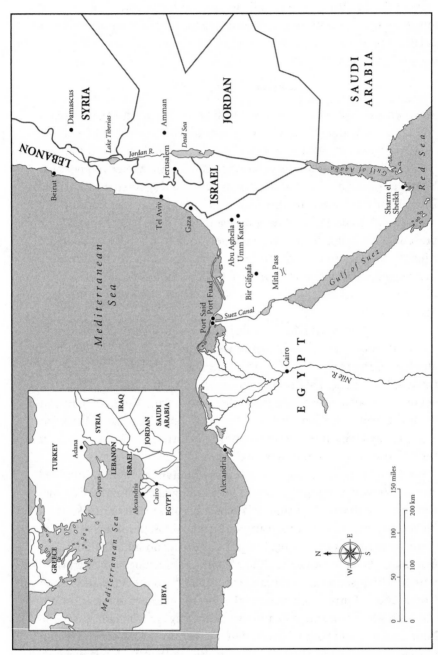

Map 19. The Levant

and Wellington preferred to keep their forces closer to home. The most that London could achieve was the Baghdad Pact of 1955, in which Britain joined with a northern tier of states—Turkey, Iraq, Iran, and Pakistan—in a loose alliance against the Soviet Union. The United States supported but would not join the pact. Once again, as so often since 1945, Britain was the little red hen in the childhood story, a hen that received no help planting, raising, and baking the wheat of regional security that everyone else wanted to eat.

Meanwhile, the forces of change made Western influence in the Middle East increasingly tenuous. As part of the general decline of empires, Britain and France granted independence to their colonies while trying to maintain influence and military bases. Iranian Prime Minister Mohammed Mossadeq nationalized the Western oil companies in his country in March 1951, although two years later the CIA and the SIS facilitated a coup that overthrew Mossadeq and put Shah Reza Pahlavi back in power.[5]

Egypt, which had always been the British center of gravity in the Middle East, became the greatest threat to Western influence in the region. In July 1952, a group of army officers overthrew the monarchy of King Farouk; Lieutenant Colonel Gamal Abdel Nasser soon emerged as the new leader and began the process of eliminating British influence from the country.

Nasser was an enormously charismatic, energetic man who believed in both Pan-Arab nationalism and social programs to improve the condition of the poor in Egypt. As such, he became a hero to many in the Arab world. Because Radio Cairo broadcast messages of support to the rebels in Algeria and provided shelter to the FLN leaders, many French officers and officials believed, simplistically, that the rebellion would wither without Egyptian aid.[6] For them, as for many Arabs, Nasser personified the future of the Middle East. In 1954, he added to his reputation by reaching an agreement with Great Britain whereby the British evacuated their troops from the Suez Canal but left equipment behind, maintained by contractors, in case of future war. The canal itself remained under British-French civil administration, while Britain was forced to shift its remaining forces in the region to Libya and Cyprus.

Nasser regarded the British and other former colonial powers as a continued threat to Arab independence. Unfortunately for the West, he had no desire to be part of a regional defense structure oriented against the USSR—for him, the objective was to gain true independence, which included keeping the former colonial powers out of the region. As such, Nasser refused to join pro-Western security agreements, choosing instead to identify his country with nonaligned states such as Yugoslavia and India. He also tried to bring other Arab states together on common concerns, including Israel.[7] This attitude frustrated a number of Western leaders, particularly British Prime Minister Eden and U.S. Secretary of State Dulles. For these men, the Cold War was a clear-cut competition between good and evil, and they could not understand Nasser's decision to treat the two sides as morally equivalent.

SEIZURE OF THE CANAL

Nasser's popularity and neutrality meant that both the West and the Soviet Union courted his support. The United States and Britain promised loans to construct the Aswan High Dam, an ambitious project intended to revolutionize Egyptian agriculture by taming the Nile River. However, the West refused to sell modern weapons to Egypt, arguing that such weapons were an unnecessary expense for nations that needed to solve basic social and economic problems.[8] So, in 1955, Egypt heightened the Cold War rivalry by turning to the Soviet Union for arms. The Soviets, acting through Czechoslovakia, agreed to provide Egypt with large numbers of relatively modern military aircraft and weapons—including MiG-15 fighters, T-34 tanks, and BTR-152 armored personnel carriers—in return for rice and cotton. Moscow also suggested that it might finance the Aswan High Dam, an offer that the Egyptians attempted to use as leverage to gain better loan terms from the United States. The Eisenhower administration was skeptical of Egypt's ability to repay any loan for the dam and was irked at the Egyptian efforts to "play the field" between Washington and Moscow. There was also considerable opposition in Congress, where Southern cotton growers, anticommunists, and supporters of Israel cooperated to block any loans to Egypt. On July 19, 1956, therefore, Secretary of State Dulles announced that the United States was withdrawing its financing offer, and Britain followed suit. Dulles made the announcement in a blunt, almost insulting manner, hoping that this setback would damage Nasser's public image and perhaps lead to his fall from power.[9]

Dulles's announcement should have ruined Nasser, but instead the Egyptian leader asserted his independence; on July 26th, he announced the nationalization of the British and French-owned Suez Canal, intending to use the profits of that canal to pay for the dam. Nasser's reputation skyrocketed in Egypt and throughout the Arab world.

The Suez Canal was a key link in world trade, and many Western governments feared that the Egyptian government would not maintain the canal properly. For the British, the seizure of the canal was also a grave challenge to their interests in the region; Anthony Eden's government wished to reassert its influence in the Middle East. Eden invited the American chargé d'affaires in London to his first crisis meeting on the canal and the next day wrote directly to President Eisenhower, seeking American support and predicting that only military action would rectify the situation.[10] That same day, the U.S. Joint Chiefs of Staff directed the Joint Strategic Plans Committee to study various courses of action concerning the canal. The committee staffers replied, quite correctly, that military intervention was undesirable because it would anger the other Arab states while stretching limited U.S. resources. The Joint Chiefs themselves were much more bellicose about the situation, an opinion initially shared by Dulles.[11] For a brief period, British-French-U.S. talks considered a tripartite action against Nasser.

However, Eisenhower had clear criteria for the use of force and concluded that Western military action in this case would be counterproductive.[12] He therefore directed Dulles to seek a diplomatic solution by calling a diplomatic conference to internationalize the canal. The British reluctantly cooperated, although Eden believed that once the conference failed, the United States would allow Britain a free hand in dealing with Egypt. Instead, Dulles tried delaying tactics between August and October, hoping that so much time would elapse that the British and French would find it politically impossible to invade. In particular, he arranged for interested nations to create a Suez Canal Users Association (SCUA) that offered a neutral administration of the canal. In September 1956, Egypt rejected the SCUA proposal. Like Dulles, Nasser believed that as time passed and Egypt demonstrated its ability to operate the canal, world and especially British public opinion would make military intervention impossible.[13]

The French government was much less concerned about U.S. views. Like Britain, France considered itself a Great Power that could and should take action to restore its standing in the Middle East. In addition to reasserting national prestige, many French officials and officers believed that overthrowing the Egyptian government was a necessary step to defeating the rebels in Algeria.

PRELIMINARY PLANNING

In practice, however, both the British and French armed forces were overextended, so that neither state felt able to take military action on its own. A British joint estimate for war with Egypt called for three divisions, a parachute brigade, three aircraft carriers, and eighteen air squadrons.[14] Yet, most of the deployable British and French armed forces were committed to counterinsurgency campaigns in their former colonies. In 1956, Britain had major troop deployments in Malaya, Kenya, and Cyprus, while the bulk of the French Army was embroiled in Algeria. Each government experienced difficulties in assembling enough troops and transport for even a limited invasion of Egypt. Each had only a handful of amphibious landing vessels, plus sufficient transport aircraft to drop only one parachute battalion at a time. Therefore, the French government approached London, offering to subordinate all French forces to British commanders if the two states attacked Egypt together.

Throughout August 1956, while the United States continued its diplomatic efforts to resolve the issue, British and French officers met secretly in London to develop an invasion plan. This planning process was painful because of the different military cultures of the two partners. Instead of an integrated command structure like the French, the British were used to having a committee of three coequal component commanders for ground, air, and sea. General André Beaufre, the French land forces commander-designate, was irritated by the British staff planning process:

> So, at this first session [August 14, 1956], we embarked on the tedious process which the British call "planning." The method is as follows; instead of the commander doing his work and making the overall decision, after which the staff does the drafting, the staff gets to work first; it produces a draft, which is then submitted to the "committee" formed by the three commanders, Land, Naval, and Air. One therefore

arrives knowing nothing of what will be proposed and one then hums and haws over each paragraph, the general idea still remaining obscure.[15]

Eventually, the two groups developed a plan, codenamed Musketeer, for a combined British-French airborne-amphibious landing at Alexandria, to be followed by an advance on Cairo that would trigger the collapse of Nasser's government. If that collapse did not occur, the invaders would have to attack across the Nile River and defeat the main Egyptian Army outside the capital. In late August and early September, the British and French military ran several small-scale exercises to work out details.

Meanwhile, the First Sea Lord, the enormously influential Lord Louis Mountbatten, was adamantly opposed to intervention, to the point where General Templer, by now chief of the Imperial General Staff, called the admiral "yellow." After various efforts to communicate through the responsible civilian ministers of war and defense, Mountbatten finally told Eden of his concerns in a meeting on September 7. In particular, the admiral feared that invading the city of Alexandria would cause huge civilian casualties and that Egyptian resistance would be so prolonged that it would take the invaders more than three weeks to advance to Cairo. Templer and the Middle East theater commander, General Sir Charles Keightley, endorsed this estimate.[16] Moreover, because Cyprus lacked port facilities, the invasion fleet would have to be based on Malta, producing an inevitable delay of several days between issuing an ultimatum and actually invading Egypt. As a result, Eden decided that he had to avoid Alexandria and make the invasion appear to be tied specifically to the canal issue. The British and French governments instructed their planners to produce a "Revised Musketeer" that envisioned prolonged psychological warfare and bombing operations prior to an amphibious landing at Port Said and Port Fuad, at the northern entrance to the canal. These ports had a much smaller shipping capacity than Alexandria, and the defenders could easily isolate the landing sites by destroying canal embankments outside the towns. In any event, such a limited attack was unlikely to achieve the implied strategic objective of eliminating Nasser's government. By this time, however, Eden felt so harassed that he refused to discuss the desired outcome of the invasion with Mountbatten.[17] Thus the political ends and military means became fatally disconnected. The military command structure was equally confused, consisting of three coequal components with a British commander and French deputy at every level (see table 1).

After Britain and France had reached preliminary agreement on the invasion plan, a third government—Israel—became involved. Although Israel had survived its war of independence in 1948–1949, by 1956 the fledgling Jewish state felt besieged on all sides. Egypt blocked Israeli ships from sailing through the Suez Canal and the Straits of Tiran, preventing any trade with Asia and East Africa. Palestinians based in the Gaza Strip (under Egyptian control) and the West Bank (held by Jordan) continued to harass the Israeli border regions. In response, Israel assumed a fiercely belligerent posture. Israeli troops patrolled right up to the frontier lines, leading to frequent firefights with their Arab counterparts. Israel also conducted punitive raids against Palestinian towns and bases along its borders; such attacks sometimes caused as many civilian casualties as the Palestinian efforts. At first, a small, ad hoc commando group known as Unit 101, under the command of then-Major Ariel Sharon, made the retaliation raids. For larger operations, Israel's airborne troops were often used.[18]

The Czech arms deal of 1955 threatened to upset this uneasy stalemate. Because of Western reluctance to sell arms, the Israel Defense Forces (IDF) were armed with a hodgepodge of aging equipment, including World War II–era Sherman tanks recovered from junkyards. Only France, which regarded Israel as a natural ally in the region, was willing to provide modern arms. For the Israelis, the arrival of Soviet weapons was thus a grave change in the military balance—although it would take Egypt time to train on the new aircraft and tanks, this weaponry would ultimately outclass that of the IDF. Tel Aviv believed it must act before the Egyptians had absorbed the Soviet aid package.[19]

The governments of France and Israel both regarded Nasser as a major threat to their security. Given these considerations, France secretly traded intelligence and technology information with Tel Aviv, increased arms shipments to Israel, and negotiated for a possible Israeli-French war against Egypt.[20] Yet, despite the apparent confluence of interests, Britain opposed Israeli participation in Musketeer. Given their recent history when Britain had occupied Palestine, the British and Israelis deeply distrusted each other. More importantly, Eden believed correctly that a British-Israeli attack on Egypt would outrage

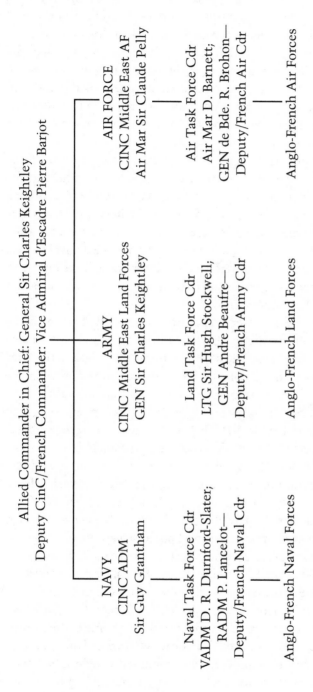

Allied Commander in Chief: General Sir Charles Keightley
Deputy CinC/French Commander: Vice Admiral d'Escadre Pierre Barjot

NAVY
CINC ADM
Sir Guy Grantham

Naval Task Force Cdr
VADM D. R. Durnford-Slater;
RADM P. Lancelot—
Deputy/French Naval Cdr

Anglo-French Naval Forces

ARMY
CINC Middle East Land Forces
GEN Sir Charles Keightley

Land Task Force Cdr
LTG Sir Hugh Stockwell;
GEN Andre Beaufre—
Deputy/French Army Cdr

Anglo-French Land Forces

AIR FORCE
CINC Middle East AF
Air Mar Sir Claude Pelly

Air Task Force Cdr
Air Mar D. Barnett;
GEN de Bde. R. Brohon—
Deputy/French Air Cdr

Anglo-French Air Forces

(Assault Forces: RADM D. Holland Martin; Aircraft Carriers: VADM M. L. Power)

FIGURE 1. Operation Musketeer chain of Command, 1956. Adapted from A. J. Barker, *Suez: The Seven Day War* (London, 1967), 26.

345

the Muslim world. To avoid this reaction, the three governments eventually agreed on an ingenious, if thin, cover story; Israel would attack Egypt first, advancing across Sinai as if to threaten the Suez Canal, after which Britain and France would intervene to protect the canal. This gave Anthony Eden a plausible excuse for invasion despite U.S. objections, although the participants were remarkably naïve to believe that their collusion would go undetected. The Israeli attack would also draw Egyptian reserves away from the landing areas for Revised Musketeer.

The origins of this agreement are often debated, but the three powers finally reached agreement in a secret conference held in the palace of Sevres, outside Paris, on October 22-24, 1956.[21] For its part, Israel provided a further deception plan, convincing Cairo that it was about to attack Jordan, whereas in fact it was massing forces against Egypt. As part of the agreement, France quietly provided naval vessels off the Israeli coast together with two squadrons of fighters on Israeli airfields to protect the Jewish state in the interval between the Israeli attack and the allied intervention.

Although Israeli intervention seemed to provide both military assistance and political pretext for Musketeer, that intervention also reinforced the need to shift the objective from Alexandria to the Suez Canal. If, in theory, the British and French were acting to protect the canal, then their invasion must be focused on that site rather than directly threatening the capital of the Egyptian government. To reduce the appearance of using force, the British insisted, as described above, on conducting several days of air strikes and psychological operations before landing troops. Moreover, to maintain the fiction of an independent intervention to secure the canal, the British invasion force could not sail from Malta until *after* the Israeli attack began.

Britain had declared a partial mobilization on August 2, although the selective call of reservists increased public debate about the possible use of force against Egypt. The parachute brigade in Cyprus had to stop hunting EOKA in order to brush up on its airborne operations. Meanwhile, the British Army faced a series of problems, especially with regard to inadequate wartime stocks. The French Army, actively engaged in Algeria, was more combat ready than some British units, but the French also experienced difficulties when they had to reequip and retrain two divisions, previously dismounted as light infantry for counterinsurgency operations, so that they were again prepared for conventional operations.[22] Such delays in preparation and execution not only robbed the Revised Musketeer plan of any surprise but also ultimately doomed the entire expedition by allowing time for Soviet, American, and other diplomatic pressure against the invaders.

OPERATION KADESH

Israel launched Operation Kadesh on the evening of October 29, 1956, with an airborne insertion of the 1st Battalion, 202nd Parachute Brigade, at the eastern end of the Mitla Pass, halfway across the Sinai. Sixteen C-47 transports dropped 375 paratroopers, who suffered only minor injuries in the operation. The Israeli chief of staff, General Moshe Dayan, had selected Mitla Pass as part of a careful balance of political factors. On the one hand, this site was close enough to the canal to give the appearance of threatening the waterway, thereby giving the British and French their pretext for intervention. On the other hand, Dayan did not wish to provoke the Egyptians into attacking Israeli population centers. He hoped, in fact, that Cairo would interpret the airborne drop as another in the series of punitive raids that Israel had launched against its neighbors. For the same reasons, Dayan did not conduct an initial air strike against the Egyptian Air Force. He also planned a phased introduction of ground forces along the border with Egypt and the Gaza strip. In violation of Dayan's deception plan, however, on the first day of the war, the Israeli commander in the Sinai committed 7th Armored Brigade against Egyptian defenses at Abu Agheila. This early commitment of Israeli armor easily could have compromised the cover story that the Israelis were conducting a retaliatory raid.[23]

The Egyptian commander in the Sinai quickly realized that he was facing a major Israeli operation, but Dayan's deception plan did work to the extent that his opponents did not make a serious effort to bomb Tel Aviv. Without waiting for its intelligence service to analyze the situation, the Egyptian general staff dispatched the 4th Armored Division, the strategic reserve, toward the road junction of Bir Gifgafah, about seventy kilometers into the northern Sinai Desert, from which the division would be able to counterattack any significant Israeli advance. Meanwhile, the Egyptian 3rd Infantry Division gave a good account of itself in the defense of northeastern Sinai. The division's 6th Infantry Brigade, commanded by Brigadier General Sami Yassa

Boulos, was particularly effective in retaining the key defenses and road junctions around Abu Agheila-Umm Katef. Boulos had been in command long enough to understand his troops and prepare his defenses, and his brigade was still equipped with familiar if obsolescent British weapons rather than the newer Soviet arms. The Egyptians had placed combat outposts to provide warning of attack and were well established in mutually supporting positions. The main weakness to Boulos's plan was that his reserve force was small and unarmored. The net result was a stalemate; although a battalion task force of the Israeli 7th Armored Brigade penetrated the Egyptian rear area on October 31, the defenders stubbornly retained their positions against repeated but poorly coordinated attacks by three Israeli brigades.[24]

Elsewhere, Egyptian performance was mixed. The long, narrow Gaza Strip was difficult to defend, and much of the 8th (Palestinian) Division surrendered after being cut off northeast of Gaza City. At the same time, the Israeli paratroops at Mitla Pass, reinforced over land by the rest of the 202nd Airborne Brigade, became involved in a bitter struggle for the pass. Once again, Egyptians in prepared defenses resisted effectively, killing thirty-eight paratroops and wounding 120 on October 31–November 1.[25] Otherwise, however, the Israeli offensive went on schedule.

While these battles occurred in the desert, the French Navy intercepted Egyptian attempts to attack Israel while French fighters, as promised, operated out of Israeli airfields. However, the British government delayed its initial air attacks both to maintain the fiction that it had not colluded with Israel and to ensure that the attacks occurred at night. This unexplained delay infuriated the Israelis, who felt that they were exposed to Egyptian retaliation while Britain had yet to enter the war. All the Israeli suspicions of British duplicity resurfaced. Indeed, the British government failed to inform its own theater commander, General Keightley, of the Sevres Protocol or, in fact, of any relationship with Israel. Thus, when Tel Aviv sent two officers to Cyprus for liaison purposes, the French hid these officers from the British to avoid incidents. Eventually, French officers convinced Keightley that the allies must coordinate with the Israelis for operational reasons. Even then, Keightley dealt with the Israeli liaison officers only through the French staff so that he could maintain deniability. In fact, when a British pilot bailed out near Israeli forces, other Royal Air Force (RAF) aircraft fired warning shots to discourage the Israelis from helping the pilot! As Prime Minister David Ben-Gurion remarked when Dayan questioned him about possible British actions against Israel, "[A]bout the British, I do not know, but about the British Foreign Office I am prepared to believe anything."[26]

The carefully developed cover story of Israeli "aggression" unraveled quickly. Anguished British officials had warned their American counterparts of a coming invasion, and the JCS favored deposing Nasser, but Eisenhower and Dulles, outraged by British duplicity, excluded the military from management of the crisis.[27] As early as October 30, British and French maneuverings in the U.N. Security Council caused the Eisenhower administration to suspect collusion. In a presidential meeting that day, Undersecretary of State Herbert Hoover, Jr., noted:

> The British and French may feel that they have forced us to a choice—between themselves and the Arabs. . . . The President wondered if the hand of Churchill might not be behind this—inasmuch as this action is in the mid-Victorian style. . . . [H]e did not see much value in an unworthy and unreliable ally and that the necessity to support them [Britain and France] might not be as great as they believed.[28]

That same day, Dulles offended French Ambassador Hervé Alphond by comparing the British and French ultimatum to the Soviet action in Budapest.[29]

Meanwhile, the British and French assembled a force that included two French divisions (the 10th Parachute and 7th Mobile Mechanized) plus the British 3rd Infantry Division, 16 Parachute Brigade, and 3rd Royal Marine Commando, as well as elements of the British 10th Armored Division. After a series of political delays, the two allies conducted air attacks beginning on the night of November 1, followed on November 5–6 by the invasion at Port Said and Port Fuad. Because of limited airlift assets, only two battalions—3rd Battalion The Parachute Regiment and 2e Regiment de Parachutistes Coloniaux (2nd Colonial Parachute Regiment)—landed on the morning of November 5. They quickly captured the small airfield and other key sites in the area. After a further French airborne drop that afternoon that included heavy weapons, the seaborne invasion began on November 6. Number 45 Commando, Royal Marines, was mounted in helicopters as the tactical reserve. In practice, the marines landed after the beaches had been secured.[30]

The British-French air raids finally alerted the Egyptian government to the true scope of its danger. Nasser ordered a general retreat from the Sinai in order to defend the canal. This order disheartened and disorganized the defenders, who did not understand why they should retreat from positions that they had defended so successfully. The Egyptian withdrawal greatly facilitated the Israeli advance, while Egyptian air power was hamstrung by the fact that only thirty pilots were trained to fly its new MiG-15s. Although the regular Egyptian forces had little success against the British and French, Nasser boldly used loudspeaker trucks and distributed arms to mobilize popular resistance in Port Said. He also had ships sunk in the canal to deny its use to the invaders and seriously considered leading a resistance movement if the invaders succeeded in occupying the country.[31]

COMBINED FAILURE

While those invaders were successful tactically, they had lost the political/strategic initiative. The governments of Israel, Britain, and France disagreed frequently about the details of the campaign, resulting in political disconnects. British public opinion, which had favored intervention when Nasser first seized the canal, was by now divided about the value of a war. As both Dulles and Nasser had anticipated, the long delay between nationalization and invasion had reduced popular support for Musketeer and gave Egypt credibility as the operator of the canal. The Soviet Union also reacted strongly, sending an ultimatum to the three invading countries that hinted at military action in response. Perhaps most disheartening from Eden's point of view was the fact that the United States disassociated itself from the British and French.

With the United Nations General Assembly meeting to demand a cease-fire, it was apparent as early as November 3 that hostilities might cease at any moment. By this time, the IDF was advancing across Sinai with little opposition, but it still needed to secure the Straits of Tiran. On November 2, the Israeli 9th Infantry Brigade began to push south along the western coast of the Gulf of Aqaba. Paratroop units, operating primarily in trucks but also conducting a two-company airborne drop, protected the western flank of this advance. An Egyptian rear guard at Ras Nurzani, just north of the objective, held up part of 9th Brigade for about eighteen hours on November 4–5. However, the remainder of the exhausted brigade reached Sharm el Sheikh early on the morning of the 5th. The defenders inflicted significant casualties, but the IDF secured the straits by noon on November 5, the same day that the British and French began their landings at the Suez Canal. Thus, Israel had achieved its tactical objectives before the Soviet ultimatum, although in February 1957, Tel Aviv had to follow Paris and London in abandoning its military positions to the UN.[32]

President Eisenhower was furious that the British would flout public opinion by such a blatant use of force, especially when their collusion with Israel would alienate the Arab world. Moreover, the Suez Crisis occurred on the very eve of presidential elections and almost simultaneously with the Soviet Army crushing the Hungarian uprising. Eisenhower was therefore unwilling to tolerate the British-French adventure. When London needed U.S. help to stop panic selling of British currency, Secretary Dulles made that aid contingent upon the invaders accepting a UN cease-fire. Eden reluctantly agreed to halt hostilities at 0200 local time on November 7, and the French had to follow suit. The British-French invasion forces never left their beach-heads but had to turn over their positions to a UN force that withdrew under Egyptian threats eleven years later, leading to renewed war.

Although Israel had gained a decade of breathing room, the 1956 failure was a great shock both to British and French prestige, and to the Western alliance. As Mohamed Heikal, Nasser's political advisor, noted, "Suez had many losers, and two clear victors—President Nasser and the Americans."[33] Nasser gained even more prestige among Arab states, and the United States felt obliged to assume the lead in organizing containment in the Middle East.

In retrospect, many participants and observers concluded that the entire concept of Operation Musketeer was a faulty one—seeking to use military force to resolve an essentially political problem and believing that the Egyptian government would collapse under the pressure of invasion. London and Paris had begun the operation with the belief that by overthrowing Nasser and reoccupying the canal, they could restore their traditional influence in the region. Instead, Musketeer exposed the limits of British and French military power while further damaging their political standing in the Middle East. Perhaps the only positive military outcome was that both the U.S. and British military authorities focused their planning on rapid deployment of coordinated forces for future emergencies in the region.

The Road to American Intervention

In the years after the Suez Crisis, President Nasser continued to pursue his policies of Pan-Arab nationalism, culminating in February 1958 with the creation of the United Arab Republic (UAR), a federated union with Ba'ath Party Syria. Still smarting from his rebuff and attack by the West, Nasser tended to closer ties with the Soviet Union and other Marxist countries that provided him with favorable terms for weapons and development loans.

These policies prompted Secretary Dulles and the Eisenhower administration generally to agree with Britain that "Nasserism" was a stalking horse for increased communist influence in the Middle East.[34] The issue was not defense of Israel, which the United States still held at arm's length, nor simply access to oil, but maintaining stability and containment. Having permanently damaged British and French influence in the region, Eisenhower and Dulles felt that they had created a power vacuum that could only be filled by the United States or its communist adversaries. On January 5, 1957, the president sent a message to Congress that became known as the Eisenhower Doctrine. Citing traditional Russian desires for control of the Middle East, he proposed both economic and military assistance to countries in the region and indicated that, if requested, the United States would intervene to defend states threatened by pro-Soviet aggression.[35] In the first application of the doctrine during mid-1957, ships of the U.S. Sixth Fleet deployed to the eastern end of the Mediterranean after an alleged attempt to overthrow the king of Jordan.

The true test case was Lebanon. This former French mandate had been remarkably prosperous and stable, due in large measure to a complicated constitution that shared power between the various religious confessions. Since 1943, this arrangement meant that the Lebanese President was a Maronite Christian, the premier was a Sunni Muslim, and the speaker of parliament was a Shi'ite. The Maronite president from 1952 to 1958 was Camille Chamoun (or Kamil Sham'un), who was constitutionally precluded from reelection. Early in 1958, Chamoun sought American, British, and French support to change the constitution in this regard.[36] Not only did he want to retain power for its own sake, but he was also concerned by the rise of Pan-Arab sentiment in Lebanon, especially after its neighbor Syria joined Nasser's UAR. Chamoun and his foreign minister, Charles Malik, agitated for

U.S. intervention and complained to both the Arab League and the UN Security Council of Syrian interference in Lebanon. Although Chamoun had great popularity, he also faced considerable opposition from various groups, including General Fu'ad Chehab (or Shihab), the military commander-in-chief. This opposition was due not so much to sectarian differences as to concern about allowing any one man to be too powerful. By May, a low-level civil war had broken out in the once-peaceful country, and Chamoun was desperately seeking foreign intervention. Chehab tried to keep the military neutral in this fighting and rebuffed offers to make him prime minister. One mob attacked the U.S. Information Service Library in Beirut. Nasser's government kept up a barrage of Pan-Arab propaganda that the American ambassador in Beirut, Robert McClintock, called "audio-visual aggression."[37]

Beginning in 1957, the U.S. and British military developed a joint contingency plan for possible intervention, and Eisenhower certainly wished to support Chamoun, but both governments were well aware that such an intervention, especially after the Suez debacle, would alienate most Arabs. Eisenhower was reluctantly willing to intervene to maintain order but not to take sides in the political struggle.[38]

Events elsewhere forced his hand. Early on the morning of July 14, 1958, a Pan-Arab sympathizer, Brigadier General Abdul Karim al-Kassim, launched a coup that assassinated the king and crown prince of Iraq as well as its pro-British prime minister. In a single stroke, British influence and defense plans in the region evaporated. Rumors of similar actions in Lebanon and Jordan gave Chamoun the leverage to finally achieve foreign intervention. Eisenhower felt that he had to act to prevent further defections from the West and to avoid the appearance of doing nothing.

Planning Operation Blue Bat

The original contingency plan, code-named Swaggerstick, called for deployment of the U.S. Army's newly formed Strategic Army Corps (STRAC), consisting of the 101st Airborne and 4th Infantry Divisions, as well as a Composite Air Strike Force (CASF) of fighters, bombers, and reconnaissance aircraft from the U.S. Air Force's Tactical Air Command. Unfortunately, Swaggerstick would have consumed 76 percent of the total airlift in the U.S. inventory, including civilian airliners with a contingency commitment to the Air Force (the Civilian Reserve Air Fleet).[39]

Instead, in 1956, the Joint Chiefs directed that the Commander-in-Chief, U.S. Navy Forces, Eastern Atlantic and Mediterranean (CINCNELM) plan to use marine elements of Sixth Fleet, already in the Mediterranean, and troops of Seventh U.S. Army in Germany. If implemented, CINCNELM would become the head of a new Specified Command, Middle East (SPECOMME). (A specified command was a joint headquarters designed to perform a specific function rather than be responsible for a geographic area.)

The resulting plan was called Blue Bat, involving both U.S. Marine Corps (USMC) and U.S. Army units. At any given time, two or more USMC battalion landing teams (BLTs) were afloat in the Mediterranean, available to make the initial landing on the beaches around Beirut. A BLT was an infantry battalion reinforced with other small units to form a combined arms force. In such a circumstance, the marines could seize a lodgment area, and the army force could land unopposed. However, these BLTs could not remain off the coast of Lebanon indefinitely, so that the plan envisioned a possible airborne landing by two Pentomic battle groups (reinforced battalions) of the 11th Airborne Division, deploying from Germany. Regardless of how the army combat units arrived, subsequent echelons would include a brigade-sized logistical element known as the 201st Logistical Command, plus a tank battalion and other heavy equipment deployed by sea. Task Force (TF) 201 would command this entire army element. To further complicate matters, some versions of the plan envisioned a British brigade based on Cyprus making the initial landing if the marines were not on station.[40]

In reality, this complicated plan was subject to a number of additional limitations. First, in 1957 the 11th Airborne Division was redesignated as 24th Infantry Division. Although it retained two airborne battle groups, the 24th's reorganization severely reduced support elements such as parachute riggers, the essential specialists who packed parachutes and prepared heavy equipment to be dropped. Second, 201st Logistical Command and most of the support elements of this plan existed mostly on paper. Third, Blue Bat required fourteen different headquarters to conduct staff planning under conditions of strict secrecy, making coordination difficult. Fourth, the 322nd Air Division in Germany was in the process of converting from C-119 to newer

C-130 transport aircraft. Yet, even if the 322nd had concentrated all of its 146 transport aircraft in one place, that would have been insufficient to move all of TF 201. There was considerable interservice friction because the USAF planners did not comprehend nor resolve this shortfall.[41] Finally, the plan was for a purely military deployment, with little thought as to the political situation or requirements that the force might encounter. As so often before and since, a deployed military force had no clear guidance on how to execute a delicate political task.

Deployment to Lebanon

As the pressure built in Beirut, the United States and Britain alerted their forces and assembled their headquarters. In mid-May, Brigadier General Sidney S. Wade and the staff of the 2nd Provisional Marine Force flew from Camp Lejeune, North Carolina, to join the headquarters of Sixth Fleet's amphibious task force off the coast of Crete. Brigadier J.W.C. Williams and the staff of Middle East Land Forces joined Wade on the 21st; Brigadier General David Grey, the commander-designate of TF 201, also visited to coordinate.[42] There followed the pattern of alerts and cancellations so common to all veterans of the Cold War, such that, despite two months of preparations, TF 201 was not ready to deploy when finally ordered to do so. At Furstenfeldbruck Air Force Base, near Munich, Germany, a frantic scene ensued on July 15–16, as the few available riggers packed equipment while the USAF planners tried to locate enough aircraft to move the force.[43]

Meanwhile, on the evening of July 14, President Eisenhower directed that the first troops land in Beirut by 0900 Eastern Time on the 15th, the hour at which he would announce the action on television. This gave American forces less than fifteen hours to react. By dint of much effort, the 2nd Battalion, 2nd Marines, sailed from Cyprus and landed its advance elements near the Beirut International Airport, south of the city, at the prescribed time. Landing vehicles disgorged four companies of fully equipped troops. They were met by bikini-clad sunbathers, young children, and soft drink vendors. As one marine commented, "It's better than Korea, but what the hell is it?"[44]

The artillery battery, underwater demolition team, and other key support elements of this BCT were absent because the supporting Landing Ship, Dock (LSD) was en route to Malta for repairs. On the

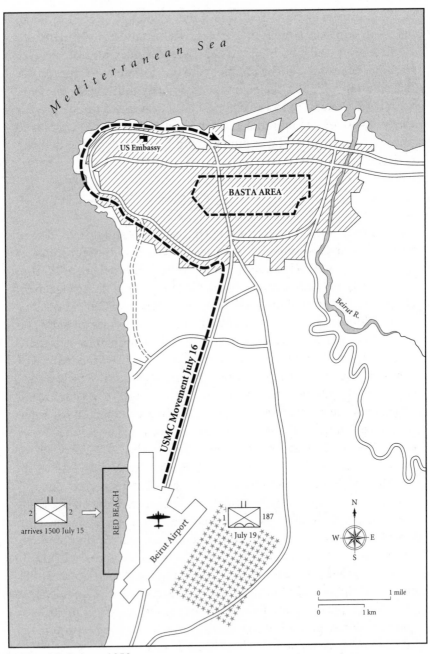

MAP 20. Beirut, 1958

evening of the 15th, however, the LSD that supported 3rd Battalion, 6th Marines, arrived offshore. Even that did not end the confusion, for Ambassador McClintock impractically asked that 2/2 Marines re-embark and land in the harbor of Beirut.[45] The next morning at 0400, Admiral James Holloway, Jr., CINCNELM and now the commander of the newly activated SPECOMME, arrived by air, followed two-and-a-half hours later by a second BLT, the 3rd Battalion, 6th Marines. Once this battalion landed, Lieutenant Colonel Harry Hadd's 2nd Battalion moved north toward the city of Beirut, satisfying McClintock's desire to protect the embassy and the port area. The Americans soon encountered a Lebanese Army roadblock, but negotiations between Shehad, McClintock, Holloway, and Wade enabled the marines to reach their objective by the evening of July 16. Over the next week, yet another BLT, 1/8 Marines, arrived offshore, while the infantry components of a fourth BLT arrived by air from the United States. Meanwhile, on July 15, TF 201 and the 201st Logistical Command formally came into being and began loading aircraft from Furstenfeldbruck and from Evreux Air Force Base, France. The 1st Battle Group, 187th Airborne, did not finish loading until 0300 on the 16th and was further delayed by weather and the need for clearance to fly over neutral Austria. Still, by 2300 on July 16, General Grey and this first army echelon had reached Adana Air Force Base in Incirlik, Turkey. There, Colonel Adam Meetze, commander of the 201st Logistics Command, and his staff officers arrived to coordinate logistical support, borrowing rations and equipment from air force stocks at Incirlik.[46]

While the marines and soldiers continued their hasty deployment, the U.S. Air Force was experiencing its own difficulties in moving CATF Bravo from the United States to Adana. Commanded by Major General Henry Viccellio, this collection of ninety-four fighter-bombers, transports, and reconnaissance aircraft had to deploy much farther than TF 201. When its designated fighter-bomber squadrons proved unready to deploy from New Mexico, the Air Force turned to the 354th Tactical Fighter Wing in Myrtle Beach, South Carolina. Given only seven hours' notice, the 354th had to dispatch two squadrons of F-100s to Adana. This wing was trained to deliver tactical nuclear weapons rather than close air support and lacked equipment and training for long-range deployment. Nonetheless, the 354th attempted to fulfill its orders. In the first squadron, one aircraft crashed, seven landed en route with various maintenance problems, and only four reached

Adana on schedule. Despite such delays, by the end of July 17 there were 165 aircraft of CATF Bravo and TF 201 parked on the taxiways at Adana. Not surprisingly, in the confusion of this deployment General Viccellio had scant time to coordinate with his army counterpart, Grey.

The further deployment of TF 201 to Beirut was also complicated. Despite the fact that the operation was done at the request of the Lebanese government, Lebanese air traffic controllers insisted that the U.S. aircraft wait their turn along with civilian airliners for the use of the one active runway at Beirut. Moreover, when Grey arrived, he discovered that the Lebanese Army had failed to provide the promised trucks and parking space at the airport.[47] The tiny USAF aerial port unit was overwhelmed, so that the 187th Airborne had to provide a labor detail to unload and sort aerial cargo. Needless to say, such a detail would not have been available in the event of active combat operations.

Because Operation Blue Bat had envisioned such operations, the support plan called not only for the 201st Logistics Command but also for massive supplies of all types to be shipped by sea from the United States and Germany. Battalions of combat engineers, construction engineers, and transportation troops arrived over the next several weeks. The U.S. Army's deputy chief of staff for logistics had ordered a support exercise four weeks before the actual deployment, but outloading by ship took much longer than anticipated. Then, when these supplies reached Beirut, the army had considerable difficulty unloading and storing the vast quantities involved. The same fate hampered the deployment of 3rd Battalion, 35th Armor, from Bremerhaven, Germany, to provide more combat power. The civilians at the port insisted on loading the vessels commercially, that is, using every possible space aboard rather than loading complete unit sets of equipment. Even the specially designed roll-on, roll-off ship *USNS Comet* was misloaded. Its two lower holds had insufficient clearance for M48 tanks, and the vehicles that were deck-loaded by crane proved difficult to offload in Lebanon. Huge dumps of equipment and supplies took weeks to sort out on the ground.[48]

EMPLOYMENT

While the U.S. troops unloaded, Arab radios in Cairo, Damascus, and Baghdad condemned the intervention. The Eisenhower administration was well aware of this but lacked the resources to conduct an effective information campaign. A Voice of America medium-wave radio, transmitting from a U.S. vessel anchored near the island of Rhodes, reached only 150 miles inland and could not compete with the Arab radios for power or coverage. Shortwave coverage was somewhat better, but the United States was in no position to influence Arab public opinion beyond Beirut.[49]

At first, the massive flow of American forces overawed the local population. The commanders had little intelligence about the political situation in Beirut, and General Grey later claimed that he learned more from the wife of an American oil executive, a longtime president of Lebanon, than from any official source. Instead of actively supporting President Chamoun, the United States adopted a neutral attitude, trying to maintain order while waiting for a peaceful change of power. This required great discipline on the part of the soldiers and marines, who became frustrated at the restrictions placed on them when they encountered sniper fire.[50] On August 1, a sniper killed Sergeant James Nettles near the Basta rebel area in northern Beirut; this proved to be the only fatality in the entire operation. Three weeks later, renewed firing wounded the French vice consul and an American soldier; the next day, August 22, American embassy personnel were pinned down by machine-gun fire from the Basta, but no one was hurt.

A new commander dealt with the problem. By July 21, Admiral Holloway had concluded that he was too involved to supervise the land forces because of his overall responsibilities as CINC, which included coordination with Ambassador McClintock and the JCS representative on the spot, Admiral Burke. Holloway therefore recommended that the Joint Chiefs create a land forces headquarters. On July 23, 1958, the Department of the Army designated General Paul Adams, the commander of Seventh Army's support forces, as commander, American Land Forces (AMLANFOR), Lebanon. In response to Adams's request for a soldier qualified in the local languages, Captain Fuab Chehab, USA, a nephew of General Shehab, accompanied Adams to Beirut.[51] To further cement the relationship, General Chehab assigned Colonel Yusuf Simaan, a 1958 graduate of the U.S. Army Command and General Staff College, as liaison officer to AMLANFOR. Such liaison officers often defused potential confrontations during the operation. By mutual agreement between Generals Adams and Grey, the available staff of TF 201 was divided into an American Land Forces staff and the headquarters for the army troop units, a unit redesignated as 24th Airborne Brigade. The marines provided eight additional officers, including Adams's chief of staff, to form the joint headquarters.[52]

General Adams had a reputation as an uncompromising commander, but he proved to be remarkably tactful with both Lebanese and U.S. officials. After analyzing his mission, he issued the tough rules of engagement described at the start of this chapter. To discourage Lebanese harassing fire, he found a low-key solution. On August 23, Adams invited a number of Lebanese Army leaders to witness a training exercise in which American artillery, tanks, armored personnel carriers, bulldozers, and helicopters leveled a simulated roadblock in short order. As Adams had anticipated, the Lebanese visitors spread the word to rebel leaders, and violence declined temporarily. Later, when the tank battalion arrived from Germany, Adams sometimes sent platoons of tanks cruising through the streets of Beirut. At random intervals, these tanks would halt, traverse their turrets toward the sea, and fire their main guns into the water. The abundance of ammunition shipped to Beirut made such demonstrations cheaper than waiting for casualties to occur. As Adams later summarized his activities, military operations in Lebanon were "a show of force with psychological overtones."[53]

With the USMC and U.S. Army in control of Beirut, American diplomacy could seek a more permanent solution. Deputy Under Secretary of State Robert D. Murphy, the legendary wartime American diplomat in French Northwest Africa, became President Eisenhower's political advisor to CINC SPECOMME. Holloway and Murphy rapidly agreed that there was no communist threat and that the U.S. intervention had negated any remote possibility of UAR involvement in Lebanese affairs. Beginning in late July, Murphy set out to convince the various Lebanese factions that they must work together to resolve the presidential succession so that the U.S. forces would depart. On July 31, the Lebanese Parliament elected General Chehab as president, with his term scheduled to begin on September 23. Upon taking office, the previously neutral general chose a cabinet composed primarily of ex-rebel leaders, further mollifying public opinion. By this time, the USMC had already withdrawn one battalion and planned further redeployments. On October 8, the Eisenhower administration announced that all U.S. forces would withdraw from Lebanon.[54] After considerable effort to remove the backlog of supplies, the troops departed smoothly.

Operation Blue Bat gave all the appearances of a success, and Lebanon remained quiet for another decade. However, no limited deployment of American troops could resolve the fundamental instability of the Middle East. As Senator Hubert Humphrey observed during hearings on the matter, "I think we are acting like the Metternich of the twentieth century. And I don't believe we are really dealing with the problems. We are dealing with symptoms."[55] As a result, the 1958 intervention gave American policy makers a false sense of their capability to control events and concealed the huge blank check implied in the Eisenhower Doctrine.

Twilight East of Suez

After the coup in Iraq, King Hussein of Jordan declared himself the ruler of both states, based on a loose federation with his relative, the murdered King Faisal, but he was in no position to enforce that claim. In fact, Secretary Dulles and other Americans suspected that Hussein, too, was likely to be overthrown. Prime Minister Harold Macmillan felt bound to protect the last pro-British government in the region and hoped to get American support in reversing the coup in Baghdad. On July 17, therefore, the British Army began Operation Fortitude, sending 2,000 troops of 16 Parachute Brigade from Cyprus to Amman, Jordan, to support Hussein's government.[56]

Unlike their American allies, the British had troops and supplies based in the region and had considerable knowledge of the country to which they deployed. Nonetheless, the deployment started out badly, with Israeli fighters turning back most of the British transports because Whitehall had failed to arrange transit across Israeli airspace! Ben Gurion shared Macmillan's concern about the Baghdad coup, but Britain was so unpopular in Israel that the deployment resumed under tight restrictions, eventually requiring RAF aircraft to transit Israel only at night.[57]

Upon arrival at the Amman airfield, the British brigade found itself in an exposed position, with few heavy weapons, a tenuous supply chain, and a Jordanian Army whose loyalty seemed suspect. With instincts developed while fighting on Cyprus, the paratroopers were very suspicious of the Jordanians and fatally shot a civilian on July 28. Although No. 208 Squadron, RAF, eventually reached the airfield with Hunter fighter-bombers, the British had no air warning radar, as

MAP 21. The Middle East, 1958–1962

demonstrated when six Syrian fighters flew overhead on the first afternoon. The U.S. Navy provided a combat air patrol until a British carrier, HMS *Eagle*, could arrive on station. Flying from Adana, USAF transports also delivered vehicles and supplies to the British, but this only reemphasized the limits of Britain's shrinking military reach. General Templer, the combative chief of the Imperial General Staff, found that his warnings about reducing the armed forces had come true, for this single brigade represented all that Britain could deploy to the critical region. Eventually, the Royal Navy transported an additional infantry battalion from Aden, a twenty-five-pounder artillery battery, and more supplies to Aqaba, opening up a surface line of communications. Yet, the British remained almost as wary as King Hussein himself, waiting for further action by the Nasserite forces.[58]

The forceful UN secretary-general, Dag Hammarskjöld, was suspicious of British motives and sought to end the intervention peacefully. After the General Assembly passed a vague resolution (1237) on August 21, calling on Arab states to respect each other's independence, Hammarskjöld toured the Middle East, seeking to defuse the situation. He pressured Nasser into reducing the propaganda aimed at King Hussein. This plus American and British aid to arm another Jordanian brigade reassured the king, allowing the British to depart from Amman in late 1958.[59]

Macmillan had tried to recruit Eisenhower for a joint intervention in Iraq, and indeed the United States had dispatched two marine landing teams to the Persian Gulf in preparation for such a move, as well as to reassure friendly states. However, Eisenhower rightly felt that such a deep deployment was legally and logistically impractical. On July 18, the new dictator of Iraq, General Kasim, publicly promised to fulfill all previous commitments, including securing the oil fields, thereby reducing the need for Western intervention. Unfortunately, Khrushchev wrongly concluded that it was his strong protests that had deterred the West, an idea that misled him in future crises.[60]

Kasim's coup removed the keystone from the Baghdad Pact, forcing London and Washington to try yet again to shore up defenses against a possible Soviet advance into the vital oil region. Britain also lost its remaining airbases in Iraq, and the pact's planning staff moved to Turkey. Despite requests from the remaining members of the alliance, the United States never officially joined the pact or its successor, the

Central Treaty Organization (CENTO) of 1959. Eisenhower and the Joint Chiefs felt that America lacked conventional forces to contribute and were reluctant to make unrealistic promises. The United States did increase military aid and participated in the military committee of CENTO, but it remained the weakest of the regional security organizations in the Cold War.[61]

Despite the Suez and Iraq disasters, London attempted to maintain its military presence and fulfill its obligations in the region during the early 1960s. In July 1961, the British dispatched 6,000 troops to Kuwait in a show of force that discouraged Iraqi pretensions to that tiny state; this proved to be the last British operation using conscripts, who were being phased out as the British Army returned to an all-volunteer status. For some time thereafter, the British kept a battalion task force in Bahrain for deterrent purposes, but in the long run this proved too difficult to maintain.[62]

As Kenya and the rest of East Africa gained independence, the British planned to use the crown colony of Aden, in the southwest corner of the Arabian Peninsula, as a final base in the region.[63] The concept was to locate a brigade in this desolate place, but Yemen had an historic claim to Aden, while the local trade unions had both socialist and Pan-Arab influences. Just outside Aden itself, local sheikhs and other rulers formed a weak government known as the Federation of Arab Emirates of the South, with four battalions of British-officered local troops.

Trouble actually began in neighboring North Yemen, where in November 1962 Colonel Abdullah al-Sallal overthrew the hereditary imam. Sallal, who was influenced by Nasser's Pan-Arabism, declared a Yemen Arab Republic. He soon had to ask for Egyptian troops to assist in a civil war against supporters of the former ruler, a rebellion that probably received covert aid from Britain and Saudi Arabia.

Aden itself faced three interrelated threats. In addition to an internal socialist party and cross-border guerrilla raids, both of which sought the merger of the federation with Yemen, there was also the Quteibi tribe, which revived its traditional practice of collecting protection money from travelers along the border. The situation came to a boil on December 10, 1963, when a grenade attack killed two people and wounded fifty-three, including the British high commissioner. The federal rulers demanded action, and Britain declared an emergency. General Sir Charles Harington arrived as commander-in-chief Middle East.[64]

Harington launched the local Federal Army, with British support, in a show of force along the northern border (Operation Nutcracker, January 1964), but this had little effect. As soon as the troops withdrew, both the insurgents and the brigands returned. Clearly, the Federation Army could not handle the situation by itself. During the spring of 1964, British troops built up to a total of five battalions (three infantry, one parachute, one Royal Marine Commando) plus elements of the Special Air Service, all commanded by a brigade headquarters. These troops received excellent support from RAF fighter-bombers and Royal Navy helicopters. The troops performed remarkable tactical feats, culminating in the seizure of Jebel Huriyah, an almost vertical hill 5,500 feet high. Again, however, shows of force of this kind could only repress rather than eliminate the unrest.

While the troops patrolled the hinterlands, terrorist attacks escalated in Aden. After a grenade attack wounded British schoolchildren in September 1965, a frustrated British high commissioner suspended the local government and imposed direct rule in the crown colony. Two of the three opposition groups merged to form the Front for the Liberation of Occupied South Yemen (FLOSY) in January 1966, and terrorist attacks continued to mount.[65]

Britain had previously announced its decision to grant independence to South Arabia effective in 1968, but in 1966 London reversed with regard to its presence after that date, indicating that it would no longer maintain defense facilities in the area. This decision encouraged the various insurgent groups. The following year, Nasser claimed that British forces were involved on Israel's side in the disastrous Six-Day War, further reducing hopes for a peaceful region. When the British had to repress a mutiny of local troops in June 1967, cooperation between the security forces deteriorated further.

By the end of 1967, Britain had suffered fifty-seven killed and 651 wounded in five years with no progress to show for it.[66] Strategically, Britain could not afford to continue such an open-ended commitment to an area that had proven to be a burden rather than a base for regional influence. Reluctantly, the British withdrew at the end of the year, leaving many local leaders and tribesmen in the lurch. The FLOSY declared the People's Republic of South Yemen, an increasingly Marxist regime that became involved in a prolonged struggle with its neighbor to the north.

By the time that Nasser seized the Suez Canal in 1956, military analysts recognized the severe limitations upon French and British ability to influence the Middle East. The abortive Suez invasion simply demonstrated these limitations to the world. Having thwarted his allies' attempt to reassert themselves, Eisenhower felt obliged to fill the resulting power vacuum. The Eisenhower Doctrine and the 1958 intervention in Lebanon completed the changing of the guard and gave an impression of America's ability to maintain order. Unfortunately, the spreading influence of Pan-Arabism, Arab nationalist socialism, and (to a lesser extent) Soviet-backed Marxism soon demonstrated the fallacies of that image. The situation worsened in 1967 when Israel humiliated its Arab neighbors in the Six-Day War. Within a few years, President Richard Nixon made an informal alliance with Tel Aviv, setting the stage for the political and economic upheaval that characterized the Middle East for the next four decades.

13

NUCLEAR NIGHTMARES

There is no geopolitical problem so complex that it cannot be resolved by the correct yield and placement of a thermo-nuclear device.

Attributed to a Soviet general officer[1]

TYURATAM, KAZAKHSTAN S.S.R., 6:50 P.M., OCTOBER 24, 1960

The experimental R-16 missile sat on launchpad 21, leaking brown nitrate fumes and sullenly refusing to take off. Three years earlier, the Soviet government had triumphantly announced that it had developed an intercontinental ballistic missile (ICBM) and launched the first artificial earth satellite, *Sputnik*. In fact, behind Khrushchev's bluffs, the Soviet ICBM program was far behind schedule, consisting of only a few unreliable prototypes. Marshal Mitrofan Ivanovich Nedelin, commander of the fledgling Strategic Rocket Forces, was under extreme pressure to deliver a more effective ICBM, as was Mikhail Kuzmich Yangel, the head of the R-16 design team.

The launch had already had repeated delays over the previous day and a half. In frustration, the normally methodical and cautious Nedelin installed a stool at the base of the rocket, from which he personally directed repairs and final checks before a renewed attempt to launch. In the haste to complete these checks, a technician in the blockhouse tried to test an electric circuit to the missile, but the electrical impulse accidentally ignited the second-stage rocket motors. These, in turn, instantly touched off the huge fuel tanks of the first stage, creating a fireball whose heat was estimated at 3,000 degrees Centigrade. This incinerated Nedelin instantly, and many of the technicians who attempted to flee were consumed when freshly laid asphalt around the pad caught fire. Although Yangel and a few others survived, nearly 120 technicians and engineers—the bulk of the missile design team—burned to death, leaving behind only the outlines of their bodies and of noncombustible items such as keys. The few remains were secretly buried in a mass grave.[2]

In the race for nuclear superiority and space exploration, the United States suffered many failures in the full glare of news cameras. The Tyuratam disaster was far worse but did not become public knowledge until 1990. Without a reliable ICBM, Khrushchev turned to a risky substitute that created the Cuban Missile Crisis.

THE THERMONUCLEAR ARMS RACE

While third world conflicts dominated the headlines during the 1950s, both Washington and Moscow continued to develop their nuclear weapons and delivery options. As noted in Chapter Four, the first Soviet atomic detonation in 1949 forced the Truman administration to make a decision about whether or not to develop the fusion or hydrogen bomb, often referred to informally as the "super bomb." Councils were divided, especially in the Atomic Energy Commission (AEC), and George Kennan, the first to articulate an intellectual basis for the Cold War, opposed the idea. However, Truman and his other advisors correctly feared that Stalin would seek such a weapon regardless of what the United States did. On January 31, 1950, Truman directed the AEC to develop the hydrogen bomb.[3]

The JCS initially saw little need for such a large weapon because it was still focused on counteracting the Soviet superiority in conventional weapons. However, the sense of being in a technological race with Moscow soon caused the JCS to refocus their atomic thinking and conclude that the United States could not fall behind in the H-bomb effort.[4]

Because this weapon was still only a concept, Truman authorized simultaneous efforts to continue refining fission weapons. Meanwhile, physicist Edward Teller pushed hydrogen development forward rapidly.

A primitive UNIVAC computer simplified the myriad of mathematical calculations involved in the design.[5] The principles of fusion were tested in early May 1951 on Eniwetok, a Pacific atoll, and Teller used this experiment to convince Robert Oppenheimer and other scientific leaders in the nuclear program. Despite continued debate within the administration, the president authorized a full-scale test that occurred on November 1, 1952, less than a month after the first British atomic explosion. This U.S. MIKE test was an experimental device rather than a true bomb, but it proved the concept. MIKE generated a force of more than ten megatons, completely destroying the island of Elugelab in the Eniwetok atoll. Against the advice of most senior officials, Truman announced this development in a somber statement that emphasized that nuclear war was "not a possible policy for rational men."[6] Seventeen months later, the United States detonated a deliverable hydrogen bomb.

As the Truman administration had surmised, their Soviet counterparts were hotly pursuing the same goal. On August 12, 1953, the Soviet Union initiated a detonation which the United States labeled "Joe-4." Both sides considered this to be the first Soviet thermonuclear device, a complicated layering of different materials meant to achieve the intense heat necessary for fusion. The Soviets reportedly adopted this "layer cake" principle because Lavrenti Beria had misunderstood the MIKE test, wrongly concluding that the United States was using such a design. In retrospect, some have argued that Joe-4 was not really a hydrogen explosion, and certainly the Soviets never again used that particular design. Nuclear weapons designers Thomas Reed and Danny Stillman contend that another spy inside the U.S. program provided the key concept of radiation explosion to put the Soviet effort back on schedule. In November 1955, the Soviet designers, including Yuli Khariton and Andrei D. Sakharov, achieved success by dropping a "super bomb" from an aircraft; the blast was so strong that two people died despite all precautions.[7]

Thereafter, both sides continued testing at a rapid pace. The Soviet Union scored a propaganda coup in March 1958 by announcing a unilateral moratorium on nuclear testing in the atmosphere. It shattered its own moratorium in October 1961 when it detonated the largest thermonuclear device ever used, exceeding fifty megatons of force. France, China, and other governments joined the nuclear testing race in the same period.

More nuclear weapons meant increased extraction of uranium ore and greatly increased production of fissionable materials. Under the combined impetus of the Soviet A-bomb and the Korean War, the Truman administration appropriated $8 billion in just three fiscal years (1951 through 1953) and sought to double uranium extraction in Canada, the Belgian Congo, and elsewhere. Vast plants, such as Hanford in the state of Washington and Savannah River in Georgia, produced highly enriched uranium and plutonium. The U.S. inventory grew from about 250 atomic bombs in 1947 to 18,000 nuclear weapons by 1960.[8]

The Soviet Union lagged well behind these figures but made production a high priority during the 1950s. After the deaths of Stalin and Beria, the nuclear program was institutionalized under the Ministry of Medium Machine Building. The research institute at Arzamas-16, 500 kilometers east-southeast of Moscow, continued to be the primary design point for nuclear devices. In 1955, a second weapons design laboratory began work at Chelyabinsk-70, an installation in the Ural Mountains. Another plant, Chelyabinsk-40, refined plutonium and tritium, while to the north the Sverdlovsk-44 and Sverdlovsk-45 sites produced enriched uranium. Series production of tactical nuclear weapons began in 1954.[9]

Years of extraction, production, and testing had two major radiation effects. On the one hand was worldwide radioactive contamination in water supplies and the upper atmosphere. Many of the early tests were surface blasts, in the sense that some portion of the fireball touched the earth's surface, thereby picking up large amounts of material that became irradiated and carried aloft by winds. By the end of the 1950s, any form of snow, sleet, or rain might well bring fallout back to earth, creating a significant hazard to people everywhere, including heightened rates of leukemia. In the Soviet Union, where precautions were at first nonexistent, nuclear materials production also led to a series of chain reactions and radiation leaks. Discharge of radioactive waste into the Techa River near Chelyabinsk led to the evacuation of twenty-two towns.[10]

As early as the 1946 tests on Bikini Atoll, U.S. military observers had concluded that the effects of radiation made the new weapon different from all others.[11] The armed services of both sides wanted to determine how their conventional forces would interact with nuclear weapons, especially the smaller-yield tactical shells, bombs, and warheads intended for battlefield use. To do this, the United States and Soviet Union conducted experiments to measure the psychological and radiological effects of exposing troops to atomic detonations. The Defense Department later estimated that at least 250,000 service members were used as experimental subjects between 1945 and 1963. Some of these men were in armored vehicles or prepared defenses that significantly attenuated the direct radiation involved, while others were completely exposed. The AEC issued warnings, but in the absence of definitive medical data, many soldiers received radiation doses that far exceeded modern safety standards. Feeling compelled to accumulate the data, Defense Department officials repeatedly insisted that the tests were safe. Meanwhile, the Marshall Islanders and residents of western U.S. states developed hyperthyroidism and other diseases because of their exposure to frequent nuclear tests. Although the Soviet Union's secrecy concealed most of its own radiation concerns, it apparently had a major disaster at a facility in Chelyabinsk, in the southern Ural Mountains, in late 1957.[12]

Not all applications of nuclear energy were so risky, of course. In addition to the development of nuclear reactors for civilian use, the AEC and Navy Department pioneered the development of nuclear propulsion for ships. In late 1954, the first nuclear-powered submarine, USS Nautilus, entered commission, revolutionizing undersea warfare. Rear Admiral Hyman G. Rickover micromanaged this program, not only controlling design and production but also hand selecting the officers involved in order to minimize the risks of the new technology. By eliminating the need to recharge batteries on the surface, nuclear propulsion made possible the first true submarine, able to operate underwater for weeks on end.[13] The United States continued to produce nuclear submarines throughout the 1950s and in 1960 launched the first nuclear-propelled aircraft carrier, USS Enterprise.

Prior to the appearance of the Nautilus, the Soviet Navy had made only limited investments in conventional submarines, despite capturing advanced German designs at the end of the war. Experiments with hydrogen peroxide-propelled subs and primitive cruise missiles apparently led to poor results, although large numbers of conventional, oceangoing submarines (known to NATO as the Foxtrot and Romeo classes) appeared in the later 1950s. Eventually, the Soviets began producing nuclear-propelled submarines, of which the first, Leninsky Komsomol, was commissioned in April 1958. The Hotel and Echo classes of nuclear-propelled submarines followed, armed with short-range missiles to engage American carrier groups.[14]

DELIVERY SYSTEMS: BOMBERS

Nuclear weapons required reliable delivery systems, which initially meant bombers that were large enough to lift the primitive weapons and that had both the range and the combat survivability to strike targets in the middle of the Eurasian and North American land masses. The Korean conflict demonstrated the vulnerability of the B-29 (and by implication its Russian copy, the Tu-4), accelerating the retirement of these aircraft from active service. The potential development of air-to-air missiles by both sides made bombers seem even more vulnerable. The U.S. B-36, which replaced the B-29 during the early 1950s, had much greater lifting capacity and unrefueled range. However, the B-36 was only marginally superior in speed (435 miles per hour versus 365 for the B-29) and was such a huge, complex aircraft that its survivability against the PVO-Strany (Soviet national Air Defense Forces) was debatable.

Thus, even before the B-36 entered service, the all-jet B-47 medium bomber had begun test flights, achieving a respectable 557 miles per hour with greater maneuverability than its predecessors. Although capable of air-to-air refueling, the B-47 had a shorter range (4,000 miles or 6,400 kilometers) than the B-36, and it therefore operated out of forward bases such as Guam, Alaska, and Britain. Moreover, the B-47 suffered significant teething problems, both because it was rushed into production without adequate testing and because the air force made constant design changes. Early versions did not even have ejection seats, and the vacuum tube technology of the K-2 navigation and bombing system often failed under rough usage. Spare parts could not keep up with production, affecting unit readiness, and at high altitude fuel sometimes boiled away, forcing the introduction of a new, more stable fuel, JP-4. A shortage of aircrews and airbases also caused serious readiness problems for the Strategic Air Command (SAC) in 1952, although this was eventually overcome.[15]

Ultimately, SAC acquired a second generation of jet bombers, including the B-52 heavy bomber and the smaller B-58. Once again, the B-52 experienced significant design problems, to the point in 1947 where Secretary of the Air Force Stuart Symington had to overrule an effort to cancel the program. Even after this, the B-52 suffered significant issues in the design of its bomb sight and in the instability of the aircraft when the bomb bay doors were open. All these issues led to a major overhaul in the procurement system, a change that served the air force well in later years.[16] The first (A) model B-52s entered service in 1954, followed six years later by the B-58. The latter was remarkably fast (Mach 2) for a bomber but had limited range. The secret to survivability of both aircraft, however, was not speed but the electronic countermeasures they carried to confuse and defeat enemy defenses.

Great Britain had achieved a hydrogen detonation on November 8, 1957; thereafter, renewed cooperation led the British to use American bomb designs.[17] In an effort to acquire its own nuclear jet bombers as quickly as possible, the Royal Air Force authorized three competing aircraft designs: the Vickers Valiant, the delta-wing Avro Vulcan, and the Handley-Page Victor. The most conventional of these three V-bombers, the Valiant, entered squadron service in 1954, but the ultimate winner of the competition was the Victor, which remained in service in various roles, including aerial tanker, until the end of the Cold War.[18]

The RAF sought to increase the survivability of the V-bombers by the addition of an air-to-ground missile that would allow the bombers to launch their weapons several hundred miles away from the intended targets. To conserve funds, in 1960, the British government decided to focus on the Skybolt, a missile then under development by the U.S. Air Force. However, the Kennedy administration became concerned that this program was increasingly expensive and unreliable. In 1962, the United States cancelled the Skybolt, influenced in part by a State Department belief that the British nuclear deterrent only served to encourage France and Germany to seek their own independent forces.[19] The resulting political controversy underlined the lack of coherence on NATO nuclear employment. Instead, in 1963, the RAF deployed a simpler design for an air-to-ground missile, the Blue Steel, with a limited range of 150 miles (240 kilometers).[20]

Because of its lack of forward bases to attack North America, the Soviet Air Force faced a most difficult task in bomber aircraft design. As noted in Chapter Four, the Soviets had been disappointed with the Mya-4 (NATO designation Bison), a four-engine jet bomber that to NATO eyes appeared quite formidable. Other efforts at developing a supersonic strategic bomber, such as the Tupolev Tu-22 (Blinder) or

Myasishchev M-50 (Bounder,) proved even less successful. Instead, Soviet Long-Range Aviation had to settle on the Tupolev Tu-95, which entered service in 1957. The Tu-95 (NATO designation Bear) was phenomenally fast for a propeller aircraft, achieving speeds of up to 565 miles (905 kilometers) per hour in some models; later versions such as the Bear-H had a range of 1,865 miles (3,000 kilometers). Even this was inadequate for a round-trip strategic mission to the United States, but it was the best that Soviet design and production could achieve. Not until the mid-1960s did the Bear acquire an effective stand-off missile (the AS-5 Kelt) to increase its range and survivability.[21]

At the time, the United States had little knowledge of the weaknesses of these aircraft. The CIA and SAC assumed that the Soviets would follow the American example, producing up to five hundred Bear bombers by the late 1950s. The possibility of such a massive Soviet force gave rise to the so-called "Bomber Gap," a subject of much debate in the United States in 1956 and a factor that drove ever-increasing target lists based on assumed Soviet nuclear growth. At congressional hearings, USAF officers argued for additional expenditures to close the perceived gap. Yet in reality, the Soviet Air Force had perhaps 150 obsolescent intercontinental bombers at a time when the USAF had 1,306 B-47s, 247 B-36s, and the first 97 B-52s. Given the huge investment in these aircraft by the three nuclear powers, calls for further expansion inevitably involved major budgetary disruptions. Eisenhower resisted the demand as much as possible, agreeing to a supplemental appropriation of $1 billion and a slight increase in B-52 production. By 1960, SAC had retired its propeller bombers and fielded 538 B-52s and 19 B-58s in addition to 1,178 B-47s. The Bomber Gap would be only the first of several controversies about nuclear preparedness.[22]

Delivery Systems: ICBMs

The Soviet Union had taken an early interest in rocketry, leading in 1938 to the famous *katyusha* multiple-rocket system. Like the Americans, in 1945, the Soviets benefited from capturing German scientists and technology associated with the liquid-fueled V-weapons. Initially, however, the need to rebuild the Soviet economy and develop the atomic bomb left Soviet missile development in limbo. In 1946, the

Commissar for Armaments, Dimitri F. Ustinov, needed a major project as an institutional justification to continue weapons research in peacetime. He convinced Stalin to assign missile development to Ustinov as an artillery weapon. Factory No. 88, outside of Moscow, became the center of an unusual collaboration between researchers, a collaboration that eventually produced the USSR's intercontinental ballistic missiles and space program.[23]

Within two years, Ustinov used both German and Soviet designers to begin mass production of the R-1 missile, an improved V-2 that ultimately evolved into the famous R-11 Scud, which in turn was the basis of the Al Hussayn missiles fired at Israel in 1991. Other Soviet missiles followed, although the technical problems of developing a truly intercontinental missile, with a range of 8,000 kilometers (5,000 miles), took a decade to resolve. When the design of a single large rocket motor proved too difficult, the Soviet designers combined four smaller engines, each derived from the German V-2, to produce the requisite thrust. The result in 1956 was the R-5 (NATO designation SS-3 Shyster), a missile that could fly 1,200 kilometers (750 miles) and carry a nuclear warhead. The R-5 went into service production and was based in the western USSR for use in a European conflict. In December 1958, the first twelve R-5Ms deployed north of Berlin in East Germany, giving Moscow the means to threaten London and Paris but not New York.[24]

By this time, however, Khrushchev and the other Soviet leaders were aware of the limitations of their bombers and sought an ICBM as soon as possible. While some Soviet engineers continued to develop longer-range theater weapons based on the R-5, Sergei P. Korolev led a design team that produced the first true ICBM, designated R-7. Because Soviet thermonuclear weapons were still relatively large and bulky, Korolev planned a 325-ton launch vehicle that would generate enormous amounts of thrust. Following on the same cluster principle used in the R-5, the first stage of the R-7 not only had four rocket engines of its own but also was assisted by four strap-on booster modules, each with another four engines. The result was clumsy and experienced numerous failures during 1957, most of which were monitored by U.S. radar stations in Turkey. By August, however, a partially successful missile flew from the Tyuratum (Baikonur) test facility in Kazakhstan to the Kamchatka Peninsula at the eastern edge of Siberia, allowing Moscow to announce that it had an ICBM. Then, on the night of October 4–5, 1957, the Soviets used an R-7 to launch *Sputnik I,* the first artificial satellite.[25]

Sputnik was not only an enormous propaganda coup but suggested a quantum leap in the entire nuclear arsenal. Alarmists feared that the Soviets would produce a large number of R-7s, which would not only imperil the U.S. bomber arsenal but reduce the warning of possible nuclear attack from hours to minutes. The Bomber Gap of 1956 gave way to the Missile Gap, an issue that lingered in American politics into the early 1960s.

The U.S. intelligence community knew enough about the Soviet testing program to be confident that the R-7 was still at an early stage of development. The Soviets undoubtedly achieved an intercontinental missile at a time when the United States had not yet perfected the first stage of its own liquid-fueled ICBM, the Atlas, but that was not the same as a fully fielded delivery system. Even as the R-7 gradually became more reliable, its liquid fuel meant that it required several hours to prepare for launch and could not be maintained indefinitely in a fueled condition. In 1959, the Eisenhower administration publicized the conclusions of an accurate intelligence estimate, assessing that the Soviets were still several years away from an effective missile.[26]

Like their adversaries, the U.S. defense services had pursued a multipronged rocketry program, producing surface-to-air missiles (the Nike series) as well as a family of missiles of various range capacities, and even primitive cruise missiles like the Navy Talos (range up to one hundred miles) and the air force's experimental Snark, with a projected range of 5,500 miles. From 1954, the highest priority had gone to the SM-65 Atlas ICBM, followed by the Titan, a more advanced design that could be placed in hardened launch silos. A 1955 panel chaired by James R. Killian, president of MIT, helped convince the Eisenhower administration that nuclear warheads could be sufficiently small to justify simultaneous development of both the Atlas and simpler, intermediate-range ballistic missiles (IRBMs) that could fly 1,500 miles (2,400 kilometers). Because all three services argued their need for such weapons, in 1955 Defense Secretary Charles Wilson authorized simultaneous programs by the USAF and a joint army-navy effort, leading eventually to the Air Force Thor, Army Jupiter and Redstone, and Navy Polaris.[27]

Missiles for Europe

Such missiles were useful only if they could be deployed within range of likely targets, and in May 1956 the JCS urged basing negotiations with a number of allies from Norway to Japan. In March of the following year, Prime Minister Harold Macmillan and President Eisenhower agreed informally that Britain would provide missile bases in return for Eisenhower's efforts to gain a congressional exception permitting the United States to again share nuclear information with Britain.[28]

Sputnik brought new urgency to this issue. Along with increased funding for Atlas, Washington sought to deploy IRBMs around the USSR as a stop-gap substitute for true ICBMs, a precedent that reappeared during the Cuban Missile Crisis. On February 22, 1958, the United States and Britain finalized an agreement to deploy sixty Thors on four RAF bases. Britain provided the facilities and manpower, while the two countries had to make a joint decision to launch.[29] Despite much political opposition in Britain, No. 77 Squadron, RAF, became the first operational Thor unit that same year. Such missiles served to reassure Europe concerning the U.S. commitment to NATO but were only a temporary measure while true ICBMs completed development.

Other NATO allies were less willing to host the missiles, not least because Moscow threatened to target any country that did so. To reduce the appearance of the United States dictating to its allies, Eisenhower turned to General Norstad, USAF, who served as SACEUR from 1956 to 1963. Norstad was to canvas NATO members and recommend missile deployments based at least theoretically on military requirements. Given its forward location and political sensitivity, Germany was obviously reluctant to accept these missiles, although Adenauer continued to seek equality of arms with other NATO members. Eventually, only Italy (fifteen Jupiter missiles) and Turkey (thirty Jupiters) were willing to accept the expense and risk of hosting additional IRBMs. Norstad also attempted to negotiate for NATO members to build more mobile, survivable missiles using U.S. technical information but could not reach agreement.[30]

Some members, such as France, demanded that the United States provide nuclear weapons to them directly, a decision fraught with legal and diplomatic consequences. Instead, Norstad cleverly pioneered the concept of a NATO nuclear stockpile, with the United States controlling weapons that would be released to members in wartime on the basis of a NATO decision. Thus began the odd history of so-called "custodial detachments," small groups of American artillery and ordnance soldiers and airmen who were responsible for controlling an arsenal of tactical nuclear weapons. In addition to Jupiter warheads, these detachments eventually controlled the nuclear warheads for surface-to-air missiles, nuclear artillery ammunition, and atomic demolitions, the latter intended to detonate underground to destroy predetermined targets such as highway interchanges. For decades, these detachments faced the dual task of securing their weapons against Soviet attack and ensuring that the non-U.S. NATO members received those weapons only after a political decision had been authenticated properly down the chain of command.

American Nuclear Strategy

Against the backdrop of the rapid development of weapons and delivery systems, the major powers groped blindly toward a strategy that would accommodate the revolutionary facts of nuclear armament. Immediately after the Hiroshima and Nagasaki bombings, many had concluded that warfare was no longer possible between major states. As the distinguished theorist Bernard Brodie wrote in 1946, "Thus far the chief purpose of our military establishment has been to win wars. From now on its chief purpose must be to avert them."[31] Brodie eventually argued that the *threat* of a nuclear attack might have more coercive effect than the *act* of making such an attack, by deterring an opponent without actual warfare.

The Korean conflict quickly demonstrated that conventional warfare was indeed still possible but must be limited. If a nuclear power concluded that it was losing a conventional conflict so badly that its vital interests were threatened, that power was likely to employ nuclear weapons with potentially disastrous consequences.

This requirement for limits was not immediately apparent to all, however. As described above, Foster Dulles became the spokesman for the Eisenhower administration's avowed plan of Massive Retaliation, using atomic weapons to raise the ante and thereby deter future aggression of the Korean type. Dulles was expressing a diplomatic position, attempting to convince his Soviet counterparts that the United States would, in fact, use nuclear weapons if its vital interests were threatened.[32]

Yet Dulles was not involved in the details of America's evolving nuclear plans, which recognized that atomic weapons were not a permanent solution to strategic problems. In October 1953, the Eisenhower administration incorporated this new reality into NSC-162/2, "Review of Basic National Security Policy." While NSC-162/2 discussed the possibility of Massive Retaliation, it also acknowledged that this option would diminish over time:

> [paragraph 6] b. When both the USSR and the United States reach a stage of atomic plenty and ample means of delivery, each will have the probable capacity to inflict critical damage on the other, but is not likely to be able to prevent major atomic retaliations. This could create a stalemate, with both sides reluctant to initiate general warfare; although if the Soviets believed that initial surprise held the prospect of destroying the capacity for retaliation, they might be tempted into attacking.
>
> c. Although Soviet fear of atomic reaction should still inhibit local aggression, increasing Soviet atomic capability may tend to diminish the deterrent effect of U.S. atomic power against peripheral Soviet aggression. It may also sharpen the reaction of the USSR to what it considers provocative acts of the United States. If either side should miscalculate the strength of the other's reaction, such local conflicts could grow into general war, even though neither seeks nor desires it. To avoid this, it will in general be desirable for the United States to make clear to the USSR the kind of actions which will be almost certain to lead to this result.[33]

The advent of the hydrogen fusion bomb and the ICBM made the question of nuclear strategy both more complex and more urgent because the destruction would be so overwhelming and the response times when the nation was attacked would be so short. The window of American nuclear superiority described by NSC-162/2 had apparently closed, leading to a ferment of Western theoretical efforts during the 1950s.[34]

In a landmark article published in January 1959, the influential analyst Albert Wohlstetter identified the risks inherent in the evolving concept of mutual deterrence. Building on previous research into airbase dispersal, he argued that the apparent balance of nuclear weapons and delivery systems did not automatically mean that each side could deter the other: "To deter an attack means being able to strike back in spite of it. It means, in other words, a capability to strike second."[35] Wohlstetter identified a number of factors that later became commonplace, such as the need for a survivable command structure to direct nuclear retaliation and for the hesitation to launch a missile which, unlike a bomber, could not be recalled. In particular, he noted the fallacy of forward-basing bombers and IRBMs; such bases reduced warning time of enemy attack while being vulnerable to shorter-range enemy weapons, and might actually increase the tendency of the opponent to attack in a crisis in which there seemed to be a danger of no-notice missile launches from such bases.

A key issue related to deterrence was the question of targeting, and here the United States reprised the evolution of strategic bombing during World War II. Between the World Wars, both the USAAF and the RAF had planned to target specific industries rather than terror attacks on civilians. Unfortunately, the state of navigation and bombing made such precision targeting impossible, and thus both air forces shifted to area bombing of industrial cities, arguing that killing skilled workers would neutralize industry just as effectively as destroying machine tools. Early plans for the employment of atomic weapons again targeted industries, but this meant attacking population centers. In January 1951, LeMay convinced the Joint Chiefs that isolated targets would be so difficult to locate and hit that his targets should be primarily industry within urban areas. With the advent of H-bombs, however, nuclear war appeared to be so destructive that economists rejected the traditional approach of targeting industry as being irrelevant, while the thought of deliberately attacking populations remained repellent. In fact, Brodie had suggested as early as 1952 that one might announce in advance a policy of *not* targeting cities, thereby giving the opponent something to lose and a reason to negotiate after an initial nuclear exchange aimed at each other's delivery systems.[36]

The obvious alternative to targeting industry and population (euphemistically termed "counter-value" targeting) was to attack the enemy's missile and bomber bases, many of which were dispersed in rural areas. Again, however, the accuracy of bombers and early ICBMs/IRBMs could not guarantee destruction of all of an opponent's delivery systems. Moreover, such "counter-force" targeting could easily be misinterpreted as American planning for a preemptive first strike, which in turn might increase the chance of a Soviet attack in a crisis.

All this nuclear theorizing, produced by a new generation of mostly civilian analysts, had far outrun the reality of military planning for nuclear war. Prior to 1960, the Joint Chiefs established targeting priorities as an annex to the Joint Strategic Capabilities Plan. Then, each of the U.S. unified commanders-in-chief or CINCs (responsible for specific regions of the world) and some specified CINCs (especially the commander-in-chief of SAC) developed their own separate war plans. In 1955, for example, SAC produced a concept Plan Bravo (for blunting the enemy's atomic capability), which involved attacks on 645 Soviet airfields plus twenty-five atomic weapons aimed at the Soviet nuclear industry. By contrast, Plan Delta (for disruption of war making) called for attacks on 118 of 134 major Soviet cities and expected to inflict sixty million casualties. A Romeo Plan to retard the Soviet conventional conquest of Europe had the lowest priority. Although various committees of the Joint Staff reviewed such plans, operational planning remained in SAC hands. Typically, each year, SAC combined the target lists into a single Emergency War Plan that sought to destroy the optimum mixture of Bravo and Delta targets in a single, massive strike; such a strike would presumably minimize the casualties among SAC aircraft conducting the offensive. The number of targets grew rapidly, although a 1957 review of these plans found that many of these targets were so close together that the blast radii would overlap.[37]

In 1957, a joint army-navy study (Project Budapest) critiqued the SAC plans as excessive, using unnecessarily mega tonnage that would create enormous destruction and radioactive fallout. Instead, the other two services proposed an "alternative undertaking," asking the CINCs to nominate targets on the assumption that most Soviet nuclear weapons would already be launched before the U.S. attack occurred. Similarly, in 1959, the Joint Chiefs had a committee chaired by Lieutenant General Thomas Hickey attempt to draw up three different target sets: military, urban-industrial, and an optimum mixture of the two. Meanwhile, the navy, and particularly Chief of Naval Operations Arleigh Burke, argued that the advent of submarine-launched ballistic missiles would allow the United States to develop a truly secure retaliatory force, one that, although small, would be so inviolable that it would

382   A MILITARY HISTORY OF THE COLD WAR, 1944–1962

deter any enemy attack on the United States. However, air force leaders continued to argue for a much larger capability.[38]

In August 1960, Eisenhower decided that the Strategic Air Command had the data, experience, and computer support to produce a true national-level plan for strategic nuclear conflict. The resulting Joint Strategic Target Planning Staff had representatives from the other services, but SAC ideas prevailed. The resulting plans carried the label of SIOP (single integrated operational plan) plus the fiscal year in which the plan would be effective, in this case SIOP-62. Although there were various options within SIOP-62, all versions called for attacks on every state in the communist bloc, including not only the USSR and PRC but also the Warsaw Pact, North Korea, and North Vietnam. The plan involved the expenditure of 3,267 U.S. nuclear bombs and warheads against an estimated five hundred Soviet weapons. Needless to say, such an attack would truly create Armageddon.[39]

Although SIOP-62 was top secret, it reflected the Eisenhower administration's Massive Retaliation approach to strategic nuclear war. In fact, it took Massive Retaliation to a logical extreme, so that even Eisenhower and the Joint Chiefs proved unable to curb the air force approach to massive overkill.[40] This approach, or perhaps more accurately a caricature of Massive Retaliation, was one of numerous defense issues during the 1960 presidential campaign. John F. Kennedy was elected to office in part because he espoused a broader approach to defense issues, based loosely on the Flexible Response concept associated with Maxwell Taylor.

The Berlin Wall crisis (see Chapter Fourteen) presented the new administration with a classic instance in which strategic nuclear weapons were almost irrelevant to the immediate problem. Frustrated with the inflexibility of SIOP-62, Defense Secretary Robert S. McNamara directed a revision with more options. The resulting SIOP-63 provided some flexibility in the scope and targeting of nuclear attacks but still involved huge casualties. In June 1962, McNamara publicly endorsed Brodie's policy of not initially targeting cities, shifting the focus of war plans to counterforce.[41] By this point, the defense secretary realized that the United States had so many nuclear weapons that it had guaranteed or "assured" the destruction of the Soviet Union even if the Soviets attacked first. Only gradually did McNamara and other U.S. planners come to accept that they were in a situation of Mutually Assured Destruction (MAD), in which each side retained sufficient capacity to devastate the other even after a first strike.

There was still much debate over what constituted MAD, however. McNamara argued for 1,000 ICBMs as a minimum force, while the USAF wanted 3,000. Kennedy himself used the worst-case scenario to justify continued U.S. weapons production and forward deployment of new systems to retain nuclear superiority.[42] During the early 1960s, the Kennedy administration, building on its predecessors' efforts, evolved the Nuclear Triad, a balance of three different delivery systems to provide both survivability and flexibility in a crisis. Bombers were the most vulnerable, uncertain delivery means, but in a crisis, the bomber force could fly to predetermined "Fail Safe" points without committing the nation to war. ICBMs were the most accurate means of delivery, yet their launch was irrevocable, and their hardened silos would eventually become vulnerable to highly accurate enemy nuclear warheads. Both Atlas and Titan missiles entered effective service in 1962, but their liquid fuel meant that they could not be launched in the fifteen-minute minimum warning time allowed by a surprise enemy missile attack. Thus, although 126 Atlases and 54 Titans I's became operational in the early 1960s, they were eventually replaced by the solid-fuel Minuteman ICBM.[43]

The third leg of the triad was seaborne missiles, of which the first example was the Polaris. The original A-1 model had a range of only 1,200 miles (1,920 kilometers), which meant that the launching vessel had to be relatively close to the target country. The target date for Polaris to enter service was 1963, but after *Sputnik* the Eisenhower administration pushed this date forward. At one point, the navy considered installing Polaris missiles on cruisers or even a partially completed battleship hull, but such a surface installation remained highly vulnerable. Over Admiral Rickover's strenuous objections, a nuclear attack submarine was cut in half to permit the installation of a section of vertically mounted missile-launching tubes. The resulting *USS George Washington* test-fired a Polaris while submerged on July 20, 1960, and entered operational service in November of that same year. Initially, there was considerable debate within the Joint Chiefs as to whether Polaris should be part of the SIOP or allocated to regional CINC targets, and the navy pushed for a large number of such submarines even before the missile system had completed testing. Eisenhower resisted this drive, although he did authorize research to lengthen the range to 2,500 miles (4,000 kilometers). Eventually, Polaris became an integral component of the strategic nuclear plan. The Kennedy administration continued to accelerate this program to the point where nine ballistic missile submarines were operational by the time of the 1962 Cuban Missile Crisis (see Chapter Fifteen).[44] Such submarines became the final guarantee that anyone who attacked the United States would inevitably suffer a retaliatory strike, thereby completing the triad. Moscow, London, and Paris later followed suit with their own versions of this triad.

SAC Alert

Despite the confidence inspired by the triad, in the age of ICBMs the U.S. nuclear forces lived at a sustained level of semialert.

The first component of this alert was defensive. When Eisenhower took office, the United States had no integrated air defense command, limited radar coverage of North America, and only twenty interceptor squadrons equipped with all-weather jets. Both the USAF and the Joint Chiefs wanted to emphasize offensive nuclear forces, but the 1953 Soviet hydrogen detonation caused considerable public outcry for defensive measures. Eisenhower had to reassure the public but insisted that defensive measures must not overwhelm budgetary requirements.[45] In May 1958, the United States and Canada agreed to create the North American Air [later Aerospace] Defense Command, or NORAD, a combined headquarters responsible for warning and air defense of North America. A string of radar sides known as the Distant Early Warning (DEW) Line rose in remote sectors of Alaska, the Canadian Arctic, and Greenland. Other radar facilities, such as the mid-Canada line, plus low-altitude radars around the continent and picket ships at sea gradually filled in the blind spots in this defense, giving both countries early warning of an impending attack. Such warnings went to hardened command posts, such as Cheyenne Mountain, Colorado, and North Bay, Ontario, where early punch-card computers helped process and display the resulting information.

For missile attack, NORAD's main function was simply to provide warning to SAC headquarters, the Defense Department, and the president. Air-breathing Soviet bombers, however, would have been met by several layers of defenses. For decades, Royal Canadian and U.S. Air Force fighter interceptors stood in isolated shelters at the ends of runways, waiting to scramble into the air and intercept unidentified intruders. Tacticians planned to have such fighters, which would presumably be outnumbered by the Soviet bomber force, engage at extremely long ranges using airborne radar and early missiles. Beginning in 1957, some of these fighters even carried the MB-1 Genie air-to-air missile, designed to knock down bomber formations with a 1.5-kiloton nuclear airburst! By 1964, there were thirty-nine USAF and twenty-one air national guard squadrons on alert.[46]

In addition, major American cities were ringed with surface-to-air missiles, beginning in 1954 with the Nike Ajax (MIM-3) and succeeded in 1958 with the longer-range Nike Hercules (MIM-14). In April 1956, Eisenhower authorized the air defense commanders to use nuclear-armed defensive missiles immediately in the event of surprise attack, a rare exception to the presidential control over all nuclear weapons. By 1964, the U.S. Army had ninety-seven active and forty-four National Guard Nike firing batteries. Although sharply reduced from 1965 onward, these missile defenses continued until 1974.[47]

Meanwhile, bombers and missiles had to remain at a constant state of readiness. Some bombers stayed aloft at all times, but the expense and maintenance strain of this limited it to a small percentage of the total force. Instead, in SAC bases across the country, signs would light up in movie theaters and chapels when the alert crews were to report to the airfield, crash-start their engines, and roll down the runways right behind the NORAD fighters. In turn, refueling aircraft followed the bombers to extend their range and endurance. The air police securing these alert aircraft also underwent constant drills against mock intruders, creating a somewhat paranoid atmosphere reflected in motion pictures such as *Strategic Air Command* (1955) and the black comedy *Dr. Strangelove* (1964). For the navy, Polaris duty meant long submerged patrols, with two crews assigned to each submarine in order to minimize time spent in port.

Inevitably, this grueling pace of constant alerts and deployments under all weather conditions produced false alarms and accidents. On October 5, 1960, the U.S. warning radar at Thule, Greenland, wrongly identified the rising moon as a missile attack, causing a brief alert.[48] Perhaps the most serious incident, however, occurred on January 17, 1966, when a KC-135 refueling aircraft collided with a B-52 over Palomares, Spain, resulting in the deaths of seven of the eleven crewmen involved. Safety devices prevented the four B-28 thermonuclear bombs from exploding, but one was lost at sea and not located for several months, and the entire community was exposed to high amounts of radioactivity. Similar "Broken Arrow" incidents occurred repeatedly, including weapons that were never recovered after falling into the Savannah River in Georgia (February 1958) and over Goldsboro, North Carolina (January 1961); in the latter case, an airborne alert B-52 suffered structural collapse, killing three crewmen and losing two weapons.[49]

Tactical Nuclear Weapons: The Ultimate Oxymoron

Yet, even as the strategic nuclear competition settled into an uneasy and sometimes fatal balance of terror, American politicians, theorists, and soldiers continued to seek ways to use the atomic weapon on the battlefield. This was true even of Eisenhower, who was determined to deter a general war without excessive defense costs.[50] As he remarked publicly in 1955, "Where these things are used on strictly military targets and for strictly military purposes, I see no reason why they shouldn't be used just exactly as you would use a bullet or anything else."[51]

Quite apart from the usual American fascination with advanced technology, tactical nuclear weapons were the obvious means of redressing the balance between Western conventional forces, especially in NATO, and their Soviet counterparts. As identified in NSC-68 and reinforced by the Eisenhower New Look, American leaders believed that in order to survive over the long haul of containment, the United States had to minimize the economic distortions of the Cold War, and that in turn meant limiting the expense and manpower devoted to standing defense forces. When compared to the seemingly unlimited hordes of Soviet, Chinese, and satellite soldiers, the Western military wanted tactical nuclear weapons to serve as an essential deterrent and equalizer. Even critics of the Massive Retaliation approach, such as General Taylor and the Kennedy administration, regarded "Tac Nukes" as one of the key stages along a spectrum of low- to high-intensity military action. Once nuclear weapons went beyond the first stage of extreme scarcity during the 1940s, there were hundreds and eventually thousands of such weapons available for tactical use. During the mid-1950s, the United States deployed first the 280mm cannon and then various nuclear-tipped rockets to both Europe and the Far East. With the Kennedy administration's emphasis on Flexible Response, the number of tactical nuclear weapons in Western Europe increased by 60 percent between 1961 and 1964.[52]

The problem lay in defining the difference between strategic and tactical nuclear weapons. For most American observers, the distinction was geographical: using weapons of limited size and range in Asia or Europe but outside the confines of the United States or USSR should qualify as tactical employment. Unfortunately, this distinction was far less self-evident to a European or Soviet leader, who might find such a "tactical" nuclear attack occurring in his front yard. Moreover, military commanders could never be certain whether or when the NATO governments would authorize the use of such weapons; until such permission arrived, they had to be prepared to fight a conventional conflict while vastly outnumbered.

Quite apart from the tactical use of such weapons to destroy enemy troop concentrations, their presence complicated the already-elaborate gaming theory of nuclear confrontation. For Thomas Schelling, one of Brodie's major competitors during the 1950s, the growing variety of nuclear weapons permitted one to threaten or inflict measured amounts of violence in order to coerce an opponent to reach an accommodation.[53] Herman Kahn, a longtime RAND analyst who had studied how the two World Wars had begun, came to advocate nuclear weapons as one aspect of a deliberate policy of escalation, seeking to deal rationally with an opponent even after the nuclear threshold had been passed. In a 1965 book, *On Escalation*, Kahn famously described an escalation ladder of forty-four steps, with nuclear weapons being used first at step fifteen![54]

Such elaborate theories assumed that all adversaries in a confrontation were led by rational, calculating leaders who shared a strong desire to avoid a total or "spasm" strategic nuclear exchange. Fortunately for world peace, these assumptions proved to be true in the instances in which Washington and Moscow confronted each other directly. However, this idea of graduated escalation—raising the ante progressively until one's opponent decided that the cost was too high—did not always fit other Cold War confrontations. In particular, when the United States attempted to conduct graduated escalation in a limited war to defend South Vietnam during the 1960s, it encountered the Hanoi government, an opponent that placed a much higher value on victory than did the United States and was therefore willing to absorb almost any degree of coercive damage.

British and French Nuclear Strategy

If nuclear weapons lured American administrations because of their promise of cheap military power, those same weapons proved irresistible to their British counterparts. The strain of overseas defense commitments from 1939 into the 1950s had left the London government nearly bankrupt and desperate for alternatives that might protect vital interests with fewer troops and expenditures. When Winston Churchill returned as prime minister in 1951, he urged the military to consider nuclear weapons, both strategic and tactical, as an economical alternative. During the summer of 1952, the British chiefs of staff reached agreement on a strategy involving conventional forces in Western Europe primarily to gain time, in the event of Soviet attack, for NATO to launch a nuclear counterstrike. As the Chief of the Air Staff and heir to the RAF's doctrine of strategic bombardment, Air Marshal Sir John Slessor was an enthusiastic proponent of this new strategy. However, because the British proposal arose at the height of American efforts to obtain European rearmament, Slessor's American counterparts naturally regarded the British idea as an attempt to renege on defense commitments to NATO.[55]

Five years later, after further counterinsurgency efforts and the fiasco of the Suez Crisis, Britain finally implemented the essence of the 1952 plan. Defence Minister Duncan Sandys issued a white paper that endorsed Massive Retaliation and in turn proposed major reductions in conventional forces. Over the next five years, Britain planned to cut its uniformed strength from 690,000 to 375,000, reducing troops in Germany from 77,000 to 64,000. This finally permitted Britain to end conscription while focusing on development of missiles for an independent nuclear deterrent.[56]

French motivations for entering the nuclear arms race were more complex. Diplomatically, France sought to maintain its prestige and reassert leadership in Europe after the disasters of Dien Bien Phu and Suez. Militarily, France like its allies wanted nuclear weapons to restore the balance against larger enemies, whether German or Soviet. Before he lost command for opposition to the European Defense Community, Marshal Juin had begun the process by which France, like the United States, converted to smaller, lighter divisions that could operate in a dispersed, flexible manner on a nuclear battlefield. Eventually, such tacticians sought battlefield nuclear weapons to complete this concept of future war.[57]

Because the coalition cabinets of the Fourth Republic were divided on this and other issues, French premiers publicly disclaimed a desire for nuclear weapons. Secretly, however, the French government refocused its nuclear program toward military applications in 1956–1957. This date was no coincidence, for it marked the period when the Suez Canal Crisis had exposed the limits of both French conventional power and the American nuclear guarantee to France. General de Gaulle in particular concluded that France needed an independent nuclear capability because the Soviet-American nuclear stalemate meant that in a crisis, the United States might be unable to protect its allies.[58]

On February 13, 1960, France detonated its first nuclear device in a remote corner of Algeria. (According to some accounts, the French scientists shared much of their knowledge with the fledgling Israeli nuclear program, giving Tel Aviv a head start that may have produced primitive bombs as early as 1967.[59]) By 1966, France had a force of fifty Mirage IV supersonic bombers, each carrying one sixty-kiloton bomb for an unrefueled distance of 2,500 kilometers (1,550 miles). Given the short warning time available in the event of Soviet attack, however, these bombers were quite vulnerable. To resolve this problem, France began constructing missile silos in southeastern France and in 1973 produced its own ballistic missile submarine, *L'Inflexible*. Unlike the British missile submarines, the French vessels were developed without American technical cooperation.[60] Given the fact that NATO did not, as de Gaulle anticipated, wither after France withdrew its forces from coalition control, the enormous expense of this French "Dissuasion Force" proved largely irrelevant.

Soviet Nuclear Planning

As K. S. Tripathi has observed, "[T]he year 1945 was a turning point in the history of strategy but the Soviet strategy under Stalin failed to turn."[61] For the next four years, there was little Soviet discussion of the effects of atomic weapons. Initially, while the Soviet Union secretly labored to close the gap in such weapons, it took the public position that they were overrated and did not change the fundamental rules of warfare. Stalin, after all, had asserted his own genius by describing what he called "the Permanently Operating Factors" that regarded war as a vast struggle of attrition between the mass armies of industrial powers.[62] More fundamentally, the Marxist leadership of the USSR had long assumed that war with the capitalist West was inevitable; this assumption required revision if one acknowledged that atomic weapons made it impossible to win such a conflict.

During the final years of his life, Stalin did permit a few trial balloons. In 1949, Georgi Malenkov publicly acknowledged that the Bomb might change the basic nature of strategy. In 1952, Stalin's final theoretical work reaffirmed the inevitability of conflict *between* capitalist states but left open the question of capitalist versus Soviet warfare.[63]

Tentative public discussion of nuclear warfare's implications began almost before the dictator's body was cold. As noted in Chapter Eight, Zhukov like his Western counterparts changed military structure during the mid-1950s, seeking more mobile and survivable troop units on an atomic battlefield. Yet, it was Nikita Khrushchev who fully embraced the idea of nuclear weapons both to provide a strategic balance and to substitute for some of the huge conventional forces of the Soviet Army. Trying to solve the economic woes of the Soviet system, in December 1959 Khrushchev proposed a phased reduction of the Soviet forces in favor of greater reliance on atomic weapons. After a strenuous debate, the Soviet government and military arrived at a compromise that reduced the army from 3.5 million men in 180 divisions (the peak reached in 1958) to two million in 138 divisions a decade later.[64] Meanwhile, Khrushchev made the Strategic Rocket Forces an equal and separate branch of the armed forces.

At the time, however, the Soviet premier was betting on a capability that did not yet exist, as indicated by the Tyuratam disaster. While the Soviet Union continued to work on a reliable ICBM, it did not overlook other options. Like its American counterpart, the Soviet Navy had experimented with various small cruise missiles launched from surfaced submarines. However, combining the technical problems of both liquid-fueled missiles and submarines was a highly risky proposition. By late 1958, the Soviets had converted several 611-series conventional submarines (NATO designation Zulu V) by installing two vertical launch tubes in the conning tower, probably using modified R-11 (Scud) missiles that had problems of safety and reliability. The next effort, the Hotel class nuclear submarines, first deployed in 1961 with four R-13 (SS-N-4) atomic-tipped missiles. Not only were these missiles limited to a range of six hundred kilometers, but the vessels themselves were experimental, giving rise to the famous reactor disaster on board the submarine K-19 in July 1961. Not until 1966 did the Soviet Navy field the first of the Yankee class of submarines, and even these still relied on liquid fuel. As late as 1986, a Yankee sub-marine sank off Bermuda after a fire in the missile compartment.[65]

Thus, in the early 1960s, the U.S. arsenal of both nuclear weapons and strategic delivery vehicles was far ahead of the Soviet inventory. Yet, despite the efforts of Eisenhower, the Joint Chiefs, and McNamara, American planners continued to use worst-case scenarios involving huge expenditures of nuclear weapons. This contributed to Soviet nervousness in the series of confrontations that erupted at that time.

14

FOUR CONFRONTATIONS, 1960–1962

Four different issues—the downing of a U-2 aircraft over the Soviet Union, the failed invasion of Cuba at the Bay of Pigs, the construction of the Berlin Wall, and the civil war in Laos—dominated the Cold War rivalry during the period 1960–1962. Although these issues were largely unrelated to each other, collectively they stoked an atmosphere of antagonism, contributing to the near-fatal 1962 confrontation over Soviet offensive missiles in Cuba.

AERIAL RECONNAISSANCE

Ironically, the first of these issues, the U-2, arose because of a U.S. intelligence program that had largely defused the so-called Bomber and Missile Gaps.

From an early stage in the Cold War, the United States had conducted two types of aerial reconnaissance against its adversaries. On the one hand were aircraft flying outside of Soviet airspace but collecting information either through electronic eavesdropping or oblique (angled) photographs of Soviet territory. Although such operations were within existing international law,[1] the bitter memory of German air reconnaissance prior to the 1941 invasion made the already-secretive Soviet government extremely sensitive to these border flights. Soviet fighters fired at such aircraft as early as October 15, 1945,[2] but the first known shoot-down of an intelligence aircraft occurred on April 8,

1950, when Soviet La-11 propeller fighters destroyed a USN PB4Y-2 Privateer collecting electronic intelligence over the Baltic Sea. This was part of a program called Special Electronics Airborne Search Projects designed to provoke Soviet radars and determine their characteristics and coverage. Ten American crew members died in this incident. After a brief suspension to review this program, President Truman approved its resumption provided that the aircraft involved were armed for self-defense.[3] In other instances, both borders and navigation were often less than precise, leading to unintended airspace violations. The most significant of these incidents involved another signals intelligence collector, this time a C130A-II modified cargo plane flying along the Turkish-Soviet border on September 2, 1958. When the C130A accidentally crossed into Soviet Armenia, MiG-17 fighters shot it down, killing all seventeen crew members.[4]

The second form of aerial reconnaissance, involving direct overflight of an adversary's sovereign territory, was unquestionably illegal. Yet, throughout the late 1940s and 1950s, the United States found such overflights invaluable for both operational and strategic intelligence purposes.

Many such flights involved shallow incursions designed to provide warning of possible enemy actions. As early as 1949, Far East Air Force RF-80As (the R prefix indicated a reconnaissance version) took photographs of the Soviet Kurile and Sakhalin islands. Once the Korean conflict began, President Truman authorized aerial reconnaissance of the Chinese coastline, to determine if Beijing was preparing to invade Taiwan, and of Soviet airbases in Siberia, to investigate signals intercepts indicating that Stalin's Tu-4s regularly deployed to those locations. In coordination with the United States, the RAF also flew a number of Spitfire reconnaissance missions out of Hong Kong. In 1954–1955, the Soviets shot down two U.S. Navy patrol planes and a USAF RB-29 off the Far Eastern coast.[5]

Seeking target data, SAC and its RAF counterparts continued such cross-border flights for years. In one instance, an RB-47E flying out of England to photograph northern Russian installations suffered cannon damage from MiG-17s but escaped with the desired images on May 8, 1954.[6] Other reconnaissance aircraft, including several belonging to the Republic of [Nationalist] China Air Force over mainland China (1958 and 1959) and at least one USAF RB-47B over Siberia (April 1955), were less fortunate when intercepted.[7]

Such limited incursions could not, however, accurately assess the extent of Soviet nuclear weapons and strategic delivery programs. Despite effective espionage, radar, and other collection programs, the Eisenhower administration became convinced that it needed more systematic coverage to determine the extent of the Soviet nuclear threat. Using conventional air force platforms to conduct such deep penetrations was an obvious act of war that Eisenhower sought to avoid, however, so the United States tried several alternative means. During January and February 1956, the United States launched a total of 448 WS-119L high-altitude, unmanned balloons with photographic capsules from West Germany, hoping that the jet stream would carry these balloons over the USSR to be recovered near Japan. Although this project Genetrix provided considerable imagery to establish a baseline of information about the Soviet Union, the Soviets soon figured out how to intercept the balloons and protested strongly, causing Eisenhower to end the operation. A smaller number of balloons failed in July 1958 for various reasons, including a faulty timing device that caused many of the capsules to land in the Soviet Union.[8]

The alternative was the U-2, one of the strangest products to come out of Lockheed Aviation's notorious "Skunk Works" design facility. In 1953, Clarence "Kelly" Johnson, the designer of various aircraft including the F104 fighter-interceptor, developed a revolutionary single-engine aircraft based on the F104 fuselage but with a huge, eighty-foot wingspan that would permit it to achieve unprecedented altitudes. The air force had originally rejected this design in favor of a more conventional twin-engine one that became the RB-57D, a variant of the British-designed Canberra that eventually captured the official altitude record of 70,000 feet. Fortunately for Johnson, the same Killian technology panel that energized development of American ICBMs was also seeking intelligence solutions to reduce the chance of nuclear attack. To determine Soviet nuclear capabilities, therefore, members of Killian's panel urged Eisenhower to pursue what became the U-2 design. In the fall of 1954, the president approved the controversial program but specified that it should not be handled by the Defense Department, perhaps because he was sensitive about overruling the air force. The obvious alternative was to operate the program under the CIA, at that time headed by the secretary of state's brother Allen Dulles. Reluctantly, the younger Dulles took on the Aquatone

(U-2) program as a joint CIA-USAF venture, with much of the funding coming from the CIA.[9]

The U-2 possessed a remarkable altitude in excess of 70,000 feet (21.3 kilometers). However, such extreme altitudes required a very lightweight, fragile aircraft that had to be operated within a narrow band of six knots per hour if it were not to stall or buffet, risking loss of wings or tail.[10] Moreover, the leaders of the Aquatone program engaged in wistful thinking in a number of ways. First, they believed that Soviet radars, based on U.S. World War II technology, would be unable to track aircraft above 40,000 feet. In practice, although Soviet air defense initially had difficulties in this regard, it quickly learned how to track the new aircraft. Of equal significance, Dulles and others assured the president that in the event the aircraft were shot down or otherwise lost, neither the pilot nor the plane would survive to provide evidence of its intelligence function. The CIA therefore developed a cover story to be used in the event of a lost U-2, claiming that it was a weather research aircraft that had gone off course. Yet, as early as April 1957, a fatal U-2 accident in Nevada indicated that both cameras and signals intelligence equipment might survive a crash.[11]

During the first two U-2 flights over the Soviet Union in July 1956, PVO-Strany had trouble tracking the aircraft, and more than twenty MiG fighters experienced engine flameout in failed efforts to reach the intruder's altitude. When Moscow protested these flights, Eisenhower promptly halted them. In a vain effort to reduce the aircraft's radar signature, Lockheed changed paint schemes and flight surfaces, but this reduced effective altitude without solving the detection problem. During the next four years, U-2s flew far more missions over the Middle East and Asia than over the Soviet Union, providing valuable intelligence during the Suez Crisis and other events. Eisenhower personally controlled the few flights permitted over the USSR, flights that provided essential information concerning the Soviet nuclear, bomber, and missile programs.[12]

When Khrushchev failed to raise the U-2 issue in summit meetings, Eisenhower concluded that the Soviet leader was tacitly acquiescing to the flights. In fact, Khrushchev was outraged by these violations of Soviet security and sovereignty, and repeatedly shook up the PVO-Strany hierarchy in an effort to halt them. During the later 1950s, the Soviet Union pushed development of the MiG-17 fighter and especially the S-75 air defense missile (NATO designation SA-2 Guideline).

The S-75 shot down a Chinese Nationalist RB-57D over Beijing in October 1959, although the West did not know the reason for that aircraft's loss. By the time of Francis Gary Powers's notorious flight on May 1, 1960, PVO-Strany had not only fielded S-75s but identified the likely flight paths and imagery objectives of future U-2 missions.[13]

President Eisenhower had authorized one additional flight, across the entire Soviet Union from Pakistan to Norway, to obtain more data prior to his scheduled May 13 summit meeting with Khrushchev in Paris. A series of delays meant that Powers actually took off on the communist May 1 holiday, an unintended coincidence that further enraged the Soviet leadership. This time, PVO-Strany was prepared, tracking the aircraft even before it entered Soviet airspace. An S-75 battalion near Sverdlovsk achieved a near-miss on the U-2, damaging the rear control surfaces and forcing Powers to eject. In the confusion, the defenders did not initially realize they had succeeded, and another S-75 battalion launched a volley that killed the pilot of a MiG-19 interceptor. The Soviet authorities captured both Powers and components of his crashed airplane, although they did not announce this publicly until six days later, by which time the U.S. government had issued its unconvincing cover story of an off-course weather aircraft.[14]

This announcement embarrassed the Eisenhower administration and disrupted the summit conference. It also ended overflights of the Soviet Union but by no means ended aerial collection. On the contrary, two months after the Powers incident, an over-zealous MiG pilot shot down an RB-47H signals intelligence aircraft flying off the shores of the northern USSR; four of the six crewmen died, and the other two fell into Soviet hands. Meanwhile, a redesigned, larger aircraft, the U-2R, continued to fly for the CIA, USAF, and NASA for decades. U-2s even qualified for operations off navy carriers in 1964.[15]

The May 1, 1960, incident had another, unintended consequence— one of the first nuclear alerts of the Cold War. In 1959, the Defense Department had standardized on five levels or gradations of alert, known as Defense Conditions, with DEFCON 5 being normal, peacetime activities and DEFCON 1 being the highest level of alert. Different unified and specified commands might be at different DEFCONs at the same time, depending upon their missions, but SAC and NORAD DEFCONs had the most immediate implications for nuclear warfare because the Soviet Union might misinterpret a higher alert posture in those two commands. Late on the evening of May 15, 1960, when the Paris conference was falling apart, Defense Secretary Thomas S. Gates, Jr., tried to conduct a "quiet" increase in alert posture as a precaution. General Nathan S. Twining, Chairman of the JCS, apparently misinterpreted the message, and by 2:23 A.M. on May 16 all elements of the Defense Department had gone to DEFCON 3, with news of the alert leaking to the press. When the Soviet Air Force commander learned of the U.S. alert, he ordered all Soviet bombers to return to base so that, if necessary, they could upload their atomic bombs. Fortunately, both sides ended their alerts at an early stage, but this mistake exacerbated the U-2 crisis and set an unfortunate precedent for later confrontations.[16]

Ironically, on the same day that a Soviet court convicted Powers of espionage, August 19, 1960, the USAF successfully recovered the first capsule from an orbiting photographic satellite, giving the United States more consistent imagery coverage than air-breathing craft had ever been able to provide. Aerial incidents along the Soviet coast fell off sharply, although there were still numerous confrontations when Soviet and U.S. aircraft intercepted each other at sea.[17]

The Cuban Revolution

If American flights over the Soviet Union infuriated Nikita Khrushchev, the rise of a pro-Marxist regime in Cuba, on the doorstep of the United States, equally angered Dwight Eisenhower and his successor, John F. Kennedy. Moreover, Fidel Castro's rise to power, while superficially similar to Maoist insurrections elsewhere, was sufficiently unusual that it altered both sides' perceptions of the nature of insurgency.

Since 1898, the United States had assumed considerable political as well as economical control over the nominally independent island of Cuba. By midcentury, American-owned industries, especially in sugar and tobacco, distorted the Cuban economy and increased social inequalities.

Although Fidel Castro was an angry young man, searching for some means of gaining power and influence, he was not initially a Marxist.[18] The son of a well-to-do Cuban farmer, Castro was at various times influenced by Falangist, Peronist, and traditional liberal ideas, without having any clear ideological focus. This changed in 1952,

MAP 22. Cuba, 1956–1961

when Fulgencio Batista seized power. Having already controlled the country from 1933 to 1944, Batista inspired the younger officers of the Cuban Army to revolt against the corrupt and privileged regime in Havana. He arrested many opposition politicians, but the young attorney Castro was too minor a figure to concern the new dictator.

On July 26, 1953, Castro organized an attempt to seize weapons in the Moncada army barracks in Santiago de Cuba. As a program for revolution, his "five revolutionary laws" went no farther than restoring the 1940 constitution and giving land to sharecroppers and small farmers. The revolt failed and Castro was arrested, but this action made him a household name and gave his efforts both impetus and a name—the 26th of July Movement. Like Adolf Hitler after the failed Munich Putsch, Castro used his trial as a platform for political revolution and obtained a lenient sentence. Released in May 1955, Castro went to Mexico.[19]

Castro raised funds from other exiles to begin forming an invasion force. A handful of veterans of the U.S. and Spanish armies provided rudimentary training for the would-be rebels, but neither these instructors nor Castro knew anything about guerrilla warfare. In November 1956, Castro led a tiny force on board the yacht *Granma*, aiming to land in southeastern Cuba. A series of delays meant that the rising designed to support him had failed before he disembarked in the wrong place in early December. Castro struggled off to the Sierra Maestra Mountains, barely escaping the Cuban Army units that deployed to the area.[20] The surviving rebel force numbered only a handful of men, including Castro, his brother Raul, and the Argentinean physician Ernesto "Che" Guevara.

After their success, Guevara and the other survivors created a myth of a tiny group of revolutionaries inspiring a rural insurrection. In fact, even before the *Granma* landing, a large number of urban professionals and students had plotted against Batista. Throughout the next two years, while Castro operated in the mountains, this urban faction made major contributions to discrediting the regime, including a general strike in April 1958. The mountain rebels had to cooperate with a coalition of other opposition groups, including a separate rebel movement in western Cuba.[21]

Although concerned by the rising violence in Cuba, Foster Dulles suspended military aid to Batista in March 1958 because of the dictator's continued repressive actions. A Cuban Army sweep in July almost defeated Castro, but thereafter the government forces fell prey to poor leadership and morale. When the rebels besieged various government outposts, the army did little to rescue its troops. In late November 1959, Batista foiled a military plot against him, but within a month he recognized that he had lost control and fled into exile on December 31, 1958. Castro emerged as the leader of the new revolutionary republic.[22]

This legend of a rural insurrection without Mao Tse-tung's extensive political preparation misled its authors as much as outside observers. Batista had far less legitimacy than most rulers, as indicated by the fact that only 867 people died in twenty-five months of war.[23] Coming from Argentina, Guevara did not realize that the rebellion was based on decades of liberal opposition in Cuba. Instead, the medical student turned Marxist claimed to have developed a new form of insurgency, focoism, involving a small revolutionary group that discredits the government by extreme violence. Focoism would supposedly produce the kind of quick victory that Castro had achieved in Cuba. This naive doctrine produced a number of failures, including Guevara's death in Bolivia in 1967.[24]

Once in power, Fidel Castro expressed the widespread Cuban nationalist sentiment against U.S. domination, irritating the Eisenhower administration. Although Guevara and Raul Castro were obviously Communists, American officials were divided in their evaluation of Fidel. When the new leader visited Washington in April 1959, Vice President Nixon described him as "either incredibly naïve about Communism or under Communist discipline—my guess is the former."[25] In May, the Cuban cabinet issued a reform law that broke up large land holdings and specified that only Cubans might own plantations. Eventually, most Americans lost their property in Cuba, including Mafia-controlled clubs in Havana. Castro also began to support rebel movements against the Dominican Republic and other American states, further alarming Washington.

Castro's reforms promised land, education, and medical care for the Cuban population. At the same time, however, his regime brutally repressed any opposition, producing a steady stream of refugees fleeing to Miami. These refugees found the U.S. government quite willing to believe that Castro was a hated dictator with little popular support. The communist menace had seemingly escaped American efforts to contain it in Asia and Europe.

"Covert" Action

As early as December 1959, the CIA began to recruit a group of exiles to become trainers and leaders of an anti-Castro insurgency. On March 17, 1960, President Eisenhower approved a plan to focus diplomatic, propaganda, military, economic, and intelligence efforts to undermine the Castro regime. The 5412 Committee, so named for the NSC directive that created it in 1955, was a group of senior officials who met weekly to supervise this and other covert activities, thereby insulating the president from direct connection to these plans.[26] The actual coordinator was Richard Bissell, deputy director for plans of the CIA. A Yale-educated economist, Bissell had previously led the U-2 project, during which he had developed an aversion to what he considered the selfish and bureaucratic military manner of management.[27]

While the Americans and their exile allies prepared to overthrow the regime, Castro began to receive weapons and training from the Soviet bloc. This motivated his opponents to hasten their preparations, before the Cuban armed forces became too strong, and made the original plan for a few hundred infiltrators seem inadequate. An improved Cuban Air Force would also imperil planned airdrops of supplies to insurgents. On November 4, 1960, the CIA transmitted a decision from the 5412 Committee to its action officers training the exiles in Guatemala. From that point onward, only sixty men would continue guerrilla training. The rest of the force would expand to prepare for a conventional invasion of Cuba. This force adopted the name "Brigade 2506," referring to the serial number of the first man to die in training. Its commander was Jose Perez ("Pepe") San Roman, a former regular officer of the Cuban Army who had been imprisoned by both Batista and Castro for opposing repression.[28]

The creation of this brigade had a number of unfortunate consequences. Although it was still too small to defeat the Cuban Army and revolutionary militia in a conventional fight, the brigade was also too large and heavily equipped to enter Cuba surreptitiously—its invasion would inevitably connect the U.S. government to the operation. The vast expansion of recruiting—from 300 to over 1,500 men, with a desired goal of 3,000—virtually ensured that the Castro government would learn of the plan and that the project could not be cancelled quietly. This large number also meant that the new recruits included some associated with the Batista regime and others who would be inadequately trained when the attack began.

The chosen invasion site was the Trinidad area of south-central Cuba, where there was a preexisting resistance movement and only two bridges connecting it to the capital. In the event of failure, the invaders could take refuge in the Escambray Mountains, only three miles (five kilometers) from the beach. In addition to a limited number of transport aircraft, the invaders had seventeen obsolescent B-26 bombers for air support. The CIA chose this airplane not for its tactical abilities but because it was so common in the region that the U.S. government could more easily deny responsibility for the air attacks. CIA contract pilots, including some officers of the Alabama National Guard, trained exile aircrews at Opa Locka Airfield near Miami, bringing further publicity to the operation. Meanwhile, a platoon of the exiles trained on M-41 light tanks at Fort Knox.[29]

In January 1961, the Eisenhower administration broke diplomatic relations with Castro, dispatched thirty-eight Special Forces troops to accelerate training in Guatemala, and left its action plan for the new administration to implement. When Allen Dulles briefed Kennedy on January 28, the new president was intrigued by the mystique of CIA operations but reserved final permission to launch the invasion.

Earlier that month, the Joint Chiefs of Staff (JCS) had suggested that an interagency group was necessary to formulate a coherent plan for dealing with Cuba, but this suggestion was lost in the transition between administrations. At Kennedy's direction, the Joint Chiefs of Staff reviewed the CIA plan, which that agency had repeatedly insisted was none of the JCS' concern. In a February 3 memorandum to Defense Secretary Robert McNamara, the JCS were cautiously favorable about the Trinidad operation but noted that "It is obvious that ultimate success will depend upon political factors, i.e., a sizeable popular uprising or substantial [presumably U.S.] follow-on forces."[30] However, neither the JCS nor most officials of the new administration were willing to oppose the CIA plan despite its manifest limitations. Several historians, notably Howard Jones, have argued that Kennedy did not focus on such considerations because he was counting on a parallel operation to assassinate Castro at the time of the invasion. In any event, it was impossible to halt the invasion plan at this stage without enormous embarrassment, coupled with a partisan charge that Kennedy was "soft on communism."[31]

On March 11, Bissell urged an immediate decision on the invasion, before Czech-trained pilots could arrive to make the Cuban Air Force more effective. At the same time, however, analysts concluded that the runway at Trinidad was too short to accommodate B-26s, thereby eliminating the flimsy pretense that the air attacks would be launched from Cuban soil. President Kennedy directed that Bissell make the operation more clandestine, reducing it to some form of nighttime landing in an isolated area. Bissell interpreted this to mean that the new site must accommodate the B-26s. Working feverishly, Colonel Jack Hawkins, an experienced marine involved in planning the invasion, came up with an alternative site on the Zapata Peninsula, a swampy resort region much closer to Havana. CIA planners wrongly believed that this area would be deserted in early spring and that they could improvise an airfield when, in fact, the Cuban government had already completed one in the area. The brigade would distribute its few tanks, mortars, and other heavy weapons to control the known access roads to the airfield, from which the B-26s could operate to attack electrical power and military installations. Bissell assured Kennedy that, just as with the Trinidad plan, the invaders could retreat to the mountains in case of defeat—even though there were no mountains nearby and the invaders had no guerrilla training. The JCS considered Zapata only marginally more acceptable than the original site but did not voice criticisms of a plan that was outside their control.[32]

Thus, the invasion became an oxymoron; Kennedy wished that an operation designed to inspire a national uprising would occur clandestinely in an area with few citizens to arouse. The invaders were supposed to conduct an amphibious landing and offload supplies entirely in darkness, an unprecedented complication. Worse was to come. As part of Kennedy's desire to reduce the signature of the event, Bissell cut the initial air strike, scheduled for D-2 (April 15, 1961,) from seventeen B-26s to only nine, of which one did not attack but instead flew to Florida to announce its planned "defection" from the Cuban Air Force as a cover story for the others. Predictably, eight aircraft were inadequate to destroy the Cuban Air Force on the ground, a vital prerequisite to the landing. Instead, the D-2 attack eliminated only five Cuban aircraft at a cost of one B-26 shot down and another that crash-landed in Florida. Worse still, the initial optimistic reports of the damage inflicted by this raid prompted Kennedy to cancel four further air strikes in an effort to further conceal American involvement. Despite strong protests from Colonel Hawkins and other military experts, who threatened to resign over the matter, Secretary of State

Dean Rusk and project leader Bissell did not intervene to convince the president of the need for further air attacks. Meanwhile, a planned diversionary landing near the site of Castro's 1957 invasion aborted when it found that Raul Castro had a large military force waiting for the landing.[33]

The main invasion fleet sailed on April 16.[34] It was built around two armed Landing Craft, Infantry (LCI), but also included seven commercial freighters and a total of seven smaller landing craft, the latter transported for most of the voyage by a U.S. Navy Landing Ship, Dock. These vessels carried not only Brigade 2506 itself but also enough weapons and supplies for a force of 15,000 rebels. Most of the exile soldiers did not learn their exact destination until they were at sea, but the American advisors continued to assure them that they would have ample support. Once this small armada approached Cuba, however, the exiles were on their own. Based on Kennedy's desire to avoid American involvement, Admiral Arleigh Burke, the Chief of Naval Operations, issued very restrictive rules of engagement, requiring that the twenty-two U.S. warships in the area, including both the fleet carrier *Essex* and the marine helicopter carrier *Boxer*, remain at least thirty miles (forty-eight kilometers) from Cuba. The desire for deniability meant that the U.S. government and military did not even have direct communications with the invaders, a fatal flaw.

In the predawn hours of April 17, two CIA officers led frogmen to mark obstacles off the beaches, but the local militia encountered the teams, ending any chance of surprise. By 3:15 A.M., Castro learned of the Bay of Pigs location and ordered his air force to begin attacks at dawn while he moved 6,000 troops with tanks toward the beachhead. Cuban T-33 jet trainers and British-built Sea Fury fighter-bombers shot up the landing vessels, two of which had already run aground on uncharted reefs, so that very little of the supplies and heavy weapons were unloaded before the flotilla departed, planning to return that evening.

The fight was not entirely one-sided. The LCIs shot down at least two Castro Sea Furies, and the 339th Matanzas Battalion, the first government force to reach the scene, was reduced to rubble by the invader's M-41 tanks and 75mm recoilless rifles.[35] Without air cover, however, the operation was doomed. The invasion flotilla returned each evening to unload further but could not get enough ammunition to the troops. Both parachutists and supply drops went into the swamps instead of their intended locations.

Under the exasperated pressure of Admiral Burke, the president belatedly authorized *unmarked* F3H jet fighters to fly over the beaches on the morning of D+2, April 19. Through an error in timing, however, these fighters were not overhead when Castro's fighters intercepted two exile B-26s, this time piloted by Americans because the Cuban crews were exhausted. The Cubans shot down both invading aircraft, capturing and executing their crews. By midday on the 19th, the invasion was crushed, although American destroyers picked up twenty-six survivors over the next few days, and a few others escaped to the woods. Overall, Castro killed at least 114 invaders and captured 1,179 but paid for this with an estimated 1,650 killed and 2,000 wounded.[36]

His success in defeating the invasion gave Castro mythic stature in the Third World. There was more than enough blame to distribute within the U.S. government, but inevitably the CIA and JCS blamed the president and vice versa. Kennedy publicly accepted responsibility for a failure that he shared with the previous administration, but privately the president and his brother Robert savagely criticized both the CIA and the JCS, leading to further misunderstandings in future crises. The Kennedy's favorite intellectual general, Maxwell Taylor, returned from retirement first to investigate the fiasco and then to serve as the president's military representative, effectively cutting the JCS out of any contact with the White House. Meanwhile, the Kennedy administration redoubled its efforts to overthrow the Cuban regime. The new program, code-named Mongoose, was to be a full-court effort by the government, coordinated by the legendary Edward Lansdale.[37] Both Castro and Khrushchev were therefore fully justified in their belief that the United States would try again.

Berlin Again

In the interim, however, Khrushchev perceived Kennedy's performance in the Bay of Pigs as an indication of weakness, a weakness that the general secretary sought to exploit in Berlin.

East Germany was both a major economic powerhouse and a major vulnerability for the Soviet bloc. Between 1945 and 1961, approximately 3.5 million of the eighteen million residents of the east emigrated legally or illegally, most of them to the Federal Republic. Even those who remained in the east used the possibility of emigration to pressure the government for better labor and housing conditions. This growing exodus undermined the political and economic credibility of the German Democratic Republic (GDR), and Khrushchev was under great pressure to help the GDR stop the hemorrhage.[38]

The focus of this issue was, as always, Berlin. In May 1952, the Soviets had closed the interzonal border and relocated most residents to create a five-kilometer no-man's-land along that border, but some seventy-seven access routes remained between East and West Berlin. Although the USSR had supposedly transferred sovereignty to the GDR in September 1955, an exchange of diplomatic notes had promised that "temporarily, . . . pending the conclusion of an appropriate agreement," Soviet troops would guarantee traffic between the West and the three western sectors of the city.[39] In 1958–1959, however, Khrushchev attempted to force the Western allies out of Berlin by issuing an ultimatum to turn control over to the GDR.

On November 12, 1958, Soviet troops tried to inspect three U.S. Army trucks that were departing West Berlin to transit to the West. An eight-hour standoff ensued before a tank platoon from the U.S. Berlin garrison appeared and the Soviets backed down. Such incidents puzzled Western leaders, who did not realize that Mikoyan and other members of the Soviet Presidium disagreed strongly with Khrushchev's hard-line position, resulting in a vacillating, weak Soviet policy. Just as Eisenhower had not understood Khrushchev's outrage about the U-2 overflights, Khrushchev and his colleagues did not comprehend the West's emotional commitment to a free Berlin, so no real compromise was possible.[40]

At the Vienna Summit conference of June 1961, Khrushchev renewed his demands to Kennedy. Finally, on Sunday, August 13, East German military engineers with Soviet support began Operation Rose, building the infamous wall that isolated the two halves of the city and choked off most immigration. Although the entire Group of Soviet Forces went on alert and rolled out of its motor pools, the actual operation was undertaken by East German police, backed by a regiment of the GDR's 1st Motorized Rifle Division. The East Germans did resort to water cannon at the Brandenburg Gate and tear gas elsewhere to disperse West Berliners who attacked the east in protest. Yet, the only Soviet interference was to force the East Germans to cancel a one-hundred-meter no-man's-land that they attempted to impose on both sides of the wall. Undertaken in great secrecy, the wall surprised the West. Khrushchev remained cautious, however, and the

East German government described the wall as a state frontier, thereby abandoning its legal claim to West Berlin. Three days before construction, retired Marshal Konev had assured the American Military Liaison Mission in East Germany that nothing would affect Western rights in their sector of the city.[41]

Even before this crisis, the Kennedy administration had been reorganizing the Defense Department and seeking to expand its conventional forces as part of the doctrine of Flexible Response, giving itself more options below the nuclear threshold. Defense Secretary Robert McNamara attempted to reduce service duplication by creating the Defense Intelligence and Defense Supply [later Defense Logistics] Agencies. In the spring of 1961, the administration sought to modify the Eisenhower budget for the next fiscal year to increase spending for Polaris missiles, civil defense shelters, and army and marine corps equipment. In addition, however, McNamara at Kennedy's behest tried to increase reserve readiness, so that two National Guard divisions and eighteen separate battalions would be available to deploy within two weeks, rather than months, of mobilization. Congress increased the defense budget from $41.8 billion to $46.6 billion but included more manned bombers than the administration wanted.[42]

The Vienna Summit brought the question of conventional forces to the forefront. The JCS recommended mobilizing 559,000 reserve component troops and spending an additional $30.9 billion over the next two years to improve general readiness. Kennedy was not prepared for such a massive effort, and both JCS Chairman Lemnitzer and SACEUR Norstad advised that even this large force would not permit the defense of Western Europe without using nuclear weapons. Instead, the president sought a modest increase to send a message to the Soviets, something Eisenhower had avoided because he had no intention of risking war over Berlin. In addition to increasing conscription, in September 1961, Kennedy authorized the one-year mobilization of two National Guard divisions (32nd Infantry and 49th Armored) with supporting forces, for a total of 75,000 men. Even this was meant to be a temporary measure while the army trained more conscripts to eventually replace these reserve component units during 1962. Moreover, this mobilization carried with it a political cost and inhibited Kennedy from further such actions later in his term. While the army guard units reported for duty, eleven air guard fighter squadrons deployed to Europe, along with the 3rd Armored Cavalry Regiment and two battle groups of the 4th Infantry Division. The army also began the long-term process of prepositioning equipment in Europe so that two divisions could move their personnel by air from the United States. Even this modest, measured reinforcement of NATO achieved its purpose by surprising Khrushchev, who had somehow expected to overawe the Americans.[43]

Although the United States had accepted the wall, it chose to dispute GDR attempts to limit movement of American officials between the two halves of the city, rejecting Khrushchev's threats to turn the city over to the GDR. On October 22, 1961, East German police (Volkspolizei or Vopos) stopped a car carrying E. Allen Lightner, the State Department representative in Berlin, on his way to see a theater performance in East Berlin. U.S. policy was that official vehicles had a right to unfettered access, so Lightner refused to show his diplomatic passport to representatives of a government the United States did not recognize. When the Vopos would not call a Soviet officer or permit him to pass, the diplomat withdrew to the western sector. Three days later, however, a squad of military policemen escorted an American official past the Vopos to enforce his right to cross.[44]

Retired General Lucius Clay, who had great influence with both the West Germans and President Kennedy because of his role in previous confrontations, prodded the American garrison (redesignated the Berlin Brigade in the midst of this crisis) to escalate matters. Clay apparently sought to force the Soviets to acknowledge that they were East Germany's controllers. On October 27, six U.S. M-48 tanks parked a few meters from the border at the critical crossing point, Checkpoint Charlie. Ten unmarked T-54/T-55 tanks appeared on the opposite side, and an American reporter who interviewed the crews established that they spoke Russian rather than German. Eventually, the entire tank company of the Berlin Brigade faced an equal number of Soviet tanks in the most direct confrontation since the dogfights of the Korean War. In this as in other instances, however, Khrushchev displayed a realism that was at odds with his blustering public persona— he quietly ordered the withdrawal of the Soviet tanks on the 28th, defusing this particular issue but not the overall crisis. The U.S. tanks withdrew twenty minutes after the Soviet ones.[45]

Shortly thereafter, the Soviets resumed harassment of Allied aircraft in the air corridors over East Germany. The Soviets tried to reserve certain altitudes for themselves, which the Allies studiously ignored.

MiG fighters buzzed civilian aircraft and dropped metal chaff to jam radars. Gradually during 1962, the petty harassment declined; while it lasted, it may have been intended in part to distract Allied attention from Soviet actions in Cuba (see chapter 15).[46]

Khrushchev's diplomatic failure may also have encouraged contemplation of forcible solutions. In March 1961, Khrushchev had committed the Warsaw Pact to modernize the satellite armies, although the expense delayed this process for years. Meanwhile, Soviet theorists had been studying the use of nuclear weapons on the battlefield, and the crisis seemed an opportune time to exercise this application. Command Post Exercise Buria (September 28–October 10, 1961) postulated that a Western attempt to reopen land access to Berlin would lead to nuclear war in twenty-four hours. In the exercise, the Warsaw Pact theoretically employed almost a thousand atomic weapons, assuming that it had destroyed 75 percent of NATO's own nuclear weapons and 60 percent of conventional troop units. One purpose of Buria may have been to convey Soviet seriousness to watching Western intelligence services, but thereafter Soviet planners assumed that almost any conflict would involve a large-scale use of nuclear fires.[47]

LAOS

When the 1954 Geneva Accords divided French Indochina into four states, the kingdom of Laos was left in an unenviable situation.[48] Although the country was supposedly neutral, Pathet Lao Communists controlled the two northernmost provinces, which they quickly turned into a pro-Vietnamese enclave. A small French advisory mission also remained in the country, but its resources were insufficient to support the Lao Armed Forces (Forces Armées du Laos, or FAL), let alone remnants of the wartime Mixed Airborne Commandos. Beginning in late 1955, therefore, the United States operated a Programs Evaluation Office (PEO) in the embassy in Vientiane. This office funneled U.S. money, weapons, and advisors into the country using the CIA-backed airline Civil Air Transport and its successor, Air America. C-46 and C-47 transports together with small L-19s and L-20s provided tenuous supply lines and, on occasion, transport for the two Laotian airborne battalions—the most potent force to counter the Pathet Lao. These battalions were often key tools in factional struggles within the Laotian government.

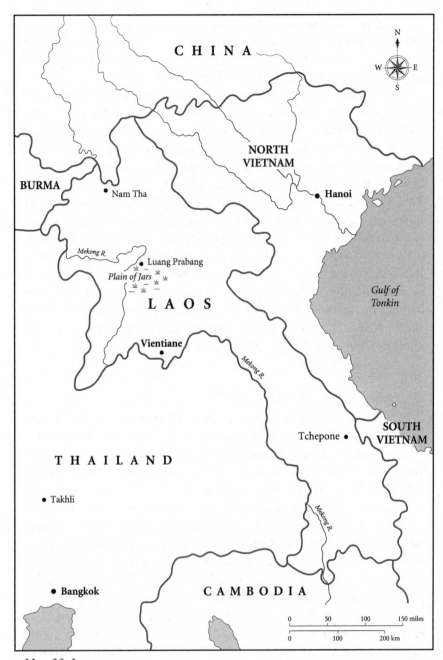

MAP 23. LAOS

Because Laos was officially neutral, the PEO was staffed with "civilians" who were often reserve or retired officers, such as Brigadier General John A. Heintges, who headed PEO in 1958–1959. In the fall of 1959, Heintges arranged for 107 instructors from the 77th Special Forces Group (Airborne) to provide weapons training for the FAL. Conveniently, these instructors became temporary civilians, disappearing from U.S. Army rolls for the duration of each six-month deployment. The Joint Chiefs objected that it was difficult to conceal the instructors and that their "civilian" status reduced their effectiveness in the eyes of their students. Moreover, the leadership and staff work of the FAL was persistently poor, making it difficult for Vientiane to coordinate its defenses. Still, the combination of French and American instructors gave the FAL some minimum military capacity, and U.S. funds allowed its expansion to 29,000 full-time troops as well as self-defense militia.[49]

In August–September 1959, however, Laos came to a crisis. North Vietnam apparently sought to reassert its influence and force the reintroduction of the international control commission required by the Geneva Accords, thereby hampering U.S. military aid. To this end, Hanoi provided additional arms and advisors, and concentrated a division on the border. With this support, the Pathet Lao made such progress against the royal forces that the Eisenhower administration seriously contemplated overt intervention. Joint Task Force 116 would be built around a marine regiment and a composite air group, with support from three carrier battle groups in the South China Sea. The marines would deploy by air from Japan to secure airheads at Vientiane and Seno, providing backup for the hard-pressed FAL. The plan was hampered not only by the practical difficulties of projecting forces into a landlocked country but also by a confused political situation in which only Thailand agreed with the U.S. view—the French and other members of SEATO thought the United States was overreacting. Nonetheless, Eisenhower authorized preparations for the deployment, including loading ships, concentrating carriers, and assembling aircraft in Japan. Fortunately for the peace, a temporary halt in the Pathet Lao advance permitted the United States to shelve this plan, but Washington remained sensitive to Laos as the weakest link in its containment strategy.[50]

The Eisenhower administration passed the Laotian hot potato to the Kennedy administration along with the Bay of Pigs plan. Khrushchev had originally resisted Chinese and Vietnamese efforts to widen the war but eventually turned to Laos as another way to pressure the United States about Berlin.[51] In January 1961, eighteen Soviet transport aircraft shuttled munitions from Hanoi to Pathet Lao–held areas on the Plain of Jars; Vietnamese advisors soon achieved a considerable improvement in the combat performance of the Pathet Lao. The Joint Chiefs again recommended an overt military assistance advisory group on the Greek pattern to help the Laotian forces. The recurring instability within the Vientiane government meant that neither Britain nor France would support SEATO operations in the crisis, and Moscow could plausibly argue that it was supporting a legitimate regime. Both American administrations sought to avoid military involvement, and the incoming secretary of state, Dean Rusk, expressed concern that Korea might flair up as a diversion. Nonetheless, Eisenhower and Kennedy were agreed that the United States must take action to encourage anticommunist groups in the region.[52]

In April 1961, eighteen B-26s, manned by a mixture of USAF and Air America pilots, assembled at Takhli Air Base, in central Thailand, to strike airfields and Pathet Lao forces inside Laos (Operation Mill Pond). Six USAF F-100s also deployed from the Philippines to Thailand to cover the B-26s if necessary, beginning a USAF presence in Thailand that continued for more than a decade. At the last minute, the White House, alarmed by the Bay of Pigs failure, cancelled the attack. Instead, on April 19, 1961, Kennedy accepted the advice of a recent visitor to the scene, Lieutenant General Thomas J. Trapnell, to convert the PEO into an acknowledged military advisory group and fund seven additional Laotian battalions. Meanwhile, groups of Thai police commandos with their CIA advisors, eventually joined by Special Forces A-teams known as White Star, had considerable success in organizing guerrillas among the Hmong or Meo mountain tribesmen of northeastern Laos.[53]

The JCS was understandably reluctant to either send more military aid or commit large U.S. forces to Laos, fearing that either course of action would limit U.S. ability to respond elsewhere. At the same time, Laos had to compete, unsuccessfully, with Cuba and Berlin for presidential attention. In a May 2, 1961, memorandum to the president, Secretary McNamara, with the support of JCS Chairman General Lyman Lemnitzer, laid out options for Laos, urging Kennedy to consider such unpalatable choices as permitting Laos to fall or using nuclear weapons in the event of a major Chinese and North Vietnamese attack. Great Power negotiations in Geneva failed when the Pathet Lao violated a cease-fire, but in June 1961 three Laotian princes began to form a neutralist coalition government. Distracted by the famine resulting from the Great Leap Forward program, Beijing was unwilling to press a confrontation with the United States.[54]

Over the course of the next year, the United States continued to increase Thai and American advisors in Laos, as well as funding and aerial reconnaissance. The Laotian army, redesignated as the Forces Armées Royales, rotated eight battalions through a retraining camp in Thailand. However, the Laotian commanders remained too dependent on indirect fire support and resisted American tactical advice that smacked, to them, of a return to their colonial status. At the same time, the CIA with Thai assistance encouraged the Meo tribesmen of the mountain regions of Laos to engage in a guerrilla war against the Pathet Lao. For the Meo, the Pathet Lao were not only ethnically different but also very repressive and demanding, so the insurgents willingly risked their lives and families to free themselves.[55]

Seeking to end the continuing ulcer, in September 1961 the JCS proposed a conventional land campaign to restore royal rule throughout Laos, using four U.S. and eleven other SEATO divisions, a total of 278,000 men, operating from Thailand. Such a proposal was obviously unrealistic in the context of other world issues, but it probably contributed to the Kennedy administration's willingness to settle for a neutralized Laos. In May 1962, the U.S.-backed forces of General Phoumi Nosavan provoked and lost a struggle for the village of Nam Tha near the Chinese border, creating a crisis in which the United States deployed 5,000 troops to Thailand, and Kennedy briefly considered military intervention to control the Mekong River Valley. Unfortunately, the air, rail, and road facilities into Laos would not support the 40,000 total troops required for such an operation. Instead, in July, the Great Powers agreed to a renewed neutralization of Laos. As expected, North Vietnam kept most of its troops in the country in violation of the agreement, although the United States honored its commitment, reducing the MAAG to a much smaller advisory operation in the defense attaché's office in Vientiane. CIA-controlled advisors and assistance also continued but without public acknowledgement.

For the next eight years, Laos remained de facto a divided land while Hanoi continued to use the country to funnel troops and supplies into South Vietnam.[56]

The United States seemed less sensitive about the neighboring neutral state of Cambodia, even though it, too, had to tolerate the growing use of its territory as part of the Ho Chi Minh Trail. In 1958, for example, Diem's Republic of [South] Vietnam seized a small, disputed portion of Cambodian territory, but the United States refused to intervene. In response, Cambodian King Norodom Sihanouk recognized the Beijing government of China and threatened to ask for Chinese military aid unless he got continuing French and American assistance. As chairman of the JCS, General Twining tried to limit Sihanouk's personal power by improving professional contacts with the Cambodian military, a policy that may have contributed to an abortive 1959 military coup against the king. Sihanouk continued his uneasy neutrality until overthrown in 1970 by a U.S.-backed revolt.[57]

Individually, the U-2 loss, the Bay of Pigs, the renewed Berlin Wall crisis, and the ongoing civil war in Laos were significant issues, but none reached the level of a casus belli. Collectively, however, these confrontations created an atmosphere of growing pressure that increased frustrations in Moscow and Washington while encouraging dissention among their regional allies. The military forces on both sides ratcheted up their capabilities, especially in strategic nuclear weapons. The Cold War again appeared to be a global, zero-sum competition in which neither side could afford to show weakness—the same type of atmosphere that had ignited World War I. The Cuban Missile Crisis and the second war in Indochina can be understood only in the context of this oppressive sense of confrontation and crisis.

15

THE CUBAN MISSILE CRISIS

S ince October 1, 1962, the U.S. Defense Department had been secretly preparing for possible war over Soviet nuclear delivery systems in Cuba. The secrecy ended on the evening of October 22, when President Kennedy gave a television broadcast in which he announced the presence of those weapons and instituted a "quarantine" of the island.

That afternoon, several hours prior to the broadcast, Kennedy had ordered that the armed forces increase their alert status to Defense Condition (DEFCON) 3, code-named "Round House."[1] General Powers, the head of Strategic Air Command (SAC), had begun dispersing some of his aircraft to preselected civilian and non-SAC military airfields several days ahead of time, so he formally initiated Round House only as the president began his speech. SAC Headquarters at Offutt Air Force Base sent out the alert order "in the clear"—that is, without encryption—so that any party (including the Soviet Union) monitoring that frequency could understand its meaning. For the newly activated 341st Strategic Missile Wing around Malmstrom Air Force Base in Montana, the first Minuteman I ICBMs needed no further preparation; elsewhere, SAC continued its dispersal of bombers and tankers. Meanwhile, General Norstad, as commander of U.S. European Command, had tactical nuclear weapons uploaded on F-100 fighter bombers.

Castro, who had anticipated a crisis for some days, declared general mobilization while Kennedy was still speaking. Khrushchev consulted with his chiefs of staff and ordered his nuclear forces moved to "increased" readiness. For the Strategic Rocket Forces, this meant marrying the warheads to their missile boosters but not actually placing liquid fuel in those boosters; even after the warheads were in place, fueling would require a further two to four hours before launching. The Soviet Air Force as a whole "stood down" from normal operations so that its aircraft could prepare for a surge of flying if ordered to war.[2] In Cuba, the United States, and the Soviet Union, millions of people expected thermonuclear conflict.

Two days later, early on the morning of the 24th, SAC moved to DEFCON 2 ("Fast Pace"). At any given time, one-eighth of the B-52s (fifty-six aircraft) and tankers (sixty-one) were now airborne, the former carrying nuclear weapons. Six hundred seventy-two other B-52 and B-47 bombers, 381 tankers, and 90 Atlas and 46 Titan ICBMs were on heightened ground alert. SAC remained at this hair-trigger level for the next four weeks.[3] Although far less dramatic, the other armed forces were equally poised for war, loading out equipment onto ships and prepositioning troop transport aircraft and fighter bombers to invade Cuba.

THE CARIBBEAN CRISIS

Traditionally, Americans have thought of the Bay of Pigs and the Cuban Missile Crisis as two separate incidents, but Soviet historiography is probably more accurate when it describes the entire period as a unified "Caribbean Crisis" over the future of the island. For the Kennedy administration, the Castro regime was an outpost of the Soviet Union, a threat to national security that spewed anti-American rhetoric while encouraging insurrection throughout the Third World.[4]

As spring turned into summer in 1962, U.S. activity concerning Castro increased in a number of ways. As the Department of Defense action officer for Operation Mongoose, General Lansdale worked tirelessly through youth, labor, and religious groups within Cuba to create an active opposition to the dictator. Yet, Castro's control was so effective that the organized opposition developed more slowly than Washington had hoped. Simultaneously, the CIA's Task Force W, named for its chief, William K. Harvey, continued to plan assassinations.[5] On July 25,

1962, Lansdale tried to get a decision on future policy by laying out four possible options for Mongoose, ranging from simply isolating Cuba (Option A) to U.S. military intervention (Option D). Still, although the administration continued to press for a change in regime, after the Bay of Pigs fiasco President Kennedy shied away from overt intervention, at least in the short run. Some analysts have suggested that he would have been satisfied if the threat of Mongoose intimidated Castro from further adventures supporting Latin American rebels. In either case, Kennedy's National Security Action Memorandum (NSAM) 181, dated August 23, 1962, directed "Plan B plus" for Mongoose, meaning that the United States would use nonmilitary means to formulate an anti-Castro revolt that might ultimately lead to U.S. intervention.[6]

The United States also conducted a series of amphibious landings and readiness exercises; Lantphibex 1-62, for example, culminated in late April with a full marine assault on the island of Vieques, off Puerto Rico. On one level, these exercises represented the implementation of the administration's pledge to develop a broad spectrum of military capabilities known as Flexible Response. Indeed, one of these major joint exercises—Three Pairs—was scheduled to occur around Fort Hood, Texas, between October 18 and 28, indicating that the United States did not contemplate an immediate invasion. However, Lantphibex 1-62 was at least partially intended as a dress rehearsal for possible Cuban action, further stoking the sense of crisis in Washington, Moscow, and Havana.[7]

CODEWORD SCABBARDS

Meanwhile, the Defense Department continued its planning for such an operation. Contingency plans by themselves do not represent a policy decision but rather a prudent military preparation to anticipate future possibilities. Nonetheless, the family of military options with regard to Cuba was the highest priority within the staffs involved, strongly suggesting impending action.

To understand this planning process, one must first review the Byzantine command structure that existed in 1962. The 1958 amendment to the National Security Act made the unified and specified commanders-in-chief, the "CINCs," responsible for various portions of the world or special capabilities such as SAC, into the direct subordinates of the president and the secretary of defense. In practice, however, civilian officials still passed decisions through the Joint Chiefs of Staff for implementation.

In October 1961, the Defense Department had created a new unified headquarters, U.S. Strike Command (STRICOM), at MacDill Air Force Base in Tampa, Florida. The very name STRICOM reflected the Kennedy administration's commitment to Flexible Response and activism in foreign affairs; this headquarters was to be the single provider of all nonnuclear forces required by regional CINCs in a crisis. In turn, STRICOM had two subordinate component headquarters to prepare and provide such forces—U.S. Continental Army Command (CONARC) for ground combat troops and the Air Force Tactical Air Command (TAC) for fighter, reconnaissance, and some airlift units. Both CONARC and TAC also had administrative, training, and doctrinal responsibilities within their respective services, responsibilities that fell outside STRICOM's authority. Technically, therefore, when conducting joint planning and operations for STRICOM, these two headquarters were the army and air force components of that command, or ARSTRIKE and AFSTRIKE, respectively. In turn, CONARC had six subordinate army headquarters, each responsible for schools, troop units, and installations in an area of the country. The Third U.S. Army, headquartered at Fort McPherson, Georgia, was critical to the Cuban situation because it was responsible for the southeastern United States, including XVIII Airborne Corps at Fort Bragg, North Carolina, and various support bases in Georgia and Florida.

However, the unified command responsible for receiving forces from STRICOM and then *executing* actions in the Caribbean was the U.S. Atlantic Command (LANTCOM) at Norfolk, Virginia. In peacetime, LANTCOM had virtually no units from the other services; unlike overseas commands, it had no component headquarters for army and air elements. Thus, in the event of wartime operations in the LANTCOM area, CONARC and TAC would also become the army and air force elements of Atlantic Command, or ARLANT and AFLANT, respectively. General Herbert B. Powell, commanding general of CONARC, wore additional "hats" as Commander-in-Chief, ARSTRIKE and ARLANT (CINCARSTRIKE and CINCARLANT); depending on what functions he was performing at the moment, he had to report to three different headquarters. (See Chain of Command, Operation Scabbards, below.)

In addition to this structural confusion, the first CINCSTRIKE was, appropriately enough, General Paul Adams, the successful joint commander during the 1958 Lebanon intervention. Adams was a relatively junior officer, and his sudden promotion understandably irritated General Powell and other more senior flag officers.

Another personality issue was the lingering suspicion that President Kennedy and his close advisors felt with regard to the JCS, based on a perceived failure during the Bay of Pigs crisis. Only the soldier-intellectual General Maxwell D. Taylor had real access to Kennedy, first as military assistant to the president and then, in September 1962, as chairman of the JCS. On May 27, 1961, the president did sit down with the Joint Chiefs to explain his view of their relationship, asking them to consider political, economic, and psychological, as well as military, aspects of any situation while giving him "direct and unfettered" advice. Perhaps, however, this discussion simply increased Kennedy's frustration when the Joint Chiefs subsequently gave him advice that he found unpalatable. In particular, the abrasive and profane air force chief of staff, Curtis LeMay, irritated Kennedy to the point that he avoided contact with the general. This isolation contributed to disconnects between the White House and the armed services during the crisis. General Taylor and Secretary McNamara did not always understand the naval and nuclear weapons implications of their decisions.[8]

In February 1962, the Joint Chiefs instructed the Commander-in-Chief, Atlantic (CINCLANT), Admiral Robert L. Dennison, to make revision of the existing Cuban contingency plans his highest priority, with a goal of reducing the preparation time to execute such plans.[9] LANTCOM went through twenty revisions and four major changes to the Cuban invasion plans in the year before the missile crisis; such frequent changes increased the probability that subordinate headquarters would be working on the wrong guidance or version of a plan when a new one was approved.

The group of operations plans (OPLANs) for Cuba, a group collectively referred to as Scabbards, included three plans; in each instance, the suffix "-62" indicated the fiscal year in which the plan took effect. OPLAN 312-62 included a variety of options for air strikes against Cuba, ranging from destroying air defense sites to a full campaign to achieve air supremacy. OPLAN 314-62 called for a deliberate invasion of Cuba. The II Marine Amphibious Force, consisting of a marine

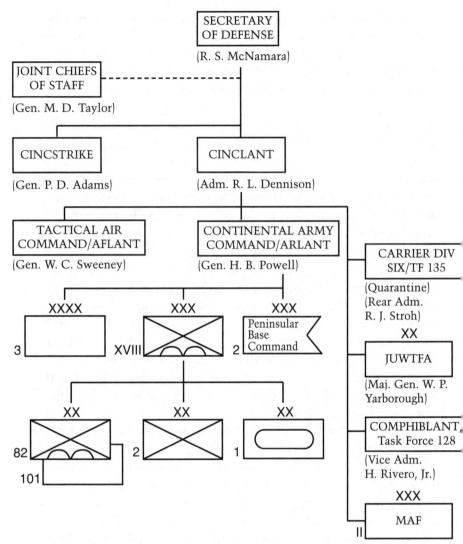

FIGURE 2. Operation Scabbards chain of command, 1962.

division and its supporting elements plus one or more regiments transferred from the Pacific, would land near the existing base at Guantanamo Bay, while XVIII Airborne Corps would parachute the 82nd and 101st Airborne Divisions onto four airfields around Havana. Airborne engineers would repair runway damage to permit the arrival of further troops and supplies; thereafter, the two airborne divisions would secure the port of Mariel, on the northern coast, through which an armored brigade (Task Force Charlie) would land to provide heavy weapons against the Cuban armed forces. The remainder of that armored division, plus most of 2nd Infantry Division from Fort Benning, would put to sea as a floating reserve. Once the marine and army lodgment areas were secure, Lieutenant General Hamilton Howze, commander of XVIII Airborne Corps, would become commander, Joint Task Force (JTF) Cuba, for the balance of the campaign. The Joint Unconventional Warfare Task Force, Atlantic (JUWTFA), headquartered at Opa Locka Airfield in Florida, would deploy Special Forces teams and Cuban exile elements to support a native uprising against Castro. Even this was an improvisation, however, since the headquarters of the Army Special Warfare Center at Fort Bragg was "dual-hatted" as the JUWTFA.

OPLAN 316-62 was intended for execution on much shorter notice—initially, 314 called for eighteen days to mount, while 316 was to commence within five days of warning. Under such circumstances, the 316 plan depended almost entirely on airborne assault, since a marine landing would require too long to prepare. As CINCLANT, Admiral Denison stressed the development of OPLAN 314, believing that two airborne divisions would be insufficient to defeat the Soviet-armed Cuban Army. Generals Adams, Powell, and Howze objected that the delay required to assemble an amphibious fleet would sacrifice surprise and expose the army and marine troops to possible Soviet nuclear attack in their assembly areas. After months of discussion, on October 17, 1962, the JCS directed a compromise whereby OPLAN 316 would involve a simultaneous air and amphibious assault on seven days' warning. Considering that such a warning had already been issued, the argument had become moot.[10]

Codeword Anadyr

Nikita Khrushchev faced two problems in 1962: defending Cuba from forthcoming U.S. attack, and finding an effective nuclear deterrent that could reach the United States. As described in chapter 13, Khrushchev had reduced the conventional Soviet armed forces on the argument that the newly created Strategic Rocket Forces could provide sufficient security against Western aggression. Unfortunately, the Soviet deterrent was woefully inadequate for the job. The marginally effective Tu-95 bombers and a handful of unreliable liquid-fueled boosters could reach the United States, but disasters such as the Tyuratam explosion

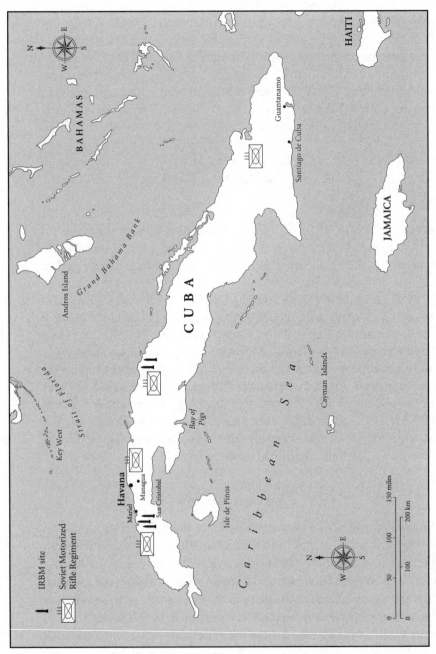

MAP 24. Cuba, 1962

and the K-19 submarine failure had placed the rest of the Soviet missile program far behind schedule. In February, Khrushchev learned that the troubled R-16 ICBM program was still no match for the American Minuteman missiles.[11]

Khrushchev's solution to both problems came to him in May 1962, while he was visiting a Black Sea resort in Bulgaria: deploy shorter-ranged, more reliable missiles to Cuba, thereby assuring both Cuban and Soviet security. Havana eagerly agreed to the plan, which eventually assumed the code name Anadyr, the name of a Siberian town chosen because it was completely unrelated to deploying Soviet forces to the tropics. To promote this deceptive name, some of the units involved received skis and winter equipment! As finally constituted, Operation Anadyr created a Group of Soviet Forces, Cuba (GSFC,) with at least 42,000 troops, extensive R-75 (SA-2) air defense batteries, fifty-six IL-28 light bombers (of which six had racks to carry nuclear weapons), twenty-four R-12 and sixteen R-14 missile launchers, sixty ballistic missile boosters, and 158 warheads and nuclear bombs. The R-12 (NATO designation SS-4 "Sandal") missile had a range of 2,000 kilometers, sufficient to reach most of the eastern United States, including SAC headquarters in Omaha as well as New York and Washington, from northwestern Cuba. The R-14 (SS-5 "Skean") could reach most of North America with its maximum range of 4,500 kilometers; fortu-nately or unfortunately, the Soviets had experienced developmental problems even with this missile and were unable to produce enough of them in time for deployment. When Kennedy made the crisis public, the R-14 launchers were in Cuba, but the missiles themselves were still en route.[12]

The GSFC staff came from the 44th Missile Army headquarters, but its commander was an unlikely choice. The General Staff had pro-posed the name of Lieutenant General Pavel B. Dankevich, a missile expert and commander of the 44th, but Khrushchev instead chose Army General Issa Alexandrovich Pliyev. Born in 1903, Pliyev was an "old war horse," having served forty years in the Soviet cavalry by the time he went to Cuba. Fighting against both the Germans and the Japanese, he had commanded cavalry-mechanized groups, a unique Soviet combination of horses and armor designed to operate over very difficult terrain that was impassible to more conventional forces. Pliyev had no technical background for something as complex as nuclear missiles. Dankevich became his deputy, but the missile general found the old cavalryman so irritating that he played tennis daily rather than focusing on the missile installations. Pliyev also had difficulty dealing with the Castro brothers.[13] Still, his wartime commands had given him experience in independent actions behind enemy lines, which may have been his best recommendation to Khrushchev and other leaders of the same generation. Pliyev established his headquarters in Managua, south of Havana.

In addition to the ballistic missiles, Pliyev controlled the 12th Air Defense Division in western Cuba, the 27th Air Defense Division in eastern Cuba, a crack regiment of MiG-21 interceptors, and four motorized rifle regiments (MRRs). Drawn from the Leningrad Military District, these regiments were ordinary units of conscripts and professional officers. Each consisted of about 2,500 men in three small mechanized infantry battalions, one battalion of thirty-one T-34 or T-55 tanks, ten 100mm self-propelled assault guns, and a battery of six 122mm howitzers. The four regiments were neither organized under a higher tactical headquarters nor integrated with the Cuban Army; in effect, they were four scattered units, with the 106th MRR located at Holguin, north of the U.S. base at Guantanamo in eastern Cuba.[14]

Finally, the Soviet force included FKR-1 (Frontoviye Krilatiye raketi, known to NATO as SS-2A) coastal anti-ship missiles as well as "Luna" Free Rocket Over Ground (FROG, probably the FROG-5) tactical weapons, both intended to defend the island against invasion rather than to attack the United States. Long after the crisis was over, the Soviet staff officer who planned the deployment, Anatoli Ivanovich Gribkov, created consternation by announcing that Pliyev had authority to launch these short-range tactical nuclear missiles without permission from Moscow. Doctrinally, that assertion may have been true for the Soviet Army as a whole, and Gribkov was probably correct about the initial orders. However, as soon as the crisis broke, Moscow realized the risks involved; Defense Minister Malinovsky explicitly denied Pliyev such authority on October 22 and again on the 27th, ordering the GSFC to repel American landings without using nuclear weapons. In practice, the warheads were stored up to three hundred kilometers away from their launchers.[15]

Working with its customarily tight security, the Soviet General Staff had to deal with an unprecedented problem of strategic force projection and logistics. Most of the troops were crowded inside ordinary cargo ships and suffered considerable hardships, including illnesses

and at least one death, on the long voyage. Whenever American surveillance aircraft or other prying eyes appeared, the soldiers had to
remain below decks, suffering in the heat of summer. Many of the
ships carried anti-aircraft guns covered by wooden false decks, and
Khrushchev ordered the ships to return fire if attacked. Upon arrival
in Cuba, the men, most of them clothed in poorly made civilian clothing
in a vain effort to hide their nationality, worked frantically to establish their various operating positions. Soviet staff officers naturally
chose wooded areas as the sites for the air defense and ballistic missile
batteries, but these palm trees provided little concealment from overhead observation and many difficulties for installation. The porous tree
trunks increased the relative humidity to unbearable levels, and the
rocky ground resisted efforts to dig firing positions and trenches.
Although the Cuban Army provided security for these sites, the Soviets
did not permit the Cubans to assist in construction. In short, the Soviet
troops lived a miserable existence and soon fell behind schedule in
making their missiles operational.[16]

DISCOVERY

Khrushchev apparently intended to announce both his defensive treaty
with Castro and his nuclear missiles in November, once the latter were
fully in place. He seems to have believed that the United States would
accept such a *fait accompli*. In this respect, however, he was as blind
about American attitudes as Kennedy was about Soviet and Cuban
perceptions. Quite apart from the political challenge posed by the
Soviet ballistic missiles, their presence in Cuba, left unchecked, would
have been profoundly destabilizing. After the so-called Bomber and
Missile Gaps, the Kennedy administration had realized that it actually
had a significant advantage in both categories. Given the short flight
time of missiles launched from Cuba, however, that advantage would
have disappeared. Indeed, had the missiles remained in Cuba, in some
future crisis the United States might well have been forced to "launch
on warning," initiating a full nuclear strike in the few minutes before
the SS-4s and SS-5s could reach American bomber and missile bases.
Thus, the Cuban missiles would have eliminated any time for delibera-
tion in a future confrontation, although few contemporaries realized
this at the time.

Throughout the summer of 1962, hundreds of unconfirmed agent
reports indicated that the Soviets had begun a massive military buildup

in Cuba, possibly including offensive nuclear missiles. In response, the CIA increased the number of U-2 surveillance flights, but the approaching hurricane season often interfered with these operations. Although Director of Central Intelligence John A. McCone raised the possibility of offensive missiles, for months there was no confirmation of the agent reports. In their absence, the U.S. government tended to assume that Soviet interest in Cuba was primarily for propaganda rather than offensive purposes. A National Intelligence Estimate of September 19, 1962, correctly identified most of the Soviet buildup, including 40,000 troops, Komar guided missile boats, MiG-21 fighters, and twelve batteries of SA-2 air defense missiles. However, the tenor of the entire report focused on the defense of Cuba rather than any threat to the United States. The report projected that the Soviets "would almost certainly estimate" a strong U.S. reaction to the presence of offensive missiles. It came closest to the truth when it projected the likely deployment of IL-28s, saying that once such bombers were identified, the United States would have to decide whether or not to consider them an offensive threat.[17]

Nonetheless, CIA and especially DIA analysts were concerned by the Soviet buildup and increased both reconnaissance flights and signals intelligence; for the latter, the USS *Oxford*, a World War II–era Liberty ship converted for intelligence collection, began to monitor communications in the area. In August, intelligence analysts briefed the JCS on the evidence of possible offensive missile deployment to Cuba, but General Taylor remained skeptical. Meanwhile, the high tempo of exercises continued, and a detachment of navy F8U Corsair fighters moved to Key West to bolster air defense against possible Soviet bombers.[18]

Traditional accounts of the Cuban Missile Crisis date events from an October 14 U-2 flight that imaged completed IRBMs, but common sense suggests that the U.S. military could not have achieved its massive war preparations in only eight days (October 14 to 22). In fact, the situation came to a boil at least two weeks earlier. On September 29–30, naval surveillance of Soviet freighters suggested that IL-28s were being shipped to Cuba, while a U-2 mission over western Cuba noted the presence of eight SA-2 firing batteries. On October 1, 1962, McNamara and the Joint Chiefs heard this information as part of their weekly meeting. At the same time, a photographic interpreter argued, correctly, that an offensive missile site was nearing completion in the San Cristobal area of western Cuba even though no launchers were yet visible. McNamara ordered the Joint Chiefs to intensify preparations for a variety of contingencies, ranging from blockade to air strikes to invasion. He followed this up the next day with a detailed memorandum, listing six contingencies "under which military action against Cuba may be necessary." There was strong evidence that two of these possibilities had already come to pass—"the positioning of [Soviet] bloc offensive weapons systems on Cuban soil" and "Cuban armed assistance to subversion in other parts of the western hemisphere." In short, without ordering any immediate actions, the defense secretary told the Joint Chiefs to prepare for war.[19] This sequence of events explains why the military was planning offensive action long after the president's civilian advisors had discarded such measures.

Preparations

On October 8, General Taylor transmitted McNamara's note to all senior commanders in the Defense Department, asking for suggestions on implementation. Joint Staff planners hosted several conferences, including an October 12 logistical meeting that raised the supply priority of all units designated for OPLANs 314 and 316.[20]

In response to the defense secretary's guidance, on October 1, the CINCLANT, Admiral Dennison, had already directed his subordinate army and air force headquarters to prepare to execute OPLAN 312 at any time on or after October 20; five days later, he extended this warning order to include forces for 314 and 316. Without an actual execution order, the units involved were still under STRICOM control, so Dennison could only suggest that the CONARC and TAC forces consider prepositioning units in the southeast. Although General Adams insisted that responses to this warning order go through him, in practice preparations went forward rapidly.

During this same period of covert preparations, the federal government had to enforce the enrollment of James H. Meredith in the segregated University of Mississippi in Oxford. President Kennedy federalized the Mississippi National Guard on September 30, and for the next several weeks XVIII Airborne Corps, the primary ground headquarters for OPLANs 314 and 316, had to devote much of its staff attention and combat troops to Mississippi. General Hamilton Howze, the corps commander, headed Operation Rapid Road in Oxford until the situation relaxed on October 10, and even after that numerous military police units scheduled for the Cuban operations remained in Mississippi.[21] During early October, however, fifty-six support units prepositioned troops and heavy equipment closer to their designated Florida bases. Joint communications between Washington and Florida bases required planning and practice. Although the number of communications circuits increased by almost 400 percent, they still were insufficient to support the anticipated traffic of an actual war.[22]

The Fleet Marine Force, Atlantic, was similarly hampered by the Mississippi question, delaying the return of a helicopter group from Oxford to New River, North Carolina, until October 11. The next day, the 4th Marine Expeditionary Brigade, consisting of three battalion landing teams with support troops and air elements, began to board ship for an amphibious exercise (PHIBRIGLEX-62) that also served as a cover story for Cuban precautions. The brigade sailed for the area of Puerto Rico on October 17, while the marines also prepared to move elements of 5th Amphibious Brigade by air from the West Coast to reinforce Guantanamo.[23]

Beginning on September 18, Tactical Air Command moved more than 140 fighter-bombers to Florida to practice simulated bombing attacks on Cuba. In response to Dennison's October 1 warning order, the TAC Commander, General Walter C. Sweeney, Jr., increased this deployment to a total of five hundred aircraft from six tactical fighter wings, all scheduled to arrive by the October 20 suspense date. Meanwhile, on the 3rd, CINCLANT issued an operations plan for the projected blockade of Cuba.

Thus, the Defense Department began preparations for a confrontation long before October 14, when a U-2 flight confirmed the presence of offensive missiles near San Cristobal. Coincidentally, the October 14 mission was the first one flown under SAC rather than CIA control, and indeed it was delayed for two days because of the need to train air force pilots and ground controllers on the CIA version of the aircraft, which had different engines from that flown by SAC.[24] This flight was followed by multiple missions over the next two days. The Soviets in Cuba were well aware that this overflight had detected them, and they redoubled their efforts to complete installation.[25]

As the tension built to a crescendo, a number of issues arose within the American armed services. First, Secretary McNamara and President Kennedy were clearly concerned that a subordinate unit might accidentally precipitate a conflict, and they therefore demanded highly centralized control of any operation. In response, on October 19, Admiral Dennison announced a major reorganization of his command structure for OPLANs 314 and 316. Instead of allowing Second Fleet headquarters to control operations as Joint Task Force 122, as originally planned, he announced that his own headquarters in Norfolk would control operations directly through its component headquarters, ARLANT (CONARC) and AFLANT (TAC). Previously, although the two components were to provide forces to CINCLANT, XVIII Airborne Corps and Nineteenth Air Force had been the operational planners and designated tactical headquarters for any operations. In effect, therefore, Dennison had inserted an extra command level between himself as joint commander and the two tactical headquarters. Moreover, there was now no joint commander on the scene, either afloat or in Florida, to coordinate the four services.[26]

General Powell, the CONARC commander, therefore concluded that he needed a field headquarters, to be known as ARLANT (Forward), in Florida to coordinate with General Sweeney, who had installed a small command post at Homestead Air Force Base. This, in turn, meant dividing the CONARC staff in half, draining much of its experience and complicating the communications and logistics network. In a ripple effect, CONARC then borrowed other officers without warning from nearby subordinate headquarters. Moreover, to control the Third Army logistical elements in Florida, on October 24 General Powell directed the 2nd Logistical Command, a headquarters element at Fort Lee, Virginia, to move to Florida and act as the Peninsula Base Command (PBC). The Army's Signal School at Fort Gordon improvised additional communications nodes, using students and equipment needed by the school.[27] Overall, the desire for centralized control proliferated headquarters and made further deployments necessary.

There was also acute competition for space in Florida. Army planners had always assumed that the air strikes of OPLAN 312 would precede invasion under either 314 or 316, but TAC planners had developed their versions of these three plans in isolation from each other, so that fighter-bombers and paratroop transports were planned to occupy identical spaces on parking aprons. Despite extensive coordination in planning and during the buildup, the air force bases in Florida proved to be overcrowded when called upon to prepare for both 312 and 316. As Dennison later described it, by mid-October the presence of USAF, marine, and navy aircraft meant that "Florida looked like the deck of an aircraft carrier. Every bit of cement in the state . . . had an aircraft on it." The admiral had no choice but to accept the TAC recommendation to substitute Tyndall and Eglin Air Force Bases for MacDill and McCoy as airborne staging locations. This change forced recomputation of the entire airborne plan because of different flight times from the airbases to drop zones in Cuba, and because longer flight times meant more fuel and hence less cargo capacity for each transport aircraft. Meanwhile, the air force had to yield use of Opa Locka airport to the joint unconventional warfare operators.[28]

For a number of reasons Third Army was hard-pressed to provide the troops for OPLANs 314 and 316. Troop units in the Continental United States traditionally had a lower priority for personnel and equipment than overseas units, a situation exacerbated in 1962 by the first deployments of helicopter and signal units to South Vietnam. Even the high-priority Strategic Army Corps units were only 80 percent of authorized strength, and across the board CONARC lacked key experts in aviation, medicine, civil affairs, and military intelligence. The 5th and 7th Special Forces Groups were short of Spanish-speaking green berets, having previously transferred most of their qualified personnel to Mongoose-related black operations.[29]

In August 1962, the army had released the National Guard and reserve units mobilized the previous year for the Berlin Wall crisis. The Kennedy administration would find it politically difficult to recall reserve component units again so soon after the previous mobilization, although it eventually did call up some air force troop transports.

In addition, the army was undergoing a number of reorganizations in 1962. Effective July 1, the traditional army system whereby support units were divided into separate quartermaster, transportation, ordnance, and similar service branches was replaced by a more functional approach to logistics. When the Cuban crisis began, CONARC's staff had shifted to this new approach while large portions of Third Army were still on the older branch model. This created confusion about procedures for requisitions and repairs. Moreover, as part of the development of a broader spectrum of defense capabilities, several divisions were reorganizing from the Pentomic concept, with five battle groups per division, to the Reorganization Objective Army Division (ROAD) built around three flexible brigades. The 2nd Armored Division at Fort Hood, Texas, which was earmarked to provide the heavy forces for Task Force Charlie, was still structured under the

Pentomic format. General Powell therefore concluded that this division would be better suited to reinforce 7th Army in Europe, which was also still under the older structure. By contrast, the 1st Armored Division, also at Fort Hood, was organized under ROAD. However, it had only activated in February 1962. In order to justify the release of the guard divisions, CONARC as well as political authorities had pressured 1st Armored to declare itself combat ready after only six months of existence. On October 18, General Powell decided to switch the wartime assignments of the two armored divisions. This was the genesis of the confused deployment of the fledgling 1st Armored Division from Fort Hood to Georgia during the Cuban crisis, a thirty-six-train movement that was so muddled it became notorious in army folklore.[30]

To further compound matters, the Defense Department did not transfer control of the appropriate CONARC and TAC forces from CINSTRIKE to CINCLANT, which should have happened when execution of the operations plans appeared imminent. On October 18, the JCS issued a warning order to General Adams (CINCSTRIKE) directing increased readiness for units involved in OPLAN 316. Adams passed on this order to Powell (CONARC) but told him not to interfere with the armored divisions involved in the Three Pairs exercise, an exercise to which Adams had devoted much effort. Only two days later did the JCS specifically direct release of OPLAN 316 units from Three Pairs, and even then reports were supposed to go through STRICOM in Florida, despite the fact that the gaining headquarters, LANTCOM, was very close to the CONARC and TAC headquarters in Virginia.[31]

On October 8, navy and air force interceptors began to arrive in Florida to bolster air defenses. However, not until ten days later did the gravity of the situation raise the issue of ground-based air defense for the airfields. CONARC scraped together all available air defense units, including a training battery of automatic weapons from Fort Bliss; because these units were not included in the operations plans, they had no logistical support for some time after reaching Florida. Perhaps the most difficult case involved the 6th Missile Battalion (HAWK), 65th Artillery. In October 1962, this battalion, with its new and highly effective air defense missiles, was still forming at Fort Meade, Maryland. On October 19, a JCS message transferred the 6th Battalion to the control of Continental Air Defense Command and directed CONARC to have it operational in Florida by midnight, five days later. The battalion loaded onto railcars and moved south, but it lacked live or service missiles. Civilian workers at Letterkenny Arsenal in Pennsylvania dutifully loaded such missiles onto tractor trailers for delivery, but at the first truck weighing station in Virginia, state policemen turned the trucks back because they were 2,000 pounds overweight! Given the secrecy of the movement, it took several hours to correct this situation, but the 6th Battalion had two batteries operational at Key West on October 27.[32]

When the JCS disseminated the order for DEFCON 3, General Powell directed the movement of 1st Brigade, 1st Armored Division, and other elements of Task Force Charlie from Fort Hood to Fort Stewart, Georgia, near the port of Savannah, from which they would load out. Given the option, General Ralph Haines decided to move his entire division rather than split it. As a cover story, this half-trained division was hastily added to STRAC and was ostensibly conducting a deployment exercise. Because of the secrecy of the deployment, normally simple tasks such as passing convoy schedules between installations became difficult. Nonetheless, the division arrived at Fort Stewart between October 25 and November 10. Because further deployment might occur on short notice, Haines wanted to keep his vehicles loaded onto their 660 railroad flatcars, yet Fort Stewart had siding space for only 138 such cars. There was adequate space at nearby Hunter Air Force Base, but the local commander would not accept army railcars on a SAC base until the army's deputy chief of staff for operations appealed directly to the air force chief of staff.[33]

PARTIAL EXECUTION

For three weeks, the U.S. armed forces had operated in an atmosphere of secrecy and frantic haste, following McNamara's guidance to prepare for war. General Taylor told the Joint Chiefs in overall terms about deliberations of the famous Executive Committee (EXCOM) in the White House and reportedly offered to arrange meetings with the president. The only such meeting occurred on October 18, with General LeMay arguing forcefully for an air strike even if the Soviets responded in Berlin. Taylor found this meeting unproductive, later recording that "the meeting may not have been particularly helpful to the President, but it certainly made the Chiefs feel better." To clarify the risks of an air attack, the president called in General Sweeney, commander of TAC, to brief OPLAN 312. Sweeney honestly conceded that no attack could guarantee complete destruction of the Soviet weapons.[34]

Yet the Joint Chiefs did not learn in detail about the decision for a quarantine rather than an air attack until October 20. Taylor at that point noted that the president realized that the JCS would be unhappy with that decision, but even then Taylor indicated that the air strike might well occur soon after the president's public warning to the Soviets.[35] This is the origin of the perception that the JCS were a group of warmongers—President Kennedy, Secretary McNamara, and General Taylor had not fully informed them, let alone involved them, in the deliberations leading to the quarantine but instead had directed them to continue preparing for a major conflict. Moreover, the professional officers were acutely aware that the SS-4s and SS-5s were almost ready, at which point the situation would become even more dangerous.

President Kennedy decided on the risky move of challenging the missiles in public rather than private, announcing on October 22 that any missile launched from Cuba would be considered as an attack by the Soviet Union on the United States. Nonetheless, he refrained from specifying any time limit or ultimatum, allowing the Kremlin some diplomatic maneuvering room. Because a blockade was legally an act of war, Kennedy instead announced a "quarantine," a linguistic prevarication that did not change the fact that the U.S. Navy had orders to block further military shipments to Cuba starting on October 24 at 10 A.M. The blockading force originally took station approximately eight hundred miles (1,220 kilometers) from the island, just outside the operational range of IL-28s. Before the effective date of the quarantine, however, the British ambassador apparently convinced the president to move the intercept line three hundred miles (420 kilometers) closer to Cuba in order to allow the Soviets more time to reconsider. The first intercept, on October 26, was of a Panamanian vessel operating under Soviet charter, further reducing the chance of confrontation with Moscow. In fact, the United States actually boarded only one Soviet vessel during the entire crisis and in several instances allowed Soviet and other ships to continue onward to Cuba without a search.[36]

The president and defense secretary were understandably concerned about the possibility of a lethal mistake in the process of stopping and boarding communist bloc vessels en route to Cuba. Moreover, as veterans of the highly informal, temporary World War II forces of torpedo boats and army air force bombers, these two men probably had some antipathy for "brass hats" and did not realize how professional the armed forces had become after fifteen years of continuous semimobilization. As a result, McNamara wanted to micromanage details in a manner foreign to the military service culture. Admiral George W. Anderson, the Chief of Naval Operations (CNO), made no secret of being offended by what he considered the defense secretary's interference in operations. The admiral recalled that McNamara expected him to personally check on the execution of a previous order to put Russian-speaking officers on board each of the intercept ships, something that Anderson trusted Admiral Dennison, the CIN-CLANT, and his subordinates to accomplish without supervision. More significantly, McNamara's concern produced an incident that has been consistently represented (based on McNamara's recollections twenty-five years later) as an example of military rigidity and civil-military tension. On the evening of October 24, the defense secretary came to the Navy Command Center in the Pentagon, asking numerous questions about the details of the quarantine. According to Anderson's recollection, he answered all McNamara's questions and then, as the secretary turned to leave, made a well-meaning attempt to reassure McNamara that his orders would be implemented: "'It's all right,' I said. 'Mr. Secretary, you go back to your office, and I'll go to mine and we'll take care of things.'" Regardless of Anderson's intent, McNamara interpreted this ill-phrased remark as the admiral telling him to mind his own business; as he departed, the secretary reportedly commented to his deputy, Roswell Gilpatric, that Anderson would not be reappointed as CNO.[37]

While McNamara was perturbed, Castro and Khrushchev were outraged when Kennedy publicly called them on the missile issue. The Cuban dictator seemed to welcome an open confrontation with the United States and insisted that the nuclear weapons were essential to defend Cuba's freedom. Khrushchev was enraged and initially decided to have the Soviet ships continue on course, blaming the United States for any resulting controversy. Deputy Premier Anastas Mikoyan talked him out of this, but as late as October 25 the Soviet leader still hoped that he could stonewall the Americans into tolerating the forty-two R-12 missiles that had already reached Cuba.[38]

For all his bluster, however, Khrushchev was sufficiently realistic to proceed cautiously and eventually back down rather than risk nuclear war. Like McNamara, he worried that someone would go too far in the crisis atmosphere. A particular sore point were the frequent U.S. reconnaissance flights, both U-2 and tactical, over the Soviet positions. The Soviet MiG-21 squadron attempted to force one USAF aircraft to land by boxing it in. More seriously, the Cuban anti-aircraft gunners fired in vain at various U.S. aircraft, contributing to the siege mentality of their Soviet comrades. Lieutenant General Stepan Grechko, the head of Soviet air defense on the island, apparently believed that hostilities had already commenced. On October 27, therefore, he directed the 27th Air Defense Division to shoot down a U-2F flown by Major Rudolf Anderson. The Soviet gunners launched three SA-2s and Anderson died, further escalating the crisis. Although the EXCOM had previously recommended that such a shoot down would be cause for an immediate air strike, the president backed off. Believing the first report that the Cubans were responsible, Khrushchev strongly criticized Castro; once the actual facts emerged, Defense Minister Malinovsky only mildly rebuked the Soviet commanders.[39]

The story of the diplomatic resolution of the missile crisis is well known. Both governments operated outside normal diplomatic channels by talking to journalists, at least one of whom was a GRU agent, cutting their ambassadors out of the discussion. On the 26th, Khrushchev wrote to UN Secretary-General U Thant, indicating that Soviet vessels would temporarily avoid Cuba, preventing a confrontation at the quarantine line. Two days later, Khrushchev agreed to withdraw the offensive missiles in return for private assurances that the United States would not invade Cuba and would match the missile withdrawal by pulling its own Jupiter IRBMs out of Turkey. Kennedy had, in fact, decided to withdraw these missiles in August, as reflected in the same NSAM that directed Mongoose to implement "Plan B Plus;" with the new Minuteman and Polaris missiles coming on line, the United States no longer needed the Jupiters but found it difficult politically to persuade Ankara to release them. In the crisis, each superpower acted without consulting the ally that hosted its IRBMs; the Cuban government never forgave Khrushchev for what it regarded as a betrayal. To mollify the Turks for the loss of their obsolescent missiles, Washington soon deployed Polaris submarines to the eastern Mediterranean, including a port call by USS Sam Houston to Izmir in April 1963.[40] For that matter, Khrushchev's public withdrawal encouraged the internal opposition that eventually forced him out of office. Overall, however, the final arrangement was a fairly equal trade—Castro's regime remained in office, but the missiles returned to the Soviet Union.

Yet conventional accounts that end on October 28 overlook the fact that the mobilization, including SAC's DEFCON 2 alert, continued for weeks thereafter. The military forces on both sides remained ready for possible war.

At sea, the 69th Brigade of the Soviet Navy, consisting of five Romeo-class diesel submarines and one older Zulu, had sailed from various locations in early October, headed for Cuba.[41] Just as for the land forces, this strategic projection into unfamiliar waters placed an enormous strain on the Soviet sailors, especially with regard to fresh water for human consumption as well as for their storage batteries. Moreover, each of these submarines carried one Type 53-58 nuclear torpedo with a ten-kiloton warhead. Moscow had authorized the use of such torpedoes if attacked by the U.S. Navy. This latter instance was subject to interpretation; after much discussion, the president had authorized the use of *practice* depth charges as a warning to submerged Soviet subs, but the stressed Soviet commanders might well have misinterpreted the small explosive charges involved. The Zulu and one of the Romeos eventually turned back, but the presence of the other four submarines further complicated the quarantine operations in late October. Throughout the Cold War, U.S. destroyer captains habitually prosecuted their antisubmarine operations with great intensity, locating and maintaining contact with Soviet submarines as a risky form of live training exercise. Both sides knew that diesel-powered submarines would eventually need to surface to recharge batteries and life support. On October 27, U.S. destroyers forced Captain Valentin Savitsky to surface the submarine B-29 with her batteries exhausted and carbon dioxide building up inside. The harassed Savitsky apparently considered using his torpedoes but was dissuaded by his other officers as well as by the incongruous sound of a jazz band playing onboard one of the hovering American ships! On October 29–31, Commander Charles P. Rozier of the destroyer USS *Charles P. Cecil* and maritime patrol aircraft pinned down the submarine B-36, eventually forcing its captain to surface, at which point he refused assistance from the Americans and departed after recharging.

While SAC aircraft remained on constant alert, and photo reconnaissance covered Cuba on a daily basis, preparations for possible invasion of the island continued. On October 27, Kennedy approved McNamara's suggestion to mobilize twenty-four air force reserve squadrons of C-119 and C-123 troop carrier aircraft, sufficient to lift the first wave of 34,800 paratroopers from Forts Bragg and Campbell. The previous day, the Military Sea Transport Service began to contract for additional Landing Ships, Tank (LSTs) and commercial vessels to support the army and marine amphibious operations.[42]

Having finished its long odyssey from Fort Hood to Fort Stuart, 1st Armored Division had to continue its movement, loading one brigade (Task Force Charlie) on ships in Savannah and the Everglades. Literally overnight, army engineers built the necessary landing slips to accommodate LSTs, completing construction in the early evening of October 31. The only two vessels specifically built to handle military equipment, USNS *Comet* and *Taurus*, arrived in Savannah together with the army's only vessel designed to discharge vehicles onto a beach, the *John Page*. When these vessels were loaded on November 4, however, problems identified during the 1958 Lebanon intervention reappeared. *Comet's* two lower holds had ceilings too low to house M48 tanks or 2 ½ ton trucks, and when the tanks were loaded on deck, the vessel became so unstable that the master refused to put to sea. Eventually, the M48s were loaded only by removing the commander's cupola from each one, rendering them unfit for service until they were reassembled and the associated machine guns were resighted for firing. Further experiments indicated that the *Page* could not transfer equipment from ship to shore in heavy seas. This meant that XVIII Airborne Corps would have to capture the port of Mariel intact to unload Task Force Charlie at dockside rather than over the beach.[43] Had the United States actually invaded Cuba, it would have had considerable difficulty landing sufficient U.S. armor to battle the Soviet and Cuban mechanized units.

By October 30, the II Marine Amphibious Force, the largest amphibious assembly since Korea, was at sea between Guantanamo and Vieques Island. Two Marine infantry battalions, a Marine HAWK battalion, and a regimental headquarters moved by air from California to Guantanamo, where they were joined by another battalion from the Fleet Marine Force, Atlantic.

Senior U.S. military leaders remained skeptical of the October 28 agreement. That same afternoon, Kennedy belatedly invited the Joint Chiefs to the White House to thank them for "your advice and your counsel and your behavior" even though he had been insulated from much of that advice and counsel. He was flabbergasted when Admiral Anderson dismissed Khrushchev's promise as a trick and General LeMay suggested "[W]hy don't we go in and make a strike on Monday [the 29th] anyway?"[44] The generals' skepticism seemed confirmed when imagery over the next several days showed no dismantling, prompting the Joint Chiefs to propose reimposition of the quarantine.

A high state of readiness continued for much of November, complicated by Castro's failure to cooperate with the Soviet withdrawal. He refused to permit UN inspectors to verify the missile removal, which meant that the United States had to be satisfied with imaging missile-shaped crates onboard ships leaving the island. The Cuban dictator became even more incensed when Khrushchev agreed, under American pressure, to withdraw the IL-28s that had first alerted the United States.[45]

CONSEQUENCES

Kennedy officially ended the alert and quarantine on November 21, and by the end of the month most of the units concentrated in the southeastern United States were moving back to their home bases. Only the air defense units remained, searching the empty skies for an attack that never came. One such unit, the 2nd Battalion (NIKE-HERCULES), 52nd Artillery, remained in southern Florida until 1979.[46]

Most historians regard the Cuban Missile Crisis as the closest approach to nuclear exchange experienced during the Cold War. Although there were other tense incidents, notably in 1973 (the Yom Kippur War) and 1983 (Exercise Able Archer), October 1962 usually appears as a watershed event that caused the United States, USSR, and other major states to step back and reconsider the hothouse international competition that had preceded it. As a result, according to the usual argument, John Kennedy, Nikita Khrushchev, Robert McNamara, and other key leaders recognized the risks they had been running and set out to reduce tensions and build confidence between the adversaries. In 1963, for example, the Moscow-Washington "Hotline," a system of teletypes (not telephones) between the Kremlin and the Pentagon, came into being for direct communication in future confrontations. That same year, the two sides agreed to a ban on nuclear tests in the atmosphere.

All of this is true, but this conclusion focuses solely on the diplomatic aspects of a military-diplomatic crisis. On the military side, both the United States and the USSR overcame great practical obstacles to deploy their forces, but the result in both cases was too incomplete and improvised to constitute a reliable military option if diplomacy had failed. Each had to rely on mid-ranking officers to make decisions, from shooting down an aircraft to pursuing a submerged submarine, that could easily have led to conflict had those officers been less disciplined and professional.

Moreover, the missile crisis further abraded civil-military relations in both capitals. The two political leaders believed that they had performed well in the crisis, achieving a fair settlement and bolstering mutual understanding. Their military advisors were much more critical, not because they wanted war but because they had a professional responsibility to evaluate the military consequences if the other side did not live up to its agreements. For the Soviet Army, Khrushchev's withdrawal only compounded officer resentment and criticism of a man who had reduced the size of the armed forces below what it considered to be a minimum safe level. Khrushchev fought back bureaucratically, forcing the chief of the General Staff, Marshal Matvei Zakharov, into early retirement in 1963 for criticizing the general secretary's interference in military affairs. The Soviet military was quite willing to see Khrushchev himself be forced to retire.[47]

The missile crisis reinforced President Kennedy's antagonism toward his military commanders, with the exception of General Taylor. In mid-November 1962, he expressed this distrust openly to a reporter, remarking that "The first advice I'm going to give my successor . . . is to watch the generals and to avoid feeling that just because they were military men their opinions on military matters were worth a damn."[48] Although this feeling is understandable, it contributed to a continuing lack of communication that carried over into future decisions concerning Vietnam. The JCS were performing their professional duty by expressing their concerns about national security policy, and as a practical matter they always executed Kennedy's decisions, including support for the test ban treaty. Both sides share responsibility for this estrangement, and General Taylor clearly believed that he was representing the military advisors effectively during the missile crisis. Yet, Ronald Carpenter has dissected the transcripts of the EXCOM meetings and concluded that the general deliberately shifted his position to suit his perception that the Kennedys were not interested in forcible solutions. On several critical occasions, Carpenter noted, Taylor referred to the JCS as "they" rather than "we" when presenting their recommendations, distancing himself from the professionals he was supposed to represent.[49] What is noteworthy in retrospect is that a president who prided himself upon being open to multiple advisors and viewpoints, upon bypassing the senior leader in an organization to consult the next level down, nonetheless chose to make his national security decisions while excluding all but one professional soldier from the table. He went through the motions of consulting the Joint Chiefs twice during the crisis but made his decisions based solely on the EXCOM recommendations. The successful outcome in the case of Cuba does not excuse a prejudiced practice that could well have led to disaster under other circumstances.

CONCLUSION

D rawing conclusions from a broad historical survey is at best a
difficult task. There are, however, a number of generalizations that
stand out clearly from the mass of detail in the foregoing narrative.

MULTIPLE ACTORS

The first such generalization involves the pivotal military roles performed by actors *other* than the United States and the Soviet Union.
Preeminent among these other actors was Great Britain, the ubiquitous
participant in military actions from Greece to Saigon, from Cyprus
to Malaya, and innumerable locations in between. During the later
1940s, when the United States could genuinely claim to be the sole
world power of the era, it was Britain that provided police and counterinsurgent forces throughout that world. Regardless of which party
was in power in Whitehall, the British followed a consistent policy of
engagement that in the long run minimized the violence and disorder
inherent in the emergence of so many new nation-states. Although
one may criticize the decisions made by individual British commanders and governors, overall this influence was remarkably enlightened
and beneficent.

Almost equally important in this regard were the two governments,
nationalist and Maoist, of China. These rival regimes not only fought
the bloodiest conflict of the Cold War era but also involved themselves

in regional struggles in both Southeast and Northeast Asia. Although some Westerners made the mistake of assuming that the People's Republic was a Soviet satellite, that government followed its own policies in French Indochina, Korea, Laos, and the offshore islands. In the process, Mao Tse-tung repeatedly disagreed with his counterparts in Moscow while risking U.S. nuclear attack.

Other powers, great or minor, were also crucial to the story of the early Cold War. France, Portugal, and the Netherlands fought rearguard colonial wars of remarkable efficiency and persistence, if not always with a clear view of public opinion in their colonies. The French were also pivotal in the question of German rearmament and the European Defense Community. Having failed to seize South Korea by insurgency during the later 1940s, North Korea's 1950 invasion unwittingly provoked the first effective test of United Nations collective security and the greatest sustained direct conflict between the Soviets (masquerading as Korean or Chinese volunteer pilots) and the Americans. Finally, revisionist Western historians have been surprised to discover "just how intimately Cuba was bound up not only with the genesis and management of the missile crisis, but with the last thirty years of superpower conflict."[1] Fidel Castro's deceptively easy victory against the Batista regime inspired numerous future conflicts, both revolutionary and conventional, that lasted for the remainder of the Cold War, as the second volume of this study will explore.

ECONOMIC COSTS

These conflicts, whether victorious or not, carried with them an enormous price tag. Indeed, the human, financial, and industrial expenses of a half century of semimobilization are incalculable. Oddly enough, the United States was the richest nation in the history of the world and the only intact industrial economy of 1945, yet it probably sacrificed less than most of its allies and opponents. Presidents Truman and Eisenhower repeatedly accepted military risks to ensure their long-term economic health, cutting their defense forces far below what their generals considered necessary for security and relying on the risky prospect of nuclear weapons to replace conventional forces. Eisenhower succeeded in this calculated risk, while the U.S. armed forces paid for Truman's cuts on the hills of Korea. Finally, although the selective service law was in effect, with one brief hiatus, from 1940 to 1972, Washington demanded large numbers of conscripts only when engaged in major conflict in Korea and Vietnam.

The Soviet Union wisely avoided direct involvement in the conflicts of the early Cold War, but the economic and social cost of sustaining military competition with the West not only delayed recovery from World War II but also ultimately doomed the Soviet regime. The unlikely peacemaker Nikita Khrushchev perceived this clearly. He sharply reduced his conventional armed forces and took the enormous risk of placing missiles in Cuba as the only means to save the Soviet economy and provide a better life for its peoples. Both of these actions contributed to his fall from power.

Just as other actors played key roles in military operations, those same actors paid a major economic price for those roles. Great Britain was virtually bankrupt in 1945 yet continued for a dozen years to invest a disproportionate part of its manpower and treasure in policing the world. Only when the Suez Crisis demonstrated the limits of British power did Whitehall belatedly adjust its defense establishment to the strategic and economic realities of the 1950s, and even then the British insisted upon maintaining an independent nuclear force, worldwide navy, and deployable army. Even in the 1960s, the British continued to fight brush fires in their former colonies.

Having suffered through civil and world war for two decades, the newly sovereign People's Republic of China absorbed a million casualties in Korea and delayed its own economic recovery indefinitely. The French and Portuguese virtually bankrupted themselves and provoked major internal political crises while seeking to defend their status as worldwide powers.

INSURGENCY AND COUNTERINSURGENCY

Despite its label as the "Cold" War, this era saw every form of military action short of nuclear conflict and in several cases approached even that precipice. Participants undertook everything from a show of force, such as the 1958 intervention in Lebanon, to conventional war, such as the Korean conflict and the last two years of the Chinese Civil War. Overall, however, the most common form of conflict was insurgency, frequently but not always resembling the Maoist, peasant-based guerrilla conflict found in China.

Given the recent preoccupation with revolutionary insurgencies in Iraq, Afghanistan, and elsewhere, it is fashionable to assume that the rebels always win such conflicts. The reality, as demonstrated by the many conflicts in this survey, is far different. With the partial exception of China, protracted revolutionary wars usually succeeded only when the rebels had not only popular support but also extensive foreign advisors, arms, and sanctuaries. The examples of Greece, Malaya, the Philippines, and Kenya demonstrate that the counter-insurgent power could indeed win if it acted promptly, isolated the rebels from outside aid, and then provided an alternative solution to the grievances that had inspired the uprising. There were anomalies, of course. In the case of Cyprus, a skilled and ruthless professional soldier manipulated domestic and foreign public opinion against a clumsy counterinsurgent commander. More typically, the French in Algeria demonstrated that the armed forces could achieve military security and stability by controlling the population and suppressing their opponents but could not prevent the rebels from exploiting domes-tic and international perceptions of government abuse. In this regard, just as today, the insurgent's best allies are information manipulation and greater patience than his opponents—the French, Portuguese, and occasionally British all lost domestic support before their well-motivated opponents.

CIVIL-MILITARY RELATIONS

Since at least the time of the Greek city-states, civil-military conflict has been an unavoidable part of any political system in which the head of state was not also the field commander. During the Cold War, however, such conflict became especially commonplace as the boun-daries between civilian and military responsibilities grew more porous than ever before. It is no coincidence that theorists such as Samuel Huntington would feel the urgent need to delineate this dividing line just as it began to break down.[2]

This breakdown occurred for at least two reasons. On the one hand, governments conducting prolonged military operations needed soldiers to assume duties such as allied diplomatic coordinator or regional military expert, duties that required knowledge of and decisions in areas that heretofore had been almost exclusively civilian. One may argue that naval commanders in remote areas had always had to make such decisions, but the advent of the Cold War, with its constant state of semimobilization, required proconsuls, such as Douglas MacArthur,

Gerald Templer, and Konstantin Rokossovsky, and indispensable specialists, such as Edward Lansdale, Harold Briggs, and Anatoli Gribkov. Yet the prevalence of instantaneous communications made the decisions of such soldiers subject to the "six-thousand-mile screwdriver" of government supervision and micromanagement. As indicated in the preface, political leaders attempted to impose their own preferences on situations despite the military consequences of such actions: Zachariadis in choosing conventional tactics in Greece, Eden in changing the invasion plan at Suez, Khrushchev in reorganizing the Soviet military and shipping missiles to Cuba, Mao in launching attacks in Korea and on the offshore islands, Kennedy and McNamara in a series of confrontations, and other leaders all engaging in what appears, in retrospect, as wishful thinking. All of these political leaders had the legal authority to make such decisions, but the results varied from military failure to armed coups and the risk of nuclear holocaust. While generals as a group are no more prescient than politicians, the armed forces and indeed the entire nation paid the price when political leaders did not give due consideration to professional military advice.

Political scientist Dale Herspring has argued persuasively[3] that the conflict was greatest when political leaders violated military cultural norms and exhibited lack of respect for their generals and admirals. Yet, the political leaders with the greatest experience in those cultural norms, such as de Gaulle and Eisenhower, often had the greatest difficulty in this regard because they were least tolerant of dissenting opinions among their military subordinates. Perhaps, in fact, the World War II experiences of various civilian leaders gave them exaggerated conceptions of their own military judgment.

At the same time, of course, civilian "defense experts" appeared in unprecedented numbers, particularly in the theory of nuclear warfare, a type of conflict in which no soldier had any experiential advantage over his civilian counterpart. Both civilians and soldiers were groping for solutions in a new environment where total war might lead to annihilation, and where the limits and desired end states of limited conflict were ill defined.

In addition, the intensely political nature of revolutionary warfare required officers on both sides to become far more politically conscious than their predecessors. For Mao and the other Marxist-nationalist insurgent leaders, politics was so preeminent that the very concept of a professional, apolitical officer was anathema. For their opponents, understanding insurgency required military officers to study the political dimensions of revolution and the problem of satisfying the political and economic needs of the population. It was only a short step from political awareness to political partisanship, with disastrous effect in the French and Portuguese societies. In the French case, at least, the only apparent solution was to rebuild the professional, apolitical officer corps by removing political concerns from the duties of officers.

INTERSERVICE RIVALRIES

Closely related to such civil-military conflicts were circumstances in which different armed services wrangled for scarce resources. The most obvious instance of this was the Revolt of the Admirals, when the U.S. Navy's uniformed leaders argued that the administration and the U.S. Air Force were distorting the defense budget and weakening national defense under the belief that nuclear-armed aircraft could provide all the security that the nation required. James Forrestal tried in vain to broker a compromise between the services concerning military functions and budgets. Western intelligence analysts caught faint echoes of similar disagreements within the Soviet Union, where the successful generals of World War II felt that Khrushchev was endangering national security by his reliance on nuclear-armed missiles and corresponding reductions in the conventional forces. Soviet admirals also paid a heavy price for trying to build a blue-water navy, something that Khrushchev considered a luxury until the absence of such a navy hampered him in the Cuban Missile Crisis. Finally, the well-connected Lord Louis Mountbatten outraged both his service counterparts and British politicians who felt that he had overstepped his bounds in advising the government against the Suez intervention of 1956.

Most of these disagreements, like the more direct challenge to civilian authority posed by MacArthur, were the unavoidable problems of senior leaders performing what they perceived to be their professional duty even when the politicians were unwilling to hear the resulting message. More fundamentally, however, such conflicts again represented the clash between short-run defense requirements and the long-run economic viability of the states those defenses protected. Under President Kennedy, Robert McNamara used an authority that Forrestal had never sought nor received to rationalize service budgetary

needs. To do this, McNamara established a programming and budgetary process that analyzed U.S. defense needs in terms of required
capabilities (conventional forces, nuclear forces, transportation, etc.)
rather than the traditional and sometimes duplicative elements of
the four separate armed services.[4] Some of McNamara's efforts in
this regard reflected his own blindness about genuine service needs,
but he at least opened the way to a more rational method of planning
defense needs and expenditures. Ultimately, however, Congress had
to intervene in this process through the Goldwater-Nichols Act of 1986,
which required senior officers to acquire education and experience
working with the other services.

INTELLIGENCE

The intelligence agencies of the opposing powers achieved considerable
successes in the early Cold War. Espionage accelerated the development
of Soviet nuclear weapons, while the British and American intelligence
services had similar if less well-known achievements in intelligence,
psychological warfare, and covert operations. Despite such achievements,
the major powers often acted like blind men in attempting to understand their world.

Predicting adversary objectives and intentions was critical to
success in both limited war and counterinsurgency, yet such predic-
tions required a cultural knowledge and independence of thought that
was rare among civil or military leaders. Men in Washington, Moscow,
Beijing, and elsewhere consistently misread their opponents as well
as the popular desires of a number of rebellious nations, resulting in
strategic surprise, military defeat, and increased civil-military friction.
In Korea, for example, the communist states thought they were continuing a civil war parallel to that in China, while the United States
and its allies regarded the twin communist interventions of 1950 as
open aggression against a sovereign state. Both the Soviets repressing
Hungary and the colonial powers fighting Third World insurgencies
blamed Cold War agitators for their problems rather than perceiving
the nationalistic and economic issues of those uprisings. Finally, Soviet
rulers repeatedly failed to predict American reactions to their actions
in Berlin, Cuba, and elsewhere.

Some of these miscommunications were simply the product of
Cold War rhetoric. In other instances, however, both military and

civilian leaders lacked the cultural and historical perspective to understand their opponents. Even sophisticated intelligence analysts had difficulty comprehending such nuances, let alone explaining those beliefs to their masters. Their armies paid for such failures in Korea, Hungary, Vietnam, Cyprus, and Egypt.

Watershed

It is traditional to regard the Cuban Missile Crisis as a watershed event, a terrifying approach to Armageddon that prompted the political leaders of both sides to step back and reconsider the risks involved. As such, it is a logical point at which to split this study into two parts. October 1962 marked a climax not only of East-West competition and the nuclear arms race but also of many of the other trends noted above. The political, military, budgetary, and economic strain of the later 1950s and early 1960s had ratcheted up friction not only between Washington and Moscow but also between each government and its military advisors, and even between the different armed services of each major power. Kennedy, Khrushchev, and their generals continued to miscommunicate and misunderstand, while the nuclear forces of each power were the foci of interservice rivalries. Both sides had to depend upon mid-level professional soldiers to make decisions that might have had catastrophic consequences. It would be simplistic to contend that just as Kennedy and Khrushchev came to know and somewhat trust each other, so their military subordinates also made peace within their respective hierarchies. To the contrary, the Cuban Missile Crisis contributed to ongoing civil-military friction for at least the next decade. Yet, after the Soviets withdrew their missiles, the form of rivalries, both between and within governments, shifted somewhat. What followed were two decades of insurgency, counter-insurgency, and sustained if soft-pedaled confrontation before the Cold War again came to a boil beginning in 1979.

Acronyms, Abbreviations, and Other Terms

AAF	U.S. Army Air Forces, 1942–1947
AEC	U.S. Atomic Energy Commission
AK	Armia Krajowa, Polish resistance Home Army in World War II
ALN	Armée de Liberation Nationale, military arm of the Algerian revolution. See FLN.
AVH	Allamvedelmi Hatosag, the Hungarian State Security Police
BCT	Battalion Combat Team, especially in Philippine armed forces
BLT	U.S. Marine Corps battalion landing team—a battalion task force afloat—prepared for landing alone or as part of a larger amphibious force
CASF	U.S. Air Force Composite Air Strike Force, a group of designated units prepared for rapid deployment in a crisis. See also STRAC.
CCF	Chinese Communist Force, the UN term for the "Chinese Volunteers" of the Korean War
CCP	Chinese Communist Party
CIGS	British Chief of the Imperial General Staff
CINC	Commander-in-Chief, the senior military officer in charge of a particular group of forces or military functional area

CINCLANT   Commander-in-Chief, Atlantic, the U.S. unified commander for the area of the Atlantic and Caribbean

CINCNELM   Commander-in-Chief, U.S. Navy Forces, Eastern Atlantic and Mediterranean, the headquarters responsible for the 1958 deployment to Lebanon

CINCPAC   Commander-in-Chief, Pacific, the U.S. unified commander for that region

CNO   Chief of Naval Operations, the senior uniformed head of the U.S. Navy

COMECON   Council for Economic Cooperation, the Soviet-dominated Eastern European equivalent (1949–1991) of ERA and the Marshall Plan

COMINFORM   Communist Information Bureau, founded in 1947 as the Soviet-dominated mechanism for aligning Marxist states and parties, the de facto successor to COMINTERN Communist International Working Man's Association

CONARC   Continental Army Command, the headquarters for U.S. Army units in the Continental United States, 1955–1973

CPSU   Communist Party of the Soviet Union

CTs   Communist Terrorists; British term for the rebels in Malaya

DA   Dal'nyaya Aviatsiya, Soviet long-range aviation command

DAG   (Communist) Democratic Army of Greece during the civil war; the original Greek term was Demokratikos Stratos Eliados

DCI   U.S. Director of Central Intelligence, head of the Central Intelligence Agency and (1947–2004) coordinator of the intelligence community

DEFCON   Defense Condition, one of five readiness conditions in the U.S. military

DGS   Direcção General de Segurança, Portuguese General Security Direction

DIA   US Defense Intelligence Agency, created in 1961 to provide unified joint military intelligence for the Department of Defense

DRV	Democratic Republic of [North] Vietnam
ECSC	European Coal and Steel Community, forerunner of the European Economic Community and European Union
EDC	European Defense Community
ELAS	Greek National Popular Liberation Army during World War II
EOKA	Ethniki Organosis Kyprion Agoniston, National Organization of Cypriot Fighters
ERA	European Recovery Administration, aka the Marshall Plan
FEAF	U.S. Far East Air Forces, the air component subordinate to FEC
FAL	Laotian armed forces, or Forces Armées du Laos
FEC	U.S. Far East Command, responsible for the occupation of Japan and Northeast Asia
FLN	Front de Liberation Nationale, political arm of the Algerian revolution (see ALN)
FNLA	Frente Nacional de Libertacao de Angola, National Front for the Liberation of Angola. Successor organization to UPA.
FRELIMO	Frente de Libertacao de Mocambique, Mozambique Liberation Front
FRG	Federal Republic of [West] Germany
GCMA	Groupements de Commandos Mixtes Aéroportés, French organization of anticommunist guerrillas in Indochina
GDR	[East] German Democratic Republic
GNA	Greek National Army
GRU	Glavnoye Razvedovatel'noye Upravlenie, Main Intelligence Directorate, Soviet military intelligence within the Ministry of Defense rather than the NKVD or KGB
GSFC	Group of Soviet Forces, Cuba
GSFG	Group of Soviet Forces, Germany
ICBM	Intercontinental ballistic missile, with a range of 8,000 kilometers (5,000 miles) or more
IDF	Israel Defense Forces
IRBM	Intermediate-range ballistic missile, with a range of 3,000–5,500 kilometers (1,865–3,420 miles)

JCS
: U.S. Joint Chiefs of Staff, the senior uniformed officers of the four service branches plus for much of its history a chairman (CJCS)

JUSMAG
: Joint U.S. Military Assistance Group, a common organization for providing weapons and advisors to assist friendly armed forces

JUSMAPG
: Joint U.S. Military Advisory and Planning Group, an early form of JUSMAG sent to Greece in 1947

KAR
: King's African Rifles

KATUSA
: Korean Augmentation to the U.S. Army

KCA
: Kikuyu Central Association, Jomo Kenyatta's organization in Kenya

KGB
: Komitet Gosudarstvennoy Bezopasnosti, Soviet Committee for State Security, intelligence and clandestine operation after 1954. See NKVD.

KKE
: Kommounistikó Kómma Elládas, the Greek Communist Party

KMT
: Kuomintang, older transliteration of the Chinese Nationalist Party, also known as GMD

KNP
: [South] Korean National Police

LANTCOM
: U.S. Atlantic Command, 1947–1993; a primarily naval command responsible for operations in the Atlantic and Caribbean

LOK
: Lochos Oreinon Katadromon, Greek National Army commando units

LCI
: Landing Craft, Infantry; capable of landing 180–210 troops on a beach

LST
: Landing Ship, Tank, a vessel twice the size of an LCI, capable of landing twenty or more tanks or other vehicles with crews on a beach

MAY
: Rural self-defense forces created by the Greek government during civil war

MCP
: Malayan Communist Party

MGB
: Ministerstvo Gosudarstvennoi Bezopasnosti; Soviet Ministry for State Security, especially involved in controlled annexed territories, 1946 to 1954, when it merged with other organizations in the KGB

MiG
: Aircraft designation derived from the Soviet Mikoyan-Gurevich design bureau, as in MiG-15

MPLA	Movimento Popular de Libertacao de Angola, Popular Movement for the Liberation of Angola
MRLA	Malayan Races Liberation Army
NATO	North Atlantic Treaty Organization, the allied command structure established to implement the North Atlantic Treaty of 1949
NCO	Noncommissioned officer
NKGB	Narodny komissariat gosudarstvennoi bezopasnosti, the Soviet People's Commissariat for State Security, 1943–1946; became MGB in 1946
NKPA	North Korean People's Army
NKVD	Narodnyy Komissariat Vnutrennikh Del, Soviet People's Commissariat for Internal Affairs, 1934–1946, and used informally until 1954. See KGB.
NORAD	North American Air [later Aerospace] Defense Command, the U.S.-Canadian headquarters responsible for air defense and warning against nuclear attack
NSA	(1) National Security Act of 1947; (2) National Security Agency, established 1952
NSC	National Security Council. When followed by a number, it refers to a particular policy document of the NSC, such as NSC-68.
OAS	Organisation de l'Armée Secrète, French military conspiracy against de Gaulle
OPC	Office of Policy Coordination, a U.S. covert action organization of the early Cold War
OPLAN	Operations Plan; in American usage, an Operations Plan is just that—a contingency plan to conduct a possible military operation, which is purely for planning purposes unless the appropriate authority directs its execution. By developing OPLANs in advance, military staffs can identify issues and greatly facilitate actual operations.
OSS	Office of Strategic Services, U.S. clandestine intelligence in World War II
PAIGC	Partido Africano da Independencia da Guine et Cabo Verde, African Party for the Independence of Guinea and Cape Verde

PCA	Parti Communiste Algerien, Communist Party of Algeria
Pentomic	Public relations term for the U.S. Army's restructuring in the later 1950s
PKP	Partido Komunista ng Pilipinas, Communist Party of the Philippines
PLA	Chinese People's Liberation Army
PLAAF	Chinese People's Liberation Army Air Force
PRC	People's Republic of China
PVO-Strany	Protivovozdushnoi Oborony Strany, Soviet air defense forces
RAF	British Royal Air Force
RCT	Regimental Combat Team, an infantry regiment reinforced by attached elements of artillery, medical, engineer, and other branches for self-sufficiency
ROC	Republic of [Nationalist] China
ROCAF	Republic of China Air Force
ROK	Republic of [South] Korea
ROKA	Republic of Korea Army
RVN	Republic of [South] Vietnam
SAC	(1) Supreme Allied Commander, one of two NATO positions (SACEUR for European land and air operations, SACLANT for Atlantic naval operations); (2) U.S. Strategic Air Command, the specified command responsible for most strategic nuclear weapons and planning, 1946–1992
SAS	Sections Administratives Specialisées, system of local offices for French military control of the population in Algeria
SEATO	Southeast Asia Treaty Organization (1954–1977)
SIOP	Single integrated operating plan, designation for various U.S. nuclear war plans
SIS	British Secret Intelligence Service, sometimes called MI6
SOE	British Special Operations Executive, a World War II special operations organization
SRF	Soviet Strategic Rocket Forces, the separate armed force responsible for strategic nuclear missiles and planning

STRAC	(1) U.S. Army Strategic Army Corps, a group of high-priority units for rapid deployment during the 1950s–1970s; (2) By extension, a slang term for any unit or equipment that was highly efficient and prepared for action. See also CASF.
STRICOM	U.S. Strike Command, 1961–1972; a unified (i.e., multiservice) military command responsible both for providing U.S.-based forces to other regional commands and for acting as the overall headquarters for U.S. operations in the Middle East and Northeast Asia. Its head was Commander-in-Chief, Strike Command or CINCSTRIKE. Indirectly, the forerunner of U.S. Central Command (1983–present).
TAC	USAF Tactical Air Command, 1946–1992
TF	Task Force
TNI	Tentara Nasional *Indonesia*, Armed Forces of Indonesia
UNITA	Uniao Nacional para a Independencia Total de Angola, National Union for the Total Independence of Angola
UPA	Uniao das Populacoes de Angola, Union of Angolan Peoples
USAAF	United States Army Air Forces, a component of the Army and War Department 1942–1947
USAF	United States Air Force
USAFE	USAF in Europe
USAREUR	U.S. Army, Europe
USMC	U.S. Marine Corps
YIAFAKA	Unarmed support structure of the Greek Communists

Notes

PREFACE

1. See, for example, Campbell Craig and Fredrik Logevall, *America's Cold War: The Politics of Insecurity* (Cambridge, MA, 2009).

CHAPTER 1

1. This description of the aerial resupply of Warsaw is based on Neil Orpen, *Airlift to Warsaw: The Rising of 1944* (Norman, OK, 1984), esp. 81–82, 86–101. See also Norman Davies, *Rising '44: The Battle for Warsaw* (New York, 2003), esp. 307–317.

2. Orpen, *Airlift to Warsaw*, 95, 136–137.

3. This explanation of the Warsaw Uprising is based on Jan M. Ciechanowski, *The Warsaw Rising of 1944* (London, 1974), and Janusz K. Zawodny, *Nothing but Honour: The Story of the Warsaw Uprising, 1944* (Stanford, CA, 1978). For a more detailed description, see Davies, *Rising '44*.

4. Ciechanowski, *Warsaw Rising*, 3–5.

5. Dimitri Volkogonov, *Stalin: Triumph and Tragedy* (Rocklin, CA, 1992), 359–360. After the collapse of the Soviet Union, the Russian government supplied the Poles with full documentation of the massacres.

6. Quoted in Ciechanowski, *Warsaw Rising*, 227.

7. Zawodny, *Nothing but Honour*, 27 (quotation), 26 (figures); see also Ciechanowski, *Warsaw Rising*, 225–226.

8. Davies, *Rising '44*, 211–213.

9. Zawodny, *Nothing but Honour*, 102–105.

10. Ciechanowski, *Warsaw Rising*, 237–243. For the decision making in Warsaw, see Wladzimierz Borodeziej, *The Warsaw Uprising of 1944* (Madison, WI, 2006), esp. 62–73.

11. Zawodny, *Nothing but Honour*, 56–57, 62–63; on Back-Zelewski in the Holocaust, see Richard Rhodes, *Masters of Death: The SS-Einsatzgruppen and the Invention of the Holocaust* (New York, 2002), 226, 277.

12. David M. Glantz and Jonathan M. House, *When Titans Clashed: How the Red Army Stopped Hitler* (Lawrence, KS, 1995), 212–214.

13. Quoted in Winston S. Churchill, *The Second World War*, Vol. 6: *Triumph and Tragedy* (Boston, 1953), 131.

14. For the argument that the Soviets did attempt to aid the rising, see Geoffrey Roberts, *Stalin's Wars: From World War to Cold War, 1939–1953* (New Haven, CT, 2006), 214–217.

15. Quoted in Churchill, *Triumph and Tragedy*, 133.

16. Zawodny, *Nothing but Honour*, 134–136; Mark J. Conversino, *Fighting with the Soviets: The Failure of Operation FRANTIC, 1944–1945* (Lawrence, KS, 1997), 130–160.

17. Zawodny, *Nothing but Honour*, 210–211.

18. Roberts, *Stalin's Wars*, 214.

19. Harold R. Alexander, *The Alexander Memoirs, 1940–1945* (London, 1962), 141–142.

20. Churchill, *Triumph and Tragedy*, 311.

21. Edgar O'Ballance, *The Greek Civil War 1944–1949* (New York, 1966), 29; David H. Close, *The Origins of the Greek Civil War* (New York, 1995), 14–27.

22. André Gerolymatos, *Red Acropolis, Black Terror: The Greek Civil War and the Origins of Soviet-American Rivalry, 1943–1949* (New York, 2004), 39–40, 49.

23. Evangelos Averoff-Tossizza, *By Fire and Axe: The Communist Party and the Civil War in Greece, 1944–1949* (New Rochelle, NY, 1978), 98–105; Close, *Origins of the Greek Civil War*, 103–109; Gerolymatos, *Red Acropolis, Black Terror*, 91.

24. Averoff-Tossizza, *By Fire and Axe*, 105 ff; for the ELAS view, see the memoirs of commander Stefanos Safaris, *ELAS: Greek Resistance Army.* (London, 1980), esp. 492–493.

25. Quoted in Churchill, *Triumph and Tragedy*, 286–287.

26. The percentage agreement on spheres of influence is described in Churchill, *Triumph and Tragedy*, 227–232; Roberts summarizes the Soviet version of this discussion in *Stalin's Wars*, 217–225; Peter J. Stavrakis provides a convincing analysis of Soviet policy in *Moscow and Greek Communism, 1944–1949* (Ithaca, NY, 1989), 11–12, 28–38.

27. Safaris, *ELAS*, 479, 487–496; Churchill, *Triumph and Tragedy*, 287–288; O'Ballance, *Greek Civil War*, 94–95. On withdrawal of the SOE officers who had deliberately recruited leftists for the resistance, see Gerolymatos, *Red Acropolis, Black Terror*, 142.

28. Averoff-Tossizza, *By Fire and Axe*, 114–115; Safaris, *ELAS*, 500; Gerolymatos, *Red Acropolis, Black Terror*, 102–105; Churchill to Scobie, 5 December 1944, quoted in Churchill, *Triumph and Tragedy*, 289.

29. O'Ballance, *Greek Civil War*, 93, 95.

30. Safaris, *ELAS*, 402 (troop strength), 506–512 (battle against EDES); O'Ballance, *Greek Civil War*, 106–109; Gerolymatos, *Red Acropolis, Black Terror*, 176.

31. Lawrence S. Wittner, *American Intervention in Greece, 1943–1949* (New York, 1982), 37; Stavrakis, *Moscow and Greek Communism*, 23–28.

32. Alexander, *Alexander Memoirs*, 142; O'Ballance, *Greek Civil War*, 101–102; Churchill, *Triumph and Tragedy*, 307–309.

33. Averoff-Tossizza, *By Fire and Axe*, 119–122; see also Wittner, *American Intervention in Greece*, 23–28.

34. Churchill, *Triumph and Tragedy*, 313–319; Averoff-Tossizza, *By Fire and Axe*, 123–126.

35. Averoff-Tossizza, *By Fire and Axe*, 125–126; O'Ballance, *Greek Civil War*, 103 ff.

36. Churchill, *Triumph and Tragedy*, 321–322; Averoff-Tossiza, *By Fire and Axe*, 126.

37. On the Varzika Agreement, see Safaris, *ELAS*, 522–523; Averoff-Tossizza, *By Fire and Axe*, 144–146.

38. Casualty figures are from O'Ballance, *Greek Civil War*, 108.

39. This section is based on Peter M. Dunn, *The First Vietnam War* (New York, 1985), 4–63, 140–223; and Ronald H. Spector, *Advice and Support: The Early Years, 1941–1960* (Washington, 1983), 5–68.

40. Bernard B. Fall, *Street without Joy* (New York, 1972), 22–24.

41. Dunn, *First Vietnam War*, 18–19.

42. On the Allied command structure for Southeast Asia, see Charles F. Romanus and Riley Sunderland, *Time Runs Out in CBI* (Washington, 1959), esp. 12–15, 259–261. On Americans blocking the Free French, see Dunn, *First Vietnam War*, 28–35.

43. Spector, *Early Years*, 45–53. For the British interpretation of this disagreement, and the resulting loss of Royal Air Force (RAF) aircraft, see Dunn, *First Vietnam War*, 84–93, 117–118. General Albert C. Wedemeyer barely mentions Indochina in his memoirs, *Wedemeyer Reports* (New York, 1958), 340–343.

44. Dunn, *First Vietnam War*, 119–139.

45. Even Ho's sympathetic biographer William J. Duiker concluded his study by leaving the motivational question open: "There is ample evidence that, whether or not he was an orthodox Marxist, under his patriotic exterior beat the heart of a dedicated revolutionary. . . . In Ho's brave new world, patriotism would be replaced by the Leninist concept of a future global federation of Communist societies." *Ho Chi Minh* (New York, 2000), 570. This unresolved mixture of nationalism and Marxism was quite common in the Third World and contributed to Western misperceptions throughout the Cold War.

46. Spector, *Early Years*, 24–27, 38–43; Dunn, *First Vietnam War*, 14–15. See also Dixie Bartholomew-Feis, *The OSS and Ho Chi Minh: Unexpected Allies in the War against Japan* (Lawrence, KS, 2006).

47. Dunn, *First Vietnam War*, esp. 16–19, 41–43; Spector, *Early Years*, 56–67.

48. Dunn, *First Vietnam War*, 39–48.

49. Gallagher, quoted in Russell Steller's introduction to Vo Nguyen Giap, *The Military Art of People's War: Selected Writings of General Vo Nguyen Giap* (New York, 1970), 24. For the text of the declaration of Vietnamese independence, see Ho Chi Minh, *On Revolution: Selected Writings, 1920–66* (New York, 1967), 143–145.

50. Dunn, *First Vietnam War*, 49, 21–22; Spector, *Early Years*, 66.

51. Spector, *Early Years*, 66–67.

52. Dunn, *First Vietnam War*, 194–199, 203.

53. Spector, *Early Years*, 67; Dunn, *First Vietnam War*, 215–222, provides an exhaustive analysis of the incident.

54. Dunn, *First Vietnam War*, 331–341.

CHAPTER 2

1. John L. Gaddis, *The Cold War: A New History* (New York, 2005), 6.

2. Ghulam D. Wardak, *The Voroshilov Lectures: Materials from the Soviet General Staff Academy*, Vol. 1: *Issues of Soviet Military Strategy*, Ed. Graham H. Turbiville, Jr. (Washington, 1989), 120–122.

3. F. F. Liu, *A Military History of Modern China, 1924–1949* (Princeton, 1956), 22–29. On Stalin's ideological myopia for revolution in the nonindustrialized regions, see Roberts, *Stalin's Wars*.

4. See Thomas M. Huber (ed.), *Compound Warfare: That Fatal Knot* (Fort Leavenworth, KS, 2002).

5. In 1949, the U.S. Army assigned Russell Volkmann, a veteran of the resistance in the Philippines, to write the first doctrine on guerrilla and counterguerrilla warfare. Volkmann produced an excellent study that addressed causes of local discontent, but his analysis was heavily influenced by World War II, especially German struggles against Soviet partisans. See Andrew J. Birtle, *U.S. Army Counterinsurgency and Contingency Operations Doctrine, 1942–1976* (Washington, 2006), 131–142.

6. The literature for the theory of Revolutionary Warfare is voluminous. For an overview of its principles, see Giap, *Military Art of People's War*, esp. 91–105; O'Ballance, *Greek Civil War*, 18; John Shy and Thomas W. Collier, "Revolutionary War," in Peter Paret (ed.), *Makers of Modern Strategy: From Machiavelli to the Nuclear Age* (Princeton, 1986), 815–862; Douglas S. Blaufarb, *The Counterinsurgency Era: U.S. Doctrine and Performance, 1950 to the Present* (New York, 1977), 3–14.

7. See Roger Trinquier, *Modern Warfare: A French View of Counterinsurgency*, Trans. Daniel Lee (London, 1964) 14–15, 33.

8. This discussion is based primarily on Randall B. Woods and Howard Jones, *Dawning of the Cold War: The United States' Quest for Order* (Athens, GA, 1991), esp. 3–32. See also R. Craig Nation, *Black Earth, Red Star: A History of Soviet Security Policy, 1917–1991* (Ithaca, NY, 1992), 145, 156–160, 170; Melvyn P. Leffler, *A Preponderance of Power: National Security, the Truman Administration, and the Cold War* (Stanford, CA, 1992); Hugh

Thomas, *Armed Truce: The Beginnings of the Cold War, 1945–1946* (New York, 1987); and Roberts, *Stalin's Wars*, esp. 245–249, 296–311.

9. Woods and Jones, *Dawning of the Cold War*, 11; see also Gregor Dallas, *1945: The War That Never Ended* (New Haven, CT, 2005), esp. 516–533.

10. Anthony Farrar-Hockley, "The Post-War Army, 1945–1963," in David G. Chandler (ed.), *The Oxford History of the British Army* (Oxford, UK, 1994), 316–317; and Michael Dewar, *Brush Fire Wars: Minor Campaigns of the British Army since 1945* (New York, 1984), 14–15.

11. Farrar-Hockley, "Post-War Army," 318; Dewar, *Brush Fire Wars*, 14.

12. Christopher Andrew, *Her Majesty's Secret Service: The Making of the British Intelligence Community* (New York, 1986), 488–493.

13. Thomas D. Boettcher, *First Call: The Making of the Modern U.S. Military, 1945–1953* (Boston, 1992), 3–5.

14. For the classic discussion of U.S. manpower tradeoffs, see Maurice Matloff, "The 90-Division Gamble," in Kent R. Greenfield (ed.), *Command Decisions* (Washington, 1959), 365–381.

15. Jeffrey G. Barlow, *From Hot War to Cold: The U.S. Navy and National Security Affairs, 1945–1955* (Stanford, CA, 2009), 46–51.

16. Bruce A. Elleman, *Modern Chinese Warfare, 1795–1989* (London, 2001), 225.

17. William W. Epley, *America's First Cold War Army, 1945–1950* (Arlington, VA, 1993), 4; Steven L. Rearden, *History of the Office of the Secretary of Defense*, Vol. 1: *The Formative Years, 1947–1950* (Washington, 1984), 12.

18. See Charles Chesterfield, "American Insecurity: Dissent from the 'Long War,'" in Andrew J. Bacevich (ed.), *The Long War: A New History of U.S. National Security Policy since World War II* (New York, 2007), 470–472.

19. www.treasurydirect.gov/govt/reports/pd/histdebt/histdebt_histo3.htm. Although $269 billion appears insignificant in comparison to the $13 trillion national debt of 2010, in proportion to the U.S. population and gross national product of 1946, it was indeed cause for alarm.

20. Rearden, *Formative Years*, 439.

21. For a detailed discussion of the dissolution of the OSS, see William R. Corson, *The Armies of Ignorance: The Rise of the American Intelligence Empire* (New York, 1977), esp. 228–247.

22. Harry H. Ransom, *Central Intelligence and National Security* (Cambridge, MA, 1958), 72–79.

23. Anne Karalekas, *History of the Central Intelligence Agency* (Laguna Hills, CA, 1977), 6.

24. Woods and Jones, *Dawning of the Cold War*, 18–21; Thomas, *Armed Truce*, 120, 129.

25. Woods and Jones, *Dawning of the Cold War*, esp. 12–15.

26. G. F. Krivosheev (ed.), *Soviet Casualties and Combat Losses in the Twentieth Century* (London, 1997), 94 gives the official, traditional figures; see Evan Mawdsley, *Thunder in the East: The Nazi-Soviet War, 1941–1945* (London, 2005), 404–405 for revisionist figures including the civilian deaths.

27. See Steven J. Zaloga, *Target America: The Soviet Union and the Strategic Arms Race, 1945–1964* (Novato, CA, 1993).

28. Brian Moynahan, *Claws of the Bear: The History of the Red Army from the Revolution to the Present* (Boston, 1989), 208–209.

29. Nation, *Black Earth, Red Star*, 156. The idea of Stalin as old fashioned in his view of strategy comes from my colleague Bruce Menning.

30. Roberts, *Stalin's Wars*, 311 and passim.

31. Ibid., 308–309.

32. Vladislav M. Zubok and Constantine Pleshakov, *Inside the Kremlin's Cold War: From Stalin to Khrushchev* (Cambridge, MA, 1996), 4.

33. Woods and Jones, *Dawning of the Cold War*, 22–23. For a detailed analysis of the Marxist world view, see Dick Combs, *Inside the Soviet Alternative Universe: The Cold War's End and the Soviet Union's Fall Reappraised* (University Park, PA, 2008), 139–153.

34. John Erickson, "The Ground Forces in Soviet Military Policy," *Strategic Review* 4:2 (April 1976), 65–66; Norman Friedman, *The Fifty-Year War: Conflict and Strategy in the Cold War* (Annapolis, 2000), 117–118. See also Nation, *Black Earth, Red Star*, 171.

35. For a detailed description of this structure, see the early chapters of Christopher Andrew and Vasili Mitrokhin, *The Sword and the Shield: The Mitrokhin Archive and the Secret History of the KGB* (New York, 1999).

36. Milstein quoted in Zubok and Pleshakov, *Inside the Kremlin's Cold War*, 14.

37. For an excellent introduction to this espionage and the decryption effort, see Robert L. Benson and Michael Warner (eds.), *Venona: Soviet Espionage and the American Response, 1939–1957* (Washington, 1996).

38. Thomas, *Armed Truce*, 326–328.

39. Ibid., 328–329; Anthony Beevor, *The Fall of Berlin, 1945* (New York, 2002), 140–146.

40. Thomas, *Armed Truce*, 149.

41. The Soviets withdrew from Bornholm in April 1946. Friedman, *Fifty-Year War*, 13–14, 51.

42. For a good survey of the condition of Europe in 1945, see Ibid., esp. 217–301. On the Soviet proconsuls, see Zubok and Pleshakov, *Inside the Kremlin's Cold War*, 113–117.

43. Bojan Dimitrijevic, "Yugoslav–Soviet Military Relations, 1945–1948," *Journal of Slavic Military Studies* 9:3 (September 1996), 581–583.

44. This discussion of Trieste is based on Roberto G. Rabel, *Between East and West: Trieste, the United States, and the Cold War, 1941–1954* (Durham, NC, 1988); and Alfred C. Bowman, *Zones of Strain: A Memoir of the Early Cold War* (Stanford, CA, 1982). Bowman was chief of staff of the British XIII Corps, which conducted the occupation.

45. Rabel, *Between East and West*, 47–54.

46. Bowman, *Zones of Strain*, 40–49, 114–115, 129–130.

47. David M. Glantz, *August Storm: The Soviet 1945 Strategic Offensive in Manchuria*, Leavenworth Papers No. 7 (Fort Leavenworth, KS, 1983).

48. Thomas, *Armed Truce*, 120–122.

49. See, for example, Edward J. Drea, *In the Service of the Emperor: Essays on the Imperial Japanese Army* (Lincoln, NE, 1998), 58–59, 202, 210, 215.

50. Allan R. Millett, *The War for Korea, 1945–1950: A House Burning* (Lawrence, KS, 2005), 48–49.

51. Boettcher, *First Call*, 45–47; Millett, *War for Korea, 1945–1950*, 50–59.

52. Elleman, *Modern Chinese Warfare*, 212–215, 223–224.

CHAPTER 3

1. Averoff-Tossizza, *By Fire and Axe*, 154–156; Wittner, *American Intervention in Greece*, 32; Stavrakis, *Moscow and Greek Communism*, 66–67.

2. O'Ballance, *Greek Civil War*, 113–116; Close, *Origins of the Greek Civil War*, 151–170.

3. O'Ballance, *Greek Civil War*, 116–117; Wittner, *American Intervention in Greece*, 44–46.

4. Quotation from Wittner, *American Intervention in Greece*, 46. The official name of the DAG was Demokratikos Stratos Eliados, but the English equivalent is used here for clarity. On Yugoslav-DAG cooperation, see Averoff-Tossizza, *By Fire and Axe*, 171, and O'Ballance, *Greek Civil War*, 121–122. O'Ballance asserts (122) that Stalin approved the creation of the DAG, but even if true, his policies at the time suggest that he intended it to be a minor irritant to gain leverage with the West, rather than to overthrow the Greek government. Stavrakis argues in *Moscow and Greek Communism*, 94–99 and 123–127, that Stalin favored a dual policy, keeping the armed option open but trying to avoid a crisis that might bring the United States into the struggle. Similarly, Andre Gerolymatos, *Red Acropolis, Black Terror*, 209, suggests that the initial armed attacks in 1946 were only meant to force concessions from the Greek government.

5. Averoff-Tossizza, *By Fire and Axe*, 166–170, 173; Wittner, *American Intervention in Greece*, 39–44; on the 1945 partial amnesty, see Gerolymatos, *Red Acropolis, Black Terror*, 194. The legitimacy of the 1946 elections is the key question in determining the popularity of the ensuing insurgency. Some authors, notably Dominique Eudes, *The Kapetanios: Partisans and Civil War in Greece, 1943–1949* (New York, 1972), 257 and passim, insist that most of the population supported the left in 1946. Close (*Origins of the Greek Civil War*, 174–176) argues that the elections were a sham, with up to 29 percent of the votes being invalid. Regardless of the degree to which these elections were rigged, however, the failure of the rebels to recruit sufficient troops (see note 9) suggests that the government had more legitimacy than the Communists.

6. O'Ballance, *Greek Civil War*, 122–123; Averoff-Tossizza, *By Fire and Axe*, 177.

7. Averoff-Tossizza, *By Fire and Axe*, 173–175.

8. O'Ballance, *Greek Civil War*, 129; Averoff-Tossizza, *By Fire and Axe*, 189–191; Greek Army General Staff, *The Nation's Battle: The Struggle of the Greek Nation against Communism till 19th August 1949* (Athens, 1952), 16–17.

9. Estimates of motivation and troop strength are highly subjective. See Greek Army General Staff, *Nation's Battle*, 13–15; Averoff-Tossizza, *By Fire and Axe*, 199–200 and passim; O'Ballance, *Greek Civil War*, 128, 199–203. On the arms supply, see Stavrakis, *Moscow and Greek Communism*, 177–178.

10. Wittner, *American Intervention in Greece*, 64–68, describes the British decision making in detail, contending that Bevin had no intention of withdrawing from Greece but wanted American help in paying for Greek defense. See also Robert Frazier, "Did Britain Start the Cold War? Bevin and the Truman Doctrine," *The Historical Journal* 27:3 (September 1984), 715–727.

11. Michael J. Cohen, *Fighting World War Three from the Middle East: Allied Contingency Plans, 1945–1954* (London, 1997), 51–57.

12. Leffler, *Preponderance of Power*, 142–146, and James A. Huston, *Outposts and Allies: U.S. Army Logistics in the Cold War, 1945–1953* (Cranbury, NJ, 1988), 132–136. Before launching this appeal publicly, on February 25, 1947, Truman invited the congressional leadership to the White House, after which Senator Hoyt Vandenberg, a Republican isolationist, endorsed the policy. Boettcher, *First Call*, 123–124.

13. Woods and Jones, *Dawning of the Cold War*, 145.

14. Wittner, *American Intervention in Greece*, 81–102.

15. Ibid., 87–88, 102–105. On the military aid program, see Huston, *Outposts and Allies*, 178–190.

16. Ibid., 224, 228, 230–131.

17. On Army morale and attitudes, see Close, *Origins of the Greek Civil War*, 201. For Operation Terminos, see Averoff-Tossizza, *By Fire and Axe*, 221–222; Greek Army General Staff, *Nation's Battle*, 21; Eudes, *Kapetanios*, 291–292, and other pro-DAG sources that claim the offensive was ineffective.

18. O'Ballance, *Greek Civil War*, 139–143; on female soldiers, see 1152 and Gerolymatos, *Red Acropolis, Black Terror*, 200.

19. The attempted kidnapping of General Scobie is recounted in Eudes, *Kapetanios*, 297.

20. O'Ballance, *Greek Civil War*, 144–145. Stavrakis argues in *Moscow and Greek Communism*, 161–165, that the attempt to gain a capital was based on the belief that, given the shortage of weapons and recruits, the DAG needed to take quick action before the correlation of forces turned even further against it.

21. Averoff-Tossizza, *By Fire and Axe*, 237–240 239 (Dovas quotation).

22. Wittner, *American Intervention in Greece*, 137–147; O'Ballance, *Greek Civil War*, 148; Close, *Origins of the Greek Civil War*, 189–192, 215.

23. On King Paul, see Eudes, *Kapetanios*, 291; Wittner, *American Intervention in Greece*, 119–125.

24. Griswold protested Chamberlin's interference in a letter to Major General Henry Vaughan, aide to the president, dated October 14, 1947, Truman Library, Official File [hereafter OF] 206–E, Box 779.

25. O'Ballance, *Greek Civil War*, 154–155; Wittner, *American Intervention in Greece*, 231–234; Rearden, *Formative Years*, 150.

26. Rearden, *Formative Years*, 151; Wittner, *American Intervention in Greece*, 234–236.

27. Rearden, *Formative Years*, 151.

28. Averoff-Tossizza, *By Fire and Axe*, 245–252; O'Ballance, *Greek Civil War*, 160–161.

29. Averoff-Tossizza, *By Fire and Axe*, 245–246; Eudes, *Kapetanios*, 307–308.

30. Averoff-Tossizza, *By Fire and Axe*, 271–278; Eudes, *Kapetanios*, 324–325.

31. Averoff-Tossizza, *By Fire and Axe*, 256–258.

32. O'Ballance, *Greek Civil War*, 166–167; Wittner, *American Intervention in Greece*, 241–242.

33. Wittner, *American Intervention in Greece*, 242–247; Memorandum, Secretary of State to President, July 29, 1948, and Letter, President to Griswold, September 15, 1948, Truman Library OF 206-E, Box 779.

34. Averoff-Tossizza, *By Fire and Axe*, 258–259; O'Ballance, *Greek Civil War*, 168. On the Air Force, see M. A. Campbell, E. W. Downs, and L. V. Schuetta, "The Employment of Airpower in the Greek Civil War, 1947–1949" (Maxwell AFB, AL, 1964), 40–41.

35. Averoff-Tossizza, *By Fire and Axe*, 281–284; O'Ballance, *Greek Civil War*, 171; Campbell et al, "Employment of Airpower," 44–45.

36. Averoff-Tossizza, *By Fire and Axe*, 285–290; O'Ballance, *Greek Civil War*, 171–173.

37. Eudes, *Kapetanios*, 330–331.

38. Zubok and Pleshakov, *Inside the Kremlin's Cold War*, 127–128, 131.

39. O'Ballance, *Greek Civil War*, 181–182; Averoff-Tossizza, *By Fire and Axe*, 254–255. Charles R. Shrader argues that the rebels could not compete in materiel terms with their U.S.-backed opponents; see *The Withered Vine: Logistics and the Communist Insurgency in Greece* (Westport, CT, 1999), esp. 263–266.

40. Wittner, *American Intervention in Greece*, 163; Eudes, *Kapetanios*, 317–318.

41. Averoff-Tossizza, *By Fire and Axe*, 292–294.

42. O'Ballance, *Greek Civil War*, 174–178; Averoff-Tossizza, *By Fire and Axe*, 280, 295–297.

43. Averoff-Tossizza, *By Fire and Axe*, 309–313.

44. Wittner, *American Intervention in Greece*, 248–250; Averoff-Tossizza, *By Fire and Axe*, 314–315; Close, *Origins of the Greek Civil War*, 218–219. On reform and military control, see D. Michael Shafer, *Deadly Paradigms: The Failure of U.S. Counterinsurgency Policy* (Princeton, NJ, 1988), 199–200.

45. O'Ballance, *Greek Civil War*, 188–193; Averoff-Tossizza, *By Fire and Axe*, 330–338.

46. Averoff-Tossizza, *By Fire and Axe*, 317–323; Wittner, *American Intervention in Greece*, 251–252, 270, 279. See Stavrakis, *Moscow and Greek Communism*, 179–184, on the Macedonian issue.

47. Averoff-Tossizza, *By Fire and Axe*, 339–345; Greek Army General Staff, *Nation's Battle*, 27–28; Campbell et al, "Employment of Airpower," 52–53.

48. O'Ballance, *Greek Civil War*, 197–200; Averoff-Tossizza, *By Fire and Axe*, 345–348. Stavrakis, *Moscow and Greek Communism*, 182, contends that Stalin ordered the border of Albania sealed to forestall a Greek incursion.

49. Memorandum, Truman to Secretary of Defense, May 27, 1950, in Truman Library, OF 206-F, Box 779.

50. Averoff-Tossizza, *By Fire and Axe*, 349–352.

51. On the reasons for the communist failure in Greece, see esp. O'Ballance, *Greek Civil War*, 204–219; Wittner, *American Intervention in Greece*, 253,

281. On the postwar effects of American aid on Greece, see Close, *Origins of the Greek Civil War*, 220–222.

52. James E. Miller, *The United States and the Making of Modern Greece: History and Power, 1950–1974* (Chapel Hill, NC, 2009), esp. 131–196.

53. Shrader, *Withered Vine*, 254. For the Italian case, see Chester J. Pach, Jr., *Arming the Free World: The Origins of the United States Military Assistance Program, 1945–1950* (Chapel Hill, NC, 1991), 138–142.

CHAPTER 4

1. This discussion is based on George Q. Flynn, *The Draft, 1940–1973* (Lawrence, KS, 1993), esp. 88–100.

2. Truman Library, OF 190-R, Box 815.

3. Flynn, *The Draft*, 95–98.

4. Epley, *America's First Cold War Army*, 4–6.

5. John B. Wilson, *Maneuver and Firepower: The Evolution of Divisions and Separate Brigades* (Washington, 1998), 214–221.

6. Abbott A. Brayton, "American Reserve Policies since World War II," *Military Affairs* 36:4 (December 1972), 140. For the problems of National Guard units after World War II, see William M. Donnelly, *Under Army Orders: The Army National Guard during the Korean War* (College Station, TX, 2001), 3–20.

7. Ibid., 14–15.

8. Hodge quoted in Millett, *War for Korea, 1945–1950*, 105.

9. Clarence G. Lasby, *Project Paperclip: German Scientists and the Cold War* (New York, 1971), esp. 27–44; Linda Hunt, *Secret Agenda: The United States Government, Nazi Scientists, and Project Paperclip, 1945 to 1990* (New York, 1991), esp. 25–50.

10. This section is based primarily on Michael T. Isenberg, *Shield of the Republic: The United States Navy in an Era of Cold War and Violent Peace, 1945–1962* (New York, 1993), esp. 80–97.

11. Ibid., 80, 89–91.

12. Barlow, *From Hot War to Cold*, 163–166.

13. Harry R. Borowski, *A Hollow Threat: Strategic Air Power and Containment before Korea* (Westport, CT, 1982), 28. This discussion of the origins of SAC is based largely on Borowski.

14. Kenneth Schafel, *The Emerging Shield: The Air Force and the Evolution of Continental Air Defense, 1945–1960.* (Washington, 1991), 54.

15. For the uploading procedure, see Richard H. Campbell, *The Silverplate Bombers: A History and Registry of the Enola Gay and Other B-29s Configured to Carry Atomic Bombs* (Jefferson, NC, 2005), 34–37.

16. Steven T. Ross, *American War Plans, 1945–1950: Strategies for Defeating the Soviet Union* (London, 1996), 14–17. The number of A-bombs is from Rearden, *Formative Years*, 439.

17. William S. Borgiasz, *The Strategic Air Command: Evolution and Consolidation of Nuclear Forces, 1945–1955* (Westport, CT, 1996), 3.

18. Ibid.

19. Ronald E. Powaski, *March to Armageddon: The United States and the Nuclear Arms Race, 1938 to the Present* (Oxford, UK, 1987), 30–33.

20. Rearden, *Formative Years*, 424–432.

21. Borowski, *Hollow Threat*, 74–87.

22. Boettcher, *First Call*, 23–30, 103–108. On Truman's attitude toward professional soldiers, see Michael D. Pearlman, *Truman and MacArthur: Policy, Politics, and the Hunger for Honor and Renown* (Bloomington, IN, 2008), 17–23.

23. Boettcher, *First Call*, 82–84; Rearden, *Formative Years*, 19–20.

24. On the problems of RAF-Royal Navy control, see Geoffrey Till in Williamson Murray and Allan R. Millett, *Military Innovation in the Interwar Period* (Cambridge, UK, 1996), esp. 208–211.

25. Leffler, *Preponderance of Power*, 197–176.

26. The Eberhardt Plan was published by the Senate Committee on Naval Affairs: "Report to the Honorable James Forrestal, Secretary of the Navy, On Unification of the War and Navy Departments and Post-War Organization for National Security," 79th Congress, 1st session, October 22, 1945.

27. Rearden, *Formative Years*, 21.

28. This discussion of NSA 1947 is based on Ibid., 23–26.

29. Ibid., 24.

30. See, for example, Andrew J. Bacevich, "Elusive Bargain: The Pattern of U.S. Civil-Military Relations since World War II," in Bacevich (ed.), *Long War*, 217–222.

31. Douglas T. Stuart, *Creating the National Security State: A History of the Law that Transformed America* (Princeton, NJ, 2008), 145–161, 278.

32. Leffler, *Preponderance of Power*, 171, 178; Boettcher, *First Call*, 169–171; Stuart, *Creating the National Security State*, 260.

33. Leffler, *Preponderance of Power*, 179.

34. Thomas, *Armed Truce*, 121–122; Boettcher, *First Call*, 188.

35. Leffler, *Preponderance of Power*, 20–21, 64–67.

36. Ibid., 159–163.

37. Roberts, *Stalin's Wars*, 314–317; Zubok and Pleshakov, *Inside the Kremlin's Cold War*, 104–107.

38. Rearden, *Formative Years*, 312. This defense budget included $4.6 billion for the army (half of it earmarked for the air force elements that were still in the process of separating from the army), $3.7 billion for the navy and marine corps, $1.5 billion for the air force, and $6 million for the Office of the Secretary of Defense.

39. David T. Fautua, "The 'Long Pull' Army: NSC-68, the Korean War, and the Creation of the Cold War U.S. Army," *Journal of Military History* [hereafter *JMH*] 61:1 (January 1997), 102–105.

40. Ibid., 106–107.

41. Rearden, *Formative Years*, 316–321.

42. Ibid., 310.

43. Jeffrey G. Barlow, *Revolt of the Admirals: The Fight for Naval Aviation, 1945–1950* (Washington, 1998), esp. 113–136. Much of this discussion is based on Barlow. See also Tami D. Biddle, "Sword and Shield: U.S. Strategic Forces and Doctrine Since 1945" in Bacevich (ed.), *Long War*, 143.

44. Boettcher, *First Call*, 168, 176.

45. Barlow, *Revolt of the Admirals*, 165.

46. Rearden, *Formative Years*, 136–137.

47. Barlow, *Revolt of the Admirals*, 123–124, 264–266. On relations between the air force and army aviation, see Frederic A. Bergeron, *The Army Gets an Air Force: Tactics of Insurgent Bureaucratic Politics* (Baltimore, 1980), esp. 53–55.

48. Barlow, *Revolt of the Admirals*, 130; Rearden, *Formative Years*, 398–401.

49. Keith D. McFarland and David L. Roll, *Louis Johnson and the Arming of America: The Roosevelt and Truman Years* (Bloomington, IN, 2005), 58–104.

50. Rearden, *Formative Years*, 44–48.

51. James E. Hewes, Jr., *From Root to McNamara: Army Organization and Administration, 1900–1963* (Washington, 1975), 271.

52. Letter, Navy Secretary Sullivan to Defense Secretary Johnson, April 26, 1949, Truman Library, OF 1285-C, Box 1625.

53. Barlow, *Revolt of the Admirals*, 185–191, 204–206, 223. See also Dale R. Herspring, *The Pentagon and the Presidency: Civil-Military Relations from FDR to George W. Bush* (Lawrence, KS, 2005), 65.

54. Barlow, *Revolt of the Admirals*, 226–233.

55. Quoted in Ibid., 253.

56. Ibid., 274–280; See also Herspring, *Pentagon and the Presidency*, 66–67.

57. Laurence W. Martin, "The Market for Strategic Ideas in Britain: The 'Sandys Era,'" *American Political Science Review* 56:1 (March 1962), 23–24; Nigel Hamilton, *Monty: Final Years of the Field Marshal, 1944–1976* (New York, 1986), 660–665.

58. S. A. Tyushkevich, *The Soviet Armed Forces: A History of Their Organizational Development* (Washington, 1984), 371.

59. Richard E. Simpkin, *Mechanized Infantry* (Oxford, UK, 1980), 31.

60. Erickson, "Ground Forces in Soviet Military Policy," 65–66; on NSC-57, see Powaski, *March to Armageddon*, 52.

61. Tyushkevich, *Soviet Armed Forces*, 373.

62. David Holloway, *Stalin and the Bomb: The Soviet Union and Atomic Energy, 1939–1956* (New Haven, CT, 1994), 78; Steven J. Zaloga, *Target America: The Soviet Union and the Strategic Arms Race, 1945–1964.* (Novato, CA, 1993), 1–2. Much of the following discussion of the Soviet atomic program is based on Zaloga's seminal work.

63. Holloway, *Stalin and the Bomb*, 83; on Fuchs, see Robert C. Williams, *Klaus Fuchs, Atom Spy* (Cambridge, MA, 1987), esp. 39–47.

64. Ibid., 14, 19.

65. Bruce Craig, "A Matter of Espionage: Alger Hiss, Harry Dexter White, and Igor Gouzhenko—the Canadian Connection Reassessed," *Intelligence and National Security* 15:2 (Summer 2000), 211–224; see also H. Montgomery Hyde, *The Atom Bomb Spies* (New York, 1980), 7–18. The scope of the Soviet espionage effort exceeds the focus of this book—for details, see Katherine A. S. Sibley, *Red Spies in America: Stolen Secrets and the Dawn of the Cold War* (Lawrence, KS, 2004).

66. Thomas B. Cochran, Robert S. Norris, and Oleg A. Bucharin, *Making the Russian Bomb: From Stalin to Yeltsin* (Boulder, CO, 1995), 15.

67. Zaloga, *Target America*, 44–45. For a contrary view, arguing the importance of espionage for both the Soviet and Chinese atomic programs, see Thomas C. Reed and Danny B. Stillman, *The Nuclear Express: A Political History of the Bomb and its Proliferation* (Minneapolis, 2009), 29–45, 87.

68. Reed and Stillman, *The Nuclear Express*, 37–62; Zubok and Pleshakov, *Inside the Kremlin's Cold War*, 147–151.

69. Robbin F. Laird, *The Soviet Union, the West, and the Nuclear Arms Race* (New York, 1986), 5.

70. Powaski, *March to Armageddon*, 53–57.

71. Zubok and Pleshakov, *Inside the Kremlin's Cold War*, 138–142.

72. Williams, *Klaus Fuchs*, 79, 95–96. The transfer of information was complicated by the 1946 McMahon Act, which limited sharing such information after the first revelations of espionage involving British scientists. See S. J. Ball, "Military Nuclear Relations between the United States and Great Britain under the Terms of the McMahon Act, 1946–1958," *The Historical Journal* 38:2 (1995), 439–454.

73. Brian Cathcart, *Test of Greatness: Britain's Struggle for the Atom Bomb* (London, 1994); Reed and Stillman, *Nuclear Express*, 46–48.

74. Tyushkevich, *Soviet Armed Forces*, 376.

75. Alexander Boyd, *The Soviet Air Force since 1918* (New York, 1977), 205–210.

76. Ibid., 212–214; Kenneth R. Whiting, *Soviet Air Power* (Boulder, CO, 1986), 37–38.

77. Boyd, *Soviet Air Force*, 220. For the effect of the blockade, see Friedman, *Fifty-Year War*, 80.

78. Boyd, *Soviet Air Force*, 215–216; Whiting, *Soviet Air Power*, 40.

79. Whiting, *Soviet Air Power*, 40–41; Boyd, *Soviet Air Force*, 223–224.

80. Roberts, *Stalin's Wars*, 321–322.

81. Ibid., 322–323; Boyd, *Soviet Air Force*, 216–217, 222; Von Hardesty, *Red Phoenix: the Rise of Soviet Air Power* (Washington, 1982), 213.

82. Robert W. Pringle, "SMERSH: Military Counterintelligence and Stalin's Control of the USSR," *International Journal of Intelligence and Counter-Intelligence* 21:1 (Spring 2008), 126. The role of SMERSH in discrediting Zhukov may have contributed to the elevation of its chief, General Viktor S. Abakumov, to succeed Beria as state security minister when the latter took control of the Soviet nuclear weapons program.

83. Harold Shukman (ed.), *Stalin's Generals* (New York, 1993), 103, 357–358. See also Roberts, *Stalin's Wars*, 32.

84. Roger R. Reese, *Red Commanders: A Social History of the Soviet Army Officer Corps, 1918–1991* (Lawrence, KS, 2005), 182–183.

CHAPTER 5

1. Nation, *Black Earth, Red Star*, 165.

2. For the trials of U.S. occupation in Austria, see James J. Carafano, *Waltzing into the Cold War: The Struggle for Occupied Austria* (College Station, TX, 2002).

3. See Bojan Dimitrijevic, "The Mutual Defense Aid Program in Tito's Yugoslavia, 1951–1958, and its Technical Impact," *JSMS* 10:2 (June 1997), 19–33. The author describes how Tito had to convince the United States that he needed conventional rather than guerrilla weapons. Thereafter, the United States provided many obsolescent armored vehicles, aircraft, and other weapons. When Stalin's successors offered improved relations, Tito broke off his cooperation with the West, which he found ideologically galling (30–31).

4. Zubok and Pleshakov, *Inside the Kremlin's Cold War*, 104, 125–133.

5. Josef Korbel, *The Communist Subversion of Czechoslovakia, 1938–1948: The Failure of Coexistence* (Princeton, 1959), 58.

6. Ibid., 67–72.

7. Ibid., 116, 166–168; Karel Kaplan, *The Short March: The Communist Takeover in Czechoslovakia, 1945–1948* (New York, 1987). Despite his role in the 1948 takeover, Svoboda was disgraced and imprisoned in 1951–1952 when his rival accused him of a pro-Western attitude and failure to reorganize the Czech armed forces along Soviet lines. He was eventually released as part of Khrushchev's de-Stalinization. See Mikhail Stefanski, "Soviet Impact on the Czechoslovak Armed Forces," in Robert S. Rush and William W. Epley, *Multinational Operations, Alliances, and International Military Cooperation: Past and Future* (Washington, 2006), 95–96.

8. For a good survey of the Czech position in 1945–1948, see the Secret cable from the U.S. Ambassador to Prague, No. 309, dated April 30, 1948. Reproduced in U.S. Department of State, *Foreign Relations of the United States* [hereafter *FRUS*], *1948, Volume 4: Eastern Europe, The Soviet Union* (Washington, 1974), 747–754.

9. Korbel, *Communist Subversion of Czechoslovakia*, 3–5; Rearden, *Formative Years*, 279–280.

10. Declaration reproduced in *FRUS, 1948, Volume 4*, 738.

11. Flynn, *The Draft*, 101–102; Leffler, *Preponderance of Power*, 209.

12. Flynn, *The Draft*, 100, 102–104.

13. Epley, *America's First Cold War Army*, 17.

14. Adrian R. Lewis, *The American Culture of War: The History of U.S. Military Force from World War II to Operation Iraqi Freedom* (New York, 2007), xix, 27–29.

15. Thomas, *Armed Truce*, 333.

16. Ibid., 320.

17. On Soviet occupation policy, see Norman M. Naimark, *The Russians in Germany: A History of the Soviet Zone of Occupation, 1945–1949* (Cambridge, MA, 1995), esp. 9–44, 71–90.

18. Timothy P. Ireland, *Creating the Entangling Alliance: The Origins of the North Atlantic Treaty Organization* (Westport, CT, 1981), 12–14. For details of planning for the occupation, see Kenneth O. McCreedy, "Planning the Peace: Operation Eclipse and the Occupation of Germany," *JMH* 65:3 (July 2001), 713–739.

19. Michael D. Haydock, *City under Siege: The Berlin Blockade and Airlift, 1948–1949.* (Washington, 1999), 22–24, 28–29.

20. Ann and John Tusa, *The Berlin Airlift* (New York, 1998), 29–48.

21. Ibid., 74; On the SED leadership, Stalin, and Berlin, see Zubok and Pleshakov, *Inside the Kremlin's Cold War*, 51–52.

22. Haydock, *City under Siege*, 7–8.

23. Ibid., 33–35.

24. On French policy, see U.S. Department of State, *FRUS, 1947, Volume 2: Council of Foreign Ministers, Germany and Austria* (Washington, 1972), 1073–1079.

25. Lucius D. Clay, *Decision in Germany* (Westport, CT, 1970), 132–133.

26. *FRUS, 1947, Volume 2*, 977, 1117–1128.

27. Leffler, *Preponderance of Power*, 117–121. The first Truman administration was weakened by the rapid departure of the leaders who had guided the United States through World War II. Some of these departures were the natural result of overwork for many years, but others were inspired by resentment against Truman's position and leadership style. For a complete list of the personnel during this period, see Boettcher, *First Call*, xiii–xv.

28. Leffler, *Preponderance of Power*, 198–199.

29. Bevin quoted in Leffler, *Preponderance of Power*, 208.

30. Tusa, *Berlin Airlift*, 92–93.

31. Ibid., 201 and following; Clay, *Decision in Germany*, esp. 354–357.

32. Clay to Chamberlin, March 5, 1948, quoted in Rearden, *Formative Years*, 281. For the status of the U.S. Constabulary in 1948, see Hofmann, *Through Mobility We Conquer*, 439–441.

33. Rearden, *Formative Years*, 280–283.

34. Avi Shlaim, "Britain, the Berlin Blockade and the Cold War," *International Affairs* 60:1 (Winter 1983–1984), 3–4.

35. Tusa, *Berlin Airlift*, 94–95.

36. Haydock, *City under Siege*, 125–127.

37. Tusa, *Berlin Airlift*, 116–117.

38. Quoted in Thomas Parrish, *Berlin in the Balance: 1945–1949: The Blockade, The Airlift, The First Major Battle of the Cold War* (Reading, MA, 1998), 157.

39. Ibid., 138–142.

40. Shlaim, "Britain, the Berlin Blockade," 3–4.

41. Clay, *Decision in Germany*, 365.

42. Haydock, *City under Siege*, 30–32.

43. Ibid., 365–366; Rearden, *Formative Years*, 288; Tusa, *Berlin Airlift*, 143–150.

44. Rearden, *Formative Years*, 292–293; Timothy J. Botti, *Ace in the Hole: Why the United States Did Not Use Nuclear Weapons in the Cold War, 1945 to 1965* (Westport, CT, 1996), 10.

45. Rearden, *Formative Years*, 292–293, 295 (quotation); Haydock, *City under Siege*, 143–145; Tusa, *Berlin Airlift*, 173.

46. Clay, *Decision in Germany*, 372–373.

47. Tusa, *Berlin Airlift*, 192–195; Haydock, *City under Siege*, 181.

48. Haydock, *City under Siege*, 158–159, 164, 180–181; Parrish, *Berlin in the Balance*, 193.

49. Tusa, *Berlin Airlift*, 168, 179, 236 and passim; Rearden, *Formative Years*, 288–290.

50. Tusa, *Berlin Airlift*, 168; Haycock, *City under Siege*, 173.

51. Parrish, *Berlin in the Balance*, 271.

52. Tusa, *Berlin Airlift*, 222–228, 249, 305; Haydock, *City under Siege*, 224, 238.

53. Tusa, *Berlin Airlift*, 248–249, 308; Haydock, *City under Siege*, 213–218, 293–294. For a list of U.S. fatalities, see James E. Wise, Jr., and Scott Baron, *Dangerous Games: Facts, Incidents, and Casualties of the Cold War* (Annapolis, 2010), 36–40.

54. Parrish, *Berlin in the Balance*, 251, 305; Tusa, *Berlin Airlift*, 235.

55. Tusa, *Berlin Airlift*, 235, 242–243, 308.

56. Parrish, *Berlin in the Balance*, 315–321; Roberts, *Stalin's Wars*, 355.

57. Rearden, *Formative Years*, 304–305.

58. Victor Gobarev, "Soviet Military Plans and Actions during the First Berlin Crisis, 1948–49," *JSMS* 10:3 (September 1997), 5–14.

59. Ibid., 7, 20–21.

60. Naimark, *Russians in Germany*, 369–373.

61. Ross, *American War Plans, 1945–1950*, 25–48; David A. Rosenberg, "American Atomic Strategy and the Hydrogen Bomb Decision," *Journal of American History* 66:1 (June 1979), 63–64; Friedman, *Fifty-Year War*, 63–65.

62. Cohen, *Fighting World War Three*, 132–139, 170–194, and passim.

63. Ross, *American War Plans, 1945–1950*, 54–56.

64. Ibid., 59–62. Rosenberg, "American Atomic Strategy," 69–77, argues that the budgetary cuts of the late 1940s forced the JCS to turn to a nuclear strategy. He also suggests that Secretary Johnson prevented President Truman from seeing the Harmon Committee Report (May 12, 1949), which asserted that nuclear attacks on Soviet cities would not necessarily achieve decisive victory, and might inspire greater resistance.

65. Scott D. Sagan, *Moving Targets: Nuclear Strategy and National Security* (Princeton, 1989), 15–17; David A. Rosenberg, "The Origins of Overkill: Nuclear Weapons and American Strategy, 1945–1960," *International Security* 7:4 (Spring 1983), 14–25.

66. Ireland, *Creating the Entangling Alliance*, 4–5.

67. Leffler, *Preponderance of Power*, 202–203; Rearden, *Formative Years*, 458–462.

68. Rearden, *Formative Years*, 464–469; Ireland, *Creating the Entangling Alliance*, 102–104, 122.

69. Quoted in Rearden, *Formative Years*, 474.

70. Rearden, *Formative Years*, 472–475; Ireland, *Creating the Entangling Alliance*, 122, 128–148.

71. Lawrence S. Kaplan, *The United States and NATO: The Formative Years* (Lexington, KY, 1984), 2.

CHAPTER 6

1. The Xi'an or Sian Incident figures prominently in most accounts of the Chinese Civil War. This summary is based on the following: Xu Youwei

and Philip Billingsley, "Behind the Scenes of the Xi'an Incident: The Case of the Lixingshe," *The China Quarterly* 154 (June 1998), 283–307; Elleman, *Modern Chinese Warfare*, 199–201; Jonathan Fenby, *Chiang Kai Shek: China's Generalissimo and the Nation He Lost* (New York, 2003), 1–13; and Tien-Wei Wu, "New Materials on the Xi'an Incident: A Bibliographic Review," *Modern China* 10:1 (January 1984), 115–141. On Zhang's difficulties with the Japanese, see Akira Iriye, "Chang Hsueh-Liang and the Japanese," *The Journal of Asian Studies* 20:1 (November 1960), 33–43.

2. Fenby, *Chiang Kai Shek*, 2–8.

3. Ibid., 6–13

4. Elleman, *Modern Chinese Warfare*, 201.

5. Youwei and Billingsley, "Behind the Scenes of the Xi'an Incident," 288–291.

6. John W. Garver, "The Soviet Union and the Xi'an Incident," *The Australian Journal of Chinese Affairs* 26 (July 1991), 145–175.

7. For a summary of the problems confronting China, see James P. Harrison, *The Long March to Power: A History of the Chinese Communist Party, 1921–72* (New York, 1972), 5–16.

8. Ibid., 46–49.

9. Liu, *Military History of Modern China*, 4–27.

10. Ibid., 37–46.

11. Fenby, *Chiang Kai Shek*, 145–161; Elleman, *Modern Chinese Warfare*, 171–174.

12. Elleman, *Modern Chinese Warfare*, 174–187.

13. Fenby, *Chiang Kai Shek*, 257–264

14. See, for example, John M. Nolan, "The Long March: Fact and Fancy," *Military Affairs* 30:2 (Summer 1966), 77–90.

15. Mark Selden, "Karl Marx, Mao Ze-Dong, and the Dialectics of Socialist Development," *Modern China* 3:4 (October 1977), 407–417; the linguistic observation is from Harrison, *Long March to Power*, 6.

16. William Wei, "'Political Power Grows Out of the Barrel of a Gun': Mao and the Red Army," in David A. Graff and Robin Higham (eds.), *A Military History of China* (Boulder, CO, 2002), 231.

17. Edward L. Katzenbach, Jr., and Gene Z. Hanrahan, "The Revolutionary Strategy of Mao Tse-Tung," *Political Science Quarterly* 70:3 (September 1955), 323–324.

18. Mao Tse-tung, *Selected Writings of Mao Tse-Tung* (Peking: Foreign Language Press, 1972), 64.

19. Ibid., 72.

20. Katzenbach and Hanrahan, "Revolutionary Strategy," 324–325. See also the classic analysis by Michael Elliott-Bateman, *Defeat in the East: The Mark of Mao Tse-tung on War* (London, 1967), esp. 82–106, 122–153.

21. Elleman, *Modern Chinese Warfare*, 208; on PLA training, see Steven I. Levine, *Anvil of Victory: The Communist Revolution in Manchuria, 1945–1948* (New York, 1987), 127–128; and William W. Whitson with Chen-Hsia Huang, *The Chinese High Command: A History of Communist Military Politics, 1927–71* (New York, 1973), 82–83.

22. Liu, *Military History of Modern China*, 149, 229, 248. The percentage of trained junior officers comes from Chang Jui-te, "The National Army from Whampoa to 1949," in Graff and Higham, *Military History of China*, 199.

23. For a contemporary analysis of KMT corruption, see Theodore H. White and Annalee Jacoby, *Thunder out of China* (New York, 1946).

24. Wedemeyer, *Wedemeyer Reports*, 301–309.

25. Philip Short, *Mao: A Life* (New York, 1999), 396–400.

26. Levine, *Anvil of Victory*, 30–32.

27. Odd Arne Westad, *Cold War and Revolution: Soviet-American Rivalry and the Origins of the Chinese Civil War* (New York, 1993), 29–52.

28. Donald G. Gillin and Charles Etter, "Staying On: Japanese Soldiers and Civilians in China, 1945–1949," *The Journal of Asian Studies*, 42:3 (May 1983), esp. 497–500.

29. Westad, *Cold War and Revolution*, 83–87; weapons numbers are from Liu, *Military History of Modern China*, 227–228.

30. Westad, *Cold War and Revolution*, 81–85.

31. Ibid., 88–90; Liu, *Military History of Modern China*, 229–230.

32. Benis M. Frank and Henry I. Shaw, Jr., *Victory and Occupation: History of the U.S. Marine Corps Operations in World War II*, Vol. 5 (Washington, 1968), 561, 570.

33. Henry I. Shaw, Jr., *The United States Marines in North China, 1945–1949* (Washington, 1960), 5, 9.

34. Frank and Shaw, *Victory and Occupation*, 533.

35. Shaw, *United States Marines in North China*, 1–8; Frank and Shaw, *Victory and Occupation*, 566–567.

36. Wedemeyer, *Wedemeyer Reports*, 360. See also Charles M. Dobbs, "American Marines in North China, 1945–1946," *South Atlantic Quarterly* 76:3 (1977), 318–331.

37. Shaw, *United States Marines in North China*, 5.

38. Boettcher, *First Call*, 52–53; John R. Beal, *Marshall in China* (Toronto, 1970), xxi. At Marshall's suggestion, the nationalist government appointed Beal as a consultant on the effects of their policies in America; his commentary is therefore a superb source.

39. Quotation from Eric Larrabee, *Commander in Chief: Franklin Delano Roosevelt, His Lieutenants, and Their War* (New York, 1987), 150. On Marshall's development, see especially Forrest C. Pogue, *George C. Marshall: Education of a General, 1880–1939* (New York, 1963), esp. 39–128.

40. Leffler, *Preponderance of Power*, 127–128.

41. Beal, *Marshall in China*, 25–26; Forrest C. Pogue, *George C. Marshall: Statesman, 1945–1959* (New York, 1987), 80–87. The details of the political and military agreements appear in Lionel M. Chassin, *The Communist Conquest of China: A History of the Civil War, 1945–1949* (Cambridge, MA, 1965), 72–75.

42. Pogue, *George C. Marshall: Statesman*, 113–116; Beal, *Marshall in China*, 350–351. For the long story of military aid to Chiang in the 1940s, see Chester J. Pach, Jr., *Arming the Free World: The Origins of the United States Military Assistance Program, 1945–1950* (Chapel Hill, NC, 1991), 64–86, 160–195.

43. Harold M. Tanner, "Guerrilla, Mobile, and Base Warfare in Communist Military Operations in Manchuria, 1945–1947," *JMH* 67:4 (October 2003), 1187. This section is based primarily on Tanner.

44. Ibid., 1196.

45. Ibid., 1192–1193, 1198.

46. Quoted in Ibid., 1196.

47. Levin, *Anvil of Victory*, 23, 40, 47.

48. Ibid., 77–82; O. Edmund Clubb, "Military Debacle in Manchuria," *The Army Quarterly and Defence Journal* 75:2 (January 1958), 222.

49. Whitson and Huang, *Chinese High Command*, 37.

50. Fenby, *Chiang Kai Shek*, 475.

51. Levin, *Anvil of Victory*, 107–120, 144–158.

52. Odd A. Westad, *Decisive Encounters: The Chinese Civil War, 1946–1950* (Stanford, CA, 2003), 128–137.

53. Clubb, "Military Debacle in Manchuria," 223.

54. Chassin, *Communist Conquest of China*, 121–126.

55. Jerome Chen, *Mao and the Chinese Revolution* (London, 1965), 286.

56. Ibid., 287–288; Liu, *Military History of Modern China*, 244–249; James C. Hsiung and Steven I. Levine, *China's Bitter Victory: The War with Japan 1937–1945* (Armonk, NY, 1992), 167–170.

57. Graff and Higham, *Military History of China*, 204–205.

58. Quoted in Lloyd E. Eastman, *Seeds of Destruction: Nationalist China in War and Revolution, 1937–1949* (Stanford, CA, 1984), 160.

59. Aid figures from U.S. Department of State, *The China White Paper, August 1949* (Stanford, 1967), 225–229.

60. Gary J. Bjorge, "Compound Warfare in the Military Thought and Practice of Mao Zedong and the Chinese People's Liberation Army's Huai Hai Campaign (November 1948–January 1949)" in Huber (ed.), *Compound Warfare*, 189–192. The author is indebted to Professor Bjorge for his guidance on Chinese military organization and for numerous helpful comments on this chapter.

61. Chassin, *Communist Conquest of China*, 46–49.

62. Bjorge in Huber (ed.), *Compound Warfare*, 182–187.

63. Jung Chang and Jon Halliday, *Mao: The Unknown Story* (New York, 2005), 296–299.

64. Ibid., 301–303; Westad, *Decisive Encounters*, 150–154. See also Peng Dehuai, *Memoirs of a Chinese Marshal–The Autobiographical Notes of Peng Dehuai (1898–1974)* (Beijing, 1984), 453–457.

65. Westad, *Decisive Encounters*, 168–172.

66. Shaw, *United States Marines in North China*, 15–17. For a detailed account of the Anping ambush, see Frank and Shaw, *Victory and Occupation*, 610–613.

67. Shaw, *United States Marines in North China*, 20–25.

68. Clubb, "Military Debacle," 224; Levine, *Anvil of Victory*, 129–132.

69. Clubb, "Military Debacle," 225–226.

70. Westad, *Decisive Encounters*, 173–176.

71. Ibid., 175–178; State Department, *China White Paper*, 318–319, 325.

72. Westad, *Decisive Encounters*, 177–178.

73. Ibid., 193–194.

74. Levine, *Anvil of Victory*, 134–136; Chassin, *Communist Conquest of China*, 187–189.

75. Levin, *Anvil of Victory*, 136; Chassin, *Communist Conquest of China*, 189–192; Westad, *Decisive Encounters*, 196–197.

76. Gary J. Bjorge, *Moving the Enemy: Operational Art in the Chinese PLA's Huai Hai Campaign*, Leavenworth Paper No. 22 (Fort Leavenworth, KS, 2004), 1, 55.

77. Westad, *Decisive Encounters*, 244–245; on the *Amethyst*, see also William Roger Lewis, "Hong Kong: The Critical Phase, 1945–1949," *American Historical Review* 102:2 (October 1997), 1076.

78. Lewis, "Hong Kong," 1080–1081.

CHAPTER 7

1. Clay Blair, *The Forgotten War: America in Korea, 1950–1953* (New York, 1987), 48–50. This account of Taejon is based on Blair and T. R. Fehrenbach, *This Kind of War: A Study in Unpreparedness* (New York, 1963), esp. 97–146, unless otherwise indicated.

2. Charles E. Heller and William A. Stofft (eds.), *America's First Battles, 1776–1965* (Lawrence, KS, 1986), 274.

3. Ibid., 288.

4. Blair, *Forgotten War*, 132–139.

5. The casualty figures and medal of honor citation are in Richard E. Ecker, *Korean Battle Chronology: Unit-by-Unit United States Casualty Figures and Medal of Honor Citations* (Jefferson, NC, 2005), 5–7.

6. William Stueck, *Rethinking the Korean War: A New Diplomatic and Strategic History* (Princeton, 2002), 1.

7. Allan R. Millett, "Korea and the End of the Cold War," in Malcolm Muir, Jr. (ed.), *From Détente to the Soviet Collapse: the Cold War from 1975 to 1991* (Lexington, VA, 2006), 114.

8. Millett, *War for Korea, 1945–1950*, 11–33.

9. Ibid., 85–91.

10. Chong-Sik Lee, "Politics in North Korea: Pre–Korean War Stage," *The China Quarterly* 14 (April–June 1963), 3–16; Charles K. Armstrong, *The North Korean Revolution, 1945–1950.* (Ithaca, NY, 2003), esp. 13–30.

11. Leffler, *Preponderance of Power*, 89–90, 251–253.

12. Millett, *War for Korea, 1945–1950*, 140–141.

13. Ibid., 142–150, 170–171, and passim.

14. Ibid., 200–234.

15. Roy E. Appleman, *South to the Naktong, North to the Yalu (June-November 1950)* (Washington, 1961), 8–9. On the transfer of Japanese equipment, see Sergei N. Goncharov, John W. Lewis, and Xue Litai, *Uncertain Partners: Stalin, Mao, and the Korean War* (Stanford, CA, 1993), 133.

16. Millett, *War for Korea, 1945–1950*, 243, 249–250; see also William G. Robertson, *Counterattack on the Naktong, 1950.* Leavenworth Papers No. 13 (Fort Leavenworth, KS, 1985), 5, 19–20.

17. Goncharov et al, *Uncertain Partners*, 130–136.

18. Ibid., 139–140; Roberts, *Stalin's Wars*, 366–369; Stueck, *Rethinking the Korean War*, 31, 72–73; see also Kathryn Weatherby, "Soviet Aims in Korea and the Origins of the Korean War, 1945–1950: New Evidence from Russian Archives," *Cold War International History Project Working Papers, No. 8* (Washington, 1993).

19. Doris M. Condit, *History of the Office of the Secretary of Defense*, Vol. II: *The Test of War, 1950–1953* (Washington, 1988), 45, 8.

20. Appleman, *South to the Naktong*, 12–17; Millett, *War for Korea, 1945–1950*, 240.

21. Weatherby, "Soviet Aims in Korea," 25.

22. On Soviet involvement in the North Korean plan, see Stueck, *Rethinking the Korean War*, 75; on the plan itself, see Appleman, *South to the Naktong*, 19–21, and Map I.

23. Chen Jian, *Mao's China and the Cold War* (Chapel Hill, NC, 2001), 87–88 and passim.

24. Robert F. Futrell, "USAF Intelligence in the Korean War," in James E. Dillard and Walter T. Hitchcock (eds.), *The Intelligence Revolution and Modern Warfare* (Chicago, 1996), 171–172. See also Allan R. Millett, *The War for Korea, 1950–1951: They Came from the North* (Lawrence, KS, 2010) 39–43.

25. Appleman, *South to the Naktong*, 31–33.

26. Stueck, *Rethinking the Korean War*, 62–65.

27. David C. Skaggs, "The KATUSA Experiment: The Integration of Korean Nationals into the U.S. Army, 1950–1965," *Military Affairs* 38:2 (April 1974), 53.

28. Reporters who researched this incident nearly fifty years later insisted on the accuracy of their version. There is no doubt that the No Gun Ri incident occurred, but the details and the intent of the American soldiers on the ground remain in dispute. See Charles J. Hanley, Sang–Hun Choe, and Martha Mendoza, *The Bridge at No Gun Ri: A Hidden Nightmare from the Korean War* (New York, 2001), and U.S. Department of the Army, Inspector General, *No Gun Ri Review* (Washington, 2001).

29. Inspector General, *No Gun Ri Review*, 97–98.

30. For an extensive discussion of the reinforcement issue, see James F. Schnabel, *Policy and Direction: The First Year* (Washington, 1972), 86–94.

31. Ibid., 93–94.

32. Ibid., 124–125. For the problems of National Guard mobilization, see Donnelly, *Under Army Orders*, esp. 21–88. By the end of the conflict, 43 percent of the Guard (138,600 men) had been called to active duty, 182.

33. Harry S. Truman, "Statement by the President of the United States (Truman) on the Korean Question, June 27, 1950," reproduced in *International Organization* 4:3 (August 1950), 551.

34. James A. Field, Jr., *History of United States Naval Operations Korea* (Washington, 1962), 62–67.

35. Charles Messenger, *History of the British Army* (Novato, CA, 1986), 201–202; Farrar-Hockley, "Post-War Army," 318–328; and Colin McInnes, *Hot War Cold War: The British Army's Way in Warfare, 1945–95*. (London, 1996), 34–46.

36. Condit, *Test of War*, 55–58.

37. Appleman, *South to the Naktong*, 252–255, 262–265.

38. On Chromite, see: Lynn Montross and Nicholas A. Canzona, *U.S. Marine Operations in Korea, 1950–1953*, Vol. 2: *The Inchon-Seoul Operation* (Washington, 1955); Appleman, *South to the Naktong*, 488–512; Field, *United States Naval Operations Korea*, 82–210; Shelby L. Stanton, *America's Tenth Legion: X Corps in Korea, 1950* (Novato, CA, 1989); and Robert D. Heinl, Jr., *Victory at High Tide: The Inchon-Seoul Operation* (Philadelphia, 1958). The results of these and other sources are synthesized in Jonathan M. House, *The United States Army in Joint Operations, 1950–1983* (Washington, 1992), 17–41.

39. U.S. Far East Command, CINCFE Operations Plan 100B, Draft No. 4, dated 12 August 1950.

40. Montross and Canzona, *Inchon-Seoul Operation*, 321–322.

41. Ernest F. Fisher, Jr., "Historical Resumé Concerning Intra-theater Airlift since World War II," unpublished transcript (1968) in Center of Military History.

42. Blair, *Forgotten War*, 273.

43. Appleman, *South to the Naktong*, 542–572.

44. Blair, *Forgotten War*, 269.

45. Stueck, *Rethinking the Korean War*, 103–104.

46. Appleman, *South to the Naktong*, 592–597, and Map VIII; Blair, *Forgotten War*, 307–316.

47. Blair, *Forgotten War*, 310–311.

48. Stueck, *Rethinking the Korean War*, 88–89; Condit, *Test of War*, 676–68.

49. Appleman, *South to the Naktong*, 655–659.

50. Zhou quotation from Goncharov et al, *Uncertain Partners*, 175; the Panikkar discussion is repeated in many accounts, including Stueck, *Rethinking the Korean War*, 89. The classic analysis in terms of Chinese self-defense is Allen S. Whiting, *China Crosses the Yalu: The Decision to Enter the Korean War* (Santa Monica, CA, 1960).

51. Stueck, *Rethinking the Korean War*, 101, 114–115.

52. Goncharov et al, *Uncertain Partners*, 159–163; Chen, *Mao's China*, 87–90. For a less aggressive interpretation of Mao's conduct, see Zhihua Shen and Danhui Li, *After Leaning to One Side: China and its Allies in the Cold War* (Washington, 2011), 40–50.

53. Goncherov et al, *Uncertain Partners*, 172–174.

54. Ibid., 187–195; Chen, *Mao's China*, 89–90. The red star removal is in Anthony Farrar-Hockley, "A Reminiscence of the Chinese People's Volunteers in the Korean War," *The China Quarterly* No. 98 (June 1984), 293.

55. Peng, *Memoirs of a Chinese Marshal*, 472–474.

56. Blair, *Forgotten War*, 279–280.

57. Ibid., 350–351; Appleman, *South to the Naktong*, 729–931, and Map XXV; Stanton, *America's Tenth Legion*, 146–170, 201.

58. Appleman, *South to the Naktong*, 672, 737–738.

59. Roy E. Appleman, *Defeat in Korea: The Chinese Confront MacArthur* (College Station, TX, 1989), 18–19; on Chinese weaknesses, see Xiaobing Li, Allan R. Millett, and Bin Yu (trans. and eds.), *Mao's Generals Remember Korea* (Lawrence, KS, 2001), 14.

60. Appleman, *South to the Naktong*, 673–675; for the Chinese side, see Xiaobing et al, *Mao's Generals Remember Korea*, 14.

61. Appleman, *Defeat in Korea*, 20–21; Blair, *Forgotten War*, 380–385.

62. Appleman, *Defeat in Korea*, 21–22.

63. Xiaobing et al, *Mao's Generals Remember Korea*, 15.

64. CIA memorandum for the President, Oct. 12, 1950, Enclosure A: "Threat of Full Chinese Communist Intervention in Korea;" National Intelligence Estimate Number 2, "Chinese Communist Intervention in Korea," 6 November 1950; and CIA Historical Staff, "Study of CIA Reporting on Chinese Communist Intervention in the Korean War, September-December 1950," October 1955, Top Secret; declassified June 2001. Page 2 of the latter study concludes that the principal problem was a U.S. misunderstanding of Chinese and Soviet strategy. All three reports are available from the CIA Freedom of Information Act Reading Room, www.foia.cia.gov/browse_docs.asp," accessed December 12, 2011.

65. Condit, *Test of War*, 75–76.

66. The Truman White House kept much of the relevant correspondence on this issue in a single file for reference. See Truman Library, President's Secretary's Files, Box 206, Korean War General Data.

67. Appleman, *Defeat in Korea*, 43–47; for order of battle, see Billy C. Mossman, *Ebb and Flow: November 1950–July 1951* (Washington, 1990), 26–29.

68. Mossman, *Ebb and Flow*, 22.

69. See Appleman, *South to the Naktong*, 759–770; David Halberstam, *The Coldest Winter: America and the Korean War* (New York, 2007), 372–383; and Fehrenbach, *This Kind of War*, 295–297.

70. Appleman, *Defeat in Korea*, 49–62.

71. Xiabing et al, *Mao's Generals Remember Korea*, 16; Fehrenbach, *This Kind of War*, 303–348. The classic analysis of this debacle is Samuel L. A. Marshall, *The River and the Gauntlet: Defeat of the Eighth Army by the Chinese Communist Forces November, 1950, in the Battle of the Chongchon River, Korea* (New York, 1953). After claiming impossible numbers of enemy vehicles destroyed or captured, Peng claimed that the UN forces were able to escape because they were so mechanized. See Peng, *Memoirs of a Chinese Marshal*, 475–47772. Mossman, *Ebb and Flow*, 47, 88–90. For the Almond-Wright debate and the roads, see Patrick C. Roe, *The Dragon Strikes: China and the Korean War: June–December 1950* (Novato, CA, 2000), 242–248, 260.

73. There are many accounts of the Changjin or Chosan Reservoir battle; this summary is from Stanton, *America's Tenth Legion*, 207–297, and Mossman, *Ebb and Flow*, 90–104, 128–150.

74. Lewis, *American Culture of War*, 114.

75. Totals derived from Ecker, *Korean Battle Chronology*, 62–63, 70.

76. Reportedly, Zhou Enlai decided that Mao had too much on his mind to be told of his son's death. The Chinese leader learned of his loss several months later when General Peng, visiting the capital to confer with Mao, blurted out an apology for Anying's death. See Short, *Mao: A Life*, 433–434.

77. Xiabing et al, *Mao's Generals Remember Korea*, 17–18, 21. On Mao's motives, see Chen, *Mao's China*, 95–97.

78. Appu K. Soman, *Double-Edged Sword: Nuclear Diplomacy in Unequal Conflicts: the United States and China, 1950–1958* (Westport, CT, 2000), 70–71.

79. Mossman, *Ebb and Flow*, 156–159.

80. Matthew B. Ridgway, *The Korean War: How We Met the Challenge; How All-Out Asian War Was Averted; Why MacArthur Was Dismissed; Why Today's War Objectives Must Be Limited* (Garden City, NY, 1967), 79–80.

81. Ibid., 85–91; Roy E. Appleman, *Ridgway Duels for Korea* (College Station, TX, 1990), 7–14; Mossman, *Ebb and Flow*, 183.

82. Mossman, *Ebb and Flow*, 184–217; Appleman, *Ridgway Duels for Korea*, 38–89.

83. Xiabing et al, *Mao's Generals Remember Korea*, 19–20, 34; see also Pearlman, *Truman and MacArthur*, 157.

84. Mossman, *Ebb and Flow*, 237–247.

85. Ibid., 285–299.

86. Xiaobing et al, *Mao's Generals Remember Korea*, 21, 35. For a slightly different translation, see Peng, *Memoirs of a Chinese Marshal*, 479.

87. Mossman, *Ebb and Flow*, 335–343.

88. Roger M. Anders, "The Atomic Bomb and the Korean War: Gordon Dean and the Issue of Civilian Control," *Military Affairs* 52:1 (January 1988), 1; Soman, *Double-Edged Sword*, 75; for details of the bomb cores, see Reed and Stillman, *Nuclear Express*, 133.

89. Condit, *Test of War*, 100–101.

90. Schnabel, *Policy and Direction*, 320–330.

91. See Michael D. Pearlman, "Korean War Anthology: Truman and Mac-Arthur: The Winding Road to Dismissal" (Fort Leavenworth, KS, 2003), and Pearlman, *Truman and MacArthur*.

92. There are many accounts of the decision to relieve MacArthur; one of the best is Condit, *Test of War*, 100–108. See also Bacevich (ed.), *Long War*, 223, for the civil-military context.

93. Mossman, *Ebb and Flow*, 351–362. By the spring of 1951, U.S. Army signals intercept units were able to penetrate Chinese communications, providing warning of the fifth offensive. Later that year, disguised KMT intelligence officers came to Korea to assist in the COMINT effort. See Matthew M. Aid, "American Comint in the Korean War (Part II): From the Chicom Intervention to the Armistice," *Intelligence and National Security* 15:1 (Spring 2000), 23–26, 33–34.

94. S. P. MacKenzie, "A Failure of Intelligence? The 29th Independent Infantry Brigade Group and the Battle of the Imjin, 1951." Paper read at the 76th annual meeting of the Society of Military History, Murfreesboro, TN, April 4, 2009, and provided by Professor MacKenzie.

95. Ibid., 410–428; Farrar-Hockley "Post-War Army," 324–328.

96. Peng's mission statement, quoted in Chandler (ed.), *Oxford History of the British Army*, 324.

97. U.S. Army Forces, Far East, and Eighth Army (Rear), *Logistics in the Korean Operation* (Tokyo, no date), Vol. 2, 124–125.

98. Mossman, *Ebb and Flow*, 378–379.

99. Xiaobing et al, *Mao's Generals Remember Korea*, 22.

100. Samuel L. A. Marshall, *Pork Chop Hill: The American Fighting Man in Action, Korea, Spring, 1953* (New York, 1956), 47, 196; Walter G. Hermes, *Truce Tent and Fighting Front*, U.S. Army in the Korean War Series (Washington, 1966), esp. 285–291. It is worth noting that this was a National Guard division.

101. Xiaoming Zhang, *Red Wings over the Yalu: China, the Soviet Union, and the Air War in Korea* (College Station, TX, 2002), 61, 84–85. Xiaoming indicates that the Soviets sent MiG-15s because of a shortage of MiG-9s, but Goncharov et al claim that Mao appealed directly to Stalin for new aircraft (*Uncertain Partners*, 200–201).

102. Xiaoming, *Red Wings*, 88–94.

103. Krivosheev, *Soviet Casualties and Combat Losses*, 281.

104. Xiaoming, *Red Wings*, 201–202. On the unauthorized overflights, see Conrad C. Crane, *American Airpower Strategy in Korea, 1950–1953* (Lawrence, KS, 2000), 165–167.

105. Crane, *American Airpower Strategy in Korea*, 77–79.

106. Ibid., 114–125, 168–172.

107. The classic but sensationalized study of American collaboration in captivity is Eugene Kinkead, *In Every War But One* (New York, 1959), esp. 17–21, 77–78, 159–165.

108. Hermes, *Truce Tent*, 233–240, 271.

109. Ibid., 240–262.

110. Soman, *Double-Edged Sword*, 86–100.

111. Rosemary J. Foot, "Nuclear Coercion and the Ending of the Korean Conflict," *International Security* 13:3 (Winter 1988–1989), esp. 94–99; Richard M. Leighton, *History of the Office of the Secretary of Defense*, Vol. III: *Strategy, Money and the New Look* (Washington, 2001), 1–4.

112. Foot, "Nuclear Coercion," 104–109. For the Chinese negotiating position, see Chen, *Mao's China*, 109–115.

113. Hermes, *Truce Tent*, 514–515.

114. Xiaobing et al, *Mao's Generals Remember Korea*, 6.

115. Chen, *Mao's China*, 2–4.

CHAPTER 8

1. President Eisenhower to General Alfred Gruenther, his successor as Supreme Allied Commander, Europe, October 27, 1953, classified Secret; declassified May 28, 1982, Eisenhower Library, Ann Whitman Papers, Administrative Series, Box 16.

2. Hamilton, *Monty*, 720–721, 728–729.

3. Ireland, *Creating the Entangling Alliance*, 169.

4. Quoted in Hamilton, *Monty*, 754–755.

5. Ireland, *Creating the Entangling Alliance*, 146–147.

6. Ibid., 123–129, 157.

7. U.S. Department of State, *FRUS, 1950, Volume 4: Central and Eastern Europe; The Soviet Union* (Washington, 1980), 684–695. See also John A. Reed, Jr., *Germany and NATO* (Washington, 1987), esp. 36–46. See Adenauer's concerns about rearmament in his *Memoirs 1945–53* (Chicago, 1966), 299–304.

8. Jean Monnet, *Memoirs*, trans. Richard Mayne (Garden City, NY, 1978), 342–347; Edward Fursdon, *The European Defence Community: A History* (London, 1980), 84–92.

9. Clarence C. Walton, "Background for the European Defense Community," *Political Science Quarterly* 68:1 (March 1953), 48–57.

10. Ibid., 42; Condit, *Test of War*, 329–335, 390–393.

11. Richard H. Immerman (ed.), *John Foster Dulles and the Diplomacy of the Cold War* (Princeton, 1990), 79–86; Kevin Ruane, *The Rise and Fall of the European Defence Community: Anglo-American Relations and the Crisis of European Defence, 1950–55* (New York, 2000), 152–165.

12. Andrew J. Birtle, "Rearming the Phoenix: American Military Assistance to the Federal Republic of Germany, 1950–1960," Ph.D. Dissertation, Ohio State University, 1985, esp. 162–205.

13. For the discussion of German rearmament problems, I am indebted to my colleague James S. Corum and especially to his paper, "Adenauer, Amt Blank, and the Founding of the Bundeswehr, 1950–1956," presented at the 75th Society for Military History Conference, Ogden, Utah, April 19, 2008.

14. Montecue J. Lowry, *The Forge of West German Rearmament: Theodor Blank and the Amt Blank* (New York, 1990), 56, 108.

15. Corum, "Adenauer, Amt Blank," 6–13.

16. David C. Large, *Germans to the Front: West German Rearmament in the Adenauer Era.* (Chapel Hill, NC, 1996), 97–99.

17. Ronald Smelser and Edward J. Davies II, *The Myth of the Eastern Front: The Nazi-Soviet War in American Popular Culture* (Cambridge, UK, 2008), 74–76.

18. James S. Corum, "Starting from Scratch: Establishing the Bundesluftwaffe as a Modern Air Force, 1955–1960," *Air Power History* 50:2 (Summer 2003), 21–26.

19. Lowry, *Forge of West German Rearmament*, 306.

20. Corum, "Starting from Scratch," 28.

21. Ireland, *Creating the Entangling Alliance*, 184–185, 215.

22. On the early history of the Supreme Headquarters, Allied Powers Europe (SHAPE) staff, see: William A. Knowlton, "Early Stages in the Organization of 'SHAPE'," *International Organization* 13:1 (Winter 1959), 1–18; Andrew J. Goodpaster, "The Development of SHAPE: 1950–1953," *International Organization* 9:2 (May 1955), 257–262; and Robert J. Wood, "The First Year of SHAPE," *International Organization* 6:2 (May 1952), 175–191.

23. Knowlton, "Early Stages," 11–14.

24. For the original command structure, see Wood, "First Year of SHAPE," 189–191.

25. Louis Galambos, Daun Van Ee, Elizabeth S. Hughes, and Robert J. Brugger (eds.), *The Papers of Dwight David Eisenhower*, Vol. 12: *NATO and the Campaign of 1952* (Baltimore, 1989), xvii, 64–69, 125–129, and passim.

26. Fautua, "'Long Pull' Army," 111–116.

27. Huston, *Outposts and Allies*, 162–165.

28. Ibid., 169; "North Atlantic Treaty Organization," *International Organization* 7:3 (August 1953), 433–435.

29. John S. Duffield, *Power Rules: The Evolution of NATO's Conventional Force Posture* (Stanford, CA, 1995), 75–121.

30. Galambos et al (eds.), *Papers*, Vol. 12, 621.

31. John Garnett, "BAOR and NATO," *International Affairs (Royal Institute of International Affairs)* 46:4 (October 1970), 674. Duffield, *Power Rules*, 88–89.

32. Huston, *Outposts and Allies*, 167–168; the $10 billion figure is from Goodpaster, "Development of SHAPE," 260.

33. Barlow, *From Hot War to Cold*, 322–325.

34. Cohen, *Fighting World War Three*, 261–269.

35. See, for example, Galambos et al (eds.), *Papers*, Vol. 12, 592–595, 594 (JCS quotation).

36. Goodpaster, "Development of SHAPE," 259–260.

37. Leffler, *Preponderance of Power*, 313–314, 355–360. For the general context of NSC-68, see Samuel F. Wells, Jr., "Sounding the Tocsin: NSC 68 and the Soviet Threat," *International Security* 4:2 (Autumn 1979), 116–158. Fautua, "'Long Pull' Army,"114–116, contends that NSC-68 provided the army with the political justification for its effort at restoring conventional warfare.

38. Acheson quoted in Ernest R. May (ed.), *American Cold War Strategy: Implementing NSC 68* (Boston, 1993), 98.

39. NSC-68 is quoted in Ibid., 23–28, 28 (quotation).

40. For a discussion of the implications of NSC-68, see Condit, *Test of War*, 6–11, 227–233.

41. John Lewis Gaddis and Paul Nitze, "NSC 68 and the Soviet Threat Reconsidered," *International Security* 4:4 (Spring 1980), 166.

42. Condit, *The Test of War*, 33–36.

43. Ibid., 225, 238–241.

44. Ibid., 229–240, 276–279.

45. Robert R. Bowie and Richard H. Immerman, *Waging Peace: How Eisenhower Shaped an Enduring Cold War Strategy* (Oxford, UK, 1998), 11, 125–145.

46. Saki Dockrill, *Eisenhower's New Look National Security Policy, 1953–61.* (New York, 1996), 3, 268.

47. Samuel F. Wells, Jr., "The Origins of Massive Retaliation," *Political Science Quarterly* 96:1 (Spring 1981), 31–35.

48. Duffield, *Power Rules*, 108–111; Cohen, *Strategy and Politics*, 123. On the JCS proposal for redeployment, see Leighton, *Strategy, Money and the New Look*, 147–179.

49. Condit, *Test of War*, 225.

50. Isenberg, *Shield of the Republic*, 341–344.

51. Karalekas, *History of the CIA*, 11–12, 30–33.

52. James Bamford, *The Puzzle Palace: A Report on America's Most Secret Agency* (New York, 1982), 15–17.

53. Wilson, *Maneuver and Firepower*, 242–247.

54. Ibid., 244–245.

55. Ibid., 252–253.

56. Leighton, *Strategy, Money and the New Look*, 421–422.

57. See, for example, Brian M. Linn, *The Echo of Battle: The Army's Way of War* (Cambridge, MA, 2007), 166–168; Fautua, "'Long Pull' Army," 118; Leighton, *Strategy, Money and the New Look*, 211–214, 365.

58. Maxwell D. Taylor, *The Uncertain Trumpet* (New York, 1959).

59. Mary T. Cagle, "History of the Basic (M31) Honest John Rocket System, 1950–1964 (U)," Historical Monograph AMC 7M, Part 1, Redstone Arsenal, AL, April 7, 1964.

60. This discussion of the Pentomic Division is based on: Theodore C. Mataxis and Seymour L. Greenberg, *Nuclear Tactics, Weapons, and Firepower in the Pentomic Division, Battle Group, and Company* (Harrisburg, PA, 1958), esp. 103–112; John H. Cushman, "Pentomic Infantry Division in Combat," *Military Review* 37 (January 1958), 19–30; Letter, U.S. Continental Army Command, January 8, 1959, Subject: Changes in ROCID TOE (U), with supporting Command and General Staff College documentation. See also Andrew J. Bacevich, *The Pentomic Era: The U.S. Army between Korea and Vietnam* (Washington, 1986); and Donald A. Carter, "From G.I. to Atomic Soldier: The Development of U.S. Army Tactical Doctrine, 1945–1956," Ph.D. Dissertation, Ohio State University, 1987.

61. Duffield, *Power Rules*, 3, 128–129, 132–134.

62. Zubok and Pleshakov, *Inside the Kremlin's Cold War*, 80.

63. May, *American Cold War Strategy*, 124.

64. Vojtech Mastny, Sven G. Holtsmark, and Andreas Wenger (eds.), *War Plans and Alliances in the Cold War: Threat Perceptions in the East and West* (London, 2006), 17.

65. Leffler, *Preponderance of Power*, 457–458; Roberts, *Stalin's Wars*, 356–359; Vojtech Mastny, "Learning from the Enemy—NATO as a Model for the Warsaw Pact" in Gustav Schmidt (ed.), *A History of NATO—the First Fifty Years*, Vol. 2 (New York, 2001), 158.

66. Andrew A. Michta, *Red Eagle: The Army in Polish Politics, 1944–1988* (Stanford, CA, 1990), 43.

67. See, for example, Jeno Gyorkei and Miklos Horvath (eds.), *Soviet Military Intervention in Hungary, 1956* (Budapest, 1999), 5–7; Mastny, "Learning from the Enemy," 159; and Robin A. Remington, *The Warsaw Pact: Case Studies in Communist Conflict Resolution* (Cambridge, MA, 1971), 10–16.

68. The text of the Warsaw Pact is available from Fordham University's Modern History Sourcebook, www.fordham.edu/halsall/mod/1955warsaw pact.html.

69. Mastny, "Learning from the Enemy,"159–168. On Hungary, see Tamas Nagy, "Hungary's Role in the Birth of the Warsaw Pact," in Rush and Epley, *Multinational Operations*, 119–121.

70. Mastny et al (eds.), *War Plans and Alliances*, 203.

71. Pal Germuska, "From Commands to Coordination; Defense Industry Cooperation within the Member-States of the Warsaw Pact, 1956–1965," in Rush and Epley, *Multinational Operations*, 101–107. On Stalin's "law," see Arnulf Baring, *Uprising in East Germany: June 17, 1953*, trans. Gerald Onn (Ithaca, NY, 1972), 5.

72. For the postwar evolution of the Soviet Army, see Jonathan M. House, *Combined Arms Warfare in the Twentieth Century* (Lawrence, KS,

2001), 191–196; John Erickson, "Soviet Combined-Arms: Theory and Practice" (Edinburgh, 1979), 55–58; Erickson, "Ground Forces in Soviet Military Policy," 66–68; and Tyushkevich, *Soviet Armed Forces*, 387–389.

73. Tyushkevich, *Soviet Armed Forces*, 389–391, 411; Erickson, "Ground Forces in Soviet Military Policy," 57–62; David M. Glantz, "Soviet Offensive Military Doctrine since 1945," *Air University Review* 34 (March-April 1983), 25–34. See also U.S. Department of the Army, Assistant Chief of Staff for Intelligence, Intelligence Research Project No. A-1729, "Soviet Tank and Motorized Rifle Division" (Washington, 1958).

74. Malcolm MacIntosh, *Juggernaut: A History of the Soviet Armed Forces* (New York, 1967), 291–296. Zhukov, an ardent nationalist, also disagreed with his government's 1956 compromise with the Polish leadership, as described below. See also Yosef Avidar, *The Party and the Army in the Soviet Union* (University Park, PA, 1983), 132–137, 148–173.

75. John Erickson, "Rodion Yakovlevich Malinovsky," in Shukman (ed.), *Stalin's Generals*, 121–123. On the Zhukov-Khrushchev relationship, see John Erickson, "The 'Military Factor' in Soviet Policy," *International Affairs* 39:2 (April 1963), esp. 218–219.

76. Avidar, *The Party and the Army*, 179–197.

77. George E. Hudson, "Soviet Naval Doctrine under Lenin and Stalin," *Soviet Studies* 28:1 (January 1976), 42–60.

78. Ibid., 61–65; Donald W. Mitchell, *A History of Russian and Soviet Sea Power* (New York, 1974), 474–476.

79. Aleksandr Fursenko and Timothy Naftali, *Khrushchev's Cold War: The Inside Story of an American Adversary* (New York, 2006), 76–77.

80. Ibid., 477, 518–519; George E. Hudson, "Soviet Naval Doctrine and Soviet Politics, 1953–1975," *World Politics* 29:1 (October 1976), 92–95, 102; MacIntosh, *Juggernaut*, 293.

81. Tad Szulc, *Czechoslovakia since World War II* (New York, 1971), 107–109.

82. Baring, *Uprising in East Germany*, 5–20.

83. Christian F. Ostermann (ed.), *Uprising in East Germany. 1953: The Cold War, the German Question, and the First Major Upheaval behind the Iron Curtain* (Budapest, 2001), 200.

84. See Soviet situation reports in Ibid., 196–219; the Brandenburg Gate incident is described on 217.

85. Baring, *Uprising in East Germany*, 133; Michta, *Red Eagle*, 50–51; Mark Kramer, "The Soviet Union and the 1956 Crises in Hungary and Poland: Reassessments and New Findings," *Journal of Contemporary History* 33:2 (April 1998), 168–170.

86. Szulc, *Czechoslovakia*, 134–138; Michta, *Red Eagle*, 50–51; Kramer, "Soviet Union and the 1956 Crises," 169–173.

87. See, for example, Kramer, "The Soviet Union and the 1956 Crises," 175–179, and Tibor Meray, *Thirteen Days that Shook the Kremlin* (New York, 1959), 5–23.

88. Jeno Gyorkei and Miklos Horvath (eds.), *Soviet Military Intervention in Hungary, 1956* (Budapest, 1999), 7–14; Szulc, *Czechoslovakia*, 139–140.

89. Gyorkei and Horvath, *Soviet Military Intervention*, 21–40, 58–59, 137, 234.

90. Ibid., 42–43.

91. On trouble elsewhere, see Kramer, "The Soviet Union and the 1956 Crises," 191–195. On Nagy, see Meray, *Thirteen Days*, 169–171. For General Kiraly, see Gyorkei and Horvath, *Soviet Military Intervention*, 85–87.

92. Gyorkei and Horvath, *Soviet Military Intervention*, 265–266; Kramer, "The Soviet Union and the 1956 Crises," 184–185.

93. Gyorkei and Horvath, *Soviet Military Intervention*, 104–107, 253.

94. Ibid., 158, 252, 261.

95. Ibid., 163–178, 262.

96. Ibid., 182, 204–205, 273.

CHAPTER 9

1. Gordon H. Chang, *Friends and Enemies: The United States, China, and the Soviet Union, 1948–1972* (Stanford, CA, 1990), esp. 99–109, provides an excellent discussion of these pressures.

2. See Brian M. Linn, *The Philippine War, 1899–1902* (Lawrence, KS, 2000).

3. Lawrence M. Greenberg, *The Hukbalahap Insurrection: A Case Study of a Successful Anti-Insurgency Operation in the Philippines—1946–1955* (Washington, 1987), 9–11; See also Uldarico S. Baclagon's anticommunist account in *Lessons from the Huk Campaign in the Philippines* (Manila, 1960), 243–246.

4. Luis Taruc, *He Who Rides the Tiger: The Story of an Asian Guerrilla Leader* (New York, 1967), 14–20.

5. A. H. Peterson, G. C. Reinhardt, and E. E. Conger (eds.), *Symposium on the Role of Airpower in Counterinsurgency and Unconventional Warfare: The Philippine Huk Campaign* (Santa Monica, CA, 1963), 2–3.

6. Robert R. Smith, "The Hukbalahap Insurgency: Economic, Political, and Military Factors," (Washington, 1963), 28–45.

7. Greenberg, *Hukbalahap Insurrection*, 26–33.

8. Shafer, *Deadly Paradigms*, 211–213.

9. Benedict J. Kerkvliet, *The Huk Rebellion: A Study of Peasant Revolt in the Philippines* (Berkeley, CA, 1979), 169.

10. Ibid., 166–169.

11. Peterson et al, *Symposium on the Role of Airpower*, 10–14.

12. Greenberg, *Hukbalahap Insurrection*, 69–74.

13. Kerkvliet, *Huk Rebellion*, 210–211.

14. See, for example, Shafer, *Deadly Paradigms*, 213–219.

15. Ibid., 74–77; Peterson et al, *Symposium on the Role of Airpower*, 34–35.

16. Kerkvliet, *Huk Rebellion*, 179–188, 216–223.

17. Greenberg, *Hukbalahap Insurrection*, 79–82.

18. Cecil B. Currey, *Edward Lansdale: the Unquiet American* (Washington, 1998), 6–51, 62–63, 70–74.

19. Ibid., 87, 128.

20. Ambassador to the Philippines (Cowen) to the Secretary of State, September 19, 1951, *FRUS, 1951, Volume 6, Part 2*, 1567.

21. Peterson et al, *Symposium on the Role of Airpower*, 17–18; Baclagon, *Lessons from the Huk Campaign*, 31.

22. Greenberg, *Hukbalahap Insurrection*, 132–133.

23. Smith, "Hukbalahap Insurgency," 119–123.

24. Blaufarb, *Counterinsurgency Era*, 31–38.

25. Kerkvliet, *Huk Rebellion*, 239; Peterson et al, *Symposium on the Role of Airpower*, 29–31.

26. Shafer, *Deadly Paradigms*, 235.

27. Currey, *Edward Lansdale*, 105–110.

28. Greenberg, *Hukbalahap Insurrection*, 134–138.

29. Kerkvliet, *Huk Rebellion*, 244.

30. See *FRUS 1951, Volume 6, Part 2*, 1541, 1549, and passim.

31. Taruc, *He Who Rides the Tiger*, 82.

32. Ibid., 91–92, 112–113.

33. Ibid., 133–145; Kerkvliet, *Huk Rebellion*, 247–248.

34. See, for example, Shafer, *Deadly Paradigms*, 205.

35. Smith, "Hukbalahap Insurgency," 115–118.

36. Joyce Kallgren, "Nationalist China's Armed Forces," *The China Quarterly* No. 15 (July-September 1963), 36–37.

37. Soman, *Double-Edged Sword*, 118–120.

38. Ibid., 117; Chang, *Friends and Enemies*, 81–90. On the F-84G question, see *FRUS, 1952–1954, Vol. 14, China and Japan*, Part 1, 168–170, 185–186. The same volume of *FRUS* contains an Appendix to NSC-148 (175–179), dated April 6, 1953, which stated that the United States would continue to seek either regime change in China or a distancing of Beijing from Moscow.

39. Soman, *Double-Edged Sword*, 123–126; "Memorandum of Discussion at the 213th Meeting of the National Security Council, Washington, September 9, 1954," *FRUS 1952–1954, Volume 14, Part 1*, 583–595.

40. Kenneth W. Allen, Glenn Krumel, and Jonathan D. Pollack, *China's Air Force Enters the 21st Century* (Santa Monica, CA, 1995), 56–58.

41. Soman, *Double-Edged Sword*, 121–123.

42. Isenberg, *Shield of the Republic*, 611.

43. Allen et al, *China's Air Force*, 58–61.

44. Isenberg, *Shield of the Republic*, 613–614.

45. Ibid., 614. On the secret guarantee of Quemoy and Matsu, see Chang, *Friends and Enemies*, 124.

46. Immerman, *John Foster Dulles*, 3–6, 235–238.

47. Chang, *Friends and Enemies*, 126–128, 132.

48. See, for example, O. Edmund Clubb, "Formosa and the Offshore Islands in American Policy, 1950–1955," *Political Science Quarterly* 74:4 (December 1959), 526–529. On Dulles's motives, see Soman, *Double-Edged Sword*, 149–153; and Chang, *Friends and Enemies*, 136–137.

49. Isenberg, *Shield of the Republic*, 615–623.

50. Chang, *Friends and Enemies*, 117; see also Huston, *Outposts and Allies*, 203, 220–221.

51. Kallgren, "Nationalist China's Armed Forces," 37–38.

52. Robert J. Watson, *History of the Office of the Secretary of Defense*, Vol. IV: *Into the Missile Age, 1956–1960* (Washington, 1997), 222–228.

53. Allen et al, *China's Air Force*, 62–63; see also the order of battle totals in Watson, *Into the Missile Age*, 224.

54. Allen et al, *China's Air Force*, 61–62; Christensen, *Useful Adversaries*, 9, 229–231; Soman, *Double-Edged Sword*, 169; Chang, *Friends and Enemies*, 173, 183–184, 186–187; Chen, *Mao's China*, 175–187.

55. Watson, *Into the Missile Age*, 224; Soman, *Double-Edged Sword*, 169, 174; Chang, *Friends and Enemies*, 187.

56. Soman, *Double-Edged Sword*, 175; Chen, *Mao's China*, 182–184; Allen et al, *China's Air Force*, 65–66.

57. Soman, *Double-Edged Sword*, 179–181.

58. Watson, *Into the Missile Age*, 230; Isenberg, *Shield of the Republic*, 623.

59. Chang, *Friends and Enemies*, 185, 188–190.

60. Watson, *Into the Missile Age*, 232–237; Chang, *Friends and Enemies*, 192.

61. Allen et al, *China's Air Force*, 66–67.

62. Ibid., 67; Watson, *Into the Missile Age*, 238–139; Isenberg, *Shield of the Republic*, 624.

63. On Mao, see Allen S. Whiting, "New Light on Mao, 3: Quemoy, 1958: Mao's Miscalculations," *China Quarterly* No. 62 (June 1975), esp. 265; the Immerman quotation is from his *John Foster Dulles*, 37.

64. Stephen E. Ambrose, *Eisenhower: Soldier and President* (New York, 1990), 379–382.

65. Huston, *Outposts and Allies*, 247–250.

66. Ibid., 249–251.

67. Watson, *Into the Missile Age*, 630–631. The remainder of this section is based on Watson.

68. Ibid., 622–628.

CHAPTER 10

1. This account is based on Jean Pouget's fictionalized memoirs, *Bataillon R.A.S., Algérie 1956* (Paris, 1981; reprinted 2007), especially 15–17. See also Alexander Zervoudakis, "A Case of Successful Pacification: The 584th Bataillon du Train at Bourdj de l'Agha (1956–57)," *Journal of Strategic Studies* 25:2 (June 2002), 54–65.

2. Carl von Clausewitz, *On War*, ed. and trans. by Michael Howard and Peter Paret (Princeton, 1976), 87.

3. Pouget, *Bataillon R.A.S.*, 17.

4. Martin Shipway, *The Road to War: France and Vietnam, 1944–1947* (Providence, RI, 1996), 1–5, 104, 160–161.

5. For periodization and conceptualization of this conflict, see Russell H. Fifield, "The Thirty Years War in Indochina: A Conceptual Framework," *Asian Survey* 17:9 (September 1977), 857–879.

6. Shipway, *Road to War*, 241–243. See also Alain-Gerard Marsot, "The Crucial Year: Indochina 1946," *Journal of Contemporary History* 19:2 (April 1984), 337–354.

7. Mark A. Lawrence and Fredrik Logevall (eds.), *The First Vietnam War: Colonial Conflict and Cold War Crisis* (Cambridge, MA, 2007), 102–103.

8. Ibid., 83–87, 100–101. On Chinese instruction, see Qiang Zhai, *China and the Vietnam Wars, 1950–1975* (Chapel Hill, NC, 2000), 11–12.

9. Lawrence and Logevall, *First Vietnam War*, 152, 160–161.

10. Ian F. W. Beckett and John Pimlott (eds.), *Armed Forces and Modern Counter-insurgency* (New York, 1965), 49–51.

11. Raoul Salan, *Indochine Rouge: Le message d'Ho Chi Minh* (Paris, 1975), 25–26; Beckett and Pimlott, *Armed Forces*, 55–56. On domestic opposition to the war, see Jacques Dalloz, *The War in Indo-China, 1945–54* (Dublin, 1990), 117–122.

12. Lawrence and Logevall, *First Vietnam War*, 8–9.

13. Salan, *Indochine Rouge*, 27.

14. Ibid., 29–30, 103.

15. United States, Office of the Chairman of the Joint Chiefs of Staff, *The Joint Chiefs of Staff and the First Indochina War, 1947–1954* (Washington, 2004), 36–37, 41–43. This study provides an excellent survey of the French difficulties in creating autonomous states in Indochina. On U.S. and French policy considerations, see Mark A. Lawrence, *Assuming the Burden: Europe and the American Commitment to War in Vietnam* (Berkeley, CA, 2005), 2–9.

16. Chen Jian, "China and the First Indo-China War, 1950–54," *The China Quarterly* No. 133 (March 1993), 86–88.

17. Qiang Zhai, "Transplanting the Chinese Model: Chinese Military Advisors and the First Vietnam War, 1950–1954," *JMH* 57:4 (October 1993), 693–699. Chen and Qiang used similar sources, primarily Chinese memoirs, to construct their analysis of the Chinese involvement.

18. Ibid., 701–702.

19. Dalloz, *War in Indo-China*, 113, 125–127; Fall, *Street without Joy*, 32–33.

20. Dalloz, *War in Indo-China*, 127–128, 144.

21. Michel Goya and Philippe Francois, "The Man Who Bent Events: 'King John' in Indochina," *Military Review* 87:5 (September-October 2007), 52–56.

22. Dalloz, *War in Indo-China*, 140, 143.

23. Goya and Francois, "Man Who Bent Events," 56–57; Fall, *Street without Joy*, 36–39.

24. Fall, *Street without Joy*, 41–46; Goya and Francois, "Man Who Bent Events," 58–59; Beckett and Pimlott, *Armed Forces*, 52–53.

25. Fall, *Street without Joy*, 49–59.

26. Beckett and Pimlott, *Armed Forces*, 53.

27. Qiang, "Transporting the Chinese Model," 704–707. On Bigeard, see Fall, *Street without Joy*, 66–71.

28. On the GCMA, see Bernard Fall's introduction to Roger Trinquier, *Modern Warfare: A French View of Counterinsurgency*, trans. Daniel Lee (London, 1964), 1–2; and Fall, *Street without Joy*, 269–278. For the Chinese involvement, see Dalloz, *War in Indo-China*, 148.

29. Dalloz, *War in Indo-China*, 155–157.

30. For details of the Navarre Plan, see *FRUS, 1952–1954, Volume 13: Indochina, Part 1* (Washington, 1982), 647–652, 744–747, 745 (quotation).

31. John Prados, *The Sky Would Fall. Operation Vulture: The U.S. Bombing Mission in Indochina, 1954* (New York, 1983), 19–24.

32. Ibid., 56–59; Beckett and Pimlott, *Armed Forces*, 54–55.

33. Chen, "China and the First Indo-Chinese War," 101–102.

34. This analysis is based upon Beckett and Pimlott, *Armed Forces*, 53–56; and Fall, *Street without Joy*, 162–172.

35. Fall, *Street without* Joy, 327–328.

36. Giap, *Military Art of People's War*, 130–138.

37. Office of the Chairman, *The Joint Chiefs of Staff and the First Indochina War*, 142–143; Eisenhower's explanation to the press is reproduced in *FRUS, 1952–1954, Volume 13*, 1034–1035.

38. Office of the Chairman, *The Joint Chiefs of Staff and the First Indochina War*, 154–162; Marilyn B. Young, *The Vietnam Wars, 1945–1990* (New York, 1991), 33–34. Prados, *The Sky Would Fall*, 44, 121, 147.

39. George C. Herring and Richard H. Immerman, "Eisenhower, Dulles, and DienbienPhu [sic]: 'The Day We Didn't Go to War' Revisited," *Journal of American History* 71:2 (September 1984), 343–363; Prados, *The Sky Would Fall*, 89–103, 115 (the domino analogy), 123–142.

40. Dalloz, *War in Indo-China*, 172–173; Beckett and Pimlott, *Armed Forces*, 54.

41. Dalloz, *War in Indo-China*, 188–197.

42. Young, *Vietnam Wars*, 42–45; Currey, *Unquiet American*, 156–165.

43. For an excellent analysis of French counterinsurgency, see Peter Paret, *French Revolutionary Warfare from Indochina to Algeria: The Analysis of a Political and Military Doctrine* (New York, 1964), esp. 20–79. See also Donn A. Starry, "La Guerre Révolutionnaire," *Military Review* 47:2 (February 1967), 61–70; John S. Ambler, *The French Army in Politics, 1945–1962*. (Columbus, OH, 1966), 308–327; and Frederic Guelton, "The French Army 'Centre for Training and Preparation in Counter-Guerrilla Warfare' (CIPCG) at Arzew," in Martin S. Alexander and J. F. V. Keiger, *France and the Algerian War: Strategy, Operations and Diplomacy* (London, 2002), 10–11. The Alexander and Keiger book first appeared as a special issue of the *Journal of Strategic Studies* 25:2 (June 2002).

44. Quoted in Dalloz, *War in Indo-China*, 183; on Faure, see Ambler, *French Army in Politics*, 215.

45. Ambler, *French Army in Politics*, 133–136, 192–195.

46. Alistair Horne, *A Savage War of Peace: Algeria 1954–1962* (London, 1979), 35.

47. Ibid., 33; Edgar O'Ballance, *The Algerian Insurrection, 1954–1962* (Hamden, CT, 1967), 28–33.

48. Horne, *Savage War of Peace*, 62–64.

49. See, for example, André Beaufre, *The Suez Expedition, 1956*, trans. Richard Barry (New York, 1969) 18. Beaufre was the French land commander for the Suez invasion.

50. John Talbott, *The War without a Name: France in Algeria, 1954–1962* (New York, 1980), 38–39.

51. O'Ballance, *Algerian Insurrection*, 40–41, 53.

52. Horne, *Savage War of Peace*, 85.

53. Jean Nicot, "Les S.A.S. et la Pacification en Algerie," *Revue Historique des Armées*, 1992 (4), 26–39; see also O'Ballance, *Algerian Insurrection*,

95; on revolutionary war, see Trinquier, *Modern Warfare*; and Alexander and Keiger, *France and the Algerian War*, 10–11.

54. Zervoudakis, "A Case of Successful Pacification," 54–64.

55. Starry, "Guerre Révolutionnaire," 61–70. See also Guelton, "French Army, " in Alexander and Keiger, *France and the Algerian War*, 35–53.

56. Horne, *Savage War of Peace*, 261–263; Alexander and Keiger, *France and the Algerian War*, xiii.

57. Keith Sutton, "Army Administration Tensions over Algeria's Centres de Regroupement, 1954–1962," *British Journal of Middle Eastern Studies* 26:2 (November 1999), 243–270.

58. Alexander and Keiger, *France and the Algerian War*, xi.

59. CIA World Factbook entry for Algeria, www.cia.gov/library/publications/the-world-factbook/geos/ag.html. Accessed December 12, 2011.

60. Paul Aussaresses, *The Battle of the Casbah: Terrorism and Counter-Terrorism in Algeria, 1956–1957*, trans. Robert L. Miller (New York, 2002); see also Horne, *Savage War of Peace*, 183–207; and Jacques Massu, *La Vraie Bataille d'Alger* (Paris, 1971). Massu commanded the 10th Parachute Division, with Aussaresses and Trinquier as his intelligence officers. For a summary of the battle, see Robert J. Kee, "Algiers—1957: An Approach to Urban Counterinsurgency," *Military Review* 54:4 (April 1974), 73–84.

61. Pouget, *Bataillon R.A.S.*, 91–92, 201–204; for the pro-torture view, see the comments of various officers in Massu, *La Vraie Bataille*, 151–162.

62. Ted Morgan, aka Sanche de Gramont, *My Battle of Algiers* (New York, 2005), 170–173.

63. Lou DiMarco, "Losing the Moral Compass: Torture and Guerre Révolutionnaire in the Algerian War," *Parameters* 36:2 (Summer 2006), 63–76.

64. O'Ballance, *Algerian Insurrection*, 60–61.

65. David Galula, *Pacification in Algeria, 1956–1958* (Santa Monica, CA, 2006; original, 1963), 6.

66. Matthew Connelly, "Rethinking the Cold War and Decolonization: The Grand Strategy of the Algerian War for Independence," *International Journal of Middle East Studies* 33:2 (May 2001), 221–245.

67. Horne, *Savage War of Peace*, 281–295. An excellent early reconstruction of the events of May 1958 is in Philip Williams, "How the Fourth Republic Died: Sources for the Revolution of May 1958," *French Historical Studies* 3:1 (Spring 1963), 1–40.

68. Williams, "How the Fourth Republic Died," 8–10.

69. Francois-Marie Gougeon, "The 'Challe' Plan, Counter-insurgency Operations in Algeria 12/1958–04/1960," MMS thesis, USMC Command and Staff College, 2005, esp. 14–24.

70. Connelly, "Rethinking the Cold War," 224–231.

71. Alexander and Keiger, *France and the Algerian War*, xiv–xvi.

72. Quoted in Ambler, *French Army in Politics*, 114.

73. Alexander and Keiger, *France and the Algerian War*, xvii–xviii.

74. Paret, *French Revolutionary Warfare*, 76–79; Beckett and Pimlott, *Armed Forces*, 67–73.

CHAPTER 11

1. The following account is based on Thurston Clarke, *By Blood and Fire: The Attack on the King David Hotel* (New York, 1981). See also Benny Morris, *1948: A History of the First Arab-Israeli War* (New Haven, CT, 2008), 8–61.

2. This discussion of Indonesia is based generally upon Cornelius W. A. J. Van Dijk, The American Political Intervention in the Conflict in the Dutch East Indies, 1945–1949, MMAS Thesis, U.S. Army Command and General Staff College, 2009.

3. Frances Gouda and Thijs Brocades Zaalberg, *American Visions of the Netherlands East Indies/Indonesia: US Foreign Policy and Indonesian Nationalism 1920–1949* (Amsterdam, 2002), 118–120.

4. Robert J. McMahon, *Colonialism and Cold War: The United States and the Struggle for Indonesian Independence, 1945–1949* (Ithaca, NY, 1981), 107–109.

5. Van Dijk, American Political Intervention, 32–34.

6. McMahon, *Colonialism and Cold War*, 168–171.

7. Ibid., 241–243; Gouda and Brocades Zaalberg, *American Visions*, 270–274.

8. Van Dijk, American Political Intervention, 79–82.

9. Michael Carver, *War since 1945* (New York, 1981), 12–13.

10. Anthony Short, *The Communist Insurrection in Malaya, 1948–1960* (New York, 1975), 26–27.

11. For an excellent discussion of British security problems, see Peter Dennis and Jeffrey Grey, *Emergency and Confrontation: Australian Military Operations in Malaya and Borneo 1950–1966* (St. Leonards, New South Wales, 1996), 7–9.

12. Richard Stubbs, *Hearts and Minds in Guerrilla Warfare: The Malayan Emergency 1948–1960* (Singapore, 2004), 253. For MCP labor efforts, see Richard Clutterbuck, *Conflict and Violence in Singapore and Malaysia 1945–1983* (Boulder, CO, 1985), esp. 45–81 and 195–210.

13. On British strategy in Malaya, see Ritchie Ovendale, "Britain, the United States, and the Cold War in South-East Asia, 1949–1950," *International Affairs* (Royal Institute of International Affairs) 58:3 (Summer 1982), 447–464; and Phillip Deery, "Malaya, 1948: Britain's Asian Cold War?" *Journal of Cold War Studies* 9:1 (Winter 2007), 29–54.

14. Short lays out the case for foreign direction of the insurgency in *The Communist Insurrection in Malaya*, 43–57; for the opposing argument, see Deery, "Malaya, 1948," 33–40.

15. Julian Paget, *Counter-Insurgency Operations: Techniques of Guerrilla Warfare* (New York, 1967), 46–47.

16. C. C. Chin and Karl Hack (eds.), *Dialogues with Chin Peng: New Light on the Malayan Communist Party* (Singapore, 2004), 135–136.

17. Ibid., 49, 51–54.

18. Stubbs, *Hearts and Minds*, 254–255; on the problem of distinguishing friend from foe, see Short, *Communist Insurrection*, 160–161.

19. Gurney to Commissioner of Police, December 12, 1948, quoted in Short, *Communist Insurrection*, 166.

20. Dennis and Grey, *Emergency and Confrontation*, 12.

21. The MCP Central Committee plan is quoted in Short, *Communist Insurrection*, 207.

22. Chandler (ed.), *Oxford History of the British Army*, 330–332; Short, *Communist Insurrection*, 114.

23. Chin and Hack, *Dialogues with Chin Peng*, 147–148.

24. Paget, *Counter-Insurgency Operations*, 54–55. On tactical sweeps, see John A. Nagl, *Counterinsurgency Lessons from Malaya and Vietnam: Learning to Eat Soup with a Knife* (Westport, CT, 2002), 79.

25. Paget, *Counter-Insurgency Operations*, 56–60.

26. Quoted in Short, *Communist Insurrection*, 235, 240.

27. Chin and Hack, *Dialogues with Chin Peng*, 153.

28. Karl Hack, "Corpses, Prisoners of War, and Captured Documents: British and Communist Narratives of the Malayan Emergency, and the Dynamics of Intelligence Transformation," in Richard J. Aldrich, Gary D. Rawnsley, and Ming-Yeh T. Rawnsley (eds.), *The Clandestine Cold War in Asia, 1945–65: Western Intelligence, Propaganda, and Special Operations* (London, 2000), 211, 215.

29. Paget, *Counter-Insurgency Operations*, 61; Dennis and Grey, *Emergency and Confrontation*, 18. The insurgent version of this incident is described in Chin and Hack, *Dialogues with Chin Peng*, 156–157.

30. On Templer's personality and appointment, see John Cloake, *Templer: Tiger of Malaya; The Life of Field Marshal Sir Gerald Templer* (London, 1985), esp. 200–205.

31. Dennis and Grey, *Emergency and Confrontation*, 19.

32. Paget, *Counter-Insurgency Operations*, 65.

33. Cloake, *Templer*, 283–288.

34. Ibid., 67–71.

35. Stubbs, *Hearts and Minds*, 256; Dennis and Grey, *Emergency and Confrontation*, 21 (for force numbers), 24–25, and passim.

36. Revisionists have suggested that the situation was already well in hand before Templer arrived. See Simon C. Smith, "General Templer and Counter-Insurgency in Malaya: Hearts and Minds, Intelligence, and Propaganda," *Intelligence and National Security* 16:3 (Autumn 2001), 60–78; and Kumar Ramakrishna, "'Transmogrifying' Malaya: the Impact of Sir Gerald Templer (1952–54)," *Journal of Southeast Asian Studies* 32:1 (February 2001), 79–82.

37. Ramakrishna, "'Transmogrifying' Malaya," 83–88; Cloake, *Templer*, 236–243, 268–269.

38. Nagl, *Counterinsurgency Lessons*, 96–97. Nagl also argues that many successful innovations emerged because the British regimental system was a learning institution that encouraged decentralized, independent ideas. However, the performance of line British units such as the Scots Guards provided little evidence to support this thesis, which is contrary to the historiography on the British Army in previous wars. Instead, Nagl cites former Special Operations Executive or Special Air Service experts as well as Lieutenant

Colonel Walter Walker, who as a Gurkha officer had many of the same attitudes later found in U.S. Special Forces about culture and working with foreign troops. Such examples do not appear to be typical of the British regimental system. 97, 192–194.

39. Chin and Hack, *Dialogues with Chin Peng*, 160–163.

40. Robin Neillands, *A Fighting Retreat: The British Empire 1947–1997* (London, 1996), 144–159.

41. Paget, *Counter-Insurgency Operations*, 72; on the aborigines, see Cloake, *Templer*, 256–258.

42. Jay G. Simpson, "Not by Bombs Alone: Lessons from Malaya," *Joint Force Quarterly* No. 22 (Summer 1999), 94–95, 97–98.

43. Ibid., 95–97; on S-55 helicopters, see Cloake, *Templer*, 245.

44. Ramakrishna, "'Transmogrifying' Malaya," 89; Smith, "General Templer," 66.

45. Deery, "Malaya, 1948," 54.

46. Ramakrishna, "'Transmogrifying' Malaya," 91; Cloake, *Templer*, 255.

47. Hew Strachan, "British Counter-Insurgency from Malaya to Iraq," *Journal of the Royal United Services Institute for Defence Studies* [hereafter *Journal of the RUSI*], 152:6 (December 2007), 9.

48. On the troubled history of Cyprus, see Nancy Cranshaw, *The Cyprus Revolt: An Account of the Struggle for Union with Greece* (London, 1978), 20–37.

49. Cranshaw, *Cyprus Revolt*, 67–75.

50. George Grivas, ed. Charles Foley, *The Memoirs of General Grivas* (New York, 1964), 2–23.

51. Ibid., 16; James S. Corum, *Training Indigenous Forces in Counterinsurgency: A Tale of Two Insurgencies* (Carlisle, PA, 2006), 27–28.

52. Carver, *War since 1945*, 55, 59.

53. Ibid., 52–53.

54. Corum, *Training Indigenous Forces*, 29–33, 33 (quotation); see also Panagiotis Dimitrakis, "British Intelligence and the Cyprus Insurgency, 1955–1959," *International Journal of Intelligence and CounterIntelligence* 21:2 (Summer 2008), 378–381. On the Turkish mob, see Grivas, *Memoirs*, 73–74.

55. Dewar, *Brush Fire Wars*, 73; Crawshaw, *Cyprus Revolt*, 176.

56. Carver, *War since 1945*, 56–57; Grivas, *Memoirs*, 77–81.

57. Dimitrakis, "British Intelligence," 383–389.

58. Miller, *The United States*, esp. 93–112, 177–194.

59. Fred Majdalany, *State of Emergency: The Full Story of Mau Mau* (Boston, 1963), 40–42.

60. Ibid., 58, 70.

61. David W. Throup, "The Origins of Mau Mau," *African Affairs* 84:336 (July 1985), esp. 403–408; Anthony Clayton, *Counter-Insurgency in Kenya: A study of military operations against Mau Mau* (Manhattan, KS, 1984), 1–2, 7, 21.

62. For servant betrayal and Mau Mau atrocities, see Neillands, *Fighting Retreat*, 176–186.

63. John Lonsdale, "Mau Mau of the Mind: Making Mau Mau and Remaking Kenya," *The Journal of African History* 31:3 (1990), 405–408.

64. Clayton, *Counter-Insurgency in Kenya*, 13–15.

65. For a detailed discussion of the Lari massacre, see Majdalany, *State of Emergency*, 138–147.

66. Ibid., 5–9; Carver, *War since 1945*, 33–36.

67. Carver, *War since 1945*, 36–37. The AT-6, known to the RAF as the "Harvard," is commonly labeled the "Texan." On the Kenya Police Reserve Airwing, see Majdalany, *State of Emergency*, 178–180.

68. Alan R. Waters, "The Cost of Air Support in Counter-Insurgency Operations: The Case of the Mau Mau in Kenya," *Military Affairs* 37:3 (October 1973), 96–98.

69. Clayton, *Counter-Insurgency in Kenya*, 23–26; Carver, *War since 1945*, 39–40.

70. Clayton, *Counter-Insurgency in Kenya*, 29–30; Majdalany, *State of Emergency*, 174–177.

71. Carver, *War since 1945*, 42–43.

72. Ibid., 43. On security abuse, see Clayton, *Counter-Insurgency in Kenya*, 37–59.

73. This introduction to the Portuguese conflicts is based primarily on John P. Cann, *Counterinsurgency in Africa: The Portuguese Way of War, 1961–1974* (Westport, CT, 1997), esp. 5–26.

74. Douglas L. Wheeler, "The Portuguese Army in Angola," *Journal of Modern African Studies* 7:3 (1969), 426–430.

75. John Marcum, *The Angolan Revolution*, Vol. 1: *The Anatomy of an Explosion (1950–1962)* (Cambridge, MA, 1969), 7–8, 47; the Labor Regulation of 1899 made it a crime for an African to be unemployed, facilitating forced labor. Rona M. Fields, *The Portuguese Revolution and the Armed Forces Movement* (New York, 1976), 20.

76. Cann, *Counterinsurgency in Africa*, 5, 20–22.

77. Willem Van der Waals, *Portugal's Wars in Angola, 1961–1974* (Rivonia, South Africa, 1993), 55–68; Cann, *Counterinsurgency in Africa*, 26–28.

78. Van der Waals, *Portugal's Wars*, 71–75, 79.

79. Thomas H. Henriksen, "Lessons from Portugal's Counter-insurgency Operations in Africa," *Journal of the RUSI* 123:2 (June 1978), 31–32; Henriksen, "People's War in Angola, Mozambique, and Guinea-Bissau," *Journal of Modern African Studies* 14:3 (September 1976), 378; Neil Bruce, "Portugal's African Wars," *Conflict Studies* No. 34 (March 1973), 2–4, 7–9.

80. Al J. Venter, *Portugal's War in Guinea-Bissau* (Pasadena, CA, 1973), 2, 82.

81. Thomas H. Henriksen, "Some Notes on the National Liberation Wars in Angola, Mozambique, and Guinea-Bissau," *Military Affairs* 41:1 (February 1977), 32–34; on PAIGC's success, see Henriksen, "People's War" 388, 397; and Piero Gleijeses, *Conflicting Missions: Havana, Washington, and Africa, 1959–1976* (Chapel Hill, 2002), 185–209.

82. Bruce, "Portugal's African Wars," 1.

83. Henriksen, "Lessons from Portugal's Counter-insurgency Operations," 32; Edgar O'Ballance, "To Turn His Coat—Or Not?" *Journal of the RUSI* 118:1 (March 1973), 87.

84. Thomas H. Henriksen, *Revolution and Counterrevolution: Mozambique's War of Independence, 1964–1974* (Westport, CT, 1983), 48–49; Van der Waals, *Portugal's Wars*, 70.

85. Henriksen, "Some Notes on the National Liberation Wars," 34.

86. Michael Calvert, "Counter-Insurgency in Mozambique," *Journal of the RUSI* 118:1 (March 1973), 82–83; O'Ballance, "To Turn His Coat," 85–87; for defectors in Mozambique, see Henriksen, *Revolution and Counterrevolution*, 104–108.

87. This discussion of resettlement is based primarily on Gerald J. Bender, "The Limits of Counterinsurgency," *Comparative Politics* 4:3 (April 1972), 331–360.

88. Henriksen, "Lessons from Portugal's Counter-insurgency Operations," 33.

89. Bender, "Limits of Counterinsurgency," esp. 337–345.

90. On counterinsurgency doctrine, see Cann, *Counterinsurgency in Africa*, esp. 51–54; the phrase "conquering hearts and minds" is quoted in Bruce, "Portugal's African Wars," 15.

91. Van der Waals, *Portugal's Wars*, 75; Bruce, "Portugal's African Wars," 7.

92. Calvert, "Counter-Insurgency in Mozambique," 83.

93. Venter, *Portugal's War*, 67.

94. Van der Waals, *Portugal's Wars*, 84–86.

95. Fields, *The Portuguese Revolution*, 37–56; the decline in exports is described in Douglas Porch, *The Portuguese Armed Forces and the Revolution* (London, 1977), 12.

96. Fields, *The Portuguese Revolution*, 2, 10.

97. Ibid., 2.

98. This comparison of the French and Portuguese military motivations is based on Porch, *The Portuguese Armed Forces*, 17–23, and Fields, *The Portuguese Revolution*, 2–10, 69–72, although the conclusions are my own.

99. Porch, *The Portuguese Armed Forces*, 22.

CHAPTER 12

1. General Paul D. Adams, interview with Colonel Irving Manclova and Colonel Martin Long, May 7–8, 1975 (transcript on file in U.S. Army Military History Institute), 25–29.

2. For the loss of Suez, see Cohen, *Fighting World War Three*, 124–138, 290–297, and 321; for Britain's strategic problem, see Cohen, *Strategy and Politics*, 11–33, 39–73, and passim.

3. Watson, *Into the Missile Age*, 48–50.

4. This account is based on David R. Devereux, *The Formulation of British Defense Policy towards the Middle East, 1948–56* (New York, 1990), esp. 40–73, 77–92.

5. Stephen E. Ambrose, *Ike's Spies: Eisenhower and the Espionage Establishment* (Jackson, MS, 1981), 189–214.

6. See Beaufre, *Suez Expedition*, 19, 31; and Donald Neff, *Warriors at Suez: Eisenhower Takes America into the Middle East* (New York, 1981), 161–162.

7. Mohamed H. Heikal, *Cutting the Lion's Tail: Suez through Egyptian Eyes* (New York, 1987), 34–40, 52–62.

8. In a 1950 tripartite declaration, the Western powers had agreed not to provide major weapons to either side in the Arab-Israeli conflict, although after the Czech arms deal, the United States quietly sold helicopters and scout cars to Israel and tolerated a Canadian decision to export twenty-four F-86s to Tel Aviv. U.S. Department of State, *FRUS, 1955–1957, Volume 16, Suez Crisis July 26–December 31, 1956* (Washington, 1990), 23–25.

9. Neff, *Warriors at Suez*, 256–263. For an alternative explanation that blames Egypt, see Herman Finer, *Dulles over Suez: The Theory and Practice of His Diplomacy* (Chicago, 1964), 47–52.

10. Eden to Eisenhower, July 27, 1956, quoted in *FRUS 1955–1957, Volume 16*, 9–11.

11. Ibid., 21–22; Watson, *Into the Missile Age*, 52–53.

12. On Eisenhower's policies, see Richard M. Saunders, "Military Force in the Foreign Policy of the Eisenhower Presidency," *Political Science Quarterly* 100:1 (Spring 1985), 97–116.

13. Heikal, *Cutting the Lion's Tail*, 119.

14. Saul Kelly and Anthony Gorst (eds.), *Whitehall and the Suez Crisis* (London, 2000), 35.

15. Beaufre, *Suez Expedition*, 34.

16. Eric Grove and Sally Rohan, "The Limits of Opposition: Admiral Earl Mountbatten of Burma, First Sea Lord and Chief of Naval Staff," in Kelly and Gorst (eds.), *Whitehall and the Suez Crisis*, 98–99, 104 (quotation), 108–109.

17. Kelly and Gorst (eds.), *Whitehall and the Suez Crisis*, 36. Mountbatten reportedly asked Eden for a letter holding the military blameless for the war and threatened to resign when Eden refused. Cohen, *Strategy and Politics*, 161.

18. Avi Shlaim, *The Iron Wall: Israel and the Arab World* (New York, 2001), 32, 38–39, 49–53, 62–76. Shlaim embodies the revisionist interpretation that Israeli leaders were as responsible as their Arab counterparts for the failure to reach a peace agreement in the early 1950s. On Israeli retaliations, see Ze'ev Schiff, *A History of the Israeli Army, 1874 to the Present* (New York, 1985), 73–76.

19. Mordechai Bar-On, *The Gates of Gaza: Israel's Road to Suez and Back, 1955–1957* (New York, 1994), 1–12, 15–20, 32–35, 201–207.

20. Reed and Stillman, *Nuclear Express*, 73–75.

21. Shimon Peres, "The Road to Sevres: Franco-Israeli Strategic Cooperation," in Selwyn I. Troen and Moshe Shemesh (eds.), *The Suez-Sinai Crisis 1956* (New York, 1990), 140–149; see also W. Scott Lucas, "Redefining the Suez 'Collusion,'" *Middle East Studies* 26:1 (January 1990), 88–112. According to Bar-On (*Gates of Gaza*, 240–243), Eden never intended to acknowledge the agreement and was furious when he learned that a British diplomat had signed a document with the Israelis and French.

22. Roy Fullick and Geoffrey Powell, *Suez: The Double War* (London, 1979), 45–51.

23. Moshe Dayan, *Diary of the Sinai Campaign* (New York, 1966), 62–63, 77–89, 91–93.

24. George W. Gawrych, *Key to the Sinai: The Battles for Abu Agheila in the 1956 and 1967 Arab-Israeli Wars*, Research Survey No. 7 (Fort Leavenworth, KS, 1990), 14–19, 44–59; Kenneth M. Pollack, *Arabs at War: Military Effectiveness, 1948–1991* (Lincoln, NE, 2004), 30–35.

25. Dayan, *Diary of the Sinai Campaign*, 100–103. Dayan insists that the 202nd Brigade commander, Ariel Sharon, had exceeded his instructions and should not have entered the pass without careful reconnaissance.

26. Quotation in Dayan, *Diary of the Sinai Campaign*, 163. For the air strike delay and liaison issues, see Motti Golani, "The Sinai War, 1956: Three Partners, Three Wars," in David Tal (ed.), *The 1956 War: Collusion and Rivalry in the Middle East* (London, 2001), 171–178. See also Dayan, *Diary of the Sinai Campaign*, 161–162.

27. Cohen, *Strategy and Politics*, 159, 165–166.

28. Memorandum of Conference with the President, October 30, 1956, classified Top Secret; declassified September 11, 1978, Eisenhower Library, John Foster Dulles Papers, White House Memoranda Series, Box 4.

29. Finer, *Dulles over Suez*, 6.

30. Fullick and Powell, *Suez: The Double War*, 19, 109–117, 128–136, 144–150; Beaufre, *Suez Expedition*, 103–109.

31. Pollack, *Arabs at War*, 35–36; 39; Gawrych, *Key to the Sinai*, 59–60; Heikal, *Cutting the Lion's Tail*, 180–181, 194.

32. Bernard B. Fall, "The Two Sides of the Sinai Campaign," *Military Review* 37: 4 (July 1957), 19–20; Dayan, *Diary of the Sinai Campaign*, 163–166, 184–186.

33. Heikal, *Cutting the Lion's Tail*, 201.

34. Charles A. Kupchan, "American Globalism in the Middle East: The Roots of Regional Security Policy," *Political Science Quarterly* 103:4 (Winter 1988–1989), 589–590.

35. On the Eisenhower Doctrine, see Finer, *Dulles over Suez*, 497–500. The evolution of this doctrine and supporting congressional resolutions is traced in U.S. Department of State, *FRUS, 1955–1957, Volume 12: Near East Region; Iran; Iraq* (Washington, 1991), esp. 437–439.

36. Various memoranda and reports in U.S. Department of State, *FRUS, 1958–1960, Volume 9: Lebanon and Jordan* (Washington, 1992), esp. 5–14. The situation is traced in this volume of *FRUS* and in Irene L. Gendzier, *Notes from the Minefield: United States Intervention in Lebanon and the Middle East, 1945–1958* (New York, 1997).

37. Quoted in Roger Spiller, *Not War but Like War: The American Intervention in Lebanon*. (Fort Leavenworth, KS, 1981), 14.

38. *FRUS 1958–1960, Volume 9*, esp. 27–51.

39. Gary H. Wade, *Rapid Deployment Logistics: Lebanon, 1958*, Research Study No. 3 (Fort Leavenworth, KS, 1984), 8–9.

40. Ibid., 11–15, 85–91; Spiller, *"Not War,"* 10–13. The following account of Lebanon is based on these two sources plus U.S. Army, Europe (USAREUR), Historical Division, *The U.S. Army Task Force in Lebanon* (Heidelberg, FRG, 1959). See also David W. Gray, *The U.S. Intervention in Lebanon, 1958: A Commander's Reminiscence* (Fort Leavenworth, KS, 1984).

41. Wade, *Rapid Deployment Logistics*, 27.

42. Jack Shulimson, "Marines in Lebanon, 1958," (Washington, no date), 7–8.

43. Spiller, *"Not War,"* 16. For the scene at Furstenfeldbruck, see Gray, *U.S. Intervention in Lebanon*, 14–16.

44. Shulimson, "Marines in Lebanon," 12–13.

45. Ibid., 13–15.

46. Wade, *Rapid Deployment Logistics*, 31–33.

47. Ibid., 33–34.

48. Ibid., 35–41.

49. Memorandum for the President, Subject: Radio Coverage for the Middle East, Karl G. Harr, Jr., dated July 23, 1958, classified Secret; declassified September 6, 1996, Eisenhower Library, Whitman Papers, International Series, Box 40.

50. Spiller, *"Not War,"* 39–42.

51. Adams Interview with Manclova and Long.

52. Ibid.; USAREUR Historical Division, *U.S. Army Task Force in Lebanon*, 38–39.

53. COMLANFOR After-Action Report, quoted in Shulimson, "Marines in Lebanon," 32.

54. Ibid., 33–35.

55. Quoted in Grendzier, *Notes from the Minefield*, 329.

56. Chandler, *Oxford History of the British Army*, 340.

57. Stephen Blackwell, *British Military Intervention and the Struggle for Jordan: King Hussein, Nasser, and the Middle East Crisis, 1955–1958* (New York, 2009), 127–129.

58. Ibid., 130–140. The British plan and limitations are discussed in Department of State, Memorandum of Conversation, July 17, 1958, classified Top Secret; declassified October 23, 1992, Eisenhower Library, Whitman Papers, International Series, Box 40.

59. Blackwell, *British Military Intervention*, 160.

60. Fursenko and Naftali, *Khrushchev's Cold War*, 165–171, 182.

61. Cohen, *Strategy and Politics*, 205–219.

62. Chandler (ed.), *Oxford History of the British Army*, 341.

63. This discussion of Aden is based primarily on Ibid., 344–345, and Carver, *War since 1945*, 62–82.

64. Carver, *War since 1945*, 65–66.

65. Ibid., 71–73.

66. Ibid., 81.

CHAPTER 13

1. During the 1980s and 1990s, this unsourced quotation hung on the wall of the Soviet analytical section of the J2 (Intelligence) staff of the Joint Chiefs of Staff in the Pentagon. Even if the quotation itself is apocryphal, it reflects the attitude of many planners during the Cold War.

2. Zaloga, *Target America*, 193–197.

3. Gerald H. Clarfield and William M. Wiecek, *Nuclear America: Military and Civilian Nuclear Power in the United States, 1940–1980* (New York, 1984) 128–134.

4. Rosenberg, "American Atomic Strategy," 80–85.

5. Reed and Stillman, *Nuclear Express*, 51.

6. Condit, *Test of War*, 477–481, 481 (quotation).

7. Cochran et al, *Making the Russian Bomb*, 17–19; Reed and Stillman, *Nuclear Express*, 38–42.

8. Cochran et al, *Making the Russian Bomb*, 472–473; weapons numbers are from Sagan, *Moving Targets*, 19.

9. Cochran et al, *Making the Russian Bomb*, 20, 33–35; Friedman, *Fifty-Year War*, 136.

10. Cochran et al, *Making the Russian Bomb*, 98–102.

11. "Preliminary Report Following the Second Atomic Bomb Test. Report of the Joint Chiefs of Staff Evaluation Board for the Atomic Bomb Tests," dated July 30, 1946, Truman Library, OF 692-G, Box 1533.

12. This discussion is based primarily on Clarfield and Wiecek, *Nuclear America*, 201–223.

13. Isenberg, *Shield of the Republic*, 386–405.

14. Jan Breemer, *Soviet Submarines: Design, Development and Tactics* (Coulsdon, Surrey, UK, 1989), 78–104.

15. Borgiasz, *Strategic Air Command*, 93–97.

16. Ibid., 99–104.

17. Friedman, *Fifty-Year War*, 147.

18. A. G. Trevenen James, *The Royal Air Force: The Past 30 Years* (London, 1976), 51–52, 61, and passim.

19. Lawrence S. Kaplan, Ronald D. Landa, and Edward J. Drea, *History of the Office of the Secretary of Defense*, Vol. V: *The McNamara Ascendancy 1961–1965* (Washington, 2006), 375–384.

20. Trevenen James, *Royal Air Force*, 97–98.

21. R. A. Mason and John W. R. Taylor, *Aircraft, Strategy, and Operations of the Soviet Air Force* (London, 1986), 130–137, 237–242.

22. Clarfield and Wiecek, *Nuclear America*, 161–162. SAC aircraft figures for 1956 are from Norman Polmar (ed.), *Strategic Air Command: People, Aircraft, and Missiles* (Annapolis, 1979), 44, 66.

23. Asif A. Siddiqi, "Russians in Germany: Founding the Post-War Missile Programme," *Europe-Asia Studies* 56:8 (December 2004), 1131–1156.

24. Alan J. Levine, *The Missile and Space Race* (Westport, CT, 1994), 22–23.

25. Ibid., 45–46, and Fursenko and Naftali, *Khrushchev's Cold War*, 194, 211; for details of the test series, see "R-7 ICBM(8K7) Family" at www.russianspaceweb.com/r7.html. See also James C. Dick, "The Strategic Arms Race, 1957–61: Who Opened a Missile Gap?" *The Journal of Politics* 34:4 (November 1972), 1064–1071.

26. Dick, "Who Opened a Missile Gap?" 1067–1069. On how the United States assessed the Soviet nuclear and ICBM programs, see Curtis Peebles, *Shadow Flights: America's Secret Air War against the Soviet Union* (Novato, CA, 2000).

27. Watson, *Into the Missile Age*, 157–164.

28. Ibid., 167; David N. Schwartz, *NATO's Nuclear Dilemmas* (Washington, 1983), 64–65.

29. Schwartz, *NATO's Nuclear Dilemmas*, 66–67.

30. This section is based primarily on Ibid., 67–81.

31. Bernard Brodie, quoted in "The Development of Nuclear Strategy," *International Security* 2:4 (Spring 1978), 65.

32. Lawrence Freedman, *The Evolution of Nuclear Strategy*, 3rd ed. (Houndsmill, Hampshire, UK, 2003), 80–83.

33. NSC-162/2, October 30, 1953, "Review of Basic National Security Policy," reproduced from the Gravel Edition of the Pentagon Papers, Vol. 1, document 18; available at www.mtholyoke.edu/acad/intrel/pentagon/doc18.htm.

34. Marc Trachtenberg, "Strategic Thought in America, 1952–1966," *Political Science Quarterly* 104:2 (Summer 1989), 302–303.

35. Albert Wohlstetter, "The Delicate Balance of Terror," *Foreign Affairs* 37:2 (January 1959), 213.

36. Trachtenberg, "Strategic Thought in America," 306–310; on LeMay and urban targeting, see Rosenberg, "Origins of Overkill," 18.

37. Sagan, *Moving Targets*, 23–24; Friedman, *Fifty-Year War*, 202–204; for detailed discussions of this targeting, see David A. Rosenberg and W. B. Moore, "'Smoking Radiating Ruin at the End of Two Hours:' Documents on American Plans for Nuclear War with the Soviet Union, 1954–55," *International Security* 6:3 (Winter 1981–1982), 3–38.

38. Rosenberg, "Origins of Overkill," 50–60.

39. Sagen, *Moving Targets*, 25–27; Rosenberg, "Origins of Overkill," 4–8; see also Powaski, *March to Armageddon*, 95.

40. Rosenberg, "Origins of Overkill," 68–70.

41. Sagan, *Moving Targets*, 28–31.

42. Powaski, *March to Armageddon*, 96–98.

43. Levine, *Missile and Space Race*, 81–83.

44. Ibid., 84–85; Watson, *Into the Missile Age*, 374–379, 477–482.

45. Leighton, *Strategy, Money, and the New Look*, 114–137.

46. On the Zuni missile, see Directory of U.S. Rockets and Missiles, www.designation-systems.net/dusrm/r-2.html. The fighter interceptor figures are listed in *History of Strategic Air and Ballistic Missile Defense*, Vol. 2: 1956–1972 (Washington, 2009), 162.

47. *History of Strategic Air and Ballistic Missile Defense*, 156, 163–172. On Eisenhower's nuclear authorization, see Rosenberg, "Origins of Overkill," 43.

48. Friedman, *Fifty-Year War*, 207.

49. For a list of such accidents, see Center for Defense Information, www.cdi.org/Issues/NukeAccidents/Accidents.htm.

50. Bowie and Immerman, *Waging Peace*, 179, 247–248, and passim.

51. Quoted in Freedman, *Evolution of Nuclear Strategy*, 73.

52. Ingo Trauschweizer, *The Cold War U.S. Army: Building Deterrence for Limited War* (Lawrence, KS, 2008), 39, 123. In 1951, Robert Oppenheimer and other civilians at the California Institute of Technology produced "Project Vista," a Defense Department-funded study of the use of nuclear weapons

for a variety of battlefield tasks; the air force and especially SAC rejected this challenge to the strategic focus of nuclear weapons. See David C. Elliot, "Project Vista and Nuclear Weapons in Europe," *International Security* 11:1 (Summer 1986), 163–183.

53. Thomas C. Schelling, *Arms and Influence* (New Haven, CT, 1967), 1–4, summarizing his earlier views.

54. Herman Kahn, *On Escalation: Metaphors and Scenarios* (New York, 1965), pages 41–50, esp. 44.

55. Ibid., 75–76.

56. Schwartz, *NATO's Nuclear Dilemmas*, 46–48; Sir John Slessor, "British Defense Policy," *Foreign Affairs* 35:4 (July 1957), 556–563.

57. Wolf Mendl, *Deterrence and Persuasion: French Nuclear Armament in the Context of National Policy, 1945–1969.* (New York, 1970), 33–74.

58. Ibid., 78–79; see also Mendl's "The Background of French Nuclear Policy," *International Affairs* 41:1 (January 1965), 22–29.

59. Reed and Stillman, *Nuclear Express*, 71–80.

60. Robert J. Lieber, "The French Nuclear Force: A Strategic and Political Evaluation," *International Affairs* 42:3 (July 1966), 422.

61. K. S. Tripathi, *Evolution of Nuclear Strategy* (Delhi, 1970), 93.

62. David M. Glantz, *The Military Strategy of the Soviet Union: A History* (London, 1992), 174–176; Freedman, *Evolution of Nuclear Strategy*, 56–58.

63. Jean-Christophe Romer, *La Guerre Nucléaire de Staline a Khroucht-chev: Essai sur la constitution d'une culture stratégique en URSS (1945–1965)* (Paris, 1991), 18–19, 55–60.

64. Ibid., 76–141; Tripathi, *Evolution of Nuclear Strategy*, 94–96; figures from Glantz, *Military Strategy*, 191.

65. Breemer, *Soviet Submarines*, 92–95, 110–113.

CHAPTER 14

1. Oliver J. Lissitzyn, "Some Legal Implications of the U-2 and RB-47 Incidents," *American Journal of International Law* 56:1 (January 1962), 135–142.

2. David F. Winkler, *Cold War at Sea: High-Seas Confrontation between the United States and the Soviet Union* (Annapolis, 2000), 10–11.

3. Ibid., 12–13; Norman Polmar, *Spyplane: The U-2 History Declassified* (Osceola, WI, 2001), 6.

4. Peebles, *Shadow Flights*, 219–221, 283–284.

5. Ibid., 8–37; Winkler, *Cold War at Sea*, 17–20.

6. Philip Taubman, *Secret Empire: Eisenhower, the CIA, and the Hidden Story of America's Space Espionage* (New York, 2003), 3–10.

7. Peebles, *Shadow Flights*, 217, 249, 124.

8. Ibid., 113–123, 207–215.

9. Taubman, *Secret Empire*, 79–109.

10. Polmar, *Spyplane*, 70–72.

11. Peebles, *Shadow Flights*, 101–103, 166.

12. Ibid., 149–197.

13. Ibid., 245, 256–258.

14. Ibid., 262–272; Francis Gary Powers with Curt Gentry, *Operation Overflight: The U-2 Spy Pilot Tells His Story for the First Time* (New York, 1970), 73–83.

15. Polmar, *Spyplane*, 207–211.

16. Scott D. Sagan, "Nuclear Alerts and Crisis Management," *International Security* 9:4 (Spring 1985), 100–106. For the Soviet side, see Bruce G. Blair, *The Logic of Accidental Nuclear War* (Washington, 1993), 23.

17. Taubman, *Secret Empire*, 320–321; Winkler, *Cold War at Sea*, 172 and passim.

18. This discussion is based on Robert E. Quirk, *Fidel Castro* (New York, 1993), 3–43.

19. Andrés Suarez, "The Cuban Revolution: The Road to Power," *Latin American Research Review* 7:3 (Autumn 1972), 6–9.

20. Quirk, *Fidel Castro*, 104, 119–127.

21. Julia A. Sweig, *Inside the Cuban Revolution: Fidel Castro and the Urban Underground* (Cambridge, MA, 2002), 7–10, 114–161.

22. U.S. Embassy in Cuba to Department of State, March 23, 1959, Subject: Military Causes for the Collapse of the Batista Regime, in U.S. Department of State, *FRUS, 1958–1960, Volume 6, Cuba* (Washington, 1991), 434–440.

23. Grayston L. Lynch, *Decision for Disaster: Betrayal at the Bay of Pigs* (Washington, 1998), 7.

24. Shy and Collier, "Revolutionary War," in Paret (ed.), *Makers of Modern Strategy*, 849–850.

25. Quoted in *FRUS, 1958–1960, Volume 6*, 476.

26. Don Bohning, *The Castro Obsession: U.S. Covert Operations against Cuba, 1959–1965*. (Washington, 2005), 5–6.

27. Richard M. Bissell, Jr., with Jonathan E. Lewis and Frances T. Pudlo, *Reflections of a Cold Warrior: From Yalta to the Bay of Pigs* (New Haven, CT, 1996), 99–111.

28. Haynes Johnson et al, *The Bay of Pigs: The Leaders' Story of Brigade 2506* (New York, 1964), 33–34, 53–56.

29. Howard Jones, *The Bay of Pigs* (Oxford, UK, 2008), 35–37; Lynch, *Decision for Disaster*, 26.

30. JCS Memorandum 57–61, quoted in Maxwell D. Taylor, *Operation Zapata: The "Ultrasensitive" Report and Testimony of the Board of Inquiry on the Bay of Pigs* (Frederick, MD, 1981), 9.

31. Jones, *Bay of Pigs*, 39–40, 50. See also Lucien S. Vanderbroucke, "Anatomy of a Failure: The Decision to Land at the Bay of Pigs," *Political Science Quarterly* 99:3 (Autumn 1984), 471–491.

32. Bohning, *Castro Obsession*, 28, 31–32. For details of the planned use of the new site, see Lynch, *Decision for Disaster*, 41–43.

33. Ibid., 34–40; Jones, *Bay of Pigs*, 76–88.

34. This summary is based on Jones, *Bay of Pigs*, 95–125; and Lynch, *Decision for Disaster*, 51–139.

35. Lynch, *Decision for Disaster*, 100–101, 109, 118.

36. Jones, *Bay of Pigs*, 118–122.

37. Bohning, *Castro Obsession*, 7–8.

38. Corey Ross, "Before the Wall: East Germans, Communist Authority, and the Mass Exodus to the West," *The Historical Journal* 45:2 (June 2002), 459–480.

39. Quoted in Elisabeth Barker, "The Berlin Crisis 1958–1962," *International Affairs (Royal Institute of International Affairs)* 39:1 (January 1963), 59.

40. Fursenko and Naftali, *Khrushchev's Cold War*, 200–209; 215–217, 285.

41. Ibid., 381–386; and Barker, "Berlin Crisis," 69. On the construction of the wall, see Peter Wyden, *Wall: The Inside Story of Divided Berlin* (New York, 1989), 127–176.

42. Kaplan et al, *McNamara Ascendancy*, 54–69.

43. Ibid., 151–164; Fursenko and Naftali, *Khrushchev's Cold War*, 386.

44. Wyden, *Wall*, 265–266; Fursenko and Naftali, *Khrushchev's Cold War*, 402.

45. Wyden, *Wall*, 260–265, 267; Kaplan et al, *McNamara Ascendancy*, 165–166.

46. Kaplan et al, *McNamara Ascendancy*, 167–168.

47. Mastny et al (eds.), *War Plans and Alliances*, 46–58.

48. This introduction to Laos is based on Kenneth Conboy and James Morrison, *Shadow War: The CIA's Secret War in Laos* (Boulder, CO, 1995), esp. 13–20.

49. Ibid., 20–22; Memorandum from the Joint Chiefs of Staff to the Secretary of Defense, September 4, 1959, quoted in U.S. Department of State, *FRUS, 1958–1960, Volume 16: East Asia-Pacific Region; Cambodia; Laos* (Washington, 1992), 588–589.

50. *FRUS, 1958–1960, Volume 16*, 558–605; Conboy and Morrison, *Shadow War*, 20–33.

51. Fursenko and Naftali, *Khrushchev's Cold War*, 424–425.

52. U.S. Department of State, *FRUS, 1961–1963, Volume 24: Laos Crisis* (Washington, 1994), esp. 12–25.

53. Conboy and Morrison, *Shadow War*, 51–66; Kaplan et al, *McNamara Ascendancy*, 238–241.

54. Kaplan et al, *McNamara Ascendancy*, 233–247. The May 2 memorandum is reproduced in *FRUS, 1961–1963, Volume 24*, 166–168. Qiang, *China and the Vietnam Wars*, 97–100.

55. Conboy and Morrison, *Shadow War*, 67–68; Blaufarb, *Counterinsurgency Era*, 128–142.

56. Kaplan et al, *McNamara Ascendancy*, 247–258.

57. Mona K. Bitar, "Bombs, Plots, and Allies: Cambodia and the Western Powers, 1958–59," *Intelligence and National Security* 14:4 (Winter 1999), 149–180.

CHAPTER 15

1. Numerous sources describe the DEFCON changes for the Cuban crisis. See Sagan, "Nuclear Alerts," 106–122; Norman Polmar and John D. Gresham, *DEFCON-2: Standing on the Brink of Nuclear War during the Cuban Missile Crisis* (Hoboken, NJ, 2006), 127–130, 144; Raymond L. Garthoff, *Reflections on the Cuban Missile Crisis* (Washington, 1987), 37–38. It is

unclear whether the unencrypted SAC alert message was normal procedure or a special warning; in either event, this broadcast ensured that the Soviets would be aware of the change in status.

2. Blair, *Logic of Accidental Nuclear War*, 24.

3. Sagan, "Nuclear Alerts," 109.

4. James G. Blight, Bruce J. Allyn, and David A. Welch, *Cuba on the Brink: Castro, the Missile Crisis, and the Soviet Collapse* (New York, 1993), 44–45.

5. Curry, *Edward Lansdale*, 239–250; see also Anatoli I. Gribkov and William Y. Smith, *Operation ANADYR: U.S. and Soviet Generals Recount the Cuban Missile Crisis*, ed. Alfred Friendly, Jr. (Chicago, 1994), 106–107.

6. Lansdale Memorandum for the Special Group (Augmented), Subject: Review of Operation Mongoose, July 25, 1962, Top Secret; redacted and declassified January 5, 1989; NSAM 181, August 23, 1962, Top Secret; declassified. Both available from National Security Archive, "The Cuban Missile Crisis, 1962—The Documents," www.gwu.edu/~nsarchiv/nsa/cuba_mis_cri/docs.htm. See also James G. Hershberg, "Before 'The Missiles of October,'" *Diplomatic History* 14:2 (Spring 1990), 176–184; Blight et al, *Cuba on the Brink*, 19–20.

7. Herschberg, "Before 'The Missiles of October,'" 181–182; for Exercise Three Pairs, see General Paul D. Adams, senior officer's debriefing by Colonel Irving Monclova and Lieutenant Colonel Marlin Long, May 8, 1975; transcript on file in Military History Institute (MHI).

8. Jeffrey G. Barlow, "President John F. Kennedy and His Joint Chiefs of Staff," Ph.D. Dissertation, University of South Carolina, 1981, 164, 177–207; and General George H. Decker, senior officer's debriefing interview with Lieutenant Colonel Dan H. Ralls, December 18, 1972, 12; transcript on file in MHI. Ronald H. Carpenter, *Rhetoric in Martial Deliberations and Decision Making: Cases and Consequences* (Columbia, SC, 2004), 70. The May 27, 1961, meeting between the president and the Joint Chiefs is mentioned in Maxwell D. Taylor, *Swords and Plowshares* (New York, 1972), 268; and in Herspring, *Pentagon and the Presidency*, 133–134.

9. This discussion of U.S. planning is based on Headquarters, U.S. Atlantic Command, *CINCLANT Historical Account of Cuban Crisis—1963* [*sic*] (U), typescript, April 29, 1963, esp. 17–23 (sanitized September 5, 1986); and Jean R. Moenk, *USCONARC Participation in the Cuban Missile Crisis, 1962* (U), Headquarters, U.S. Continental Army Command, October 1963, redacted and declassified, October 11, 1988, 6–19. See also House, *U.S. Army in Joint Operations*, 75–84.

10. Moenk, *USCONARC Participation*, 16–19; see also Adams debriefing, 12.

11. Fursenko and Nafali, *Khrushchev's Cold War*, 412–429.

12. Polmar and Gresham, *DEFCON-2*, 6, 28–31.

13. Gribkov and Smith, *Operation ANADYR*, 24–26, 58, and passim.

14. Ibid., 27.

15. Mark Kramer, "Tactical Nuclear Weapons, Soviet Command Authority, and the Cuban Missile Crisis: A Note," *International History Review* 15:4

(November 1993), 740–747. Malinovsky's Order to Pliyev, October 22, 1962, is reproduced and translated on the National Security Archive, "The Cuban Missile Crisis, 1962—The Documents." See also Gribkov and Smith, *Operation ANADYR*, 43, 62–66.

16. Gribkov and Smith, *Operation ANADYR*, 30–41, 53–57.

17. Central Intelligence Agency, Special National Intelligence Estimate 85-3-62, "The Military Buildup in Cuba," September 19, 1962, Secret; declassified July 1999, available from National Security Archive, "The Cuban Missile Crisis, 1962—The Documents." See also Gribkov and Smith, *Operation ANADYR*, 97–102.

18. Joseph F. Bouchard, "Use of Naval Force in Crises: A Theory of Stratified Crisis Interaction," Ph.D. Dissertation, Stanford University, 1988, 516, 518, 527.

19. Ibid., 527–530; the October 2 memorandum is quoted extensively in this work. The collection of information concerning IL-28s and missile sites remains obscure. The data described by Bouchard are missing from the CIA's after-action report: James Q. Rever, Memorandum for Deputy Director of Central Intelligence, Subject: "Historical Analysis of U-2 Overflights of Cuba, 24 October 1962," classified Top Secret; released December 2005, available through CIA Freedom of Information Act Reading Room. The IL-28 discovery and possible missile site are also discussed in Polmar and Gresham, *DEFCON-2*, 83–84.

20. The following discussion of the buildup is derived from a variety of sources, primarily available in the Naval Historical Center: *CINCLANT Historical Account of Cuban Crisis*; Moenk, *USCONARC Participation*; Headquarters, Third U.S. Army, "Historical Narrative on the Cuban Crisis, 1962 (U)," 26 June 1963, Secret; declassified 13 December 1987; and Adam Yarmolinsky, "Department of Defense Operations during the Cuban Missile Crisis," 13 February 1963, sanitized version edited by Dan Caldwell in *Naval War College Review* 32:4 (June–July, 1979), 83–99.

21. Headquarters, 82d Airborne Division, "The Role of the 82d Airborne Division in the Cuban Missile Crisis, 1962 (U)," typescript report, April 12, 1983, 5.

22. *CINCLANT Historical Account of Cuban Crisis*, 24–27.

23. Ibid., 2, 155.

24. Lieutenant General Marshall S. Carter, Memorandum for Record, Subject: Reconnaissance Overflights of Cuba, October 12, 1962, Top Secret; declassified December 2005, CIA Freedom of Information Act Reading Room. Although the USAF had its own U-2s, the pilots required additional training on the J-75 powered version, and Carter as deputy director of the CIA worried that the USAF ground stations were not familiar with the control process.

25. Gribkov and Smith, *Operation ANADYR*, 52–54.

26. *CINCLANT Historical Account of Cuban Crisis*, 10–11, 49–50.

27. Third Army "Historical Narrative," 2–4 and Appendix 7 (Signal) to Annex C (Logistics).

28. Admiral Dennison's quotation is from Barlow, "President John F. Kennedy," 227; the planning implications are in Moenk, *USCONARC*

Participation, 104–105; on Opa Locka, see *CINCLANT Historical Account of Cuban Crisis*, 47.

29. Moenk, *USCONARC Participation*, 141–142. *CINCLANT Historical Account of Cuban Crisis*, 65, describes the shortage of Spanish-speaking special forces as a result of sending a company to the Caribbean Command in July.

30. Moenk, *USCONARC Participation*, 115; Joseph R. Wisnack, "'Old Ironsides' Response to the Cuban Crisis," *Army* 13:9 (April 1963), 26–30.

31. Moenk, *USCONARC Participation*, 12, 108–111; Wisnack, "'Old Ironsides,'" 27–30.

32. Moenk, *USCONARC Participation*, 99, 117; Third Army, "Historical Narrative," Appendix 5 to Annex C (Logistics), 3.

33. Third Army, "Historical Narrative," 3 and Appendix 8 (Transportation) to Annex C (Logistics), 4; Moenck, *USCONARC Participation*, 120–121.

34. Taylor, *Swords and Plowshares*, 269; Herspring, *Pentagon and the Presidency*, 137.

35. "Notes taken from transcripts of meetings of the Joint Chiefs of Staff, October/November 1962, Dealing with the Cuban Missile Crisis," compiled in 1976 and originally classified Secret, available from National Security Archive; Taylor, *Swords and Plowshares*, 269.

36. Dan Caldwell, "A Research Note on the Quarantine of Cuba, October 1962," *International Studies Quarterly*, 22:4 (December 1978), 625–633; for the first intercept, see Barlow, "President John F. Kennedy," 236. See also Carpenter, *Rhetoric in Martial Deliberations*, 102–104.

37. George W. Anderson, "As I Recall . . . The Cuban Missile Crisis," *U.S. Naval Institute Proceedings*, 113:9 (September 1987), 44–45; Kaplan et al, *McNamara Ascendancy*, 212, gives the more confrontational version of these encounters, including McNamara's comment to Gilpatric. Anderson flatly denied ever referring to John Paul Jones, contrary to McNamara's recollection—Anderson quoted in Carpenter, *Rhetoric in Martial Decision Making*, 100–101.

38. Quirk, *Fidel Castro*, 431–437; Raymond L. Garthoff, "Cuban Missile Crisis: The Soviet Story," *Foreign Policy* 72 (Fall 1988), 70–71.

39. Gribkov and Smith, *Operation ANADYR*, 57, 66–69; Barlow, "President John F. Kennedy," 240–243.

40. NSAM 181, August 23, 1962, available from National Security Archive, "The Cuban Missile Crisis, 1962—The Documents;" Blight et al, *Cuba on the Brink*, 23–24; on Turkey, see Polmar and Gresham, *DEFCON-2*, 262–263.

41. This discussion of the 69th Naval Brigade is based on Polmar and Gresham, *DEFCON-2*, 157–168.

42. Yarmolinsky, "Department of Defense Operations," 88, 92; *CINCLANT Historical Account of Cuban Crisis*, 156–158.

43. Moenk, *USCONARC Participation*, 129–134.

44. Incident quoted in Gribkov and Smith, *Operation ANADYR*, 148.

45. Quirk, *Fidel Castro*, 444–448. Kennedy told one reporter that the Soviets had to realize that any deception about the withdrawal would lead to U.S. invasion; Benjamin C. Bradlee, *Conversations with Kennedy* (New York,

1975), 119–120. For their part, the Soviet troops felt ashamed that they had to uncover the missiles for U.S. aerial inspection during the withdrawal. Such actions fueled the sense that Khrushchev had capitulated to the United States; Gribkov and Smith, *Operation ANADYR*, 73.

46. Yarmolinsky, "Department of Defense Operations," 94; Moenk, *USCONARC Participation*, 213; Charles Kirkpatrick, "History of the 52d Air Defense Artillery," unpublished 1983 typescript on file in Center of Military History, 10–15.

47. Reese, *Red Commanders*, 190–191.

48. Bradlee, *Conversations with Kennedy*, 122.

49. Carpenter, *Rhetoric in Martial Deliberations*, 79–85, 97–101.

CONCLUSION

1. Blight et al, *Cuba on the Brink*, 8.

2. Samuel P. Huntington, *The Soldier and the State: The Theory and Politics of Civil-Military Relations* (New York, 1957), esp. 72–79.

3. Herspring, *Pentagon and the Presidency*, 409–415.

4. Kaplan et al, *McNamara Ascendancy*, 72–95.

BIBLIOGRAPHY

ARCHIVAL SOURCES

Central Intelligence Agency Freedom of Information Act Reading Room,
  http://www.foia.cia.gov
Combined Arms Research Library, Fort Leavenworth, KS
Dwight D. Eisenhower Presidential Library, Abilene, KS
  Ann Whitman Papers
    Administration Series
    International Series
    International Meetings Series
    Miscellaneous Series
    National Security Council Series
  John Foster Dulles Papers
    Subject Series
    Chronological Series
    White House Memoranda Series
National Security Archive. "The Cuban Missile Crisis, 1962—The Docu-
  ments." www.gwu.edu/~nsarchiv/nsa/cuba_mis_cri/docs.htm.
Harry S. Truman Presidential Library, Independence, MO
  National Security Council Files
  Official Files Series
  President's Secretary's Files
U.S. Army Center of Military History, Washington, DC
U.S. Army Military History Institute, Carlisle, PA
  Edward M. Almond Papers
U.S. Navy Historical Center, Washington, DC

PUBLISHED SOURCES

Adenauer, Konrad. *Memoirs 1945–53*. Trans. Beate Ruhm von Oppen. Chicago: Henry Regnery Co., 1966.

Aid, Matthew M. "American Comint in the Korean War (Part II): From the Chicom Intervention to the Armistice," *Intelligence and National Security* 15:1 (Spring 2000), 14–49.

Aldrich, Richard J., Gary D. Rawnsley, and Ming-Yeh T. Rawnsley (eds.). *The Clandestine Cold War in Asia, 1945–65: Western Intelligence, Propaganda, and Special Operations*. London: Frank Cass, 2000.

Alexander, Harold R. *The Alexander Memoirs, 1940–1945*. Ed. John North. London: Cassell, 1962.

Alexander, Martin S., and J. F. V. Keiger. *France and the Algerian War: Strategy, Operations and Diplomacy*. London: Frank Cass, 2002.

Allen, Kenneth W., Glenn Krumel, and Jonathan D. Pollack. *China's Air Force Enters the 21st Century*. Santa Monica, CA: RAND, 1995.

Ambler, John S. *The French Army in Politics, 1945–1962*. Columbus: Ohio State University Press, 1966.

Ambrose, Stephen E. *Eisenhower: Soldier and President*. New York: Simon and Schuster, 1990.

———. *Ike's Spies: Eisenhower and the Espionage Establishment*. Jackson: University Press of Mississippi, 1981.

Anders, Roger M. "The Atomic Bomb and the Korean War: Gordon Dean and the Issue of Civilian Control," *Military Affairs* 52:1 (January 1988), 1–6.

Anderson, George W. "As I Recall . . . The Cuban Missile Crisis," *U.S. Naval Institute Proceedings*, 113:9 (September 1987), 44–45.

Andrew, Christopher. *Her Majesty's Secret Service: The Making of the British Intelligence Community*. New York: Viking, 1986.

——— and Vasili Mitrokhin. *The Sword and the Shield: The Mitrokhin Archive and the Secret History of the KGB*. New York: Basic Books/Perseus Books, 1999.

Appleman, Roy E. *Defeat in Korea: The Chinese Confront MacArthur*. College Station: Texas A&M University Press, 1989.

———. *Ridgway Duels for Korea*. College Station: Texas A&M University Press, 1990.

———. *South to the Naktong, North to the Yalu (June–November 1950)*. United States Army in the Korean War Series. Washington, DC: Office of the Chief of Military History, 1961; reprinted Center of Military History, 1986.

Armstrong, Charles K. *The North Korean Revolution, 1945–1950*. Ithaca, NY: Cornell University Press, 2003.

Aussaresses, Paul. *The Battle of the Casbah: Terrorism and Counter-Terrorism in Algeria, 1956–1957*. Trans. Robert L. Miller. New York: Enigma Books, 2002.

Averoff-Tossizza, Evangelos. *By Fire and Axe: The Communist Party and the Civil War in Greece, 1944–1949*. Trans. Sarah Arnold Rigos. New Rochelle, NY: Caratzas Brothers, 1978.

Avidar, Yosef. *The Party and the Army in the Soviet Union.* Trans. Defna Allon. The Pennsylvania State University Press, 1983.

Bacevich, Andrew J. *The Pentomic Era: The U.S. Army between Korea and Vietnam.* Washington, DC: National Defense University Press, 1986.

——— (ed.). *The Long War: A New History of U.S. National Security Policy since World War II.* New York: Columbia University Press, 2007.

Baclagon, Uldarico S. *Lessons from the Huk Campaign in the Philippines.* Manila: M. Colcol and Company, 1960.

Ball, S. J. "Military Nuclear Relations Between the United States and Great Britain under the Terms of the McMahon Act, 1946–1958," *The Historical Journal* 38:2 (1995), 439–454.

Bamford, James. *The Puzzle Palace: A Report on America's Most Secret Agency.* New York: Penguin, 1982.

Baring, Arnulf. *Uprising in East Germany: June 17, 1953.* Trans. Gerald Onn. Ithaca, NY: Cornell University Press, 1972.

Barker, A. J. *Suez: The Seven Day War.* London: Faber & Faber, 1967.

Barker, Elisabeth. "The Berlin Crisis 1958–1962," *International Affairs (Royal Institute of International Affairs)* 39:1 (January 1963), 59–73.

Barlow, Jeffrey G. *From Hot War to Cold: The U.S. Navy and National Security Affairs, 1945–1955.* Stanford University Press, 2009.

———. "President John F. Kennedy and His Joint Chiefs of Staff." Ph.D. Dissertation, University of South Carolina, 1981.

———. *Revolt of the Admirals: The Fight for Naval Aviation, 1945–1950.* Washington, DC: Brassey's, 1998.

Bar-On, Mordechai. *The Gates of Gaza: Israel's Road to Suez and Back, 1955–1957.* New York: St. Martin's Press, 1994.

Bartholomew-Feis, Dixie R. *The OSS and Ho Chi Minh: Unexpected Allies in the War against Japan.* Lawrence: University Press of Kansas, 2006.

Beal, John R. *Marshall in China.* Toronto: Doubleday Canada, 1970.

Beaufre, André. *The Suez Expedition, 1956.* Trans. Richard Barry. New York: Frederick A. Praeger, 1969.

Beckett, Ian F. W., and John Pimlott (eds.). *Armed Forces and Modern Counter-Insurgency.* New York: St. Martin's Press, 1965.

Beevor, Anthony. *The Fall of Berlin, 1945.* New York: Viking, 2002.

Bender, Gerald J. "The Limits of Counterinsurgency," *Comparative Politics* 4:3 (April 1972), 331–360.

Benson, Robert L., and Michael Warner (eds.). *Venona: Soviet Espionage and the American Response, 1939–1957.* Washington, DC: National Security Agency and Central Intelligence Agency, 1996.

Bergeron, Frederic A. *The Army Gets an Air Force: Tactics of Insurgent Bureaucratic Politics.* Baltimore: The Johns Hopkins University Press, 1980.

Birtle, Andrew J. "Rearming the Phoenix: American Military Assistance to the Federal Republic of Germany, 1950–1960." Ph.D. Dissertation, Ohio State University, 1985.

———. *U.S. Army Counterinsurgency and Contingency Operations Doctrine, 1942–1976.* Washington, DC: U.S. Army Center of Military History, 2006.

Bissell, Richard M., Jr., with Jonathan E. Lewis and Frances T. Pudlo. *Reflections of a Cold Warrior: From Yalta to the Bay of Pigs.* New Haven, CT: Yale University Press, 1996.

Bitar, Mona K. "Bombs, Plots, and Allies: Cambodia and the Western Powers, 1958–59," *Intelligence and National Security* 14:4 (Winter 1999), 149–180.

Bjorge, Gary J. *Moving the Enemy: Operational Art in the Chinese PLA's Huai Hai Campaign.* Leavenworth Paper No. 22. Fort Leavenworth, KS: Combat Studies Institute, 2004.

Blackwell, Stephen. *British Military Intervention and the Struggle for Jordan: King Hussein, Nasser, and the Middle East Crisis, 1955–1958.* New York: Routledge, 2009.

Blair, Bruce G. *The Logic of Accidental Nuclear War.* Washington, DC: The Brookings Institute, 1993.

Blair, Clay. *The Forgotten War: America in Korea, 1950–1953.* New York: Times Books/Random House, 1987.

Blaufarb, Douglas S. *The Counterinsurgency Era: U.S. Doctrine and Performance, 1950 to the Present.* New York: Free Press/Macmillan, 1977.

Blight, James G., Bruce J. Allyn, and David A. Welch. *Cuba on the Brink: Castro, the Missile Crisis, and the Soviet Collapse.* New York: Pantheon Books, 1993.

Boettcher, Thomas D. *First Call: The Making of the Modern U.S. Military, 1945–1953.* Boston: Little, Brown, 1992.

Bohning, Don. *The Castro Obsession: U.S. Covert Operations against Cuba, 1959–1965.* Washington, DC: Potomac Books, 2005.

Borgiasz, William S. *The Strategic Air Command: Evolution and Consolidation of Nuclear Forces, 1945–1955.* Westport, CT: Praeger, 1996.

Borodeziej, Wladzimierz. *The Warsaw Uprising of 1944.* Trans. Barbara Harshav. Madison: University of Wisconsin Press, 2006; original, Frankfurt: S. Fischer Verlag GmbH, 2001.

Borowski, Harry R. *A Hollow Threat: Strategic Air Power and Containment before Korea.* Westport, CT: Greenwood Press, 1982.

Botti, Timothy J. *Ace in the Hole: Why the United States Did Not Use Nuclear Weapons in the Cold War, 1945 to 1965.* Westport, CT: Greenwood Press, 1996.

Bouchard, Joseph F. "Use of Naval Force in Crises: A Theory of Stratified Crisis Interaction." Ph.D. Dissertation, Stanford University, 1988.

Bowie, Robert R. and Richard H. Immerman. *Waging Peace: How Eisenhower Shaped an Enduring Cold War Strategy.* Oxford University Press, 1998.

Bowman, Alfred C. *Zones of Strain: A Memoir of the Early Cold War.* Stanford, CA: Hoover Institution Press, 1982.

Boyd, Alexander. *The Soviet Air Force since 1918.* New York: Stein and Day, 1977.

Bradlee, Benjamin C. *Conversations with Kennedy.* New York: W. W. Norton, 1975.

Brayton, Abbott A. "American Reserve Policies since World War II," *Military Affairs* 36:4 (December 1972), 140.

Breemer, Jan. *Soviet Submarines: Design, Development and Tactics*. Coulsdon, Surrey, UK: Jane's Information Group, 1989.

Brodie, Bernard. "The Development of Nuclear Strategy," *International Security* 2:4 (Spring 1978), 65–83.

Bruce, Neil. "Portugal's African Wars," *Conflict Studies* No. 34 (March 1973).

Cagle, Mary T. "History of the Basic (M31) Honest John Rocket System, 1950–1964 (U)." Historical Monograph AMC 7M, Part 1. Redstone Arsenal, AL: U.S. Army Material Command, April 7, 1964.

Caldwell, Dan. "A Research Note on the Quarantine of Cuba, October 1962," *International Studies Quarterly*, 22:4 (December 1978), 625–633.

Calvert, Michael. "Counter-Insurgency in Mozambique," *Journal of the Royal United Services Institute for Defence Studies* [hereafter *Journal of the RUSI*] 118:1 (March 1973), 81–85.

Campbell, M. A., E. W. Downs, and L. V. Schuetta. "The Employment of Airpower in the Greek Civil War, 1947–1949." Typescript. Maxwell AFB, AL: U.S. Aerospace Studies Institute, December, 1964.

Campbell, Richard H. *The Silverplate Bombers: A History and Registry of the Enola Gay and Other B-29s Configured to Carry Atomic Bombs*. Jefferson, NC: McFarland & Co., 2005.

Cann, John P. *Counterinsurgency in Africa: The Portuguese Way of War, 1961–1974*. Westport, CT: Greenwood Press, 1997.

Carafano, James J. *Waltzing into the Cold War: The Struggle for Occupied Austria*. College Station: Texas A&M University Press, 2002.

Carpenter, Ronald H. *Rhetoric in Martial Deliberations and Decision Making: Cases and Consequences*. Columbia: University of South Carolina Press, 2004.

Carter, Donald A. "From G.I. to Atomic Soldier: The Development of U.S. Army Tactical Doctrine, 1945–1956." Ph.D. Dissertation, Ohio State University, 1987.

Carver, Michael. *War Since 1945*. New York: G. P. Putnam's Sons, 1981.

Cathcart, Brian. *Test of Greatness: Britain's Struggle for the Atom Bomb*. London: John Murray, 1994.

Chang, Gordon H. *Friends and Enemies: The United States, China, and the Soviet Union, 1948–1972*. Stanford, CA: Stanford University Press, 1990.

Chang, Jung and Jon Halliday. *Mao: The Unknown Story*. New York: Alfred A. Knopf, 2005.

Chassin, Lionel M. *The Communist Conquest of China: A History of the Civil War, 1945–1949*. Trans. Timothy Osato and Louis Gelas. Cambridge, MA: Harvard University Press, 1965; original, Paris, 1952.

Chen, Jerome. *Mao and the Chinese Revolution*. London: Oxford University Press, 1965.

Chen Jian. "China and the First Indo-China War, 1950–54," *The China Quarterly* No. 133 (March 1993), 85–110.

———. *Mao's China and the Cold War*. Chapel Hill: University of North Carolina Press, 2001.

Chin, C. C. and Karl Hack (eds.). *Dialogues with Chin Peng: New Light on the Malayan Communist Party*. Singapore University Press, 2004.

Churchill, Winston S. *The Second World War*, Vol. 6: *Triumph and Tragedy*. Boston: Houghton Mifflin Co., 1953.

Ciechanowski, Jan M. *The Warsaw Rising of 1944*. Cambridge: Cambridge University Press, 1974.

Clarfield, Gerard H. and William M. Wiecek. *Nuclear America: Military and Civilian Nuclear Power in the United States, 1940–1980*. New York: Harper & Row, 1984.

Clarke, Thurston. *By Blood and Fire: The Attack on the King David Hotel*. New York: G. P. Putnam's Sons, 1981.

Clay, Lucius D. *Decision in Germany*. Westport, CT: Greenwood Press, 1970; original, Garden City, NY: Doubleday & Company, 1950.

Clayton, Anthony. *Counter-Insurgency in Kenya: A study of military operations against Mau Mau*. Manhattan, KS: Sunflower University Press, 1984.

Cloake, John. *Templer: Tiger of Malaya; The Life of Field Marshal Sir Gerald Templer*. London: Harrap Limited, 1985.

Close, David H. *The Origins of the Greek Civil War*. New York: Longman Publishing, 1995.

Clubb, O. Edmund. "Formosa and the Offshore Islands in American Policy, 1950–1955," *Political Science Quarterly* 74:4 (December 1959), 517–531.

———. "Military Debacle in Manchuria," *The Army Quarterly and Defence Journal* 75:2 (January 1958), 221–232.

Clutterbuck, Richard. *Conflict and Violence in Singapore and Malaysia 1945–1983*. Boulder, CO: Westview Press, 1985.

Cochran, Thomas B., Robert S. Norris, and Oleg A. Bucharin. *Making the Russian Bomb: From Stalin to Yeltsin*. Boulder, CO: Westview Press, 1995.

Cohen, Michael J. *Fighting World War Three from the Middle East: Allied Contingency Plans, 1945–1954*. London: Frank Cass, 1997.

———. *Strategy and Politics in the Middle East, 1954–1960*. London: Frank Cass, 2005.

Combs, Dick. *Inside the Soviet Alternative Universe: The Cold War's End and the Soviet Union's Fall Reappraised*. Pennsylvania State University Press, 2008.

Conboy, Kenneth and James Morrison. *Shadow War: The CIA's Secret War in Laos*. Boulder, CO: Paladin Press, 1995.

Condit, Doris M. *History of the Office of the Secretary of Defense*, Vol. II: *The Test of War, 1950–1953*. Washington, DC: Office of the Secretary of Defense, 1988.

Connelly, Matthew. "Rethinking the Cold War and Decolonization: The Grand Strategy of the Algerian War for Independence," *International Journal of Middle East Studies* 33:2 (May 2001), 221–245.

Conversino, Mark J. *Fighting with the Soviets: The Failure of Operation FRANTIC, 1944–1945*. Lawrence: University Press of Kansas, 1997.

Corson, William R. *The Armies of Ignorance: The Rise of the American Intelligence Empire*. New York: Dial Press/James Wade, 1977.

Corum, James S. "Adenauer, Amt Blank, and the Founding of the Bundeswehr, 1950–1956." Paper presented at the 75th Society for Military History Conference, Ogden, Utah, April 19, 2008.

———. "Starting from Scratch: Establishing the Bundesluftwaffe as a Modern Air Force, 1955–1960," *Air Power History* 50:2 (Summer 2003), 16–29.

———. *Training Indigenous Forces in Counterinsurgency: A Tale of Two Insurgencies*. Carlisle, PA: Strategic Studies Institute/U.S. Army War College, 2006.

Craig, Bruce. "A Matter of Espionage: Alger Hiss, Harry Dexter White, and Igor Gouzhenko—the Canadian Connection Reassessed," *Intelligence and National Security* 15:2 (Summer 2000), 211–224.

Craig, Campbell and Fredrik Logevall. *America's Cold War: The Politics of Insecurity*. Cambridge, MA: Belknap Press/Harvard University Press, 2009.

Crane, Conrad C. *American Airpower Strategy in Korea, 1950–1953*. Lawrence: University Press of Kansas, 2000.

Cranshaw, Nancy. *The Cyprus Revolt: An Account of the Struggle for Union with Greece*. London: George Allen and Unwin, 1978.

Currey, Cecil B. *Edward Lansdale: the Unquiet American*. Washington, DC: Brassey's 1998.

Cushman, John H. "Pentomic Infantry Division in Combat," *Military Review* 37 (January 1958), 19–30.

Dallas, Gregor. *1945: The War That Never Ended*. New Haven, CT: Yale University Press, 2005.

Dalloz, Jacques. *The War in Indo-China, 1945–54*. Trans. Josephine Bacon. Dublin: Gill and Macmillan, 1990.

Davies, Norman. *Rising '44: The Battle for Warsaw*. New York: Viking Penguin, 2003.

Dayan, Moshe. *Diary of the Sinai Campaign*. New York: Harper & Row, 1966.

Deery, Phillip. "Malaya, 1948: Britain's Asian Cold War?" *Journal of Cold War Studies* 9:1 (Winter 2007), 29–54.

Dennis, Peter and Jeffrey Grey. *Emergency and Confrontation: Australian Military Operations in Malaya and Borneo 1950–1966*. St. Leonards, New South Wales: Allen & Unwin with the Australian War Memorial, 1996.

Devereux, David R. *The Formulation of British Defense Policy towards the Middle East, 1948–56*. New York: St. Martin's Press, 1990.

Dewar, Michael. *Brush Fire Wars: Minor Campaigns of the British Army since 1945*. New York: St. Martin's Press, 1984.

Dick, James C. "The Strategic Arms Race, 1957–61: Who Opened a Missile Gap?" *The Journal of Politics* 34:4 (November 1972), 1062–1110.

Dillard, James E. and Walter T. Hitchcock (eds.). *The Intelligence Revolution and Modern Warfare*. USAF Academy Military History Symposium Series, Vol. 3. Chicago: Imprint Publications, 1996.

DiMarco, Lou. "Losing the Moral Compass: Torture and Guerre Revolutionnaire in the Algerian War," *Parameters* 36:2 (Summer 2006), 63–76.

Dimitrakis, Panagiotis. "British Intelligence and the Cyprus Insurgency, 1955–1959," *International Journal of Intelligence and CounterIntelligence* 21:2 (Summer 2008), 375–394.

Dimitrijevic, Bojan. "The Mutual Defense Aid Program in Tito's Yugoslavia, 1951–1958, and its Technical Impact," *Journal of Slavic Military Studies* [hereafter *JSMS*] 10:2 (June 1997), 19–33.

————. "Yugoslav-Soviet Military Relations, 1945–1948," *JSMS* 9:3 (September 1996), 581-593.

Dobbs, Charles M. "American Marines in North China, 1945–1946," *South Atlantic Quarterly* 76:3 (1977), 318–331.

Dockrill, Saki. *Eisenhower's New Look National Security Policy, 1953–61.* New York: St. Martin's Press, 1996.

Donnelly, William M. *Under Army Orders: The Army National Guard during the Korean War.* College Station: Texas A&M University Press, 2001.

Drea, Edward J. *In the Service of the Emperor: Essays on the Imperial Japanese Army.* Lincoln: University of Nebraska Press, 1998.

Duffield, John S. *Power Rules: The Evolution of NATO's Conventional Force Posture.* Stanford University Press, 1995.

Duiker, William J. *Ho Chi Minh.* New York: Hyperion, 2000.

Dunn, Peter M. *The First Vietnam War.* New York: St. Martin's Press, 1985.

Eastman, Lloyd E. *Seeds of Destruction: Nationalist China in War and Revolution, 1937–1949.* Stanford University Press, 1984.

Ecker, Richard E. *Korean Battle Chronology: Unit-by-Unit United States Casualty Figures and Medal of Honor Citations.* Jefferson, NC: McFarland & Company, 2005.

Elleman, Bruce A. *Modern Chinese Warfare, 1795–1989.* London: Routledge/Taylor & Francis, 2001.

Elliot, David C. "Project Vista and Nuclear Weapons in Europe," *International Security* 11:1 (Summer 1986), 163–183.

Elliott-Bateman, Michael. *Defeat in the East: The Mark of Mao Tse-tung on War.* London: Oxford University Press, 1967.

Epley, William W. *America's First Cold War Army, 1945–1950.* Land Warfare Papers No. 15. Arlington, VA: Association of the United States Army, 1993.

Erickson, John. "The Ground Forces in Soviet Military Policy," *Strategic Review* 4:2 (April 1976), 64–79.

————. "The 'Military Factor' in Soviet Policy," *International Affairs* 39:2 (April 1963), 214–226.

————. "Soviet Combined-Arms: Theory and Practice." Unpublished typescript, University of Edinburgh Defence Studies, September 1979.

Eudes, Dominique. *The Kapetanios: Partisans and Civil War in Greece, 1943–1949.* Trans. John Howe. New York: Monthly Review Press, 1972.

Fall, Bernard B. *Street Without Joy.* New York: Schocken Books, 1972.

————. "The Two Sides of the Sinai Campaign," *Military Review* 37: 4 (July 1957), 3–23.

Farrar-Hockley, Anthony. "A Reminiscence of the Chinese People's Volunteers in the Korean War," *The China Quarterly* No. 98 (June 1984), 287–304.

————. "The Post-War Army, 1945–1963," in David G. Chandler (ed.), *The Oxford History of the British Army.* New ed.: Oxford University Press, 1994.

Fautua, David T. "The 'Long Pull' Army: NSC-68, the Korean War, and the Creation of the Cold War U.S. Army," *Journal of Military History* [hereafter *JMH*] 61:1 (January 1997), 93–120.

Fehrenbach, T. R. *This Kind of War: A Study in Unpreparedness.* New York: Macmillan, 1963; reprinted 1989.

Fenby, Jonathan. *Chiang Kai Shek: China's Generalissimo and the Nation He Lost.* New York: Carroll & Graf, 2003.

Field, James A., Jr. *History of United States Naval Operations Korea.* Washington, DC: Department of the Navy, 1962.

Fields, Rona M. *The Portuguese Revolution and the Armed Forces Movement.* New York: Praeger, 1976.

Fifield, Russell H. "The Thirty Years War in Indochina: A Conceptual Framework," *Asian Survey* 17:9 (September 1977), 857–879.

Finer, Herman. *Dulles Over Suez: The Theory and Practice of His Diplomacy.* Chicago: Quadrangle Books, 1964.

Fisher, Ernest F., Jr. "Historical Resumé Concerning Intra-Theater Airlift since World War II." Unpublished transcript (1968) in U.S. Army Center of Military History.

Flynn, George Q. *The Draft, 1940–1973.* Lawrence: University Press of Kansas, 1993.

Foot, Rosemary J. "Nuclear Coercion and the Ending of the Korean Conflict," *International Security* 13:3 (Winter 1988–1989), 92–112.

Frank, Benis M. and Henry I. Shaw, Jr. *Victory and Occupation: History of the U.S. Marine Corps Operations in World War II*, Vol. 5. Washington, DC: Headquarters, U.S. Marine Corps, 1968.

Frazier, Robert. "Did Britain Start the Cold War? Bevin and the Truman Doctrine," *The Historical Journal* 27:3 (September 1984), 715–727.

Freedman, Lawrence. *The Evolution of Nuclear Strategy*, 3rd ed. Houndsmill, Hampshire, UK: Palgrave Macmillan, 2003.

Friedman, Norman. *The Fifty-Year War: Conflict and Strategy in the Cold War.* Annapolis, MD: Naval Institute Press, 2000.

Fullick, Roy and Geoffrey Powell. *Suez: The Double War.* London: Leo Cooper, 1979.

Fursdon, Edward. *The European Defence Community: A History.* London: Macmillan Press, 1980.

Fursenko, Aleksandr and Timothy Naftali. *Khrushchev's Cold War: The Inside Story of an American Adversary.* New York: W. W. Norton, 2006.

Gaddis, John Lewis. *The Cold War: A New History.* New York: Penguin Press, 2005.

—— and Paul Nitze. "NSC 68 and the Soviet Threat Reconsidered," *International Security* 4:4 (Spring 1980), 164–176.

Galambos, Louis, Daun Van Ee, Elizabeth S. Hughes, and Robert J. Brugger (eds.). *The Papers of Dwight David Eisenhower*, Vol. XII: *NATO and the Campaign of 1952.* Baltimore: Johns Hopkins University Press, 1989.

Galula, David. *Pacification in Algeria, 1956–1958.* Santa Monica, CA: RAND Corporation, reissued 2006; original, 1963.

Garnett, John. "BAOR and NATO," *International Affairs (Royal Institute of International Affairs)* 46:4 (October 1970), 670–681.

Garthoff, Raymond L. "Cuban Missile Crisis: The Soviet Story," *Foreign Policy* 72 (Fall 1988), 61–80.

———. *Reflections on the Cuban Missile Crisis.* Washington, DC: Brookings Institution, 1987.

Garver, John W. "The Soviet Union and the Xi'an Incident," *The Australian Journal of Chinese Affairs* 26 (July 1991), 145–175.

Gawrych, George W. *Key to the Sinai: The Battles for Abu Agheila in the 1956 and 1967 Arab-Israeli Wars.* Research Survey No. 7. Fort Leavenworth, KS: Combat Studies Institute, 1990.

Gendzier, Irene L. *Notes from the Minefield: United States Intervention in Lebanon and the Middle East, 1945–1958.* New York: Columbia University Press, 1997.

Gerolymatos, André. *Red Acropolis, Black Terror: The Greek Civil War and the Origins of Soviet-American Rivalry, 1943–1949.* New York: Basic Books/Perseus Books Group, 2004.

Gillin, Donald G. and Charles Etter. "Staying On: Japanese Soldiers and Civilians in China, 1945–1949," *The Journal of Asian Studies* 42:3 (May 1983), 497–518.

Glantz, David M. *August Storm: The Soviet 1945 Strategic Offensive in Manchuria.* Leavenworth Papers No. 7. Fort Leavenworth, KS: U.S. Army Command and General Staff College, 1983.

———. *The Military Strategy of the Soviet Union: A History.* London: Frank Cass, 1992.

———. "Soviet Offensive Military Doctrine since 1945," *Air University Review* 34 (March-April 1983), 25–34.

——— and Jonathan M. House. *When Titans Clashed: How the Red Army Stopped Hitler.* Lawrence: University Press of Kansas, 1995.

Gleijeses, Piero. *Conflicting Missions: Havana, Washington, and Africa, 1959–1976.* Chapel Hill: University of North Carolina Press, 2002.

Gobarev, Victor. "Soviet Military Plans and Actions during the First Berlin Crisis, 1948–49," *JSMS* 10:3 (September 1997), 1–24.

Goncharov, Sergei N., John W. Lewis, and Xue Litai. *Uncertain Partners: Stalin, Mao, and the Korean War.* Stanford University Press, 1993.

Goodpaster, Andrew J. "The Development of SHAPE: 1950–1953," *International Organization* 9:2 (May 1955), 257–262.

Gouda, Frances and Thijs Brocades Zaalberg. *American Visions of the Netherlands East Indies/Indonesia: US Foreign Policy and Indonesian Nationalism 1920–1949.* Amsterdam University Press, 2002.

Gougeon, Francois-Marie. "The 'Challe' Plan, Counter-insurgency Operations in Algeria 12/1958–04/1960," Masters of Military Science Thesis, USMC Command and Staff College, 2005.

Goya, Michel and Philippe Francois. "The Man Who Bent Events: 'King John' in Indochina," *Military Review* 87:5 (September-October 2007), 52–61.

Graff, David A. and Robin Higham (eds.). *A Military History of China.* Boulder, CO: Westview Press, 2002.

Gray, David W. *The U.S. Intervention in Lebanon, 1958: A Commander's Reminiscence.* Fort Leavenworth, KS: U.S. Army General Staff College, 1984.

Greece. Army General Staff. *The Nation's Battle: The Struggle of the Greek Nation against Communism till 19th August 1949.* Athens: Greek Army General Staff, 1952.

Greenberg, Lawrence M. *The Hukbalahap Insurrection: A Case Study of a Successful Anti-Insurgency Operation in the Philippines—1946–1955.* Washington, DC: U.S. Army Center of Military History, 1987.

Gribkov, Anatoli I. and William Y. Smith. *Operation ANADYR: U.S. and Soviet Generals Recount the Cuban Missile Crisis.* Ed. Alfred Friendly, Jr. Chicago: Edition q, Inc., 1994.

Grivas, George. Ed. Charles Foley. *The Memoirs of General Grivas.* New York: Praeger, 1964.

Gyorkei, Jeno and Miklos Horvath (eds.). *Soviet Military Intervention in Hungary, 1956.* Budapest: Central European University Press, 1999.

Halberstam, David. *The Coldest Winter: America and the Korean War.* New York: Hyperion Books, 2007.

Hamilton, Nigel. *Monty: Final Years of the Field-Marshal, 1944–1976.* New York: McGraw-Hill, 1986.

Hanley, Charles J., Sang-Hun Choe, and Martha Mendoza. *The Bridge at No Gun Ri: A Hidden Nightmare from the Korean War.* New York: Henry Holt, 2001.

Hardesty, Von. *Red Phoenix: the Rise of Soviet Air Power.* Washington, DC: Smithsonian Institution, 1982.

Harrison, James P. *The Long March to Power: A History of the Chinese Communist Party, 1921–72.* New York: Praeger, 1972.

Haydock, Michael D. *City under Siege: The Berlin Blockade and Airlift, 1948–1949.* Washington, DC: Brassey's, 1999.

Heikal, Mohamed H. *Cutting the Lion's Tail: Suez through Egyptian Eyes.* New York: Arbor House, 1987

Heinl, Robert D., Jr. *Victory at High Tide: The Inchon-Seoul Operation.* Philadelphia: J. B. Lippincott Co., 1958.

Heller, Charles E. and William A. Stofft (eds.). *America's First Battles, 1776–1965.* Lawrence: University Press of Kansas, 1986.

Henriksen, Thomas H. "Lessons from Portugal's Counter-insurgency Operations in Africa," *Journal of the RUSI* 123:2 (June 1978), 31–36.

———. "People's War in Angola, Mozambique, and Guinea-Bissau," *Journal of Modern African Studies* 14:3 (September 1976), 377–399.

———. *Revolution and Counterrevolution: Mozambique's War of Independence, 1964–1974.* Westport, CT: Greenwood Press, 1983.

———. "Some Notes on the National Liberation Wars in Angola, Mozambique, and Guinea-Bissau," *Military Affairs* 41:1 (February 1977), 30–36.

Hermes, Walter G. *Truce Tent and Fighting Front.* United States Army in the Korean War Series. Washington, DC: Office of the Chief of Military Historian, 1966.

Herring, George C. and Richard H. Immerman. "Eisenhower, Dulles, and Dienbienphu [sic]: 'The Day We Didn't Go to War' Revisited," *Journal of American History* 71:2 (September 1984), 343–363.

Hershberg, James G. "Before 'The Missiles of October,'" *Diplomatic History* 14:2 (Spring 1990), 163–198.

Herspring, Dale R. *The Pentagon and the Presidency: Civil-Military Relations from FDR to George W. Bush.* Lawrence: University Press of Kansas, 2005.

Hewes, James E., Jr. *From Root to McNamara: Army Organization and Administration, 1900–1963.* Washington, DC: U.S. Army Center of Military History, 1975.

History of Strategic Air and Ballistic Missile Defense, Vol. 2: 1956–1972. Washington, DC: U.S. Army Center of Military History, 2009.

Ho Chi Minh. *On Revolution: Selected Writings,1920–66.* Ed. Bernard B. Fall. New York: Praeger, 1967.

Holloway, David. *Stalin and the Bomb: The Soviet Union and Atomic Energy, 1939–1956.* New Haven, CT: Yale University Press, 1994.

Horne, Alistair. *A Savage War Of Peace: Algeria 1954–1962.* London: Penguin Books, 1979.

House, Jonathan M. *Combined Arms Warfare in the Twentieth Century.* Lawrence: University Press of Kansas, 2001.

———. "Joint Operational Problems in the Cuban Missile Crisis," *Parameters: U.S. Army War College Quarterly* 21:1 (Spring 1991), 92–102.

———. *The United States Army in Joint Operations, 1950–1983.* Washington, DC: U.S. Army Center of Military History, 1992.

Hsiung, James C. and Steven I. Levine. *China's Bitter Victory: The War with Japan 1937–1945.* Armonk, NY: M. E. Sharpe, 1992.

Huber, Thomas M. (ed.). *Compound Warfare: That Fatal Knot.* Fort Leavenworth, KS: U.S. Army Command and General Staff College Press, 2002.

Hudson, George E. "Soviet Naval Doctrine and Soviet Politics, 1953–1975," *World Politics* 29:1 (October 1976), 90–113.

———. "Soviet Naval Doctrine under Lenin and Stalin," *Soviet Studies* 28:1 (January 1976), 42–65.

Hunt, Linda. *Secret Agenda: The United States Government, Nazi Scientists, and Project Paperclip, 1945 to 1990.* New York: St. Martin's Press, 1991.

Huntington, Samuel P. *The Soldier and the State: The Theory and Politics of Civil-Military Relations.* New York: Vintage Books, 1957.

Huston, James A. *Outposts and Allies: U.S. Army Logistics in the Cold War, 1945–1953.* Cranbury, NJ: Associated University Presses, 1988.

Hyde, H. Montgomery. *The Atom Bomb Spies.* New York: Ballantine Books, 1980.

Iatrides, John O. *Revolt in Athens: The Greek Communist "Second Round," 1944–1945.* Princeton: Princeton University Press, 1972.

Immerman, Richard H. (ed.). *John Foster Dulles and the Diplomacy of the Cold War.* Princeton: Princeton University Press, 1990.

Ireland, Timothy P. *Creating the Entangling Alliance: The Origins of the North Atlantic Treaty Organization.* Westport, CT: Greenwood Press, 1981.

Iriye, Akira. "Chang Hsueh-Liang and the Japanese," *The Journal of Asian Studies* 20:1 (November 1960), 33–43.

Isenberg, Michael T. *Shield of the Republic: The United States Navy in an Era of Cold War and Violent Peace, 1945–1962*. New York: St. Martin's Press, 1993.

Johnson, Haynes with Manuel Artime, Jose Perez San Roman, Erneido Oliva, and Enrique Ruiz-Williams. *The Bay of Pigs: The Leaders' Story of Brigade 2506*. New York: Dell, 1964.

Jones, Howard. *The Bay of Pigs*. Oxford University Press, 2008.

Kahn, Herman. *On Escalation: Metaphors and Scenarios*. New York: Frederick A. Praeger, 1965.

Kallgren, Joyce. "Nationalist China's Armed Forces," *The China Quarterly* No. 15 (July-September 1963), 35–44.

Kaplan, Karel. *The Short March: The Communist Takeover in Czechoslovakia, 1945–1948*. New York: St. Martin's Press, 1987; original, Munich: R. Oldenbourg Verlag, 1981.

Kaplan, Lawrence S. *The United States and NATO: The Formative Years*. Lexington: University Press of Kentucky, 1984.

Kaplan, Lawrence S., Ronald D. Landa, and Edward J. Drea. *History of the Office of the Secretary of Defense*, Vol. V: *The McNamara Ascendancy 1961–1965*. Washington, DC: Office of the Secretary of Defense, 2006.

Karalekas, Anne. *History of the Central Intelligence Agency*. Laguna Hills, CA: Aegean Park Press, 1977. (Originally a 1976 report to the Senate Select Committee to Study Governmental Operations with Respect to Intelligence Activities.)

Katzenbach, Edward L., Jr., and Gene Z. Hanrahan. "The Revolutionary Strategy of Mao Tse-Tung," *Political Science Quarterly* 70:3 (September 1955), 321–340.

Kee, Robert J. "Algiers—1957: An Approach to Urban Counterinsurgency," *Military Review* 54:4 (April 1974), 73–84.

Kelly, Saul and Anthony Gorst (eds.). *Whitehall and the Suez Crisis*. London: Frank Cass, 2000.

Kerkvliet, Benedict J. *The Huk Rebellion: A Study of Peasant Revolt in the Philippines*. Berkeley: University of California Press, 1979.

Khrushchev, Nikita S. *Khrushchev Remembers*. Trans. and ed. Strobe Talbott. Boston: Little, Brown, 1970.

Knowlton, William A. "Early Stages in the Organization of 'SHAPE,'" *International Organization* 13:1 (Winter 1959), 1–18.

Kinkead, Eugene. *In Every War but One*. New York: W. W. Norton, 1959.

Korbel, Josef. *The Communist Subversion of Czechoslovakia, 1938–1948: The Failure of Coexistence*. Princeton: Princeton University Press, 1959.

Kramer, Mark. "The Soviet Union and the 1956 Crises in Hungary and Poland: Reassessments and New Findings," *Journal of Contemporary History* 33:2 (April 1998), 163–214.

———. "Tactical Nuclear Weapons, Soviet Command Authority, and the Cuban Missile Crisis: A Note," *International History Review* 15:4 (November 1993), 740–751.

Krivosheev, G. F. (ed.). *Soviet Casualties and Combat Losses in the Twentieth Century*. London: Greenhill Books/Lionel Leventhal, 1997.

Kupchan, Charles A. "American Globalism in the Middle East: The Roots of Regional Security Policy," *Political Science Quarterly* 103:4 (Winter 1988–1989), 585–611.

Laird, Robbin F. *The Soviet Union, the West, and the Nuclear Arms Race.* New York University Press, 1986.

Large, David C. *Germans to the Front: West German Rearmament in the Adenauer Era.* Chapel Hill: University of North Carolina Press, 1996.

Larrabee, Eric. *Commander in Chief: Franklin Delano Roosevelt, His Lieutenants, and Their War.* New York: Harper & Row, 1987.

Lasby, Clarence G. *Project Paperclip: German Scientists and the Cold War.* New York: Atheneum, 1971.

Lawrence, Mark A. *Assuming the Burden: Europe and the American Commitment to War in Vietnam.* Berkeley: University of California Press, 2005.

Lawrence, Mark A. and Fredrik Logevall (eds.). *The First Vietnam War: Colonial Conflict and Cold War Crisis.* Cambridge, MA: Harvard University Press, 2007.

Lee, Chong-Sik. "Politics in North Korea: Pre-Korean War Stage," *The China Quarterly* 14 (April–June 1963), 3–16.

Leffler, Melvyn P. *A Preponderance of Power: National Security, the Truman Administration, and the Cold War.* Stanford University Press, 1992.

Leighton, Richard M. *History of the Office of the Secretary of Defense*, Vol. III: *Strategy, Money and the New Look.* Washington, DC: Office of the Secretary of Defense, 2001.

Levine, Alan J. *The Missile and Space Race.* Westport, CT: Praeger, 1994.

Levine, Steven I. *Anvil of Victory: The Communist Revolution in Manchuria, 1945–1948.* New York: Columbia University Press, 1987.

Lewis, Adrian R. *The American Culture of War: The History of U.S. Military Force from World War II to Operation Iraqi Freedom.* New York: Routledge, 2007.

Lewis, William Roger. "Hong Kong: The Critical Phase, 1945–1949," *American Historical Review* 102:2 (October 1997), 1052–1084.

Lieber, Robert J. "The French Nuclear Force: A Strategic and Political Evaluation," *International Affairs* 42:3 (July 1966), 421–431.

Linn, Brian McAllister. *The Echo of Battle: The Army's Way of War.* Cambridge, MA: Harvard University Press, 2007.

———. *The Philippine War, 1899–1902.* Lawrence: University Press of Kansas, 2000.

Lissitzyn, Oliver J. "Some Legal Implications of the U-2 and RB-47 Incidents," *American Journal of International Law* 56:1 (January 1962), 135–142.

Liu, F. F. *A Military History of Modern China, 1924–1949.* Princeton: Princeton University Press, 1956.

Lonsdale, John. "Mau Mau of the Mind: Making Mau Mau and Remaking Kenya," *The Journal of African History* 31:3 (1990), 393–421.

Lowry, Montecue J. *The Forge of West German Rearmament: Theodor Blank and the Amt Blank.* New York: Peter Lang, 1990.

Lucas, W. Scott. "Redefining the Suez 'Collusion,'" *Middle East Studies* 26:1 (January 1990), 88–112.

Lynch, Grayston L. *Decision for Disaster: Betrayal at the Bay of Pigs.* Washington, DC: Brassey's, 1998.

MacIntosh, Malcolm. *Juggernaut: A History of the Soviet Armed Forces.* New York: Macmillan Company, 1967.

Majdalany, Fred. *State of Emergency: The Full Story of Mau Mau.* Boston: Houghton Mifflin, 1963.

Mao Tse-tung. *Selected Writings of Mao Tse-Tung.* Peking: Foreign Language Press, 1972.

Marcum, John. *The Angolan Revolution,* Vol. 1: *The Anatomy of an Explosion (1950–1962).* Cambridge, MA: The MIT Press, 1969.

Marshall, Samuel L. A. *Pork Chop Hill: The American Fighting Man in Action, Korea, Spring, 1953.* New York: William Morrow, 1956.

———. *The River and the Gauntlet: Defeat of the Eighth Army by the Chinese Communist Forces November, 1950, in the Battle of the Chongchon River, Korea.* New York: William Morrow, 1953; reprinted *Time* Magazine, 1962.

Marsot, Alain-Gerard. "The Crucial Year: Indochina 1946," *Journal of Contemporary History* 19:2 (April 1984), 337–354.

Martin, Laurence W. "The Market for Strategic Ideas in Britain: The 'Sandys Era,'" *American Political Science Review* 56:1 (March 1962), 23–41.

Mason, R. A., and John W. R. Taylor. *Aircraft, Strategy, and Operations of the Soviet Air Force.* London: Jane's, 1986.

Massu, Jacques. *La Vraie Bataille d'Alger.* Paris: Librairie Plon, 1971.

Mastny, Vojtech, Sven G. Holtsmark, and Andreas Wenger (eds.). *War Plans and Alliances in the Cold War: Threat Perceptions in the East and West.* London: Routledge, 2006.

Mataxis, Theodore C. and Seymour L. Greenberg. *Nuclear Tactics, Weapons, and Firepower in the Pentomic Division, Battle Group, and Company.* Harrisburg, PA: Military Service Publishing Company, 1958.

Matloff, Maurice. "The 90-Division Gamble," in Kent R. Greenfield (ed.), *Command Decisions.* Washington, DC: Office of the Chief of Military History, 1959, 365–381.

Mawdsley, Evan. *Thunder in the East: The Nazi-Soviet War, 1941–1945.* London: Hodder Arnold, 2005.

May, Ernest R. (ed.). *American Cold War Strategy: Implementing NSC 68.* Boston: Bedford Books of St. Martin's Press, 1993.

McCreedy, Kenneth O. "Planning the Peace: Operation Eclipse and the Occupation of Germany," *JMH* 65:3 (July 2001), 713–739.

McFarland, Keith D. and David L. Roll. *Louis Johnson and the Arming of America: The Roosevelt and Truman Years.* Bloomington: Indiana University Press, 2005.

McInnes, Colin. *Hot War Cold War: The British Army's Way in Warfare, 1945–95.* London: Brassey's, 1996.

McMahon, Robert J. *Colonialism and Cold War: The United States and the Struggle for Indonesian Independence, 1945–1949.* Ithaca, NY: Cornell University Press, 1981.

Mendl, Wolf. "The Background of French Nuclear Policy," *International Affairs* 41:1 (January 1965), 22–36.

———. *Deterrence and Persuasion: French Nuclear Armament in the Context of National Policy, 1945–1969*. New York: Praeger, 1970.

Meray, Tibor. *Thirteen Days that Shook the Kremlin*. Trans. Howard L. Katzander. New York: Frederick A. Praeger, 1959.

Messenger, Charles. *History of the British Army*. Novato, CA: Presidio Press, 1986.

Michta, Andrew A. *Red Eagle: The Army in Polish Politics, 1944–1988*. Stanford, CA: Hoover Institution Press, 1990.

Miller, James E. *The United States and the Making of Modern Greece: History and Power, 1950–1974*. Chapel Hill: University of North Carolina Press, 2009.

Millett, Allan R. *The War for Korea, 1945–1950: A House Burning*. Lawrence: University Press of Kansas, 2005.

———. *The War For Korea, 1950–1951: They Came from the North*. Lawrence: University Press of Kansas, 2010.

Mitchell, Donald W. *A History of Russian and Soviet Sea Power*. New York: Macmillan, 1974.

Monnet, Jean. *Memoirs*. Trans. Richard Mayne. Garden City, NY: Doubleday and Co., 1978.

Montross, Lynn and Nicholas A. Canzona. *U.S. Marine Operations in Korea, 1950–1953*, Vol. 2: *The Inchon-Seoul Operation*. Washington, DC: Headquarters, U.S. Marine Corps, 1955.

Morgan, Ted, aka Sanche de Gramont. *My Battle of Algiers*. New York: Harper Collins and Smithsonian, 2005.

Morris, Benny. *1948: A History of the First Arab-Israeli War*. New Haven, CT: Yale University Press, 2008.

Mossman, Billy C. *Ebb and Flow: November 1950–July 1951*. United States Army in the Korean War Series. Washington, DC: U.S. Army Center of Military History, 1990.

Moynahan, Brian. *Claws of the Bear: The History of the Red Army from the Revolution to the Present*. Boston: Houghton Mifflin, 1989.

Muir, Malcolm, Jr. (ed.). *From Détente to the Soviet Collapse: the Cold War from 1975 to 1991*. Lexington: Virginia Military Institute, 2006.

Murray, Williamson and Allan R. Millett. *Military Innovation in the Interwar Period*. Cambridge: Cambridge University Press, 1996.

Nagl, John A. *Counterinsurgency Lessons from Malaya and Vietnam: Learning to Eat Soup with a Knife*. Westport, CT: Praeger, 2002.

Naimark, Norman M. *The Russians in Germany: A History of the Soviet Zone of Occupation, 1945–1949*. Cambridge, MA: Belknap/Harvard University Press, 1995.

Nation, R. Craig. *Black Earth, Red Star: A History of Soviet Security Policy, 1917–1991*. Ithaca, NY: Cornell University Press, 1992.

Neff, Donald. *Warriors at Suez: Eisenhower Takes America into the Middle East*. New York: Simon & Schuster, 1981.

Neillands, Robin. *A Fighting Retreat: The British Empire 1947–1997*. London: Hodder and Stoughton, 1996.

Nicot, Jean. "Les S.A.S. et la Pacification en Algerie," *Revue Historique des Armées*, 1992 (4), 26–39.

Nolan, John M. "The Long March: Fact and Fancy," *Military Affairs* 30:2 (Summer 1966), 77–90.

"North Atlantic Treaty Organization," *International Organization* 7:3 (August 1953), 433–441.

O'Ballance, Edgar. *The Algerian Insurrection, 1954–1962*. Hamden, CT: Archon Books, 1967.

———. *The Greek Civil War 1944–1949*. New York: Praeger, 1966.

———. "To Turn His Coat—Or Not?" *Journal of the RUSI* 118:1 (March 1973), 85–87.

Orpen, Neil. *Airlift to Warsaw: The Rising of 1944*. Norman: University of Oklahoma Press, 1984.

Ostermann, Christian F. (ed.). *Uprising in East Germany. 1953: The Cold War, the German Question, and the First Major Upheaval behind the Iron Curtain*. Budapest: Central European University Press, 2001.

Ovendale, Ritchie. "Britain, the United States, and the Cold War in South-East Asia, 1949–1950," *International Affairs* (Royal Institute of International Affairs) 58:3 (Summer 1982), 447–464.

Pach, Chester J., Jr. *Arming the Free World: The Origins of the United States Military Assistance Program, 1945–1950*. Chapel Hill: University of North Carolina Press, 1991.

Paget, Julian. *Counter-Insurgency Operations: Techniques of Guerrilla Warfare*. New York: Walker and Company, 1967.

Paret, Peter. *French Revolutionary Warfare from Indochina to Algeria: The Analysis of a Political and Military Doctrine*. New York: Frederick A. Praeger, 1964.

Parrish, Thomas D. *Berlin in the Balance: 1945–1949: The Blockade, The Airlift, The First Major Battle of the Cold War*. Reading, MA: Addison Wesley, 1998.

Peng Dehuai. *Memoirs of a Chinese Marshal—The Autobiographical Notes of Peng Dehuai (1898–1974)*. Trans. Zheng Longpu; ed. Sara Grimes. Beijing: Foreign Language Press, 1984

Pearlman, Michael D. "Korean War Anthology: Truman and MacArthur: The Winding Road to Dismissal." Fort Leavenworth, KS: Combat Studies Institute, 2003.

———. *Truman and MacArthur: Policy, Politics, and the Hunger for Honor and Renown*. Bloomington: Indiana University Press, 2008.

Peebles, Curtis. *Shadow Flights: America's Secret Air War against the Soviet Union*. Novato, CA: Presidio Press, 2000.

Peterson, A. H., G. C. Reinhardt, and E. E. Conger (eds.). *Symposium on the Role of Airpower in Counterinsurgency and Unconventional Warfare: The Philippine Huk Campaign*. RAND Memo RM-3652-5R. Santa Monica, CA: RAND Corporation, 1963.

Pogue, Forrest C. *George C. Marshall: Education of a General, 1880–1939*. New York: The Viking Press, 1963.

———. *George C. Marshall: Statesman, 1945–1959*. New York: Viking-Penguin, 1987.

Pollack, Kenneth M. *Arabs at War: Military Effectiveness, 1948–1991.* Lincoln: University of Nebraska Press, 2004.

Polmar, Norman. *Spyplane: The U-2 History Declassified.* Osceola, WI: MBI, 2001.

———, (ed.). *Strategic Air Command: People, Aircraft, and Missiles.* Annapolis: Nautical and Aviation Publishing Company of America, 1979.

——— and John D. Gresham. *DEFCON-2: Standing on the Brink of Nuclear War during the Cuban Missile Crisis.* Hoboken, NJ: John Wiley and Sons, Inc., 2006.

Porch, Douglas. *The Portuguese Armed Forces and the Revolution.* London: Croom Helm, 1977.

Pouget, Jean. *Bataillon R.A.S., Algérie 1956.* Paris: Presses de la Cité, 1981; reprinted 2007.

Powaski, Ronald E. *March to Armageddon: The United States and the Nuclear Arms Race, 1938 to the Present.* Oxford University Press, 1987.

Powers, Francis Gary with Curt Gentry. *Operation Overflight: The U-2 Spy Pilot Tells His Story for the First Time.* New York: Holt, Rinehart, and Winston, 1970.

Prados, John. *The Sky Would Fall. Operation Vulture: The U.S. Bombing Mission in Indochina, 1954.* New York: The Dial Press, 1983.

———. *Vietnam: The History of an Unwinnable War, 1945–1975.* Lawrence: University Press of Kansas, 2009.

Pringle, Robert W. "SMERSH: Military Counterintelligence and Stalin's Control of the USSR," *International Journal of Intelligence and Counter-Intelligence* 21:1 (Spring 2008), 122–134.

Qiang Zhai. *China and the Vietnam Wars, 1950–1975.* Chapel Hill: University of North Carolina Press, 2000.

———. "Transplanting the Chinese Model: Chinese Military Advisors and the First Vietnam War, 1950–1954," *JMH* 57:4 (October 1993), 689–715.

Quirk, Robert E. *Fidel Castro.* New York: W. W. Norton, 1993.

Rabel, Roberto G. *Between East and West: Trieste, the United States, and the Cold War, 1941–1954.* Durham, NC: Duke University Press, 1988.

Ramakrishna, Kumar. "'Transmogrifying' Malaya: the Impact of Sir Gerald Templer (1952–54)," *Journal of Southeast Asian Studies* 32:1 (February 2001), 79–82.

Ransom, Harry H. *Central Intelligence and National Security.* Cambridge, MA: Harvard University Press, 1958.

Rearden, Steven L. *History of the Office of the Secretary of Defense,* Vol. 1: *The Formative Years, 1947–1950.* Washington, DC: Historical Office, Office of the Secretary of Defense, 1984.

Reed, John A., Jr. *Germany and NATO.* Washington, DC: National Defense University Press, 1987.

Reed, Thomas C. and Danny B. Stillman. *The Nuclear Express: A Political History of the Bomb and its Proliferation.* Minneapolis: Zenith Press, 2009.

Reese, Roger R. *Red Commanders: A Social History of the Soviet Army Officer Corps, 1918–1991.* Lawrence: University Press of Kansas, 2005.

Remington, Robin Alison. *The Warsaw Pact: Case Studies in Communist Conflict Resolution.* Cambridge, MA: MIT Press, 1971.

Rhodes, Richard. *Masters of Death: The SS-Einsatzgruppen and the Invention of the Holocaust.* New York: Alfred A. Knopf, 2002.

Ridgway, Matthew B. *The Korean War: How We Met the Challenge; How All-Out Asian War Was Averted; Why MacArthur Was Dismissed; Why Today's War Objectives Must Be Limited.* Garden City, NY: Doubleday & Company, 1967.

Roberts, Geoffrey. *Stalin's Wars: From World War to Cold War, 1939–1953.* New Haven, CT: Yale University Press, 2006.

Robertson, William G. *Counterattack on the Naktong, 1950.* Leavenworth Papers No. 13. Fort Leavenworth, KS: Combat Studies Institute, 1985.

Roe, Patrick C. *The Dragon Strikes: China and the Korean War: June-December 1950.* Novato, CA: Presidio Press, 2000.

Romanus, Charles F. and Riley Sunderland. *Time Runs Out in CBI.* U.S. Army in World War II Series. Washington, DC: Office of the Chief of Military History, 1959.

Romer, Jean-Christophe. *La Guerre Nucléaire de Staline a Khrouchtchev: Essai sur la constitution d'une culture stratégique en URSS (1945–1965).* Paris: Publications de la Sorbonne, 1991.

Rosenberg, David A. "American Atomic Strategy and the Hydrogen Bomb Decision," *Journal of American History* 66:1 (June 1979), 62–87.

———. "The Origins of Overkill: Nuclear Weapons and American Strategy, 1945–1960," *International Security* 7:4 (Spring 1983), 3–71.

——— and W. B. Moore. "'Smoking Radiating Ruin at the End of Two Hours:' Documents on American Plans for Nuclear War with the Soviet Union, 1954–55," International Security 6:3 (Winter 1981–1982), 3–38.

Ross, Corey. "Before the Wall: East Germans, Communist Authority, and the Mass Exodus to the West," *The Historical Journal* 45:2 (June 2002), 459–480.

Ross, Steven T. *American War Plans, 1945–1950: Strategies for Defeating the Soviet Union.* London: Frank Cass, 1996.

Ruane, Kevin. *The Rise and Fall of the European Defence Community: Anglo-American Relations and the Crisis of European Defence, 1950–55.* New York: St. Martin's Press, 2000.

Rush, Robert S. and William W. Epley (eds.). *Multinational Operations, Alliances, and International Military Cooperation: Past and Future, Proceedings of the Fifth Workshop of the Partnership for Peace Consortium's Military History Working Group.* Washington, DC: U.S. Army Center of Military History, 2006.

Safaris, Stefanos. *ELAS: Greek Resistance Army.* London: Merlin Press, 1980.

Sagan, Scott D. *Moving Targets: Nuclear Strategy and National Security.* Princeton: Princeton University Press, 1989.

———. "Nuclear Alerts and Crisis Management," *International Security* 9:4 (Spring 1985), 99–139.

Salan, Raoul. *Indochine Rouge: Le message d'Ho Chi Minh.* Paris: Presses de la Cité, 1975.

Saunders, Richard M. "Military Force in the Foreign Policy of the Eisenhower Presidency," *Political Science Quarterly* 100:1 (Spring 1985), 97–116.

Schafel, Kenneth. *The Emerging Shield: The Air Force and the Evolution of Continental Air Defense, 1945–1960.* Washington, DC: Office of Air Force History, 1991.

Schelling, Thomas C. *Arms and Influence.* New Haven, CT: Yale University Press, 1967.

Schiff, Ze'ev. *A History of the Israeli Army, 1874 to the Present.* New York: Macmillan, 1985.

Schmidt, Gustav (ed.). *A History of NATO—the First Fifty Years,* Vol. 2. New York: Palgrave/St. Martin's Press, 2001.

Schnabel, James F. *Policy and Direction: The First Year.* United States Army in the Korean War Series. Washington, DC: U.S. Army Center of Military History, 1972; reprinted 1988.

Schwartz, David N. *NATO's Nuclear Dilemmas.* Washington, DC: Brookings Institution Press, 1983.

Selden, Mark. "Karl Marx, Mao Ze-Dong, and the Dialectics of Socialist Development," *Modern China* 3:4 (October 1977), 407–417.

Shafer, D. Michael. *Deadly Paradigms: The Failure of U.S. Counterinsurgency Policy.* Princeton: Princeton University Press, 1988.

Shaw, Henry I., Jr. The United States Marines in North China, 1945–1949. Washington, DC: Headquarters, U.S. Marine Corps, 1960.

Shen, Zhihua, and Danhui Li. *After Leaning to One Side: China and Its Allies in the Cold War.* Washington, DC: Woodrow Wilson Center and Stanford University Press, 2011.

Shipway, Martin. *The Road to War: France and Vietnam, 1944–1947.* Providence, RI: Berghahn Books, 1996.

Shlaim, Avi. "Britain, the Berlin Blockade and the Cold War," *International Affairs (Royal Institute of International Affairs)* 60:1 (Winter 1983–1984), 1–14.

———. *The Iron Wall: Israel and the Arab World.* New York: W. W. Norton, 2001.

Short, Anthony. *The Communist Insurrection in Malaya, 1948–1960.* New York: Crane, Russak & Co., 1975.

Short, Philip. *Mao: A Life.* New York: Henry Holt, 1999.

Shrader, Charles R. *The Withered Vine: Logistics and the Communist Insurgency in Greece.* Westport, CT: Praeger, 1999.

Shukman, Harold (ed.). *Stalin's Generals.* New York: Grove Press, 1993.

Shulimson, Jack. "Marines in Lebanon, 1958." Washington, DC: Headquarters, U.S. Marine Corps, no date.

Shy, John and Thomas W. Collier. "Revolutionary War," in Peter Paret (ed.), *Makers of Modern Strategy: From Machiavelli to the Nuclear Age.* Princeton: Princeton University Press, 1986, 815–862.

Sibley, Katherine A. S. *Red Spies in America: Stolen Secrets and the Dawn of the Cold War.* Lawrence: University Press of Kansas, 2004.

Siddiqi, Asif A. "Russians in Germany: Founding the Post-War Missile Programme," *Europe-Asia Studies* 56:8 (December 2004), 1131–1156.

Simpkin, Richard E. *Mechanized Infantry.* Oxford, UK: Brassey's, 1980.

Simpson, Jay G. "Not by Bombs Alone: Lessons from Malaya," *Joint Force Quarterly* No. 22 (Summer 1999,) 91–98.

Skaggs, David C. "The KATUSA Experiment: The Integration of Korean Nationals into the U.S. Army, 1950–1965," *Military Affairs* 38:2 (April 1974), 53–58.

Slessor, Sir John. "British Defense Policy," *Foreign Affairs* 35:4 (July 1957), 556–563.

Smelser, Ronald and Edward J. Davies II. *The Myth of the Eastern Front: The Nazi-Soviet War in American Popular Culture.* Cambridge: Cambridge University Press, 2008.

Smith, Robert R. "The Hukbalahap Insurgency: Economic, Political, and Military Factors." Washington, DC: Unpublished typescript, Office of the Chief of Military History, 1963.

Smith, Simon C. "General Templer and Counter-Insurgency in Malaya: Hearts and Minds, Intelligence, and Propaganda," *Intelligence and National Security* 16:3 (Autumn 2001), 60–78.

Soman, Appu K. *Double-Edged Sword: Nuclear Diplomacy in Unequal Conflicts: the United States and China, 1950–1958.* Westport, CT: Praeger, 2000.

Spector, Ronald H. *Advice and Support: The Early Years, 1941–1960.* U.S. Army in Vietnam Series. Washington, DC: U.S. Army Center of Military History, 1983.

Spiller, Roger. *"Not War But Like War:" The American Intervention in Lebanon.* Leavenworth Papers No. 3. Fort Leavenworth, KS: Combat Studies Institute, 1981.

Stanton, Shelby L. *America's Tenth Legion: X Corps in Korea, 1950.* Novato, CA: Presidio Press, 1989.

Starry, Donn A. "La Guerre Révolutionnaire," *Military Review* 47:2 (February 1967), 61–70.

Stavrakis, Peter J. *Moscow and Greek Communism, 1944–1949.* Ithaca, NY: Cornell University Press, 1989.

Strachan, Hew. "British Counter-Insurgency from Malaya to Iraq," *Journal of the RUSI* 152:6 (December 2007), 8–11.

Stuart, Douglas T. *Creating the National Security State: A History of the Law that Transformed America.* Princeton: Princeton University Press, 2008.

Stubbs, Richard. *Hearts and Minds in Guerrilla Warfare: The Malayan Emergency 1948–1960.* Singapore: Eastern Universities Press, 2004; original, Oxford University Press, 1989.

Suarez, Andrés. "The Cuban Revolution: The Road to Power," *Latin American Research Review* 7:3 (Autumn 1972), 5–29.

Stueck, William W. *Rethinking the Korean War: A New Diplomatic and Strategic History.* Princeton: Princeton University Press, 2002.

Sutton, Keith. "Army Administration Tensions over Algeria's Centres de Regroupement, 1954–1962," *British Journal of Middle Eastern Studies* 26:2 (November 1999), 243–270.

Sweig, Julia A. *Inside the Cuban Revolution: Fidel Castro and the Urban Underground.* Cambridge, MA: Harvard University Press, 2002.

Szulc, Tad. *Czechoslovakia since World War II.* New York: The Viking Press, 1971.

Tal, David (ed.). *The 1956 War: Collusion and Rivalry in the Middle East.* London: Frank Cass, 2001.

Talbott, John. *The War without a Name: France in Algeria, 1954–1962.* New York: Alfred A. Knopf, 1980.

Tanner, Harold M. "Guerrilla, Mobile, and Base Warfare in Communist Military Operations in Manchuria, 1945–1947," *JMH* 67:4 (October 2003), 1177–1222.

Taruc, Luis. *He Who Rides the Tiger: The Story of an Asian Guerrilla Leader.* New York: Frederick A. Praeger, 1967.

Taubman, Philip. *Secret Empire: Eisenhower, the CIA, and the Hidden Story of America's Space Espionage.* New York: Simon and Schuster, 2003.

Taylor, Maxwell D. *Operation Zapata: The "Ultrasensitive" Report and Testimony of the Board of Inquiry on the Bay of Pigs.* Introduction by Luis Aguilar. Frederick, MD: Aletheia Books/University Publications of America, 1981.

———. *Swords and Plowshares.* New York: W. W. Norton, 1972.

———. *The Uncertain Trumpet.* New York: Harper and Brothers, 1959.

Thomas, Hugh. *Armed Truce: The Beginnings of the Cold War, 1945–1946.* New York: Athenium, 1987.

Thompson, Robert. *Revolutionary War in World Strategy, 1945–1969.* New York: Taplinger Publishing Co., 1970.

Throup, David W. "The Origins of Mau Mau," *African Affairs* 84:336 (July 1985), 399–433.

Tien-Wei Wu. "New Materials on the Xi'an Incident: A Bibliographic Review," *Modern China* 10:1 (January 1984), 115–141.

Trachtenberg, Marc. "Strategic Thought in America, 1952–1966," *Political Science Quarterly* 104:2 (Summer 1989), 301–334.

Trauschweizer, Ingo. *The Cold War U.S. Army: Building Deterrence for Limited War.* Lawrence: University Press of Kansas, 2008.

Trevenen James, A. G. *The Royal Air Force: The Past 30 Years.* London: Macdonald and Jane's, 1976.

Trinquier, Roger. *Modern Warfare: A French View of Counterinsurgency.* Trans. Daniel Lee; Introduction by Bernard Fall. London: Pall Mall Press, 1964; reprinted Fort Leavenworth: U.S. Army Command and General Staff College, 1985.

Tripathi, K. S. *Evolution of Nuclear Strategy.* Delhi: Vikas Publications, 1970.

Troen, Selwyn I. and Moshe Shemesh (eds.). *The Suez-Sinai Crisis 1956.* New York: Columbia University Press, 1990.

Truman, Harry S. "Statement by the President of the United States (Truman) on the Korean Question, June 27, 1950," *International Organization* 4:3 (August 1950), 551.

Tusa, Ann and John. *The Berlin Airlift.* New York: Sarpedon, 1998.

Tyushkevich, S. A. *The Soviet Armed Forces: A History of their Organizational Development.* Washington, DC: Government Printing Office, 1984; original, Moscow, 1978.

U.S. Department of the Army, Assistant Chief of Staff for Intelligence, Intelligence Research Project No. A-1729, "Soviet Tank and Motorized Rifle Division." (Washington, 1958)

U.S. Department of the Army, Continental Army Command, January 8, 1959, Subject: Changes in ROCID TOE (U), with supporting Command and General Staff College documentation. (Combined Arms Research Library No. N-17935.62-U)

U.S. Army, Europe, Historical Division. *The U.S. Army Task Force in Lebanon.* Heidelberg, FRG: 1959. Declassified report. (CARL)

U.S. Army Forces, Far East, and Eighth Army (Rear). *Logistics in the Korean Operation.* Typescript, four volumes (Tokyo, c. 1955).

U.S. Department of the Army, Inspector General. *No Gun Ri Review.* Washington, DC: Department of the Army, 2001.

U.S. Department of State. *The China White Paper, August 1949.* Reprinted Stanford University Press, 1967.

———. *Foreign Relations of the United States, 1947, Volume 2: Council of Foreign Ministers; Germany and Austria.* Washington, DC: Government Printing Office, 1972.

———. *Foreign Relations of the United States, 1948, Volume 4: Eastern Europe, The Soviet Union.* Washington, DC: Government Printing Office, 1974.

———. *Foreign Relations of the United States, 1950, Volume 4: Central and Eastern Europe; The Soviet Union.* Washington, DC: Government Printing Office, 1980.

———. *Foreign Relations of the United States, 1951, Volume 6: Asia and the Pacific, Part 2.* Washington, DC: Government Printing Office, 1977.

———. *Foreign Relations of the United States, 1952–1954, Volume 13: Indochina, Part 1.* Washington, DC: Government Printing Office, 1982.

———. *Foreign Relations of the United States, 1952–1954, Volume 14: China and Japan, Part 1.* Washington, DC: Government Printing Office, 1985.

———. *Foreign Relations of the United States, 1955–1957, Volume 12: Near East Region; Iran; Iraq.* Washington, DC: Government Printing Office, 1991.

———. *Foreign Relations of the United States, 1955–1957, Volume 16: Suez Crisis July 26–December 31, 1956.* Washington, DC: Government Printing Office, 1990.

———. *Foreign Relations of the United States, 1958–1960, Volume 6: Cuba.* Washington, DC: Government Printing Office, 1991.

———. *Foreign Relations of the United States, 1958–1960, Volume 9: Lebanon and Jordan.* Washington, DC: Government Printing Office, 1992.

———. *Foreign Relations of the United States, 1958–1960, Volume 16: East Asia-Pacific Region; Cambodia; Laos.* Washington, DC: Government Printing Office, 1992.

———. *Foreign Relations of the United States, 1961–1963, Volume 24: Laos Crisis.* Washington, DC: Government Printing Office, 1994.

U.S. Far East Command, CINCFE Operations Plan 100B, Draft No. 4, dated 12 August 1950. Copy in Edmond M. Almond Papers, U.S. Army Military History Institute (MHI), General Files X Corps.

U.S., Office of the Chairman of the Joint Chiefs of Staff. *The Joint Chiefs of Staff and the First Indochina War, 1947–1954.* Washington, DC: Office of the Chairman of the Joint Chiefs of Staff, 2004.

U.S., Senate Committee on Naval Affairs, "Report to the Honorable James Forrestal, Secretary of the Navy, On Unification of the War and Navy Departments and Post-War Organization for National Security," 79th Congress, 1st session, October 22, 1945.

Vanderbroucke, Lucien S. "Anatomy of a Failure: The Decision to Land at the Bay of Pigs," *Political Science Quarterly* 99:3 (Autumn 1984), 471–491.

Van der Waals, Willem. *Portugal's Wars in Angola, 1961–1974*. Rivonia, South Africa: Ashanti, 1993.

Van Dijk, Cornelis W. A. J. "The American Political Intervention in the Conflict in the Dutch East Indies, 1945–1949," Master of Military Art and Science Thesis, U.S. Army Command and General Staff College, 2009.

Venter, Al J. *Portugal's War in Guinea-Bissau*. Pasadena, CA: Munger Africana Library, 1973.

Volkogonov, Dimitri. *Stalin: Triumph and Tragedy*. Rocklin, CA: Prima, 1992.

Von Clausewitz, Carl. Ed. and trans. by Michael Howard and Peter Paret. *On War*. Princeton: Princeton University Press, 1976.

Vo Nguyen Giap. *The Military Art of People's War: Selected Writings of General Vo Nguyen Giap*. Ed. Russell Steller. New York: Monthly Review Press, 1970.

Wade, Gary H. *Rapid Deployment Logistics: Lebanon, 1958*. Research Survey No. 3. Fort Leavenworth, KS: Combat Studies Institute, 1984.

Walton, Clarence C. "Background for the European Defense Community," *Political Science Quarterly* 68:1 (March 1953), 42–69.

Wardak, Ghulam D. *The Voroshilov Lectures: Materials from the Soviet General Staff Academy*. Vol. 1: *Issues of Soviet Military Strategy*. Ed. Graham H. Turbiville, Jr. Washington, DC: National Defense University, 1989.

Warsaw Pact, aka Treaty of Mutual Friendship, Co-operation, and Mutual Assistance, May 1, 1955. available from the Fordham Modern History Sourcebook at www.fordham.edu/halsall/mod/1955warsawpact.html.

Waters, Alan R. "The Cost of Air Support in Counter-Insurgency Operations: The Case of the Mau Mau in Kenya," *Military Affairs* 37:3 (October 1973), 96–100.

Watson, Robert J. *History of the Office of the Secretary of Defense*, Vol. IV: *Into the Missile Age, 1956–1960*. Washington, DC: Office of the Secretary of Defense, 1997.

Weatherby, Kathryn. "Soviet Aims in Korea and the Origins of the Korean War, 1945–1950: New Evidence from Russian Archives," *Cold War International History Project Working Papers, No. 8*. Washington, DC: Woodrow Wilson International Center for Scholars, November 1993.

Wedemeyer, Albert C. *Wedemeyer Reports*. New York: Henry Holt, 1958.

Wells, Samuel F., Jr. "The Origins of Massive Retaliation," *Political Science Quarterly* 96:1 (Spring 1981), 31–52.

———. "Sounding the Tocsin: NSC 68 and the Soviet Threat," *International Security* 4:2 (Autumn 1979), 116–158.

Wenger, Andreas. *Living With Peril: Eisenhower, Kennedy, and Nuclear Weapons.* Lanham, MD: Rowman & Littlefield Publishers, 1997.

Westad, Odd Arne. *Cold War and Revolution: Soviet-American Rivalry and the Origins of the Chinese Civil War.* New York: Columbia University Press, 1993.

———. *Decisive Encounters: The Chinese Civil War, 1946–1950.* Stanford University Press, 2003.

Wheeler, Douglas L. "The Portuguese Army in Angola," *Journal of Modern African Studies* 7:3 (1969), 425–439.

White, Theodore H. and Annalee Jacoby. *Thunder out of China.* New York: William Sloane Associates, 1946.

Whiting, Allen S. *China Crosses the Yalu: The Decision to Enter the Korean War.* Project RAND Study R-356. Santa Monica, CA: RAND Corporation, 1960.

———. "New Light on Mao, 3: Quemoy, 1958: Mao's Miscalculations," *China Quarterly* No. 62 (June 1975), 170–263.

Whiting, Kenneth R. *Soviet Air Power.* Boulder, CO: Westview Press, 1986.

Whitson, William W. with Chen-Hsia Huang. *The Chinese High Command: A History of Communist Military Politics, 1927–71.* New York: Praeger, 1973.

Williams, Philip. "How the Fourth Republic Died: Sources for the Revolution of May 1958," *French Historical Studies* 3:1 (Spring 1963), 1–40.

Williams, Robert C. *Klaus Fuchs, Atom Spy.* Cambridge, MA: Harvard University Press, 1987.

Wilson, John B. *Maneuver and Firepower: The Evolution of Divisions and Separate Brigades.* Washington, DC: U.S. Army Center of Military History, 1998.

Winkler, David F. *Cold War at Sea: High-Seas Confrontation between the United States and the Soviet Union.* Annapolis: Naval Institute Press, 2000.

Wise, James E., Jr., and Scott Baron. *Dangerous Games: Facts, Incidents, and Casualties of the Cold War.* Annapolis: Naval Institute Press, 2010.

Wisnack, Joseph R. "'Old Ironsides' Response to the Cuban Crisis," *Army* 13:9 (April 1963), 26–30.

Wittner, Lawrence S. *American Intervention in Greece, 1943–1949.* New York: Columbia University Press, 1982.

Wohlstetter, Albert. "The Delicate Balance of Terror," *Foreign Affairs* 37:2 (January 1959), 211–234.

Wood, Robert J. "The First Year of SHAPE," *International Organization* 6:2 (May 1952), 175–191.

Woods, Randall B. and Howard Jones. *Dawning of the Cold War: The United States' Quest for Order.* Athens: University of Georgia Press, 1991.

Wyden, Peter. *Wall: The Inside Story of Divided Berlin.* New York: Simon and Shuster, 1989.

Xiaobing Li, Allan R. Millett, and Bin Yu (trans. and eds.). *Mao's Generals Remember Korea.* Lawrence: University Press of Kansas, 2001.

Xiaoming Zhang, *Red Wings over the Yalu: China, the Soviet Union, and the Air War in Korea*. College Station: Texas A&M University Press, 2002.

Xu Youwei and Philip Billingsley. "Behind the Scenes of the Xi'an Incident: The Case of the Lixingshe," *China Quarterly* 154 (June 1998), 283–307.

Yarmolinsky, Adam. "Department of Defense Operations during the Cuban Missile Crisis," February 13, 1963, sanitized version edited by Dan Caldwell in *Naval War College Review* 32:4 (June-July, 1979), 83–99.

Young, Marilyn B. *The Vietnam Wars, 1945–1990*. New York: Harper Collins, 1991.

Zaloga, Steven J. *Target America: The Soviet Union and the Strategic Arms Race, 1945–1964*. Novato, CA: Presidio Press, 1993.

Zawodny, Janusz K. *Nothing but Honour: The Story of the Warsaw Uprising, 1944*. Stanford, CA: Hoover Institution Press, 1978.

Zervoudakis Alexander. "A Case of Successful Pacification: The 584th Bataillon du Train at Bourdj de l'Agha (1956–57)," *Journal of Strategic Studies* 25:2 (June 2002), 54–65.

Zubok, Vladislav M. and Constantine Pleshakov. *Inside the Kremlin's Cold War: From Stalin to Khrushchev*. Cambridge, MA: Harvard University Press, 1996.

INDEX

Marshal of the Soviet Union is abbreviated as MSU.